Unanimous praise for A.N. Wilson
and
TOLSTOY

"His imaginative approach to the mysteries of personality is a good reminder that consistency is for peanut butter, not for geniuses who exploit their conflicts in creative acts. Wilson's *Tolstoy* is the story of the literary titan's relationships with three subjects: God, Russia and women."

Time

"A fascinating exploration of the fiction Tolstoy created about himself and turned into his great novels . . . A. N. Wilson shows how a biographer can demythologize a great imagination without diminishing its grandeur and truth. This may be regarded as one of the best biographies of our century."

Leon Edel

"Must surely rank among the most impressive intelligent biographies ever written."

The Economist

"A. N. Wilson brings to his *Tolstoy* a bracing mix of insight, skepticism, wry wit and clean prose. Moreover, he has the tools vital to a work of this sort—a knowledge of Russian history and literature and, above all, the ability to read Tolstoy in the original rather than through the scrim of translation. . . . Wilson brilliantly explores the forces that shaped and nurtured his genius."

New York Newsday

"Highly readable and worth reading."

USA Today

Tolstoy

A. N. Wilson

FAWCETT COLUMBINE • NEW YORK

A Fawcett Columbine Book
Published by Ballantine Books
Copyright © 1988 by A. N. Wilson

All rights reserved under International and Pan-American Copyright
Conventions. Published in the United States by Ballantine Books, a
division of Random House, Inc., New York.

Library of Congress Catalog Card Number: 89-90645

ISBN: 0-449-90449-0

This edition published by arrangement with W. W. Norton & Company, Inc.

Cover design by Richard Aquan

Cover painting by N.E. Ge, 1884, courtesy of SCR

Manufactured in the United States of America

First Ballantine Books Edition: October 1989

10 9 8 7 6 5 4 3 2 1

To my wife and daughters

Contents

Acknowledgements

This book began in 1967 when I heard R. V. Sampson talking about Tolstoy. His lecture started with a Jewish proverb. 'If God came to live on earth, people would smash his windows.' Professor Sampson went on to say that people had been smashing Tolstoy's windows ever since he had enunciated his great principles of life. I was amazed that anyone could speak of a novelist as if he were divine, but pretty quickly became excited by the Tolstoyan ideals which Professor Sampson expounded. That excitement, and that amazement, continue to this hour. I have never got over Professor Sampson's lecture. He will certainly regard the present book as an exercise in window-smashing, but I feel that I owe him a great debt.

If it is true that I should never have begun the book without R. V. Sampson, I should never have finished it without several wonderful pieces of good fortune. One of these was going to New College, Oxford, and having as my tutor the man who has written the best critical study of Tolstoy in English, John Bayley. Another of these was finding myself, rather later, living within a stone's throw of the Slavonic branch of the Taylorian Library. The staff there have been unfailingly kind and helpful, as have the staffs of the Bodleian Library and the London Library.

Another piece of luck was finding in Jennifer Baines a teacher who was patient enough to devote hours of her time to helping me achieve a reading knowledge of Russian. The benefits of this far outstretch even the broad confines of Tolstoy. But I could certainly not have contemplated writing this study without her.

Thanks, too, for conversational help from Marina Stepanovna Douglas, and for the kindness of those who showed me Yasnaya Polyana and the Tolstoy Museum in Moscow.

I am grateful to Michael Holman of Leeds University for his help with a number of the illustrations; to Susan Rose-Smith for her skilful picture research; to James Woodall, Christopher Sinclair-Stevenson and Star Lawrence for all their editorial help; and to Douglas Matthews for compiling the index.

I am, finally, fortunate in having Virginia Llewellyn Smith as a critic and near-neighbour, who overcame her lively detestation of my old hero to read the typescript and who made many invaluable suggestions. The dedicatees of this book will know whether I am any easier to live with than its subject; they have the supreme virtue of being totally unlike any of the women of Yasnaya Polyana.

Oxford, October 27, 1987

A Note on Dates and Transliterations

The dates in this book are given in the 'old style'. That is to say, they follow the Julian Calendar, which was used in Russia until 1917. The Julian Calendar was twelve days behind the Gregorian Calendar in the nineteenth century and thirteen days behind in the twentieth century. There are some inevitable inconsistencies, however, caused by the fact that Tolstoy did not always remain within the territories where the Julian Calendar was operative. Thus, when he visits London, or Switzerland, or takes part in battles against Englishmen or Frenchmen, the occasional Gregorian date slips in.

I have attempted to follow the system of transliteration from Cyrillic to Roman script recommended by the Slavonic and East European Review, but I have departed from those guidelines in a number of particulars. This is largely in the area of proper names, where a literal transliteration looks merely odd to an English eye. So, we read here of Alexander, not Aleksandr. I have rendered the name of Tolstoy's wife Sofya, rather than Sof'ya. In general, I have not transliterated 'hard' and 'soft' signs. Initial or inter-vocalic *e* I have rendered *Ye* (Dostoyevsky, Yevgeny) but in other positions, *e* is rendered *e* (Onegin). I have spelt the ending of proper names with a *y*, whether in Cyrillic script this corresponds to и or й or ий . Not everyone will agree with my Nikolay for Nikolai, Dmitry for Dmitri or Tolstoy for Tolstoi but there are no fixed rules for transliteration, and though I am guilty of inconsistencies, I hope that all my transliterations are intelligible. My aim has been to make things easy for the eye of a reader who has no Russian.

List of Illustrations

List of Illustrations

Chronology of Tolstoy's Life and Times

1825   Accession of Nicholas I; December 14, Decembrist Rising defeated. Prince Sergey Grigoryevich Volkonsky, a cousin of Tolstoy's mother, is sent into Siberian exile for his part in the rebellion.

1828   August 28, birth of Lev Nikolayevich Tolstoy (hereafter LNT).

1830   September 7, death of LNT's mother   Pushkin finishes first draft of *Yevgeny Onegin.*

1832   Foundation of the 'Ant Brotherhood': the secret of earthly happiness is written on a green stick and buried at Yasnaya Polyana.

1837   Death of LNT's father   Pushkin killed in a duel

1838   Death of LNT's grandmother

1841   Death of LNT's Aunt Alexandra (Countess Osten-Saken): LNT with his orphan brothers and sister move to Kazan to live with another aunt, Pelageya Yushkova.   Death of Lermontov in a duel

1842 LNT loses his virginity; starts to read Rousseau.

Procurator of Holy Synod, N. A. Pratasov, forbids Metropolitan Filaret of Moscow to write a Russian commentary on the Bible.

1844 LNT matriculates at Kazan University.

Count Mikhail Vorontsov becomes Viceroy of the Caucasus.

1845

Russian infiltration into the Caucasus continues; invasion of Chechnya.

1846

Dostoyevsky's *Poor Folk* published

1847 LNT gets V.D. Comes into his inheritance, leaves Kazan and goes back to Yasnaya Polyana.

Dombey and Son published in Russia

Herzen leaves Russia, never to return.

1848

Year of revolutions

1849 LNT spends some time in St. Petersburg; passes two law exams at university there; becomes local magistrate in Tula; lives there for a while.

Russian invasion of Hungary

Dostoyevsky sentenced to death; last-minute reprieve; sent to convict prison of Omsk, Siberia.

1850 LNT living in a Moscow apartment; reads Sterne; partly in love with Volkonsky cousin; writes *The History of Yesterday.*

Publication of *David Copperfield*

1851 April 20, leaves Yasnaya Polyana for Caucasus; goes as volunteer on expedition from Starogladovsk.

November in Tiflis writing *Childhood*

1852 February, LNT enters army.

The Raid published in *The Contemporary*

1853

February, Prince A. S. Menshikov in Constantinople to assert Russian predominance over 'the sick man of Europe'

October 8, Turkey declares war on Russia.

1854 LNT receives his commission. After leave at Yasnaya Polyana reaches army at Bucharest.

Boyhood appears in *The Contemporary.*

November, LNT reaches Sebastopol.

March, France and England declare war on Russia: battles of Inkerman and Balaclava; Charge of the Light Brigade; Siege of Sebastopol.

Dostoyevsky released from Omsk prison

1855 April-May, LNT serves in Sebastopol.

Publishes *Recollections of a Billiard Maker; Sebastopol in December; Sebastopol in May; The Woodfelling*; disastrous losses at cards.

November, LNT returns to St. Petersburg, meets Afanasy Fet, a lifelong friend, and rest of literary set — Nekrasov, Turgenev, Goncharov, etc.

September 8, Malakhov captured by French; surrender of Sebastopol.

Death of Nicholas I; accession of Alexander II, the reforming Tsar.

Turgenev's *Rudin* published

1856 January 21, death of LNT's brother Dmitry

February, LNT photographed with his fellow *Contemporary* authors

Publishes *The Snowstorm, Two Hussars, A Russian Landlord*

November 26, leaves army

March, peace signed between Russia, Turkey, France and England

1857 *Youth* published

February, visits Paris with
Turgenev and Nekrasov; sees a
man guillotined; leaves Paris in
disgust. April, goes to
Switzerland and gets to know his
cousin Alexandra Alexandrovna
Tolstaya (Alexandrine) on
holiday in Lucerne with her
sister; lifelong friend and
confidante. August, returns to
Yasnaya Polyana.

1858 Visits St. Petersburg

Begins long-standing relationship with one of his peasant-
serf's wives, Aksinya Bazykina

Committees set up to persuade local
nobility to prepare for emancipation of
serfs

Publication of Turgenev's *Home of
the Gentry* and Goncharov's *Oblomov*

1859 Publishes *Three Deaths* and
Family Happiness

Starts to organise a school at
Yasnaya Polyana

Publication of Turgenev's *On the Eve*

1860 LNT's second (and last) visit
abroad: goes to see his brother
Nikolay, who dies at Hyères,
October; emotionally profoundly
affected; financially rescued,
having lost most of own
inheritance through gambling
debts.

December, goes to Rome
where LNT meets his Decembrist
cousin, Prince Sergey Volkonsky

1861 LNT revisits Paris.

February-March in London;
hears Dickens read; meets
Matthew Arnold, Herzen.

February 19, emancipation of serfs
from the personal ownership of
landowners

To Brussels where he meets Proudhon and sees his book, *La Guerre et la Paix*; April, returns to Russia.

April 26, challenges Turgenev to duel

June, works as Arbiter of the Peace

1861-2 At work on the school at Yasnaya Polyana.

Birth of LNT's son Timofey, a future coachman

1862 February, Yasnaya Polyana magazine published; May, gives up being Arbiter of the Peace; May-June to Samara to take the *kumys* cure; police raid on Yasnaya Polyana

August, renews contact with Bers family; September 16, proposes marriage to Sofya Andreyevna Bers; September 23, marries her.

1863 Publication of *The Cossacks;* starts to write *War and Peace.*

Son Sergey born

1864 Birth of daughter Tatyana

Publication of Dostoyevsky's *Notes from the House of the Dead* and Turgenev's *Fathers and Children*

Polish rebellion crushed; many former Russian liberals, such as Katkov, become reactionary.

Institution of local assemblies — the *zemstvo*; rudimentary jury service begins in Russia. Student unrest in Kazan; five students shot.

Marx's First International formed in London

Publication of Dostoyevsky's *Notes from the Underground*

1865 *1805* published (i.e. first part of *War and Peace*)

Dostoyevsky's *Crime and Punishment* and Leskov's *Lady Macbeth of Mtsensk* published

1866 Birth of son Ilya

LNT counsel for the defence (unsuccessful) in the hopeless Shabunin court martial

Publication of Dostoyevsky's *The Gambler*

Konstantin Pobedonostsev succeeds Count Dmitry Tolstoy as Procurator of the Holy Synod.

1867 Work on *War and Peace* continues.

Tanya Bers (the model for Natasha Rostova) marries Alexander Kuzminsky and becomes a near neighbour of the Tolstoys at Yasnaya Polyana.

Ethnographic exhibition in Moscow; the big Slav section encourages growth of Slavophilism.

Turgenev's *Smoke* published

1869 Birth of son Lev

War and Peace finished

A *nuit de feu* at Arzamas, when LNT confronts death

Dostoyevsky's *The Idiot* published

1870 Reading philosophy, especially Schopenhauer; reads all the major dramatists. Recurrent bouts of illness.

Starts work on *Peter the Great* and learns Greek

Franco-Prussian War; Third Empire overthrown; defeat of the Paris Commune.
Death of Herzen

Birth of Vladimir Ilyich Ulyanov (Lenin)

1871 Birth of daughter Masha

LNT takes *kumys* cure in Samara

ABC book published

Dostoyevsky's *The Devils* published

1872 LNT reopens school at Yasnaya
Polyana

Publication of *A Prisoner in the
Caucasus* and *God Sees the
Truth but Waits*

June 13, birth of son Pyotr

September, LNT put under
house arrest by investigating
magistrate

1873 Takes family to Samara; in the
summer there is a famine; LNT
launches an appeal; abandons
Peter the Great novel.

An eight-volume *Collected
Works* of LNT is published.

Death of son Pyotr

1874 Death of 'Auntie' Toinette

1875 First instalments of
Anna Karenina published; a new
ABC book; summer spent in
Samara horse-racing.

November, daughter Varvara
born dead; December, death of
Aunt Pelageya Yushkova;
LNT's obsession with death,
temptation to commit suicide,
grow stronger.

1876 January-April and December,
further instalments of *Anna
Karenina*

Visits Samara and Orenburg;
begins to practise the Orthodox
Faith.

Leskov's *Cathedral Folk* published

First publication in Russian of
Marx's *Capital*

Large strike in Odessa, supported by
Union of South Russian Workers, the
first working-class organisation in
Russia

Panslavism rampant; June 30, Serbia
declares war on Turkey; demonstrations by revolutionary students in
St. Petersburg.

Publication of Turgenev's *Virgin Soil*

1877 January-April, final instalments of *Anna Karenina*;
Katkov refuses to print the final
part of the novel; major quarrel
with LNT.

LNT's belief in Orthodoxy
strained

Birth of son Andrey

April 24, Russia declares war on
Turkey; patriots like Dostoyevsky are
loud in their belief that Constantinople
belongs by right to Orthodox Russia.

1878 March, visits the Peter and Paul
fortress where the Decembrists
were imprisoned

Abandons attempt to believe
in Orthodoxy

Reconciliation with Turgenev;
exchange of visits in summer.

Peace signed between Russia and
Turkey; creation of Bulgaria; more
student riots in St. Petersburg.

1879 Continues work on *The
Decembrists,* begun previous
year; writing *A Confession.*

Son Mikhail born

Abandons *The Decembrists* and
starts *What I Believe*

Assassination of Prince Kropoktin,
governor of Kharkov; several attempts
to assassinate Tsar.

Birth of Osip Vissarionovich
Djugashvili (Stalin)

1880 Working on *Critique of
Dogmatic Theology*

Fourth edition of *Collected
Works* (now in eleven volumes)

Death of Empress; Alexander II
marries his mistress, Princess
Catherine Dolgorukaya.

Oil drilling begins in Azerbaidzhan;
big programme of railway-building
begins.

Dostoyevsky makes his famous speech
at the unveiling of the Pushkin
memorial.

Publication of *The Brothers
Karamazov*

1881 Letter to the Tsar

Working on *Synthesis of the Four Gospels* and *What Men Live By*; visits Optina monastery.

Son Alexey born

Death of Dostoyevsky

Assassination of Alexander II; accession of Alexander III and the beginning of real power for his former tutor, Pobedonostsev. Reactionary ministers like Pobedonostsev and Ignatyev drive out reformers such as Loris-Melikov; Jewish pogroms.

1882 LNT's wife persuades him to buy house in Moscow.

Studies Hebrew; tries to drop the use of his title; threatens to leave home.

Riots in the Universities of St. Petersburg and Kazan. Tightening of censorship laws.

1883 Writes *What I Believe*; refuses to do jury service.

LNT hands over to wife power of attorney to conduct all matters concerning his property. Vladimir Grigoryevich Chertkov visits the Tolstoys and immediately becomes LNT's intimate and disciple.

New laws governing membership of religious sects; persecution of minorities steps up.

Plekhanov publishes *Socialism and the Political Struggle* and founds the Marxist Liberation Group in Geneva.

Turgenev dies. The last thing he writes, a few days before death, is a letter to LNT imploring him to return to art.

1884 LNT starts bootmaking.

What I Believe forbidden by censor: *The Decembrists* fragment published.

His wife concentrates her attention on the *Collected Works*, now in effect her property and source of family income.

June 18, daughter Sasha born

Otechestvennye zapiski (Notes for the Fatherland) is the first serious casualty of the censorship laws; paper closed.

1885 LNT revisits the Crimea. He
becomes a vegetarian and a
teetotaller, gives up hunting and
smoking; Chertkov more and
more an influence, as well as a
follower. Together LNT and
Chertkov found *The Intermediary.*

Publication of *Where Love Is,
God Is*

LNT's wife converts a shed near
their Moscow house into a
warehouse and publishing office
for her husband's *Collected Works.*

1886 Death of son Alexey

What Then Must We Do? and
The Death of Ivan Ilyich
published

Archbishop of Kherson
denounces LNT as a heretic.

Chekhov's first volume of stories
published

1887 LNT writes *On Life*

Five students are hanged for trying to
kill the Tsar. One of them is Lenin's
brother.

1888 LNT's play *The Power of
Darkness* performed in Paris

Birth of son Ivan (Vanichka)

1889 Publishes *The Kreutzer Sonata*

S. A. Tolstaya brings out her
twelve-volume *Collected Works*
of LNT. Dispute about *The
Kreutzer Sonata* (SAT objects
both to the content and to the
fact that it is banned by censor).

1890 Repin's painting, *Tolstoy in his Room*

SAT petitions the Tsar in person and gains permission to publish *The Kreutzer Sonata* as Volume XIII in the *Collected Works.*

June 12, more laws; number of peasant representatives on *zemstvo*s reduced; Jews forbidden to sit on a *zemstvo.*

1891 LNT attacks smoking and alcohol in *Why Do Men Stupefy Themselves?* Renounces copyrights and divides proportico among his family. Son Lev has mental breakdown.

September famine: LNT leads relief; opens soup kitchens in famine districts; raises money etc.

Famine; failed harvest.

1892 Articles on famine; continues famine relief work. Writes essay on vegetarianism, *The First Step.*

Repin's painting, *Tolstoy Ploughing*

Death of Fet

Maxim Gorky's first published story

Sergey Yulyevich Witte becomes Minister of Finance.

1893 *The Kingdom of God is Within You* published

1894 *Christianity and Pacifism* published

Death of Alexander III; accession of Nicholas II and his unpopular German wife.

Peasants denied passports and forbidden to travel within the Empire without permit.

Stalin enters theological seminary at Tiflis.

1895 February 23, death of son Ivan

Master and Man published; begins to work on *Resurrection.*

Nicholas II dismisses the idea of representative government as 'senseless dreams'.

Lenin with companions arrested and imprisoned; nearly dies of pneumonia; exiled briefly to Switzerland where he meets Plekhanov. On his return to Russia, Lenin is sent to Siberia.

1896

Khodynka catastrophe; thirteen hundred crushed to death. Strikes and demonstrations.

Pobedonostsev urges the Tsar to imprison LNT.

1897 Starts *What Is Art?*

Biryukov, LNT's future biographer, and Chertkov arrested and sent into exile

SAT's passion for the musician Taneyev at its embarrassing height

1898 Finishes *What Is Art?*

Son Sergey accompanies two thousand Dukhobors to Canada, largely paid for by LNT.

Works on *Father Sergius*

1899 More Dukhobor migration

LNT finishes *Resurrection*

Student riots; all universities in Russia temporarily closed.

Stalin leaves seminary and starts to mix with disgruntled revolutionary groups.

1900

Russian language made compulsory in Finland. Marxist RSDLP brings out its first paper, *Iskra* (*The Spark*).

Lenin's Siberian exile ends. He goes abroad.

1901 LNT excommunicated by Orthodox Church; in March issues *A Reply to the Synod's Edict*.

Chekhov's *Three Sisters* first performed

An unsuccessful attempt is made on Pobedonostsev's life.

Illness; goes to Crimea to recover; meets Gorky, Chekhov,

Starts to write *Hadji Murat*

1902 LNT finishes *What Is Religion?*

More assassinations: governor of Kharkov, Minister of the Interior et al; many estates plundered.

Starts to reread Shakespeare

1903 *After the Ball* published

Split between Mensheviks and Bolsheviks

Easter: Jews massacred at Kishinyov.

1904 Death of Brother Sergey

Death of Chekhov

Bethink Yourselves!, LNT's protest against the Japanese war, published

War with Japan; Port Arthur attacked; Russian fleet annihilated in Tsushima Straits.

Lenin launches his newspaper *Vperyod! (Forward!)*.

1905 *The One Thing Needful* and other articles seized by police

Son Andrey leaves the army for 'nervous reasons'.

January, general strike. Tsar's uncle Grand Duke Sergey assassinated. Mutiny of battleship *Potemkin*. Treaty of Portsmouth ends war. The Manifesto: 1905 'Revolution'. Witte becomes, in effect, the first Prime Minister in Russian history.

November, Nicholas II and Empress get to know a 'man of God' called Rasputin.

1906 LNT finishes *The Circle of Reading.*

Serious illness of wife; death of daughter Masha.

Formal inauguration of the *Duma* (Parliament)

1907 Police raid on Yasnaya Polyana; seizure of LNT's books.

SAT's brother murdered by striking dock workers. Marauders rampage at Yasnaya Polyana. Much to LNT's dismay, his wife protects their property with an armed police guard.

Stalin stops using his native language (Georgian) and begins to write in Russian.

1908 *I Cannot Be Silent* etc. published

Arrest and banishment of N. N. Gusev, Tolstoy's secretary.

Return of Chertkov, who builds a house three miles from Yasnaya; battles with SAT over ownership of LNT's MSS, diaries, copyrights etc.

1909 Chertkov expelled from his estate for subversive activity and compelled to go to Moscow; Chertkov and Sasha persuade LNT to make a secret will.

1910 More quarrels about copyright, wills, diaries; SAT increasingly mad.

October 28, LNT leaves home; November 7, dies at Astapovo.

Upon death of LNT, street demonstrations and strikes

November 9, buried at the place of the green stick in Yasnaya Polyana; first public funeral since conversion of Russia to Christianity which was not attended by religious rites.

Rasputin urges the Empress to dissolve the *Duma.*

Foreword

The first thing to strike any foreigner about Russia is its immensity. We all know from our schoolbooks that the modern Soviet Union, like the Empire of Catherine the Great, occupies roughly one sixth of the world's surface. Comparatively few, however, make this knowledge real by attempting to travel across its surface. Even to retrace, in a train or a car, the journey of Napoleon from Warsaw to Moscow is to cover a huge distance — a seemingly interminable journey across flat, unvarying countryside. To have reached Moscow, as a glance at the map shows us, is to have covered only the tiniest part of this extraordinary land mass which, for various historical reasons, speaks of itself as a single political entity.

Peter the Great is rightly deemed the father of modern Russia. But it was really the German Princess Catherine the Great, Empress of Russia from 1762 to 1796, who was responsible for what Russia became in the following century. Catherine had the foreigner's view that Russia was too big, paradoxically combined with the monomaniac's desire to make it even bigger. She annexed Poland, she extended its territories southward to the Black Sea. She created the map of Russia more or less as we know it today. At the same time, she had a fear of it being unmanageably large, a fear based on ignorance. 'What interest. . . . could the young German princess take in that *magnum ignotum*, that people, inarticulate, poor, semi-barbarous, which concealed itself in villages, behind the snow, behind bad roads, and only appeared in the streets of St. Petersburg like a foreign outcast, with its persecuted beard, and prohibited dress — tolerated only through contempt?' The question was Alexander Herzen's, the first truly great Russian radical, perhaps the greatest, to fall foul of the bureaucracy which Peter had created, which Catherine had sustained, and extended, and which was to grow like a self-perpetuating monster throughout the nineteenth century.

Towards the close of the eighteenth century, liberty and self-government became the political ideals of the West. The United States came into being, having thrown off the monarchical and colonial principles of the British Crown. The French *bourgeoisie* established, by violent revolution, its right to overthrow the outmoded hierarchy of monarch and aristocrat. Catherine, who had flirted with the ideas and the authors of the Enlightenment, left a legacy in Russia which was violently opposed to it. With systematic thoroughness, she managed to build up a system — precisely because of the enormous size of her Empire — which was almost incapable of reform.

Apart from her expansion of the borders of Russia, two hugely important measures, both of which had a tremendous bearing on the future, should be mentioned.

The first was her extension of serfdom throughout the Empire. In the Ukraine, for example, where the peasantry had hitherto been free, Catherine enacted a system of laws which forbade peasants to leave an estate without their landlord's permission. The landlord became their owner. Estimates vary, but it is thought that by the end of her reign well over half the population of the Russian Empire had become a slave class, every bit as subjugated as the negro slaves of America.

The other reform, which went hand in hand with this extension of slavery, was a strengthening and ossifying of the gentry. In other European countries, aristocratic status, initially reflecting a position of political power, was to evolve into an inchoate position, difficult to define in terms of strength or importance. In England, for example, a duke at the beginning of the nineteenth century would certainly be rich, but he would not necessarily exercise any political power. And, by the middle of the Victorian age, his power would be yet more questionable. As for the members of the lesser gentry in England, their titles were no more than mementoes of favour granted to an ancestor by the Sovereign.

Such an evolution was impossible in Russia, since Catherine established a strict hierarchical system of government in which only members of the aristocracy could exercise power. Membership of the aristocracy was a discernible political status. Not only was the highly organised system of local government entirely in the hands of the local gentry. They were given certain privileges which made them different in kind from their non-gentry neighbours. Not merely were they exempt from tax, and certain legal penalties, such as corporal punishment, but also, they alone could receive a full university education. They alone could aspire to occupy senior bureaucratic positions in central Government. To be deprived of 'gentry' status was, therefore, the equivalent of being disenfranchised.

Between the gentry and the serfs, Catherine also established the town merchants as a separate estate with fixed, recognised privileges and social duties.

When she died in 1796, she left an Empire which was completely top-heavy in terms of its powerbase. The Crown, and the bureaucracy with which it was surrounded, had the means to exercise an absolute control over every citizen and every institution within its dominion. Once the system got going, with bureaucrats multiplying bureaucrats, as in the comedies of Gogol, it was hard to see how it could be reformed without being destroyed altogether. And this explains why the monarchy, again and again, throughout the nineteenth century, resisted reform for fear that even quite minor changes would bring down the whole system.

Curiously enough, considering the fact that Catherine and perhaps most of the leading aristocrats of her day were privately 'modern' in their religious views, her reforms had the effect of making Russia into a theocracy, whose levels of tolerance would make the Spanish Inquisition look like a Democratic Party convention. This was because, in her Germanic thoroughness, she had totally secularised the power of the Church, bringing even *that* within the power of the state. She had not only taken possession of Church lands. She had confirmed that the Church, as a religious body, should actually be run by the state. Not only the appointment of bishops but even the propagation of doctrine were brought into the jurisdiction of the secular civil service. The Procurator of the Holy Synod was a layman, entitled to lay down the law about liturgy, worship and theology to the Patriarch of Moscow himself.

It was a strange paradox that Catherine, with no ounce of Russian blood, should have enacted policies which led to an increase in Russian isolationism from the rest of the world. With such an inheritance, many Russians had no chance of travelling about within the boundaries of the Empire, let alone travelling outside it, or reading foreign books.

Nevertheless, there were changes in the wind. Some of them came about, fortuitously, by virtue of the Napoleonic Wars. With Russian troops moving about in Poland, Germany, France and Austria, there was no possibility of the state exercising the power of their minds which it was able to do in the stable conditions of peacetime. The Emperor at the time of Napoleon, Alexander I, was in any case a liberal. But, even if he had not been on the side of moderate reform, he would have been unable to stop the Russian soldiers meeting foreigners and seeing the way that things were done abroad. Their French prisoners of war, after Napoleon's retreat from Moscow, would have been able to tell them of a republic, where each citizen was regarded as the equal of the next. Englishmen could tell them of their own political compromises, and the possibility of a constitutional monarchy, with an elected legislative chamber. In all the farms and fields through which the armies of Alexander I marched, they were able to meet farmers and their wives and children who may not have been rich, but who were not *owned* by anyone, and who would have regarded serfdom as the most appalling throwback to the Middle Ages.

Self-conscious Russians, at the beginning of the nineteenth century, would have felt, in addition to shame at their political backwardness, an acute awareness of cultural inadequacy. Throughout the Continent of Europe, in the first two decades of the last century, there was an extraordinary abundance of genius. These were the years that produced the finest plays and lyrics of Schiller, some of Goethe's best poetry, the *Méditations poétiques* of Lamartine, the best operas of Rossini, the novels of Scott, the poems of Byron and Shelley: but nothing comparable in Russia. It looked as though Russia was doomed to be a backwater, as far as the history of literature was concerned.

The appearance of the great Russian writers of the nineteenth century is something only paralleled in the history of literature by the emergence of English poets during the reign of Queen Elizabeth I. Nothing prepares us for it. Suddenly, there they are — Lermontov, Gogol, Belinsky, Griboyedov. Above all, there, for the tragically brief period of 1799-1837, is Alexander Pushkin, perhaps the most varied and intelligent poet in the world, a genius of world class, after whom Russia — not just Russian literature — would never be the same again. Pushkin showed that it was not necessary, as almost all the educated class in Russia did, to speak in French in order to be clever, moving, witty, inventive. Pushkin also showed that it was possible to be authentically Russian, while being totally opposed to all the cruelties and absurdities of the Russian system of government.

Pushkin, even more than Goethe or Scott, was remarkable for the ease with which he moved from one literary form to the next and effortlessly transformed them all. He is the closest thing that literature has to Mozart. A tender lyricist, a flippant satirist, a great dramatist, a master of the short-story form, he also, in his long poem *Yevgeny Onegin*, effectively invented the Russian novel. Thereafter, whatever magnificent things the Russians did with that most fluid of literary forms, they trod, willy-nilly, in Pushkin's footsteps. He was killed in a duel in 1837. Perhaps it is the greatest single tragedy in the history of literature. There is no knowing what masterpieces we have lost by that death.

After Pushkin, there were to be many magnificent Russian poets, and a long line of great Russian novelists. Among these novelists, there is one who stands out, for most Russians, as the greatest of them all. In terms of sheer volume and monumental size he is, if anything, a larger figure even than Pushkin himself. Ninety volumes of his work fill the shelves of the Russian library. His name was Count Lev Nikolayevich Tolstoy.

*　　　*　　　*　　　*

Tolstoy was peculiarly the product of the Russia which we have been describing. He could not have written or lived as he did had he not been born in a particular time and place and situation. He was born on August 28, 1828, and he died on November 7, 1910. Though most Russian writers of the nineteenth century were technically of the gentry class — how else could they have had the education or the leisure to practise their craft? — Tolstoy was alone, among great writers, in being born into the very highest social rank. On both his parents' sides he was not merely an aristocrat, he was a member of the old *seigneurial* class, the sort who did not just rule over local government, but who had a place at Court, and the ear of princes.

By the accident of his parents' poverty and early death, however, Tolstoy never exercised his rights as a grand courtier or a diplomat or a senior army officer. The only thing which his high aristocratic status conferred upon him was the sort of freedom which might have

5

been enjoyed by any writer born at the same time in, let us say, France or the United States.

To be a free man in a country where everyone else is in bondage conveys a strange unreality of status. Tolstoy never fully appreciated his luck. Nor, perhaps, did he ever realise how much he was cut off from the experience of other writers, let alone of the merchant class or of the enslaved peasantry. Yet it was in the company of peasants that he spent the greater part of his life. His sorties into the outside world were brief. He served as a soldier in the Crimean War. He made two short visits to Europe, seeing Italy, France, Germany and England. But, even within Russia, his experience of travel was limited. He came to hate the intellectuals of St. Petersburg as much as he despised the rich houses of Moscow. Until his late middle age, he had very few friends outside his own family circle, and most of his time was spent on his country estate, some one hundred and thirty miles from Moscow.

His isolation, and the privilege of his birth, partly explain why, in the second half of his career, Tolstoy managed to get away with being such a trenchant and violent opponent of the Government. At various points in the last two decades of his life, it seriously began to look as though Tolstoy's was the only voice which the Russian Government did not dare to muzzle. The socialist revolutionaries had very largely been locked up, or killed, or sent into exile. Many of the religious dissidents were breaking salt in the mines of Siberia, or silently cowering before the censor. Tolstoy, with a simplicity which seems almost childish, mysteriously got away with denouncing the cruelty of the army — indeed, the unlawfulness of war itself — the inequality of the social hierarchy, the squalor and oppression of the urban poor, the destitution of the starving, the criminality of the censor. He got censored. But, as will inevitably happen unless a government actually takes the step of killing a writer, his hand went on steadily moving across the page. Even though the solutions which he preached to the problems of the nineteenth century were ones which only a small proportion espoused — pacifism, vegetarianism, reading the Gospels and knitting your own clothes — he stood for something much bigger and more important than just himself or his ideas. So long as he was there, huge numbers of Russians felt that it was not quite impossible to believe in the prospect of individual liberty, the survival of individual dignity in the face of a cruel, faceless, bureaucratic tyranny. It was for this reason that, when he died, there were demonstrations all over Russia. Students rioted. Anarchists were rounded up by the police. Thousands of people followed his coffin to its place of burial. And, after the death of Tolstoy, Russia looked for more desperate solutions to its difficulties.

But the chief reason why the Government had left him alone is to be found in the reverence which the Russians feel for literary genius. With the reverence, there goes, on behalf of governments, suspicion and fear. The word has power in Russia, which is why its greatest exponents have nearly always ended up behind bars or dying in exile.

In Tolstoy, successive Tsars and their advisers recognised that they had a literary monument too large to dislodge. He had begun his career gently, with a few semi-autobiographical scenes from childhood, with short stories based on his experience in the army, and with sketches of the suffering at the siege of Sebastopol. His fellow writers, such as Turgenev and Dostoyevsky, Fet and Nekrasov, recognised that a great practitioner had arrived in their midst. But nothing was to prepare the world for his two greatest achievements, *War and Peace* and *Anna Karenina*. In the latter novel, he wrote one of the great love stories of the world. But, in *War and Peace*, there was something much grander. The novel in fact evolved out of Tolstoy's purely private preoccupations and fantasies with his own family. But its first episodes had no sooner appeared than his readers knew that he had done something much more. He had created a national epic to which all Russians could respond. In telling the story of Napoleon's invasion and retreat from Moscow, Tolstoy had become a national institution. It was a story to which every patriotic Russian could and does respond. In the accuracy of its portraiture, in all its emotional faithfulness, in its abundant vivacity, it is also one of the great works of literature of the world.

The life of this author is full of contradictions and puzzles. The paradoxes of Tolstoy are numberless. For instance, this most Russian of novelists was almost entirely influenced not by Russians but by English and French writers. His vision of Christianity owes much more to American Quakers and French rationalists than it does to Russian Orthodox spirituality. And yet he believed himself to be speaking, for much of the time, with the authentic voice of the Russian peasant. There have been many who have turned from Tolstoy's later work — his advocacy of political anarchism, for example, or his condemnation of Shakespeare — with something like hatred. Others, inspired by the Christian simplicity of his later writings, have been disillusioned to discover, upon reading about his life, that the great prophet of peace lived in an atmosphere of domestic hatred perhaps unrivalled in the history of matrimony.

And yet, for all these contradictions and paradoxes, the sheer stature of Tolstoy is never diminished. The Russian painter who has left us the largest number of portraits of Tolstoy was Ilya Repin. He has also left us various unforgettable prose portraits of the novelist, as well as those which he put on canvas. He spoke of Tolstoy's towering moral presence, and hypnotic spiritual aura. 'Often a day or two after a conversation with him when your own mind begins to function independently, you find that you cannot agree with his views, that some of his thoughts, which seemed at the time incontrovertible, now appear improbable. . . .' For all that, what remained for Repin was the sense of Tolstoy as a giant. Once, when riding with Tolstoy through the woods near his house, Repin saw him with a vision of particular clarity, 'like Raphael's God in the vision of Ezekiel, with forking beard and a kind of special grace and agility characteristic of a warrior or a Circassian, manoeuvring among the branches, now pushing aside the twigs with his hand'. What arrested the painter was not just the speed, but a vivacity which was almost divine. Some such awe is only fitting when approaching such a figure. If the portrait which follows is less flattering than a canvas by Repin, it is painted, nevertheless, with no small sense of the subject's grandeur.

Chapter One
Origins

1828 - 1841

Бывало, нами дорожили,
Бывало....

[There was a time when we were highly
esteemed; there was a time. . . .]
Pushkin, *My Genealogy*

'And on they went, singing "Eternal Memory". . . .' Tolstoy's story begins, like Doctor Zhivago's, with a woman's funeral. Only, when Tolstoy's mother died on August 4, 1830, he was too young to remember her. Born on August 28, 1828, he lost his mother when he was barely two. He could never remember her face, and no portrait of her survives. Both facts are of profound significance in the story of Tolstoy's inner life.[1]

His mother's name was Marya Nikolayevna Volkonskaya — that is, Mary, the daughter of Nicholas Volkonsky. She was born in 1790, the only child of an eccentric, choleric prince who, at the time of her birth, was eminent in the service of the Empress Catherine the Great. The Volkonskys were an ancient family, who traced their grand descent back to Prince Ryurik. They considered themselves grander than the Romanovs, and Prince Nikolay Sergeyevich had added the distinction of military achievement to that of a noble inheritance. He first rose to prominence in the Turkish campaign of 1780, and in 1793 a successful career in the army was rewarded with the gentler life of the diplomat. He was Russian Ambassador to Berlin in 1793. Prince Nikolay was an outspoken man, and nobody could call him sycophantic in relation to his royal patrons. When Catherine suggested to him that he should marry the 'niece' (and mistress) of her stern favourite Potemkin, Volkonsky had replied, 'What made him think I should marry his whore?' With the death of Catherine the Great in 1796, his career came to an end.

Catherine was succeeded by the mad Emperor, Paul, who dismissed Prince Volkonsky from the army for failing to appear at a review.

Conscious that all his Court were plotting against him, Paul had the classic paranoid tendency to develop particular hatreds for old friends and favourites, whether at court or in the field of foreign diplomacy. An example of Paul's military wisdom is his idea, in January 1801, that twenty thousand Cossacks should march from Orenburg to India in order to defeat the British there. A few months after Paul had proposed this scheme, he was strangled by a group of senior army officers and replaced by Alexander I. By then Prince Nikolay Volkonsky had already, for a number of years, been leading a life of retirement, like Yevgeny Onegin's uncle, quarrelling with the servants, gazing through the windowpanes and squashing flies.

Tolstoy's mother had lost her mother when she was two. When he left the army and retired to his country estate one hundred and thirty miles south of Moscow, Prince Volkonsky devoted himself to his young daughter's education. By then she was seven. A true follower of Catherine the Great, and a son of the Enlightenment, Prince Volkonsky, unlike his grandson, believed both in the education of women and in the superiority of European culture over Russian. They spoke to one another in French, the father and his child. He ensured that she knew German and Italian, and that she had a good grounding in music and history. They read Rousseau together, and works of the French Encyclopaedists. As befitted a former ambassador, who had been given the rank of General by the Emperor Paul before his dismissal, Prince Volkonsky was entitled to keep two armed sentinels. They stood guard, more like toy soldiers, or something in the fantasies of Tristram Shandy's Uncle Toby, at the towers which flanked the entrance to the estate of Yasnaya Polyana. (The name means 'Bright Glade'.) Life in the great house became more and more isolated from the world, and from the current of public events. In all observable aspects, Yasnaya Polyana remained in the eighteenth century throughout Prince Nikolay's days.

Yasnaya Polyana is a place of great beauty, as the modern tourist can discover. Indeed, as one of Tolstoy's kinsmen has observed in a recent book, 'not a little of the attraction of Yasnaya Polyana, at least for its Russian visitors, lies in the solitary physical evocation in the Soviet state of the old manorial way of life, preserved through the chance of Tolstoy's being not only a great writer, but also the inheritor of an aristocratic demesne'.

The modern visitor sees a low-lying range of white buildings not dissimilar from the colonial style of architecture to be encountered in

Carolina or Virginia. It is set in well-planted, gently undulating countryside. The village still survives, where Tolstoy's peasants struggled to maintain their existence. Even today, dressed up as a show-place for trippers, it feels remote and primitive, though it is not much more than a hundred miles from Moscow and close to the main road.

As a crow would measure, these shabby houses and hutments are less than a mile from their master's house, across fields which are still cultivated, and across the abundant orchards. Spiritually, the distance seems almost infinite between these humble abodes and the house, filled as it is with Tolstoy's extensive library, with a grand piano and portraits of ancestors painted in the western manner. Though by the standards of a European aristocratic house, Yasnaya Polyana is austere, it remains most distinctly the house of a European aristocrat. And yet we do not feel, as we might when visiting a castle on the Loire or the Rhine, that this is part of the landscape it inhabits. Even in the days when Russia was full of manorial estates and rich houses, they must have seemed like islands in an alien sea.

All around the Europeanised house (which is only a wing of the mansion inhabited by Tolstoy's grandfather Volkonsky) stretches the land which was to exercise so strong a hold on the novelist. Here are the abundant birchwoods which in spring and summer have a feathery, delicate green against which the house looks particularly splendid. In winter, everything seems white — the barks of the trees, the house itself, the snow-covered fields and paths, the frozen ponds and lakes. You feel something more than just the close physical proximity of nature in this place. More, there is this sense of displacement, of incompatibility between house and land, as though the pretensions and claims of civilised man would inevitably, in the face of nature, break down. Who could be said to *own* these trees, these pieces of ice, these fields? These were questions which were to haunt the young heir of Yasnaya Polyana, Lev Tolstoy.

For any reader of *War and Peace*, however, the place has an instantly recognisable quality as well. We feel as much at home as in any place which a writer has encapsulated in imaginative form. Just as it might be impossible to travel through certain bits of Civil War country without being reminded of Faulkner's *The Unvanquished*, so at Yasnaya Polyana we are instantaneously transported to the 'Bald Hills' of Tolstoy's greatest novel.

It was here, at Yasnaya Polyana, that Tolstoy's grandfather pursued the legendarily bad-tempered existence which Tolstoy was to myth-ologise in *War and Peace*. Tolstoy changed just one letter of his grandfather's name — a V to a B — when 'inventing' the figure of Prince Bolkonsky. In his early appearances in that novel there is something very grand about Prince Bolkonsky: 'Everyone sitting in the ante-chamber experienced the same feeling of respect and even terror when the enormously high study door opened and showed the figure of a rather small old man, with powdered wig, little withered hands, and bushy grey eyebrows which, when he frowned, sometimes hid the gleam of his clever, youthfully glittering eyes.'[2]

Much of the Bald Hills drama, in the initial stages of *War and Peace*, revolves around the Mr. Woodhouse-ish question of whether a selfish old man can spare his daughter's hand in matrimony. 'Life without Princess Marya, little as he seemed to value her, was unthinkable to him. "And why should she marry?" he thought. "To be unhappy for sure. . . ."'[3] All this has small enough importance in terms of the book's plot, but the personal significance for Tolstoy is obvious. In depicting her in his novel, he changed one letter in his mother's surname, and left her Christian name unaltered. What he was contemplating, in the grand military sweep of his epic, were huge questions such as the causes of war and peace, the rise and fall of empires, the past of Europe, the future of Russia. But, as he reconstructed Prince Bolkonsky's selfish reflection, Tolstoy was contemplating the (to him) no less important historical mystery of his own birth.

Tolstoy never saw his Volkonsky grandfather. The old man died in 1821, leaving his daughter a spinster — by now thirty-one years old and unmarried. Worried about the inheritance, she suggested, in a general sort of way, to the rest of the family that she might marry a cousin, Prince Mikhail Alexandrovich Volkonsky. Nothing came of this idea. Prince Mikhail got married to someone else in Moscow that April, and Princess Marya attended the ceremony. There she met a less eligible bachelor, Prince Nikolay Ilyich Tolstoy, five years her junior, and the two families immediately entered into discussions with their lawyers. A marriage was arranged and shortly took place. If Princess Marya intended to have heirs, there was some element of hurry. They were married on July 9, 1822. Her dowry was eight hundred male 'souls', serfs in the Tula and Oryol districts, and the estate of Yasnaya Polyana.

Count Nikolay Ilyich Tolstoy was an ex-army officer. His father was the governor of Kazan, a town four hundred miles to the east of Moscow, and the old man's financial affairs were so chaotic that Nikolay had felt obliged to leave the army, lest at any point he might be shamed into admitting that he was too poor to buy himself further promotion. (He was a lieutenant-colonel when he resigned his commission.) Marriage to a rich woman was the obvious answer to his difficulties and, since the Tolstoys were also an ancient and highly esteemed Russian family,[4] the Volkonskys agreed to the match.

The Tolstoys had five children, Nikolay, Sergey, Dmitry, Lev and lastly a daughter, Marya, who was born in March 1830. Princess Marya never really recovered from this confinement, and died five months later.

Tolstoy died seven years before the revolution of the proletariat; he was born three years *after* the revolution of the nobility. It is almost as if he was cocooned between the two revolutions, that of December 1825 and that of October 1917. There had been assassinations and palace revolutions in plenty throughout the history of the Romanov royal house, but the uprising on December 14, 1825 was different in kind. It has been called 'the first truly political movement ever to be directed against the established system' in Russia.[5] It was a political movement with wide adherence, and a history dating back a decade. The first formal structure taken by the would-be reformers was the foundation in 1816 of the Union of Salvation or Society of True and Faithful Sons of the Fatherland. This was a group of Guards officers, inspired by the ideas and events of the previous thirty years in Europe, who dreamed of converting the absolutist autocracy of the Russian Emperor into an enlightened constitutional monarchy, advised by assemblies. The dreamers, or conspirators, were wildly different in their views and aims, which was one reason for their failure. Some looked to England as an ideal model, to a country really governed by an aristocratic oligarchy, but retaining the ancient forms of monarchy and religion. Others looked to France, its Revolution, its commitment to a republic. Some were Freemasons, or dabblers in the new and cranky creeds which from time to time caught the imagination of the St. Petersburg salons. Some of the conspirators wanted to emancipate the serfs, though they were not all agreed on what terms. But their movement seems by the standards of later revolutionary movements amateurish and dilettante. Their plots were, as Pushkin said, hatched between claret and champagne to the accompaniment of satirical songs and friendly arguments.

Their opportunity for action was given to them upon the death of Alexander I in Taganrog on November 19, 1825. The questions arose: should he be succeeded by the second Imperial brother, Constantine, at that moment in Warsaw, or by the third, the Grand Duke Nicholas? Alexander I had, in 1822, declared Nicholas (who had a son, and who was loyal to Orthodoxy) to be his heir rather than Constantine. This was because Constantine, after a long exile, was imagined by friends and enemies alike to have a number of 'liberal' views that in all probability he never possessed. The Northern and Southern Societies of conspirators, whose activities were of course known to the Imperial police, declared themselves in favour of Constantine's succession, but they had less than a month in which to popularise their point of view in the ranks of the army. The military was the chief source of their strength; not only were the majority of them officers, but the Grand Duke Nicholas was in any case unpopular with the army. On December 14, the Grand Duke was declared Tsar Nicholas I, and the army reviewed on the Senate Square in St. Petersburg. The day was a war of nerves between the new Emperor and his army. It seemed as though some three thousand troops had come out in favour of revolution, leaving about nine thousand loyal to the new regime. There were exciting moments, as when old Alexander Yakubovich, a veteran of the Caucasus, paraded in front of the mutinying troops and cried, 'Constantine and a Constitution!'; but, when the orders were given for the Moscow regiment to load, the old hero developed a violent headache and was nowhere to be found. The Governor-General of St. Petersburg was sent out to reason with the mutineers and was shot dead. Then followed the Metropolitan Serafim, splendid in cope and the crown-like mitre of the Eastern Church. The rebels told him to go back into the cathedral and pray for their souls. Finally, the Grand Duke Michael tried to plead with them, and they told him to return to the Winter Palace since he was endangering his life. But, by the end of the day, Nicholas I's patience had run out. He ordered his troops to fire on the rebels, and they fled without putting up any resistance. For the next thirty years, the Russian Empire was to be dominated by this huge and ferocious despot, who devoted himself to a confident and calculated policy of reaction against the faintly liberalising trends of Alexander I.

As for the Decembrists,[6] as the conspirators of December 1825 came to be called, they were rounded up. About six hundred were questioned, a hundred and twenty-one were put on trial: five were condemned to death, thirty-one were exiled to Siberia for life, and eighty-five for a shorter term. Of the Siberian exiles, few were more romantically attractive than Tolstoy's second cousin, Major-General Prince Sergey Grigoryevich Volkonsky,[7] who was stripped of lands, titles and estates before being dragged in chains in front of the Tsar, who shouted at him, 'You are a fool, Major-General Prince Volkonsky! You should be ashamed of yourself!' But his young wife did not think so. Abandoning their little son, she followed her husband into exile, and stayed with him for the next thirty years before spoiling things and running off with another man. She had been originally wooed by Pushkin, who wrote a poem about her heroic exile:

> Во глубине сибирских руд
> Храните гордое терпенье,
> Не пропадет ваш скорбный труд
> И дум высокое стремленье...

> [In the depths of the Siberian mines
> Maintain your proud patience,
> Your sorrowful labour will not be wasted,
> Nor your high aspiration of mind. . . .][8]

When Nicholas I died in 1855, there was every reason for Russian dissidents and malcontents to rejoice. But Volkonsky, hearing the news in Siberia, *wept*. He wept because his Emperor was dead, and he wept for Russia, because thirty years of exile (a shorter spell was to teach similar lessons to Dostoyevsky) had made him wonder what alternatives there were to the repressive and reactionary form of government which, as a young man, he had so vigorously opposed. He wrote:

And when will our national consciousness be rid of this fatal confusion between power and national welfare, that has brought so much falsehood into every sphere of national life, falsehood which has coloured our politics, our religious and social thought, our education? Falsehood has been the principal ailment of Russian politics, along with its usual companions, hypocrisy and cynicism. They run through our whole history. Yet surely life's goal must not be just to exist, but to exist with *dignity*. And if we want to be frank with ourselves, then we must admit that if Russia cannot exist

17

otherwise than she did in the past, then she does not *deserve* to survive. And as of now, we have had no proof that the country can be run along different lines.[9]

This Prince Volkonsky was a kinsman of Tolstoy's mother, Princess Marya Nikolayevna Volkonskaya. After the amnesty granted by Alexander II, Tolstoy was able to meet him — though in Italy, not Russia. Throughout the first half of his life Tolstoy had a preoccupation with the Decembrist Rising which bordered on obsession. He was acutely aware that he had been born too late for it; acutely aware, also, that had it succeeded the whole of Russian history would have been different. For Tolstoy, always, the destiny of Russia and the destiny of his own family were inseparable, and both are not merely 'ingredients' of his art. They are its primary force, motivation, inspiration. Gorky was right to stress that Tolstoy is a 'whole world', his bigness stemming partly from the fact that his family had been helping to shape the national destiny since the time of Prince Ryurik, and partly stemming from his own enforced remoteness from his immediate ancestors. For him, the process of discovering who he was, and who they were, and what Russia was, were all intimately linked. The 'world' which is Tolstoy is, as Gorky said, intensely national, intensely Russian, and yet — to Lenin's infuriation — supremely individualistic. Too late for one revolution and too soon for the next, his existence is both one of detachment from the fabric of his national history, and a challenge to the society which, all around him, pursued a course so much at variance with the direction which he wanted to take. 'I could hardly imagine Russia, or my relationship with her, without my Yasnaya Polyana.' Viewed in some lights, Tolstoy seems like the archetypal Romantic egotist, the ardent reader of Rousseau, whose mind was sufficiently big to enable him to sit out the nineteenth century, unaffected by its changes and chances. In another aspect, however, Tolstoy seems more caught up in the movements of history than any other imaginative artist. The involvement and the detachment were, like everything about him, in a perpetual state of contradiction and struggle.

*   *   *   *

Tolstoy was to grow up and become a great novelist, that is to say a great liar. Novels are works of art which arrive at truth by telling untruths. Novelists are frequently men and women who have been compelled, by some inner disaster, to rewrite the past, to refashion their memories to make their existence more interesting or more explicable to themselves. This self-mythologising process had begun in Tolstoy before conscious memory, which is why we can only guess at the truth of what he tells us about his childhood. The novella which he entitled *Childhood*, and which some biographers have taken to be an almost photographic record of how the infant Tolstoy passed his days, was, by his own confession, a complete fabrication.

Nevertheless, there is an obvious interest in Tolstoy's own recollections, spoken or written. One of the things which makes him such a memorable writer is his extra-consciousness, or super-consciousness, of existence itself. Although there was nothing, absolutely nothing, in his first twenty years of life to suggest that he would become a great genius in any sphere, the clue to what makes him special resides in this preternatural ability to be aware. We all know that there is such a thing as life, that we are alive, that the world is there, full of sights and sounds. But, when we read Tolstoy for the first time, it is as if, until that moment, we had been looking at the world through a dusty window. He flings open the shutters, and we see everything sharp and clear for the first time. This super-awareness came to him, he informs us, when he was still a baby.

I lie bound and wish to stretch out my arms, but cannot. I scream and cry and my screams are disagreeable to myself, but I cannot stop. . . .[10]

These recollections purport to relate to a time when Tolstoy was a baby in swaddling clothes, still being fed at the breast. The wonder is that he did not remember the exact texture of his wet-nurse's nipples, and the mixture of sensual greed and spiritual revulsion which, as a six-month-old boy, they awoke in him. St. Augustine, whose egotistic journey offers so many parallels to Tolstoy's own, comes close to having such a 'memory', or at least to wishing that he had had it.

The next impression, remembers Tolstoy, is a pleasant one.

I am sitting in a tub and am surrounded by a new and not unpleasant smell of something with which they are rubbing my tiny body. . . .[11]

The 'tiny' is the giveaway. His novel *Childhood* is full of such details, as when, in the opening scene, the narrator draws stockings on to his 'tiny feet'. As children, we are not aware of having tiny bodies. Only a child who had become an artifact, a memory in an older mind, could be aware of having a tiny body as he sat in his tub.

> Probably it was the bran put into my bathwater; the novelty of the sensation caused by the bran aroused me, and for the first time I became aware of, and liked, my own little body with the visible ribs on my breast, and the smooth, dark, wooden tub, the bared arms of the nurse, the warm, steaming, swirling water, the noise it made, and especially the smooth feel of the wet rim of the tub as I passed my hands along it.[12]

Some people have such perfect pitch that almost all music is intolerable to them; others have a heightened colour sense, or a peculiarly sensitive sense of smell. This or that person, notoriously, has a different level of erotic awareness. In Tolstoy, *consciousness itself* was overdeveloped. In a non-Wordsworthian sense, the world was 'too much with him'.

The other great quality which all readers notice in Tolstoy is his moral directness and simplicity. This, too, he believed, stretched back to the time of his childhood. When he was five years old, he was called by his elder brother Nikolay to join the other children. Nikolay, who was aged ten at this stage, was always the leader in their games, their entertainer and their mentor. He would tell them ghost stories and fairy tales. But, on this particular occasion, he had something rather more important to divulge to the five-year-old Lev, and to Sergey, Dmitry and Marya. Nikolay had discovered the secret by which all men would become happy. There would be no more disease, no trouble, no anger. Everyone would love one another, and they would be called the Ant Brothers. In Russian the word for 'ant' is *muravey*; almost certainly, Nikolay had heard of the Christian denomination (who, incidentally, had such an effect on John Wesley) known as the Moravian Brotherhood. He had also, no doubt, vaguely heard of Freemasons, and their aspirations to unite mankind with some form of universal wisdom. Hence the Ant Brotherhood.

As Lev Tolstoy grew older, the game of the Ant Brotherhood exercised a powerful hold over his imagination. Not until much later in life, when he had become a figurehead of dissent and a religious guru, were Tolstoy's friendships ever ideological. The family, not the like-minded *kruzhok* (little circle), supported him. Intellectually and emotionally, there was always the mythology of the Ant Brotherhood behind him.

> The Ant Brotherhood was revealed to us, but not the chief secret — the way for all men to cease suffering from any misfortune, to leave off quarrelling and being angry, and become continuously happy — this secret he said he had written on a green stick buried by the road at the edge of a certain ravine, at which spot (since my body must be buried somewhere) I have asked to be buried in memory of Nikolenka.[13]

Yasnaya Polyana, where this stick is buried, was potent with legends in Tolstoy's own personal mythology, and with unremembered national and family 'memories' on which he was brought up. If the great *political* legend in nineteenth-century Russian history was the Decembrist Rising of 1825, then the great national event was the invasion of Russia by Napoleon in 1812: an event exactly parallel in nineteenth-century Russian imaginations to the invasion by Hitler in 1941 in the imaginations of twentieth-century Russians. In both cases, there are the same ingredient elements of shock, fury, awe, and national pride. But, in the Napoleonic case, there was no memory to compare with it. To the outsider, looking at a map of the Russian Empire in the time of Alexander I, or the Soviet Union in the era of Stalin (diminished as that had been by the humiliating terms agreed by Trotsky at Brest-Litovsk), the perennial Russian fear of invasion strikes a note which is difficult to comprehend. The country is so vast, the distances covered by any invader would have to be so enormous, that only a madman or a genius would contemplate a military operation of such audacity. Yet twice such madmen have arisen, bringing with them at each date scenes of carnage unparalleled in Russian history. Borodino, the battle which immediately preceded the French occupation of Moscow in September 1812, inaugurated new horrors in the history of warfare. Napoleon called it the most terrible of all his battles. The casualties were greater than at any battle before in the history of the world: thirty thousand French and forty thousand Russians in a single day. Tens of thousands more French were to die in the winter retreat which followed, the whole campaign emphasising with hideous and inescapable force the sheer futility of the pursuit of power, and the hollowness of military glory.

21

Of the war, Princess Marya thought as women do think about war. She was afraid for her brother, who was there, and without understanding it, she was amazed in the face of human cruelty, impelling people to kill one another. But she did not understand the significance of this war, which seemed to her like all previous wars. . . .[14]

These are the reflections of Princess Marya Bolkonsky in *War and Peace* as she hears the rumours of the Napoleonic invasion in her father's estate.

Prince Andrey, a few chapters later, on the road from Smolensk, turns off to inspect the place, and finds it already in a state of dilapidation. His mother and sisters have fled to Moscow, the peasants are in a state of despondency and financial ruin, three regiments of Russian dragoons have already billeted themselves there. On route marches, the ornamental gardens have been spoilt, some of the windowpanes have been smashed, already there is grass growing on the paths. There are few more vivid moments, before Borodino, of the emotional impact of Napoleon's war.

Yasnaya Polyana, and the whole of Russia, after Napoleon's invasion, were to live again, a deliverance on which Tolstoy was to meditate. So much is going on inside a novelist's subconscious when he creates his characters that no simple identification of people in the books and people in 'real life' will ever make complete sense. Nevertheless, it seems to be beyond question that in the figure of old Prince Bolkonsky, Tolstoy was thinking of his Volkonsky grandfather; that the young Prince Andrey Volkonsky contains a good bit of Tolstoy's father, and Prince Andrey's virtuous sister Marya Bolkonsky is Tolstoy's mother Marya Volkonsky. In so far as there is truth in these simple identifications, they are full of psychological importance. By making his parents into a brother and sister, Tolstoy, with classic Oedipal jealousy, has removed his mother from his father's bed. But one could not take any of this very far without realising the central fallacy of the approach. It would be impossible, with any hope of historical plausibility, to use *War and Peace* as an accurate picture of what Tolstoy's parents or grandfather were like. We have only the 'fictional' descriptions of life at Bald Hills to study: almost no authentic documentation for life at Yasnaya Polyana at the time of 1812. We will never know how much is embellishment, and how much the truth. *War and Peace* is not only a great historical novel. It is also a monument to his obsession with his own personal history. Readers of the novel who turn back to Tolstoy's early life feel in a thousand ways that they have *been there before*.

*   *   *   *

Left a widower at the age of thirty-five, Tolstoy's father had tried to manage efficiently the estates which he had inherited from his wife. There was little enough Tolstoy money. Since the old governor of Kazan had died in 1820, Nikolay Ilyich had struggled with inherited debts and a host of extravagant female dependants.

His occupations were farming and lawsuits, chiefly the latter. These lawsuits frequently obliged him to leave home, and besides that, he used often to go hunting and shooting. Beyond this, Count Nikolay Ilyich was a literate man, with a well-stocked library, but the times when he was at home with his children were few.

'I remember him in his study, when we went to say "good night", or sometimes simply to play, where he sat on the leather divan, smoking a pipe, and caressed us, and sometimes to our great joy let us climb on to the back of the divan while he either continued to read, or talked to the clerks standing at the door, or to my godfather who often stayed with us.'[15] Tolstoy's recollections of his father are full of admiration and affection. He recalls his handsomeness, his frock coat and narrow trousers or, in the country, his exuberance on the hunting field. But like all aristocratic children of the period, they saw very little of their father. It would seem that they felt a certain closeness towards their Tolstoy grandmother, a silly, affectionate spendthrift, very decidedly of the *ancien régime*. One of Tolstoy's earliest memories was of her sitting in a yellow cabriolet underneath a clump of hazel bushes. The footmen were lowering branches to her so that she could pluck nuts without getting out of her seat.

In 1837, the children lost their father. He had gone into Tula to see about one of his lawsuits, and dropped dead in the street. He was forty-two years old. Some of the family immediately suspected his servants of having murdered him. Others thought that he had had an epileptic fit. Both of these speculations, however interesting, are groundless. Dostoyevsky's father actually *was* murdered and the event was a turning point in his life. But the nine-year-old Tolstoy did not have fits when he heard of his father's death. The event passed in a dazed blur of grief, followed the next year by the death of his old Tolstoy grandmother.

The children were now put under the guardianship of an aunt, the late count's sister, the Countess Alexandra Ilyinichna Osten-Saken, a woman who could easily have stepped out of Dostoyevsky's pages. Her husband had been a mad Baltic count who had tried to cut out her tongue, and on another occasion had shot her. She found consolation in a pious exercise of the Orthodox religion. She was never happier than when reading the lives of the saints or, when she could not read about them, going to meet them. When in the country on her late sister-in-law's estates at Yasnaya Polyana, she frequently entertained the strange, half-crazed, wandering pilgrims who traipsed the mud roads that connected town with town in those pre-railway days. 'From time immemorial, such wanderers have existed in Russia, nomads, homeless and hearthless, possessing no earthly ties, following no trade, driven onwards by some nameless thought. Leading the life of gypsies, and yet not of the gypsy class, they roamed over the vast territories of Russia, from village to village, from country to country. . . . Nobody knew the meaning of their pilgrimages. I am convinced that had any of them been asked whither he was going and why, not one could have answered. . . . Perhaps they were escaping nothing more tangible than *toska*, that nostalgia only Russians experience, utterly indescribable, utterly incomprehensible, and often without motive.'[16]

Tolstoy was not unique in being fascinated by these curious figures, but perhaps, because of his aunt's spiritual predilections, he was exposed to rather more contact with them than were other boys of his class. Grisha, the *yurodivy* (holy idiot) whom he described in *Childhood*, was one such: filthy, wild-eyed, misshapen and incoherent. Grisha was in fact a made-up character, a composite of many different tramps who must have arrived at Yasnaya Polyana during Tolstoy's childhood. In old age, he recalled that he had been less impressed by any of the professional holy fools than by an actual idiot, a gardener's boy, whom he overheard praying in a hot-house adjoining the drawing room, 'and who really amazed me by his prayer, in which he spoke to God as if he were a living person. "You are my doctor, you are my apothecary," he said with impressive conviction.'[17]

We can be sure that his aunt Alexandra (who was so holy that she did not wash, and gave off 'a specific acid smell') imparted her piety to the children. His favourite Bible story was that of Joseph and his brethren, the story of a younger son being cast out by his brothers and sold into a strange land, and then, when he is reunited with them in grown-up life, being able to lord it over them and being able to reward

24

them with grain and gold and treasures. The appeal to the young orphan of this tale is obvious; likewise, the appeal of a story in which a 'dreamer' and an idler manages to make a worldly success out of his inner life. Every novelist who has enjoyed great popularity and success must have tasted the rewards of Pharaoh's house.

Not that the Bible could have as great a role in the upbringing of an Orthodox child as it did in that of a western Protestant. It was only in 1818, ten years before Tolstoy's birth, that there existed a New Testament in modern Russian as opposed to Old Church Slavonic. An English child of the period, for its religious instruction, would have very little besides the Bible, the Catechism and perhaps (in the stricter households) Fox's *Book of Martyrs*. But a little Russian boy could feast his imagination on twinkling lamps, dark icons, and muttered prayers at home; in church, on the great sense of everyone praying together, rich and poor alike, standing in the body of the church, lighting tapers, bowing, crossing themselves, and joining in the chanting of the voluntary choir. In an Orthodox liturgy, unlike anything seen in the West, we witness the whole people of God doing their liturgy together, the doll-like priest, a bearded figure stiff in vestments, doing his stuff behind the screen, and only appearing from time to time, to bless, to exhort or to distribute the Sacrament. In all this, there is not much exercise of the intellect. There are no analytical sermons, as there might have been in Scotland or Switzerland or France. Probably the priest is barely literate. It was not a Church which had produced as many great scholars as the Churches of the West, and its attitude to knowledge was, by the standards of Western Europe, obscurantist and superstitious. But it had produced saints.

Tolstoy's aunt Alexandra cannot have failed to tell him the stories of the saints and heroes of the Russian Church. She would have told him of how the Russian people had been converted to Christianity by Prince Vladimir of Kiev (who died in 1015) inviting the missionaries from Constantinople. Before his conversion, Vladimir was a lecher, a drunkard, and a soldier. After his baptism, he abandoned his habits of feasting and rich living, and lived among the poor, opening his gates to invalids and beggars. He who had previously shed blood so freely in battle became convinced that it was wicked to take human life. Throughout his great dominions, he abolished the death penalty for criminals, and when the Greek bishops told him that he was wrong to do so, he remained convinced that torture and capital punishment had no place in a Christian kingdom.

Nor can she have failed to tell her nephews about the sons of Prince Vladimir, Boris and Gleb, the first two canonised saints of the Russian Church. When Vladimir died, his eldest son, Svyatopolk, tried to get rid of his other brothers and become the sole ruler of Russia. First he attacked Prince Boris, his younger brother, who was leading a detachment of his father's troops. But Boris believed the words of Our Lord that it is wrong to resist violence with violence, and he allowed himself to be butchered by Svyatopolk. By his action (for Svyatopolk wanted only his death) Boris spared the lives of all his troops. A few days later another brother, Gleb, followed Boris's example. 'The story of Boris and Gleb shows that the seeds of the Christian religion fell on fertile soil in Russia, and that the nation accepted wholeheartedly the new teaching. It also reveals that Christianity was understood by Russian people neither as a system of doctrines, nor as an institution, but primarily as a way of life.'[18]

These stories sank into Tolstoy's consciousness as a child, but they can hardly have been more vivid to him than the fact of death. When he was nine and his father died, Tolstoy tells us, he found it impossible to believe that Count Nikolay Ilyich no longer existed. When walking the streets of Moscow he stared at every stranger that he passed, hoping that it would be his father — a detail which he later used when little Seryozha was missing his mother Anna Karenina. His father's non-existence was imaginatively unabsorbable; not so God's. When, at about this time, a schoolfriend of his brother's told them that he had made a great discovery, they all gathered round to hear. This child, Volodenka Milyutin, was a sage twelve year old studying at the *Gymnasium* near the Tolstoy house in Moscow. In the course of his studies, the secret had been revealed to him, that *God does not exist*. Everything, moreover, that grown-ups taught about Him was a mere fiction. The Tolstoy brothers debated the matter, and decided that, on balance, what Milyutin had told them was true. The non-existence of God does not seem to have disconcerted them particularly. Perhaps if Aunt Alexandra had lived longer, she might have influenced the children to be more conventionally pious. Perhaps not. A figure who was much closer to all the children, and in particular to Tolstoy himself, was a distant kinswoman, Tatyana Alexandrovna Yergolskaya.

In his earliest memory of her, she was already over forty. 'She must have been very attractive, with her enormous plait of crisp, black, curly hair, her jet-black eyes and vivacious, energetic expression. . . .' he wrote. Then he drew back. 'I never thought about whether she was beautiful or not.' The hero of *Resurrection*, Nekhlyudov, looks at a portrait of his mother in the room where she died. He is sickened by the particular care with which the painter has depicted the outline of her breasts, and the cleavage between them showing over the low-cut gown. There was something revolting and blasphemous to him about contemplating his mother as a half-nude painter's beauty. 'It was the more disgusting that, in this very room three months since, this woman had lain, dried up like a mummy, and at the same time filling, with an excruciatingly oppressive smell which nothing would stifle, not just the room, but the whole house.'[19] Even 'innocent' images of maternity in Tolstoy are complicated by feelings of sex and death. Cultures more highly-charged than our own need to be tasted for Tolstoy's youthful psyche to come into focus. (Was it St. Aloysius who was so holy that he would not remain in the same room alone with his mother lest she inflamed him with lust?) Incestuous feelings for the mother he never had were to torment Tolstoy throughout his life.

Meanwhile, Tatyana Alexandrovna Yergolskaya, the beloved Tante Toinette, provided a mother-substitute. 'Probably she loved my father and he loved her, but she did not marry him when they were young, because she thought he had better marry my wealthy mother, and she did not marry him subsequently because she did not wish to spoil her pure poetic relations with him and with us.'[20]

Family legends harden and ossify. We shall never really know, any more than Tolstoy really knew, what was going on in his father's heart at the time of his mother's death. We can be fairly certain that whatever prevented Count Nikolay and Tante Toinette from marrying, it was not the peculiarly Tolstoyan notion that her relations with the children would have been more 'pure' and 'poetic' had she not shared their father's bed. We do not even know that she did not. For Tolstoy, it was important to establish his 'little aunt's' purity. Her kisses and caresses were reserved for him. It was from her, and perhaps only from her, that he had any displays of physical affection when he was a young child. It was from her that he learnt 'the spiritual delight of love'. Moreover, as we have already said, she taught him 'the charm of an unhurried, tranquil life'.

It is a lesson which any child in that peculiar household would have done well to absorb. But their chances of imbibing it were to be severely cut short. Tatyana was with them all at Yasnaya Polyana in the summer of 1841 while Aunt Alexandra made one of her frequent visits to the celebrated Kaluga hermitage, an offshoot of the Optina Pustyn monastery which Dostoyevsky was to make famous in *The Brothers Karamazov*. In August, there came the news that Aunt Alexandra had died there. Tatyana set out for the monastery to arrange the funeral, and the younger children stayed behind in the country with servants and tutors, occupying themselves by building a throne for their dog. (It fell from this contraption and injured its paw.)

None of them understood at once what the significance of Aunt Alexandra's death was to be. It was the fourth major death in Tolstoy's first thirteen years of life, and in terms of his destiny over the next six years, it was the most crucial. The losses of his parents and his grandmother were incalculable. But the loss of his mildly mad aunt Alexandra actually displaced him, his brothers and his sister. It uprooted them from the familiar scenes of Yasnaya Polyana and Moscow, and it wrenched them away from the one person for whom they all felt the warmest affection. For their 'aunt' Tatyana was in fact only a very distant relative, and she had no legal right over the children. Their guardianship passed naturally to their father's only surviving sister, the Countess Pelageya Ilyinichna Yushkova.

Tolstoy's eldest brother, Nikolay Nikolayevich, was by now eighteen and acutely aware of the family's shortage of cash until they attained their majority. He begged their aunt Pelageya (whom none of them really knew) to do what was possible. What the children did not realise was that there were 'emotional undercurrents'. Years before, Colonel Yushkov, Aunt Pelageya's incurably womanising husband, had taken a shine to Tatyana Alexandrovna Yergolskaya. He had even, in his bachelor days, proposed to her. For the boy Tolstoy, Aunt Toinette's love was pure and delightful. His aunt Pelageya had keener, jealous memories of the 'enormous plait of crisp black curly hair', and the jet-black flirtatious eyes, which had beguiled both her brother and her husband. It was not something which, even twenty years later, she felt able to live with. The children could come and live with the Yushkovs in Kazan, but Tatyana Alexandrovna (though now of an age when she was unlikely to excite the Colonel into an indiscretion) was to be left behind.

'It is a cruel and barbaric thing to separate me from the children for whom I have cared so tenderly for nearly twelve years,' she confided in a correspondent.

Countess Pelageya Ilyinichna was no Miss Murdstone, but the whole thing has the relentless poignancy of a Victorian novel. She and her bluff, jolly husband believed that they were doing the best for the Tolstoy children, as indeed they were. That was just the trouble. The best — at that particular moment — was not what they needed or wanted. The ramshackle and rather crazy grandeur of life under the tutelage of Aunt Alexandra was to be replaced by the moneyed 'comfort' of life with her worldly sister. Mud tracks in the country or the pavements of Moscow: now the provincial streets of Kazan. They were leaving behind the lice-infested pilgrims and the religious maniacs with whom one aunt surrounded herself, to encounter another aunt's powdered flunkeys and socialite nobodies who, because they were in Kazan, were somebodies. *The Way of the Pilgrim* was sealed off, and *Vanity Fair* was built in its stead.

Chapter Two

Joseph and his Brethren

1841 - 1847

Me voilà en Asie!

Catherine the Great

*T*olstoy lived in Kazan from 1841 to 1847.[1] Though there were visits to various family estates during this period, his teens were a kind of exile. Opinions of the place have varied. Catherine the Great, staying there in 1767, had written to Voltaire, '*Me voilà en Asie*.'[2] Sergey Aksakov, whose unforgettable schooldays were spent in Kazan, remembered during the winter months, how the 'ice on the great lake Kaban was the scene of famous encounters with fists between Tartars and Russians. They lived on opposite sides of the lake.'[3] Alexander Herzen recalled 'the veiled faces of the Tartar women, the high cheekbones of their husbands, the mosques of true believers standing side by side with the churches of the Orthodox faith — it all reminds one of the East. At Vladimir or Nizhny the neighbourhood of Moscow is felt; but one feels far from Moscow at Kazan.'[4] The most entertaining of English travellers in Russia, Sir D. Mackenzie-Wallace, however, having told us that Kazan was once the capital of an independent Tartar *khanatel*, later in the century warns that 'the town as a whole has a European rather than an Asiatic character. If anyone visits it in the hope of getting a "glimpse of the East", he will be grievously disappointed.'[5]

Tolstoy's paternal grandfather had been the governor of Kazan. Because of its position on the Volga, and its being on the borderlands between European and Asiatic Russia, the two had a certain importance, but it was far from being large, and as Mackenzie-Wallace would remind us, it only seems interesting by comparison with other provincial towns on the Volga.

At the time of Tolstoy's residence there, its population was not more than thirty thousand. It was a lively little place, and the aunt and uncle were at the centre of things. If your happiness derived from dinners, card games, masquerades and *tableaux-vivants*, then the Yushkovs' was a merry enough household in which to grow up. And, much of the time, Tolstoy did revel in these things. But his adolescence was rendered an agony by shyness, and by the sense that his thick nose and springy hair made him hideously unattractive to girls. There were hours of silent agony in front of the looking-glass, and equally ghastly spells of lust, which tormented him almost from the moment he arrived in Kazan. There was a maid in his aunt's house called Masha who first aroused him; he was too shy to do anything about it, and shortly after that his brother Sergey introduced him to brothels.

The brothers Tolstoy, and their sister Marya, remained very much a family, but already the Brotherhood was in evolution and dissolution. Nikolay passed through Kazan University and joined the army. The other two brothers provided Lev Nikolayevich with contrasting influences. Sergey was a worldling. With him you could drink and dance and talk about sex. Dmitry, the one closest in age to Lev, was at this stage a very different sort of youth. Lev, only about a year his junior, envied Dmitry's 'large, dark, serious eyes', and his ability not only to make girls laugh, but also to impress them with the belief that he was deeply serious. In extreme old age, Tolstoy remembered Dmitry as a Dostoyevskian innocent during the Kazan phase. While Sergey and Nikolay were dissolute and worldly, Dmitry 'never suffered from the usual vices of youth. He was always serious, thoughtful, pure and resolute, though hot-tempered.' Like the eldest, Nikolay, Dmitry was quite indifferent to how he was regarded by the rest of the world; he cared nothing for dress, rank, or personal appearance: all the things which really obsessed the adolescent Lev.

At this stage, the Tolstoys had an extraordinary poor relation called Lyubov Sergeyevna. 'When I knew her, she was not only pitiable but hideous. I do not know what her illness was, but her face was swollen as if it had been stung by bees. Her eyes were just narrow slits between swollen shiny cushions without eyebrows. Similarly swollen, shiny and yellow were her cheeks, nose, lips and mouth. She spoke with difficulty (having probably a similar swelling in her mouth). In summer, flies used to settle on her face and she did not feel them, which was particularly unpleasant to witness. Her hair was still black but scanty and did not hide her scalp. A bad smell always came from her, and in her little room, the windows of which were never opened, the odour was stifling. And this Lyubov Sergeyevna became Dmitry's friend. He began to go and listen to her, talk to her and read to her. And we were morally so dense that we only laughed at it, while Dmitry was morally so superior, so free from caring about people's opinion, that he never by word or hint showed that he considered that what he was doing was good. He simply did it. And it was not a momentary impulse but continued all the time we lived in Kazan.'[6]

As befitted a Dostoyevskian innocent, Dmitry was profoundly pious, though his piety differed from that of their aunt Pelageya. She (who ended her days as a nun when the Colonel was dead) had particular interest in the stuffs and golden cloths with which the priests were vested, and she was a generous benefactor of churches. Dmitry was fired with the romance of Christ's poor. His peculiarity first showed itself during his first fast in preparation for Holy Communion. He prepared not at the fashionable University church, but at the prison church. At this church, there was a very pious, strict priest who used during Holy Week to read through the whole of the Gospels — something which is prescribed but seldom done in the Orthodox liturgy. Dmitry used to stand throughout these recitations.

The church was built so that the prisoners were separated from the rest of the congregation by a glass partition with a door in it. Once, when one of the prisoners wanted to pass something to one of the deacons — either some money or a taper to be lit — nobody would do it for him; but Dmitry 'with his serious face' stepped forward and handed it over.

The image of this prison church was to haunt Tolstoy forever. It was to inspire his most powerful and tasteless attack on the Orthodox faith, written forty years after Dmitry had died. But for a short time, when he was about sixteen, Tolstoy was inspired by Dmitry to feelings of piety. He confessed his sins, he went to Holy Communion, he wallowed in the rich liturgical atmosphere of the Kazan churches. In addition to the prison church, there were many splendid fanes where the young believer could worship, above all the Cathedral with its three renowned and wonder-working icons of Saints Yury (i.e. George), Varsonofy and Herman. Yet, in spite of the fact that religion was in his bones and blood, his mind was never really very happy with it for long. He tells us that once, on the day of a university exam, he walked near the Black Lake and prayed to God to let him pass the exam. But, nevertheless, while learning the Catechism, 'I saw clearly that the whole Catechism was false.'

It was almost exactly at this date that he began to read Jean-Jacques Rousseau,[7] a writer who — if this title belongs to anyone — was the greatest single influence on the development of Tolstoy's thought. He used to say later that, as a young teenager, he so idolised Rousseau that he wished he could have worn his portrait round his neck in a locket, like a holy icon.[8] In other conversations, he would imply that this actually had been his practice. If so, neither the locket, nor anyone else's memory of it, survives. Also, as an old man, he liked to say that he had read the whole of Rousseau many times, even his *Dictionary of Music.* But it is hard to establish how much of the Genevan *philosophe* Tolstoy had managed to get hold of in Kazan.

Family legend had it that his mother's favourite reading was *Emile,* which would have made it into a sacred text so far as Tolstoy was concerned, regardless of content. Almost certainly, he did read *Emile* in his teens, and absorbed the simple piety of the Savoyard priest's creed (in Book IV). This priest, born a peasant, and ordained before he has given himself the chance to question the doctrines of the Catholic Church, becomes preoccupied with a quest for truth at about the same time as getting into trouble for his inability to keep his vows of celibacy. 'My perplexity was increased by the fact that I had been brought up in a church which decides everything and permits no doubts, so that having rejected one article of faith, I was forced to reject the rest; as I could not accept absurd decisions, I was deprived of those which were not absurd.'[9]

The Savoyard priest does not reject God, but finding all manifestations of the supernatural, and all ideas of the future life, quite unknowable, he prefers to concentrate on those elements in religion which do immediately concern him: that is, matters of morality and conscience as they impinge on his own soul: 'I am aware of my soul; it is known to me in feeling and thought: I know what it is without knowing its essence. . . . Our first duty is towards ourself. . . . Conscience is the voice of the soul, the passions are the voice of the body. . . . Conscience! Conscience! Divine instinct, immortal voice from heaven; sure guide for a creature ignorant and finite indeed, yet intelligent and free.'[10]

At various crucial moments of his life, Tolstoy found himself rediscovering the faith of the Savoyard priest; the oftener he discovered it, the more certain he became that it was his own inner vision: hence the confusion he sometimes felt about whether he or Rousseau had written the works of Rousseau. Rousseau's appeal to him need not be laboured: the acceptance of the near ungovernability of sexual passions; the idea that though the dogmas of the old religion be false, the kernel of moral truth contained within them can be rediscovered and made new; the love of simplicity, rural life, and the idea that virtue is best practised in retirement from society: how exciting all this must have seemed when read in an upstairs room in the Yushkov household. Rousseau, early associated in Tolstoy's mind with his mother, was the exact opposite of everything Aunt Pelageya stood for. Her household and her way of life emphasised social distinctions in the crudest possible manner. Rousseau taught the equality of all men. Her *soirées,* where you could hardly hear yourself speak above the silly chatter, were full of loud, noisy, happy people; the gloomy adolescent Lev Nikolayevich read in Rousseau that wisdom was best learnt in solitude. Pelageya believed that religion consisted in obedience to the Church and a love of her rituals; Rousseau, that true religion consisted in a rejection of church dogmas, and a contemplation of one's own inner soul and conscience.

Meanwhile, though, with the inconsistency which marks almost any adolescent character, he continued to attach extreme importance to wearing smart clothes and uniforms, getting drunk, riding an expensive horse, and asserting his social superiority whenever he came across children of the lesser nobility or of yet lowlier rank. All memories of him at this date, his own and other people's, call back a young blade of fairly insufferable arrogance and conceit, who, for all his moral posturings, devoted most of his waking hours to various sorts of upper-class horseplay.[11]

But this would be a misleading impression. Nineteenth-century Russians, just as much as modern ones, were expected to 'serve'. The poor anti-hero of Pushkin's *Bronze Horseman* 'serves' somewhere or another in an office in the gleaming metropolis erected by the great tyrant Peter, his demented attempts to run away from Peter's statue being suggestive, as all readers of the poem so terrifyingly feel, of the complete impotence of ordinary, private individuals in the presence of an overwhelmingly strong autocracy. The higher ranks of the aristocracy, no less than the dreary, nameless little Yevgenys of Pushkin's imagination, were expected to 'serve' and it was with this in mind that the Tolstoys' education was planned and organised. The oldest, Nikolay, was bound for a military career. The Tolstoys were in a position to 'serve' in important and high-ranking capacities. This, for Lev, was what gave such delightful poignancy to the innocent Dmitry's feeble attempts to get into Government service. Presenting himself at the Secretary of State's office at the Second Department of the Civil Service in St. Petersburg, Dmitry did not try to pull any kind of strings. His brothers imagined that he must be the only man in Russia who took the word 'serve' quite literally. Humble and patriotic, he was not wanting to use his name, or the fact that both his mother's and his father's family had played an important part in the history of Russia in the last three centuries. He merely told the Secretary his rank, and explained that he had decided to offer his services in the field of legislation.

'Your name?'

'Count Tolstoy.'

'You have not served anywhere?'

'I have only just finished my course and I simply wish to be useful.'

'What post do you want?'

'It is all the same to me — one in which I can be useful.'

Poor Dmitry was too good for this world. No wonder his attempts to 'serve' ended so calamitously! (Having wasted his short life, he was to die in a sordid hotel bedroom in the arms of a prostitute.) Lev Nikolayevich was to become a diplomat, like generations of Tolstoys before him, a decision which must have had something to do with the fact that he had a great capacity for languages. With the tutor brought with them to Kazan, the younger Tolstoy boys perfected their French and German. Once arrived in the place, Lev studied Arabic and Turko-Tartar in the local *Gymnasium* or grammar school, before entering the University at the age of sixteen. Kazan, both geographically and historically, was well-placed for the study of such Oriental languages, and his first year as a student was spent thus engaged. In Tolstoy's second year he changed to Law, and gave up the idea of becoming a career diplomat.

These sentences convey almost nothing, if by 'university' we imagine something like the institution which now flourishes in Kazan, with its large well-stocked libraries, its hideous physics block and badly dressed students — things largely indistinguishable from anything which might be found in Harvard, Paris or Oxford.[12] As Tolstoy first went up the hill towards Kazan University in May 1844, he would have seen a beautiful white building with a green roof and a golden cupola. But he soon lost any illusions about the beauty of the life there. A modern western historian[13] has likened the University of Kazan at this date to Dotheboys Hall, and the educational principles of the Director to those of Mr. Squeers. State scholars, for example, were obliged to do tough manual labour. The University grounds were divided into allotments, exactly divided up according to the number of students. In Aksakov's memory, the buildings seemed 'like terrible enchanted castles such as I read of, or a prison where I was to be shut up as a convict. The great door between the columns at the top of the high flight of steps, when it was opened by an old pensioner, I felt had swallowed me up — the two broad, high staircases, lit from the cupola and leading from the hall to the first and second floors — the shouting and confused noise of many voices which came from all the classrooms. . . . all this I saw and heard and understood for the first time.'[14]

At the *Gymnasium*, and even more at the University, Tolstoy would have first become aware of the actual structure of life in Russia, life outside his own family, life as directly affected by the policies and character of Imperial autocracy.

Kazan had only been a university since 1804 when a decree of Alexander I elevated the grammar school there to university status. The lecturers in early years were nearly all ushers or hacks from the old school and, of the seven professors in the original University, most were German because there simply were no Russians capable of teaching to the required standard. Where Russians did display intellectual prowess, they could be sure of vigorous persecution from the Government. The outstanding Russian mathematician of the early nineteenth century, for example, was N. I. Lobachevsky, whose pioneering work on non-Euclidian geometry was acclaimed by scientists all over the world. But not in Russia. Almost all Lobachevsky's energies, as Professor of Mathematics at Kazan from 1827-1846, had to be devoted to defending himself and his colleagues from the assaults of the University Curator, M. L. Magnitsky. This figure had hoped for the chair of Mathematics himself, and when he failed to get it, he managed to get the Government post of University Curator. He was based in St. Petersburg, and was persistently unsympathetic to Kazan. Indeed, his first report to the Minister of Education about the University was that it should be abolished. Having failed in that resolve, he kept up a series of attacks on all the teachers there, reporting back on them to the Minister of Education, Count S. S.

Uvarov, himself no model of progressive liberalism. This took such underhand forms as examining students' lecture notes for evidence of sedition on the part of the lecturers. And sedition, as defined by Uvarov's Ministry, was almost impossible to avoid.

Tolstoy, as we have seen, decided to specialise in his first year at Kazan in Oriental languages. But it was considered highly damaging if students read anything which exposed their minds to the fact that not everyone shared the doctrines of the Russian Orthodox Church. Lecturers in the Oriental Faculty were forbidden to 'enter into the details of the religious beliefs and customs of the Mohammedan peoples'. Influence, if there was to be influence, was to be all the other way around. Uvarov defined the Oriental Faculty at Kazan in these terms: 'the half-savage sons of the steppes of Mongolia eagerly accept the fruitful seeds of enlightenment.'[15]

Fair's fair. There was at least one Buryat Mongol student in the faculty in Tolstoy's time: and though they expected students of Arabic not to read anything with a Moslem reference there were Moslems at Kazan University. At this period in Oxford, you could not even enter the University, let alone take a degree, unless you belonged to the Church of England. Uvarov's remarks about the half-savage sons of the steppes are no sillier than Samuel Johnson's about driving cows out of the garden, as a justification for expelling Methodists from Oxford.

Some explanation should perhaps be offered for what the Minister of Education meant by the 'seeds of enlightenment', lest by 'enlightenment' the modern reader supposes that the University lecturers were encouraging their students to read Kant, Rousseau, Diderot or Voltaire. If you read philosophy at Kazan in Tolstoy's time, the set books were St. Paul's epistles to the Colossians and to Timothy. This was at the insistence of Magnitsky, famous in private conversations for his cynical expressions of atheism, but who, in his public role, was determined to stamp out from the universities 'the fine poison of unbelief and of hatred for the lawful authorities'.[16]

Philosophical inquiry, in such an atmosphere, was therefore almost inevitably bound not only to be anti-Church, but also anti-Government. Since the Government of Nicholas I chose to view itself as the very embodiment of Orthodoxy — and Orthodoxy of a stridently oppressive, ignorant and superstitious kind — it was hard to depart from those superstitions without declaring yourself against the Government.

Tolstoy was to become one of the most notable of nineteenth-century Russian dissidents, one whom both the Government and, subsequently, Lenin recognised as more than half-doing the revolutionaries' work for them while always remaining an anomaly in the political spectrum. Much of this must be explained in terms of Tolstoy's own personality, and in terms of who he was and who his family were. But much stems, too, from the accident of his having gone to university at Kazan, rather than St. Petersburg or Moscow, both at this period hotbeds of liberalism, anarchism and general discontent with the Government.

Kazan in Tolstoy's day knew none of the 'student unrest' which was beginning to trouble it when Lenin's father studied there a decade later. By the time Lenin was himself a student at Kazan in the 1880s, there were even public demonstrations against the University Inspector: it was for his part in such a riotous assembly that Lenin was sent down in 1887. In Tolstoy's day, the discipline was unchallenged, as is shown by the shock which his own arrogant behaviour caused his fellow students. When he and an undergraduate were late for a history lesson, they were locked up together for the night in the lecture room, and the other young man was amazed at the cool way in which Tolstoy inveighed against the absurdity both of the University system and of its syllabus. In Moscow, no such amazement would have been felt, and it would have been the norm from an enlightened and rebellious young nobleman. Kazan completely lacked, in the 1840s, the atmosphere of political discontent which could have produced, say, an Alexander Herzen. All Herzen's radicalism was learnt, in embryo, while he was an undergraduate at Moscow in the 1830s. After he had left his beloved University, he fostered his radical ideas with a small group of like-minded college friends. It was only when this *kruzhok* began to diminish under the persecutions of the autocracy, and after he had himself suffered prison and Siberian 'internal exile', that Herzen finally left Russia forever in January 1847. While Tolstoy was lying in the University clinic at Kazan, the father of Russian socialism was making his way across a Europe which was on the brink of revolutions; and though he never saw many of the *kruzhok* again, they remained with Herzen, in his memories and his writings, throughout the period of his exile. Although a passionate individualist in his convictions, Herzen, like all those radicals and revolutionaries in Russia who looked to him as to a king over the water, was sustained by the thought of a little gang. Tolstoy, whose way of being a rebel was to be analogous but, in the end, totally different, had no such reassuring sense of belonging, in his youth, to an intellectual circle.

He is frank in his declaration that he chose his university friends because of their looks. He would rather ride in a sleigh wrapped up in a rug with some handsome young blade than discuss how to set the world to rights. Late nights were devoted to drinking and wenching, not to the niceties of political argument. Political engagements, as opposed to unspecified discontent, a sense that the world was out of joint, could hardly have dawned on Tolstoy in such a place as Kazan unless there had been a considerable politicised student movement. There was none.

When we consider the statistical facts, his isolation seems almost more exaggerated than he could feel it, or make it, himself. While he was a student at Kazan, the population of the Empire was in the region of sixty million. A census taken five years earlier (and there is no reason to suppose that there was a dramatic increase in university numbers in the years 1842-1847) showed that there were three thousand four hundred and eighty-eight students in the whole Empire attending universities. Of that number, in 1842, only seven hundred and forty-two took degrees.

Higher education which, in the Soviet Union, as in the modern West, is an ideal held out to all who can attain it, was something which affected only the tiniest proportion of the population of Russia in Tolstoy's day. And, after a year of reading Oriental languages, Tolstoy switched to Law. This put him in an even smaller elect, for only higher-ranking members of the aristocracy were allowed to study Jurisprudence in Russian universities of the *ancien régime*.

Tolstoy's professor at this date was a man called D. I. Meyer who, curiously enough, in 1849, before Tolstoy had become famous, noted down his impression of the boy. 'I gave him an exam today and noticed that he had no desire to study at all. He has such expressive facial features and such intelligent eyes, that I am convinced that with good will and independence he can develop into a remarkable person.'[17]

Inspired by Professor Meyer, Tolstoy decided that he wanted to study very much indeed. Just as Dmitry's piety momentarily persuaded him that he wanted to be a devout Orthodox and Sergey's debauchery made him want to act the part of a rake, Tolstoy's admiration for the Professor of Law (the first and only person teaching at Kazan to inspire such devotion) made him want to pass his exams. 'For me the chief sign of love is the fear of offending or not pleasing the object of one's love: simply, fear.'

Meyer had asked Tolstoy to prepare a dissertation comparing Catherine the Great's *Instructions to the Commission for the Composition of a Plan for a New Code of Laws* with Montesquieu's *Spirit of Law*. His diaries at this time show that Tolstoy considered this an extremely profitable exercise. There is nothing in his notes to suggest the later positions he was to adopt, the advocacy of anarchy and so on. There is no whiff of criticism of the notion of a purely autocratic system of government. As we have already indicated, it would have been inconceivable for an undergraduate of this period to have voiced criticisms of the Government in a formal piece of work without getting himself and his tutor into trouble. But to judge from the private jottings he made, there is nothing to suggest that Tolstoy felt such hostility. The only hint of the man he was to become is seen in his condemnation of capital punishment; but nothing could be less 'Tolstoyan' than his belief that good laws should be interchangeable or synonymous with morals.

One might ask how a disciple of Rousseau *could* have accepted the despotic notions of Catherine the Great, a lady whom in later life Tolstoy castigated as a 'stupid illiterate and lewd wench'. The answer must be that at nineteen, Tolstoy was unformed. More than the generality of nineteen year olds, he was many things: both a Romantic revolutionary, and a man who wanted a career in Government service; a free-thinking nature-worshipper and, on occasion, a guilt-ridden Orthodox.

The guilt was sexual. It is typical of Tolstoy, who loved to keep things in the family, that the introduction to whoring came from his brothers. It would seem that he was about fourteen years old when he was first taken to a brothel by his elder brother Sergey. He tells us that after he had 'accomplished this act' he stood by the bed and wept.[18]

There is no way of knowing whether or not this was true. Historians have also been baffled by Tolstoy's memory that this momentous event in his personal history took place in a room set apart for the purpose in one of the monasteries in Kazan.

Tolstoy was to have plenty of subsequent experiences which could complement the first disillusioning moment with the Kazan tart: parlour maids, gipsies, peasants, eventually a wife were all to share his bed and witness the violent contradictions between his animal appetites and his sense of spiritual revulsion against the sexual act. There is a sort of Manichean appropriateness about it, if he really lost his virginity in a monastery. Whether or not they are true, the images which old age supplied him — of his uncontrollable desires, of a brother egging him on, of the lure of the woman followed by the lachrymose shame of it all — these tell their own ineradicable story. He wept but he took. Few artists have had a more exaggerated sense of sexual guilt; few have been more clumsy of their handling of it in private life, nor more creative in their literary use of it.

Some of the reasons for his tormented feelings about sex are probably buried in the Freudian irrecoverable past — perhaps even before the death of his unremembered mother. But others are more superficially obvious, none more so than the fact that three years of sleeping with prostitutes left Tolstoy infected with gonorrhoea. A V.D. clinic is a better place than most to form feelings of hatred for one's own body. Just at the moment when his studies seemed to be going well for him, Tolstoy developed the dreaded symptoms of discharge and stinging, and was taken off to the University clinic for treatment.

The fact that there was a University V.D. clinic in a little place such as Kazan is indicative of the prevalence of the problem. Nineteenth-century Russia, no less than the countries of the West, was plagued by venereal diseases. Indeed when you consider the medical history of the last century, with its dazzling array of distinguished syphilitics from Abraham Lincoln to Baudelaire, you might think that celibacy was the only prophylactic. Tolstoy's father may well have had syphilis — his own sudden death and the hyperactivity of his children have been advanced as possibly syphilitic symptoms — but there is no evidence here to go on. Tolstoy himself was lucky, comparatively speaking, to have the highly unpleasant, but much less dangerous, clap.

The mercury treatment which sufferers from gonorrhoea underwent was no joke. One of the dangers attaching to the disease is urethral stricture — an inability to pass urine and a subsequent poisoning of the body. It was this that killed James Boswell, Samuel Johnson's biographer, and a lifelong sufferer from gonorrhoea. Mercury was supposed to cleanse and open up the passages. But liquid metal does not easily get into those bodily regions on its own. It has to be injected through the male member. It is surely a reassuring tribute to the power of nature that the famous lechers of history like Boswell and Tolstoy lost none of their appetite for the chase in spite of the fact that one bit of bad luck could land them once more in the clinic with its primitive syringes and scarcely competent medics.

We have remarked on Tolstoy's isolation in the world. History had made him a minority member of a minority class while withholding from him many of the privileges of that class. Thus, he was a member of one of the senior aristocratic families, but an impoverished branch of that family. Parentless, he was growing up neither in the old-fashioned, solid world of Moscow society nor in the exciting metropolitan atmosphere of St. Petersburg.

Now, at the age of nineteen, he was physically isolated in the clinic. It was the first time in his life when he had been completely alone. Even at lectures, or going for walks, Tolstoy, like most well-born youths, was accompanied by a servant. (Herzen was the same — he had a lackey to carry his books all the time he was at Moscow University.) Tolstoy had made a friend of his lackey, who was called Vanyusha. Now even he was removed. There were no brothers, no cousins or aunts, no noisy friends. Just the pain, and the shame, and the blank walls of the clinic looking down on him. It was in this enforced solitude that Tolstoy first began to keep a diary. Its first words are, 'It is six days since I entered the clinic. . . . I have had gonorrhoea, from the source where you usually get it.'

It is on the day that he wrote those words that the true history of Tolstoy may be said to have begun. After all, the reason we value him and find his story of interest is as an imagination. Tolstoy was to have some adventures — he saw a man's head being chopped off in Paris, he took part in the Crimean War. But, for the most part, the outward circumstances of his life were no more interesting than any other Russian nobleman of the nineteenth century. What singles him out is what happened when he began to keep a diary, a record which was to develop, eventually, into the practice of fiction.

With many gaps, he was to remain a compulsive diarist until his last days of life. The diary was a confessional, a notebook, a catalogue of moral laws. It was never to be the chatty, observant sort of diary kept by a Boswell or a Pepys. It was not a diary which focused much attention on other people. Centre stage, always, and for the rest of his life, was Tolstoy himself.

Because of this, the diary is a vehicle less of self-record than of self-projection. He is not giving an account of what he is actually like, so much as projecting a version of what he would like to be like: it is in this process of projection and transformation that the origins of Tolstoy's fiction are found.

On April 17, he was asking his diary 'what is the purpose of a man's life?' and deciding that it was 'development' — whatever that was supposed to mean — 'the development of everything that exists'. It appears to mean that Tolstoy felt that he must realise all his potential and talents, for he adds, 'I would be the unhappiest of men if I could not find a purpose for my life — a purpose both general and useful — useful because my immortal soul when fully mature will pass naturally into a higher existence and one that is appropriate to it. So my whole life will be a constant and active striving to achieve this one purpose. . . .'[19]

Nothing about his examinations, which were forthcoming; nothing about leaving the University either. Yet two days later, on April 19, 1847, he petitioned the University authorities to be allowed to go home 'on the grounds of ill health and domestic circumstances'. On the date of this petition to go down from Kazan, he merely notes in his diary. 'Got up extremely late and only made up my mind at two o'clock what to do during the day.'[20] Read out of context, this would sound like a day of idle lounging. Because it coincides with the date of his petition to the governing body of Kazan University to be allowed to go down, we must assume that the 'resolution' formed at two o'clock was in fact the decision to go home, that is, to go to Yasnaya Polyana. No explanation.[21]

By this date, Tolstoy had left the clinic, and was living once more with his brothers Sergey and Dmitry. Some time before, they had moved out of the Yushkov house, and were living with their servants in a separate apartment. Whether Colonel Yushkov had had enough of their rowdy ways, or whether they had got bored with his, is not recorded. Perhaps there was not enough room for them. The Yushkov house is not particularly large.

So, between April 17, when Tolstoy was expressing his urgent desire to 'study the whole course of law necessary for my final examination at the University' and his petition of leave on April 19, what had happened?

Two facts have to be borne in mind. In the previous year's examinations, Tolstoy had done disastrously badly. Having mastered Arabic and the rudiments of some other Oriental languages, he had then 'flunked' on some simple geographical questions which were put to him in the *viva voce* parts of the examination. What were the chief ports of France? He had not the faintest idea, and showed an equal ignorance of the simplest facts of Russian history. It may well have been that when it came to the point, he did not wish to go through that humiliation again. After all, in those days it was perfectly usual to attend a university without taking a degree.

The second fact is much more crucial; and that is, that on April 11, 1847, Tolstoy had come into his inheritance. The first experience of solitude in the clinic had been both desolating and exciting, a time when, perhaps as never before, he realised that his life was his own. The revealing thing about his childhood fondness for the story of Joseph and his brethren is the extreme ambivalence of that story, in which the second youngest member of a great family, after a period of separation from them all, achieves such eminence that he becomes their lord and master, holding in his hands their life and destiny. But this achievement only comes after a period of separation, when Joseph is away from his brethren, proving himself in Egypt.

Nikolay had already gone into the army. Sergey was coming to the end of his course at Kazan, which would have left Tolstoy with his brother Dmitry, the 'holy idiot'. And although he idolised Dmitry in his memory, it is significant that he hardly ever saw him between the time when he left Kazan in 1847 and Dmitry's death.

The complicated business of sharing out their parents' inheritance had been under discussion since the previous summer with the trustee of their father's will. In particular, they were anxious that Marya should not be impoverished. The executor wrote to Nikolay, posted in the Caucasus, 'I know your brotherly love towards Marya Nikolayevna, who loves you like a father.'

The final agreement left Marya with Pirogev, an estate of some one hundred and fifty serfs, and nine hundred and fifty-eight *desyatinas* of land. (A *desyatina* is about 2.7 acres.) The other estates and serfs were divided up among the brothers. It is remarkable how equitably they divided it. For example, Nikolay got a larger estate, Plotits'na, with rather more than a thousand *desyatinas*, and three hundred and seventeen serfs; Sergey, who loved riding, got the stud farm, and the prize estate of the inheritance, Pirogovo, with about two thousand and seventy-five *desyatinas*. But these brothers paid their younger brothers compensation in 'roubles silver'. Nikolay paid Lev two thousand five hundred silver roubles; Sergey paid him one thousand five hundred silver roubles. Dmitry got seven thousand silver roubles from Sergey, while inheriting three hundred and thirty-one serfs of his own and an estate of a thousand *desyatinas*.

In addition to his roubles, Lev inherited various estates in the Tula province: Yasenky, Yagodnoya and Mostovoya Pushotsh, as well as one called Malaya Vorotinsk. It was a convention that the youngest son inherited the estate where the family had grown up, and so Lev also inherited the Volkonsky estate of Yasnaya Polyana. Altogether he came into about one thousand four hundred and eighty-five *desyatinas* of land and the ownership of three hundred and thirty peasants — 'souls', as they were always called.

It is quite hard to translate these statistics into tangible or imaginable realities. That is, how rich was Tolstoy? A lot poorer than his extravagant old Tolstoy grandfather had been, the governor of Kazan. The richer families in Russia, such as the Sheremetyevs, had incomes in the region of seven hundred thousand roubles a year, and owned two hundred thousand 'souls'.[22] In general the upper ranks of the nobility, to which both Tolstoy's parents belonged, the grand seigneurial class, might have been expected to own over a thousand souls, whereas the 'gentry' would own in the region of five hundred. If you owned less than a hundred 'souls' you were considered to belong to the 'impoverished' *dvoryane*.[23] Tolstoy's family had most distinctly come down in the world in the last twenty years. On the other hand, to inherit at the age of nineteen four thousand roubles, three thousand acres and three hundred and thirty slaves was not exactly poverty.

*　　　　*　　　　*　　　　*

The inheritance was made formal on April 11, 1847, shortly after Tolstoy left the clinic. The exams still loomed up, and he had resolved to work hard for them. But his resolution lasted precisely a week. On the 19th, he asked for permission to withdraw from the University and, leaving Dmitry and Sergey still studying there, he left Kazan for Yasnaya Polyana.

To speak of Tolstoy 'deciding' to abandon his university studies or 'making up his mind' to leave Kazan implies both a finality and a rationality which were not present. The only rational explanation for his departure is that there *was* no explanation. On impulse, he decided to go back to 'Auntie'. Not for the last time in his tempestuous existence, inner crisis was resolved by flight.

Chapter Three
The History of Yesterday

1847 - 1850

We feel our vocation only after we have once mistaken it. . . .

A Landlord's Morning

Spring was just beginning to burst when Tolstoy came home in April 1847.[1] Around, nestling in pleasant, rolling country, was the estate, its villages, farms and outbuildings. Dodging ruts and pot-holes in the mudtrack which nineteenth-century Russians might have recognised as a road, the coach would pass between those two turrets constructed by old Prince Volkonsky in Napoleonic times. The whitewash on them was flaky now and after only thirty years their brickwork looked seedy. The turrets passed, the coach drove down the avenue of silver birches, almost a cliché of patriotism and nostalgia in Russian literature; and at the end of the birch avenue stood the two-storeyed, white-painted house, initially reminiscent of New England colonial architecture. Nearby stood the no less elegant one-storey servants' quarters, built by Grandfather Volkonsky and equipped with accommodation for the house serfs, as well as with workshops, looms for weaving and carpet-making, sewing rooms and lace-making rooms.

The peasants who came to peer at the arrival of their new landlord were indescribably filthy and poverty-stricken. Even the big house itself, when you got closer, showed all the signs of dilapidation and decay. The English garden, planted long since by old Volkonsky, had gone to seed. The paths were unswept, unweeded. The roof looked in a bad state. The woodwork of the verandah, with pretty carved fretwork, was rotting and splintered. But waiting for him on the verandah would have been Aunt Tatyana. After nineteen years of emotional and geographical upheaval, this was a homecoming.

For some, the actual place of their birth is of almost no significance. For Tolstoy, however, the Volkonsky inheritance was infinitely more than a collection of wooden buildings and muddy avenues. The house, too, was much more than just a place. To date, it had been the one constant thing in his life. His family fortunes had changed with appalling violence and rapidity since he was two years old, taking him now to Moscow, now to Kazan, now to this aunt, now to that. Yasnaya, like Aunt Tatyana, remained a constant, and to Yasnaya, for summer holidays, they had always tried to return. Its significance for him was found less in the memories it contained than in those events and personages which were beyond memory's grasp. The recovery of the Volkonskys and their world was no merely whimsical interest in family history; it was an urgent, emotional necessity. The fact that the search always eluded him is an essential ingredient in his art. Even in old age, when he had lived continuously at Yasnaya for many years, his diary finds him walking in the garden and thinking of his mother. 'Yes, my dear mother whom I never called by that name, since I couldn't talk. Yes, she is my highest conception of pure love — not a cold, or divine, but a warm, earthly, maternal love. This is what attracts my bitter, weary soul. Mummy dear, caress me.'[2]

Inside the house was the green leather sofa where Tolstoy himself was born and where (often at great pain and inconvenience to his wife) he insisted that so many of his children should be brought to birth. The fetish has such obvious importance that it does not need to be stressed. It tells its own tale. Wandering about the cold, dusty rooms, the nineteen-year-old possessor of his inheritance would have seen the portraits of Tolstoys and Volkonskys looking down upon him; uncles, cousins, grandparents, but no mother. ('By some strange chance no portrait of her has been preserved, so that as a real physical being I cannot picture her to myself. I am in a way glad of this, for in my conception of her there is only her spiritual figure, and all that I know about her is beautiful.')[3] The uniformed men who stared from the walls of landings and dining room, however, had all too physical a presence, and they looked upon the young Tolstoy with gloomy disdain. Yasnaya Polyana had known better days. Russia had known better days. The family — this branch of it at least — had known better days. In the time of Catherine the Great they had been generals, diplomats, ministers of the Crown. There were still Volkonskys and Tolstoys at court, but they were cousins of some distance, and their existence only made Tolstoy's poverty and lack of direction a further cause for self-doubt and reproach.

We need feel no surprise that Tolstoy felt the urgent need to *do* something about Yasnaya Polyana; something to improve the estates and the physical well-being of his serfs. Nicholas I himself, no dangerous liberal, had addressed the Council of State in 1842 and admitted that 'there is no doubt that serfdom in its present situation in our country is an evil, palpable and obvious for all'. But Nicholas argued that to give them their freedom and to introduce reforms all at once would in fact cause hardship and social disorder. Like later governments in history, he pleaded for a 'gradual transition to a different order' and blamed a lot of the trouble on those foolish landowners who tried to educate their serfs beyond their station. To this noble band, Tolstoy soon aspired to belong. He felt an instinct to tidy things up, to improve their living conditions, to give them more say in how their affairs were run. But the gulf between the serfs and their new young landlord was enormous; and Tolstoy soon began to reflect, in his own small area, on this nineteenth-century Russian malaise. Those who were equipped, by breeding or education, to govern the country were not given the power to do so by the autocracy. But even if they could not hope to take part in the processes of government, they tended to drift to the towns. The reward for their status, however, was the possession of land and serfs. Russia was therefore scarred by a multitude of neglected estates whose owners were either incompetent or unwilling to take the responsibility for them. Sometimes the estates were left in the hands of an agent; sometimes, they were just left, while the 'souls' owned by these absentee or negligent landlords could go to the devil. Tolstoy, at the age of nineteen, was forced into the dilemma himself by the fact of his inheritance; and the fact that his estate was a place charged with so much important emotional significance did not make it easier for him. As well as schemes for the estate, he was full of schemes for what to do with himself. He was a wild mixture of extreme indolence and wistful ambition. Life, so far, had been a mess. For the next two years he planned:

(1) To study the whole course of law necessary for my final examination at the University. (2) To study practical medicine, and some theoretical medicine. (3) To study languages: French, Russian, German, English, Italian and Latin. (4) To study agriculture, both theoretical and practical. (5) To study history and geography. (6) To study mathematics, the grammar-school course. (7) To write a

dissertation. (8) To attain a degree of perfection in music and painting. (9) To write down rules. (10) To acquire some knowledge of the natural sciences. (11) To write essays on all the subjects that I shall study.[4]

Quite a programme. No wonder that he did not include time for writing a novel. In fact, it never crossed his mind. The list shows (medicine, agriculture) that he did partly want to study so that he could become a responsible landlord. One of the very impressive things about Tolstoy's life, taken as a whole, is that he carried out this demanding course of study pretty thoroughly. To the languages, he also could add competence in Turkish and Arabic and, in later life, Greek and Dutch. Perhaps he never achieved perfection in painting. But in all the other areas, he was to become competent, chiefly, no doubt, because of his acute consciousness that in his youth it had been emotionally impossible to settle down to being educated. Nor was it realistic to imagine, as a nineteen year old alone in the country with a favourite 'Auntie', that he would find either the necessary stimulus to begin or the external disciplines to continue such a course of study. For the first few months at Yasnaya Polyana, he was tasting freedom from Kazan, and a strong sense of homecoming: there was the rediscovery of the haunts of childhood, as well as the various experiences of poking a disgusted nose into the peasant *izbas* (cottages), of hunting animals and entertaining country neighbours and relations. None of the resolutions at this stage had any chance of being carried out: except perhaps, his resolutions to write down rules. He was good at that. There were rules for controlling the emotions, rules for subordinating the will to the feeling of love ('Keep away from women' — small hope of that!), rules for exciting feelings of universal love, rules for developing various faculties, such as the ability to draw conclusions, poured from his pen. But no conclusions were drawn in life.

As we have said, one obvious reason why Russia was in such a mess was that the owners of estates found it too boring to live on them. The tastes and aspirations reflected by Tolstoy's rules would obviously not be satisfied by Auntie (clever and stimulating as she was) nor by the peasants (fascinating as he found them imaginatively and sexually). Tolstoy needed companionship, drawing rooms, concert halls, libraries: in short, he needed town. Rousseau's cult of the rural and the primitive had seized his imagination while surrounded by the bustling and noisy atmosphere of Kazan. Nor was Tolstoy ever disloyal to Rousseau's vision in principle. In practice, though, after his first few months there, Yasnaya Polyana bored him terribly.

His cousin (and future brother-in-law) Valeryan Petrovich Tolstoy came to stay towards the end of the summer, before returning to complete a spell of Government service in Siberia. As Valeryan's *tarantas* (coach) pulled away, Lev Nikolayevich impulsively jumped in to join him, perfectly prepared, on the spur of the moment, to go and pass the winter in Siberia. Why not? What else was there to do? Valeryan pointed out that though Lev Nikolayevich had brought a little hand luggage, he had no hat on his head, and that this might be uncomfortable in Siberia. Tolstoy stopped the coach and got out again.

The little story reveals the complete aimlessness and lack of direction in his life at this juncture. *We* know that he is Tolstoy and that one day he will write *War and Peace*. But no such knowledge was vouchsafed to the young man himself. When he inherited Yasnaya Polyana he was quite as genuinely at a loose end as any of the Romantic heroes of early nineteenth-century Russian literature, as indolent as Chatsky or Olenin. What a good example, incidentally, of how dangerous it can be to make uncritical use of the fiction as a source for Tolstoy's biography. No one questions, for example, that the novel which he later planned, but never completed, to be entitled *A Russian Landlord*, draws heavily on this period for its memory and inspiration. 'Yes,' said old man Tolstoy, pausing for a walk round the estates with his German biographer Löwenfeld, 'here we are in the very *selo* [village] where the young landowner experienced all his disappointments.'[5]

But, far from being a drifter like Tolstoy himself, the hero of the novel is seen in vividly decisive terms. On the very first page we meet a nineteen-year-old prince who has completed his course at the University (unlike Tolstoy) and who, after a summer spent on his estate, writes to his favourite aunt that he intends to devote himself to bettering the lives of his peasants.

As I wrote to you before, I found affairs here in indescribable disorder. Wishing to put them in order and understand them, I discovered that the chief evil lies in the very pitiable and impoverished condition of the peasants, and that this is an evil that can only be remedied by work and patience. If you could only see two of my peasants, David and Ivan, and the way they and their families live, I am sure that the mere sight of those two unfortunates would do more to convince you than anything I can say to explain my intention. Is it not my sacred and direct duty to care for the welfare of these seven hundred men?[6]

Tolstoy, one notices, has quietly doubled the size of his inheritance for the purposes of fiction. He is not only more decidedly altruistic than in real life; he is also richer.

Yevgeny Onegin, and other heroes, have similar feelings of charity about the 'souls' in their ownership; and there is no reason to suppose that Tolstoy was anything but earnestly sincere in his desire to better the lot of such as Ivan and David. In Gogol, Leskov and other writers, we get used to the tragi-comic figure of the liberal landlord, trying to improve the life of his peasants and being viewed with a profound suspicion which would never have been directed towards the heartless, old-style agents and landlords who maltreated or abused them. In Leskov's tale of the emancipation, *A Spiteful Fellow*, the idiotic peasants take a great dislike to their liberal English steward, Mr. Denn. 'He wouldn't give me a flogging,' one of them complains. They are not happy until they have burnt down the distillery which Denn had built for them, nor until some of their number have been flogged, put on a chain gang, or sentenced to penal servitude in Siberia; then they know where they are.

Tolstoy attempted no such crude ironies in the fragment *A Landlord's Morning*, but it quite obviously reflects his dismay at the hopelessness of peasant conditions as he confronted them in the summer of 1847. Dismay, however, is not all that he felt when confronted by the great gulf fixed between himself and his peasants. A profound imbibing of Rousseau inclined him to a belief in the noble savage, while something deeper drew him towards the peasants in a startlingly unusual manner. The fragment ends on a typically Tolstoyan note, wishing that he *was* a peasant, and not just any peasant, but a particular one called Ilya. There is nothing here of Marie Antoinette. What Tolstoy envies in Ilya is his supposed ability to respond to life spontaneously and naturally. It is not Ilya's Christian virtue so much as his pagan self-abandonment which so attracts Prince Nekhlyudov: ruddy of cheek, fair of curls, a latter-day King David, the peasant has arrived on his cart outside an inn:

Ilya broadly exchanges greetings with a fair-faced, broad-bosomed hostess, who asks 'Have you come far? And how many of you will want supper?' and with her bright, kindly eyes looks with pleasure at the handsome lad. Now having seen to his horses he goes into the hot, crowded house, crosses himself, sits down before a full wooden bowl, and chats merrily with the landlady and his comrades. And here, under the penthouse, is his place for the night, where, in the open, starry sky is visible and where he will lie on scented hay near the horses which, changing from foot to foot and snorting, pick out the fodder from the wooden mangers. He goes up to the hay, turns to the east, and crossing his broad, powerful chest some thirty times, and shaking back his fair curls, repeats, 'Our Father' and 'Lord have Mercy' some twenty times, covers himself, head and all, with his coat and falls into the healthy, careless sleep of strong, young manhood. And now he dreams of the towns: Kiev with its saints and throngs of pilgrims, Romen with its traders and merchandise, Odessa and the distant blue sea with its white sails, and Tsargrad [i.e. Constantinople] with its golden houses and white-breasted, dark-browed Turkish women — and thither he flies freely and easily further and further and sees below him golden cities bathed in bright radiance, and the blue sky with its many stars and the blue sea with its sails; and it is gladsome and gay to fly on, further and further. . . .

'Splendid!' Nekhlyudov whispered to himself, and the thought came to him, 'Why am I not Ilya?'[7]

The crazy question was to return to Tolstoy again and again in the course of his life. Even on his deathbed (though by then the thought had become encrusted with doctrine) he was studiously wondering what it would feel like to be spontaneous, and uniting this wonder with his admiration for the *muzhik* (peasant).

Ilya, like a number of the noble savages in the young Tolstoy's imagination, feels no sexual guilt. He is able to shake back his curls, and make the sign of the cross over his beautiful chest, and then dream, with no torment, of the full breasts of Turkish women. But it was not so for Lev Nikolayevich, whose attitude to sex alternated between insatiable sexual appetite and morbid self-reproach. His diary, when he could bestir himself to write in it, is a catalogue of 'rules' punctuated with pompously juvenile generalisations: 'From whom do we derive sensuality, effeminacy, frivolity in everything and a multitude

57

of other vices, if not from women? Who is to blame for the fact that we lose our innate feelings of boldness, resolution, judiciousness, justice etc. if not women? A woman is more receptive than a man; and therefore women were better than us in virtuous ages; but in the present depraved and corrupt age, they are worse than us.'

These feelings of revulsion are very marked whenever he can bring himself in the diaries to allude to the sexual act itself rather than resorting to such code-language as 'I am not pleased with myself,' for a lapse into unchastity. For example, in the spring of 1851, we find him writing, 'I beckoned to something pink, which in the distance seemed to be very nice, and opened the door at the back. I couldn't see her. It was vile and repulsive. I even hate her because I've broken my rules on her account.'

There was plenty of this in the years of indolence after he first left Kazan. In the first summer at Yasnaya Polyana, he was in love with a maid called Dunyasha. She had lately got married to a steward called Orekhov and the young landlord had the pair sleep in the room next to him, so that he could imagine on the other side of his bedroom wall, and perhaps, in a tormented way, even listen to the guiltless happiness of the couple. Another year, it was a maid of his Aunt Tatyana, a girl called Gasha, whom he got pregnant. The incident was one of the things which, according to his later conversations with Biryukov, got changed and dramatised into the theme of his later novel *Resurrection*. Gasha, however, unlike Maslova, did not have to drag her way through sin and shame, but was transferred to a perfectly happy life as a maid in the household of Tolstoy's sister.

But in spite, or perhaps because of, the delights and moral torment provided by maids and peasant women, life in the countryside was as dull for Tolstoy as it had been for Yevgeny Onegin.

> Потом увидел ясно он,
> Что и в деревне скука та же,
> Хоть нет ни улиц, ни дворцов,
> Ни карт, ни балов, ни стихов...

[Then he saw clearly that it could be just as boring in the country, even though there were no streets, no palaces, no cards, no balls, no verses. . . .][8]

*   *   *   *

58

For the next two years, Tolstoy spent the summer months in Yasnaya Polyana and for the winter season, he took a flat, which he shared with a friend, in the Arbat district of Moscow.

A twentieth-century Muscovite would be surprised, were he or she to return to the Moscow of 1850, by its smallness and by its newness. In 1812, it had been a largely wooden town. At the time of Napoleon's invasion, it had been burnt to the ground. More or less all that survived of the old town was within the walls of the medieval citadel, or Kremlin, with its stupendous churches, cathedrals and royal residences.

Domestic Moscow was a nineteenth-century creation. The town which Tolstoy knew consisted of avenues, squares and houses, not one of which was much more than forty years old. True cosmopolitans like Turgenev enjoyed looking down their noses at the Muscovites, who seemed to them provincial and conservative. But many of the 'good' old families had large houses there. In 1850, there was still an air of aristocratic leisure about the place. The extraordinary over-crowding and industrial expansion which dogged the old capital in the later part of the century, and which caused Tolstoy such anguish, had not yet begun.

By his own confession, the Moscow days and nights were dissipated: a lot of drinking; sorties to brothels or to 'the gipsies'; an increasing addiction to gambling. All these punctuated his presence at the *soirées* and balls of his grander relations and friends. In society, shyness still tormented him unless he was drunk. It is hard to think that the rules which he formulated for social behaviour necessarily made him the most charming of companions. '*Rules for society*. Choose difficult situations, always try to control a conversation, speak loudly, calmly and distinctly, try to begin and end a conversation yourself. Seek the company of people higher in the world than yourself. . . .'[9]

The irresolution of these years, the inability to settle or to study, or to know where his life was leading, were perhaps exacerbated by the fact that the Ant Brotherhood was now dispersed. Nikolay was absent on military service in the Caucasus. Dmitry was out of touch. Sergey was devoting himself to horses and to fornicating with gipsies. Yet, of all the four brothers, Lev Nikolayevich was the only one who had failed to complete his university course. Obviously, the original idea (or one of them) upon leaving Kazan was that he would spend his

59

time in the country to revise his law books. That idea came to nothing. Then, quite suddenly, towards the end of January 1849, he went to St. Petersburg.

There could have been no greater contrast between the essentially provincial atmosphere of Moscow, and the gracious beauty and cosmopolitan energy of St. Petersburg. It was not Tolstoy's first visit to the place, but it was his first extended stay there. For the first time, his eye took in the sheer scale of the city — the streets, the buildings, the Nevsky Prospekt, the canals, the enormous eighteenth-century palaces, the avenues and boulevards down which the people glided elegantly in their sleighs. The Neva was frozen. The snow showed off the buildings to peculiar effect. This was the city which Pushkin loved and celebrated in his poetry:

> I love your brutal winter, freezing
> the air to so much windless space;
> by broad Neva the sledges breezing;
> brighter than roses each girl's face.[10]

Here too was the world which later Dostoyevsky was to make his own — the teeming world of the poor, the eccentrics and grotesques who invariably congregate in a capital city. All sorts and conditions were here, from the Tsar and his courtiers (among them Tolstoy's own relations) to the notorious bath-houses and bars of low life. Here, too, were intellectuals, fully aware that this was the city where Peter the Great had deliberately opened a window upon Europe. It was a place where you were as likely to hear French spoken as Russian, where students might congregate in cafés, and where all the latest periodicals and publications could be devoured.

On February 13, a fortnight after his arrival, Tolstoy wrote to his brother Sergey that he intended to stay in the capital forever. First, he was going to take his law examinations, then he was going to enter Government service, as all the great Tolstoys had done. 'I know you won't believe that I've changed; you'll say "That's the twentieth time you've said it, and there's no good in you and you're the emptiest of fellows." But no, this time I've changed quite differently from the way I used to change before. Before, I'd say to myself, "I think I shall change," but now I see that I have changed and say, "I have changed." '[11]

Strange to say Tolstoy did buckle down and pass a couple of law examinations within a few months of coming to live at St. Petersburg; but the next letter to Sergey, in May 1849, tells its own sad tale. He was badly in need of three thousand five hundred silver roubles to cover gambling debts and living expenses. Would Sergey kindly sell a small estate to cover the costs? As for Lev Nikolayevich's idea of joining the Civil Service, it had evidently been forgotten or abandoned. He was now going to join the Horse Guards as a cadet. Unfortunately, he could not join up, let alone get a commission, without money. 'God willing, I'll turn over a new leaf and become a respectable person one day. . . . Don't show this letter to Auntie. I don't want to upset her.'[12]

But the next thing which Auntie heard was that Tolstoy was going to devote the summer to music. It was always a passion with him and, to help his studies along, he brought home to Yasnaya Polyana a noisy, drunken German musician, lately met in a cabaret in St. Petersburg, whose name was Rudolph.

Aunt Tatyana, who had not played the piano for years, started to practise again, and she surprised her nephew by the accuracy and beauty with which she played his favourites: Weber's Sonata in A-flat major, as well as the usual repertoire of Mozart, Haydn, Bach and early Beethoven.

But his aunt was worried about him. She wished that he would settle to something, even if it were merely to have an affair with a rich, married woman. She fantasised about his becoming an aide-de-camp to the Tsar, but as autumn began once more to set in at Yasnaya Polyana, Tolstoy had a new craze up his sleeve. He started a school for the peasants at Yasnaya Polyana. Like most of his ventures at this date, it did not come to anything. In fact, after a couple of years, it folded for want of funds. But it was the beginning of something which was to be a major preoccupation in the years to come.

Another public-spirited thing which he did in the autumn of 1849 was to become a local magistrate. On November 23, he was nominated for a post in the Chancellory of the Tula Assembly of Nobles. Tolstoy moved into Tula, the merry little provincial town some miles from Yasnaya. It was the very place where, twelve years before, his father had dropped dead in the street. Tolstoy's duties on the Assembly of Nobles can hardly have been arduous.

A photograph taken not long before he went to Tula shows a lean, extremely youthful twenty-one year old. The next twelve months were to add whiskers, flab and belligerence to the face. But in 1849, the face is sharp, wary. It looks as though it could have developed into a bony face like Alexander Pope's, or Voltaire's. The very short hair emphasises large, protuberant ears. The full lips are not merely sensuous but satirical. But the most arresting feature is the preternaturally straight brown hair which overhangs very dark, deep-set eyes. It is a face of extreme aliveness and alertness. But it stares at us, as though a complete stranger to its cravat, frockcoat and sofa. It seems to be asking, 'What in the world am I doing here?'

A sense of being a displaced person was a recurrent one in all Tolstoy's great literary precursors in Russia, in none more so than Lermontov, whose *A Hero of Our Time*, one of the most extraordinary novels in the history of the world, Tolstoy read at about this time. Pechorin, the 'hero', believes that 'in our time', happiness or moral certainty are impossible. When he has killed Grushnitsky in the duel, he proclaims, '*Finita la commedia*'. Mortals, he says in another place, can do no more than go on from doubt to doubt. Just as Onegin, in an earlier generation, was a conscious projection of Pushkin himself, so in *A Hero of Our Time*, the identification between artist and subject was absolute. Belinsky, when he first met Lermontov in 1840, declared that Pechorin *was* Lermontov.

Yet in Pushkin and Lermontov, no more than in Griboyedov, Romantic egotism differed from the solipsistic frenzy of Byron or Schiller by always, in fact, sharing something with its readership. Whereas Byron struck his poses in an essentially solitary way for the benefit of his English admirers (and, indeed, rather like Wilde, could be said to have been a martyr to them) Pushkin found, almost *malgré lui*, that to his poses every Russian bosom was returning an echo. The Romantic hero in Russian literature found, willy-nilly, that the more he wrote about himself, the more his readers felt him to understand Russia itself, and their collective moral predicaments.

A perceptive English critic has written, 'Pechorin knows that on December 14, 1825, an iron door closed upon Russia. For his generation there seems to be no way out. He is the bound athlete, the genius who could only become a bureaucrat.' All this suggests Pushkin's, and Lermontov's, strong political commitment and awareness. They were both old enough to have been actively sympathetic to the Decembrists; hardly an option for Tolstoy, who was born into the age of the 'bureaucrats'. At no stage, really, can one 'place' Tolstoy on any political spectrum, any more than you could fit him into any of the circles of literary movements of his day, or pigeonhole him as a westerniser or a Slavophil. He is truly a creation of the generation into which he was born, moving 'from doubt to doubt'; and, because he was quite cut off by upbringing and education from the intellectual circles of the capital, his journey, which began alone, was to continue for much of life as a pretty solitary trek.

The year in Tula was not really a year in Tula. In the warmer months he went back to Yasnaya Polyana. Whenever he could, he went to stay with his sister, or with friends. In the winter of 1850, he moved back to his flat in Moscow.

Что нового покажет мне Москва?
Дчера был бал, а завтра будет два.

[What new thing will Moscow show me?
Yesterday there was a ball, tomorrow there will be two.]

The familiar lines from Griboyedov's *Misfortunes of Being Clever* (*Gorye ot uma*) had already become proverbial by 1850. The play is set in 1820. 'Cleverness' ('*um*') for those twenties intellectuals was synonymous with radicalism. It was cleverness which involved Griboyedov in the Decembrist conspiracies, and cleverness which got his play censored. His early death aged thirty-four is as much of a piece with his Romanticism as were those of Pushkin and Lermontov. For some Russians, Griboyedov, not Pushkin, was seen as the master. Alexander Blok considered *Gorye ot uma* 'perhaps the greatest work in our literature. . . . unsurpassed in the literature of the world'.[13]

Western readers who are amused by Griboyedov's cynical drawing-room comedy might well find Blok's hyperbole incomprehensible. Probably not Tolstoy, though, who, not in the least 'clever' in Griboyedov's sense, would probably have found much to respond to in the comedy. Unlike Onegin or Pechorin, Griboyedov's hero Chatsky is middle-aged, a forty-five year old who has seen it all, a somewhat Proustian figure, in fact, who, wearied and even disgusted by high society, is yet unable to keep away from it.

Grand drawing rooms, rather than peasant cottages, were to provide Tolstoy with the inspiration for his first attempt at prose fiction. Throughout December, he was in Moscow, becoming increasingly fond of gambling, and going to as many parties as he could. Then, towards the end of the month, Nikolay Nikolayevich returned from the Caucasus, and the Ant Brotherhood began to reassemble. Tolstoy went to spend Christmas with Nikolay at his sister's house. They also reunited with Sergey. After the holiday, Tolstoy went back to Moscow, where the social round began again.

Increasingly, he was becoming fond of Louisa Ivanovna, the wife of his Volkonsky cousin, Alexander Alexandrovich. On March 24, he spent yet another evening at their house, playing cards, and hovering awkwardly about his hostess, and staying so late that they gave him supper before he went downstairs to greet his patient coachman and make his way home through the frosty air. That night, for some impenetrable reason, was different. Perhaps it was a trivial reason. Perhaps he was, to *just* the right degree, drunk; or, to *just* the right degree, in love with the idea of being in love with Louisa Ivanovna. The next morning, he woke up, thinking of the evening, and it seems that he spent the day alone. From 26 to 28 March, he wrote solidly, polishing it up in the next few days, before on April 1 returning to Yasnaya Polyana. It was a fragment, never to be completed, called *The History of Yesterday*.[14]

The elements in Tolstoy's genius were many-stranded, many-particled. As was the case with other prodigious literary geniuses, these elements only appeared to coalesce after a period of total indolence. *The History of Yesterday* is both a record of Tolstoy's indolence and, as it were, a snapshot of some of the undeveloped elements of his genius before they 'gelled' or came together. It is a fascinating record of how he set to work, writing up and transforming experience. On the one hand, it can be seen as a simple extension of his journal. Not only does it describe an actual evening, spent at a *soirée* of the Volkonskys' in Moscow; but it also meditates upon the diary itself. When he gets home, he indulges in a feast of self-reflection of a kind which will only be too familiar to readers of the diaries.

I have often heard it said of me — 'Hollow man, he lives without an aim.' And I have even often said it of myself, not just so as to reiterate the words of someone else, but I feel in my soul that it is bad to live like this, and that one needs to have an aim in life.

But what is one to do in order to become a man of action, and live with an aim? One can't give *oneself* an aim. I've already tried countless times, and it did not work. One needs, not to invent an aim, but to find one which is already in existence and which I have but to recognise. I think I have found some sort of aim: universal knowledge and a development of all my faculties. And one of the best means of attaining this is to keep a Franklin journal. In the diary every day, I write down what I have done wrong. . . .[15]

But *The History of Yesterday* is not really the work of a penitent; no more so than *The Confessions* of Jean-Jacques Rousseau. Tolstoy is more than a bit in love with the flirtatious 'older woman' who is his hostess. In a very Rousseauesque way, he lets the reader into the secret that she is also in love with him ('*Comme il est aimable, ce jeune homme*'), and when her husband's back is turned, their flirting becomes almost outrageous.

The hero of Tolstoy's early diary is a graceless, rather humourless fellow, whom it is hard to like. The hero of *The History of Yesterday* begins to be a deliberately comic creation. He has a strict rule not to go to bed after midnight, and so he rises from the *soirée* to leave early. He makes his adieus to his host. But *madame* urges him to stay, and he finds himself, awkwardly standing, with a hat in one hand, and the other hand resting on the back of her divan. Of course he stays to supper, but he has neither the skill nor the nerve — the *um* in fact — to carry out the lightweight conversation which is required of him. He is not Chatsky, nor was meant to be.

Her husband went out for some reason, probably to order the supper. When I am left alone with her, I always feel clumsy and awkward. When I follow those who are departing with my eyes, it is as bad for me as dancing a five-figure quadrille. I see that my partner is crossing over to the other side, and I must stand alone. I am confident that Napoleon could not have suffered more when, before Waterloo, the Saxons went over to the enemy, than I did, when, in my first youth, I watched this cruel evolution. . . .[16]

The joke may be clumsy, it may misfire, but it is there. The detachment from self of which the real diary was incapable becomes here something comically, self-consciously Sternean.

Tolstoy read *A Sentimental Journey* initially in French, but he was so bowled over by it ('an immense influence') that he soon set to work to improve his English by translating it from the original into Russian. This was a purely private enterprise. Both *A Sentimental Journey* and *Tristram Shandy* had been published in Russian before the close of the eighteenth century. At first glance, one would imagine that the gulf between *Tristram Shandy* and *War and Peace* was absolute, and that no line could be drawn which would connect their authors. At this date, there is no evidence that Tolstoy had read *Tristram Shandy*; so there is no need for us to build Shandy Hall at Yasnaya Polyana, nor to point out that Tolstoy's story, like Tristram's, was four volumes finished before he was even born; no need to draw fantastic parallels between the siege of Moscow in 1812, and Uncle Toby's misfortunes at the siege of Namur. No need, alas, to connect Tolstoy's maternal fixations with Tristram Shandy's obscene fascination with his mother's body and its various orifices.

But we do have incontrovertible evidence that *A Sentimental Journey* was what started Tolstoy off as a writer. The practice of getting up steam by reading English novels was to survive into his maturity. His wife records in her journals in 1878, 'I happen to know that when Lyovochka turns to English novels he is about to start writing himself.'[17] Nothing so crude as imitation was at work in the mature Tolstoy. Rather, the absorption in a different mind engaged in an analogous creative process released something within him, providing, when it worked, the right blend of distraction and impetus.

> He is fretful because he cannot write; this evening, while he was reading Dickens's *Dombey and Son*, he suddenly announced to me: 'Aha! I've got it!' When I asked what he meant he would not tell me at first, but eventually he said: 'Well, I've been imagining this old woman — her appearance, her manner, her thoughts — but I haven't been able to find the right feelings to give her.'[18]

He was not borrowing the feelings out of Dickens, but somehow or another, reading the work of another great writer stimulated his own daemon.

In the immature Tolstoy, something much closer to imitation was at work. The strong element of suppressed sexual desire and the *faux-naïf* flirtation between a young man and a slightly older woman owe much to Sterne. So, perhaps, do the moments of solitude, but it is in solitude that the essential differences between the two writers most sharply emerge. Tolstoy's narrator when in repose worries about the moral pointlessness of his life, he wishes that there were some great aim to follow, and like the hero of all the great Tolstoyan fictions, he strives to master, in his own weak person, the mysteries of the universe itself. Quite simply, he yearns for God. Not so the 'Yorick' with whom Sterne chose to enflesh his imagination.

> Alas, poor Yorick! cried I, what art thou doing here? On the very first onset of all this glittering chatter, thou art reduced to an atom — seek — seek some winding alley with a tourniquet at the end of it, where chariot never rolled or flambeau shot its rays. There thou mayest solace thy soul in converse sweet with some kind *grisset* of a barber's wife, and get into such coteries. . . .[19]

Sterne's huge appeal as a writer (again, to use a criterion of Henry James) was that he did not strictly speaking *write* at all. The high popularity of *A Sentimental Journey* in the last forty years of the eighteenth century stemmed from its usability as a blueprint for Romantic egotists. Stylistically, it could have been penned by some lecherous parish clerk. It arrives in your hands half finished. The reader does the writer's work for him, finding in it virtues which the reader has put there himself and therefore esteems much more highly than he would the virtues of another. Sterne not surprisingly enjoys great popularity in the twentieth century, with its mania for readers doing the work of writers, and discovering their own 'text' as they go along. Also, *A Sentimental Journey* is attractively short.

In Tolstoy's eyes, the gap between the unfinished book Sterne did not write, and the 'masterpiece' which we discover in it, was filled by his own evolving self-preoccupations. To a large degree, Tolstoy only found himself at this period as a reader. He only made sense to himself when imagined as an Onegin, a Chatsky, a Pechorin. In *The History of Yesterday*, he transposes the imagined self into a social world. The result is not without its comedy, some of it conscious, as during his shy attempts to converse with Volkonskaya, and some of it still unconscious, in the diary mode: his knowing comments about how to conduct oneself in society, his man-of-the-world poses. But there are other strands here, too. Coming out into the late Moscow night, and being met by Dmitry the coachman, the narrator creates, for perhaps a page and a half, the illusion that we are really there, listening to the crossing keepers and Muscovite coachmen shouting to each other through the frosty air. It is a glimpse of what Tolstoy was to be at his best, a glimpse of the very essence of that genius with which he enjoyed so stormy a relationship. At present, it was safe, because he had no idea that it was there. There is not the smallest trace in *The History of Yesterday* that he recognised what he was really good at: that he was possessed with a Shakespearian capacity to recreate our world, all its naturalness, all its outer reality, all the inner feelings of its human inhabitants. There is no sign that he knew what he was up to while writing *The History of Yesterday*. In all its stammering clumsiness, its mixture of unconscious comedy and high moral seriousness, it could have been penned by Pierre Bezukhov, the clumsy hero of *War and Peace*; which, in a way, it was.

> Cold is the absence of heat. Darkness is the absence of light. Evil is the absence of good. Why does man love heat, light and goodness? Because they are natural. The cause of heat and light are the sun; the cause of goodness is God. You could no more have had a bad God, than a sun which is cold and dark. We see light, and rays of light; we seek its cause and we say that it is the sun. Light and dark and the law of gravity lead us to the highest point, so the law of goodness leads us to its source — God.[20]

In his beginning was his end. In Tolstoy's best art — as, for instance, in the creation of Pierre himself — there is as much naturalness in talking about God as there is in describing frost or *barouches*. But, as in the end, at the very beginning, there is a tension between the spontaneity of his art, and the demands of soul. The fates are about to shower upon this improbable recipient imaginative gifts which are almost without parallel. He fears them, *et dona ferentes*.

The true literary irony of the piece is that it is as much a self-contradiction as anything penned by the paradoxical Sterne. Its paradox is totally unconscious. The narrator expresses regret and self-hatred because he has no aim in life, and does not know what to do. But it is precisely in writing down his predicament and fashioning it into something which is half-way to being art that his 'aim in life' is discovered. Quite unannounced and sandwiched between social engagements of stunning triviality, Tolstoy's vocation as a writer had arrived. Rightly was the aunt, in *A Landlord's Morning*, to say that we only feel our vocation when we have once mistaken it. From now onwards, Tolstoy's existence is to be understood in what he was or was not writing.

The literary historians, anxious to hurry on to Tolstoy's great works, have written slightingly of *The History of Yesterday*. But they have also written misleadingly, as though its chief interest was a freak, a false herald, promising the emergence of a Proust or a Joyce. Far from being proto-Modernist, the fragment actually suggests (with its debts and allusions to Sterne and Rousseau) a world of literary modes and models which, by the standards of Western Europe, were at least half a century out of date. But *The History of Yesterday* does herald a new star in the firmament; a novelist who has almost nothing in common with Proust or Joyce; the author, that is to say, of *Anna Karenina* and *War and Peace*.

Chapter Four

Kinderszenen in the Caucasus

1851 - 1854

Когда касаются холодных рук моих
С небрехной смелостью красавиц городских
Давно бестрепетные руки –
Наружно погружась в их блеск и суету,
Ласкаю я в душе старинную мечту,
Погибших лет святые звуки.

[When the hands of town-beauties, which have
long since ceased to tremble, touch my cold
hands with careless boldness, how often then
— outwardly absorbed in their glitter and
vanity, do I caress in my soul an old dream,
and the sounds of years gone by!]

Lermontov, 'January 1'

*I*t was three years[1] since the brothers Tolstoy had all seen one another together; all, by now, had gone very separate ways, and the effects on the immature Lev Nikolayevich had been disastrous. Since he left Kazan, he had been unable to settle to anything. Friendships had been formed, dinners eaten, maids deflowered, resolutions of good conduct written down but, time and again, broken. More disastrous than his inability to settle in Moscow, St. Petersburg or Yasnaya was Lev Nikolayevich's growing addiction to the tables. However he might be loved by his aunt Toinette, his sister Marya or his brother Sergey, the addiction — which was the ruin of so many noble families in Russia — was a menace. The idleness, the moral inertia, the sense of futility were all sure symptoms of what the Russians call *khalatnost'*: literally, 'dressing-gownness', the tendency to loll about doing nothing, and thinking futile thoughts. It is in such moods that gambling debts, desperate philosophies and suicides are hatched.

No one recognised the dangers more than the young self-improver himself, and the resolution of the difficulty — salvation through literature — had not yet formed itself in his brain.

On December 22, 1850, Nikolay Nikolayevich had come home on long leave from the Caucasus, and the means of grace — via the Ant Brotherhood — were at least reconstituted. The noise of life began again, though for a few months the brothers did not see much of each other. Nikolay had other old contacts to renew besides that with his youngest brother. Sergey had by now installed his favourite gipsy girl from Tula, Marya Shishkina, as mistress of his household. Marya

Nikolayevna and her husband Valeryan were nursing their new offspring. Lev Nikolayevich spent much of the time in Moscow buying a horse he did not need, flirting with his cousin's wife, practising gymnastics (a new craze) and having the experiences and, at last, the resolution to pen the fragmentary *The History of Yesterday*. Thus was passed the holy season of Lent.

Easter was spent in Yasnaya Polyana and, conscious of his unworthiness, he confessed his sins to the village priest and received Holy Communion. In the days after Easter, he tried to talk things over with his aunt, but the mere sight of one of the house serfs 'is making me struggle violently with passion and yield to it more and more often, just because I've already had her here'. On April 18, the diary sadly recalls, 'I could not refrain.'[2] On the following day, his brother Nikolay arrived with his sister and brother-in-law. They had come for a family reunion in the old home, to be sure. But there was also business to discuss. How were Lev Nikolayevich's debts, now standing at sixteen thousand roubles, to be paid? It was eventually agreed that one of his villages, Verotynka, should be sliced off his estate and sold. Meanwhile, what was to be done with the young prodigal? Common sense, family tradition, and Lev Nikolayevich's natural impulse to run away from difficult situations, for once, all combined. Generations of Tolstoys had served in the army and it had been on Lev's mind for some years that he might, like Nikolay, do the same. Why should he not accompany his elder brother when his leave was up, return to the Caucasus and see how he liked it? If it seemed a plausible idea, he could join up as a cadet.

The idea had everything to be said for it. Not only would it be an ideal way of taking Lev away from the drawing rooms of Moscow, which were obviously so 'bad' for him. It also had positive attractions, particularly for the newly-fledged 'literary' man, who had just scribbled his few pages of *The History of Yesterday*. Where better, for a young hero of their time, to seek a period of exile than in the Caucasus where, as Lermontov observed, the wilderness listens to God, and star speaks to star? It is important, perhaps, given the fact that *our* responses to the Caucasus are so conditioned by what Pushkin, Lermontov and Tolstoy had to say about the place, that we remember that, whatever the romantic charms of the landscape, the reasons for a Russian troop presence there were purely military. As Ronald Hingley has incisively reminded us, 'Like the English lakes, the Caucasus inspired the country's poets, but the atmosphere was less elegiac, and anything but Wordsworthian. It was neither little Lucy nor the springs of Dove that one might expect to meet round the bends of Chechnya's mountain tracks so much as a bullet in the neck.'[3]

Eighteen fifty-one was an extraordinarily exciting time for a young Russian to be embarking upon his career, and the journey to the Caucasus by a young man whose career might go either in a literary or a military direction is emblematic of the climate of things.

In intellectual circles, particularly in St. Petersburg, the march of progress was still keenly and optimistically felt, in spite of the many repressive measures of the Government of Tsar Nicholas I. Whatever the Emperor and his advisers may have wanted, Russia was by now on its way to being a fully European country, open to all the cultural and ideological conflicts which had swept through Western Europe in the previous decade. If the Decembrist generation had brought back European books and ideas as though they were some kind of guilty contraband (in the way that a modern Soviet citizen might smuggle home blue jeans after a trip to London or Paris) the present generation were less self-consciously borrowers and more surely partakers of the European inheritance.

Eighteen forty-eight had been the 'year of revolutions'. Louis-Philippe had been driven from the throne of France; Metternich had fallen in Vienna. In Berlin Frederick William IV had conceded a constitution. At about the same time, only a few weeks before the Paris revolution, a young German exile in London had published a little work called *The Communist Manifesto*, whose opening words were 'A spectre is haunting Europe.' His name was Karl Marx.

The Russians not only had intellectuals of their own to match these western developments. Their extraordinary literary renaissance showed every sign of continuing. Having played almost no part in the European scene at any previous stage in its history, there had been a sudden and extraordinary flowering. Alexander Pushkin (1799-1837) had begun to publish poems when he was fifteen which were wholly Russian in character, and yet comparable with his giant contemporaries Byron and Scott. Pushkin's appearance in the Russian sky — comparable with the emergence of Shakespeare towards the close of the sixteenth century in England — lit up a firmament of stars: his fellow poet Lermontov; the critic Belinsky; and other names no less remarkable, both those such as Alexander Herzen who were 'Europeanisers' and welcomed Russia's new contacts with the West, and those such as the Aksakov brothers who cherished the Slavic inheritance and were to be known as 'Slavophils'. Lermontov, moreover, before his tragically early death, was to write *A Hero of Our Time*. The literary bombshell which was waiting to burst upon Europe — the development of the nineteenth-century Russian novel — had started to fizz. The absurdities of Russian bureaucracy had been satirised in Gogol's hilarious *Dead Souls* (1837) and in the writings of M. E. Saltykov-Shchedrin whose novel *The Golovlyov Family* is if anything funnier than Gogol.

Tolstoy, then, belonged to the first generation in Russia to have been born into a full, vigorous literary and intellectual inheritance; to have been born into a Russia which not only received western intellectual writings as well as novels and poems, but which also now produced such writings themselves, writings of a kind which rivalled and outshone their western equivalents.

On one level, then, bliss was it in that dawn to be alive. But there was a drawback. In Russia, for intellectuals, there has always been a drawback.

Tsar Nicholas I was not, to put it mildly, an intellectual and his reaction to all this imaginative renaissance in his midst was characteristically decisive. Herzen had suffered internal exile from 1834 onwards and in the year of revolutions he found himself exiled from Russia altogether. There is not much doubt that, had Belinsky not died in 1848, and had Lermontov and Pushkin not already been dead, they would all have been locked up or silenced. Gogol's exposition of the corruption of local government officials in *Dead Souls* seems to us like pure comedy. It cost him his liberty. Even though he was profoundly Orthodox in religion and conservative in politics, Gogol was such a non-person in the Government's eyes that by the time he died in 1852, Turgenev could be put under house arrest merely for writing a kind obituary of his fellow novelist.

This, then, was the climate in which Tolstoy was growing up: a renaissance such as had never been seen in Russia before and a system of censorship which vigorously suppressed any signs of independent life among poets, journalists and novelists. It is rather as though the Government of Louis XIV, instead of persecuting Huguenots, had turned its attentions on Corneille and Racine; or as though Elizabeth I, not content with making Catholic martyrs, had sent Shakespeare, Marlowe and Spenser to the gallows. On December 22, 1849, a young genius called Fyodor Mikhaylovich Dostoyevsky was arrested and condemned to death for the crime of owning a printing press. The sentence was changed at the very last minute — even as he stood before the firing squad — and by the time Tolstoy was making his way down to the Caucasus, Dostoyevsky was doing hard labour in Siberia.

*　　　　*　　　　*　　　　*

Nicholas I felt the classic tyrant's need to compensate for disturbance at home by taking up a belligerent attitude to the countries on his border. And there were definite causes for Russian anxiety. Poland, for example, was a traditional area of concern. It had always regarded itself as an independent Catholic kingdom, profoundly hostile to the Orthodox Empire to its east. Now it had the full backing of Prussia against the borders and armies of Nicholas I. And as if this was not worrying enough for Nicholas, there had been, ever since 1848, a whiff of revolution in the air throughout Eastern Europe. Romania had had a revolution in 1848. Poland and Hungary were riddled with westernising, atheistical revolutionaries. Or so, to the Russian way of looking at things, it appeared.

In addition, Nicholas wanted to expand the borders of his Empire in three important directions — in the north-east Pacific, in Turkey (where an international crisis was brewing) and in the Caucasus.[4]

It was the Caucasian situation which, immediately, affected Tolstoy. It is somehow emblematic of what the future would hold that his literary career, which really began in the Caucasus, should have come to birth far from the salons of Moscow and St. Petersburg. It is also somehow typical that, though there were strong political reasons for his brother's fellow soldiers to be in the Caucasian mountains, for Tolstoy it was a purely personal journey. Of all the Russian writers in the last century, he is the one who fits least easily into any intellectual circle or political category. From the beginning he is alone.

By the treaty of Turkmanchay, in February 1828, Russia had acquired Persian Armenia. During the 1830s, the Russians made inroads into the main Caucasus *massif* and had ambitions of pressing on towards Turkestan and Afghanistan, in spite of continual resistance from the natives. In 1844, the Tsar appointed Count Mikhail Vorontsov as viceroy of the Caucasus. In May 1845, Vorontsov had led a force of eighteen thousand men into Chechnya. The mountaineers retreated, allowing the Russians to press on as far as Grozny, penetrating deep into the heavily (beech) wooded hill country. But it was then that the resistance from the mountain snipers could begin, and there were four thousand Russian casualties, including three generals, in the summer of 1846. There had been no peace in the Caucasus ever since, in 1799, the mad Emperor Paul had annexed Georgia, which for hundreds of years had been a little buffer state between the Ottoman and the Persian Empires.

Transcaucasia required, and received, a constant supply of Russian troops, rather as the Northwest Frontier of India and Afghanistan, at the same period, and for the next hundred years, needed the perpetual vigilance of the British army. In fact, the comparison has often been made between the relative positions of the Caucasus and India in the life and imaginations of the Russian and British Empires respectively.[5] It is probably a more helpful one than the comparison with the English lakes, though Tolstoy was to have his Wordsworthian moments in the year to come.

When the decision had been made that he should accompany Nikolay back to his unit, there was nothing to do but act upon it. They left Yasnaya Polyana on April 29, 1851, spent a few days in Moscow, and then made their way to spend a week in Kazan. In his diary at the time Tolstoy expressed his 'contempt for society', but by the simpler standards of Nikolay (founder of the Ant Brotherhood, who had spent the past five years entirely in the company of soldiers) Lev was disconcertingly, and even foolishly sophisticated. Within a day of arrival in Kazan, Lev remarked to his elder brother of some passer-by in the street, 'That man is a cad.' 'Why?' asked the baffled Nikolay. 'Because he isn't wearing gloves.' 'Why is it caddish not to wear gloves?' asked Nikolay. Lev did not have an answer.[6]

Still he was not so much of a coxcomb that he could not enjoy a return to childhood enthusiasms. One day, helpless with giggles, he climbed a tree outside his Aunt Pelageya's house and shouted at everyone through the windows. And he renewed a fairly unserious contact with a girl he had been half in love with. The girl's name was Zinaida and, unlike the maids and gipsies about whom he could only scribble secretly in his diary, this devotion could be talked about in the family. It was 'the pure yearning of two souls for one another'.[7] He even tried getting ready to be the Lermontov *de ses jours* — by writing a poem about her. It was awful.

Going to Kazan gave them the chance to make duty calls on the family. But it also provided them with the chance to travel south in the most agreeable possible manner: by barge down the Volga.

The dullness of the landscape in the initial stages of their voyage down the river was relieved by the exciting sense that, as they drew closer to Astrakhan, they were entering a new and romantic world. If the boat seemed in danger of getting stuck on shallows or sandbanks, exotically clad figures would come to haul it to rescue. Tolstoy was getting his first glimpse of the Cossacks.

Cossacks, since the seventeenth century, had been a law unto themselves, while fulfilling an essential role as border guards for the Tsars. On the Polish border, they had something of the character of Orthodox crusaders, medieval knights born centuries out of time, organised into camps, and committed to resisting the Roman Catholicism, monarchism and westernisation of the Poles. In the Tartar regions whither Tolstoy was bound, their religious obedience had, strangely enough, less fervour. Cossacks here were nominally the defenders of Christianity against Islam. But though they tended to be Old Believers (an ultra-conservative sect who had broken away from the Orthodox Church rather than accept the reforms of the Patriarch Nikon in 1653) and therefore to regard even the Orthodox as beyond the pale, their general attitude to life was unfanatical. In so far as their religion affected existence, it was very much the sort of life-worship which Tolstoy describes in his Cossacks novel.

Though they had not adopted the Mohammedanism of their foes the Tartars, they had adopted many Tartar words, costumes and customs. Unlike the Cossacks of the Polish border, the Cossacks in the Caucasus grouped themselves together in villages. And it was to such a village, Starogladkovskaya (the name means 'old and smooth') that they were bound, a tiny little place on the banks of the Terek, a border village with, on the other side of the river, hostile Moslem snipers looking down upon it. All the physical descriptions of the village in Tolstoy's later story, *The Cossacks*, are based closely on the place: the almost shocking beauty of the mountains, seen from the reedy, sandy banks of the Terek, the Oriental strangeness of the village, the low-lying, thatched houses, the beautiful women, kept firmly in their place.

But the final version of the story was not written up for another nine years. We should postpone until then, perhaps, a discussion of Tolstoy's reasons for making the hero of *The Cossacks* both so like, and so unlike, his twenty-three-year-old self. Olenin, it will be remembered, only has to glimpse the mountains before deciding, at once, to put his past behind him. (He fails to do so in the end, but his initial reaction is to feel that 'all his Moscow reminiscences, shame and repentance, and his trivial dreams about the Caucasus, vanished and did not return'.)

Tolstoy, who had no function in Starogladkovskaya, save as an awkward civilian hanger-on of his military elder brother, felt no such reassurances on his arrival in the Caucasus, if his diaries of the period tell us the truth. He realised that he would be thrown back, for company, on Nikolenka's regimental colleagues, and the prospect did not please him much. Within two days of arriving in the place, he was exclaiming 'My God, my God, what sad and melancholy days. . . . The melancholy which I feel is something which I cannot understand or imagine to myself. I have nothing to regret, almost nothing to wish for, no reason to be angry with fate. I can understand how gloriously I could live on my imagination. But no. My imagination depicts nothing for me — I have no dreams. There is a certain gloomy delight in despising people — but I am not even capable of that; I don't give them a thought at all. . . .' Six days later, he was deciding that he really had been in love with the girl in Kazan with whom he had flirted. No wonder. 'I did not say a word to her about love, but I am so sure that she knew my feelings that if she did love me, I attribute it only to the fact that she understood me. All impulses of the soul are pure and elevated to begin with. Reality destroys their innocence and charm.'[8] This was certainly true as far as sex was concerned, and it is crucially important to understand this if Tolstoy is to come into any kind of focus.

The summer months were spent as only the pure in heart could spend them. . . . gambling, fighting, womanising. If he had thought that by getting away from Moscow drawing rooms, he could cure his addiction to cards, he was not reckoning on the Russian soldier's passion for gambling. In the second half of June, he lost two hundred roubles of his own, a hundred and fifty of Nikolay's. He borrowed a further five hundred and promptly lost that, bringing his losses by the beginning of July to eight hundred and fifty roubles.

At about this period, Tolstoy had his first direct experience of military conflict, when Nikolay's unit took part in a raid on the Chechen mountain tribesmen. It was an incident which inspired one of his earliest published stories, *The Raid*, a fascinating piece of writing which foreshadows the later Tolstoy in a number of revealing ways. When it was at length published in a magazine in March 1852, Tolstoy complained to his brother Sergey that the tale had been

'simply ruined by the censor. All that was good in it had been struck
out or mutilated.' It is understandable why the censor objected to
these 'good' passages, because they represent (even at this early stage
of his career) Tolstoy's profound worry about the very allowability of
war, a worry which is made all the more powerful by his devastating
artistic ability to particularise. For this story is an enormous artistic
advance on *The History of Yesterday*. In his first (censored) paragraph,
he wrote that he was 'more interested to know in what way and under
the influence of what feeling one soldier kills another than to know
how the armies were arranged at Austerlitz and Borodino'.[9] Thus,
beside his (slightly boring) *philosophe*'s desire to define the nature of
courage there is the wonderfully realised detail of particular lives: the
captain whose old mother back in Russia believes that he has been
spared by the wonder-working icon of Our Mother Mediatrix of the
Burning Bush (in fact he has been wounded several times); the cruel-
seeming young lieutenant who models his behaviour on the heroes of
Lermontov and Marlinsky — 'but his mistress (a Circassian of course),
whom I happened to meet subsequently, used to say that he was the
kindest and mildest of men, and that every evening he wrote down his
dismal thoughts in his diary as well as his accounts on ruled paper and
prayed to God on his knees. And how much he suffered merely to
appear in his own eyes what he wished to be.'[10] The comic absurdity
of this should put us constantly on our guard, incidentally, when
approaching Tolstoy's own multifarious accounts of himself. The
literary historian Prince Mirsky was right to regard the diary, in its
own way, as much as a work of art (though with different sorts of
purpose) as the fiction.[11] Much of Tolstoy's stupendous success as a
psychological realist depends on the confidence trick — he fooled
himself as much as his readers — of appearing himself in so many
guises; the *roué* and the cynic, the penitent and the mystic, the chaste
lover of one woman, the passionate devotee of his family, the
voluptuary in the brothel, the callous society man who finds his
brothers unendurably boring. Tolstoy makes the lieutenant in *The
Raid* so real to us because to all important purposes, he *is* that
lieutenant. And it is this power of sympathy, wherever it comes from,
combined with his photographic eye for detail, which makes his moral
judgements so devastating as the justly famous, censored passage
from Chapter VI.

Who will doubt that in the war of the Russians against the

mountain tribes, justice, resulting from a feeling of self-preservation, is on our side? If it were not for this war, what would secure the neighbouring rich and cultured Russian territories from robbery, murder, and raids by wild and warlike tribes. But consider two private persons. On whose side is the feeling of self-preservation and consequently of justice? Is it on the side of this ragamuffin — some Djemi or other — who, hearing of the approach of the Russians, snatches down his old gun from the wall, puts three or four charges (which he will only reluctantly discharge) in his pouch and runs to meet the Giaours, and on seeing that the Russians still advance, approaching the fields he has sown which they will tread down and his hut which they will burn, and the ravine where his mother, his wife, and his children have hidden themselves, shaking with fear — seeing that he will be deprived of all that constitutes his happiness — in impotent anger and with a cry of despair tears off his tattered jacket, flings down his gun, and drawing his sheepskin cap over his eyes sings his deathsong and flings himself headlong on to the Russian bayonets with only a dagger in his hand? Is justice on his side or on that of this officer on the General's staff who is singing French *chansonettes* so well just as he rides past us? He has a family in Russia, relations, friends, serfs, and obligations towards them, but no reason or desire to be at enmity with the hillsmen, and has come to the Caucasus just by chance and to show his courage. . . .[12]

Since *The Raid* is more or less the earliest finished Tolstoyan fiction that there is, it is interesting to find from the beginning an instance of the apparent separation of what has been called Tolstoy's right and left hands. At first sight, it is easy to think that the Slavophil patriot, the man who loves the excitement of the military life, the amoral Tolstoy who simply loves life in all its manifestations and details, is at war with Tolstoy the 'moralist'. We are often invited to think of Tolstoy as someone who spoilt his 'art' by trying to develop as a moraliser or a thinker. But in *The Raid*, there is no such division. It is because he can so cram his short story with detail of every human and natural kind — the captain lighting up a pipeful of cheap tobacco at the mention of his mother, the flocks of wild pigeons whirling above the broad ravine, the crickets and grasshoppers and thousands of other insects filling the roadside grasses with sound — it is all this massing of detail which leads naturally to the 'moralising'. War is not an abstract thing. In *The Raid* we see a battalion of well-trained Russian soldiers, actual people with lives and personalities who are completely real to us, harrying some pathetic tribesmen. 'Can it be that there is not room for all men on this beautiful earth under these immeasurable starry heavens? Can it be possible that in the midst of this entrancing Nature feelings of hatred, vengeance, or the desire to exterminate their fellows can endure in the souls of men?'[13] To know, to know deeply and closely, is to sympathise. And at the same time, there is a callous Homeric eye in Tolstoy which can see the behaviour of the soldiers who are looting the little village and recognise this too as an emanation of nature, of life. The conclusion of the tale depends for its beautiful effect precisely on such a suspension of moral feeling so that, while sympathising, we do not judge.

> The green of the grass and trees was turning black and becoming covered with dew. The dark masses of troops moved with measured sounds over the luxuriant meadows. Tambourines, drums and merry songs were heard from various sides. The voice of the second tenor of the Sixth Company rang out with full force and the sounds of his clear chest notes, full of feeling and power, floated through the clear evening air. . . .[14]

The Raid reflects a strong dawning in Tolstoy, which war was always to effect in him, of the sense of common humanity, shared not only with Russians of the officer class, but with peasants, gipsies, Cossacks, everyone. The story must reflect some feeling which he actually had himself in the summer of 1851 when we witness him making friends with the Cossack villagers.

The Tolstoy brothers were billeted with a vast, octogenarian Cossack, called Yepishka Sekhin. As is often going to happen in the course of my book, we are confronted with the problem of how to disentangle a character in real life from what he became in fiction. Evidently Yepishka was very much like Dyadya Yeroshka in Tolstoy's *The Cossacks*. Yepishka is at first described in Tolstoy's diaries merely as a 'veteran of Yermolov's days, a Cossack, a rogue and a joker'. In the finished novella Yeroshka is a figure of Shakespearian vigour, of Falstaffian strength of personality, once met, never forgotten, with his vastly broad shoulders, his broad beard as grey as the moon; even the smell of him remains with us — 'the strong but not unpleasant blended odour of *chikhir* [Caucasian wine], vodka, gunpowder and hard-baked blood'. *The Cossacks*, when finally revised, was the result of nine years' reflecting on Tolstoy's experience in the Caucasus, and Yeroshka's almost pagan life-acceptance is placed very deliberately at variance with young Olenin's tormented, educated, urban moralism. Such a 'considered' view of Yeroshka informs and shapes what might well be half memories of real conversations with the giant Yepishka.

'God has done everything for the joy of man. There is no sin in any of it. Take an example shall we say from the wild animal. He lives both in Tartar reeds and in ours. Wherever he lands up, there is his home. What God has given, that he eats. But our people say that we shall have to lick frying pans in hell for that. I think that it is all a fraud,' he added, after a pause.

'What's a fraud?' asked Olenin.

'What the preachers say. Once, old man, we had a Cossack captain who was my *kunak*, my close friend. He was a fine lad, just like I was. He was killed in Chechnya. So, he used to say that the preachers make all that stuff up out of their own heads. When you croak, he said, the grass grows on your grave, and that's all.' The old man laughed. 'He was a desperate man.'

'And how old are you?' asked Olenin.

'God knows. I must be about seventy. When you had a *tsaritsa*, I was no longer little. You work it out, see if it's as much as seventy years.'

'It would be. And you're still a fine fellow.'

'Well, anyway, thank God, I'm healthy, completely healthy, only a woman has marred me, the witch.'

'How?'

'Oh, well, she just has.'

'So, when you die, the grass will grow,' repeated Olenin.

Yeroshka evidently did not want to express his thought clearly. He was silent for a while.

'And is that what you thought? Drink!' he shouted, with a smile, pushing over the wine to him.[15]

By the time *The Cossacks* reached its final form, Tolstoy did not wish it to appear that Olenin had enjoyed the witchlike women, who could 'mar' men in unmentionable ways. The Cossack beauties ultimately elude Olenin. In actual life, Yepishka Sekhin acted quite cheerfully as a procurer for Tolstoy. In July and August, his favourite was a gipsy girl called Katya. Her 'songs, eyes, smiles, breasts and tender words' all enchanted him. He got into the way of humming the song, 'Tell me why' — 'not one of my favourite songs, but one which Katya had taught me sitting on my knee on the very evening when she told me she loved me, and that she only showed favours to others because the gipsy choir required it of her, but that she allowed nobody but me those liberties which have to be hidden by a curtain of modesty. That evening I genuinely believed her artful gipsy chatter,' he noted on August 10, 'and I was in a good mood, as no *guest* disturbed me.'

If he wasted some tears on Katya, that certainly did not stop him from taking an interest in the other women in the village. On August 25 he 'had a Cossack girl at my place. I hardly slept all night My spirit failed.' On the 26th 'Did nothing all day. . . . Roamed around the village in the evening, staring at the girls.' 'On the 28th I was twenty-three. I set much store by this age, but unfortunately I'm just the same.'[16] In the autumn, however, under Nikolay's tutelage, he moved to Tiflis with the intention of joining up in the regular army. And in October he entered the 4th Battery (that is, Nikolay's) of the 20th Artillery Brigade, as a non-commissioned officer of the 4th class.

It was a modest beginning to a military career. Doubtless, he went to Tiflis chiefly for the purpose of taking his army exams. But he was also in need of medical treatment. For three weeks he was laid up with sores all over his tongue and the inside of his mouth, pains in his back, sleeplessness and fever. At first syphilis was suspected, but it would seem as though he had an unpleasant recurrence of the clap which had afflicted him since his teens in Kazan. In December he was able to write to Nikolay that 'the venereal infection has been cured, but the after-effects of the mercury treatment are incredibly painful (*me font souffrir l'impossible*).'[17]

This letter to Nikolay was very far from being the only production of Tolstoy's pen as he recovered in the lodgings which he had found for himself in a pleasant middle-class suburb of Tiflis, 'very pretty, surrounded by vineyards. . . . and on top of everything else, I get free practice in German'.[18]

This reference to German is explained by the fact that there was a considerable German colony in Tiflis. It appealed to Tolstoy, who wrote to his aunt that it was 'a civilised town which apes Petersburg a lot and almost succeeds in imitating it'.

To his diary, neglected since September, he confided the notorious thoughts which his wife found so offensive when she was to read them fourteen years later: 'I have never been in love with women. . . . I have very often been in love with men.' The pain of the mercury treatment has to be borne in mind when we read of his protestations that he has never loved a woman. (Entries for the diary all summer have professed his chaste love for Zinaida, in Kazan, and his adoration of Katya in the village.) He reflects in particular on his love of the Islenev* family, and his obsession, during his spell in St. Petersburg, with the youngest boy, 'externally very attractive, but' as he said later, 'profoundly immoral'.

As personal as our choice of clothes, psychosexual mores are greatly determined by fashion. We could not prove it, but we could say quite confidently that the sexual histories of Shakespeare, Oscar Wilde and Mick Jagger (say) would have been quite different if they had all swapped centuries and been born at different periods. Where sexual fashions come from it is not easy to say, any more than we can say that allegedly seminal works (*Childe Harold*, Freud's *Lectures on Psychoanalysis*, or Jack Kerouac's *On the Road*) reflect or determine the prevailing mood of a decade. One thing is certain: that Dickens is such a seminal writer, nowhere more than in Russia. All his works were translated into Russian more or less simultaneously with their English appearance, but it was *Dombey and Son* in 1847 which had the biggest success.[19] Dombey-mania overtook the *salons* of Moscow and St. Petersburg, and we can be sure that it came Tolstoy's way. *David Copperfield* was published in monthly parts in England from May 1849 to November 1850, and it was translated almost immediately into Russian. Its success outshone even the extraordinary reception of *Dombey and Son*, and it is obvious that Tolstoy read it. In a letter of December 1851, he alludes casually to Mr. Micawber in a way which suggests that his brother Sergey will know what he was talking about. It would have been surprising if the Tolstoy brothers had not, like most other reading Russians that summer, been gripped

* Alexander Islenev, the father of this family, had six children by Lyubov Alexandrovna Kozlovskaya before her divorce from her lawful husband, Prince Kozlovsky. Although they subsequently married, their union was not recognised in Russian law and the Islenev children were not allowed to bear their father's name. They were each christened Islavin. Hence the Islavin/Islenev confusion of names. Tolstoy's mother-in-law belonged to the Islenev family, but her maiden surname was Islavin.

with Copperfield-mania. In later years, he would come to say that Dickens was his favourite author and *David Copperfield* his favourite book.

It is easy to see why the novel had such a particular appeal for Tolstoy at this particular date; easy to see why, once Tolstoy had read it, *David Copperfield* became a model for his own autobiographical reflections, a helpful complement to Rousseau's *Emile*.

Dickens inherited from Rousseau (not, one would imagine, from *reading* him; he merely absorbed what the Romantic generation had absorbed of Rousseau as later generations of Freudians did not need, or bother, to read Freud) the concept of original innocence. The children in Dickens are all angels. It is the cruelty or hamfistedness of the grown ups which corrupts them: the grime of cities, the squalor of workhouses, the absurdity of classrooms.

On another level, Copperfield's feeling of hero-worship for Steerforth corresponds *exactly* to Tolstoy's feelings for the young men he has admired. Indeed, it might very well be the case that the Copperfield-Steerforth relationship suggested to Tolstoy the way he should understand these young men, whom, since Kazan days, he had 'loved' more than women. ('I fell in love with men before I had any idea of the possibility of pederasty; but even when I knew about it, the idea of the possibility of coitus never occurred to me.') What happens in Dickens (and Tolstoy was to make varied use of the fact over the next twenty years) is that rampant sexuality when seen from the male point of view is passionately attractive; but seen from the female point of view it is destructive. Copperfield adores Steerforth, and all in Steerforth which will cause the 'ruin' of Little Em'ly. But when Little Em'ly loses her purity, all readers are meant to agree that it would be better if the waters could close above her head.

Pushkin had already (both in *Yevgeny Onegin* and, tragically, in his own person) turned the Byronic persona on its head by confronting the sexual champion with the two things he could not defeat: the chastity of a good woman, and death. In the next generation, male sexuality and female purity had grown polarised. The link had been forged — not a surprising one in a generation so riddled with V.D. — between sex and death. Men in love with their own lost innocence invented perfect childhoods for themselves and mothers every bit as immaculate as the Virgin Apparition of Lourdes, who appeared eight years after the publication of *David Copperfield*.

In the most fascinating book dealing with the subject, Hugh

87

Kingsmill[20] points out that the extraordinary cult of childhood innocence was a feature of the very period when Tolstoy was coming to manhood, the early 1850s. Thackeray, for example, in the thirties and forties had referred to his schooldays at Charterhouse as the violent, horrible place it actually was. His sketches of school life were entitled *Dr. Birch's Academy*. But by the early 1850s, when he was writing *The Newcomes* (and, incidentally, when he had become syphilitic, a detail Kingsmill chastely spares us) Thackeray had submitted to the changed spirit of the age. Slaughterhouse is transmuted into Grey Friars, and for the bullies, bloods and sneaks of Dr. Birch's academy we are given 'a little red-cheeked, white-headed gown boy' to whom Colonel Newcome, a dying pensioner of the Grey Friars Hospital, takes a great fancy. The child prattles by the Colonel's bedside of a cricket match with the boys of St. Peter's, exciting the old man with reminiscences of his own cricketing feats in old days; until at last Clive Newcome thinks it advisable to dismiss the child with a sovereign to buy tarts. 'I *curre*, little white-haired gown boy!' Thackeray concludes, 'Heaven speed you, little friend!'[21]

It was in this extraordinary climate that Tolstoy began his literary apprenticeship, finding it, we need hardly emphasise, immensely congenial. In November 1851, after a longish gap, he wrote from Tiflis to his Aunt Toinette that although he had to hang about waiting for his military papers to come through, he is not in the least bored. 'Do you remember, dear Aunt, a piece of advice you once gave me — to write novels? Well, I'm following your advice and the occupations I speak of consist of composing literature. I do not know if what I am writing will ever be published, but it is a work which amuses me, and which I have persevered too long at to abandon.'[22]

He was rewriting and wholly revising the work which is known as *Childhood*. Lest the foregoing paragraphs about Dickens and Thackeray seem tangential to our biographical purpose, it is perhaps necessary to emphasise what was happening to Tolstoy at this point. We are touching on the very core of what makes it such a challenge to write the biography of a great novelist; on something, in fact, which induces a suspicion of the whole art of biography itself. Tolstoy was profoundly self-obsessed, and it is this self-obsession which made him a writer. But the truth could equally be told the other way around. It could be said that it was only through the artifice of literature that he was able to comprehend or impose a shape on the inchoate business of existence. The vast majority of the human race drifts without record from conception to extinction. Their lives go unrecorded, and it is only theology which might make us suppose that these individual lives have any previous or future existence, or indeed, during their palpable existence on earth, that they have any identifiable significance. For most, it is a tale full of sound and fury signifying nothing; but, most significant of all, it is a tale which is not told. It is only by telling the tale that we create the illusion that there is a tale to tell. The rise of the novel in literature, which came with a great resurrection in the art of biography, a passion for journals, letter writing, personal confessions and memoirs, all of which happened shortly before or during the lifetime of Rousseau, gave to articulate beings the means of creating a shape, of holding on to words and moments which would otherwise be forgotten, of creating a barricade against death. By recording Johnson's conversations, or those of Louis XIV, a Boswell or a Saint-Simon have done something which is essentially artificial. They have made marmoreal things which are essentially ephemeral. The act of record is in itself an act of artifice. The novel and the biography are not really all that different, as Tolstoy's young intelligence was very quick to recognise. He loved Rousseau's *Emile* and *The Confessions* equally; and not because they were so wonderfully distant from himself, but because to all serious purposes, he thought they were about himself. Dickens made a similar impression, influencing not merely the novels which he was to write, but the way in which he was to record his own life in the diaries.

The greatest of Tolstoy critics, Eykhenbaum, long ago asserted that it is not safe to take Tolstoy's diaries as a literal record of events, however passionately sincere he might have felt while he was writing them.[23] They are best understood when compared with the eighteenth-century models (Rousseau, Franklin) on whom he (sometimes consciously) modelled himself. Likewise, it is when his Copperfield-mania is at its height that he starts to see all his male friendships in terms of the Steerforth-young-David mould, to describe himself as having been 'almost in love' with Dyakov in Kazan, or to consider that his love for Islavin 'spoilt the whole eight months of my life in Petersburg'.[24] As, perhaps, with most such feelings, there is a very fine borderline between the homoerotic and the narcissistic. The little boy loves Steerforth because he would like to *be* Steerforth. By externalising shameless masculine energy he is able to love it without the sensations of mawkish guilt which overcome him when contemplating his own sexuality. Similarly, by making Steerforth do all the running with the Little Em'lys of this world, it leaves the self-image, the 'innocent', prepubescent Copperfield-figure, free to pursue an emotional attachment to Em'ly which is untainted by sexual desire.

We see all this process at work in the revisions Tolstoy made between the first and second drafts of *Childhood* while he was staying in the German suburb of Tiflis. The first draft of *Childhood* begins as a way of writing out his obsession with the Islenev family. The nursery recollections are those of his beloved Islavin, as are the family circumstances. The story in the first version hinges on the discovery by the children that their parents are not married. (The Islenevs are indeed illegitimate.) Stage one of the creative process has been passed through: the homoerotic. In the revision,[25] the love of Islavin becomes blatantly the contemplation of self. The details of Islavin's illegitimacy are dropped. Little Nikolay begins to be given the characteristics which Tolstoy is told — by those, like his aunt and his brother, who remembered his childhood — he had himself. He is given the memories which are just beyond Tolstoy's own reach — Yasnaya Polyana before the death of his mother. The drama of the story, the event on which it all hangs is switched: no longer the Islenev illegitimacy (that hook is abandoned) but, Copperfield-like, the death of his mother.

Critics have pointed out that in some of the crucial scenes of the story (such as the description of the young boy's grief for his mother's death) there is sentence by sentence equivalence between *Childhood* and *David Copperfield*. Other passages reveal the strange slip of timescale in the book. They show that what purports to be the feelings of a little boy are actually the feelings of a grown-up. You get this, for example, in the repeated, obsessive assertions that the narrator has no memory of his mother's face.[26] As it happens, this adds a sort of pathetic poignancy and authenticity to the narrative, since it *is* one of the features of real grief that the features of the beloved, whom one most desperately wants to recapture, remain forever elusive. Nonetheless, it is unlikely that in such circumstances one would say — of a real loss — that the face eludes the memory because they are being seen through tears, 'the tears of the imagination', as the narrator of *Childhood* does in Chapter III. These are the words of a man who is almost knowingly creating for himself a memory which he does not have, of a mother, and perhaps of a whole childhood, which were in fact for him a blank, or a shapeless series of impressions which, until they were made into art, had no coherence and meaning for him at all.

The text of *Childhood* is crammed with a like evidence that the childhood imagination is in fact that of a young man. Mention has already been made of the fact that he repeatedly speaks of his 'little limbs', clothes and so on as being 'tiny'. It is only when you are outside a body, looking in, that you are aware of its tinyness. Inside, as a child, one does not think of oneself as little; though one might think of the rest of the world as big, that is not the same thing.

Moreover — and this is a fact which biographers have been slow to pick up — the 'memories' of *Childhood* are in a large number of cases transcriptions of adult, recent experiences, things which had happened to him in the year during which the novel was composed: the experience of living with Nikolay, his slightly bossy elder brother (doubtless plenty of childhood memories passed between them as they talked); the comradeship of the soldiers; the pleasures of the hunt; the amorous dalliance with Katya; even his kindly German landlords in the suburbs of Tiflis were all 'Copperfielded' and made into distant memories. Tolstoy was a young man with a brother called Nikolay whom, to judge from the many jokey references in his letters, he was beginning to find oppressively protective. In *Childhood*, with this passion for *being* the person who obsesses him (an essential ingredient in the psychology of many novelists), he names himself Nikolay, with a tiresome elder brother called Volodya.

Memories of an actual German tutor to his elder brothers, Fyodor Ivanovich, got turned into dear old Karl Ivanich as he enjoyed the German suburbs of Tiflis. His crush on the Islenevs, and on young Islavin in particular (which happened when he was twenty), is made into a thing of infancy ('His original beauty struck me at first sight. I felt irresistibly attracted to him. To see him was sufficient to make me happy, and at one time the whole strength of my soul was concentrated on that desire.') This is almost word for word what Tolstoy had written in his diary about Islenev. It is the sort of language which besotted young men (like Shakespeare and Southampton) use of one another when they are in love, but innocent of homosexual desire. It is not the sort of feeling which ever actually crops up between ten year olds. Likewise, the vividness with which he 'remembers' the hunt surely reflects very recent memories of hunting with the regiment in the Caucasus. (One recalls that Proust used to be driven out to look at the apple blossom before being driven back at top speed to his hideous cork-lined bedroom in Paris to record the freshness of childhood memories of the stuff.) It is only in the very old that childhood

91

memories are vivid. It is precisely because they are so elusive that they appeal to us; the more so that they should appeal to someone like Tolstoy who probably in psychological terms — never having had parents or what we now call bonding — simply had not had a childhood at all. There was nothing, of a coherent kind, to remember; therefore, everything to create. It was because he could not properly remember it that it was so necessary to create it. It was equally necessary, since he was unable to take Yepishka's bluff, pagan attitude towards sex, to absolve himself through art, to sanitise his experiences, and to make them innocent. The Katya whom he had loved during the previous months, and perhaps from whom he had contracted the sores and fevers which made it necessary to undergo mercury treatment, became, in the affectionate, diminutive Katenka of *Childhood*, the twelve-year-old child of a house serf called Mimi. Katenka is still decidedly a *devochka* and not a *devushka*, a little girl, not a *demoiselle*, and yet, the scene in the ninth chapter, where the narrator, his brother Volodya, their sister Lyuba and Katenka are gathering caterpillars, would have a feeling of *Lolita* about it unless the narrator was meant to be a ten year old, or unless the grown-up narrator were actually thinking of a twenty-year-old Katenka:

> I looked over Katenka's shoulder. She was trying to lift the caterpillar on a leaf which she had placed in its path.
>
> I had noticed that many little girls had the habit of twitching with their shoulders, trying with this movement to shift their open-necked dress to its proper place when it had slipped. I remember that Mimi always got angry with this gesture and said, '*C'est un geste de femme de chambre.*' Leaning over the caterpillar, Katenka made this very gesture and just at that moment the wind lifted the little shawl from her little white shoulders. Her shoulder-strap, at that moment, was within two inches of my lips. I was no longer looking at the caterpillar. I looked and looked, and with all my strength I kissed Katenka's shoulder. She did not turn round, but I noticed that her neck and ears flushed red. Volodya, without raising his head, said scornfully, 'Why this display of affection?'
>
> There were tears in my eyes. I did not take my eyes off Katenka. For a long time, I had already been accustomed to her fresh, fair little face and I had always loved it; but now examined it much more attentively and loved it all the more.[27]

The parallels between the two young 'mavishes' on Yarmouth beach in Dickens's novel are quite unmistakeable. Katenka, like Little Em'ly, is related to a domestic employed by the narrator's mother. Their love is meant to be quite unspotted and pure, in direct contrast to anything she and Steerforth might get up to later. And yet, although Tolstoy has tried to make Katenka into his Little Em'ly, it does not quite work. Nikolay is not alone when he kisses Katenka, as David is when he kisses Little Em'ly. A scornful elder brother looks on, just as, years before, an elder brother had looked on, in a whorehouse in Kazan, while Lev Nikolayevich (not *that* much older than the narrator of *Childhood* is supposed to be) had his first experience of sex and burst into tears by the bed. Even less time had elapsed since he had pressed his lips to an actual Katenka. Since we are told in the diary that the real-life Katya liked to sit on Tolstoy's lap and assure him that he was the only man in her life, her shoulder blades will have been particularly real and vivid to him. 'Happy, happy, irrecoverable days of childhood! How can one fail to love and cherish its memories!'

It is small wonder that, when he came to reflect on his career as a novelist in old age, Tolstoy should have particularly abominated *Childhood* on the grounds that it was insincerely written, an incoherent jumble of events from his own and his friends' childhoods, nor that he should have recalled, 'that at the time of writing I as far from independent in my forms of expression, but was under the influence of two writers — Sterne (*A Sentimental Journey*) and Topffer (*La Bibliothèque de mon oncle*) who had a great effect on me just then)'.[28] It is entirely typical of Tolstoy's periodic outbursts of irrational envy of writers who might be thought to be as great as himself that he conveniently forgets Dickens at this point and drags in the much less important (and as a writer totally negligible) figure of Topffer. By the time these words had been spoken, Prospero's wand had been broken and cast aside. So had the cult of worshipping the immaculate mother, either in childhood memory or in church icons. Jesus was by then the model, and like all Tolstoy's great models, one to be slapped down and remade in Tolstoy's own image. By then, he was determined to be himself an innocent, a strong son of God. Fiction had been seen through for what it was, and his life had been seen as dividing into four great phases; the period of childhood innocence; the period devoted to ambition and above all to lust; the period of his early married life; and then the blessed period of his own rebirth, when he had cast aside the artist's laurel and assumed the prophet's mantle.

Why we should assume that the 'memories' of Tolstoy when old were any more authentic than the memories of Tolstoy when young, it is hard to say. The fact that memories come so vividly to old people (long after any witnesses who might gainsay them are dead) is not a guarantee of their accuracy. Who is to say that all memory is not a form of fiction and that the 'natural' thing to do with existence is to allow it to pass, uncluttered by history, unstamped by the ego? This was something which Tolstoy would never, could never do. The early years were too much of a fog and, one would suspect, too much of a painful fog, for that.

It would probably be more truthful, if we had to divide his life into phases, to make Tolstoy's life fit into three distinct parts. In the first phase, we have a heightened intelligence which has nothing to focus upon; passionate sensibility, who feels things so keenly that it is almost ready to explode; eyes which see more brightly, ears which hear more sharply, nostrils which smell more acutely, loins which lust more vigorously than those of ordinary mortals. The history of this sensibility is a mess. It is all false starts, dead aunts, unhappy houses. Overwhelmingly strong, it is a sensibility which lacks altogether any motive of direction and has been tugged now in this direction, now in that. Tolstoy does not know where he is going, emotionally, geographically, or in the most prosaic terms of his outward career. Is he to be a fop in St. Petersburg, or a card-playing *roué* in Moscow, or a pious country farmer? Which is to be stronger in him, his desperate need to be loved and approved of by his own sex, or his overpowering physical weakness for the opposite sex? How is it that, however he tries to impose order on this existence, it falls into chaos?

Thus, the first stage; and it is the stage which it is almost impossible to reconstruct because we can only visualise it, as it were, from the inside. It is like envisaging a tortoise without its shell. Then, with *The History of Yesterday*, there is a false start which points towards the way of salvation, and in *Childhood*, that salvation dawns. The intolerable chaos and agony of life, as well as its unmanageable pleasures and its fascinatingly irreversible history, can be mastered. Through the medium of prose fiction, it was possible to transform experience itself.

One of the extraordinary things about Dickens as a writer is the strength with which he kidnaps every reader's inner life. To some extent, those who are no more than readers of *David Copperfield* feel that David's childhood memories have been their own. For Tolstoy, the spell of nine or ten years' intense reading life — in which Rousseau, Sterne and Dickens were the most formative influences — finally took shape in his being able to write. Henry James, in one of his magnificent put-downs (as it happened to Mrs. Humphry Ward), apologised for having a low opinion of *Robert Elsmere* because he could not read novels, only write them. He spoke probably for all novelists. Tolstoy would certainly have said the same if he had had an ounce of self-awareness; but like many self-obsessed people, he was entirely lacking in self-knowledge which is why, for the next twenty years, he was able to write fiction with the self-detachment of a saint. It was only when he decided that fiction would not do, and that a saint, rather than a novelist, was what he was cut out to be, that the real trouble began.

*　　　*　　　*　　　*

On July 3, 1852, Tolstoy plucked up his courage and sent *Childhood* to a St. Petersburg editor. 'My request will cost you so little labour that I am sure you will not refuse to grant it. Look through this manuscript, and if it is not fit to publish, return it to me. Otherwise evaluate it, send me what you think it is worth, and publish it in your journal. . . .'[29]

There is something quite lordly about the tone of this letter: and this is the more surprising when we realise that he is not so much writing to *an* editor as to *the* editor, as far as literary life in the early 1850s was concerned. *The* editor, and *the* journal: *Sovremennik* (*The Contemporary*). It is worth saying a brief word about the position and history of this periodical, and about the Grub Street of St. Petersburg in the decade or so before Tolstoy began to write.

Russian intellectuals divided themselves at this period between Moscow-based 'Slavophils', who were on the whole nationalistic, religious and traditional; and St. Petersburg-based 'westernisers', whose nickname or title more or less explains itself: they were on the whole left-wing in politics, progressive in social and moral ideas, free thinking in religion. Their main periodical in the forties had been *Otechestvennye zapiski* (*Notes for the Fatherland*). Turgenev published with them; so did Herzen, Nekrasov, Bakunin, Granovsky and the young Dostoyevsky. In the mid-forties, there was a split in the ranks

95

of those who wrote for the paper, and Belinsky, the leading critic of the age, left the paper, followed by all the more radical and westernising writers — notably Herzen, Nekrasov, and Panayev. Nekrasov and Panayev managed to buy *The Contemporary*, which had the distinction of having been founded by Pushkin itself. They intended to make it a vehicle for all their (by now slightly old-fashioned) radical ideas.

They had a struggle. Herzen, who would certainly have been one of their leading contributors, was exiled in 1847; and the following year — the so-called year of revolutions in Europe had, as we have seen, made the Government of Nicholas I decidedly edgy. The Emperor appointed A. S. Menshikov as head of a committee whose function was to censor the radical and intelligent press, in particular the *Notes for the Fatherland* and *The Contemporary*. This action only increased the regard in which the two papers were held by the intelligentsia, and the educated aristocracy and gentry. Anyone who wished his writings to be taken seriously would want to be published by Nekrasov. In writing to him, Tolstoy had gone straight to the top.

As a name in literary history, Nekrasov is probably best known for his tempestuous funeral. He died in December 1877, and thousands of people, mainly university students, highbrow malcontents and radical intellectuals, followed his casket to the graveside. Dostoyevsky himself delivered an oration at the cemetery, and expressed the view that Nekrasov was worthy to be placed beside Pushkin and Lermontov in the poetic pantheon. 'Higher still than Pushkin or Lermontov!' exclaimed a young voice in the crowd. Upon which, the funeral ceremony turned into a passionate literary debate, with some people declaring Nekrasov's superiority to Pushkin, and others thinking that this was to place him too high.

Tolstoy himself was to suffer the penalty of being judged not on his literary merit, but on the grounds of what he 'stood for'. Russian writers ask for this sort of treatment; and whether they do or they don't Russian readers give it to them. It is hard for me, a wholly westernised latecomer to the debate which began at his grave, to see so much literary merit in Nekrasov. He wrote, in what seems a patronising and sentimental way, about the unhappy lot of the peasant; and he did so in verse which even one of his more indulgent Russian critics admits to be 'most unequal and. . . . unpoetical'. But with titles like *Red-Nosed Frost* and the unfinished *Can Anyone be Happy in Russia?* you could not really, in Nekrasov's day, go wrong. By the time Nekrasov had died, Tolstoy had left *The Contemporary*. But it is important to remember that he began there. It was the journal which published the extreme radical fiction of Chernyshevsky, and Goncharov's masterpiece *Oblomov*. Tolstoy aspired to stand with the great writers of the age and to align himself with the radical *chic* of the metropolis.

He had not reckoned either on the meddlesome habits of editors, nor on the intolerance of the censors. When *Childhood* appeared in *The Contemporary*, the author was outraged to discover that it had been monkeyed about with. Even the title was different: *A History of My Childhood*.

'Dear Sir,' Tolstoy wrote to Nekrasov, 'I was extremely displeased to read in *The Contemporary* Number IX a story entitled *A History of My Childhood* and to recognise it as the *novel Childhood* which I sent to you. . . . The title *A History of My Childhood* contradicts the idea of the work. Who is interested in the history of *my* childhood. . . ?'[30] In a furious catalogue the young author lists all the epithets and phrases which the editor has changed and says why he prefers the original version. But publication in *The Contemporary* made Tolstoy's reputation immediately. Turgenev was extravagant in his praise. Though so passionately Anglophile, it is interesting that he did not recognise the extent of Tolstoy's debt to *David Copperfield* and was amazed when the tales were translated into English that London reviewers thought *Childhood* just a pale imitation of Dickens. Turgenev read *Childhood* in the comparative comfort of his 'internal exile', at home in Spasskoye, having been arrested some months before for his injudiciously adulatory obituary of Gogol. Dostoyevsky also read the September issue of *The Contemporary* in his place of exile, Siberia. The thing was just signed L.N.T. Initially Dostoyevsky was overwhelmingly impressed but then the irresistible awkwardness and jealousy, which were always to characterise the two writers' refusal to have any relations with one another, overrode his literary judgement. 'I like Lev Tolstoy enormously,' he wrote later, 'but in my view he won't write much of anything else. . . .'[31]

Nothing could have been further from the truth, as Dostoyevsky's instinct must have told him. From now onwards, Tolstoy was a writer: that is, a man whose life is defined by what he is or is not writing. Over the next two years, he was writing continuously. In circumstances which were, to say the least, distracting, he produced *Boyhood*, *Youth* the *Sebastopol Sketches*, *The Snowstorm*, *A Russian*

Landlord, and most of *Family Happiness*. Even more important, he was laying the foundations of experience which would evolve into *War and Peace*.

On January 12, 1854, Tolstoy heard that he had, as requested, been transferred to the 12th Artillery Brigade, serving on the Rhine. He took a month's leave, went back to Yasnaya Polyana, and then heard from Nekrasov that he did not like his latest story *Notes of a Billiard Marker*. 'Your previous work was too promising,' wrote Nekrasov, 'to follow it up with something so undistinguished.'[32]

Tolstoy was raring to go, like a young horse that could hardly be restrained from exhausting itself at too early a stage of the ride. The diary is a record of repeated trying-on of roles. 'I'm absolutely convinced that I'm bound to achieve fame: it's actually because of this that I work so little: I'm convinced that I only need to have the wish to work upon the materials which I feel I have within me. . . . Here is a fact which needs to be remembered more often.' (By whom? we might ask.) 'Thackeray spent thirty years preparing to write his first novel, but Alexandre Dumas writes two a week.'[33] Tolstoy is aware of this tremendous gift within himself, but he does not know yet what it is. Then, as so often in his destiny, he did not have to make a decision. Rather, he yielded to the compulsion of external events.

Chapter Five

Crimea

1854 - 1855

Средь груды тлеюших костей
Кто царь, кто раб, судья или воин?

[Amid the heap of rotting bones, who is Tsar,
who is the slave, who is a judge or a warrior?]
Alexey Tolstoy, *John Damascene*

When Tolstoy, after the age of fifty, became an out-and-out pacifist, his writings on the subject of warfare were marked by a remarkable simplicity of moral outlook. Everything became black and white. As far as he was concerned, war was evil. There were no ambivalences, no circumstances where the idea of a just war might have demanded his consideration.

It is surely no accident that he developed these simplistic ideas as a veteran of the Crimean War, a war, that is to say, which was completely pointless and manifestly avoidable. This was no case of a West European despot penetrating deep into the heart of the Russian homeland. Here was no Napoleon marching on Moscow in 1812 or Adolf Hitler turning his back, for some inexplicably grandiose motive, on the Nazi-Soviet axis and attempting to tread in Napoleon's snow-bound footsteps. If Tolstoy had been involved in such a campaign as the wars against Napoleon and Hitler, in which so many heroic Russians lost their lives for an observable end, he might have wanted to say that there were some circumstances in which war was the only solution to a case of international conflict. It is easy, after all, to predict the reaction of Napoleon to a 'negotiated settlement' to the problem of 1812. Munich showed what Hitler thought of the negotiating table. If the Russians wanted to rid themselves of these despotic menaces, the only way to do so was by the means of war.

The Crimean tragi-farce is different in scale, different in degree, different in kind. What was at stake was the quarrel of five great powers — Russia, Prussia, Austria, France and Britain — quarrelling over the demise of the 'sick man of Europe', the Turkish Ottoman Empire.

The idea that the Russians had a right to move into Turkey had been growing in the Russian mind throughout the century. It was partly political — Nicholas I would have liked a warm-water port, and the strategic importance of Constantinople and the Dardanelles is obvious to anyone who has ever looked at a map of the Mediterranean. If he controlled western and southern Turkey, the Russian Emperor could move from his Black Sea ports such as Odessa and Sebastopol all the way down through the Balkans and round into the eastern Mediterranean. If he conquered the Ottoman Empire entirely, he would command the whole of the Black Sea to the north as well as all the lands which occupy modern Syria, Lebanon, Israel and parts of Egypt and Libya. It is obvious why the other superpowers wanted to stop him.

There were sentimental and religious ideas behind Nicholas's expansionist dreams, too. The Orthodox Patriarch of Constantinople had, ever since the sixteenth century, lived under the tyranny of a Muslim potentate, the Sultan. Now, with the weakening of Turkey as a political power, Russians began to hope that God would give back the Patriarchate to the Christians. While so doing, the Deity might be expected to liberate the various Slavic peoples scattered about the Baltic, such as the Serbs, who had their own autocephalous Christian churches and patriarchates, and looked to the Russian Orthodox Patriarchate of Moscow as to a friendly big brother.

The mixture of political opportunism and religious fervour suited Nicholas I's purposes well, since a foreign war is about the best way of uniting a populace at home and persuading them to forget their political discontents. While it was possible to regard Holy Russia as threatened by an unholy alliance of western Protestants and atheists and Turkish infidels, it was easier to forget the plight of intellectuals, dissidents, serfs and other such blots on the Russian landscape.

A good example of this process at work can be seen in Tolstoy's mind at this time. He was a fervent patriot, and fully on the side of his own country against the threats of the other powers. During this period he read, among other things, *Uncle Tom's Cabin*. We should expect the disciple of Rousseau and the potential anarchist to see the obvious parallels between the Negro slaves in the United States and the slaves on his own estate. But his only comment in a diary entry was, 'It's true that slavery is an evil thing, but ours is a very benevolent evil.' That was what it felt like in the wartime situation of 1853-4. Slavery, for the time being, was something that he could forget, or feel comfortable about. And that was just what Nicholas I wanted from his people.

Nobody viewed the Russian Emperor's activities in the Mediterranean with more dismay than the British. If anyone was to dominate the world scene, they wanted it to be them. They were already scheming to build a Suez canal in Egypt which would link up Europe with their vast imperial territories in India and Africa. The very last thing they needed was a powerful Russia. They therefore joined vociferously with the other powers in protesting against the Russian interference in the Balkans and the Russian invasion of Ottoman territory there.

In the early months of 1854, the Western Allies protested their concern at Russia's warlike activities and in March, Britain and France broke off diplomatic relations with Russia.

By then, Tolstoy had reached Bucharest, and he was with the Russian armies when they crossed the Danube and laid siege to Silistria.[1] On March 22, he was assigned to the 3rd Battery of the 12th Artillery Brigade. Six weeks later, he was attached to the staff of the Commander of the Artillery on the Danube, General A. O. Serzhputovsky, and towards the end of May he saw his first engagements — sporadic outbursts of fighting between Russian and Turkish troops among the network of fortifications in Silistria. Cannon thundered night and day and, although he tried to keep up an appearance of nonchalance, he was terrified. To test his nerve, a notorious practical joker in the regiment led Tolstoy through an exposed piece of terrain. The young soldier seemed impassive, but afterwards he admitted that he had felt sick with fear. For the most part, however, the strange business of war went on beneath his gaze like a ghastly sport.

'It's true,' he wrote home, 'it's a funny sort of pleasure to see people killing each other, and yet every morning and evening I would get up on to my cart and spend hours at a time watching, and I wasn't the only one. The spectacle was truly beautiful, especially at night.'[2]

Then, as arbitrarily as it had all begun, it stopped. The fighting was brought to an end by negotiation. The Prussians and the Austrians put pressure on Nicholas I, and he ordered a withdrawal of his troops from the disputed Balkan territories. Tolstoy found himself marching back across the Danube. The war, such as it was, seemed to be over.

But this was to disregard the fact that British troops, under the command of Lord Raglan, were already on their way. In the course of a swelteringly hot summer, a total of fifty thousand soldiers, English and French, with their horses and field guns were being transported across the Mediterranean. In England, there was a tremendous enthusiasm for the idea of a war. There had not been one, properly speaking, since the Battle of Waterloo, nearly forty years before. The newspapers, for the first time in history, had exercised a real power in whipping up public opinion about a subject hitherto totally absent from the English consciousness: the custody of the Holy Places in Palestine. A few reporters had given accounts of superstitious bearded monks guarding the holiest shrines of Christendom and the idea of a Protestant bishopric in Jerusalem, held jointly with the German Lutherans, began to be of great appeal. All of a sudden, Russia became the threatening bear of *Punch* cartoons and the British public longed to hold back the alleged threats to British interests in such very British places as Silistria, the Black Sea and Constantinople.

By the time the Russians had so unsportingly retreated from the disputed lands, the British were more or less committed to war. Lord Aberdeen, the Prime Minister, and Lord Palmerston, the belligerent Foreign Secretary, could hardly have brought home the troops without a shot being fired. Apart from anything else, it would have been hard to explain why more than half of them were dead before they ever saw battle — victims of dysentery, cholera, typhoid and the other inevitable diseases which assailed overcrowded troopships in a hot Mediterranean summer with no clean water supply. Reinforcements were being sent to the theatre of war before the first act. And a theatre it was, too. A flotilla of British sightseers followed the task force as it made its way through the Bosporus and up into the Black Sea. By now, all cause and justification for the war on a diplomatic level had ceased. Spurred on by the thought that, if they destroyed the Russian navy, they would remove the threat of Russian domination in the future, they made for Sebastopol and began to besiege it at the beginning of September.

Tolstoy, for the whole of that summer, had been stuck on the Danube. Like many other young men before and since, who have gone to war expecting to see action, he did absolutely nothing in the military line for three months. He wrote a certain amount. He toyed with *A Russian Landlord*. He read voraciously: Dickens, Lermontov, Goethe. He lolled about. He observed.

Then, in June, having for six weeks been troubled by fistulas, he submitted to an operation by the doctors. On June 30 he had the operation under chloroform, and 'was a coward'. Three days later, he was once more gambling, a lust which at this date possessed him like the Devil. In the intervals when he was not losing money at cards and reading, he devoted extended passages of his journal to self-flagellation and fascinated self-analysis. 'Yes, I am not modest; and that is why I am proud at heart, but bashful and shy in society.' 'What am I? One of four sons of a retired lieutenant-colonel, left an orphan at seven years of age in the care of women and strangers, having received neither a social nor an academic education and becoming my own master at the age of seventeen, without a large fortune, without any social position, without, above all, my principles.' He also described himself as 'ugly, awkward, untidy and socially uneducated'.[3]

Still, there were consolations. 'The landlady's pretty daughter was reclining at her window, leaning like me on her elbows. A barrel organ passed along the street and when the sounds of a good old waltz receding further and further into the distance had completely died away, the girl gave a deep sigh, got up and moved quickly from the window. I felt so sad, yet happy, that I couldn't help smiling and long continued to look at my streetlamp, whose light was sometimes obscured by the branches of a tree swaying in the wind, and the sky, and all these things seemed to me even better than before. . . .'[4]

*   *   *   *

There were plenty of women that summer, even if his military career was slow to get off the ground. In July, Tolstoy, through the intervention of Prince Gorchakov himself (a friend of his father's), got a transfer from the Danube to the Crimea. It was a slow journey — from Bucharest, through Russia, and from Tekucha Berlad and Aslui to Kishinyov, where he remained until November. It was not until the end of the year that he finally got his transfer to the 5th Light Battery of the 12th Artillery Brigade. In the intervening months, the journal is a simple record of tarts, remorse, and reading (*Bleak House, Uncle Tom's Cabin, Henry Esmond,* Schiller's *Die Räuber*, George Sand, Balzac, what not). In his lassitude, he alternates between thinking that he has got consumption and making religious resolutions. 'I wish to believe in the religion of my fathers and to respect it,' is one typical diary entry. Another is, 'Wrote quite well, but not much, had dinner, wrote a bit more, ran after a wench. . . .'[5] Tolstoy, like all true writers, carried his life about with him, created the very cocoon of observant detachment, indolence and sensuality in which a creative mind flourishes.

105

When he got to the Crimea, one of his commanding officers noticed this at once. The 5th Light Battery of the 12th Artillery Brigade had suffered heavy losses at the Battle of Inkerman and were now quartered some fifteen *verst*s from Sebastopol. It was rough. Each officer had a little barrack-hut knocked up for him by the soldiers out of planks. An officer senior to Tolstoy, Y. I. Odakhovsky, noticed how Tolstoy would retreat to his squalid hut. 'If I dropped in on him in his barrack, I often found him at his literary work,' this intrusive fellow informs us, 'but he did not discuss his work with anyone.'[6]

Odakhovsky, writing his memoirs after Tolstoy has become a celebrated writer, would like us to believe that he and Tolstoy got along famously. It is perfectly possible that they did, in spite of Tolstoy's observation in his diary that 'Odakhovsky, the senior officer, is a nasty, mean little Pole. . . . Filimonov, in whose battery I am, is the dirtiest creature you could imagine. . . .'[7] Like many detached minds, Tolstoy was perfectly capable of deriving enjoyment from the company of those he despised (and, conversely, capable of hating, in the pages of his diary, those whom in life he found congenial). It was a gift which was to bring him torment when he married, but as a shy young aristocrat, stuck in a mess with a miscellaneous group of men, it helped him through.

After a day of mysteriously silent scribbling in the hut, the young count would emerge and dine with his fellow officers in the mess. Odachovsky was fascinated by the subtle manner in which Tolstoy could exercise *power* over his companions. It was Tolstoy who got them playing silly nursery games. It was Tolstoy who, amid the general merriment and drunkenness, got his commanding officer Filimonov to balance on one leg on a tent peg. Moreover it was Tolstoy who was in charge of giving prizes for these japes, and they were always surprised by the fact that he had noticed, precisely, the little tastes and predilections of his companions. The man who had a particular penchant for oranges would find himself getting an orange if he stood on the tent peg for long enough; whereas the man who had hardly ever mentioned to anyone his taste for honeycake would be given some honeycake. The officers began to be aware that there was a 'chiel amang them', noticing and observing and storing things in his memory.[8]

The power of this young man had not, in Odachovsky's recollections, been of the kind you would look for in an assertive subaltern. It was in the two areas of observation and subversion that it was apparent. At dinner there was often criticism of the way the campaign was being organised, of the way the engineers had armed the fortifications, of the placement of guns. It felt good humoured. There were a lot of laughs. But Tolstoy was usually at the bottom of them. Yet he was not a *leader*. He seemed to be something of a joke. They were amused alike by the ugliness of their new companion, as by his manners; his surly silences were broken by passages of fluent and ultra-well-spoken 'dinner conversation' of a kind which would have been more appropriate at the table of a Moscow princess than in a mud hut in the Crimea. They were half amused and half troubled by his extreme moral vulnerability. Sometimes he would simply disappear and they did not know where he was. They would find him in old clothes sitting with the house serfs, or chasing girls, or playing cards.[9]

*   *   *   *

The progress of the war during the autumn of 1854 became ugly. After the unsuccessful Russian attempt to beat off the French and English at the Battle of Alma, the siege and bombardment of Sebastopol could begin in earnest.

The following month, in October, with the weather already turning cold, the fighting intensified. From October 17 onwards, British field artillery and naval batteries kept up a relentless attack on Sebastopol and its defences.

One day during that week, the London *Times* correspondent happened to meet Lord Cardigan, Colonel-in-Chief of the Light Brigade and a friend. He asked the journalist, in a ridiculous tone of voice which he adopted for mocking men he considered effeminate, 'What was the firing for last night?'

Russell, knowing of Cardigan's notoriety for picking a quarrel, said that he did not know what the firing was for and attempted to hurry past.

'You hear, Squire,' said Cardigan, to his companion, 'this Mr. William Russell knows nothing of the reason for that firing. I daresay no one does.' And then he added, 'I have never in my life seen a siege conducted on such principles.'

Since Cardigan had never in his life seen a siege of any description, nor any military engagements, this was perhaps not surprising. Only a small number of very old men in the army could remember the last war. Cardigan's best training for the events which followed had been on the hunting field, which perhaps partly explains why he led his regiment in that famous charge a week later at the Battle of Balaclava. The heroics of the Charge of the Light Brigade had about as much effect on the progress of the war as if Cardigan had stayed at home and chased foxes. As the winter set in, and the soldiers on both sides found the struggle against cold and disease quite as hard as their engagements with one another, it became more and more clear that the idea of a cavalry invasion of the Crimea by the French and the British had been totally insane. Everything hung, not on the great battles, but on the progress of the Siege of Sebastopol. And it was in the middle of that struggle that Tolstoy found himself. He had missed the famous battles of Inkerman and Balaclava, and had read the newspaper accounts of them with a mixture of rage and awe. Inkerman, from the Russian point of view, was perhaps the most shaming engagement of them all, with a numerically superior Russian army repulsed by the Western Allies and more than ten thousand Russian men killed in a single day. 'Horrible slaughter!' Tolstoy said to his diary. 'It will weigh on the souls of many! Lord forgive them!'

Here was a completely futile waste of life. In 1812, Russians had died because Napoleon wanted to take their country over. In 1854, they were dying because of the incompetence of a small band of upper-class buffoons, with no particular aim in view. None of the battles of the Crimea need have happened.

After Inkerman, Tolstoy, who was stationed at a place called Kishinyov, applied for a transfer to Sebastopol itself and his request was granted. On his way, he fell in with British and French prisoners of war. He admired them. Physically and morally they seemed more impressive to him than their Russian counterparts.

Conditions in Sebastopol were appalling. He was only a week there on this visit and frequently got lost among the labyrinth of batteries. There were five hundred big calibre guns facing the enemy to the south. Almost more than the military scale of the operation, Tolstoy was impressed by the spirit of the place. 'There wasn't so much heroism in the days of ancient Greece.' The dying and the dead lay everywhere. Women and priests brought them water, sacrament, comfort. A dogged willingness to die rather than surrender had taken possession of them all. When Vice-Admiral Kornilov, one of the chief participants of the Siege, went round among the troops and asked if they were willing to die, there was something almost gleeful about the way the soldiers shouted back, 'We'll die, your Excellency, hurrah!' Twenty-two thousand Russians had died already in the conflict and Kornilov, soon enough, was of their number.

But then again, on November 15, Tolstoy was withdrawn from Sebastopol to a small Tartar village called Eski-Simferopol, four miles away from Sebastopol. He spent the winter here and discovered among the smart Russian exiles an atmosphere almost surreal in its remoteness from the war. There was drinking, hunting, dancing, as at a Russian country houseparty in peacetime. And, most fatal attraction of all, there was gambling. Perhaps the consciousness that at any moment he might be sent into action and killed increased Tolstoy's insane passion for cards. There would be an extraordinary procedure in which, after particularly heavy losses, he would make his confession to his fellow officers, lament his folly, beat his breast. They had no idea whether he was serious or not. One thing was certain. The losses *were* serious. By January 1855, he had gambled away (*shtoss* was his particular game) all the money he owned, and a lot more besides. Then, on January 28, came the big crash. 'Played *shtoss* for two days and nights. The result is understandable — the loss of everything — the Yasnaya Polyana house. I think there's no point in writing — I'm so disgusted with myself that I'd like to forget about my existence. . . .'[10]

Dickens, Pushkin and Dostoyevsky have all given us glimpses of this self-destructive madness. Tolstoy, interestingly enough, writes very little about it. Nikolay Rostov's stupidity over gambling in *War and Peace* was nothing to Tolstoy's. He was compelled to go on playing until he had lost his birthright, the very house where he was born. The big house at Yasnaya Polyana was sold and transferred to another site to pay off all these card debts. When Tolstoy was to return there, it was not to the old memories, which in any case he did not have, of his parents, but a new world of his own invention. Was that part of the reason he gambled? The thrill of gambling, like that of religion, is precisely its offer of excitingly capricious reward, or alternatively, annihilation. The real gambler may not want to be dispossessed, but on one level, he needs to be. 'When shall I cease at last to lead a life without purpose or passion or to feel a deep wound in my heart and know of no means of healing it?' he had asked his journal in November 1854.[11]

How was the month of February spent? He had now lost his house, and was in danger of losing everything. But throughout February he played and played. Two hundred roubles on February 8. Another seventy-five on February 12. Two hundred more at the beginning of March — all to Odakhovsky, who assures us in his memories of the game that the losses were only slight. At this period an ensign's annual pay in the army of Nicholas I was two hundred and nine silver roubles.[12]

*   *   *   *

It was not the army of Nicholas I much longer. Alexander Herzen, the political exile, describes a morning in London in that spring of the Crimean War:

> On the morning of the fourth of March I went as usual at eight o'clock into my study, opened *The Times*, read a dozen times and did not understand, did not dare to understand the grammatical sense of the words at the head of the news column: *The Death of the Emperor of Russia*. Hardly knowing what I was doing, I rushed with *The Times* in my hands into the dining-room; I looked for the children and the servants to tell them the great news, and with tears of joy in my eyes gave them the newspaper. . . . I felt as though several years had rolled off my shoulders. It was impossible to stay indoors. . . . I ordered champagne. . . . In the streets, on the Exchange, in the restaurants, people were talking of nothing but the death of Nicholas: I did not see but one man who did not breathe more easily from knowing that that sore was taken out of the eye of humanity, and did not rejoice that the oppressive tyrant in the big boots had at last returned to the clay. . . .[13]

Tolstoy, now stationed at Balbek, took the oath of allegiance to the new Tsar, the reforming Tsar, Alexander II, the man to whom liberals like Herzen looked in hope for an end to the autocracy, and a crushing of the bureaucratic power of the *chinovniks*, the secret terror of the 'Third Division', ancestor of today's K.G.B. They could have no conception of the horrors which lay in store. As far as life in the Crimea was affected, it was still Nicholas I's army, and his war. Shortly after they took the oath of allegiance, the men of the 3rd moved into Sebastopol itself. For Tolstoy there followed six months of close observation of war, and soldiering in earnest.

The Crimean was one of those wars, like the First World War in

Europe, in which issues of great general principle between the nations become resolved into bloody and pointless quarrels over tiny little patches of land. It was a war which got no one anywhere; but the same could be said of the Siege of Troy. It is remarkable how much the Crimean War still — after a century in which there have been bigger wars, and more urgent wars — has its legendary power. For the British, as well as its strange legacy of woollen garments (cardigans and balaclavas being a rather sinister reminder of those frozen troops on the Inkerman heights), there is the saintly figure of Florence Nightingale, and one of the greatest celebrations of military defeat in English verse. For the Russians, there was the Siege of Sebastopol, an enterprise which called forth all their powers of endurance in the face of great agony, and the mingled pleasures of isolation from the rest of the world, and intense suffering in a totally worthless cause.

Admiral Kornilov began the formal defence of the fortress at Sebastopol with a religious procession, the clergy carrying banners, icons and crosses. The troops were all sprinkled with holy water. Religion and warfare, for the Holy Orthodox army, went hand in hand. It was part of a regimental commander's duty to make sure that his men went to confession and received communion annually. A soldier, in one contemporary officer's definition, is one 'on whose powerful shoulders lies the obligation, dear to soul and heart, to defend the holy faith, the Tsar's throne and native land; to strike down foreign foes and to wipe out domestic enemies. . . . A bad son of the Church can not be a son of the Fatherland.'[14]

Yet the piety of Russian officers did not make army life any easier for the men who served under them. One could as well have expected Lord Cardigan's nominal membership of the established Church to soften his love of military discipline. If one had to choose between serving in the British or Russian armies in the 1850s as an ordinary soldier, it is hard to know which was more horrible; but the Russians, just, have the edge on their enemies.

Nicholas I took particular pride in the fact that the death penalty, abolished in Russia by the Empress Elizabeth in the eighteenth century, had never been restored. It must have been a 'fact' of great comfort to the five Decembrists who were hanged in 1825. The army enforced discipline by means of the knout, and running the gauntlet. Once, very early in Nicholas I's reign, when two Jews tried to escape the plague by running over the Turkish border, the Emperor wrote in his own hand, 'send the guilty ones through one thousand men twelve times. God be thanked, there has been no death penalty with us, and I shall not introduce it.'[15]

This running the gauntlet meant walking between a file of one thousand men, each of whom was obliged to beat, club or kick the victim as he passed. The Jews who were trying to escape the plague in 1827 were thus sentenced to twelve thousand blows. Any man who refused to kick or beat his brother soldier as he passed would himself be given the same treatment. Running the gauntlet was a common form of punishment in the Russian army until the end of the *ancien régime*. One of the bitterest and most brilliant short stories of Tolstoy's last period, *After the Ball*, describes it happening in our century.

A contemporary officer of Tolstoy's in 1855 describes some of the other routine punishments which a soldier might expect. 'For a mistake in drill to thrash the soldier with the scabbard or the iron ramrod, so that they carry him off to the lazaret [punishment block] on his cloak — that meant nothing. To knock out some of his teeth with the guard of the sabre so that the soldier should look more cheerfully at his commander and hold his head higher, or to bore his back with the sabre so that the soldier throws his chest out — this means to know posture and how to train a soldier. If the soldier after such beatings coughs and spits blood, then he is glad. "Glory to God, your honour; in the autumn they will assign me to the unit." '[16]

Tolstoy does not, in his journals, note any particular disapproval of the way in which the army conducted discipline. It is true that many soldiers are reported as having been glad to be posted to Sebastopol, whose hardships were nothing compared to the parade ground at home. But the evidence would suggest that Tolstoy was every inch an officer of his time. Although, in fits of melancholy, he would sit in the back yard with serfs, he never mingled with his own soldiers. His own men were awkward with him, and he with them. It required in him, Odachovsky tells us, courage to go up to a man and tell him that his tunic was unbuttoned. He was revolted by his soldiers, and often beat them in fits of anger. The fastidiousness of one side of his nature hated the coarseness of army speech. Indeed, in the mess, he invented meaningless 'cuss' words to replace the filth and profanities of ordinary swear words. Yet, when he left them, his replacement learnt from his troops that there had never been such a swearer as Count Tolstoy.[17]

The contradictions in his own nature were as ridiculously marked, and as obvious to Tolstoy himself, as the contradictions in the world. Is it any wonder, as he watched the priests sprinkling the soldiers with holy water and encouraging them to kill their fellow men, that Tolstoy yearned for some form of Christianity which had cut loose from the Church? In March 1855 a conversation in the mess about religion set his mind once more on a religious bent. He went to confession, received communion, and that day he felt inspired 'with a great idea, a stupendous idea, to the realisation of which I feel capable of devoting my life. This idea is the founding of a new religion appropriate to the stage of development of mankind — the religion of Christ but purged of beliefs and mysticism, a practical religion, not promising future bliss, but giving bliss on earth.'[18]

The day after making this resolution, he lost another two hundred roubles at *shtoss*. Then he caught a heavy cold, and descended into a month of heavy self-pity, scribbling at his novella, *Youth*. After Easter he was lusting seriously after a nurse he had seen at the dressing station.[19]

*   *   *   *

The officers of the 3rd found quarters in an apartment in Katherine Street, on the main Katherine Wharf of Sebastopol. By now the Siege was in full swing, but there were not bombardments every day, nor was there useful military occupation for all the troops stationed there. The twelve guns of Tolstoy's battery were divided up. Four were placed on the Yazonov Redoubt, and eight were kept in reserve against further action or a sortie. Tolstoy, together with the 'nasty mean little' Pole, Odachovsky, and several other officers, found themselves on reserve, that is with nothing to do. By day, Tolstoy was seen to tinker with his writings. In the evening, he would have a bite to eat and drink vodka with his fellow officers. He liked to drink, but they never saw him any the worse for it. He would sit at the piano — things were more comfortable in the Katherine Street apartment than in the muddy huts of Balbek — and play for his fellow officers. Sometimes he sang jokey songs, making up the words as he went along. *Risqué* verses would alternate with sentiments of high patriotism. One of the songs which became popular among the Russian troops at this period was composed by Tolstoy at this piano.[20]

Life was, in some ways, almost eerily normal for long spells in Sebastopol. The other officers got bored with Tolstoy's card obsession. 'Comrades! He plays all the time. It's a shame! Let's give our word not to play with Count Tolstoy.' His losses, and the insane passion with which he played, had come to be a source of embarrassment in the mess. It was no skin off Tolstoy's nose. As soon as the artillery officers stopped playing with him he began to go out into the town, where he would find infantry or cavalry officers prepared to give him a game. He would almost invariably come back having lost yet further.

Jaunts in the town provided other temptations too. 'As for women, there seems to be no hope. . . . Sensuality is tormenting me. . . . Lots of pretty girls. . . .' But there are other examples in literature — Pepys and Boswell are two, Dickens was almost certainly another — of men whose powers of literary observation were actually quickened by the need for a sexual quest. It gives point to a walk about town. The man on the look-out for sexual quarry has his eyes, as the saying is, skinned. While he looks for the girls, he sees a great deal else. The Crimea was the first major war to be recorded by the camera.[21] (How very differently we would view the Napoleonic wars if there had been cameras in the Peninsula or at Waterloo.) At Sebastopol, more remarkably, there was a camera with intelligence called Tolstoy. His incomparable *Sebastopol Sketches* are *cinéma vérité* of the very highest quality.

> Soldiers, sailors, officers, women, children and tradespeople are moving about, carts loaded with hay, sacks and casks, are passing, and now and then a Cossack, a mounted officer, or a general in a vehicle. . . . Everywhere you will see the unpleasant indications of a war camp. . . . But look more closely at the faces of these people moving about around you and you will get a very different impression. Take for instance this convoy soldier muttering something to himself as he goes to water those three bay horses, and doing it all so quietly that he evidently will not get lost in this motley crowd which does not even exist as far as he is concerned, but will do his job be it what it may — watering horses or hauling guns — as calmly, self-confidently, and unconcernedly as if it were all happening at Tula or Saransk. You will read the same thing on the face of this officer passing by in immaculate white gloves, on the face of the sailor who sits smoking on the barricade, on the faces of the soldiers waiting in the portico of what used to be the Assembly Hall, and on the face of that girl who, afraid of getting her pink dress muddy, is jumping from stone to stone as she crosses the street. . . .[22]

She is not going to look at him. He must go to cheaper women for his pleasure. But her pink skirt and her little ankles, and, for the moment, her face, have alerted the all-seeing eyes of Tolstoy.

> Yes, disenchantment certainly awaits you on entering Sebastopol for the first time. You will look in vain in any of these faces for signs of disquiet, perplexity or even of enthusiasm, determination, or readiness for death — there is nothing of the kind. What you see are ordinary people quietly occupied with ordinary activities. . . .[23]

But this impression is rudely checked by a visit to the hospital, and by hearing and experiencing the noise of cannon fire and bombardment. The first of the sketches is moving in the way that accounts of London during the Blitz are moving: 'Men could not accept such conditions of life for the sake of a cross, or promotion, or because of a threat: there must be some other and higher motive power.' The patriotic fervour of 'Sebastopol in December 1854' greatly appealed to the wartime readers of *The Contemporary* back in St. Petersburg. The new Emperor, Alexander II, actually commissioned a translation into French — what a significant gesture that! For all its Russian piety, the tale would only speak to half the courtiers in the language they themselves used.

The patriotism of the first sketch is tempered in the second — 'Sebastopol in May' — by a strongly satirical sense of how absurd army life and military vanity can be; also by scenes in which the sufferings of wounded men are observed with an intolerable vividness.

The picture of Kalugia's courage and patriotism (in 'Sebastopol in May') is funnier, and more touching, than anything in the anti-war propaganda of Tolstoy's late period. 'He was ambitious and blessed with nerves of oak — in a word he was what is called brave. He recalled how an adjutant, Napoleon's he thought, having delivered an order, galloped with bleeding head full speed to Napoleon. "*Vous êtes blessé?*" said Napoleon. "*Je vous demande pardon, sire, je suis mort*," and the adjutant fell from his horse, dead. . . .'[24]

The reader has only recovered from laughing at this sentence when his eye meets the next sentence. 'That seemed to him very fine. . . .' There is the whole absurdity of the patriotic position. The May sketch — with its vision of the mortuary piled high with corpses which 'a couple of hours before had been men full of various lofty or trivial hopes and wishes'; with its Stendhalian sense that nobody, in the

115

heroic moment, even knows what is *happening*; with its picture of the little ten-year-old boy, having first the revolting stench, and then the sight of a decomposing, headless French corpse — is a very different thing from its predecessor. The sketch ends with a denunciation of the vanity and 'courage' of popinjays like Kalugia, and a tubthumping expression of amazement that Christian people, seeing the carnage they have done, are pleased, and not, as they should be, penitent. This is the strain in Tolstoy which was to dominate the second half of his life — the preacher, the prophet, the denouncer of obvious evils in an obvious way. He is not, like the artist of the first sketch (or parts of the second), a fascinated observer, prepared to stare at everyone's face, and describe things exactly as they are. He is not, except in the crudest sense, a rhetorician. But he is arrestingly certain of his own moral rightness. He did not emerge as a result of some sort of mid-life crisis after the artist had finished *Anna Karenina*. He is there from the beginning. His is an unsubtle voice, almost devoid of charm, but, unlike the scribes, he speaks with authority, and however repelled we may be by him, we stop and listen: 'The hero of my tale — whom I love with all the power of my soul, whom I have tried to portray in all his beauty, who has been, is and will be beautiful — is Truth.'[25]

The *May* sketch drew on Tolstoy's experience doing occasional duty on the guns. It was inevitable that it should be censored. The last hero you should choose in Russia, if you want to get on in the literary world, is truth. Nor would any government in modern times (eastern or western) welcome or allow, while hostilities were still in progress, revelations or reflections such as Tolstoy's *May* sketch contained. Almost as much as its obvious wrongness — killing and maiming people — Tolstoy was immediately confronted with the fact that warfare is a natural enemy of his hero truth. Few would fight in wars if at the time they knew the full truth about them, or could foresee the consequences of them. Conversely, those who in peacetime would believe themselves to be passionate champions of truth believe that, in their nation's security, almost any degree of *suppressio veri* or downright lying is justified.

The Siege of Sebastopol dragged on all through the summer of 1855 while the Powers conferred in Vienna, trying to bring the war to an end. The British and the French continued to insist on the destruction of the Russian navy as a part of the peace agreement. This was something which General Gorchakov refused to accept. Too much had already been lost at Sebastopol, too much life and too much pride, for such humiliation to be acceptable. On August 16, Gorchakov, who had walked out of the negotiations at Vienna, persuaded the new Tsar to make one last effort to relieve Sebastopol.

He attacked the French and the British in the Battle of Chornaya Rechka. The Allies lost some two thousand men in this battle and the Russians some ten thousand. It was a major Russian setback. But it was also a remarkable event in the history of literature, for it was the only large-scale military engagement which was witnessed at first-hand by Lev Tolstoy.

It was at Chornaya Rechka ('Black Stream') that Tolstoy discovered the truth of what he had already read in Stendhal's *The Charterhouse of Parma* — that one cannot tell the 'truth' about battles since all the witnesses are people who are too busy staggering about in smoke, squelching through wounded bodies, drunk with vodka, fear or courage, to have any clear sense of what is going on. Just as we lose sight of Stendhal's Fabrice on the field of Waterloo, so, for a moment we lose sight of the young Tolstoy at Chornaya. But the curious thing about the young Russian officer who sees his comrades in arms at once so detached and so engaged, so vague and yet so intermittently brave, is that he is in control. In all important senses, at least. He is not just a young man on the field of battle. He is an artist, confronting his true *métier*. A professional artillery colonel called Glebov encountered him at that period and did not know what to make of him.

On August 4 [i.e. at the battle of Chornaya] he attached himself to me, but I could not make use of his funny little guns in the battle, since I was defending a position with battery guns; on August 27, he applied to me again, but this time without his guns, so I was able to entrust him (because of the shortage of officers) with the command of five battery guns. At any rate, it is clear from that that Tolstoy is eager to smell powder — but only fitfully, like a partisan, avoiding the difficulties and privations of war. He travels about to different spots as if he were a tourist; but he no sooner hears the noise of firing than he appears on the field of battle. . . .[26]

Already, Tolstoy had recognised, and obeyed, his vocation to become a writer. But he still could not possibly have known what sort of a writer he was going to be. *War and Peace* lies in the future. But it is here that the seeds of it are sown. He was not so much collecting material (a phrase which implies conscious 'research') as mopping up an experience which was to be intensely fruitful. Moreover, the experience is to determine the form. Now here, now there, wishing to experience everything, the young Tolstoy is a man whom Colonel Glebov cannot keep track of. He is in himself as open — and from the artistic sense, as vulnerable and generous — as the book which he is one day going to write. For it is, as C. S. Lewis suggested, in its apparent lack of form that much of the book's vast moral strength lies.

> I thought that the strong narrative lust, the passionate itch to see 'what happened in the end' which novels aroused necessarily inured the taste for other, better, but less irresistible forms of literary pleasure. . . . Tolstoy, in this book, has changed all that. I have felt everywhere. . . . that sublime indifference to the life or death, success or failure, of the chief characters, which is not a blank indifference at all, but almost like submission to the will of God. . . .[27]

It is this 'sublime indifference', a Homeric quality, which was given to Tolstoy, both on the field of battle and — much more interestingly — when he held a pen in his hand. It marks the last of the *Sebastopol Sketches*, as it had been the characteristic of the first two.

It was renewed French artillery bombardment which led to the final fall of Sebastopol. When it became clear that the besieged could hold out no longer, Gorchakov ordered his troops to cross to the northern side of the harbour destroying all depots, ammunition and stores as they went. Sebastopol burnt for two days before the French and British entered it on September 10. If Gorchakov had not organised the Russian withdrawal at that point, the casualties would undoubtedly have been much worse. As it was, the final assault cost the Russians some thirteen thousand lives and the Allies nearly eleven thousand.

The ending of the war was not wholly disastrous for the Russians, for on the Caucasus front General N. N. Muravyov scored a notable victory over the British at Kars. This doubtless strengthened the Russian hand at the peace negotiations in Paris in the following spring. Nevertheless, the result of that treaty neutered Russian naval power in the Black Sea, since Alexander II was obliged to promise to keep his navy in the Baltic ports and to leave the Black Sea as a neutral zone. This unsatisfactory arrangement was to flare up several times before the century was out and to play its part in shaping not only the development of the First World War, but also, indirectly, that of the Revolution of October 1917.

By September 2, 1855, Tolstoy was apologising to his diary for a week without writing, but two sentences tell the tale. 'Lost 1500 roubles. Sebastopol has surrendered.'[28] In September, he turned for home. It was a month in which the womanising was more than usually uncontrolled, perhaps a consequence of being out of the firing line. At the beginning of October, he remarked that he had not changed his clothes for three days. He felt lazy, apathetic. For the first time in ages, he made a small win at cards — a hundred and thirty roubles, and immediately spent the money on a horse. 'What nonsense!' he told himself. 'My career is literature — to write and write!'[29]

Chapter Six

Bronchitis is a Metal

1855 - 1857

'Bronchitis is a metal.'

Tolstoy to Turgenev

There is a famous photograph,[1] taken on February 15, 1856, of a group of Nekrasov's more distinguished contributors to *The Contemporary*. On the extreme left, almost too languid to hold up his head without balancing it against his wrist, is Goncharov, whose languid hero Oblomov is a proverbial figure in Russian literature. Behind his comic inability to stir himself and do anything is a great range of half-articulated, but fundamentally serious concerns. There is a pining for simplicity, and a reverence for nature which find their echo in Tolstoy. There is the alarming thought that perhaps there is no answer to the question, 'What are days for?'* and that, in happiness or sadness, fill them how we may, we face extinction before we are given to learn the purpose of our journey. Even now, Goncharov is a neglected writer among English readers, though for Russians he is one of the most important figures in nineteenth-century literature. Beside Goncharov in the photograph, there sits Turgenev, displaying a similar air of moral exhaustion. Doubtless his expression, like Goncharov's, could be explained by the tedious atmosphere of the photographer's studio, and by the fact that the pose is taking a much longer time than had been promised. But in Turgenev's writing of the time, to an even stronger degree than in Goncharov's, there is an anguish and a moral ambivalence, about his own life, torn as he was between a domineering mother and an impossible mistress, about art, and about the future of Russia.

* На что вы, дни? , a lyric by Yevgeny Baratynsky, seems to anticipate Larkin's equally Goncharovian question.

Censorship was squeezing the life out of Russian writers at this date. Writing of the period 1849-1856, Count Uspensky said that 'one could not move, one could not even dream; it was dangerous to give any sign of thought — of the fact that you were not afraid'.[2]

Writers bore the brunt of the Government's determination that there should be no revolutionary movement in Russia comparable to those which had swept Europe eight years before in 1848. By then, Herzen was in exile, and almost every Russian writer of note had either felt the constraints, or actually (like Turgenev, or Dostoyevsky or Saltykov-Shchedrin) suffered arrest as a result of the zeal of the so-called Committee of April 2. This was a branch of the Third Department (an organisation founded by Nicholas I as a counter-revolutionary secret police). The Committee was presided over by the prodigiously reactionary D. P. Buturlin, who was in charge of all press censorship in the capital and who was credited with the immortal opinion that had it been in his power, he would have censored the Gospel because of its democratic tendencies.[3] He wasn't joking, and the seriousness of his words receive their just balance or punishment in the later years of Tolstoy.

With Goncharov and Turgenev in the photograph are a number of other *Contemporary* contributors — Druzhinin, Ostrovsky, Grigorovich, all of whom, by their mere association with the paper, ensured that their lives would be kept under constant surveillance by the police, and all of whose writings, however inoffensive, could be used against them as indictable, criminal evidence.

In those days, everyone assumed that Russia had a future, and the debate centred upon what that future should be. Between the wilder extremes of naked political solutions, there lay two broad general intellectual camps — on the one hand, the Moscow-based Slavophils, who believed that Russia should resist European influences, above all the influence of rationalism, and find its soul once more in a rediscovery of the meaning of Orthodoxy. In St. Petersburg, on the other hand, the intelligentsia for the most part dissented from the Slavophil solution and favoured an opening up of Russia, an acceptance of technological and ideological advance. These western-isers, of whom Turgenev is perhaps the most agonised and attractive example, tended to be liberal or radical in politics, and unbelieving, or at best wistful, in their religious allegiance. Neither the religious Slavophils, nor the rationalist westernisers enjoyed happy relations with the Government. The Slavophils, for example, resented the degree to which the autocracy dominated the Church and claimed for itself 'Russian' values which, by Slavophil doctrines, should have sprung naturally, as a free flowering, from the people. Had they had their way, Russia would not have accommodated itself to the attitudes and mores of the West, and with the progress of the nineteenth century, it would have become more and more foreign in relation to the nations of Europe. In some ways, they did have their reward. Had the westernisers achieved their ambition, Russia would have emancipated its serfs, modernised the conditions of the poor, and evolved, at local and national level, a system of representative government. They too had their ambitions in part fulfilled.[4]

But somehow the system was to beat both of them. However much the intelligentsia wanted a future for Russia, the power of the state, its capacity to diminish and destroy the lives of individuals, was to grow in belligerence and to some degree in strength. Ideas such as those disputed by Turgenev, Aksakov, Chernyshevsky, counted for less than the power granted to bullying secret police to wake up the thinkers in the middle of the night.

In that famous photograph of 1856, there is one figure who looks completely out of place. Five of the men in the picture have long hair growing over their ears; this figure has a short, military haircut. Five loll languidly, leaning on chairs, crossing their legs, or leaning on chairs. One stands bolt upright. Five are wearing cravats, waistcoats, watch chains, trousers, frock-coats; they could be literary gentlemen anywhere in Europe. We could superimpose upon this photograph a contemporary picture of Flaubert, Tennyson or Manzoni and they would not look out of place, as the young man standing behind Turgenev looks out of place, in his Russian military uniform.

*　　　　*　　　　*　　　　*

Tolstoy went to St. Petersburg straight from Sebastopol in the fall of 1855. The poet Fet has left an unforgettable description of his first awareness that the young genius had reached the capital. It is with good reason that all biographers repeat this old chestnut. Afanasy Afanasyevich Fet, then aged thirty-five, called on Turgenev one December day in 1855, and was impressed by the magnificent short sabre which he saw hanging on the hat-stand in the hall. The servant informed Fet that it was the property of Count Tolstoy, who was staying with his master. For the next hour, Turgenev and his guest conversed in whispers, because, although it was the middle of the day, Tolstoy was asleep in the next room. 'He's like this all the time,' said Turgenev. 'He has come from his battery at Sebastopol, is staying with me, and has gone off on a tangent. Sprees, gipsies, and cards every night: then he sleeps like the dead until two o'clock in the afternoon. I try to restrain him, but I've given up now.'[5]

The tension between Tolstoy and Turgenev probably owed its origins to quite personal concerns: Tolstoy did not much like Turgenev's interest in his sister Marya for a start. Tolstoy's coarseness grated upon the older man's graceful sensibility, but at a much deeper level there was wariness, as there often is between artists who are both playing the same game. The late nights and the boorish behaviour enabled Turgenev to label Tolstoy as a 'troglodyte', but a more damagingly percipient comment was that Tolstoy was all the time putting on an act. 'Not one word, not one movement of his is natural! He is eternally posing before us, and I find it difficult to explain in a clever man this impoverished Count's arrogance.' Turgenev was most generous in his recognition of Tolstoy's literary genius. More, perhaps, than any of Tolstoy's contemporaries, he was responsible for boosting the career of his younger rival. ('I'm not exaggerating when I say that he'll become a great writer and a splendid person,' he wrote, with a conspicuous emphasis on the future tense, to Tolstoy's sister.)[6]

But Turgenev knew that behind the exercise of fiction, there lies the simple childhood desire to pretend. Tolstoy saw it too in Turgenev, and hated the older man's political radicalism. In the light of poses and attitudes which Tolstoy was later to strike himself, it is interesting that during the first spell of their acquaintanceship, Tolstoy was simply unable to believe that someone of Turgenev's wealth and privilege should wish to impoverish himself by emancipating the serfs. Fet records for us that Tolstoy thought Turgenev was 'merely wiggling his democratic haunches'.[7]

With Fet himself, however, Tolstoy was to become a close friend, and their friendship lasted until death. Perhaps one thing which bound them together initially in the world of civvy-street intellectuals was that they were both in the army, though both were to resign their commissions soon. Much more hung on Fet's military career, from a personal point of view, than on Tolstoy's.

Poor Fet had a complicated history which could only have happened in nineteenth-century Russia. His parents were German (Johann and Charlotte Foeth). When he was fourteen years old, the authorities declared that they did not consider Fet to have been validly baptised. Having been called Afanasy Afanasyevich Shensin, after his step-father, he was obliged to take the name Fet (the Russianised version of Foeth) and to forfeit all his claims to inherit Shenshin's estate, and all his noble status. 'If you ask me what all the sufferings and all the sorrows of my life are called,' he once wrote, 'I will answer: they are called Fet.'[8] He joined the army after university in 1845, solely because cavalry officers, after reaching a certain rank, could achieve noble status. This desire to be a nobleman was not a matter of simple snobbery. If you were not classifiable as 'gentry' or 'nobility' in nineteenth-century Russia, your life was as circumscribed as that of non-Party members in the Soviet Union today. The place and extent of your residence, the job you did, the amount you were allowed to travel within Russia and abroad, all depended upon membership of a certain estate in society. By 1853, Fet had become a lieutenant, and looked certain of earning back his birthright, when a cruel law was enacted which said that only those who attained the rank of colonel could henceforth claim membership of the *dvoryanstvo* (nobility). At that point despair entered Fet's soul. He married, for money, the unappealing sister of Botkin, his most admiring critic, and for a while continued to pen lyrics to the girl he actually loved. His writings were hugely successful, and his popularity enabled him to collect enough money to buy an estate in the Mtsensk district, near where he had been born. But his treatment at the hands of the Government had silenced him. He was reduced to Oblomovism, and spent his days sitting miserably at home, reading Schopenhauer ('that Buddhist, that corpse',[9] as Herzen had called him). It is surely significant that throughout this period, Fet wrote no more poetry, but that when, at the age of fifty-four, his baptism and birth certificates were suddenly and capriciously legalised, and he was admitted once more to the legal membership of the Shenshin family (and hence of the nobility), his lyrics once more started to flow.

There is much in Fet's sad, kindly character which explains why Tolstoy responded to him so immediately, and began to call him (how is it possible to translate these diminutives and terms of affection without heightening their absurdity?) *dragotsenny dyaden'ka* — precious little uncle. Tolstoy exchanged more letters with Fet than with any other writer, and although the novelist and the poet were to diverge so extremely in middle age, there is much which the two have in common. Fet was a life-long atheist, whereas for Tolstoy the concerns of religion would ultimately overwhelm his interest in literature. Tolstoy was a self-conscious realist, whereas Fet, as has been well said, 'sang of the love he never allowed himself to have'.[10] Tolstoy, from the beginning, nursed feelings that art should be committed, if not politically, at least morally, whereas Fet tells us in his memoirs, 'I have never been able to understand art interested in anything except beauty.'[11]

Yet in Fet's poetry, as in the best of Tolstoy's fiction, there is a highly comparable simplicity. It is not simple-mindedness so much as reverence and rapture in the face of nature itself. In his 'garden' poems, Fet reveres the stars, the trees, the flowers, just for being themselves.

Царит весны таинственная сила

[The mysterious force of spring rules]

could be a line spoken by a character in *The Cossacks*. The final stanza of that poem is profoundly Tolstoyan in its sense of human littleness beneath the stars. The 'smoke' of the poem might superficially remind the reader of Turgenev, but Fet is not saying (as Turgenev's title suggests) that everything in life is pointless so much as emphasising the frailty of all human aspirations.

> А счастье где? Не здесь, в среде убогой,
>   А вон оно - как дым.
> За ним! за ним! воздушною дорогой -
>   И в вечность улетим

> [But — where is happiness? Not here amid misery.
>   But here it is — like smoke.
> After it, after it! By an airy way,
>   And we shall fly off into eternity.][12]

Like Tolstoy, Fet could not for long take his mind off the prospect of extinction — and in 1856, just as he was beginning to find his feet in the literary world.

Fet was the little uncle to Tolstoy, a closer companion, on an intellectual and spiritual level, than Tolstoy's own brothers. But it was in the early months of his friendship with Fet that Tolstoy witnessed the first of his siblings make his journey, like smoke, into nothingness.

*   *   *   *

The power of total recall is never vouchsafed, not even to the most vivid imaginations or intellects. In our personal mythologies, we select a very few characters and incidents to masquerade, in memory or half-memory, as our past. The more we articulate these 'memories', the less true they are likely to be, the more tolerable and acceptable. Tolstoy's personal myth, not unusually, was that of Paradise Lost, and his recollections of his brother Dmitry sharpen this perspective into lurid caricature. In Kazan days, Dmitry had been a holy innocent, praying, and being kind to the afflicted and the poor, while his worldling brothers played cards and chased the girls. He was some sort of image of what a part of Tolstoy wanted himself to be.

> I believe that I had already left for the Caucasus when a remarkable transformation came over Dmitry. He suddenly started to drink, smoke, squander money, and go about with women. How it happened, I don't know, and I did not see him at this period. The only thing I know is that the man who led him astray was Islenev's youngest son, outwardly very attractive but also deeply immoral.[13]

It is interesting to notice how the last sentence is contradicted by the one before it. Tolstoy had no idea how the corruption of Dmitry came about. But he was also quite sure that it happened as a result of Islenev's corrupting influence.

In the last chapter there was some discussion of the ways in which literary influences, and in particular those of Dickens, provided Tolstoy with a method of sorting out his own past, and of reading back into his childhood a laundered version of events which were in fact happening in his grown-up life. The sequence which we call *Childhood, Boyhood,* and *Youth* are apprentice pieces, and though they are the apprentice pieces of a great genius, they would not detain us long were it not for the biographical importance which they embody. Not that Tolstoy was not simply recording, or attempting to record childhood in the manner of, say, Aksakov and Herzen. He was making a series of highly significant projections. The original drafts of *Childhood,* which are not translated into English, show us a

129

rudimentary epistolary novel. The letters — from the same Nikolay Irtenev who is our narrator in *Childhood, Boyhood* and *Youth* — were a series of reminiscences, first confessing the misdemeanours of an adolescent and a young man, and then attempting to round out the picture of this young man by a series of flashbacks or *Kinderszenen*. These stories were all written in the person, not of Tolstoy, but of his friend Islavin. Any possible doubt about the matter is dispelled by the fact that in these first-draft letters, the protagonist, like Islavin, is illegitimate.

The Islavin children, of whom there were six, were the offspring of one of their less innocent neighbours at Yasnaya Polyana, A. M. Islenev. (Neighbours, that is to say, in gentry terms: his estate was twenty miles away.) These children were given the surname Islavin, and since they were much of an age with the Tolstoys, they played together quite frequently. In retrospect, he tended to make the girls symbols of purity and innocence, and the boys agents of corruption. But in spite of this mythopoeic tendency, a few realistic memories intruded. On one occasion, for example, when they were playing, he pushed one of the Islavin girls in the small of the back so hard that she fell off the balcony where they were playing. In memory, this event happened because he was trying to spare her the attentions of other little boys — but at the age of ten (and she eleven), is this probable? The incident stays in the mind, and the biographies, because this little girl, whose innocence and sexual purity he was prepared to do violence to preserve, was none other than Lyubov Islavin, later Tolstoy's mother-in-law.

Not long after this jape, the Tolstoys and the Islavins became separated. The Tolstoys went off to Kazan, only returning to Yasnaya Polyana for summer holidays. It was really not until he had left Kazan that Tolstoy rediscovered the Islavins and they became seriously important to him. They met up, not in the country, but in St. Petersburg, during that year after Kazan when he toyed with the idea of reading Law at St. Petersburg University. Having had a childhood which was, by most standards, 'emotionally deprived', Tolstoy had a great weakness for other people's families. He loved them *en groupe*, and enjoyed vicariously attaching himself to them. Cut off from his brothers, parentless and auntless, he did this to the Islavins at their St. Petersburg house during eight 'wasted' months of 1851. When they were over, he confided in his diary.

My love for Islavin spoilt the whole eight months of my life in Petersburg for me. Although not consciously, I never bothered about anything else except how to please him. All the people I loved felt this, and I noticed how hard it was for them to look at me. Often, I couldn't find that moral understanding which reason required in the object of my love, or after some unpleasantness with him or her, I would feel hostility towards them; but this hostility was based on love. I never felt this sort of love for my brothers. I was very often jealous of women. I can understand ideal love — complete self-sacrifice to the object of one's love. And that is what I experienced.[14]

For the purposes of his *Childhood*, he chose to become Islavin, intermingling Islavin's memories with his own. It is only at the end of *Youth* that the 'I' of the story can project his moral preoccupations on to his wholesome friend Nekhlyudov, Tolstoy's righteous self-image. In time, first in *A Russian Landlord*, and much later in *Resurrection*, the 'I' figure is forgotten altogether and only the moralist, only Nekhlyudov, will remain.

At this early stage, however, Islavin remains in Tolstoy's mind as a mythological tempter and, when blended into fiction, as an image of his own lost innocence. By all accounts, Islavin was a boozy, dissolute young man who liked gambling and going to brothels. So did Tolstoy, which is why they got on together so well. But Tolstoy's conscience would not let it rest there. Islavin had been more than a drinking companion. He had excited Tolstoy's love, a love which could not be distinguished from guilt. So, when he came to revise and rewrite *Childhood*, and to continue the sequence with the only intermittently successful *Boyhood* and *Youth*, Tolstoy was celebrating his love for Islavin, and trying to absolve himself from it by *being* Islavin and writing the story in his person. Later, the absolution could be perfected and completed by marrying the daughter of the child he pushed off the balcony, by leaving behind his involvement with the guilty Islavin maleness, and by entering the sugary, innocent world of their females.

That this sort of thing was going on in Tolstoy's imagination it is hard to doubt, when we look at his reaction to the death of his brother Dmitry. Dmitry, like Nekhlyudov, was someone that Tolstoy hardly ever saw after he had passed his eighteenth year. This made it all the easier to make him into a figure of complete innocence and moral rectitude, such as emotionally insecure people require their families to be. In his old-age reminiscences, Tolstoy finds it hard to account for the fact that this paragon of virtue should have died in the arms of a prostitute. There is something automatic about the explanation which he provides: that Islenev's youngest son led him astray. What? Another Tolstoy soul lost through the love of Islenev/Islavin? This seems almost too bad to be true.

*   *   *   *

The death of Dmitry is one of the most vivid examples of guilty experience which Tolstoy could only absolve by means of art. He wrote very little about it at the time. Yet, as he remembered in 1902 or 1903, when recollection of the 'vileness' of his former life caused him 'the torments of hell', he was 'particularly detestable' at the time of Dmitry's death. The scene occurred in the provincial town of Oryol. Tante Toinette had come over from Yasnaya Polyana to tend her consumptive nephew, and to help Masha, the pock-marked girl whom he had rescued from a brothel. At this stage of his life Lev Nikolayevich was intoxicated with his own advancement in the world and, after the social restrictions of military service, he was inordinately excited by the life of the metropolis. As his brother lay dying, Tolstoy records, he was unable to excite in himself any feelings of pity for him. He was disgusted by the smell of the sickroom. He felt reproached by the kindness and sheer practical goodness of the women. They knew what to do in the sickroom, and they did it. Lev Tolstoy watched as the two women sponged Dmitry, propped him up on pillows and prepared him for the visit of the priest. 'Both women knew without any doubt what life was and what death was, and though neither of them would have been able to answer, nor even to understand such questions which confronted Lev, neither of them doubted the significance of this phenomenon — and they both had exactly the same outlook upon them; an outlook which was not only theirs, but was shared by millions of other people. They knew quite certainly what death was, and the proof of that was, as they knew, without a second's hesitation, what it was necessary to do with the dying, and not to fear them. Lev and others, although they could talk about death a lot, evidently did not know a thing, for they were afraid of it, and decidedly did *not* know what you should do when people were dying.'[15]

The passage occurs in *Anna Karenina* where Tolstoy has added one syllable to his name and where Lev occurs as Levin. Otherwise the

details are remarkably similar to Dmitry's own deathbed at Oryol. In old age, Lev would remember how Dmitry had prayed after the priest held an icon in front of his face. But this too, like the practical kindness and common sense of the women, had been a reproach to Lev at the time. The death of Dmitry had been an isolating experience, one of those chilling reminders that he was not as others are. The certainty that, in having no parents, he had missed out on most of the emotional history which the world calls childhood had compelled him to construct his childhood artificially, a pastiche fashioned from Dickens out of the actual experience of the Islavins. Thereby, he could bring what he could not remember, and could not feel — the death of his mother — into a narrative framework. He could give it a life which it was denied by conscious memory. In the Caucasus, what was lacking was less memory than what sprang from the original loss of memory, and that original maternal deprivation: an inability to react to the world spontaneously, as old Yepishka did. This was to flower into his finest early work, *The Cossacks*. The death of Dmitry had meant almost nothing at the time. As a physical spectacle, he was repelled and disgusted by it. And with youthful insensitivity, and the typically crass values of a young socialite enjoying himself in the capital, he could hardly bear the thought of missing a party that week in St. Petersburg. Someone had offered to take him to a grand Court spectacle, and it seemed a pity to be missing that just because his brother was rotting away with consumption. So, after only two days in Oryol, Tolstoy abandoned Dmitry to his fate, and went back to the capital. Dmitry lingered on a little while, and finally died on January 21, 1856.

The whole experience of Dmitry dying, and of his own shabbily thoughtless part in the matter, was buried in Tolstoy's mind. We are often told by the commentators that he gives an exact account of the case in the scenes from which I have already quoted in *Anna Karenina* where Levin visits his dying brother. But the details which have been changed in that part of the book are as revealing as those which have not. In the novel, significantly, it is Kitty, Levin's wife, who tends the dying man, rather than his aunt. She had first met him at the German spa town of Soden, and it is there (Soden being a place where Russian consumptives often went to die) that she had learnt her easy sickbed manner. Soden is the town where Tolstoy's brother Nikolay was to die in 1860. There, as we shall see, there were elements of neglect and guilt. But nothing so glaring as in the case of Dmitry. He was

actually able to spare the time to be with Nikolay while he was dying. So, though the squalor of Dmitry's hotel death, and the kindly, pock-marked prostitute, and the large, bony hands which had struck Tolstoy at the time, are all recorded in *Anna Karenina*, he does not record the fact that Lev, unlike Levin, was not even patient enough to wait for the death.

The death of Dmitry is conflated with that of his elder brother, and in the book, the dying brother is called Nikolay. The girlfriend, Masha (the usual Russian diminutive for Mary — it was the familiar one used by Tolstoy for his sister), becomes dignified not merely into Marya, but Marya Nikolayevna, the full name of Tolstoy's sister. 'Nikolay' in the novel is further attended by the actual maid from Yasnaya Polyana, Agafya Mikhaylovna. Tolstoy does not even bother to change her name. What was in fact a bleak and rather guilty death becomes in the novel a strongly family affair. By the time Tolstoy was able to write it all up, he was himself a married man, so that an idealised picture of his wife could also be brought in, rather as the medieval masters, when depicting the Crucifixion, thought nothing of adding the figure of their patron (some Italian prince or Flemish burgher) to the conventional group of figures — St. John and the Virgin — at the foot of the Cross.

What scandalised Tolstoy most of all, when he looked back on the death of his brother Dmitry, was how little he had cared. It was the most appalling case of having the experience and missing the meaning. The advantage of the novelist's imagination — an imagination, anyway, cast in Tolstoy's particular mould — is that it can seize upon unacceptable scenes from the past, and replay them as the protagonist would have wished. In *Anna Karenina* he flagellates himself for his inability to rise to the occasion of the deathbed, as the women could do; and he recaptures, with lurid vividness, the stench and squalor and fear of his brother's room. Particularly unforgettable is the moment when Marya Nikolayevna needs help in turning the patient over in bed, and how, as he thrusts his hands under his brother's damp, emaciated limbs, Levin feels dreadful revulsion, made worse by the fact that his brother then wants to kiss him. It is one of the very greatest scenes in Tolstoy. But one suspects that it was only able to be brought into being precisely because it was *not* like that at the time. 'Emotion recollected in tranquillity' is another phrase for making things up after the event. The crucial theme of those particular chapters in *Anna Karenina* is not feeling, but lack of feeling. And by

conflating the death of his two brothers, Lev Nikolayevich is able to be present, body and soul, at a deathbed which in 1856 was a matter of huge indifference to him. In the novel, it even becomes rather the edifying stuff of which a man could read aloud to some Dickensian family circle, with a gulp in his throat.

> The sight of his brother and the closeness of death renewed in Levin's soul that feeling of horror in the face of the inscrutability and at the same time the nearness and unavoidability of death, which had taken possession of him on that autumn evening when his brother had paid him a visit. That feeling was now even stronger than before; even less than before did he feel able to understand the significance of death, and its unavoidability now seemed even more terrible to him; but now, thanks to the proximity of his wife, this feeling did not drive him to despair; in spite of death, he felt the necessity of living and loving. . . .[16]

All very affecting, in its place in the novel. And, as the commentators remind us, such thoughts reflect Tolstoy's own growing preoccupation with death during the 1870s when the passage was written. But it took nearly twenty years for him to get these emotions right. No wonder they seem so perfect in the case of Levin. Like a criminal who had been twenty years on the run, Tolstoy could be expected to get his lines right when the time of trial came, and he had to relive the offensive scene.

*   *   *   *

Three aspects of metropolitan life were of particular attraction as he made his retreat from his brother's deathbed and hurried back to St. Petersburg: the Court, the bath-houses, and the literary salons. That is to say, snobbery, sex and fame.

In the first, his painful shyness and clumsiness were at war with a pride in his birth, and a delight, which is reflected so exuberantly in *War and Peace*, in all the resplendent detail of high life. How very high that was, by the contemporary standards of other European countries, is revealed to any modern visitor to the armoury of the Kremlin in Moscow, or to the Winter Palace in Leningrad where, in addition to the stupendous opulence of the coaches and costumes and uniforms and furniture, the sheer size and scale of it all are overwhelming. The Russian Court, in all its imperial glory, was much the grandest thing in Europe, and far outshone the muted luxuries of Windsor or even — a phrase one does not write lightly — the Habsburg splendour of Schonbrunn.

Even those who today have seen the Winter Palace at Leningrad, and been overwhelmed by its scale and richness, have only seen the half of what Tolstoy saw when he attended court functions there. For in those days, the newly built palace was not a museum, but a living setting for imperial magnificence, room after room dripping with crystal and marble and full of people who astounded foreign visitors by the wealth of their costumes, their jewels, and their elaborate uniforms. Nor was the Winter Palace an individual showcase. There, indeed, the bureaucrats, the senior military officials and their diplomats mingled in their finery with Grand Dukes and Grand Duchesses. But the company was probably more select, and the furnishings and costumes were hardly less plutocratic in the great aristocratic houses of St. Petersburg, stunning in their wealth, size and elegance.

Into this world, in which his ancestors had moved as habitués, Tolstoy blundered with a mixture of awe and embarrassment. Everyone at such a *levée* would know 'who he was', but he belonged to no inner circle, and even his kinsfolk who were courtiers were strangers to him. The courtier with whom he was to form the closest attachment was the Countess Alexandra Alexandrovna Tolstaya, a lady in waiting to the Grand Duchess Marya of Leuchtenberg. But this friendship — one of the most important of Tolstoy's life — was only to blossom on foreign soil. In the court, as in the literary salons, he was always something of a stranger.

The fact that he got invitations to Court functions did not go unnoticed among his literary friends, and helped to mark him out from the rest. There is jealous derision in Turgenev's exclamation, yelled at some literary dinner, 'Why bother to come here? Go off and see your princesses!'[17]

Turgenev was a difficult man to get along with. At various stages of his life he had acrimonious quarrels with Dostoyevsky, Fet, Katkov and Nekrasov. Tolstoy was not alone in exciting his wrath. But Turgenev seems to have had the capacity to arouse Tolstoy's anger in return, and in their most memorable exchange one catches the flavour of their antipathy. Serious contemporaries perhaps tried to extract from these rows and quarrels some profound ideological or intellectual difference. If Tolstoy had sat at a dinner table which contained Turgenev (who, as a true European and cosmopolitan, was a friend of George Sand), Tolstoy would see that as a good opportunity to be as rude as possible about this fashionable French writer. 'I can't repeat the nonsense he talked about George Sand, it was so crudely obscene,' Turgenev wrote furiously one morning to his friend Botkin, promising never to see or speak to Tolstoy again. But then they would meet, and be friends once more, until Tolstoy thought of some new way of provoking him. One good way of getting any group of literary men on the raw is to say that you do not see any merit in Shakespeare. Tolstoy tried this one at several stages of his life, always with pleasingly apoplectic results. He perfected the technique in that season at St. Petersburg. Fet got to a dinner party where the performance had ended and Tolstoy was on his way out. 'What a pity you were late,' another friend wrote to him. 'You would have learnt that Shakespeare is an ordinary writer and that our delight and astonishment over Shakespeare are nothing more than our desire to be fashionable, and our habit of repeating foreign opinions. . . .'

Lest the reader should be tempted to believe that Tolstoy was *thinking* when he indulged in these bear-baiting exercises, one should repeat and cherish his best exchange with Turgenev. On one of these occasions, Turgenev became so angry with Tolstoy that he thought he would choke. He clutched his throat and said, 'I can't stand any more of this! I've got bronchitis!' 'Bronchitis!' said Tolstoy scornfully. And then, perhaps feeling that his words made sense, 'Bronchitis is a metal!' The remark is very mildly less absurd in Russian than in English, in so far as *bronchit* could conceivably be some word like *grafit* (graphite) which refers to a physical substance rather than a disease. Tolstoy could have misheard. But there is a surreal appropriateness in the exchange. Tolstoy would spend many years of his life trying to persuade people that Shakespeare was no good; that Jesus wasn't a Christian; that folk songs were better than Beethoven and that property is theft — in other words, preaching the important gospel that bronchitis is a metal.

Nowhere does an intelligent and independent-minded person feel more strongly the need to preach this gospel than in some little intellectual circle such as the group surrounding *The Contemporary*. The writers for this periodical all furiously debated the question: whither Russia? and all thought that they had got the answer to the question. In the latter half of the fifties they were beginning to form into opposing camps. Turgenev and the more civilised writers were liberals, who hoped for a gradual reform of the system, and dreamed as liberals always do of the coming-together of men of good will everywhere. . . .

But there were others who looked to Herzen in exile, or who read the writings of the French socialist Proudhon, and who felt that the injustices in society were so glaring, the inequalities so gross, that only a radical, and possibly a violent solution could be found. This point of view was represented by figures like Nikolay Chernyshevsky and his friend Dobrolyubov. By supporting these radicals, Nekrasov lost nearly all his great contributors. Turgenev led the way, but Botkin, Fet, Saltykov-Shchedrin, Goncharov and Tolstoy himself all left for other periodicals. The paper was closed down by the censor in 1866.

Tolstoy's aloofness to the squabbles among lesser *Contemporary* writers is highly characteristic of his attitude to intellectual controversies at other periods of his life. He was open in his rudeness about both sides. He could mock the liberalism of Turgenev as mere posing, and attack the profanity and violence of the extreme left. If such double-handed scepticism produced some explosions at a *soirée*, or even a threatened fisticuffs, so much the better. But at the same time, Tolstoy was quietly absorbing much from both points of view: and it is extremely unlikely that his life at Yasnaya Polyana would have developed as it did without this period of exposure to what the intelligentsia was thinking in St. Petersburg. But like many countrymen, he was temperamentally inclined to entrench himself, and to resist contemporary fashions. It was while he was in St. Petersburg, and not while he was at home, that he resolved to liberate his serfs. And though, when he returned for a spell of five months on his estate in the latter half of 1856, he failed to put the plan into operation, he did try to do so. He had absorbed Turgenev's guilt and *Angst* about the position of the country nobility. But equally, he had absorbed much of the extreme radicalism of Chernyshevsky, Herzen and Proudhon. It had entered his system — true son of Rousseau as he was — without effort, or without his really noticing the difference. Though he found it emotionally impossible to belong to groups or to admit that he agreed with anyone, Tolstoy was from now on a fellow traveller with those who wanted to bring the system down.

*　　　*　　　*　　　*

The third great distraction of St. Petersburg life — we have mentioned the Court and the salons — was the easily available sex. The diaries show that this period was one of unrestrained activity, both in brothels and in the bath-houses. All classes of society and both sexes frequented these bath-houses, since pre-Revolutionary plumbing in Russia was even more rudimentary than post-Revolutionary. Each enormous house in St. Petersburg, whose each block of stone would dwarf a peasant's *izba*, contained many dwellings. But they were too large for carrying water about. One English visitor remarked that the size of everything in St. Petersburg seemed 'to have been designed for the countless generations to come, rather than for the practical wants of the present inhabitants'.[18]

The most respectable citizens of St. Petersburg, therefore, as well as the least respectable, would be found of an afternoon or an evening, making their way to the bath-house. 'Terrible', 'disgusting' and 'never again' are the frequent refrains in the diary as Tolstoy made his way around the very circuit of brothels and bath-houses which, forty years on, would see the revels of Rasputin. 'I make it a rule for all time,' he wrote in May, 'never to enter a pub or a brothel.'[19] But lust kept returning, so terrible that at the sight of the other naked bodies in the bath-house, it amounted to a physical pain.

Not long after this, he took his way home to the country. At first he stayed with Turgenev at Spasskoye, and on his way there he had a religious experience (unspecified) which moved him to tears.

By the beginning of July, he was back at Yasnaya Polyana. Much had happened since he was last there, both to himself, inwardly, as a man, and to the fabric of his estate. His grandfather's great house had now been demolished and Tolstoy took up residence in the surviving wing. He had also become exercised once again (a perennial preoccupation) with the status and fate of his peasants. There was so much talk now in St. Petersburg that the Government might be on the point of liberating the serfs that Tolstoy wanted to jump the gun and set his villagers free, regardless of what the Government decided.

Old Aunt Toinette, however, who remained at Yasnaya Polyana as a link with the past and the old ways, could not be persuaded that it was a good thing to let the peasants go.

'In comparison with my former Yasnaya recollections of myself,' wrote Tolstoy, 'I feel how much I've changed in the liberal sense. Even T. A. [i.e. his aunt] displeases me. In 100 years you couldn't knock into her head the injustice of serfdom.'

Tolstoy was to spend the next five months at home, happy to be there. Clearly, in spite of the cataclysmic debts which he had allowed himself to amass during the war, they had not been brought quite to the verge of ruin. It was a sad but ghoulish fact that one factor contributing to this had been the death of Dmitry, whose inheritance was divided among his surviving brothers and sister.

Tolstoy needed this period of respite, when he sat at home, waiting to discover what direction life would lead him into. It was in some ways a happy time, when he saw a lot of his friend Dyakov, who was, as he had confided in his diary some time before, the individual with whom he had been most deeply in love. They knew each other well, and they spoke on a level of intimacy. Dyakov advised Tolstoy that he should marry his ward, Valerya Vladimirovna Arsenyeva. She was the daughter of a Yasnaya Polyana neighbour, whose father had died in 1854 leaving Tolstoy, amazingly, as the legal guardian of his three children. By the summer of 1856, Valerya, the eldest, was twenty years old and Dyakov's idea that her twenty-six-year-old guardian should marry her did not look altogether preposterous. She was pretty. She wore alluringly skimpy evening gowns. She was 'sweet'. She was 'limited and impossibly trivial'. As far as Tolstoy was concerned she was everything a woman could be. But the more he contemplated it, the less he could imagine himself having family life; or, more crucially important, sexual relations with a girl who was so 'sweet'. In September, he started to have nightmares that he had become impotent: not a fear which he had ever had before. Throughout the fall, while he awaited his discharge from the army (it came through on November 28), he bombarded Valerya with letters. They were of inordinate length and incomparable condescension but, taken together, read like an elaborate backing away from a situation which pleased neither party. In November he informed her that although it is all right for her, as a woman, to 'think and feel as the foolish man does, it would be disgraceful and sinful for me. . . . Please go for a walk every day. . . . And wear a corset. . . . and Christ be with you and may he help us to understand and love one another well. . . .'[20] he wrote to her from Moscow in November. The advice is unstoppable. Not only does he dismiss all her friends and relations ('it is incomprehensible to me how you can live with these people without being disgusted'), but he also feels moved to correct any vestiges of self-regard which, after a summer with him, Valerya might have had left. 'Alas,' he wrote to her from St. Petersburg, 'you are deluding yourself if you think that you have taste. . . . The elegance of bright colours etc. is excusable, although ridiculous, in an ugly young lady, but for you with your pretty little face it's inexcusable to make such a mistake. . . . Christ be with you. . . .'[21] 'Religion is a great thing, especially for women. . . .'[22] 'How is it that you say nothing of Dickens or Thackeray. . . . ?' 'And what is this nonsense you have been reading. . . . ?'[23]

It must have been with very mixed feelings indeed that Valerya gradually learnt that her young guardian wanted to back off from any matrimonial possibilities. His tone of voice and manner to her do not suggest that he could ever have been wholly happy married to a woman of his own class or intellectual level. Never really having known anything of family life, he shrank from it; it is hard not to feel that the hectoring bullyism, alternating with grossly sugary endearments, were a subconscious expression of how little he wanted to be drawn into the world of 'family happiness', which, if not with his mind, then with his imagination and his instinct, he always held to be an idea of hell. In January, he cut the Gordian knot, and wrote to her:

Dear Vladimirovna, That I am to blame towards myself and towards you — terribly to blame — there is no doubt. . . . I'm not capable of giving you the same feeling as your fine nature is prepared to give to me. . . . In a few days time, I'm going to Paris, and when I shall return to Russia, goodness only knows. . . .[24]

Chapter Seven
Travels

1857 - 1862

I shall pass through many places
　That I cannot understand —
Until I come to my own country,
　Which is a pleasant land!

Hilaire Belloc

*I*n the spring of 1857, anxious to continue their young friend's education, Nekrasov and Turgenev took Tolstoy to Paris.¹ The foreign capital excited in him a mixture of fear and delight. 'A new city, a new way of life, no ties, and the spring sunshine which I caught the feel of.'² In the first few February days, he suffered from indigestion, stayed too long in his shiveringly cold bedroom, and met mainly Russians. Nekrasov, who was only staying in Paris for a few days before going back to Russia, was a gloomy companion, and Turgenev was getting on Tolstoy's nerves. One day when they went, for some reason, to a shooting gallery, Tolstoy detached himself from their company and went and hired himself an apartment. Doubtless there were reasons for his desire to be independent. By the middle of February, he was picking up interesting acquaintances on the street.

But, as something to fall back on, Turgenev's companionship was welcome. The older novelist showed the younger all the sights. They saw the forest and castle of Fontainebleau. They went to Dijon and explored all the churches. 'Turgenev doesn't believe in anything, that's his trouble; he doesn't love, but loves to love.'³ They played chess together in cafés, chatted and idled away the days. In Dijon, Tolstoy recorded, 'Turgenev is a bore; I want to go to Paris, but he can't be left alone. . . . We almost quarrelled.'⁴

In March when he had returned to Paris, Tolstoy was visited by one of those *mauvais quarts d'heure* which were to assail him throughout his life. Returning from a debauch, he lay awake in his apartment and suddenly felt 'tormented by doubts about *everything*. And now, even though they don't torment me, they are still with me. Why? And what am I. . . . ?'⁶ The moment passed. A few days later, his brother Sergey appeared, and they had a happy fortnight together with their friend Obolensky. They went to Versailles. They went to the theatre. Turgenev took them to a number of balls and dinners. They managed to find women readily available. On March 30, they saw off Sergey at the station, and on April 3, Turgenev arrived at Tolstoy's lodgings and woke him up, in order to confide his worries that he was suffering from spermatorrhoea. 'But he won't have treatment and gads about. . . .'[6] So far, then, so good. Paris was turning out to be all that the young foreign visitor might expect. 'I can't foresee the time when the city will have lost its interest for me, or the life its charm,' he wrote to his friend Botkin.[7]

But the letter was unfinished. The next day, he was — by his own confession — 'stupid and callous' enough to go and witness a public execution by guillotine. It was an experience paralleled by Dostoyevsky's Idiot, Prince Myshkin, who also saw a beheading in France. When Tolstoy returned to finish his letter to Botkin he had to admit that his whole mood had changed. 'I've seen many horrible things in war and in the Caucasus, but if a man had been torn to pieces before my eyes it wouldn't have been so revolting as this ingenious and elegant machine by means of which a strong, hale and hearty man was killed in an instant.'[8]

The letter continues, in a richly Tolstoyan way, to condemn not just the killing, but the system which produced it. There are some fine generalisations: 'The Law of man — what nonsense! The truth is that the state is a conspiracy designed not only to exploit, but above all to corrupt its citizens.'[9] These sentences suggest that he had been reading Proudhon and de Maistre, or at least mixing with those who had read these authors. Later, they were to be crucial elements in his mental furniture, essential presuppositions for the Tolstoyan way of looking at things.

The disgustingness of the guillotine remained for Tolstoy one of the most vivid and life-changing experiences.

When I saw the head part from the body and how it thumped separately into the box, I understood, not with my mind, but with my whole being that no theory of the reasonableness of our present progress could justify this deed, and that though everyone from the creation of the world, on whatever theory, had held it to be necessary, I knew it would be unnecessary and bad; and therefore the arbiter of what is good and evil is not what people say and do, nor is it progress, but is my heart and I.[10]

He wrote those words twenty years after the experience. For the time being, he felt merely revolted, not least with himself for having been party to the spectacle.

Tolstoy was unable to sleep for days after he saw the execution. Paris suddenly became hateful to him. He felt no interest in the self-consciously 'literary' milieu in which Turgenev moved. And, anyway, his lodgings were noisy and uncomfortable. He was staying in a *maison garnie*, inhabited by thirty-six couples. 'Nineteen of them were illicit alliances. That infuriated me.'[11] A single person in the midst of so much noisy conjugality felt sadly alone in the world. He longed for his own kind. As a student at Kazan, he had come into his inheritance at Yasnaya Polyana, and the knowledge that he could now move solely in the world of his family had sent him rushing home to the companionship of his aunt Toinette. Once again, in Paris, ten years later, he made a similar bolt towards the bosom of the family. This time, he must have been desperate. He heard by chance that some cousins, whom he had barely met during the previous season at St. Petersburg, were spending the winter in Geneva. These were his first cousins once removed, Lisa and Alexandra Alexandrovna Tolstaya. They were ladies-in-waiting to the only daughter of Nicholas I, the Grand Duchess Marie of Leuchtenberg. Lisa had been the Grand Duchess's governess, Alexandra was to be given the charge of educating the daughter of the present Emperor, the Grand Duchess Marya Alexandrovna, who was eventually to marry Queen Victoria's son, Alfred, Duke of Edinburgh and later Duke of Saxe-Coburg.

It was therefore into a courtly little group, whom he did not know particularly well, that Tolstoy burst in the spring of 1857. 'Paris was driving me *mad*!' he exclaimed to Alexandra.[12]

For all she had known or cared, Tolstoy had been in Russia. But without explanation, he continued, 'I rushed to Geneva as soon as I knew you were here, certain that *you* could save me.'[13] Like a lot of things spoken in jest between the sexes, this was true. The two cousins began an animated and affectionate conversation which was to last for very nearly the next half-century.

Here they were just foreigners, from the same class and family and background. But being in Switzerland made it easier for them to make

147

friends. Tolstoy's clumsy Pierre Bezukhov manners made it hard for him to enjoy the company of courtiers. When he got to know her better, he could find it astonishing that Alexandrovna should wish to spend all her time with the Royal Family. 'Up the chimney,' as he called the Royal Household.

But in Switzerland, in the cold spring weather, they could walk by the lakes and mountains without the constraints which a royal drawing room would have imposed upon their happy flow of words and jokes and ideas.

> The weather was exquisite, the landscape — need I say? We gloried in it with the delight of dwellers in the plains, though Lev Nikolayevich did sometimes try to curb our enthusiasm by assuring us that this was as nothing compared to the Caucasus.
>
> Still, it was quite enough for us. . . .[14]

After a few happy days at Geneva, Tolstoy disappeared and his cousins went for a walking tour.

> After several days of wandering in the mountains and valleys we went to Lucerne, and there Lev made another of his unexpected and unpredictable appearances. He seemed to spring out of the earth. . . .[15]

Alexandra, who probably came to know Tolstoy better than anyone else in the world, including his wife, has not only left us the best reminiscences of him, but was also responsible for drawing out of him, over the next forty-five years, a stream of magnificent letters, in which he revealed more about his life and character than in any other place. They are much better than the diary: they were written for the readership of someone in whose presence it was impossible to pose. Quite simply, Alexandra Alexandrovna liked this young literary genius in the family. In her, he found a companion who was vivacious, witty, sensitive, moral, and nobly born. For a man whose experience of women had hitherto been mainly of aunts or tarts, this was heady, beautiful. Here was a woman whom he could love as a friend. She brought out the best in him. 'I'm so ready to fall in love,' he confided in his diary. 'If only Alexandrine were ten years younger.'[16]

She was forty. He was approaching his twenty-ninth birthday. All that summer, they became more fond of one another. She even half made a Christian out of Tolstoy. The diary records a number of confessions and communions. But he could not bring himself to view her as a partner in any but a spiritual, cerebral sense. All summer long, he continued to lust after one girl and then another. Sometimes his lust was gratified, sometimes not. 'I'm just a silly little boy,' he said. . . . 'Alexandrine has a wonderful smile.'[17]

Cynics could say that Alexandra had a lucky escape. They think that 'being married to Tolstoy' was an absolute condition, rather than one which was uniquely undergone, endured or enjoyed by his wife. Had he married Alexandra, he would have married a kind and mature friend, who understood him, and would have been able to laugh him out of the many calamities of the later years. There are plenty of signs that he found her physically attractive. But somehow or another, during the summer of 1857, it was decided that they were to be 'just friends'. Never just friends however. He had to play up the age difference and give her a nickname of *babushka*, the word in Russian for 'crone' or 'Granny'. It is a bit like calling her 'old girl'.

By the time of his birthday, August 28, he was back home, priding himself that he had not had a row with his sister Masha. There was much that the brother and sister did not talk about. Her marriage was going badly. She was getting on too well with Turgenev. His story *Faust*, which had appeared in *The Contemporary* the previous year, was obviously all about her. The figure of Vera is a transparent portrait of Tolstoy's sister. Now, in August 1857, she announced that she was going to stay at Spasskoye with Turgenev, alone. 'This angered me,' said Tolstoy. 'We met rather coldly. . . .'[17] But his thoughts were still with Alexandra in Ostend.

> The awful 28th is over, and I hope that you are still alive, my dear [she wrote]. I *long* for a letter from you. I am awaiting for it as if I were dealing with a reasonable, steady individual, someone capable of remembering his good resolutions. I am waiting for news of your sister, who interests me very much and whom I have often thought about since our conversations. . . . Ostend is a dreadful anthill where the sound of the sea is drowned in the noise of a horribly smart set of people who swarm on the beach from morning till night and plunge into the sea, regardless of age or sex. . . .[19]

Nobody knows for certain what happened that summer between Turgenev and Tolstoy's sister. Probably, it all remained on the level of a flirtation. In the autumn, brother and sister went to Moscow, where they enjoyed seeing Fet, and derived rather less enjoyment from some of their other social encounters. There was the 'disgusting literary atmosphere' *chez* Aksakov. And there was a dinner at the Bers household. Old Bers was a man who mingled medical skill with social climbing and amorousness. He had had an affair with Turgenev's mother, and was almost certainly the father of Turgenev's half-sister.[20] The Bers were old friends of the Tolstoys. Hitherto, Tolstoy had found them charming, but not on this occasion. Bers's wife, a woman no more than two years older than Tolstoy himself, struck him that evening as 'awful, balding and frail'.

These judgements would be of no interest for us were it not for our knowledge that this awful, bald woman would one day be Tolstoy's mother-in-law. At this period Sofya Bers was only thirteen years old. She was just one of the little girls he had always known. It was with some relief that he escaped Moscow and took the train to St. Petersburg, the journey which was to be of such significance to his most extraordinary literary heroine. In the autumn of 1857, it was more or less the only bit of railroad track in the whole Empire. (It had been completed six years previously.)

For the rest of the autumn he was in St. Petersburg. Alexandra 'is a joy and a comfort. I've never seen a woman who could hold a candle to her,' he reflected at the end of October.[21] In November 'she is definitely the woman who charms me more than any other'.[22] In December, 'She has me on a string and I am grateful to her for it. However in the evenings I am passionately in love with her, and return home full of something — happiness or sadness, I don't know which.'[23]

They were happy times in St. Petersburg. The new Emperor was a liberal. His wife was a European. For the first time since the days of Alexander I, there was hope that there might be a change for the better in Russia's political system; hope that Russia might become a place where the intellect, and freedom, and all the things for which Pushkin had lived and written, were valued.

As has happened with almost every change of regime in Russia in the last two hundred years, optimists saw signs of spring. In the first year of the new reign, for example, there had been widespread reforms and amnesties. The surviving Decembrists were allowed to return. The institution of cantonists — by which the sons of military conscripts were compelled into military orphanages, and themselves made into soldiers — was abolished, thus liberating eighty thousand children. You were no longer fined for being Jewish. The Emperor was known to favour educational reforms, the building of railroads and — most important of all — the emancipation of the serfs. 'It is better to abolish serfdom from above than to wait until the serfs begin to liberate themselves from below.' In that famous saying, the Emperor encapsulated the liberal belief that it was possible to undermine the effects of revolution by getting in with the reforms first. The liberal nobility had their hopes raised by talks of local government reforms and representative assemblies.

In not so many years, when Tolstoy's imagination had had time to absorb this period, his excitement at the reforming spirit of Alexander II's early years and his wonder at the sight of the returning Decembrists would be turned into the Francophile enthusiasm of 1805, and the free-thinking zeal of that ur-Decembrist Pierre. It was the habitual process by which Tolstoy made experience into fiction. Events and experiences of the present, or near past, were fed back into the distant past. The little boy in *Childhood* is, in many ways, really a young man in the Caucasus. That actual young man in the Caucasus would become, when the time came to revise *The Cossacks*, a much more innocent fellow than Tolstoy had been. But in the company of his cousin Alexandra a richer ore was being tapped. He had always had the *entrée* to the great world if he wanted to take it. But it was she who made it possible. *War and Peace* would be unendurable if, in all the 'peace' scenes, we saw the dinners, *levées*, balls and parties entirely through the myopic eyes of Pierre. The narrator who describes these scenes has liberated the clumsy, awkward side to Tolstoy — the side who wrote *The History of Yesterday* — and made him free — free as Jane Austen — to observe, to satirise the world of the Scherers and the Rostovs. This is the world which Alexandra opened up for Tolstoy in the winter season of 1857-1858. She quite literally brought out the best in him. It is a good thing to mix with those who like us. Alexandra liked her cousin. She civilised him in a way that Turgenev's languid manners and political *chic* could never do. It was she, too, who, in her good-humoured way, saw the essential point about Tolstoy. She saw why his moral aspirations — as they occur in his fiction, and in his life — are so moving, while his moral presumption is so repulsive. She quoted to him a sentence of Charlotte Brontë's: 'Do not think I am good: I only wish to be so.'[24] There are broad gulfs between wanting to do good and doing good, as she wrote to him in the summer of 1858. By then, she was inescapably tied up at Court and he was in the country. She describes how she and the Grand Duchess and the other ladies of the Court were bumping into each other as they rushed for the magazine tables to find anything new by their new hero. He was at Yasnaya Polyana and his attention was being more and more devoted to the peasants and to their future. But his work and his imagination would have been enormously diminished if he had not been given, through his *amitié amoureuse* with the 'old girl', a glimpse up the chimney.

*　　　*　　　*　　　*

From all that he had heard in St. Petersburg, Tolstoy knew that the emancipation of the serfs was imminent in Russia. Already, things were changing. Under the tutelage of P. D. Kiselyov, there had been considerable extensions of peasant privileges. Kiselyov made provision for peasants who were not 'gentry serfs' (i.e. privately owned) to form themselves into communes, to colonise sparsely populated regions, to make use of state forests, even to borrow capital from the state. There was to be a measure of self-administration. In the villages, a *volost'* or canton elder was to be elected to represent the interests of the community with the larger nobles and, after 1864, with a local council, the *zemstvo*.

All this involved the presupposition that someone, somewhere in a Russian village, was able to read — not always a safe assumption to make. It was obviously in the interests of reaction to keep the populace illiterate; nor could those whose livelihood depended upon tilling the soil always see the necessity for bookwork. A parish priest in the south of Russia at about this period decided to educate his parishioners, and chose to teach thirty boys from the parish how to read. At first the parents went along with the idea. But when they realised that schooling was not compulsory, they immediately came and remonstrated with the priest. 'Not only did the peasants not see any material benefit from the teaching of their children,' the priest wrote, 'but they saw this as a loss of needed work time and turned to me with the request that I assign their children a salary for attending school. . . .' In that particular parish, education ceased, and the population remained, as they wanted to be, illiterate. When, in 1861, the proposal for emancipation was published, two hundred and eighty thousand copies were printed, and more were immediately required. But this is not a high proportion in a population of sixty millions. A contemporary painting, by G. G. Myasoyedov, called 'Reading the Manifesto', depicts various peasant men, of mixed age, huddled around a little boy — presumably the only literate person in the village — who has a copy of the proclamation in his hands.[25]

Figuratively speaking, it was to that little boy that Tolstoy paid much of his attention in the coming years. Ever since a brief, abortive, attempt to start a school at Yasnaya Polyana in 1848, he had nursed the ambition of educating his peasants. It had begun as an idea straight out of Rousseau. As the century advanced, his desire to be an educator was one of the things which anchored him most closely to his country's destiny. He shared with the revolutionaries, with the Church, the Government, the emergent *intelligentsiya*, a desire to capture the uneducated minds of the peasantry. But he differed from nearly all in his desire, which anticipates a lot of twentieth-century educational theory, to allow each child to develop as an individual. He did not simply regard them as vessels to be filled up with information and ideas.

The whole history of education in Russia begins with a certain sort of crude comedy and ends in blood. In the nineteenth century, however hard educators tried to 'raise' the peasantry to a level where they would enjoy reading for some lofty purpose, even 'for its own sake', the preponderance of learners wished only to read for practical purposes. The ability to read a map, for example, gave enormous scope to those whose way of life in their own region was unsatisfactory and who wished to migrate to another part of the Empire. The jealous neighbour, who could read the deeds of a cottage or a small plot of land, had enormous power over the illiterate next door. With the ability to read, it was possible that the over-numerous children of a peasant family could go into town and read the street signs, tell one shop from another, and even get jobs in restaurants where they could now read the menu. It was on this sort of level that literacy held attractions for the populace at large.

Tolstoy had a more high-minded view of it all, but he also entered into the practical uses of literacy, and enjoyed setting up a school. It began in 1859 with about twenty children, but he soon expanded and began to take on assistant teachers. One of these, Pyotr Vasilyevich Morozov, described arriving by foot at the farm, and seeing a little swarm of peasant kids making their way towards the low-lying farm buildings which served as schoolroom at that date. On the verandah outside the building there stood a genial man with a thick, dark beard, soft boots — evidently a prosperous peasant type. 'How can I see the Count?' asked Morozov. 'I am the Count,' was the reply.[26] Tolstoy intensely enjoyed being among peasants and liked wearing peasant costume. He found the women sexually attractive and available. He loved kissing the men, too. 'Their beards smell wonderfully of spring,' he told Alexandra.[27] Among such people, he was the monarch of all he surveyed. He had no need to be as shy or belligerent as the drawing rooms of Moscow and St. Petersburg made him feel.

The foundation of a school at Yasnaya Polyana was just one gesture towards the recovery of that green stick on which was written the secret of happiness, the means to destroy evil and to build a Kingdom of Heaven on earth. In the classroom as he laughingly taught the children the alphabet, he might have felt the Ant Brotherhood was reforming.

But there were obstacles in his way. He did not know much about education: and, Europeaniser and westerniser that he was, he believed that he should travel abroad to see how they did things in Germany, France, England. Abroad, too, was where the original, embryonic Ant Brotherhood was heading in the summer of 1860. His elder brother Nikolay was suffering from tuberculosis, and his condition was becoming serious. He had already settled in Soden, the Prussian health resort. As harvest approached, and the children disappeared into the fields, Tolstoy decided to leave Yasnaya Polyana in the charge of his assistant teachers, and to go abroad himself. He went with his sister Marya, and a few weeks later they would be followed by brother Sergey. It all looks as if he could foresee what was going to happen. But he did not. Instinct may have been guiding him, but with his conscious self, he was in for a shock.

*   *   *   *

It was a summer of vivid dreams. Perhaps his brother Nikolay's illness affected him more profoundly at a subconscious level than he at first recognised. Or perhaps, merely, the German food disagreed with his repose. In one dream, he saw that the religion of his time — and his own religion — is just a belief in progress. 'Whoever said to anybody that progress is good?' In another, perhaps more prophetic, dream, he was dressed as a peasant, and his mother did not recognise him. . . .[28]

For most of the month of July and for the whole of August, he devoted himself to inspecting German schools, and to absorbing the

Geist of the place. 'Luther is great,' he wrote having seen one Church primary school. 'Just the Bible without explanations or abbreviations.'[29] The remark shows how little of Luther he had ever read. In fact, the whole of Luther's philosophy of life derived from a sense of human imperfectibility, and the need for grace. The 'pure religion and undefiled' after which Tolstoy aspired was of the sort which Luther would have regarded as purely carnal. Luther was a disagreeable man, but a brilliant and original interpreter of the Augustinian world myth. His vision of a humanity which is obliged to accept its own guilt, and even to love it, is utterly at variance with the simple moralism of Tolstoy's creed.

Lutheranism at its purest level had little effect on the way the Germans ran their primary schools, and in many of the places Tolstoy visited, he found conditions 'terrible. . . . a prayer for the King, beatings, everything by heart, frightened, morally deformed children'.[30] At the beginning of August he met Julius Froebel, nephew of Friedrich Froebel, the founder of the Kindergarten system. Froebel's account of being lectured on education by his Russian visitor sounds like any exchange between any western liberal and any Russian between that date and this. Particularly admirable is Tolstoy's ability to criticise this German system of education, and to make a virtue out of the fact that the Russians did not even have any system. The Germans, who had at least been trying to evolve a satisfactory way of preparing children for life, are thus given a left and a right. On the one hand, Tolstoy's fortnight's survey has convinced him that they are doing it all wrong. On the other, how much better these things are done, or not done, at home. 'Progress in Russia, he told me, must come out of public education, which among us will give better results than in Germany, because the Russian masses are not yet spoiled by false education. . . .'[31] Tolstoy went on to speak of the Russian masses as a 'mysterious and irrational' force from which, one day, would spring 'an entirely new organisation of the world.'[32] No one can deny that this prophecy was fulfilled, and when it did, how grateful we all were.

The meeting between Tolstoy and Froebel took place in Kissingen. A few days later, Nikolay arrived from Soden. 'He's terribly clever and clear-headed. And he wants to live,' Tolstoy told his diary, 'but he has no energy for living.'[33] Yet, although he could see the truth with one part of himself, Tolstoy was being unrealistic about how ill Nikolay was. Both brothers, moreover, had to contemplate the life style of Sergey, who had also turned up in Kissingen, having lost his entire fortune at the gambling tables. The Ant Brotherhood was no longer, in real life, very congenial. Sergey had about him 'the glitter of aristocracy' and Lev found himself going off for walks on his own, and seeking out the company of German peasants, or of the novelist Auerbach, rather than his own family. After a few days Nikolay went back to the company of Mashenka in Soden. 'I'm no use,' said Lev in his diary.[34]

Biographers of Tolstoy with a stricter moral sense than mine have expressed the feeling that Tolstoy should have been some use.[35] But what could he have done? The knowledge that those whom we love are about to die is very often cruelly withheld from us. Tolstoy had already lost one brother. Though he was only thirty he knew that we are not immortal. But he behaved as if Nikolay *was* immortal. Nikolay wrote to him, asking him to come down to Soden. He did so slowly, spending a couple of days at Frankfurt, and toying with his story *The Idyll*. When he reached Soden, he thought his brother was well, and in good spirits. But he was wrong. Nikolay died on September 20. 'What's the point of struggling and trying, if nothing remains of what used to be N. N. Tolstoy?' Lev wrote to his friend Fet:

He didn't say that he felt death approaching, but I know he followed its every step, and surely knew what still remained to him of life. A few minutes before he died, he dozed off, then suddenly came to and whispered with horror: 'What does it all mean?' He had seen it — this absorption of self in nothingness. And if he found nothing to cling to, what shall I find? Even less. And then it's most unlikely that I or anyone else would struggle with it up to the last minute quite as he did. A couple of days before I said to him, 'We'll have to put a chamber pot in our room.' 'No,' he said. 'I'm weak but not as weak as that, we'll struggle on a bit longer.' Up to the last minute he didn't give in to it; he did everything himself, continually tried to occupy himself, wrote, asked me about my writing, gave me advice. But I felt he was no longer doing all this from any inner desire, but on principle. One thing remained for him to the end — nature. The night before he died he went into his bedroom to . . . . and fell exhausted on the bed by the open window. I came in, with tears in his eyes he said: 'How I've enjoyed this whole last hour.' From the earth you came, to the earth you will return. The one thing that remains is the vague hope that there, in nature, of which you will become a part in the earth, something will remain and be discovered. All who knew and saw his last minutes say, 'How wonderfully peacefully and calmly he died,' but I know how frightfully agonising it was, for not a single feeling escaped me.[36]

It is one of the best descriptions of a deathbed that Tolstoy ever gave us. And without suggesting for a moment that Tolstoy did not feel intense grief for Nikolay, one can see that the deathbed has already become a scene in a novel. The feelings of the dying must, by any logical understanding, be theirs alone. We can't know them. But for the novelist, who knows everything, not a single feeling escapes him. One sees here, in a moment of intense personal horror, how Tolstoy's extreme egotism feeds his power of artistic sympathy. He *is* Nikolay on the deathbed, and the death which most upsets him to contemplate is not his brother's but his own. That is why he can have all Nikolay's feelings for him as well as all his own.

The elder brother whom he had so much revered and respected died in Tolstoy's arms. He was thirty-seven. Lev Nikolayevich, five years younger, could now feel his childhood sealed off. True, Sergey and Mashenka were still alive, but upon neither of his surviving siblings was it possible to foist his fantasies of family purity or childhood innocence, as had been the case with Nikolenka and the Ant Brotherhood. Indeed, the two survivors might have made him fear that he had been born into a difficult genetic inheritance.

Writing to his aunt Toinette from the Caucasus in 1852 he had confided in her a dream which he had had. 'It's a beautiful dream but it's still not all that I allow myself to dream of. I am married — my wife is a sweet, good, affectionate person; she loves you in the same way as I do. We have children who call you "Granny"; you live in the big house, upstairs — the same room that Granny used to live in; the whole house is as it was in Papa's time, and we begin the same life again. . . . If they made me Emperor of Russia, if they gave me Peru, in a word if a fairy came with her wand to ask me what I desired, my hand on my heart, I would reply that my only desire is for this to become a reality.'

With his brother Sergey, such dreams, however intensely felt, must have seemed a little far removed from reality. It was Sergey, after all, who had introduced Lev to the brothel. When they grew up, Lev used to complain that they had little in common. This could very well have meant that he feared they had too *much* in common.

He had similarly watched Marya's marriage to Valeryan collapse and the flirtation with Turgenev begin. The images of innocence with which Lev Tolstoy liked to associate his family had died with Nikolenka. From now onwards, Lev Tolstoy's imagination was free to seek its consolations in a pure mythologising of his past. He sought back, and back, beyond the time of the Ant Brotherhood, to the era of the parents' marriage, and further back still to a time when there were no Tolstoys at Yasnaya Polyana — only old Prince Volkonsky and his long-suffering daughter; a time before the Decembrist Rising, when the officers who marched on Paris returned, and brought to Russia a sense of new beginning, a time when the 'mysterious irrational force' of the Russian people seemed benign, even glorious. It is no surprise that the next lot of relations he should have visited should be Volkonskys: and Volkonskys who harked back to precisely this period of existence.

In November he made a visit to Italy. In Florence, he presented himself to the most romantic and distinguished of all the Russian emigrés there, his mother's second cousin Count Sergey Grigoryevich Volkonsky, now seventy years old. 'His outward appearance — with long grey hair — was exactly like that of an Old Testament prophet,' Tolstoy recalled. 'This was an astonishing old man, the flower of the Petersburg aristocracy, nobly born and charming. And yet, in Siberia, even after he had done his penal servitude, and when his wife had no kind of drawing room, he used to work with the men, and all kinds of peasant labourers would be lolling about in his room. . . .'[37]

It is just the sort of scene which we associate with Tolstoy himself in old age — the wife having to rub shoulders with extraordinary peasant visitors, the husband a prophetic Old Testament character with flowing grey locks. Tolstoy was not many days with his distinguished old kinsman, but it is unimaginable that they did not speak of the Decembrist Rising, and of Count Volkonsky's sufferings at the hands of the autocracy. Of his various encounters abroad, it is possible that the meeting with Volkonsky made the most impression. Tolstoy's own efforts in the prophetic vein were to occupy much of his future years, and it was the budding prophet and educator who buzzed about the capitals of Europe for the next five months. But Volkonsky had touched a deeper vein, and shaken Tolstoy's imagination.

*   *   *   *

After Italy, England.

Tolstoy was in London for only sixteen days at the beginning of March 1861. In later years, he retained a keen memory of its criminal and sordid underworld. 'I was struck when I saw in the streets of London a criminal escorted by the police, and the police had to protect him energetically from the crowd, which threatened to tear him in pieces. With us it is just the opposite, police have to drive away in force the people who try to give the criminal money and bread. With us, criminals and prisoners are "little unhappy ones".'[38]

He was fascinated by the double standards of the English, and in particular their hypocrisy about sexual matters. He very nearly admired it. He wrote knowingly to Strakhov, nine years after his visit to the English capital, 'Imagine London without its eighty thousand Magdalens! What would become of families? How many wives and daughters would remain chaste? What would become of the laws of morality which people so love to observe? It seems to me that this class of woman is essential to the family under the present complex forms of life.'[39]

It is tempting to hope that one or more of the women who plied their trade in the Haymarket attracted the custom of the future author of *The Kreutzer Sonata*. But we have no evidence that any such transaction took place. Certainly, Tolstoy had every chance to witness the 'laws of morality' being flouted in the household of Alexander Herzen who, over the previous twenty years, had experienced a series of amorous catastrophes, if possible involving a woman called Natalya. Natalya the First, whom Herzen had seduced away from her Muscovite husband, and who was to bear him children and to marry him, had been consistently unfaithful to him with one of his best friends. She had died, and after a period of several years' mourning, Herzen had received into his London home a Russian radical called Ogaryov and his wife. She was also called Natalya and she was to bear Herzen three children. At the time of Tolstoy's visit, this complicated emotional story was in full swing. A daughter by Herzen's first union — another Natalya — was such an admirer of *Childhood* that she begged her father's permission to sit in the corner of the study and listen as the two great men conversed. It should have been worth listening to: the greatest Russian novelist, and the greatest radical Russian thinker of the nineteenth century. Moreover, they had something to talk about. On March 2, the *Illustrated London News* informed its readers, 'Tomorrow morning nearly forty millions of the human family who tonight will retire to bed as slaves will rise up free. The 3rd March (Feb 19th Old Style) has been fixed upon for the emancipation of serfs throughout the Russian Empire.' It is inconceivable that the two Russians did not discuss emancipation, but not in the hearing of little Natalya. She was mortified when the servant showed in Count Tolstoy. He was dressed in new fashionable clothes, and he spoke to her father about prize fights, of which apparently he had seen a good number since his arrival in London. She never heard one word of 'good talk' between the two men.

Herzen, for his part, found Tolstoy as annoying as did most of his fellow *littérateurs*. He wrote to Turgenev that they were seeing each other most days. 'We have quarrelled. He is stubborn and talks nonsense, but is a naïve and a good man.'

It was inevitable that Tolstoy should consort with a fellow country-man, particularly one with such impeccably radical credentials as Herzen. But he also did what he could to taste English life, and see some of the great men of the time. He went to the Houses of Parliament and heard Lord Palmerston making a speech for three hours. Not surprisingly, he found it pretty boring. One wonders how well he understood spoken English. On March 14, he went to St. James's Hall in Piccadilly and heard one of Dickens's famous readings — from *A Christmas Carol*. A portrait of the great novelist was always to hang in Tolstoy's study at Yasnaya Polyana. He read and reread Dickens. As an old man he was to say, 'Dickens interests me more and more. I have asked Orlov to translate *A Tale of Two Cities*, and I will ask Ozmidov to do *Little Dorrit*. I would undertake *Our Mutual Friend* myself if it were not that I have something else to attend to.' We do not have any record of Tolstoy meeting his hero, though we have a good example of the way in which first-hand biographical 'material' is often misleading. Tolstoy told his first biographer Biryukov that he had once heard Dickens in a large hall 'lecturing on education'. It has been more or less proved that Dickens did not give any 'lectures' on education at the time of Tolstoy's visit to London. His only recorded public appearance is the reading of *A Christmas Carol*. Such a fact leaves us to draw one of two conclusions. One is that Tolstoy's English was not up to understanding the famous dramatic renderings which Dickens made of his own work. This is a tempting comic interpretation: that Dickens with all his histrionic powers was trying to recreate the Ghost of Marley and the Spirit of Christmas Past only to give to an intelligent foreigner the impression

160

that he was 'lecturing on education'. These Englishmen. Sadly, the duller alternative is probably true. Tolstoy told Biryukov that he had heard Dickens in a large public hall and Biryukov, knowing of Tolstoy's and Dickens's interests in pedagogy, supplied the deadly untruth.[40]

The impression would be an easy one to make, since Tolstoy continued, while in London, to make his survey of European educational methods. Was he not now in the land of Mr. Gradgrind himself?

A few days after his arrival in London, he set off on a tour of seven schools with a note from the Education Department in Downing Street. 'I shall feel much obliged to the teachers of the above named schools, if they will kindly enable the bearer of this, Count Leon Tolstoy, a Russian gentleman interested in public education, to see their schools, and if they will give him, as far as they can, all the explanations and information which he may desire. Count Leon Tolstoy is particularly anxious to make himself acquainted with the mode of teaching Natural Science, in those schools where it is taught. Matthew Arnold.'[41]

It is tantalising, once again, that we have no record of what passed between Tolstoy and Arnold when they met, on the occasion when this letter was composed. Arnold, as an Inspector of Schools, had an unrivalled knowledge of the Nonconformist Board Schools throughout England and therefore, perhaps, a more comprehensive experience of the English poor than any man of his class or learning. Those who know him only as a poet and critic can have no idea of how hard Arnold worked, and of how much he knew of what was going on. Tolstoy rather surprisingly left any such areas of enquiry until much later in his career. His *What Then Must We Do?* of 1881 is a horrified account of the Moscow slums. It makes it quite clear that Tolstoy in all his previous sixty years had been only dimly aware of the way that the urban poor lived. Arnold could have no such illusions.

Another reason why we should value more knowledge or information about their meeting is that Arnold, with his remarkably cosmopolitan tastes in reading, was the first Englishman to write an intelligent account of Tolstoy's novels. His essay on *Anna Karenina* remains one of the very best things ever written on Tolstoy. Perhaps if some Boswell had been present he would have found Tolstoy wanting to quiz the great poet and critic about prize fights. But I doubt it. I think they would have had something to say to each other.

Armed with Arnold's letter, Tolstoy set off for the schools. It shows how much he valued his days with the London children that he kept mementoes for the rest of his life. At St. Mark's Practising School in Chelsea, for instance, the children were asked to write an account of how they spent the day, and to present these 'compositions' to their noble foreign visitor. The little essays are preserved in the Tolstoy Museum in Moscow, and like the frozen figures of Pompeii or Herculaneum the neatly copied, little copperplate scripts carry us back at once to the scene: 'Chalkley Age 12 years, Dear Sir, When I came to school I played at marbles and lost all mine' — Tolstoy would have sympathised with that! — 'then we were called in and when we had had three lessons we came out to play again then I had some more marbles and lost them and then we went in and had Latin and Music and while we had Music there was a hailstorm but when we came out to dinner it left off raining them [*sic*] I bought some more marbles and lost them then I played at egg at [*sic*] then we were called in school for afternoon's work first we had arithmatic [*sic*] and now we are having composition which I like very much.'[42]

A German educationalist, Leopold Weise, visiting England a decade before Tolstoy, disliked what he found. There was a lack of 'unrestrained joyousness, the poetry of boyhood and youth. . . .' Even little boys in England wore hats and were 'from as early a period as their twelfth year treated in all respects as men'.[43] Tolstoy felt very likely the same, but his reading of Dickens would have convinced him that the English had seen through the faults of their own system. Rather than feeling that Dickens had got things right, he must have had the much eerier sense that the whole of London, and in particular its poor schoolchildren, had actually been conjured up by Dickens's imagination. The fact that we have an essay in Chalkley's own hand does not dissuade us of the obvious truth that Chalkley was invented by Dickens. It must have given the young novelist pause when he left London behind him and took the road for Brussels, where the French anarchist philosopher Proudhon was residing.

*   *   *   *

Proudhon later told Herzen that 'Monsieur Tolstoi' stood out with great individuality among the many Russians who had visited him. They spoke of emancipation and all it would mean to the new Russian Empire. They spoke of the Christian religion to which Proudhon was implacably opposed. One hears much of Proudhon in Tolstoy's later tones. Here is some of Proudhon's *Jesus*. 'In my own home I have seen my mother, my aunts etc., reading the Bible and following the preacher of Nazareth like the holy women; today the people no longer understand the Gospels and do not read them at all. The miracles make them laugh and all the rest is Greek to them. As for the moral side, they no longer feel it is in their hearts.'[44]

Tolstoy a little sycophantically informed the sage that he had never previously understood Proudhon's obsession with Roman Catholicism; but having seen England and France all was made clear. 'Only then did I understand how right you were.' What? In England in 1861? How did Tolstoy form that impression? Anyway it was all right, he informed Proudhon, because 'in Russia the Church amounts to zero'.[45] This may have been true in the inner life of intellectuals but it is scarcely an accurate picture of Russia, nor a helpful comparison with countries through which Tolstoy was travelling. Whatever the faults of the Wesleyan and Jewish schools which he saw in London they were not, like all Russian institutions — universities, the army, the prisons — doggedly sworn to obedience to the national religion. True, French Catholicism made various feeble attempts to win back the intellectuals from the seductive power of Renan — later of Loisy. But it was a doomed cause since the Church in France had none of the political power of the Church in Russia. Heresy was not in France, as in Russia, a criminal offence. Were these remarks meant seriously? If so, did Tolstoy have any idea of how life was lived in his own country by those who were not cocooned and protected by membership of the landed class?

His instinctive reaction to things was always that of a landed aristocrat, who enjoyed the almost monarchical independence afforded by being lord of his own estates, and governor of his own people's destiny. From time to time, he would fulminate against the autocracy, or plead with the Tsar for clemency, or in some way or another clash with the Government. But it was not really like just anyone clashing with the Government. It was done in the spirit of a man who knew that his cousins were all at Court; in the spirit of an aristocrat whose imagination was fed on the memories of the Decembrist Rising and, before that, the assassination of the mad Tsar Paul. He assumed, always, that it was the aristocrats' function to tell an autocrat when he went too far. Like all those grand families who claimed that the lineage went back to Prince Ryurik, Tolstoy — on his Volkonsky side at least — could believe himself to be of older, better family than the Romanovs themselves.

The remark about the Church is typical. 'In Russia the Church amounts to zero.' This means that the majority of writers he had met in St. Petersburg were *non-pratiquants* and that at Yasnaya Polyana churchgoing was left to people like aunts. As a remark about Russia, it means nothing at all.

Perhaps the most important idea of Proudhon's to be absorbed into the Tolstoyan world view, however, is the phrase *La propriété, c'est le vol.* This will remain truer, in Tolstoy's view, than the truth of the British constitution as long as mankind exists. On it alone, he opined in 1865, 'can the Russian revolution be based'.[46] For the purposes of Tolstoy's future development, it does not much matter that he did not mean the same by this phrase as Proudhon had done. Proudhon's main criticism of the communists was that they wished to destroy private property. He was not opposed to innocent property-owners. He denounced rather those big property owners who used their property to exploit the labours or freedom of others. In his book *What is Property?* Proudhon began by saying that if you asked 'What is slavery?' you could answer in one word — murder. 'Why then to this other question, what is property, may I not likewise answer "theft"?'

Happily, it lies quite outside the scope of this book to say whether Proudhon was right or wrong in the analyses which he proposed.[47] Nor must we recount the ways in which Proudhon backtracked and changed his mind on this and other questions. The anarchic strain in Proudhon was what appealed to Tolstoy; and when the time came, the phrase about property being theft would explode in Tolstoy's life. But Proudhon is more famous, perhaps, in the Tolstoyan connection, for having provided Tolstoy with one of his better-known phrases.

At the time of their meeting Proudhon was just finishing a book entitled *War and Peace.* The Russian chronicler of Tolstoy's days and months, who normally gives us such a full account of things, merely says, 'evidently, since he was just approaching the end of his work *La Guerre et la Paix*, Proudhon told Tolstoy about it'.[48] For many years of this century, it was barely possible to mention Proudhon in Russia because of his lamentably un-Marxian form of socialism. When Eykhenbaum was bold enough, in 1928, to express his astonishment that not one Russian literary critic had ever perceived the close association between Proudhon and Tolstoy's great novel, he received an icy reception from the establishment. This particular theory of

Luisa Volkonskaya, model for Lise
Bolkonskaya in *War and Peace*

Tolstoy's father

A sketch of Tolstoy as a student of
Kazan University (unknown artist)

Daguerreotype by V. Shenfeldt of
Tolstoy as a student, 1849

Tolstoy with his eldest brother,
Nikolay, just before they embarked
together to the Caucasus in 1851

Tolstoy in the uniform of an artillery
officer, 1854

Tsar Nicholas I (1825–1855)

Tsar Alexander II (1855–1881)

Tsar Alexander III (1881–1894)

Tsar Nicholas II (1894–1917)

The authors of *The Contemporary* (*Sovremennik*).
Left to right (seated), Goncharov, Turgenev, Druzhinin, Ostrovsky;
standing, Tolstoy, Grigorovich (1856).

The editor of *Sovremennik*, 'the
glorious Russian poet-democrat',
Nekrasov

Turgenev in old age

Fet

Tyutchev

Sofya Andreyevna Bers at the time of
her marriage to Tolstoy

Tolstoy aged about fifty

Tatyana Andreyevna Bers, Sofya's younger sister and the model for
Natasha Rostova in *War and Peace*

Tolstoy and his family at about the period when he was writing Anna
Karenina. From left: Sofya, holding infant Lev; their daughter Tatyana;
'Big Masha', daughter of Sofya's sister Tanya (in black) with two of her
children. Tolstoy's sons Ilya and Sergey are in the front row.

A page from the manuscript of *War and Peace* showing
Tolstoy's marginal corrections and doodles

Yasnaya Polyana

Tolstoy's Moscow house

Eykhenbaum's was suppressed, and the book in which it occurs was published abroad. In 1957 Eykhenbaum mysteriously renounced his former theories, urged his readers to take no notice of his own work on Tolstoy and to read only the immortally fascinating essays of Lenin.

Two things come together here: the fact that Proudhon was, from a Marxist point of view, a heretic; and the much more damaging fact that he was not Russian. Among the Russians there is an intense national pride in the novel *War and Peace*, and in its author, Lev Tolstoy, 'The Soldier and Patriot', as one Russian study published in the 1960s calls him.

There are things in Proudhon's *La Guerre et la Paix* which encourages comparison with Tolstoy. For one thing, the book, which is an indictment of war, begins on an almost epic scale, describing the great battles of the past, and admitting that war brings out the best in men, qualities of strength and courage and unselfishness. But Proudhon believed modern war is essentially a product of capitalism; its foundations were really economic. Change the nature of society, reform its economic structure, and you will have brought an end to war. War will be outgrown, 'henceforth heroism must give place to industry'.[49]

Strangely enough, although Tolstoy does appear to have absorbed many of these arguments in his later non-fictional writings about poverty — in particular *What Then Must We Do?* — he does not appear to have shared Proudhon's view of the origins of war, nor the Frenchman's definition of what was wrong with war. The most articulate and beguiling Tolstoyan of contemporary times (using the word here to mean a man who regards Tolstoy as a great thinker, and who shares his views) has demonstrated that Proudhon was not really as much of an influence as Eykhenbaum supposed. Professor Sampson points much more to the influence of three more seemingly cynical observers — Stendhal, Herzen and de Maistre. All of them were very different. But all, crucially, were men of 1812. De Maistre, who gloried in war and loved oppression, naturally saw in Napoleon a man who had changed the very nature of warfare by making it bloodier than it had ever been before. He was plenipotentiary of the King of Sardinia at Alexander I's Court at St. Petersburg. Stendhal, as an officer in Napoleon's army, had wintered in Moscow in 1812, and had been one of those who miraculously survived the retreat. For Herzen, it was the scene and time of his birth. As a newborn baby, he was left behind in the blazing city when the inhabitants set fire to Moscow. All three men could see that there was something special about the 1812 campaign. Napoleon himself said that 'Borodino was the most terrible of all my battles.' There had never been a battle of such scale or horror. Professor Sampson likens it, in Tolstoy's day, to Hiroshima in our own, an event after which it is impossible to view the world in quite the same way.[50]

Tolstoy's encounter with Proudhon reminds us of the movements of Tolstoy's mind at this period. The foreign travels of 1861 are more pregnant with the future than the earlier jaunt to Germany, because they stirred up such profound reflections upon the past. His brother Nikolay's death had torn him back to the lost world of his childhood innocence; and the encounter with the Volkonskys in Florence had reminded him of a yet remoter lost Eden — Russia before the Decembrist Rising, when aristocratic, free-thinking men such as Herzen had, or might think they had, the Emperor's ear. With Herzen himself, and with Proudhon, Tolstoy had time to reflect upon the unjust way in which the world is ordered, but with neither of their solutions was he truly in sympathy.

Doubtless there are many reasons for this, but the imaginative ones are clear. He was not a socialist for the simple reason that he did not believe in society. This had always been true, but the death of Nikolay and the isolation of abroad confirmed it. Tolstoy did not want to belong to a clique or a group or a movement or a gang. Moreover, his glimpses of 'abroad' had made him long to get settled into Russia, and in particular into Yasnaya Polyana, its immediate, local difficulties and problems. He looked back now with distaste upon his flirtation with the free-thinking, Europeanising world to which Turgenev had introduced him. (As Eykhenbaum brilliantly observes, all this rejected side of Tolstoy's own nature gets embodied, when he comes to write his novel, in Napoleon; the Bonaparte of the novel, with his free-thinking and progressive ideas, is in many ways quite different from the actual Emperor of history.) 'God has been restored,' Tolstoy wrote, as he returned home, 'hope and immortality.' In the whole course of his life, he never left Russia again.

*   *   *   *

Tolstoy both did and did not belong to the societies he inhabited. Yasnaya Polyana provided him with the security and strength and independence which would eventually enable him to write *War and Peace*. Yet in itself it was an emblem of his status as an outsider in provincial Russia. He both was and wasn't peasant-like; he both was and wasn't a St. Petersburg aristocrat; he both was and wasn't a writer, a member of the intelligentsia.

His ambivalence was apparent throughout his first year back home, and it produced conflicts, some comic, some touching, some prophetic. Tolstoy was not sure where he was, or who he was.

Before he got home, he found that he had been appointed, *in absentia*, a Justice of the Peace, with special responsibilities for supervising the new legislation which had come into force upon the emancipation of the serfs. The innocent outsider might suppose that it was a strange honour to have conferred upon a young man who was not very popular with the local gentry and whose life style had not hitherto been all that might be expected from the judicial bench. But consider the nature of his task. The marshal of the local nobility had already made representations to the governor of Tula that the traditional rights of landlords over 'their' peasants should be respected, whatever the newfangled laws might decree. But the law now allowed for the peasants to have redress in cases of injustice. They could exact financial compensation if they had been wrongfully made victims of physical punishment. In the many cases where emancipation was effectively withheld from the peasants, it was the arbiter's job to intervene and make sure that justice was done. This was the sort of task which fell to Tolstoy on his return. One of his neighbours, for instance, Kostomarov, was claiming that all his 'souls' were really his own personal house serfs and therefore not entitled to any land.

Is it any wonder that the governor of Tula gave the uncongenial task of arbiter to a young nobleman who was actually out of the country at the time of his appointment? Anyone doing the job was bound to make enemies, so why not entrust it to a young man whom the neighbourhood regarded in any case with abhorrence? The fact that he was offered the job is a tribute not to Tolstoy's powers of leadership, but to his already observable social isolation.

There were many cases like that of Mrs. Artukhov. She lodged a complaint with her local council (the *zemstvo*) that her manservant, Mark, wanted to leave her on the grounds that he was now a free man. Moreover the 'Arbiter of the Peace, Count L. N. Tolstoy' had ruled that Mark and his wife should be given, not merely their freedom, but also three and a half months' wages to compensate for the time he was wrongly held in Mrs. Artukhov's employment against his will. When she appealed to the *zemstvo*, who were all her own kind, Tolstoy's unpopular, and fair, decision was overruled.

Though the governor of Tula had thought Tolstoy's appointment would have the advantage of letting other landowners off the hook, it infuriated the others. Tolstoy was this funny mixture. They knew that he had been abroad and picked up a lot of ideas. But they would not have expected a nobleman of such breeding to side with the peasants against *them*. The magistrates' session at Tula reversed nearly all his decisions. 'I have earned the terrible indignation of the nobility,' he wrote to Botkin. 'They even want to beat me and take legal action against me. . . . I am just waiting for them to calm down and then I shall resign.'[51]

The authorities began to regard Tolstoy as a dangerous revolutionary, which he was; much more potentially dangerous than either they or he ever realised. This was abundantly clear when they came to investigate the school which he was running at Yasnaya Polyana. Having seen the schools of Italy, Germany, France, Belgium and England, he was anxious to put his own educational theories into practice. To our contemporary way of looking at things, they were remarkably advanced and enlightened. He was not a believer in treating children as the passive vehicles of information which was to be drummed into them, Gradgrind style, by repetition or by fear. Rather, he sought, as we would say, to 'draw them out'. The essays and stories which the children wrote still survive. Many of them were published in the lifetime of the children. By then Tolstoy had enlisted and enrolled a number of assistant teachers, and devised a proper curriculum. He described it all to Alexandra, who had complained to him that corresponding with the Laird of Yasnaya Polyana was like 'having a game of tennis all by oneself, throwing the ball into the haystack'. He told her not to be angry, and then painted for her an idyllic pastoral which explained why he had been too busy to write.

> When I escape from my office and from the peasants who persecute me from every part of the house, I go to the school; but, as it is under repair, the classes are installed in the garden, under the apple trees, to which one has access by stooping, the vegetation being so dense. The schoolmaster sits there, and all around the pupils, nibbling grasses and making lime and ash-leaves pop. The master teaches according to my advice, but not very well after all, which

the children feel. They love me more. And we begin conversing for three or four hours, and nobody is bored. One cannot describe these children. I have never seen the like of them amongst the children of our dear rank. Just think that during the two years, without any discipline, no boy and no girl was punished. No laziness, no rudeness, no stupid jokes, or distasteful words. The schoolhouse is nearly finished. Three large rooms — one pink, two blue — are for the use of the school. A museum besides is in one of the rooms. Along the walls, on brackets, stones, butterflies, skeletons, grasses, flowers, apparatus for physics, etc., are placed. On Sundays the museum is open for everybody and a German from Jena (who is an excellent fellow) does experiments. Once a week botanical class, and we go into the forest to search for flowers, grasses, and mushrooms. Four times a week singing class; six times drawing (again the German) and it goes very well. . . .[52]

It all sounds a little too good to be true, but the testimony of his pupils shows that there was really something very special about the Yasnaya Polyana school, and that they did genuinely love him. This thirty-two-year-old eccentric, who maddened his 'own kind' and could not fit into any of the social or intellectual stereotypes of the day, found true companionship with his young friends at the school. He spoke to them as equals. No wonder they sat and listened. 'I've been thinking,' he would say. 'Maybe I'll give up my estate and my life as Master, and live like a peasant, build a hut on the edge of the village, marry a country girl, work as you do at mowing, ploughing and all kinds of work.' While the boys and girls debated the proposition, Tolstoy made notes.

To his many other maddening characteristics, Tolstoy could add that he was good with children, and this did not go unnoticed in the neighbourhood. By the time his *Yasnaya Polyana*, a periodical based on the school experiments, was being published in the following year, the Minister of the Interior, Valuyev, was drafting a memo to the effect that 'A close perusal of the educational review *Yasnaya Polyana*, published by Count Tolstoy, inclines me to think that by advocating new teaching methods and principles for the organisation of schools for the common people, this periodical is spreading ideas which are not only false but dangerously biased. . . . The continued publication of the periodical would seem undesirable, especially as its author, who has remarkable and persuasive literary powers, is above all suspicion of criminal intention or dishonesty. . . .' Worse and worse! They could not even get him on a charge of fraud or corruption, and shut him up that way. 'What is harmful is the inaccuracy and eccentricity of his views which, set forth with exceptional eloquence, may be convincing to inexperienced teachers and may thus orient education in the wrong direction.'[53]

*   *   *   *

There is a tendency to think of Tolstoy's desire to live like a peasant as a feature of his middle and later years, a manifestation of his religious, post-literary self. But it was always there and, in the years immediately following his return from abroad, this Rousseauesque identification with the peasants was very strong. It was an important symptom of the isolation which was so necessary to him, as an artist. He could not function inside any mainstream. He had to be an outsider. With two of his brothers now dead, he was able to taste, that happy summer, some of the reassuring delights of the Ant Brotherhood. But, whether or not he was fully conscious of the fact, part of its sweetness was that it angered, not merely his neighbours, but the Government itself. It placed him out on a limb, *contra mundum*, beyond the pale. Always, in Tolstoy's life, there was this dual compulsion. On the one hand, there was the need for a little band of the faithful, who looked up to him as the Master. He found it in the Yasnaya Polyana school. When he came to marry, he tried to find it in his progeny. And he was to find it in the motley band of 'dark ones' who, in later years, followed his teachings and example.

But he had no interest in joining ready-made brotherhoods, nor in attaching himself to cliques. And the year which saw him antagonising the Department of the Interior and upsetting nearly all his landed neighbours also saw him distancing himself, irrevocably, from the literary set in St. Petersburg. His attitude to the peasants placed him in peril of siding with extreme radicals like Chernyshevsky. But he need not have worried. Chernyshevsky lambasted Tolstoy's pedagogical writings in a scathing *Contemporary* article.[54] He was anxious to prove Tolstoy's ignorance, dragging up the fact that he did not have a proper university degree, was shocked that Tolstoy did not take more seriously *chic* figures like Froebel, and took the view, common to urban radicals, that members of the aristocracy had no business to be on the side of the peasants unless they learnt from the intelligentsia how to cultivate the right attitudes. As a matter of fact, Chernyshevsky's attack on Tolstoy is a good early-warning signal of how much the serious 'political' left in Russia hated the peasants. They did not like the idea of anybody achieving independence, and this is what intelligent and independent-minded country people have always wanted. Tolstoy, for all his posturings, was actually on the side of the peasants whom he knew, and who loved him. He wanted them to be free. Chernyshevsky's doctrinaire radicalism is interestingly analogous to the response of English socialists to the Distributist movement in the 1920s. The suggestion that the poor should be liberated not only from the oppression of capitalists but also from the tyranny of the state filled such people as Shaw or the Webbs with horror; they lost no time in caricaturing the position of the Distributists as 'back to the land' and 'three acres and a cow'. These were creeds to which the poor *kulak*s clung, too. While Shaw mocked the Distributists' ideal at home, his hero Stalin was employing weapons heavier than satire and, in his collectivisation of the land, massacring peasants in their millions who failed to conform to the requirements of the Five Year Plan.

Tolstoy's row with Chernyshevsky, then, anticipates the extreme suspicion with which, in later years, the Bolsheviks would regard the 'Tolstoyans'. His quarrel with Turgenev doubtless had its roots in the same need to cut himself off from anything which might have been thought of as metropolitan fashionableness. At the same time, it went deeper than that. It was both more tragic and more farcical.

Turgenev got back from abroad in May 1861, and almost immediately invited Tolstoy to stay at his estate of Spasskoye. The meeting was happy enough, and there was a good dinner. After the meal Turgenev proudly produced the newly completed manuscript of his novel *Fathers and Children* and, placing his friend on the drawing-room sofa, put the masterpiece into Tolstoy's hands. Then he left his guest to savour the experience of reading it alone.

When Turgenev returned to the drawing room to see what impression the novel was making upon Tolstoy, he was disconcerted to see the young man stretched out on the sofa, fast asleep. Since both the participants in this marvellous scene were novelists, that is to say falsifiers, it is hard to know how much of it actually took place, and how much was a fiction in their own brains. Tolstoy improves the story by saying that he opened his eyes and was just able to see Turgenev's back slinking through the door of the room, and trying not to be noticed.

171

So much for Tolstoy's verdict on *Fathers and Children*. The next round of the combat occurred when Tolstoy chose to be singularly offensive about Turgenev's natural daughter, and offensive in precisely the same way that Chernyshevsky was offensive about him. Turgenev happened to remark that the girl had an admirable English governess who had asked him to specify how much his daughter might spend on charity. He went on to describe this governess teaching his daughter to 'mend the tattered rags of the poor'.

'And you think that's a good idea?' asked Tolstoy abruptly.

'Yes, surely. It puts her in touch with the real world.'

'Well, I think that a well-dressed girl with filthy, stinking rags on her lap is acting in an insincere theatrical farce.'

Turgenev's face became red.

'I would ask you not to say that.'

'Why shouldn't I say what I believe?'

'Then you are saying that I am educating my daughter badly?'

Tolstoy said, yes, he did think this, but it was his opinion. It did not reflect on his opinion of Turgenev personally.

'Then,' shouted Turgenev, 'if that's what you think, I'll punch your nose.'

After this well-reasoned contribution to the educational debate, Turgenev ran out of the room, returning a minute later to apologise to Fet's wife who had been the bewildered witness of it all.

'For God's sake, forgive my bad behaviour, for which I apologise most deeply,' he said, and then, like some comic character in Dickens, he ran once more from the room.

But Tolstoy was not prepared to leave it at the level of drawing-room farce. The animosity between the two writers was real, and deep. Those who witnessed it must have hoped that it would all blow over, because they had no reasonable grounds for hating one another. But they had something much stronger than that, grounds, enforced by that mysterious jealousy which is as strong as sex: literary rivalry.

Tolstoy went away, but the quarrel nagged at him, and at the first stop on his journey, he posted a note to Turgenev, reminding him that he had behaved improperly. At the next post station along the road he awaited a reply from Turgenev. There was none. Tolstoy immediately ordered pistols, and sent a second letter, announcing that he challenged Turgenev to a duel. He hoped that Turgenev would meet him in the woods at the edge of Bogoslovo, a place whose name means the Word of God.

As it happened, Turgenev had replied to the first letter, but sent it to Tolstoy's next address rather than to a changing post along the road. It suggested that they break off relations altogether — a good idea, but Tolstoy's challenge was by now in the post. It is a frightening thought that if Tolstoy had been having this quarrel with Dostoyevsky, they would almost certainly have met for this duel, killed one another, and deprived the world of the two greatest novelists of the nineteenth century. It is a good thing they never met. Turgenev sent grovelling apologies, fully admitted (which was hardly, by now, true) that he was completely to blame and wholly in the wrong, and said that Tolstoy, being wholly in the right, was justified in summoning Turgenev to justify himself with pistols. But the letter is of a kind which would have made it impossible for Tolstoy to insist on satisfaction. He asks Tolstoy's pardon. Tolstoy replied that he knew Turgenev was afraid of him. 'I scorn you and do not wish to have anything more to do with you.'

For the next few months, there was a truce, during which, inevitably, Tolstoy's conscience began to trouble him. He realised that he had gone too far, and he wrote a letter to Turgenev telling him that it was, for him, a torment that he should have an enemy. He sent the letter, to be forwarded, to Turgenev's bookseller in St. Petersburg. But Turgenev was abroad, and did not read this letter for three months. Meanwhile, rumours had reached him that Tolstoy was going round Moscow accusing him of cowardice, and circulating copies of his letter to that effect. Very well. If Tolstoy had been accusing Turgenev of cowardice, he must answer for it. When Turgenev returned to the province of Tula, he would insist upon a duel to defend his honour. Since he was at that time in Paris, and would not be returning to Russia for the rest of that year, he could not fight the duel for about eight months, but it was, as far as he was concerned, a firm date.

Even Tolstoy could see the absurdity of this. It was one thing to fight a duel on the spur of the moment when passions were running high, another to keep the resentment at an artificial heat for two thirds of a year. He wrote asking Turgenev's pardon for any offence he may have caused, and declined the challenge.

For the next seventeen years, there was to be no contact between the two men. This made complete what had been evolving over the previous two or three years: the social, political and intellectual isolation in which Tolstoy's daemon could flourish. The quarrel with

Turgenev was about nothing: it could have been patched up in half an hour if Tolstoy had wanted it. But Turgenev was at this juncture the most obvious rival to Tolstoy's latent genius. (When Dostoyevsky's genius emerged, Tolstoy simply refused to meet him.) He was by now isolated from St. Petersburg but — thanks to his activities as a magistrate and an amateur schoolmaster — isolated from the local nobility around Tula. He had already written and said enough to earn him enemies in the Government, and it would not be long before they made their appearance. All that was needed, now that his artistic isolation was assured, was some emotional cocoon in which his loneliness could be sheltered. It was time for him to get married.

Chapter Eight
Marriage

1862

Suppose you are fortunate enough to have
'fallen in love with' and married your friend.
And now suppose it possible that you were
offered the choice of two futures: 'Either you
will cease to be Lovers but remain forever joint
seekers of the same God, the same Beauty, the
same Truth, *or else*, losing all that, you will
retain as long as you live the raptures and
ardours, all the wonder and the wild desire of
Eros. Choose which you please.' Which should
we choose? Which choice should we not regret
after we had made it?

C. S. Lewis, *The Four Loves*

*I*n 1862, Tolstoy completed his first masterpiece, *The Cossacks*. It was what he called his 'Caucasian' novel[1] and it had been lying around in various versions ever since he had himself lived in the Caucasus. But a melancholy spell in Moscow at the beginning of the year brought more gambling debts, and at the beginning of February, Tolstoy was approached by Mikhayl Nikiforovich Katkov, editor of the periodical *Russkii Vestnik* (*The Russian Herald*) with the offer of a thousand pounds if Katkov, rather than Nekrasov on *The Contemporary*, could have the novel.

It was to be a momentous partnership. Katkov would publish *War and Peace* and the greater part of *Anna Karenina*. He was an interesting man, and not the mindless reactionary which some literary historians have made him out to be. In fact, his career is emblematic of much that was happening in those confusing decades of Russian history. He was ten years older than Tolstoy, and his background was Moscow intellectual. He taught philosophy at Moscow University from 1845 onwards, when it was still very much the University where Herzen had learnt and propagated his radical ideas. Katkov was a believer in constitutional government of the English pattern, but his liberalism was to be destroyed in 1863 by the Polish Uprising. Thereafter, we find him associated with extremely conservative, patriotic views — more like those of Dostoyevsky than those of Tolstoy.

Politically and intellectually, Tolstoy was as difficult to place at this period of his life as at any other. Katkov did not buy *The Cossacks* because it was the work of a fellow radical. He bought it because it was a work of genius. It is one of the most supreme examples in the Tolstoy *œuvre* of his ability to 'make strange', to use the formalist term, very familiar, old stuff. The young man riding off to the Caucasus is a cliché of early Russian Romanticism. But Olenin's relationship with Yeroshka and Maryanka is so subtly drawn that never for an instant do we feel that Tolstoy is trespassing in Lermontov or Pushkin country. These two characters, Yeroshka and Maryanka, are two of the great originals in literature. Yet, in different ways, they both illustrate the extreme separateness of their world from Olenin's. Olenin's is partly the typical isolation of the Romantic man, which Rousseau and Wordsworth might feel simply because they are so special, so much themselves, but which comes home with special force abroad where, as another poet was to feel, 'elsewhere' underwrote his existence. Tolstoy does not feel the merely Lermontovian or Byronic (or, come to that, T. E. Lawrence-ish) desire to be a member of a different race or culture. With extreme realism, he recognises that he can't be: not merely that he cannot transcend the barrier of race and class even in his love for Yeroshka and for Maryanka; but, more importantly, that he cannot make himself an innocent. In his final conversation with the old man Yeroshka condemns Russian doctors as *fal'csh* — phoney.

> Olenin did not begin to reply. He was in all too much agreement that everything was phoney in the world in which he lived and to which he was returning.[2]

It was the world, incidentally, in which Tolstoy was living while writing the story: an extremely important fact, which will emerge later in this chapter. Olenin's return, like that of Scott's Waverley in highly comparable circumstances, is a crucial part of the story. To that degree, at least, it would not be necessary to dismiss those mid-twentieth-century Soviet critics who have seen the *narod*, the people, as the collective heroes of this story. 'The idea of the superiority of the people, their consciousness, their labour-based morality over the moral worthlessness and degeneracy of the nobility is the main idea of the story.' Western critics have derided this point of view, but it is not a completely preposterous one. It is only rubbish to say that this is *all* with which the story concerns itself.

But it is an element in the story. However much Olenin tries to befriend the Cossacks, he is still just as alien from the villagers as his fellow officers; in fact, because of his squeamish sense of morals, rather more alien than a man like Beletsky. Both the Russian officers, as far as Yeroshka is concerned, come from a pampered, risible world where men depend upon dud doctors, can't hold their liquor, and are not much good either as huntsmen or in bed. To the wise Yeroshka, these are self-evident truths and he milks the friendship with Olenin for all it is worth.

Worth is the key word. In their sad moment of parting there is a truly Falstaffian touch when Yeroshka cadges, successfully, Olenin's rifle. Tolstoy manipulates language as a device to remind us of Yeroshka's extreme alienness. When we first meet him, he 'had on a ragged, tucked-in, homespun coat, on his legs tied round with string were puttees of deer's *porshny* and a dishevelled white cap. On his back he carried over one shoulder a *kobilka* and a sack with a hen and a small falcon for luring hawks. . . .'3

This description requires two authorial footnotes to tell us the meaning of the Cossack words *porshny* and *kobilka*. This is a device, incidentally, much favoured by Scott. With very similar effect he scatters his Scottish Highland scenes with Gaelic words which require the elucidation of a footnote. But Olenin (whose name reminds us of the word *olen'*, a deer) is not reading a text with footnotes, he is meeting the huntsman, the predator, for real, and he tries to identify with him by using the strange Tartar greeting. He says *koshkildy* in reply. But Yeroshka gleefully corrects him. Using the second person singular with which one would address children or inferiors, he says 'Eee lad, thou dissn't know form! Daft thing! If someone says "*koshkildy*" to thee tha sayst "*Allah razi bo sun*" — God save thee.'4

The unbridgeable gap between Olenin and the Cossack, felt powerfully enough in his dealings with Yeroshka, and with Maryanka, is even more strongly emphasised in his pathetic desire to be chums with Lukashka, to whom, rather condescendingly, he gives a horse. The differences are emphasised in almost every conversation between the two young men. We have already been told, for example, in the documentary chapter, that the Old Believers forbade smoking on the Scriptural grounds that it is not what goes into a man's mouth, but what comes out of it which corrupts him. Olenin is often to be seen puffing a nervous cigarette, which gives added pathos and comedy to Lukashka's

'What do you smoke for? . . . . Is it really as good as all that?'
He evidently said this solely because he noticed that Olenin was awkward and that he was lonely among the Cossacks.

179

'That's how it is,' Olenin replied. 'I've got used to it. Why?'
'Hm. If one of our blokes started to smoke, there'd be trouble. . . .'[5]

Lukashka feels sorry for Olenin, and condescends to him by 'making' this somewhat baffled conversation. Olenin reveres the Cossack warrior but he is very far from taking the view that he is a noble savage. In fact, he takes a very modern, Europeanised view of him, as he remembers hearing Lukashka and Maryanka kissing outside the hut that very morning, and as he dwells upon the Cossacks' proud attitude to the number of enemy snipers they have been able to kill.

> What a fine young man, thought Olenin, looking at the Cossack's cheerful face. He remembered about Maryanka and about the kiss which he had overheard beyond the gate and he felt so sorry for Lukashka, sorry for his lack of education. What sort of nonsense and muddle is this? he thought. The man has killed another man and he is happy and contented as if he had done the most splendid deed. Can it be that nothing tells him there is no cause for great joy in this? That happiness does not consist in killing but in sacrificing oneself? . . .[6]

We, with hindsight, can hear in Olenin's musings the texts from which the pacifist sage of Yasnaya Polyana was to preach his sermons to the world in the latter half of his career. True, they provide evidence that his concern with these matters was lifelong, and not merely something which occurred after Tolstoy's mid-life crisis. But, in the context of the story itself, Lukashka and Olenin are balanced. The difference between the classes is something which Tolstoy can see. He can see — here the Marxist critics are right — that the *narod*, the people, the sheer brute force of the uneducated, is a much stronger thing than the effete musings of the hero. Tolstoy sees this even though the musings of Olenin are his own. These are the early days. We see here what Lenin so admired in Tolstoy — his ability to cast off the assumptions and attitudes of his own class and reflect the outlook of the *narod*. As Lenin recognised, this was nothing to do with Tolstoy's political attitudes at any given time but to his artistic power: the power to tell the truth which specially artists have, because only in art is such detachment possible.

Tolstoy was never less concerned to push a point of view than in *The Cossacks*, and there are strong biographical reasons for this. For more than one contemporary critic, who were not in a position to compare *The Cossacks* with what was to come in Tolstoy's later *œuvre*, *The Cossacks* was ruined by the 'philosophising'. It was said that Count Tolstoy had abandoned characterisation in favour of stuffing his hero's head with a lot of thoughts about life which a person of his intelligence and background would not be able to sustain. Two things strike us about this point of view. Yes, Olenin is just a cipher, not a character in the way that the Cossacks are characters. Yes, he is the vehicle for ideas. But the dislocation occurs because he is being made a vehicle for ideas which Tolstoy was having ten years after the events described. We find a parallel between Olenin and the Tolstoy of 1862. Like a whole succession of Tolstoyan protagonists, Olenin decides that his happiness will derive from living for others. He prays to God that he will not die before doing something kind; he is baffled that anyone could enjoy killing; he longs for sexual purity and (importantly) he remains chaste. Very unlike Tolstoy himself in the Caucasus. Where Olenin differs from the later heroes — such as Pierre, Levin or the Nekhlyudov of *Resurrection* — is in his abandonment of the quest. After all, he is not elevated by his sojourn among the Cossacks. He merely knows himself a little better and trusts himself a little less. 'He no longer promised himself a new life. He loved Maryanka more than before and now knew that she could never love him.'[7]

But Olenin is not the only character in the story. In some ways, he is the least important figure in it. Yeroshka's full-bodied and illogical materialism is given as much weight as Olenin's vaguely 'spiritual' yearnings. In fact, there is much in the exuberant life-acceptance of Yeroshka which is actually closer to the later Tolstoy than Olenin's Schopenhauerian melancholy.

Soviet readings of *The Cossacks*, with their laborious emphasis on 'the people', are only half right. If the story has a point, it is not to show the superiority of the common people over the moral degeneracy of the nobility, so much as to assert the overriding, and really amoral, power of Great Creating Nature. Olenin, walking in the woods near the spot where he and Yeroshka had startled a deer, feels at first that being in the country is just impossible: the day is already hot, and he and his dog are covered in mosquitoes. But then, with almost Hindu detachment, he resigns himself to being eaten alive by insects 'and strangely enough by midday this sensation even became pleasant to him'. He goes on to have the highly 'ecological' idea that these myriads of insects went so well with the wild, with the monstrosity of rich vegetation, with this dark verdure, with this odorous hot air, with these little rivulets of turbid water, everywhere oozing from the Terek and gurgling beneath the overhanging leaves that what had before seemed to him terrible, unbearable, now became positively pleasant.[8]

Like the Ancient Mariner, ravished even at the sight of the 'thousand thousand crawling things', Olenin gives a blessing. It is his vision of nature, the whole pulsating world of it, which makes him think that it is absurd to live purely for himself. In a very few pages, which could only have been penned by Tolstoy, he has moved from irritation at mosquito-bites to self-dedication in pursuit of the good. As well as being one of the most beautiful chapters in *The Cossacks*, it is also central to a proper understanding of Tolstoy himself, as a man, as an artist, as a thinker. It will always be tempting when he starts to condemn the things of this world to set up a contrast between the moralist and that 'crude biological assertion of life which is not beyond but simply outside any moral categories'. But it is a dichotomy which we draw to make sense of what cannot, properly, be made sense of: that is, Tolstoy's capacity to tap, or to appear to tap, the very forces of nature itself. And this he does both in the later doctrinal writings, as well as in the earlier stories. It is not so much a contrast between Tolstoy's ideas and his life-acceptance, as it is a sense of hierarchy. Olenin being bitten by mosquitoes suddenly feels himself to be part of the living organism of nature: not a Russian nobleman or the relation of this or that grandee, but just a creature, like the deer and the mosquito. In the Tolstoyan scale of values, this is a life-enhancing thought. 'It's all one what I might be — an animal such as any other over whom the grass will grow and nothing more, or a frame in which has been set a part of the one deity — all the same, it is necessary to live in the best way.' We would spoil Tolstoy if we tried to suggest that his life and work were not riven with inconsistencies, but this humility before life itself, this sense of existence having a divine significance, is one of the recurrent possessions of his genius. 'Suddenly, it was as if the sun had shone into his soul.'

It is in this light that we read the love interest in *The Cossacks*. It is fascinating, from a biographical point of view. Olenin, it is hinted, has a 'past', but it is one which he leaves behind in Moscow with his drinking pals and his gambling debts. By the time he reaches the

Caucasus, his chastity has become an object of remark to his fellow officers. While Lukashka climbs in and out of windows and evidently enjoys Maryanka's favours, and while Yeroshka is happily confident that there is nothing sinful in wenching, Olenin is coy and restrained. Occasionally, he makes a pass at Maryanka but so much as holding her hand produces in him feelings of bashful self-reproach. He knows that he cannot appreciate her beauty in the same pure way that he loves the mountains and the misty mornings and the forests. He is ferociously jealous of Lukashka. He loves Maryanka not just with his mind but with his whole being. But in the end he drives away and she does not even look up at him as he passes in the cart.

In an earlier version of the story, Lukashka took to the hills leaving Maryanka free to marry Olenin, which she did. In the passages of Tolstoy's diary on which the novel is based, the contrasts are even starker. Yeroshka is plainly Tolstoy's old friend Yepishka, who gave him the idea for the book. And in his rapture at the beauties of nature, his desire to be good, his detestation of superficial city life, his Romantic fondness for Cossack customs, costumes and language, there is an obvious overlap between the two cadets, Lev Nikolayevich and Olenin, the Lion and the Fawn. But in real life, the Lion bedded almost as many Caucasian women as he shot wild boar and he spent the latter part of his year as a cadet being treated for suspected syphilis.

In other words, *The Cossacks* in its final version was an exercise in laundering the past. By the time he had finished it, he must have begun to wonder what, if any, was the true version of events. The novel is so much more vivid than the diary. When the trick worked, art provided Tolstoy with a highly satisfying method of dealing with his darker memories. But the diary, with its reminders of how he had actually behaved, and what he might actually be like, could not be discarded or destroyed. He wanted it there. His obsessive reperusal of it was perhaps less like picking an old wound than an act of wondering. What was this thing conscience which was so powerfully at work in him from time to time? In part, it was a symptom that he was not at ease with the physical world, not in harmony with things as Yepishka had been. Before the grass grew over his head, Tolstoy longed to resolve the difficulty. In his art, he could manage the various sides to his nature by parcelling it out to different characters. But in life, he wistfully yearned for innocence. When the time came to marry, he wanted to present a washed, an innocent self, to his beloved. But at the same time, he feared marriage, precisely because he knew that he was not an innocent and that what he took into the marriage chamber would be a body considerably less innocent than that of Olenin.

*　　　　*　　　　*　　　　*

Three years before, on January 1, 1859, Tolstoy had inscribed in his diary, 'I must get married this year — or not at all.' The twelvemonth passed, and Tolstoy had remained a bachelor. Considering his sister's unhappy experience of the married state with their cousin Valeryan, and his brother Sergey's sensible decision to opt out of the marriage game and live as a gipsy, it is a wonder that Tolstoy felt this pressing need for matrimony. It was not as though he lived in society. His visits to Moscow or St. Petersburg were either to family or old friends, or to writers and intellectuals whose attitude to marriage was by bourgeois standards loose and irregular. Nor was it as though he lacked either for emotional adventures, nor for the opportunity to have women. He had considered proposing marriage to the daughter of the poet Tyutchev, to either of the daughters of his friend Lvov, and to a number of others. Tyutchev's daughter, Yekaterina, would, he believed, have accepted him, but he detected in her acquiescence rather than ardour. 'She would have accepted me with studious coldness.'

One might ask — and some of his cynical St. Petersburg friends *would* have asked — 'What's wrong with that?' But Tolstoy was looking for something more in a wife. He appears to have been looking for love, what is more, an absolving love which would restore him once again to the condition of his childhood innocence. At the same time, to judge from his censure of Tyutcheva, he wanted someone who would share his highly charged erotic proclivities.

He found one near at home in the person of Aksinya Bazykina, a twenty-three-year-old married peasant with whom he had enjoyed a passionate and long-standing liaison since 1858. 'I'm in love as never before in my life,' he recorded that first summer. 'She's very pretty. . . . Today in the big wood. I'm a fool. A beast. Her neck is red from the sun.'[9] It was very usual for Russian landlords to have sexual relations with their peasants. Tolstoy's father had at least one illegitimate peasant-child, serving as a coachman at Yasnaya Polyana. It would seem as though Tolstoy himself had feelings for Aksinya which went beyond those of lust. With others, over the years, lust flared up. But

Aksinya was different. 'Continue to see Aksinya *exclusively*,' he writes a year later, in a self-contradictory paragraph which weighs up the desirability of the Lvov daughters. Before going abroad, in 1860, he had risen at five in the morning and gone in search of her in the village. 'I looked for her. It's no longer the feelings of a stag but of a husband for a wife.'[10]

By the time the school had been established, and Tolstoy's pedagogical enthusiasms were in full swing, Aksinya had provided him with at least one pupil: a son called Timofey. In later life he was to have the job of coachman to one of Tolstoy's legitimate sons — an exact repetition of the state of things at Yasnaya Polyana in the twenties.

Probably Aksinya was illiterate. Certainly, she was not gifted with the ability to pour out words and to describe her emotions — as was the woman Tolstoy actually married. So we do not know what Aksinya felt. By the time the child, Tolstoy's firstborn son, came into the world, Lev Nikolayevich had contracted a legitimate union in Moscow.

This all happened in the late summer of 1862. The Bers family had, for some time, occupied a special place in Tolstoy's interests among those whom he scrutinised for possible wife material. Old Bers was the sort of man Tolstoy describes so well in his novels in such figures as Rostov *père* or Stiva; sybaritic, *simpatico*, at ease with the world. He, it will be remembered, had been the lover of Turgenev's mother. The incident would still appear to have rankled and if, like Tolstoy, you found pleasure in tormenting Turgenev, the Bers household was a tempting one to frequent. Old Bers was a court doctor and the family lived within the Kremlin in Moscow. His wife was much younger than he was, only eighteen months Tolstoy's senior, and (here must lie an explanation for *some* of what happened next) not merely a childhood acquaintance of Tolstoy's but someone who had already been fed through his imagination in the *Childhood*, *Boyhood* and *Youth* sequence. For Bers's wife was none other than Tolstoy's childhood friend Lyubov Alexandrovna Islavina, one of the little girls whom he had pushed off a balcony in a fit of prepubescent jealousy: his brother was in love with her, and the innocent narrator of *Childhood* loved her too. Lyubov remained one of the best friends of Tolstoy's sister Marya. Here was love as Tolstoy thought he had known it before the shameful scene in the Kazan whorehouse, before the coition, and the tears, and the clap. Here too was something which always excited Tolstoy's heart, a whole family, coherent and apparently rumbustiously fond of each other. If, as is so often said, he depicted the Bers family in the Rostov scenes of *War and Peace* we can sense some of the attraction which these people held for him. It was not enough to Copperfield the past. He had to find absolution, to go back and back, if necessary before his birth, and pronounce the record clean. These wholesome, happy people provided him with the chance to do so.

It may be of significance that Tolstoy first met the woman he would marry when she was not quite twelve years old.[11] It was back in 1856. Tolstoy, newly returned from the Crimean War, had called on the Berses at their summer residence at Pokrovskoye, eight miles or so outside Moscow.

They begged Tolstoy to teach them 'The Eighth of September', one of the patriotic songs which he was rumoured to have composed during the war, and then he had sat at the piano with Tatyana Andreyevna — his future sister-in-law, then aged ten — and played duets. Then he had given place on the piano stool to the girls' uncle, and while this man played Chopin Waltzes and Mazurkas, Tolstoy had murmured to their mother, 'Ah, Lyubov Alexandrovna, do you remember how we used to dance to these tunes together when we were young?' Tatyana Bers, recalling the evening in her memoirs, misread the occasion. She thought that there was a *tendresse* between her mother and their visitor. But the operative phrase in the exchange is 'when we were young'. This was a twenty-nine year old talking to a woman of not much over thirty. What he meant was 'when you were young'. He now found Lyubov Alexandrovna hideous, bald and frail. But not so her little daughters, who awakened in him that peculiar blend of concupiscence and yearning for childhood innocence which played so big a part in explaining the success of *David Copperfield*. From the mid to late fifties onwards, Tolstoy had his eye on the Bers girls. He had his eye on many other girls too, but their mother's link with his own imaginative past, as portrayed in *Childhood*, *Boyhood* and *Youth*, is probably important. One cannot exaggerate the extent to which Tolstoy's fiction is his version of how he wanted life to be. It is not autobiography in the simple sense (if there is a simple sense of the word autobiography, and if any autobiographer ever knows, or wants, to tell the truth). But the fiction is much the more important thing, arranging events to make them tolerable to himself. Into this tortuous process the Bers daughters were now, willy-nilly, absorbed. One of the very remarkable facts about Tolstoy, when we consider how quarrelsome he was and how stormy was his relationship with his wife, is the comparative stability of his relationship with the Bers family as a whole. In their marital dealings, they were no happier than he was. The old doctor was a notorious lecher and betrayer of his wife. The daughters' marriages turned out quite poorly. Yelizaveta's first marriage ended in divorce, and little Tatyana was not very happy with her Kuzminsky cousin. But for Tolstoy, the Berses were always an image of family happiness. Because the parents were alive, they were a more plausible and close-knit family group than the Tolstoys of Yasnaya Polyana. What is more, he liked them. At least one of his brothers-in-law, for example, was to become a close friend.

There were two questions, as marriage approached. The first was whether he should marry at all. And the second question was whether, if he married a Bers girl, he should marry Yelizaveta, Sofya or Tatyana. At the beginning of 1862 these questions were all highly tentative. He was as close to marrying one of the other girls, or just opting for an irregular life with the girl he was actually in love with, Aksinya. But then, in the summer of 1862, one of those strange external events happened in Tolstoy's life which plunged him into impulsive action.

*   *   *   *

This book is primarily the story of a novelist, but not of a novelist whose works are self-contained. Rather, it is the history of a great genius whose art grew out of his three uneasy and irresolvable relationships: his relationship with God, his relationship with women and his relationship with Russia. In all cases, the relationships were stormy, full of contradictions. They were love-hate relationships, and the hate was sometimes rather hard to distinguish from the love. There will be several points, later in the story, when it looks as if the most important of those love-hate relationships is his love-hate for God. Most of Tolstoy's biographers — tempted by the profusion of diaries and letters which document the forty-year Borodino-style bombardment which constituted the Tolstoy marriage — have concentrated upon that. It can never be forgotten. But it is also a mistake to forget the relationship with Russia. This is not merely a whimsical way of speaking, nor even just an emotional matter. If old Prince Volkonsky, Tolstoy's grandfather, had not quarrelled with the Emperor Paul, if Tolstoy's father had not been so subject to *khalatnost'*, if everything had been just a little different, the Tolstoy brothers would have been great powers in the land. Their cousin Dmitry was Minister of Education and Procurator of the Holy Synod. Their cousin Alexandra was daily at Court. They were closely related to the great families, and to the men of influence; but a series of chances and the mystery of their own character had decreed a different destiny for the Tolstoy siblings. Instead of being a lady-in-waiting at Court, Marya Nikolayevna was pursuing the most extraordinary romantic adventures, having brought to an end her notoriously unsatisfactory marriage. Sergey had as little regard for the conventions, and as little desire to get on in the world. And Lev Nikolayevich himself, even if he had passed the exams at the right point in his career, and not become addicted to a way of life which made 'service' in the bureaucracy seem an unattractive option, was nowhere near exercising authority. And yet, as he surely felt, they were born to lead; and if things had gone differently — ah, all those ifs of Tolstoy's personal and national history — he would have been a legislator, not just of his little kingdom of Yasnaya, but of a wider sphere.

In terms of Tolstoy's personal mythology, life started to go wrong at puberty, with the awakening of sexual desire. In terms of the national myth, in which he and most enlightened aristocrats believed, the loss of innocence occurred with the Decembrist Rising.

He had begun to think about the Decembrists as a possible theme for a novel back in 1856, and he returned to the theme in 1860-61.[12] Having finished *The Cossacks* in 1862, he again turned back to the Decembrists, at about the same time as the Bers girls had begun to fascinate him.[13]

His story was to concern a Decembrist exile returning to Russia from Siberia in 1856. Consciously or not, he was obviously inspired by his own feelings as a young war veteran returning from the Crimea. What sort of a Russia was he returning to? But with all the fertile comprehensiveness of his mind, Tolstoy wanted to use his returning hero as a vehicle for looking at the whole of Russia. His hero would now be quite old, looking back to the days of 1825 when, already a mature, married man, he had tried to change the despotic and autocratic way in which the Empire was controlled.

But then, Tolstoy had realised that in order to understand this man, it was going to be necessary to trace his history back yet further: to the times of Napoleon and the 1812 campaign.

For the third time, then, I went back still further into the past, prompted by a feeling which to most of my readers may perhaps seem strange but which I trust will be intelligible to those whose judgement I value. This feeling can only be described in one word — shame; I felt ashamed to tell the story of our victories over Napoleon and his army without mentioning also our own disasters, our own disgraces. Who can read the many patriotic accounts of the year 1812 without feeling secret shame? . . . .[14]

The Decembrist Rising, in Tolstoy's imagination, was perhaps the greatest attempt to absolve Russia of its guilt, its shame. The autocracy itself took a different view of eccentric young aristocrats, critical of their methods or their history. Nicholas I had established his famous Third Section, which, under its various names — *Cheka* or K.G.B. — has been such a conspicuous ornament of Russian life ever since. The 'liberal' Alexander II had done nothing to abolish them. It was they who had collected the evidence to exile Herzen. It was they who had Turgenev put under house arrest for a single, tactless phrase in his obituary of Gogol. It was they who were watching Tolstoy.

He had known that they were his enemies ever since the censor had taken exception to the later *Sebastopol Sketches*. Now they began to be worried by his educational activities. Freelance schools, such as the one which he had established at Yasnaya Polyana, were forbidden by the new laws of 1861.

One of the teachers he had employed had, when a university student, been suspected of printing and distributing anti-religious works. The Tula police, when approached by the Third Section, were able to provide salacious rumours about the 'debauchery' of Count Tolstoy. No doubt Aksinya's name was carefully entered into some police file.

They did not do anything until the summer of 1862. Tolstoy, always haunted by the spectre of his tubercular brother Nikolay, had been worried by a cough, and took off to the Bashkir country of Samara for a rest cure. He left his aunt Tatyana (Tante Toinette) and his sister Marya in charge at Yasnaya Polyana. On July 6, the police descended on Yasnaya Polyana at dawn, headed by a Third Section officer called Colonel Durnovo. They terrified Tolstoy's aunt and sister, and began a thorough search of the place, turning out all drawers and cupboards. Nadezhda Mandelstam, describing the raid of her flat by the *Cheka* on May 13, 1934, tells us of how they 'burst into our poor hushed apartments as though raiding bandits' lairs or secret laboratories in which masked *carbonari* were making dynamite and preparing armed resistance'.[15] Similar feelings must have occurred to Tolstoy's aunt and sister as they watched the policemen roughing up their house. They had been told that there was a secret printing press designed for propagating seditious literature. They found a copy of Herzen's periodical *The Bell* and that only exacerbated their curiosity and suspicion. Having upturned every drawer, desk, bureau and closet in the house, one of them decided (this is the way that the minds of policemen work) that there might be something interesting in the tiny pond in the park. After an elaborate dredging operation, they discovered only weeds, mud and fish.

The invasion of his little kingdom by these oafs infuriated Tolstoy and he was outraged by the fact that they had frightened his aunt and his sister. It horrified him to think that the Government which authorised such activities was composed of members of his own family and circle, and he wrote off in high dudgeon to his cousin Alexandra in St. Petersburg.

> Fine friends you have! . . . . One of your friends, a filthy colonel, read all my letters and diaries which I thought to entrust to the person closest to me only before my death; he read over sets of my correspondence that I wished to keep hidden from the world at any price, and he left, admitting that he had found nothing *suspicious*. . . . It is my good fortune and that of your friend that I was not here. I would have killed him. Fine! Glorious! That is how your Government makes friends for itself. If you will recall my political attitude you will know that always, and especially since my love for the school, I have been entirely indifferent to the Government, and even more indifferent to the present liberals whom I scorn with all my soul. Now I can no longer say this. I possess bitterness and revulsion, almost hatred for that dear Government. . . .[16]

In essence, Tolstoy's political attitude never changed after this incident, though he did his best to cultivate the indifferentism which is the greatest privilege of a man living on a private estate and possessing independent means. But he went on loving Alexandra, and through her, the very class, and the very Government which he hated and reviled. Nothing is ever as simple, in Tolstoy's attitudes, as he wanted to make it. Nor, for the Government's part, was their attitude simple towards him. Throughout the reign of three emperors, they were to be wary of him and frightened of his capacity to stir up discontent through his writings. But there was always admiration for his genius, and something more: a vein of indulgent tolerance such as, in a family, might be felt for a wayward uncle. Tolstoy was 'one of them'.

It is interesting that, in his fury at the police raid, he should have singled out for especially indignant mention the fact that the Colonel read his private letters and diaries. Already the thought had formed itself in Tolstoy's head that these documents would be read by someone, the person closest to him. If the correspondences were so private that he really wanted no one to read them, it is curious that he had kept not one, but two copies of each letter. As for the identity of that reader — of the diaries — who was she to be? Although he told Alexandra in July that these documents were so secret that no one should be allowed to see them until he was dead, only a few weeks later he was thrusting them into the hands of an eighteen-year-old girl.

*   *   *   *

It is fairly likely that Tolstoy would have married any of the Bers family had not Lyubov Alexandrovna taken matters into her own hands. A month after the police raid on Yasnaya Polyana, there was the Bers raid. Lyubov Alexandrovna took her three daughters to stay at her father's estate of Ivitsy, thirty-five miles from Yasnaya Polyana, and one evening they all paid a call, ostensibly to see Marya Nikolayevna. The previous year, the mother had made it fairly clear that she wanted her eldest daughter married off first. Yelizaveta was now nearly twenty. The previous year, when the idea had cropped up, Tolstoy had confided in the diary, 'I daren't marry Liza.' Now, in the summer of 1862, he was aware that 'Liza seems to be quietly taking possession of me. My God! How beautifully unhappy she would be if she were my wife.'[17] Ominous words, which the sister who did eventually marry him must often have read.

The trouble was, that he really preferred the *youngest* sister Tatyana. Though barely sixteen, she possessed in abundance that animation which the poet Fet found so striking a feature of the Bers family. ('All of them, notwithstanding the watchful supervision of their mother and their irreproachable modesty, had that attractive quality which the French call *du chien*.') Tatyanchik the Imp, they called her. Passionate, enthusiastic, egotistical — she had that quality which Tolstoy so often noticed and loved in his fiction: she was brimming over with *life*.

After the Bers raid at Yasnaya Polyana, Tolstoy was bidden over to Ivitsy by Lyubov Alexandrovna, for further chances to size the girls up. Here they were in the house, not of Dr. Bers, but of old Alexander Islenev, in other words of the father in *Childhood*. There was a curious confluence of memory and desire, life and art. The visits of Count Tolstoy caused increasing excitement among the girls. It was all very seemly. It was nothing much more than music and chit-chat. But after one such visit, their aunt Olga took Tatyana on one side. 'Why has Liza told me that Lev Nikolayevich intends to marry her when my eyes tell me differently?' she enquired.

It was at Ivitsy on the night before the girls went back to Moscow that there occurred the romantic scene which Tolstoy was later to mythologise in *Anna Karenina*, in the proposal scene between Kitty and Levin. In spite of Liza's beautiful melancholy, and little Tatyanchik's animation, Tolstoy found himself being drawn inescapably to the middle sister Sofya. He considered her 'plain and vulgar but she interests me'. Obviously, there was a powerful sexual attraction between them. But, more important than that, he saw a flirtation with Sofya as a way of escaping the net which was closing around himself and Liza. He did not want to marry Liza. He did want to go to bed with Sofya. That, roughly speaking, was the position on their last evening at Ivitsy.

There was a fairly large party. Someone was playing the piano. Tolstoy was able to get snatches of conversation with Sofya. 'Why aren't you dancing?' she asked. 'Oh, I'm too old for that,' he said. The party continued. At various tables round the rooms, elderly guests played cards, and at length got up to go. When the dancing stopped, Lyubov Alexandrovna insisted that her girls be packed off to bed. The rest should be told in Sofya Andreyevna's own words:

Just as I was going to the door, Lev Nikolayevich called to me.
'Wait a moment, Sofya Andreyevna.'
'What is it?'
'Will you read what I'm going to write?'
'Very well.'
'I'm only going to write the initials. You must guess the words.'
'How can I do that? It's impossible! Oh, well, go on.'

192

He brushed the games scores off the card table, took a piece of chalk and began writing. We were both very serious and excited. I followed his big red hand, and could feel all my powers of concentration and feeling focus on that bit of chalk and the hand that held it. We said nothing.

'y.y. & n.f.h.t.v.r.m.o.m.a. & i.f.h.'

'Your youth and need for happiness too vividly remind me of my age and incapacity for happiness,' I read out. My heart was pounding, my temples were throbbing, my face was flushed — I was beyond all sense of time and reality; at that moment I felt capable of anything, of understanding everything, imagining the unimaginable.

'Well, let's go on,' said Lev Nikolayevich and began to write once more.

'y.f.h.t.w.i.a.m. & y.s.L.y. & y.s.T.m.p.m.'

'Your family has the wrong idea about me and your sister Liza. You and your sister Tanechka must protect me.' I read the initials rapidly and without a second's hesitation.

Lev Nikolayevich wasn't even surprised; it all seemed quite natural somehow. Our elation was such that we soared high above the world and nothing could possibly surprise us.

Then we heard Maman crossly summoning me to bed. We hurriedly said goodnight, extinguished the candles and went out. Behind my cupboard upstairs I lighted the stump of a candle, sat down on the floor, put my notebook on the wooden chair and began to write my diary. I wrote down the words to which Lev Nikolayevich had given me the initials and grew vaguely aware that something of great significance had occurred between us — something we were now unable to stop.[18]

*   *   *   *

If we knew all the facts in the story so far, without knowing how it continued and ended, it would still be impossible to predict what Tolstoy did next. The more we knew, the less we should be able to predict. Imagine knowing everything — not just all the evidence (which is by definition unreliable) of diaries, letters, novels — but everything. Imagine that one had a God's eye view of all that passed through Tolstoy's heart that summer. The next stage would still be surprising.

The incident with the chalk and the letters was profoundly

important to Sofya Andreyevna. If she was half in love with him before, by now she was head over heels. She began to scribble a story about an ugly, moody, older man, completely inconsistent in all his opinions, and whom she adored. The story about the initials and the chalk — which both Tolstoy and his wife came to believe — cannot possibly be true, if you think about it. No crossword-puzzle solver or expert in cryptograms was ever so telepathic as Sofya Andreyevna claims to have been. And, as so often in her diaries, she lets us see what is going on without seeing it herself.

Tolstoy was in a tight corner. He did not want to marry Liza. He was not sure whether he wanted to marry at all. But he felt a sudden surge of interest in Sofya, such as, in the past, he had felt for at least forty women: a feeling which could liberate him from the marriage bond.

When the time came for them all to return to Moscow, Tolstoy impulsively took the coach with the Bers girls. It was the sort of coach with four seats inside and two outside. Inside the coach sat Mrs. Bers, Tolstoy's sister Marya, Yelizaveta, and their youngest brother Volodya. Outside sat Tolstoy and Sofya, leaning against one another, and wrapped up in rugs as the coach made its slow way from Tula through the night. At the last changing post before Moscow, Yelizaveta pointedly said that she found the inside of the coach stuffy, and that she would like to join the Count outside. 'Oh,' he said tactlessly, 'but it is surely Sofya Andreyevna's turn to sit outside.'

For Sofya, this was the great point of the journey. For everyone else the chief drama would surely have been that of Tolstoy's sister. She had for a year now been the lover of a Swedish Viscount, Victor-Hector de Kleen. Her marriage was finished. She was about to go abroad, as she thought, forever. This event probably weighed more heavily on the minds of her brother and her old friend Lyubov Alexandrovna than who sat next to whom on the coach.

Once back in Moscow, in the last week of August, Tolstoy found that he thought less about Sofya, and more about public affairs. He drafted, and sent, a long letter of protest to the Emperor, complaining about the police raid at Yasnaya seven weeks previously. He dined with the Katkovs ('They're discussing the good of Russia all the time'). Two days before his thirty-fourth birthday, he dined with the Berses and Sofya showed him her story about the fascinating ugly man. He took it away and read it on his birthday and was impressed by what an accurate picture of him it drew. That evening, he did not visit the Bers household. He spent it as he really preferred — with the Tyutchevs, eating and chatting. He was happy to think of what he and Mlle. Tyutcheva had escaped. 'You ugly mug,' he told himself, thinking of Sofya's story, 'don't think about marriage; your vocation is different and for that you have been well endowed.'

*   *   *   *

On August 29, he travelled with Dr. Bers to their *dacha* at Pokrovskoye, and after dinner there with the girls, he records this cryptic entry. 'She made me decipher the letter. I was embarrassed, so was she.' What does this mean? 'She' in the context is undoubtedly Sofya Andreyevna, who was being attended by two suitors that evening — Messrs. Popov and Polivanov, neither of whom made Tolstoy jealous because he was by now so sure that she loved *him*. But what is this letter which needs deciphering? Surely it is more likely that this is the cryptogram, the series of initials which, in both their memories, he scribbled on a card table, and which she interpreted without fault and at once? Much more likely that Tolstoy posted her the message and that she found it incomprehensible. Her devotion to him made him feel 'you swine' — a bit like pity and sorrow.

Another week went past. He dined with the Tyutchevs once more. This time, he found their 'blue-stocking' conversation repulsive. He dined with a friend called Perfilyev, whom he had known for eight or nine years, and they got drunk together. Both in their mid-thirties, the two men felt old. They gorged themselves and lay on the floor, their faces almost touching, breathing heavily. 'Dublitsky,' said Tolstoy, calling himself by the name of the fascinatingly repulsive man in Sofya's story, 'don't intrude where youth and poetry, love and beauty are — leave that to cadets, my friend. . . . Nonsense — monastery work, that's your vocation, and from its height you can look down calmly and gladly at other people's love and happiness. . . .'

But the next day he saw Sofya again, and 'she draws me irresistibly'. He tried to cope with the passion which she aroused in him by going into the village from her *dacha* that afternoon and having a peasant girl called Sasha. But it was no use. For the rest of the week, he was in an agony of love with Sofya. He could not settle. He did gymnastics. He dined at his club. He was too frightened to act or speak. By September 13 he had resolved, 'I'll go tomorrow as soon as I get up and say everything, or I'll shoot myself.'

The next day, he did not shoot himself. Instead, he wrote a letter to Sofya proposing marriage. He did not post it. He put it in his pocket, and remained in a state of frenzy for the next twenty-four hours. He called on the Tyutchevs. He called at the Bers apartment, thrust the letter into Sofya's hand, but was unable to speak. Then he went home and went to bed. But he could not sleep. He got up again, and spent the night talking to Perfilyev about the past. He told him all about Nikolay's death. He wept. In his agitation, he decided that what he most wanted in Sofya was a confidante. 'There won't be any secrets for me alone; but secrets for two; she will read everything.'

The next day, September 16, he called on the Berses again.

The whole household had been thrown into a flurry by his visits. Liza had been with Sofya when she read the letter. 'What is it?' she had asked. '*Le Comte m'a fait la proposition*,' said Sofya. Their mother came into the room at this point. When she heard the news she asked, 'Do you *want* to marry *le Comte*?' 'Yes,' said Sofya, and together they went to tell the rest of the family.

Liza was in tears, and the parents were astonished. It was not what Lyubov Alexandrovna had intended at all. Dr. Bers's first reaction was one of anger, but as a cynical man of the world, he gave his consent. Tolstoy asked for the marriage to take place at once. It is an extraordinary fact that Sofya's parents agreed to this. The next day, September 17, was her nameday, and when all their friends came to the party, they learnt that she was to be married within a week. September 23 was set as the day! Why the rush? Apart from flirtatious conversations and silences in company over the last month, and one journey by coach, the bridal pair had had no time together. They were not even sufficiently well-acquainted to know whether they *liked* one another. Probably they never did. He found her strange and fascinating. She found him monstrous and frightening. There was a strong sexual attraction between them. On this basis, they prepared to enter upon one of the most closely documented and one of the most miserable marriages in history.

Tolstoy's present for her nameday was to give Sofya the opportunity to read his diaries. This was commoner in nineteenth-century Russia than is sometimes realised (Nicholas II and his bride did the same). But that is not to say that it was wise. He wanted to keep nothing hidden from her. Dr. Bers's permission was sought before the notebooks were presented to his daughter, and he gave it. What can he have been thinking of, to give his consent? Did he hope that, when she learnt of Tolstoy's notorious (to Bers and his circle) depravity, Sofya would call the whole thing off? She was an inexperienced eighteen year old. In 1890, twenty-eight years later, she was still poring over them, making fair copies and trying to keep them from the hands of his friends and disciples. 'I don't think I ever recovered from the shock of reading the diaries when I was engaged to him,' she wrote. 'I can still remember the agonising pangs of jealousy, the horror of that first appalling experience of male depravity.'[19] Here it all was, in one great dollop: the early whoring and wenching, the repeated doses of V.D., the gipsies, the Cossack girls, the quasi-homoerotic devotion to his student friends, the flirtations in drawing rooms — a whole catalogue of active sexual life going back twenty years. What was worst was the discovery that he had, until only a month or two before, been besottedly in love with his peasant mistress Aksinya. Yet, the wedding plans went ahead. In their first private interview after she had read the diaries, Sofya was in tears. 'Does this mean that you won't forgive me?' he asked. 'Yes, I forgive you, but it's dreadful,' she said, as she handed the books back to him. Tolstoy had aroused in her a lifelong addiction which was an essential ingredient in their relationship. They did not keep diaries all the time, but in the years when they did so, it was an irresistible game. She had to read his diaries, however hurtful or shocking they were. And, to put the record straight, she had to write her own version of events. It was as though, with a part of themselves, they did not quite exist until they had become characters on a page. On any ordinary human level, Tolstoy's action in showing her the diaries was cruel. But Tolstoy did not live on the ordinary human level. Whatever he thought he was doing when he showed her the books, he was actually putting her to the most important test of all: not, would she forgive him? but, would she *read* him? She passed the test. With a profound, intuitive intelligence, which gave her no pleasure, she latched on immediately to Tolstoy's need for absolution through the written word. It was something which bound them together very deeply, even when they felt hatred and dread of one another. She was his reader. She survived all the ups and downs of married life until this fact came to be challenged, and rival readers tried to move in and take her place. Even less than most people on their wedding day can Sofya Andreyevna have known what she was doing when she married her husband. But it is wrong to think of her as a witless victim. It hurt her very much to be in love with the monstrous hero of her own short story. But it was his monstrosity that she loved. And from the very beginning, she knew that her reading of the diaries put her in a unique position in the world. It was a position of power which she could not resist.

After an agitated week in which she and her mother bought the trousseau and made the arrangements, the day dawned. First thing in the morning, Tolstoy himself called at the Bers apartment in a state of confusion and excitement. He doubted, after all, whether they were doing the right thing. 'I have come to say,' he said, 'that there is still time. . . . All this business can be put a stop to.' Sofya started to cry. Did it mean that he was coming to cancel the wedding? 'Yes, if you don't love me.' More tears. Lyubov Alexandrovna burst into the room to find Tolstoy trying to console her daughter. All three of them must in that moment have wondered whether or not he was right. It was a crazy situation. But Lyubov Alexandrovna had the reputation of her daughter to think of. All Moscow had been told. The invitations had been sent out, the church had been booked, the presents had been received, the dresses chosen. 'You've chosen a fine time for upsetting her!' said the future mother-in-law, and banished Tolstoy from the house, reminding him of the time of the wedding that evening.

We do not know how Tolstoy spent the day. Far too late, he returned to his apartments to change, and was told by a despondent servant that there was nothing to change into. All his clean clothes, and all his linen, had been packed and sent ahead with Tolstoy's brother Sergey Nikolayevich to Yasnaya Polyana. There was not so much as a clean shirt to be found.

The wedding was scheduled for eight o'clock at night in the Kremlin church of the Nativity of Our Lady. By seven o'clock, Sofya Andreyevna was waiting in her wedding dress. The custom was for the groomsman to come and tell the bride that the groom was waiting for her at the church. An hour later, he had still not arrived. At half-past eight, she and her family had begun to despair. Tolstoy, who had seemed in the morning so wild and uncertain, had evidently decided to do a bunk. Just then, Tolstoy's manservant arrived to explain what had happened to the luggage and the shirts, followed not long after by the groomsman to say that a shirt had at last been found and that the groom was now awaiting the bride in church. An hour late, and in a state of great distress, Sofya Andreyevna went to greet her lord. As he led her to the altar, the choir sang 'Come O Dove'. There were three hundred guests, who had been waiting for over an hour to witness the extended nuptial celebrations, the lighting and snuffing of candles, the chanting, the holding of crowns over the heads of the bride and groom. Sofya Andreyevna cried during most of the service.

Afterwards, when she was about to get into the carriage and be driven away by her new husband, she turned to her mother, threw herself into Lyubov's arms, and sobbed like a child. 'If leaving your family means such great sorrow to you, then you cannot love me very much,' Tolstoy said to her, when the carriage was on the move.

*　　　*　　　*　　　*

They broke the journey at a place called Birulyevo. Tolstoy had already established in the coach that his bride knew the facts of life. The innkeeper opened up the best suite — 'The Emperor's chambers' — and the young Countess sat shy on a sofa, unable to speak. A servant brought in a samovar. Still, silence and gloom, and what Tolstoy regarded as morbid timidity. 'Well,' he said, as they sat silently and watched the steaming samovar, 'show that you are the mistress. Come on, pour the tea!' She was so shy with him that she did not even dare to call her husband by name.

She had already read the diaries. Had she noticed in Tolstoy how swiftly sexual gratification turned to feelings of intense 'morbidity' in himself? Had she noticed how self-hatred in this area so easily became hatred of the person who had first excited all these messy feelings? Or was she merely dreading becoming another name in that notebook, that sad catalogue?

*　　　*　　　*　　　*

The next day, after another long journey, the pair arrived at Yasnaya Polyana. It was only a couple of months since she had called there with her mother, a flirtatious schoolgirl. Now she returned as mistress of the place. Her brother-in-law Sergey Nikolayevich was waiting to greet them as the coach pulled up at the front door, and so was Tante Toinette who, Tolstoy noticed, was 'already preparing to suffer', now that her favourite little nephew had found himself a bride. Auntie, as the custom was, held up an icon and Sofya Andreyevna genuflected and kissed it, before greeting her new relations. Sergey stood offering them bread and salt on a tray. That night, Tolstoy had a bad dream. Whether by this he means a nightmare or a wicked dream, it is hard to tell, but two other words are added. 'Not her.'[20]

Chapter Nine
Alchemy

1862 - 1864

Or whether doth my mind, being crowned
  with you,
Drink up the monarch's plague, this flattery?
Or whether shall I say mine eye saith true,
And that your love taught it this alchemy. . . . ?
Shakespeare, Sonnet 114

An English traveller in Russia at the very end of the eighteenth century has left a memorable account of a typical provincial landowner. There is not much reason to suppose that things had greatly changed in the first sixty years of the nineteenth century.

> You will find him throughout the day, with his neck bare, his beard lengthened, his body wrapped in sheep's hide, eating raw turnips, and drinking *kvass*, sleeping one half of the day, and growling at his wife and family the other. The same feelings, the same wants, wishes, and gratifications. . . . characterise the nobleman and the peasant.[1]

This disgusted reaction is quoted by a modern historian to illustrate the truth that mere membership of the *dvoryanstvo* did not, in Russian terms, guarantee gentility.

Russia had its own brand of Squire Westerns and Sir Pitt Crawleys, neither metropolitan in habit nor polite in manners. The great families in *War and Peace*, we are told, 'are in no sense typical. They were the members of an exclusive club of some one thousand four hundred *grands seigneurs* in an empire in which a million persons claimed "noble" status of some kind.'[2]

While this is undoubtedly true, to which category did Tolstoy himself belong — was he a *grand seigneur* or an eater of raw turnips? Until he had invented, in late middle age, a special religion which made a virtue out of raw turnips and growling at the wife, Tolstoy could not be sure himself.

Certainly, he was well connected. His cousins in St. Petersburg and Moscow were somebodies. But in life style and attitudes, he was much more like any small country squire. Only in a vicarious way could he or did he want to be *grand seigneurial*. Sofya Andreyevna Bers had been accustomed to her parents' well-maintained and spacious apartment in the Kremlin, to good clothes and fine company, to constant society, and to the assistance of a staff of ten servants. Things were very different indeed at Yasnaya Polyana. The vast house where his Volkonsky grandfather had lived in such splendour had been demolished. 'Yasnaya Polyana' now meant the two remaining wings. In one of them, Tolstoy had his school, full of children from the estate. In the other, he lived with 'Auntie', Tatyana Yergolskaya. There were only three servants worthy of the name, a maid called Dunya, a manservant called Alexis, and an old man who very occasionally surfaced from bouts of extreme drunkenness to do some cooking. As soon as he was back home, Tolstoy changed his city clothes for the rough peasant shirt and belt, familiar to us from the many icons of the Master. The house, as he showed the new bride around, cannot have failed to impress her with its extreme austerity. There was almost no upholstered furniture, only hard chairs and tables. Most of the lighting was from stinking tallow candles. The bedrooms in particular were icy and bleak. There were no carpets — it was assumed that you would have felt slippers or bast shoes to wear in bed — and little in the way of bed linen. The young Countess was astounded to discover that her husband did not believe in pillow cases. He always slept with a hard old red leather pillow, which looked as though it had been wrenched from a railway carriage.[3]

It was all quite frightening for an eighteen-year-old Europeanised city girl. There was nobody there who could possibly become her friend, no substitute for her sisters, for instance, nor for the innumerable, polite, harmless, jolly people who streamed in and out of her mother's Moscow drawing room.

Fascinated by her husband, and deeply attracted to him sexually, she threw herself into the task of being a country wife. Her first visit to the cowsheds made her retch, and among the filthy, badly-tended farm buildings, the new bride was constantly in danger of meeting not just nasty smells, but also echoes of her husband's guilty past. Only a few weeks before, she had been forced to read his guilty secrets, and the phrase 'in love as never before' stuck into her mind with particular cruelty now that she was face to face with Tolstoy's peasant mistress.

Only months before, he had been telling his journal that he regarded Aksinya Alexandrovna Bazykina more or less as a wife. Now his actual wife met the earthy, common-law Aksinya and her little baby, Tolstoy's bastard. 'I think I shall kill myself with jealousy,' she told her diary. '"In love as never before" he writes. With that fat, pale peasant woman — how frightful! I looked at the dagger and the guns with joy. One blow, I thought, how easy it would be — if only it weren't for the baby. Yet to think that she is there, just a few steps away. I feel demented.'[4]

But the smell, the loneliness, and the rough ways, and the sinful past, though disgusting to her at some moments, were at others profoundly exciting on a sexual level. His very puritanism and the abruptness of his sexual approaches fascinated and attracted her, while hurting and irritating her. 'He will not let me into his room which makes me very sad,' she wrote, a fortnight after the wedding. 'All physical things disgust him.'[5] But a month later, November 13, she writes in a sated, purring mood, aware that for the previous few weeks she had been unable to concentrate on anything much except bed; and already she is pregnant. 'Over the next few years, I shall make myself a serious *female* world, and I shall love it even more than the old one because it will contain my husband and my children. . . . But I haven't settled down yet.'[6]

Visitors during the first few months were not aware of the momentary horrors which Sofya Andreyevna confided to her diary. Rather they were arrested by the palpable happiness of the pair. Her brother came to stay and, looking back on those early months, said that he 'was perhaps the closest observer of their family life. Their understanding, their friendship and their mutual love always served for me as an example and as an ideal of marital happiness. All I need say is that my parents, who, like all parents, were never satisfied with the fates of their children, frequently said, "We could not wish for anything better for Sofya."'[7]

The same quality of glowing happiness struck Fet on his visits, and that it was something which Tolstoy himself felt we know from his snatches of diary keeping during the honeymoon period. 'My happiness seems to absorb me completely,' he wrote on January 5, 1863.[8] Shortly afterwards his wife was to write in her diary that she felt nothing but self-reproach and remorse for her previous harsh thoughts, and for her husband, nothing but love. 'There is absolutely no evil in him, nothing I could ever dream of reproaching him for.'[9]

When her brother, her sister Tanya and a friend came to stay on January 9, Sofya Andreyevna could hardly bear to see them. 'I simply cannot stop crying, I would not let them see me for anything, for they are children and have never been in love. I so long to see him,' she scratched in her bedroom secrecy on to the tear-stained diary pages. 'Lord, what if he loses interest in me altogether? Now absolutely everything depends on him. What a worthless person I am; how depressing this mental pettiness is. . . .'[10]

Some readers of the letters and diaries of Countess Tolstoy have discovered in each outburst of unhappiness an offence with which to indict her husband. Others, more charitably or more gynaecologically minded, would have us note that Sergey, her eldest son, was born on June 28, 1863 — just nine months after the wedding — and that in the first eight years of marriage, Sofya Andreyevna bore her husband seven more children — a crushing emotional and hormonal upset which would have tested temperaments sturdier than her own. (In all, she was to bear thirteen children in the first twenty-six years of her marriage.)

There are two or three good books about Tolstoy's wife, but mine cannot be one of them. If this story is to remain within manageable bounds, it must concentrate largely on Tolstoy himself, and that will involve risking the appearance of indifference towards those whom he hurt, consciously or unconsciously. Even if this were not the case, it is notoriously difficult to know the truth about a marriage. Marriage as a spectator sport is a gruesome business, besides which the gladiatorial excesses of ancient Rome seem innocent. Novelists earn their living, many of them, by creating the illusion that we can see inside that most inner and private of things, the relationship between a man and a woman. Biographers and newspaper editors increase the thrill by suggesting that what we read in their pages is real, true, authentic.

The Tolstoys, as befitted such vulgar and proto-modern figures, have invited the sort of scrutiny which is given to filmstars and uncrowned heads in the American and European press. The voluminous records, in journals and letters, of their ups and downs (but chiefly of their downs) were compiled almost from the beginning, with us, the reading public, in mind. For the first fifteen years of their married life, there were not many journals. The Tolstoys were too preoccupied and, in their fashion, too happy, to bother with them. The diary-rivalry, developing into a diary-war, with prolix accounts of each other's misdemeanours, really belongs to the 'post-literary' period of Tolstoy's life, the time following *Anna Karenina* and his famous emotional crisis. Then, every tearful complaint, every barbed insult, and every incident of wounded vanity was scribbled down for the prurient gaze of posterity. Such records do not necessarily tell us the truth. People who are as closely entwined with one another as the Tolstoys, and involved in such a very long-term sexual relationship (remarkable in the extent of its passion and longevity) cannot often see the wood for the trees when they are describing their day-to-day, hour-by-hour existence. At one minute he might hate her, or she him. Another moment, while still hating, they might love each other distractedly. Like married couples who enjoy having rows at other people's dinner tables, or on street corners, they would be almost certain if they read some of the later accounts of their marriage to yell at their well-wishers and supporters, 'You keep out of this!' before returning to the enjoyable task of destroying one another.

Supporters is the word, if we are to keep the image of marriage as a spectator sport. And there have been many who have brought to the biographer's task the literary equivalent of coloured scarves, the silly, loud rattles, the flickknives and the broken bottles without which no self-respecting 'supporter' would grace the terraces. Most of these Tolstoy 'hooligans' — that is to say, biographers who seem to approach their subjects and their readers spoiling for a fight — have been on the side of 'Sonya', as they always call her. The old man, however, has a distinguished supporters' club, particularly, for some reason, among the English.[11]

In Sofya Andreyevna Bers, Tolstoy found a mate of extraordinary qualities — tenacity, energy, intelligence and a capacity for family affection. Both of them — as has often been observed by other pens — had 'difficult' temperaments, and their marriage called forth in them qualities of endurance which neither, in the end, quite possessed. Assessing the pain and personal cost on both sides would be as difficult as Pierre's task when he blundered about the battlefield of Borodino trying to see what was going on.

This book is the story of Tolstoy, as a writer and a thinker. The relevance of his marriage to that story is sometimes difficult to measure, as, to her distress, his wife was to find. But there can be no doubt of its importance in the initial stages. It does not matter whether we attribute it to the prospect of paternity, to a more balanced and regular sexual regime, to less alcohol, or to the prosaic fact that his wife was a punctilious and devoted secretary. At last, Tolstoy was able to devote himself to his proper work: *The Decembrists*.

What distinguishes the literary masters of pre-Romantic times is, in almost every case, a unique blending of a personal with a collective or national vision: the journey of their own mind, together with a discovery of their place in the *saeculum*. Dante's love of Beatrice and his love of Florence become in the end interchangeable. In the early Shakespeare, these two elements are diffuse: the narrator of the Sonnets is a man consumed by a purely personal vision, personal love and personal suffering. No wonder Proust found Shakespeare's Sonnets such an imaginative quarry, for they seem to assert the Proustian view that only art can redeem the ravages of time; tyrants' crests and tombs of brass are viewed with disdain, rather than with the Christian humanism of the later tragedies and romances. The personal vision is all: 'poor soul, the centre of my sinful earth', just as it had been for Tolstoy when he wrote the early diaries and *The History of Yesterday*. In the early history plays, Shakespeare's patriotism is formal; there is a set-piece quality about it. Only when the personal tragedy chronicled in the Sonnets has been absorbed, and real patriotism been discovered or felt, is he capable of the *Henry IV* plays in which the devotion of an unsuitable older man to a younger wag is made the occasion not merely of Shakespeare's most enduring comedy, but also of his most profoundly felt political and national emotions. In a highly analogous way, we may feel that the *Vita Nuova* and the early political writings of Dante are inchoate when compared with the completed vision of the *Divina Commedia*, where the inner vision and the grand, Homeric, national one are fused.

When Tolstoy said that *War and Peace* was not a novel, he was warning readers not merely to lap it up in the same spirit in which they might read instalments of *David Copperfield* or *Crime and Punishment*. This is not a matter of authorial self-conceit; the degree to which that was or was not felt is an irrelevance here. Tolstoy knew, just as Dante and Shakespeare must have known in their day, that he had produced a masterpiece which it would be completely unhelpful to compare with an ordinary serial novel.

In our reading of Shakespeare, almost everything is a matter of conjecture. We can only guess that the relationship between Hal and Falstaff reflects, in a jokey manner which Shakespeare's friends would have recognised at once, the friendship between the sonneteer and the 'man right fair'; and we can only see dimly how the ability to distance himself from the experience — and like Hal to 'despise his dream' — led to a deepening consciousness of England and the social order. But whereas we can only conjecture about the growth of Shakespeare's mind, in Tolstoy, the process of alchemy is transparent. Almost every particle of *War and Peace* bears a relation to something in Tolstoy's personal experience. There is in the whole book hardly an incident, conversation or character which the commentators are not able to tell us is 'autobiographical' — and in those passages which are not autobiographical in this sense, there is a conspicuous flatness (I think of Pierre's initiation into the Freemasons which Tolstoy, not a Mason himself, worked up out of books: it shows). Yet although the gossipy editors might wish to nudge our ribs at every turn and tell us that Sonya's love for Nikolay Rostov, for instance, 'is' Auntie Tatyana's love for Tolstoy's father, or that the scenes of Borodino and Austerlitz owe much to Tolstoy's own experiences on the Polish front and at Sebastopol, we don't (anyway on a first reading of the novel) pay much attention to these wiseacres. If we could tear our eyes from the page to talk to the commentators, we would rather say, what do you mean by saying that Prince Andrey's chilling thoughts about his wife, or his ruminations on the field of Austerlitz, or his love for Natasha or his cynicism or his heroism are *based on* such and such an instance in real life? For everyone who has enjoyed the experience of being completely lost in the world of *War and Peace*, such scenes *are* real life. Putting down the novel and returning to the everyday concerns of 'real life' is, in the experience of almost all readers of the book, a turning to something paler, less true than Tolstoy's art itself. And this testimony comes not just from readers being unwillingly drawn to a fireside or dinner table, but also from men and women of action. In the Second World War it was a common experience that those who read *War and Peace* were, for that week or fortnight, more interested in the campaigns of Napoleon and Kutuzov than in those of Hitler versus the Allies. I have even heard men say that they have read it on the field of battle and that the descriptions of Schön Graben or Borodino were more 'real' for them than the actual explosions and maimings and death going on around them.

It is a simple, even a 'middlebrow' point to make about *War and Peace* but it is one which is important, as it lies at the heart of its paradox. No book seems more *real*, more universal in its concerns, less self-preoccupied, and yet when the literary historian comes to unweave the strands which make up the tapestry, we find a process which is every bit as self-obsessed as Proust. The difference between the two writers is at heart a political one and a religious one. After the Dreyfus trial and the First World War, Proust could not really see any future for the society he depicts; his relationship with it, like his relationship with his own parents, is highly ambivalent, and it is with mixed feelings that we view at the end the destruction of architecture, the bombardment of Paris, and the dismantlement of the society which the narrator has analysed with such a cold eye. Tolstoy was enough of a St. Petersburg liberal — or, perhaps, enough of an old-fashioned Slavophil patriot — to be able to believe that Russia had a future. What changed in 1862 was his own life. He was now able to grasp, with his imagination, that he had a future also. Shakespeare (in Sonnet 114) remarks on the extraordinary fact that his love has taught him an alchemy

> To make of monsters and things indigest
> Such cherubims as your sweet self resemble,
> Creating every bad a perfect best
> As fast as objects to his beams assemble. . . .

It is the perfect, and most knowing assertion of the positive artistic principle — that life can be remade — almost, he hints, redeemed through the vision of an artist. For Proust, the dissolution of society, while art survives — his own art, that is — is something in which he glories; there is no alchemy, in this sense, in his obsession with Albertine. It leads on to no positive vision for humanity. The vision is wholly misanthropic. Tolstoy's marriage was what produced the Shakespearian alchemy in his imagination. Wilson Knight, commenting on Sonnet 114, wrote, 'Intellectually Shakespeare is himself baffled. But it has happened. The universe has in fact been stamped with God's signature: and that is how the works of Shakespeare were born.' That is also how *War and Peace* was born. Reading it, we feel the universe stamped with God's signature. But it is doubtful if it would have got written at all had not the manuscripts been copied and stamped with the signature, not of God, nor of Tolstoy, but of his wife.

*   *   *   *

An essential ingredient in the alchemy was the cordiality which existed between Tolstoy and his in-laws. He was in love not just with Sofya but with all the Bers family, and was very happy to spend the first Christmas holiday of his marriage in Moscow with them.

One evening Tolstoy went out, leaving Sofya behind with her sister Tatyana and their mother. Obviously, they wanted to hear all about life at Yasnaya Polyana. For the first hour or so, Sofya had nothing but praise for her husband and his *ménage*. But as time wore on, she was able to admit that life at Yasnaya was not without its difficulties. She admitted to Tanya — as they all called her — that she sometimes got fed up with being an adult. Sometimes she yearned for the company of her younger sisters; she wanted to lark about, as in nursery days, and do the sort of silly things which made Tanya say she was off her head. But if she showed high spirits in that silent house 'Auntie' Tatyana Alexandrovna would say, 'Careful! Gently, *ma chère Sophie, pense à votre enfant!*'[12]*

Sofya's loneliness, and her need for her sister Tanya's company was to provide Tolstoy with an essential catalyst when he came to write his masterpiece: not just the model for Natasha Rostova, but a whole imaginative injection of vigour and vitality.

Meanwhile, on that evening during the Christmas holidays in 1862-3, there was in evidence another, more backward-looking ingredient in the masterpiece. The women sat up talking, and talking, and eventually Sofya could not conceal her anger and alarm: Tolstoy was still not back, and it was by now one o'clock in the morning. When at length he appeared, Tolstoy was confronted with a pale, agitated Sofya in floods of tears, and a distracted mother and sister trying to console her. He had no idea why she was so upset. 'Darling girl, calm down!' He laughed, and then, as though this would console a young wife who was, apart from anything else, hurt by his neglect, said, 'I was at Aksakov's and I didn't notice the time going by. You see, I met one of the Decembrists there: Zavalishin.'[13]

One of the interesting things about this story, which occurs in the memoirs of Tanya herself, is that it is not true. Zavalishin, one of the Decembrist rebels in 1825 who had been exiled to Siberia, was not in Moscow at this time. It is impossible to know whether Tolstoy was lying, or whether Tanya misremembers the facts. It reveals, either way, that if there was anything in the family which you would

* Hereafter I shall refer to Tatyana Bers as Tanya to avoid confusion with Tolstoy's aunt Toinette, also called Tatyana.

expect to keep Tolstoy up until one in the morning, it would be an encounter with one of those doughty old liberal rebels against the autocracy.

Since 1861, when he had been to Rome and met his own distinguished Decembrist cousin, S. G. Volkonsky, Tolstoy had been toying with the idea of a novel about the Decembrists. Only three chapters got written. They are set in 1856, the year in which S. G. Volkonsky was in fact allowed to return to Moscow after his exile. As he travels back to the city, the returning exile is impressed by all the improvements which he witnesses in his country since 1825 — 'Russia's strength is not in us,' he muses (i.e. in the aristocracy), 'but in the people [*narod*].'[14] The character, who is a prototype of Pierre Bezukhov in *War and Peace*, has the name of Labazov, so clearly, though he is loosely based on Volkonsky, he is also linked in Tolstoy's mind with that other Decembrist hero Zavalishin,* his enthusiasm for whom gave a late night to the Bers household in the early days of January 1863.

*   *   *   *

The first six months of 1863 were devoted to clearing the decks in preparation for greater things. As far as Tolstoy's writing was concerned, it was a time for collecting up what he had written so far, and publishing it in four volumes — the first *Collected Works of Tolstoy*. The fourth volume contained the much revised *The Cossacks*, which was published in the beginning of 1863 in *Russkii Vestnik*, and received, on the whole, golden opinions. Tolstoy, who had published nothing for the previous three years, was now established as a major Russian writer: the author of *Childhood*, *Sebastopol Sketches* and *The Cossacks*. But he knew by now that within him there was a much greater enterprise, nothing less than the history of his own nation, seen entirely through his own imagination: or, to put it another way, the history of his own soul dressed up as the history of Russia. It needed only one spark of joy to set the whole thing going.

During this period Tolstoy wrote one of his most original and enchanting tales, *Kholstomer* or *Strider*. It is the story of a piebald

---

* The transposition of letters was a common device of Tolstoy's when drawing one of his literary portraits. So Zaval-ishin becomes Labaz-ov. The letters are reversed, and a 'v' becomes a 'b' as with his Volkonsky/Bolkonsky substitution.

horse. Then, there was a pause. The heavily pregnant Sofya, who was a naturally efficient household manager, began to get Yasnaya Polyana ready for the birth of her first child. She was, according to Fet, 'a beautiful bird who enlivened everything by her presence'. She introduced carpets and curtains into rooms where they had never before been seen. Nursery staff were engaged, and prepared. The rough old servants found themselves on the staff of a Victorian country house: a Russian house, where Auntie still muttered to the icons, and where bast-clad beggars still appeared at the windows, but one touched and enlivened by western civilisation. As June approached, all the family awaited the birth with eagerness and on June 28 Sofya gave birth to their son Sergey, her comfort by no means increased by Tolstoy's insistence that the labour and delivery should take place on the very same knobbly leather divan from which he had chosen to make his entrance into the world thirty-five years before.

Not long after this joyful event, Sofya's sister Tanya came to stay for an extended period, and Tolstoy was able to start writing his *grande œuvre*.

Tanya Bers played an extremely important role in the lives of both the Tolstoys. In the awkward days of their honeymoon, they took refuge in writing jokey letters to Tanya. By March 1863, Tanya was a close confidante of Tolstoy's. To her he could speak, as to no one else, of his worries about Sofya Andreyevna's emotional instabilities. For instance, one night he had a bad dream in which his wife had become a painted china doll. He asked her, 'Are you made of china?' and she replied 'Yes I am.' He began to touch her, and found that she was china all over. The paint was coming off her lips, and there was a piece coming off her shoulders. Her bodice was china, and so was the flesh beneath. The eyes looked real, but they weren't real. They just stared at the bed.

She obviously wanted to go to bed, and she kept rocking back and forth. I was at my wit's end, and took hold of her and tried to carry her over to the bed. My fingers made no impression on her cold, china body and, what surprised me even more, she had become light as a glass phial. And suddenly she seemed to shrink away, and she grew tiny, tinier than the palm of my hand, although she still looked exactly the same. I took hold of a pillow, stood her up in one corner, pummelled another corner with my fist and laid her down there; then I took her nightcap, folded it into four and covered her with it up to the chin. She lay there looking exactly the same. I put out the candle and laid her down to sleep under my beard. Suddenly I heard her voice from under the pillow: 'Lyova, why have I become china?' I didn't know what to reply. Again she said, 'Does it matter that I'm china?' I didn't want to upset her and said that it didn't.[15]

But it did, and it went on worrying Tolstoy even in his waking hours. Sometimes he would look up and think that the dream was true. As he looked at her, she had a way of becoming a tiny china doll. Tanya was rising seventeen when she received this confidence from her brother-in-law.

Tanya had the most electrifying effect on Tolstoy's brother Sergey, who met her on one of his visits to Yasnaya from his own estate of Pirogovo. For some years now, he had been living with his gipsy mistress Marya Mikhaylovna Shishkina and they had several children. Apparently, he felt considerable awkwardness about this arrangement and had more or less given up society, living on his stud farm, breeding horses, and seeing no one except gipsies and family.

As soon as he met Tanya Bers, he fell deeply in love with her and she with him. Here was a case of the family sticking together, if not actually an assembly of the Ant Brotherhood. Lev marries the daughter of Marya's best friend Lyubov and within months, Sergey is in love with Lyubov's other daughter Tanya. ('Ah, Lyubov Alexandrovna, do you remember how we used to dance to these tunes together when we were young?')

A wedding day was fixed. Sergey was to marry his beautiful Tanya. She, unrealistically, had only ever met him on his visits to Yasnaya Polyana which were invariably conducted alone. She was not fully aware of the commitments which he had left behind at Pirogovo.

Sergey himself decided to put Marya Mikhaylovna away and return her to her gipsy encampment. It was against his conscience to do this, but he was so much in love with Tanya he could not do otherwise. Then, one day, he arrived home before dawn. He came into the house and glanced into Marya Mikhaylovna's room. He saw her at prayer before her icon and something told him that he could not go through with his plans. That night he wrote to Tanya telling her that the gipsy woman was in despair and that he could no longer marry her, Tanya. Tanya, ever ebullient and volatile, tried to poison herself, but it was not a very successful attempt. Her misery on this occasion was all useful to Tolstoy when he came to describe the grief of Natasha Rostova for Prince Andrey in *War and Peace*.

Tolstoy, from the beginning, had been gravely suspicious of her attachment to Sergey. When she first confided her love to Lev, he wrote to her:

> In the centre of the earth is the alatyr stone and in the centre of man is the navel. How inscrutable are the ways of providence! Oh younger sister of the wife of her husband! In this centre, other objects are sometimes found as well. . . . Tanya, my dear friend, you are young, beautiful, gifted and lovable. Guard yourself and your heart. Once your heart has been given away you can't get it back again, and the mark on a tormented heart remains forever I know that the artistic demands of your rich nature are not the same as the demands of ordinary girls of your age; but Tanya, as an experienced man who loves you not just because we are relations, I'm telling you the whole truth. . . .[16]

Not long afterwards, Sergey did the decent thing by his gipsy girl and married her, giving her children legitimate status (a matter of great importance in nineteenth-century Russia). Tanya herself was to marry an unsatisfactory man called Kuzminsky, 'on the rebound'. It was not a happy marriage. But Tanya was a survivor.

Her young face still arrests us as it stares out of the photographs. She had rather big ears, and not, by the strictest canons, a beautiful face. But it is all animation. No china doll she. Tanya Bers had a quickening effect upon the Yasnaya Polyana household. As happened in the case of so many nineteenth-century marriages, devotion to the sister-in-law was an important factor, at once solidifying of affection, and dangerous. Tanya was the best friend of Tolstoy's wife, and not just her sister. It was therefore companionable that he should like her so much too. At the same time, the emotional hazards of proximity were always there, to enliven the relationship. Unlike Dickens, Tolstoy never fell overtly in love with his sister-in-law. He left that to his brother Sergey. Equally it was a matter of fascination. By being the protective friend and brother-in-law, who could warn her off too close an attachment to Sergey, Tolstoy was able to indulge as freely as he liked in the luxury of loving her himself.

In October 1863, there was a ball in Tula, the nearest provincial town of any size to Yasnaya Polyana. Alexander II was visiting the place, and the Tolstoys were invited. Sofya, who was pregnant again, and feeling unwell, could not go, and told Tolstoy that he must take Tanya. Sofya adapted a ball-gown for her little sister, and there came the moment when Tanya, flushed with excitement, appeared in her ball-finery to ask how she looked.

'You realise, don't you, Tanya, that even if I was well enough, I could not have gone to the ball?' asked Sofya.

'Why not?'

'Don't you know Lev's *views*? How could I have worn evening dress? It is unthinkable! He is always criticising married women who, as he puts it, "expose themselves".'[17]

So it was Tanya's pretty shoulders and back, and Tanya's bosom that were exposed for the gentry of Tula. Tolstoy, himself splendidly attired in a frock coat, emerged from his chamber and the pair set off. Tanya's excitement is written into the episode of *War and Peace* where Natasha Rostova goes to the ball and dances with Prince Andrey. When Tanya and Tolstoy had driven off, Sofya collapsed in tears. There were to be no more balls for her. Biographers can weep with her, but readers of *War and Peace* can be thankful. The much-needed catalyst was Tanya. It was she who got the novel on the move, it was she who released something in Tolstoy's imagination. The ingredient was a love which never really rose above the level of a flirtation. Years later, Sofya Andreyevna asked Turgenev why he had not written any fiction in the years immediately before. He confided that he could only write fiction when he was slightly in love, and that of late the ardour had cooled.[18] So, Tanya may be viewed as the 'onlie begetter' of *War and Peace* precisely because she was not deeply the object of Tolstoy's love. This, always, was Sofya. Tolstoy was neither a disloyal nor an inattentive husband. However repellent a modern reader might find Tolstoy's attitude to women, there was nothing, on its own terms, which was dishonourable about it. Not only was he true to Sofya. From the first, he owed her a dangerous amount. But she was always a wife. This meant, as far as Tolstoy was concerned, that she was his mistress, the mother of his children, and the manager of his household. It meant so much more besides. She was his confidante, his helpmeet and, after only a few months, decidedly the most powerful figure in the marriage. But it was on strange terms — terms which today, outside the stricter disciplines of old religions such as Islam, are almost unknown. She was a *wife*. Therefore, in public, she submitted; and she did not bare her arms.

If her powerful and disciplined management of all the outward circumstances of Tolstoy's life provided the setting in which *War and Peace* was able to get written, it was the good-humoured, lively Tanya who provided the book with that inexpressible liveliness — the life which is its clue.

Throughout the summer and autumn of 1863, Tolstoy worked on his book. He was still planning to write *The Decembrists*, but he now conceived the story as being of three eras. In 1856, his Decembrist hero was to return to Moscow from his Siberian exile; but before that there would have to be an extended section describing the Rising itself, in 1825. Before that again, it would be necessary to tell the story of how that generation came into contact with European egalitarian ideals and notions — through their military service in the Napoleonic wars.

But the mere contemplation of the Napoleonic wars was, for Tolstoy, a matter which called forth all the deep inconsistencies in his outlook and sympathy. With one part of himself, in adolescence and early manhood, he had been a fervent westerniser, a French rationalist, a believer in progress, liberty, and political freedom. All these things were beliefs cherished by the Decembrists, some of whom — so intense had been their devotion to French ideas — followed the invading army of 1812 back to Paris in order to imbibe the new culture. But for the majority of Russians, the invasion of their country by Napoleon had been an appalling outrage. It had led to slaughter on a scale unparalleled in the history of warfare. Memory of this invasion hardened, for so-called Slavophils, the sense that outside, European influences were essentially hostile to Russia's interest. Russia had been delivered — though at such great cost — and they should show their thanksgiving for that delivery by being as un-European as possible, by recognising that they owed their deliverance to the Christ of the Orthodox Church, to the Mother of the wonder-working icons, to the prayers of the Orthodox saints, to the valour of the Orthodox army, to the wisdom of the saintly Emperor, and to the god-sent Russian winter.

Modern visitors to the Soviet Union, or those who entertain Soviet visitors in the West, are today frequently surprised by the strength of Russian memories of the Second World War. Russians still talk about it all the time — it is not just the Second World War, but the Glorious Patriotic War. Russians find the western attitude towards the last great European war just as incomprehensible: where, among young people, there is not total ignorance of who the protagonists were, there is a tendency to be flippant about it. Not so in the Soviet Union. Whether this is because until very recently it was, by and large, a gerontic state ruled over by men whose finest hour was during the last war, or whether because of the huge numbers slain, or whether because the shock of being invaded when you live in an uninvadeable country takes several generations to live down, who can say. What a twentieth-century Russian feels about the Glorious Patriotic War against Fascism was felt just as strongly by the nineteenth-century Russian about the invasion by Napoleon. It was the great moment of national trial and national deliverance, analogous to the defeat of the Spanish Armada in Elizabethan England, exercising a similar appeal over the popular imagination, the sort of collective experience in which a nation finds itself.

By October, Sofya records that Tolstoy was now at work on a book which she calls *The History of 1812*, but it was no mere outward account of those events. A fortnight later, on November 13, she records a coolness between them and, as usual, over-reacts. 'He does not love me, I couldn't keep his love. How could I? It was fate! In a moment of grief, which I now regret, when nothing seemed to matter but the fact that I had lost his love, I thought even his writing was pointless; what did I care what Countess So-and-so said to Princess So-and-so?'[19]

These are clear indications that the masterpiece as we know it was taking shape. From the huge number of drafts, now lodged in the Tolstoy Museum in Moscow, the scholars have been unable to decide with certainty which bits were written in 1863, and which later. One of the earliest versions, perhaps written soon after Tolstoy had taken Tanya to the ball at Tula, began with a ball at a nobleman's house in St. Petersburg in 1811. A similar variant begins with the ball, but has a long preparatory paragraph describing the European situation between Tilsit and the fire of Moscow. We know that the link with the Decembrist theme was still strong in Tolstoy's mind. We know that some of the battle scenes were sketched out in 1863. But most of what he had written were family scenes — what Sofya contemptuously called 'what Countess So-and-so said to Princess So-and-so'.

Perhaps she was a little jealous that Tolstoy used her sisters, Tanya and Lisa, as secretaries while she was occupied with her baby. But it would be a mistake to imagine that Tolstoy did nothing all year except write *The History of 1812*. There were long spells when he did not write anything. It was during this year that Tolstoy made 'an important discovery': 'Managers, foremen and overseers are only a burden on a farm. You can verify this by firing all overseers, and by sleeping until ten o'clock. You will see that there will be no change for the worse. I have made this discovery and am absolutely convinced.'[20]

The discovery meant a lot of extra work, both for his wife and himself. Tolstoy supervised the fields, the forest, the vegetable-growing and the beehives. His wife was in charge of the house, the estate office, the barns, the cattle and all the hired labour. Given her initial revulsion to the filth of the cattlesheds and of the peasants themselves, her efficiency in these areas was not without heroism.

The experiment to let the peasants run the farm themselves was a complete failure.

> It is the business of the wealthy man
> To give employment to the artisan.[21]

Tolstoy would never learn this lesson and was always wasting his time in tomfool attempts to be like the peasants — which he wasn't. Though his wife was prepared to hire labour to look after the cows, she drew the line at looking after the pigs — which were Japanese hogs. Having dismissed the swineherd for drunkenness, Tolstoy was left in charge of the hogs himself. He found the task so deeply uncongenial that it led him to idle cruelty far worse than that of the sot he had dismissed: 'I would give the hogs as little food as possible to make them weak. It worked! If the next time I saw them, they were still squeaking, I gave them just a little food. Whenever they became quiet, I knew the end had come.'[22]

Tolstoy knew nothing about salting or curing a ham. In warm weather, all the hams rotted and had to be thrown out. Those which were sent to Moscow arrived in a putrefied state. So did the butter. In the fields, with Tolstoy in charge, things were in chaos. Tolstoy enlisted one of his pupils from the school, a fourteen-year-old boy, to help him tell the peasants what needed hoeing, digging or planting. Unsurprisingly, they took no notice either of Tolstoy's instructions or those of the boy. When he realised what a mess he was making of everything, Tolstoy did not go back to his desk at once and start writing *War and Peace*. On the contrary, he would go visiting. He spent more and more time with his Bers relations in Moscow, often leaving Sofya behind at Yasnaya Polyana while he was in the bosom of the very family circle for which she pined. Or he would go out hunting.

In 1864, there occurred a happy accident which, from the point of view of *War and Peace*, concentrated Tolstoy's mind wonderfully. In the September of that year, Tolstoy noted that he had written 'about a hundred and twenty printed pages' of his novel, but that he could not make progress. He was in a period of corrections and alterations. He was always an obsessive corrector and reviser, but it was only after Sofya came into his life that the evidence was kept. It was she who kept each scrap of manuscript, and bundled them into boxes, like the Apostles gathering up the fragments which remained after the feeding of the five thousand. The number of cases, too, was the exact equivalent to the number of baskets on that occasion: twelve. Twelve stout wooden cases of Tolstoy manuscripts were bound up at the time of the Revolution and sent to the Rumyantsev Museum in Moscow. For those who find the Countess Tolstoy's character unsympathetic these twelve boxes should be held up as a peace offering. Without her, we would have no picture at all of the evolution of her husband's masterpiece.

Meanwhile, back in September 1864, Tolstoy was neglecting his book and riding off to see a neighbour. He was not riding a hunter, but two of his dogs ran alongside him and, inevitably, they caught sight of a hare. Tolstoy knew that the horse was not used to jumping, but the excitement of his dogs instantly communicated itself to him. They were barking and chasing after the hare. Throwing caution to the winds, Tolstoy called out 'Sick 'em!' and gave chase. At the first jump the horse stumbled and Tolstoy was thrown. He lay in agony with his right arm broken. Sofya was heavily pregnant with their second child Tatyana, and Tolstoy felt that the shock of hearing about his accident would bring about premature labour. So when he was eventually discovered, he got himself taken to Tula without informing his wife, and had the arm set by a dud doctor there. For weeks his right arm was useless, and after the baby Tatyana's birth, he went to Moscow to have it reset. For the remaining months of the year the Tolstoys lived with the Berses, and the novel was continued by dictation to Tanya and Liza.

The original book about the Decembrists, with its portentous

Alchemy

theme (nothing less than Nekrasov's 'Who can be happy in Russia?') had been conceived when Tolstoy was still on the fringes of St. Petersburg salons and what is known as intellectual life. The book may be said to originate and to end in primarily intellectual concerns; but, as with all great minds, Tolstoy's questions were essentially simple ones — the kind which do not often interest 'intellectuals'. He was not truly interested in anything so parochial as the fortunes of Russian liberals 1812-1856. He was interested in the much simpler, deeper question — *how do we come to be here?* One way of answering this question is to examine our own personal inner histories, as he had tried to do all those years before in *The History of Yesterday*. Another was to turn to historians, who could tell us how society had evolved, how this ruler had succeeded that, and how one tyrant declared war on another.

Neither approach in the end satisfied Tolstoy. He was to be neither the Russian Darwin nor the Russian Macaulay. His approach to the question of origins was entirely distinctive and self-revelatory. It is of fundamental importance, however, that it emerged, not in an intellectual salon, but in a family. And it was after he broke his right arm, and was obliged to dictate and perform his work that the importance of that family became clear to them all. In the early drafts, the family which will be the centre of his book are called the Tolstoys. This is later changed to Prostoy, which means simple, plain, ordinary, unaffected. Later they were to become the Rostovs (pronounced, not that pronunciation matters much, with the accent on the second syllable).

After some weeks of convalescence and dictation in Moscow, Doctor Bers arranged an evening at the house of his close friends and relatives the Perfilyevs. Tolstoy was to read aloud from his novel. At first he was shy. Never in the course of his whole life would he consent to read aloud in public. He was the reverse of Dickens; his public could only be reached by writing, and he was not one, either, for making public speeches about matters of contemporary concern. He was always a private person, and here, though he had an audience, it was essentially a private audience. It was also an audience of a very singular character. At first, his reading was muted, shy. But gradually, as he got confidence, he was able to act all the different parts, and to put different intonations and characters into them ('do the police in different voices'). Here was the story of a young man bending to kiss Tanya's doll Mimi, and receiving, instead, a kiss from Tanya herself.

221

But it had become the story of Natasha Rostova kissing Boris. The more pages he read, the more vividly they all began to recognise themselves.

'Why!' exclaimed the daughter of their hostess artlessly, 'Mama, Marya Dmitriyevna Akhrosimov is you; she resembles you exactly!' They noticed more vividly than any later reader of the novel could possibly do that he had set up his easel among them and painted them to the life. But the static painting image is not a good one. For what *we* notice is the animation of the readings — Tolstoy throwing himself with equal vigour into all the parts as he reads them. A novelist is less like a painter than a puppeteer. The superficial resemblance of his characters to figures in 'real life' might be very noticeable to those characters themselves, but it is not this resemblance which gives them their life, their vigour. The imagined life comes from another source — from the artist himself. That is why the game of matching the figures in a novel to their 'real life' equivalents is at best only half satisfactory and, in the end, positively misleading. The biographers of Proust, for example, provide us with many interesting superficial parallels between the central figures of his novel, and actual figures in French society. But it would be a philistine reader, either of the novels or of the biographies, who concluded that Monsieur Swann was Charles Haas or the Baron de Charlus was Robert de Montesquiou. In each case, Proust has merely copied a shell. What gives the characters their haunting reality is the fact that Proust has apportioned to each his own passions and interests, temperament and background. To Swann he gave his all-consuming aestheticism, his experience of a great love, his knowledge that his life would be cut short by ill health and, perhaps most important of all, his Jewishness. To the Baron de Charlus, he has given the characteristics of which he was more ashamed — his pride, his snobbery, his homosexuality. In a very analogous manner, we find that Tolstoy animates the figures of his imagination. Natasha's excitement at the ball, for instance, owes quite as much to Tolstoy's excitement that he was taking Tanya as it did to Tanya's own animation. In writing his novel, he is drawing upon all the inchoate and disparate preoccupations which have existed at the back of his mind for the last thirty-five years. The immediate and superficial resemblances between the Prostoys or Rostovs to the Bers circle does not conceal from us, who have followed the story thus far, the truth which he revealed when he called them initially the Tolstoys: not the family Tolstoy, though they

222

too, like the Berses, provided the artist with his models, but the multifarious Lev Nikolayeviches who had been strutting and fretting their hour upon the stage ever since 1828. 'Lyovochka,' Tanya said to him one day, 'I can see how you are able to describe landowners, fathers, generals, soldiers, but how can you insinuate yourself into the heart of a girl in love, how can you describe the sensation of a mother — for the life of me I cannot understand.'[23] She could not understand, but she had put her finger on the very heart of his secret, the thing which made it possible for him to 'gore his own thoughts' and 'make old offences of affections new'. In Nikolay Rostov, as he was to become, we read all Tolstoy's early experiences in the army, his vacillations between sentimental love of his family, and addiction to gambling and debauchery. But Nikolay is the innocent side of Tolstoy's past. Into the less appealing characters, he can pour the memories of his darker nature — into Dolokhov and Pierre drinking themselves silly, and tying a bear to a policeman: into Anatole Kuragin, indulging in guilty love (in his case for his sister). He even pours himself into Hélène herself, whose attitude to Pierre so closely resembles Tolstoy's diary-self view of his own clumsy, stupid behaviour when out in society. . . . It *all* gets used.

So, too, does his preoccupation with his mother. All the chapters devoted to Princess Marya and her crusty old father Prince Bolkonsky (Volkonsky in early drafts) owe their origin to Tolstoy's attempt to reconstruct what his own mother's existence had been like at Yasnaya Polyana, before she married Nikolay Rostov/Prostoy/Tolstoy. It is surely revealing that while he shared the jollier Rostov passages with the Berses, it was to Sofya that he entrusted the much more intimate, almost sacred task, of transcribing the passages relating to Princess Marya.

'How I like everything about Princess Marya!' she wrote to him, when he was still in Moscow. 'You see her so clearly. Such a splendid sympathetic character.'[24] The strength and vigour of Marya as an artistic conception must have owed much of its origin to Tolstoy's own guilty awareness of what, in the first year of marriage, he was doing to his own wife. He had buried her in the country, just as Marya was a prisoner in her father's household at Bald Hills. He was perpetually irritable with her, as the old Prince Volkonsky was with his daughter, but beneath the irritability is a dependence on her which is one of the most touching things in the novel. He loves her, we are told, 'more than himself'. One of the funniest scenes in the book is when the old prince fears that Anatole Kuragin is going to come and offer Marya a proposal of marriage. Even before the Kuragins have arrived, he has lost his temper with the steward for sweeping the snow from the drive, and then there takes place the wonderfully dotty exchange in which the servants are told to shovel the snow back.

'The road's covered up?'

'Indeed sir. Thank God. Please forgive our singular stupidity.'[25]

What makes the old prince so angry and so irritable is that he is jealous of anything which threatens to separate him from Marya's love. Tolstoy was no stranger to the wildest, silliest extremes of jealousy. In her memoirs Tanya records how both her brother-in-law and her sister 'poisoned their lives with jealousy'. She tells the story of how a harmless social acquaintance of theirs, a young man called Pisaryov, once called at Yasnaya Polyana for a short stay. At tea, he happened to catch Tolstoy in the mood where anything could be interpreted in the wrong way. Pisaryov committed the cardinal sin of sitting by Sofya, who was dispensing tea from the samovar, and added insult to injury by helping her pass the cups around to the other members of the party.

'I was watching Tolstoy,' Tanya writes. 'Pale, and very much upset, he would rise, pace the floor, leave the room, only to reappear again. In some way, his nervousness was contagious. Sofya became aware of it and was at a loss what to do.

'The situation came to a sudden end the next morning when Tolstoy gave orders to get the coach ready and the manservant informed the young man that the horses were waiting. . . .'[26]

Transpose the ages of the people involved: make Tolstoy the jealous father instead of the jealous husband, and you have a scene of old Prince Bolkonsky and his daughter at Bald Hills.

In all the original versions, the old prince was simply a picture of his grandfather, and Princess Marya of his mother, solitary, as she had been in life. But as he meditated on the story, Tolstoy realised that he needed a hero to die at Austerlitz. Thus was Prince Andrey born. Sofya was not alone in the early stages in finding Andrey an unsatisfactory character. Fet, too, thought him static and tedious. 'It is true,' Tolstoy admitted, 'he is tedious, monotonous, merely *un homme comme il faut* throughout the first part. But it is not his fault, it is mine.'[27]

Andrey, who begins as mere cannon-fodder — a hero who can be killed off at Austerlitz with maximum emotional effect, and who is also, in part, a portrait of Tolstoy's brother Nikolay, and in part a portrait of their own father — becomes something much deeper: a vehicle for the self which Tolstoy might have become if he had shed his diffidence, cultivated the friendship of his cousin Alexandrine and her other friends 'up the chimney' and become, through Government or military service, a 'somebody'. In Prince Andrey there is all the loftiness and pride which Tolstoy's early St. Petersburg and army contemporaries noted in himself. Beneath the cynical exterior, however, there is hidden the soul of a profoundly sensitive man, who is alive to the agonies of love, and the deep mystery of existence. In part, Prince Andrey is a literary creation. He is like a hero of Pushkin's or Lermontov's imagination, and it is partly this fact which emboldened Tolstoy to give him some of his most hidden and most personal characteristics. Tolstoy was plagued all his life by a thorough-going scepticism which amounted to an incapacitating disease. By scepticism here we are not talking just about a Voltairean view of God or the universe, but a capacity to question the point of doing or feeling anything. It begins with Schopenhauerian pessimism. It can lead in the end to a sort of Hindu detachment. In Tolstoy's personal writings, it is summed up by the untranslatable little shrug of a phrase, *chto zh?* — so what, what then? is implied by it. He is always asking it, often with devastating effect. When Sofya wrote that she found Prince Andrey's character unsatisfactory we do not know whether he was still at this stage a figure half sketched out or whether she had begun to see in him this terrifying negativism. In no area of Prince Andrey's life is it more upsetting than in his attitude to his little wife. In his early conversations with Pierre and with his own sister he reveals complete disillusionment not only with his wife, but with himself, and with the whole condition of matrimony. 'If you get married expecting anything from yourself in the future, then at every step you will feel that everything is finished for you, everything is closed except the drawing room where you will be stood with a court lackey on one side and an idiot on the other. But what's the use. . . . ?' he says to Pierre. And to his sister, 'Know one thing, Masha, I can't reproach my wife and I never have done so. Nor will I do so, I can't even reproach myself for anything in relation to her; and that will always be the case, whatever the circumstances. But if you want to know the truth. . . . if you want to know whether I'm happy, or whether she is happy? No! Why not? I don't know. . . .'[28]

It is this gloomy, pinched, and secretly tragic Tolstoy who comes into blossom as Prince Andrey. And it is not surprising that when the Prince is wounded in battle, Tolstoy cannot bear to kill him off. Instead, he leaves him staring at the sky, confronting the greatness and the nothingness of things, as Tolstoy was so often to do himself, loving Natasha even as Tolstoy loved Tanya, and as he had loved Sofya before she became his wife.

But this is not the whole of Tolstoy's nature. For he is also, more obviously, to be found in the figure of Pierre — clumsy, awkward, sensual, vulnerable, consumed with a childish preoccupation with the great questions — why are we here? how should a man live? It is this much more blundering, rough-hewn side of Tolstoy's nature that he himself preferred, and so he rewards it in the end by marrying it off to Natasha, and makes of Pierre's and Natasha's married love an idealised version of his love for Sofya. The book was still far from being what we read as *War and Peace* but, as 1864 came to an end, it was much closer to being the thing it was destined to be.

We have noted, with a clumsiness designed to emphasise the delicate process by which imagined beings turn into characters in fiction, the processes by which Tolstoy at the same time drew from life, and animated the characters with his own daemon. But there is one completely unforgettable character in *War and Peace* whom we have not mentioned yet and who must be brought forward before this chapter ends. It would seem as though he was there from an early stage. Here he is, on one of the drafts penned in 1863 or 1864, talking about Napoleon: 'He kept on winning his battles, not because he was a genius (I am convinced he was very far from that) but on the contrary because he was more stupid than his enemies, could not be carried away by logical deductions and only bothered about seeing that his soldiers were well-fed, embittered, obedient and as numerous as possible.'[29]

In the finished version of the story, Tolstoy keeps this figure in reserve and he is not allowed to contribute to the initial discussions about Napoleon in Anna Pavlovna's salon. While the St. Petersburg gentry discuss the question of whether Napoleon is Antichrist, this figure is made to keep quiet. At first we are not aware of his presence, but then he butts in and interrupts the conversation with a remark to us — the witty observation that Anna Pavlovna is like a *maître d'hôtel* serving up as a choice delicacy bits of food which, if we had seen them in the kitchen, we should not have cared to eat. 'Even so Pavlovna dished up to her guests, first the *Vicomte* and then the *Abbé* as particularly choice morsels.'[30] It is our old friend who proclaimed that bronchitis is a metal, the man who could be relied upon to bust up any of Turgenev's dinners by shouting that Shakespeare or George Sand, or anyone else you might admire, was no good. It would be mistaken to identify this strand in Tolstoy with the narrator of *War and Peace*, for one of the extraordinary qualities of the book is that for seven-eighths of the time it does not feel as if it is being narrated at all. It is a Shakespearian, faceless presence who narrates all the most memorable scenes in the book — not just the big scenes but all the touching minor details which give it its greatness. Think of the older Countess Rostova giving Anna Mikhailovna money to pay for Boris's uniform — a moment which makes both women weep — 'because they were friends, and because they were kind-hearted and because they — friends from childhood — had to think about such a sordid thing as money, and because their youth was over. . . .' At moments like these we feel the universe stamped with God's signature.

The Tolstoy who thought bronchitis was a metal would never have known that the Countess Rostova had pretended to her husband that she was in debt because she wanted to slip her old friend the money for her son's uniform. If he had seen the two women crying, it would just have baffled him, but it would not have interested him. It would have annoyed him to think that we were eavesdropping on anything so trivial when we might have been listening to his views. What the views *were* did not matter much, so long as this hectoring bore is the only person in the room talking, and we are all listening, as the children had to listen to him in the schoolroom at Yasnaya Polyana. In those early years of marriage, when the novel was still a series of unfinished and unconnected chapters, this is just one voice among many. Tolstoy was happily, and selfishly at work in the area which was so wholly his that he was right to deny it a category and right to say it was 'not a novel'. 'Yesterday,' he wrote insensitively to Sofya from Moscow — she was stuck in the country looking after the farm and the children — 'I explained to Tanya why it is easier for me to bear a separation from you than it would be if I were not writing. Along with you and the children (I feel however that as yet I do not love them enough) I have a continual love or care for my writing. If this were not so, I really feel that I could not spend a day without you; this you will surely understand, for what writing is for me, the children must be for you.'[31]

Sofya Andreyevna did understand: that was one of the most

remarkable things about her. She was jealous, but she kept her jealousy under control, and did a great deal to nourish her husband's literary genius. But there was a less equable character looking over Tolstoy's shoulder as he wrote, and who detested, with an unconquerable jealousy, all the work of his imagination, all the figures who through the strange alchemy of art had, or were developing, a life of their own: all the Pierres, the Andreys, the Natashas, the Borises and the Dolokhovs. This figure was that belligerent bore insisting that bronchitis is a metal. For the moment, he bided his time. He was patient while Tolstoy dictated to his sisters-in-law, or while his right hand, gradually healed, passed to and fro across the page. But sooner or later he would grab the pen from Tolstoy the artist's hand and have his say.

Chapter Ten
War and Peace

1865 - 1869

Mes personnages, je ne suis aucun d'eux et je suis chacun d'eux.

Montherlant

'*I*'m very glad you love my wife,' Tolstoy wrote playfully to Fet on January 23, 1865. 'Although I love her less than my novel, still, you know, she is my wife!'[1] The joke consists in a half truth. With one part of himself, an indolent amateur farmer who was perfectly happy to let the days pass in the company of his close friends and relations, Tolstoy was without zest for literary work. He was too happy. But with a deeper part of himself, the literary work was consumingly important. All unseen, as it ordered itself in his brain, it was setting into an acceptable shape his own past, absolving his own sins, and giving himself the sort of power as a chronicler which fortune had denied him as an administrator. His forebears — generals, ambassadors, equerries — had all exercised great influence in the state, as his distant relations continued to do. (Count Dmitry Tolstoy became Minister of the Interior in the following year.) Destiny had not allowed Lev Nikolayevich Tolstoy the chance to be a man of affairs. But this did not prevent him, with his imagination, from fashioning, shaping and describing the whole story of modern Russia. Nothing less was his ambition as he planned the great epic history of 1805-1812, of 1825 and of 1856. So, though there were periods of great idleness even during these, the most creative years of his life, such idleness should not be mistaken for literary indifference. A writer is not just at work when he holds a pen in his hand. He needs to allow the work to gestate; and when the work is of the proportions of *War and Peace*, the gestation will often be long and apparently idle indeed.

Children could be born (the family had increased to four by the time the task was quite done, with the births of Ilya in 1866 and Lev in 1869). Kingdoms could rise and wane. Relations could marry and give in marriage. It was all secondary to the great literary task. As he confessed to Alexandrine that year, after a Polish rising had been put down with singular savagery by the Russians, 'It's a matter of complete indifference to me who suppresses the Poles or captures Schleswig-Holstein or delivers a speech at a *zemstvo* meeting. Butchers kill the oxen we eat, but I'm not obliged to accuse them or sympathise with them.'[2] In years to come, he would take a very different line. He would devote pages of propaganda to attacking butchers, and to questioning everybody else's right to eat meat, and to attacking governments for acts of violence against the innocent. As yet, however, as he candidly admitted to Alexandrine in the same letter, he was not a Christian, 'and still far from being one; but experience has taught me not to believe in the infallibility of my judgement'. Again, how unlike the later Tolstoy. The belligerent, argumentative Tolstoy was largely silent for these years. The gambler kept his money in his pocket. The whoremonger was faithful to his wife and, in their periods of inevitable separation, they grew very tender towards one another. After a spring of minor family illnesses, and the sense, familiar to all young mothers, that she could never be alone, and never properly rested, Sofya Andreyevna contentedly told her diary,

We are on good terms. Lyovochka is very busy with the dairy yard and is writing his novel without much enthusiasm. He is bursting with ideas, but when will he ever write them all down? He sometimes talks to me about his plans and ideas which is always a tremendous joy. I always understand him too.[3]

Katkov, who had published *The Cossacks* in *Russkii Vestnik*, agreed to take on this new historical fiction, and the first part of *1805*, as it was then called, was published in the issue of February 1865. (It is interesting to remember that Scott's *Waverley* was separated by exactly the same distance in time from the events it describes.) Tolstoy's wife worked all through Christmas and January copying and correcting three separate drafts of the book before they were deemed fit for submission to Katkov. When the proofs came back, Tolstoy made yet more corrections and additions, in a crabbed, illegible hand which blackened the page. Sofya Andreyevna alone could decipher his scribbles — truly, alone. Tolstoy himself was often unable to make out what he had written.

Her brother Stepan calculated that by the time the book was finished, Tolstoy's wife had written out the equivalent of *seven* fair copies of the whole work.[4] Nor was she a mere copyist, for at every stage, after his return from convalescing in Moscow during 1864, she advised and commented upon the work, giving intelligent reflections not only upon the content, but also its manner of presentation and publication. All this was squeezed in between her duties, as she and her husband both conceived them, as a mother and housekeeper. It is one of the most impressive partnerships in literary history. Given Tolstoy's habits of self-doubt and indolence, it is improbable whether, without his wife's help and guidance, the work would ever have reached a conclusion.

The chronology of the work, once it had began regularly, was as follows.[5] Once the agreement had been made with Katkov that *1805* would be published, the Decembrist part of the story was put on one side, and he devoted the latter part of 1864 and the beginning of 1865 to the passage which we now read as the opening part of *War and Peace*, though it did not yet have this title.

The public was enthusiastic. Here were the legends they had been brought up on, and the memories of the very old, brought to life! Strangely enough it was precisely this fact which baffled the pedantic critics. 'It is neither a novel nor a novella,' wrote one fool, as though it matters what category you put a book into, 'it is rather some sort of attempt at a military and aristocratic chronicle of the past.'[6] This anonymous writer strongly objected to the aristocratic flavour of the whole piece, and complained — as did several other reviewers — about the amount of French in the text. 'To read a book which has this mixture of French and Russian without the slightest need for it is indeed neither pleasant nor comforting; it might be all very well on the aristocratic pages of the *Russian Herald*, but in a separate edition the French texts should have been left out.'[7] In his final revision of the novel, Tolstoy did indeed cut the French, thereby spoiling the comedy of scenes such as the opening chapter.

It was inevitable that some 'literary' responses should be hostile, since Tolstoy had deliberately cut himself off from the literary set surrounding Nekrasov and Turgenev. Equally inevitably — any stick to beat a dog — they attacked him for being an aristocrat. Reviews did not mean much. Not surprisingly the power of *War and Peace* as mythology, as a reinforcement, like Tchaikovsky's 1812 Overture, of a patriotic idea long outlasted the lifetime of its first audience. One sees this most clearly when contemplating the fate of the novel in Stalinist days. Intellectual Bolsheviks like Mikhail Olminsky, whose ashes were buried in the Kremlin Wall in 1933, were probably right to dismiss *War and Peace* as a counter-revolutionary work. (Olminsky, like Tolstoy's first reviewers, stressed its link with Katkov and the ultra-right-wing *Russkii Vestnik.*) And yet, *War and Peace* went on being read and it went on being allowed. Stalin would not allow it to be suppressed. As the Bolshevik paradise unfolded, and many literary reputations (notably Dostoyevsky's) went underground, Tolstoy mysteriously survived.[8] This was partly owing to the pertinacity of his first editor, and devoted disciple, Chertkov. But it was also because the straight Russianness of his largest epic was so big a part of everyone's emotional fabric. Whether or not Sholokhov was the first great Soviet novelist or the plagiarist which his enemies believe, it is surely more than interesting that when the recent past came to be surveyed, in *Quiet Flows the Don* (1928), it was done in so Tolstoyan a pattern.

As the 1930s progressed, and the Russian authorities became more old-fashionedly xenophobic, there was something positively reassuring about the modes of Tolstoyan realism. Karl Radek told the Writer's Union in 1934 that James Joyce's writings were 'a heap of dung teeming with worms. . . .' He went on to say that 'as teachers, Balzac and Tolstoy are enough for us'.[9]

In strictly Marxist terms, Tolstoy should not have been 'enough' at that point in history. One feels the paradox, even today, in visiting Yasnaya Polyana which, as one of his kinsmen has attractively observed, appeals partly because it is 'the solitary, physical evocation of the old manorial way of life': a way of life which Tolstoy himself yearned to escape and which the Revolution succeeded in destroying. Yet there it is, artificially preserved and 'restored' (in fact largely rebuilt after being gutted and burnt by the Nazis). The shrine handbooks do not lie when they speak of Tolstoy as if he were a national monument. A quotation from Gorky reminds the visitor that 'Tolstoy is a profoundly national writer who with astounding fullness embodies in his soul all the peculiarities of the complex Russian psyche: he has the turbulent mischief of Vaska Buslayev and the gentle thoughtfulness of the chronicler Nestor, he burns with the fanaticism of Avvakum, he is a sceptic like Chaadayev, no less of a poet than Pushkin and as clever as Herzen — Tolstoy is a whole world.'[10]

It does not particularly matter that none of this is true (Tolstoy is not a better poet than Pushkin, and no one thinks he is): nor that the quotation invites anarchic parody. The list, after all, could go on forever, assuring us of Tolstoy's Russianness, telling us that he had the sexual voracity of Rasputin, the piety of St. Vladimir, the adventurousness of Yury Gagarin — all as true, or as untrue, as we care to make it. That is why, though Lenin fulminated against the falsity of Tolstoyan ideas ('Tolstoyism,' he wrote shortly before the Revolution, 'should be fought all along the line'), this did no damage to Tolstoy as a national institution.

He, and his national myth, were actually wheeled into service by Stalin as soon as Hitler broke the Nazi-Soviet axis. Within three weeks of the outbreak of hostilities, a hundred and fifty thousand copies of *Sebastopol Sketches* had been reissued, shortly followed by reprints of the 1812 passages in *War and Peace*. Relevant chapters, by Stalin's special command, were even posted up in Moscow for people to read during the blackest days of 1941-42. Not only, by then, was Tolstoy the most published author in Russia (there were more of his works in print during the war than those of Lenin) but also he was given the title the Great (*velikii*), an adjective at that time reserved, in all official publications, for Stalin alone. Nor was it the patriotism of *1812* alone which made it popular. As the party intellectuals, now safely dead, had observed, *War and Peace* is counter-revolutionary. With the threat of the invasion, Stalin reintroduced into the army all the pre-revolutionary trappings which Lenin thought he had swept away forever. Moscow in 1941 and 1942 sparkled with gilded epaulettes, scarlet and white jackets, smart tunics, trousers with piping, quite consciously modelled on the scenes in Tolstoy's novel.[11] If there is life beyond the grave, and the dead see what is happening on earth, Tolstoy could have known no worse purgatory than to witness — old pacifist anarchist as he was by the end — his work being used as part of Stalin's effective war propaganda in the Glorious Patriotic War against the Fascists.

*   *   *   *

In the course of 1865 Tolstoy began to revise all the battle scenes of his novel, then to add new ones; new chapters included those splendid ones at Schön Graben which do not appear in the earlier drafts. 'Is it

235

worthwhile noticing trifles?' asks Prince Bagration at Schön Graben.[12] The answer, if you are a novelist, is a triumphant yes. The scenes live so vividly precisely because he has laboured to build up and polish all the details with such punctilious observation: the chit-chat of the men in the mess interrupted by a whistle in the air and the firing of the first cannonball from the French lines; a horse, struggling to its feet on the battlefield when its rider has been shot dead; two soldiers dragging their comrade through the mud, his throat gurgling, his mouth dripping blood; Nikolay Rostov's marvellously touching and believable thoughts when, wounded, he watches the approach of French soldiers — 'Can they be coming at me? What for? To kill me? *Me*, whom everyone likes so much?';[13] Tushin, suddenly finding himself for no apparent reason weeping as he parts from Prince Andrey:[14] all these details seem so natural that one might think that the scenes of Schön Graben wrote themselves. They are, indeed, highly literary devices. Tolstoy conceded that in writing them he owed much to the battle scene of Stendhal's *The Charterhouse of Parma*. But mere detail is not enough to explain their vigour, their unforgettable life. Solzhenitsyn's *August 1914*, which tries to imitate them, is just an accumulation of detail with no life at all; it shows what *War and Peace* would be like if it had not been written by a great genius. Tolstoy's inner daemon and his wife's tireless penmanship were the essential ingredients which made the book possible.

But from April until November there was a silence while he rewrote and replanned the development of the epic. From the point of view of an editor, Tolstoy was not an ideal contributor, and nor was *1805* — magnificent as it is — an ideal serial novel. It is too stately in its sweep; there are too few cliffhangers — by the melodramatic standards of the nineteenth century — to guarantee that readers will buy the next issue to see what happens next. That is part of the interest of Tolstoy's story. We all want to know who Natasha will marry, but we all know what happened to Napoleon. His story really is, in this sense, epic, a retelling of national myth, which is comparable, in Russian terms, with Homer.

Katkov was fortunate, however, to have other irons in the fire. One could say that no editor of any periodical ever had such good fortune as he. For, while Tolstoy bided his time with *1805*, Dostoyevsky was sitting in Wiesbaden wondering how to extricate himself from an appalling financial crisis, the result of a gambling bout. Since marriage, Tolstoy had been largely cured of gambling; and, since the death of two of his brothers (he inherited a good share of their estates) he had a regular source of income apart from his literary work. He could afford the leisure to pause for a whole year while he considered how his novel should proceed. Dostoyevsky could not afford such luxuries. He was desperate. He had no income — no money at all to pay hotel bills. So, in September 1865, he dashed off a famous letter to Katkov suggesting to him the story of *Crime and Punishment*.[15] Katkov bought the idea. 'Later I found out,' Dostoyevsky was to write, 'that he was only too glad to accept my offer because he had nothing else for that year. Turgenev has not written anything and he has quarrelled with Lev Tolstoy.'[16] He had not exactly quarrelled with Tolstoy, though he was displeased by his inability to produce at an appropriately regular rate. Though there was a St. Petersburg rumour of a quarrel between author and editor, Tolstoy denied it in his next dispatch to Alexandrine. It was, in fact, no rumour which caused the silence. It was the commercial astuteness of Tolstoy's wife. Tolstoy was cock-a-hoop that he had got Katkov to pay twenty-five roubles for each printed page of *1805*. But Sofya Andreyevna had a belief in volume publication. This was to cause many rows in future years, when Tolstoy tried to give away copyright and generally behave, from a business point of view, like a fool. His wife always clung to the view that a writer's fortune derives from his income from *books*. Everything else, for her, was illusory. Katkov may pay a lot of money for the serial of *1805*, but a serial, once sold, is sold; a book goes on selling for years. Moreover, if everyone has run out to buy the serial, it would diminish the volume sales of *1805*. So Sofya urged Tolstoy to think again before sending any more chapters to Katkov. To supply the gap, Dostoyevsky wrote *Crime and Punishment*. Subscribers of *Russkii Vestnik* in 1866 thus enjoyed a literary feast such as has been enjoyed by few literary periodicals. January contained *Crime and Punishment*, the first twelve chapters. February, March and April had more of *1805* — taking us to the end of Part Two, Volume One in *War and Peace*. Then more *Crime and Punishment*. At this point, Tolstoy lighted upon a title for his story. He decided to call it *All's Well that Ends Well*. Prince Andrey lives, and recovers from his wounds, but when he realises how deeply his friend Pierre Bezukhov loves Natasha, he allows them to get married. Petya is not killed in battle. Sonya relinquishes Nikolay, so that he can marry Prince Andrey's sister. There is no appearance of Platon Karatayev, the peasant wiseacre whose conversation in prison leads to Pierre's spiritual awakening:

that awakening happens spontaneously. So, a very different novel in many ways was planned. Under Sofya Andreyevna's canny eye, the first volume, entitled *1805*, was published in June.

Biographers and literary historians have made surprisingly little of the fact that Dostoyevsky's and Tolstoy's masterpieces were both published at the same time, in the same periodical and by the same editor. Surprisingly little, too, has been made of the fact that there are distinct echoes each of the other in both the great books. How could they ignore each other? Each must have felt as he was writing his novel that he was bringing to birth a masterpiece such as Russian literature had never seen. In a sense, each was right. But there, in the selfsame publication, there was something of at least comparable greatness. They could not but be astonished and chagrined. The fact that they were silent about it has allowed their biographers to ignore the singular importance of this literary dog which does *not* bark in the night.

The area where we see them glancing at each other is in their reflections upon Napoleon. After the first instalment of *Crime and Punishment*, Dostoyevsky was mercilessly mocked and lampooned in a comic paper called *Iskra* (*The Spark* — not to be confused with the Communist paper of the same name founded in 1900 which survives to this day in Russia). The paper published a very funny parody of Dostoyevsky's wild, religio-sensational style, and in subsequent chapters this put rather a damper on Dostoyevsky. But, we are told by one of his most intelligent biographers, 'He felt no such constraint in dealing with the "Napoleonic" theme in the novel.'[17]

In March 1865, Napoleon III had published *The History of Julius Caesar* and the event had provoked reflections, in various European languages, upon the general theme of great men and their effect on history. Napoleon III, writing in the shadow of his distinguished grandfather, argued that providence threw up such men as Julius Caesar, Charlemagne and Napoleon to pave the path which people have to follow and thus complete in a few years the work of centuries. Such men stamp their genius on a whole era.

In the Russian press the book was greeted as a piece of self-defence by the Imperial author. But *The Contemporary*, in one of the last issues before it was closed down by the censor, carried a long review of the book in which it pointed out a fascinating moral consequence of Napoleon III's idea. If it is true that men of destiny are, as he argued, essentially different from other men, it must follow they are governed by different morals, and different logics. It would follow that there was one logic and one set of logics by which you would judge the actions of ordinary men and another set of criteria by which you would judge heroes, demigods and geniuses.

The Contemporary went on to ask the fascinating question, how can we recognise immortals? Supposing there was a man whom all his friends and acquaintances took to be an ordinary mortal but who was in fact a Napoleonic genius. Would this not secretly entitle him to disregard the ordinary laws of morality? For such a person, might it not be acceptable, for instance, to commit a murder, just as it might be permissible for a man of destiny to start a war or a revolution in which thousands of his fellow mortals would be killed? The substance of all this *Contemporary* article is absorbed entirely into *Crime and Punishment*: we find it echoed, almost word for word, in the speech of the detective Porfiry Petrovich in Part III, chapter 5; all the 'Napoleonic' theories are attributed to the criminal Raskolnikov himself. There is a good example here of how one senses Tolstoy and Dostoyevsky straining to disagree with one another through the medium not of overt public controversy but through the different artistic presentation of an idea. The differences reveal so much about both men, both as individuals and as writers. Dostoyevsky, who was by now preoccupied with an apocalyptic dread of socialism, made the 'Napoleonic' theme an occasion for meditating first on the nature of personal evil, and secondly something of a prophecy about the shape of things to come. Raskolnikov, who (before his redemption through the prostitute Sonya) scorns personal morality, and has decided that all the great men in history could be described as 'criminals', is both the terrifying emanation of a Dostoyevskian idea of human nature, and a prophetic figure. Dostoyevsky was thrilled that after he had begun the story just such a murder as Raskolnikov commits was in fact perpetrated by a student called Danilov.[18] He would have been even more thrilled and disgusted by the close resemblances between Raskolnikov and Lenin in his brutal notions of what is forgivable in a man of destiny. Dostoyevsky's use of the Napoleonic idea is terrible, melodramatic, and yet plausible. Tolstoy's hero, Pierre Bezukhov, is completely unlike the crazed murderer Raskolnikov of Dostoyevsky's imagination. Pierre (who was to become the Decembrist in the finished novel) is an idealistic fellow, who believes in the initial stages of the book that Napoleon is a great deliverer of mankind, and gets so carried away with his imagination that he actually imagines himself to *be* Napoleon.[19] But no one could be further from Raskolnikov. Here we have a case of Tolstoy making one of his characters adopt his own habit of so identifying with a character that he almost imagines himself to be that person. What is most striking of all is that Dostoyevsky, in spite of all his moral protestations, fundamentally accepts the Napoelonic idea — he accepts, that is to say, the cant that there are 'men of destiny' who change history. Tolstoy, as he laboured at his book, was to distance himself further and further from that point of view and, indeed, to rewrite history in order to establish his point of view. His idealisation of Kutuzov, who appears to sit back and let things happen, who allows the French into Moscow, who allows it to burn, knowing that the great Russian winter and the spirit of the Russian people will eventually be too much for the Napoleonic armies, is only a small part of Tolstoy's prolix attempt to distance himself from any point of view which might have come the reader's way when perusing *Crime and Punishment*. It is obsessive; in the finished version we have two appendices and numerous asides assuring us of the falsehood of the 'Napoleonic idea', and grinding on and on about 'the forces that move nations'.

> In regard to the migration of the peoples it does not enter anyone's head today to suppose that the renovation of the European world depended on Attila's caprice. The farther back in history our observation lies, the more doubtful does the free will of those concerned in the event become, the more manifest the law of inevitability.[20]

*　　*　　*　　*

There were plenty of interruptions to work, and the Tolstoys would not have been the Tolstoys if they had not, even in this period of comparative harmony, kept up a measure of marital tension. After the birth of their son Ilya in May 1866, Sofya Andreyevna plunged into a period of melancholy, and poured out her sorrows to her diary: she had difficulty in feeding the new baby, painful breasts, exhaustion. Worst of all, however, were the torments of jealousy. Tolstoy had engaged a new bailiff to manage the estate, and was spending far more time than Sofya liked in the company of the bailiff's animated young wife. 'She is an attractive young woman and a "nihilist".' Sofya was tortured by Tolstoy's fondness for this crop-headed young blue-stocking. While she imagined, each time he set foot outside the house, that Tolstoy and this Marya Ivanovna were committing adultery, he was totally insensitive to her fantasies. He returned saying how fascinated he was by Marya Ivanovna's conversation, or how sorry he felt for such a clever young woman being forced to lead such a dull life in the country. This was fine talk to the wife he had exiled from Moscow and forced to lead the life of a country bumpkin. 'She is in the drawing room with the children,' Sofya scribbled, 'and I have shut myself in my room. I simply cannot endure her. It enrages me to see her beauty and high spirits, especially in the company of Lyovochka.'[21]

It is true that Marya Ivanovna did provide a distraction from the great work, but Sofya (who in her memoirs cannot even remember Marya's surname) had no reason to fear. Tolstoy was always delighted by the company of clever, animated women, but he was not committing adultery with his new friend. In fact, he found her very slightly ridiculous. In August of that year, when the Dyakovs visited Yasnaya Polyana, he suggested that, instead of the usual charades after dinner, they should try to enact a play. He produced the manuscript of a magnificent little comedy which he had composed — a play in three acts entitled. . . . *The Nihilist*! In the play, Tolstoy reverses the sexes. A happy, conventionally married couple in the country are visited by some young people, one of whom, a student, is full of the new nihilist ideas. The husband gets the absurd idea that his wife and the student are carrying on an affair, but in the end everything is resolved. Sofya Andreyevna played the role of the husband in Tolstoy's drawing-room production, and Tanya her sister put up a spirited performance as his flirtatious wife. Dyakov, whom Tolstoy had loved so besottedly in their youth, played the beautiful student, and Tolstoy's sister Marya played the part of a religious pilgrim. Thus were their inner emotional difficulties externalised and laughed away.

Something more serious which distracted Tolstoy's attention in that summer of 1866 was a macabre real-life drama which drew him back into his military past.[22] Colonel Yunosha, a neighbour who often went riding and hunting with Tolstoy, was in charge of a court martial. The other two officers of the court were a twenty-one-year-old man called Kolokoltsov and a man called Stasyulevich, who had been with Tolstoy in the Caucasus thirteen years before. A private in the 2nd Company of their regiment (65th Moscow Infantry) had assaulted his captain. They could not find anyone to act in this man's defence. Would Tolstoy oblige? The court martial was fixed for July 16, 1866.

Private Vasily Shabunin was probably a very typical Russian soldier, and a desire to reacquaint himself with the breed, as he wrote and rewrote the military experiences of Nikolay Rostov and Prince Andrey, perhaps played some part in Tolstoy's willingness to break off his work on *War and Peace* and to do his best for the defendant in this hopeless case. Shabunin was twenty-four years old, rather overweight and red, and deeply alcoholic. He seems to have spent most of his spare time lying on his bunk drinking *sivukha*, the poisonous local brandy, and muttering psalms or passages from the Gospels. One day his cruel captain, one Yasevich, gave Shabunin a report to copy out for the battalion commander, and when the poor private had finished his labour, the captain merely crumpled it up and threw it in his face. Shabunin, understandably, hit the man in the face, with the words, 'Take that in your ugly Polish mug.' When it was reported to the Adjutant-General of the Moscow Military District, it was decreed that Shabunin be court-martialled under Article 604 of the code of military regulations. This had been introduced under the draconian Nicholas I, who had gradually come to disregard the century-old tradition that there was no death penalty in Russia. 'Raising a hand or weapon against a superior,' stated the regulation, 'is to be punished by death.'

So, Tolstoy had a case of life and death on his hands. By the time he had taken on the case of defending Shabunin, the wretched man had already signed a full confession of guilt. Tolstoy had two interviews with him before the trial, and found him dull and unresponsive.

What could Tolstoy have done to save this man? He took the line of defence — very interesting in the light of his later obsessions with suicide — that Shabunin would not have made a confession of guilt unless he had *wanted* to die. The fact that he had confessed, before the trial, and knowing that his offence was punishable by death, meant — Tolstoy averred — that Shabunin was suicidal. (The more obvious explanation, that Shabunin was just stupid, must have been clear to everyone taking part in the trial.) But if he was suicidal, Tolstoy argued, then the balance of his mind was disturbed; if he was mad, then he should have been pleading insanity and diminished responsibilities. Tolstoy bungled this line of defence. He failed to get an independent medical examination of his client, and he ignored the fact that an army doctor had already examined Shabunin and found him to be sane. He therefore failed to get the man off, and Shabunin was sentenced to death. Tolstoy wrote at once to Alexandrine in St. Petersburg to get a pardon directly from the Tsar, but, there being no grounds for such a pardon, Shabunin did not escape. He was executed by firing squad, quite near Tolstoy's home, on August 9. They did it in style, with drummers and other musicians.

Years later, in 1903, a paper called *Pravo*, trying to rake muck, carried an article by a witness of the trial, who claimed, unsurprisingly, that there was a great contrast between Tolstoy who, in 1866, argued the case in a formal way, and the old anarchist Tolstoy of the 1890s who would have disputed the right of the court martial to be convened at all. Yes, there is a contrast; but so what? When the Tolstoyan disciples found out about the Shabunin affair, they were shocked. His first biographer, Biryukov, questioned the Master about the Shabunin trial and in 1908 got an abject and gerontic account of the whole matter: 'That incident had much more influence on my life than all the seemingly more important events of life; the loss or recovery of wealth, successes or failures in literature, even the loss of people close to me.' To *Pravo* he wrote, 'It was absolutely horrible to me now to reread my pitiful, disgusting speech for the defence which you have printed. . . . Speaking of the most obvious offence against the laws of God and man which some men were preparing to commit against their brother, I did nothing better than cite some stupid words written by somebody else called laws. . . .'

We can be certain that Shabunin would have had an even smaller chance of reprieve had his defence counsel not cited these stupid things called laws in court. The pacifist saint of 1908 was disgusted by the thought of Shabunin's fate, as is the modern reader. But for Tolstoy the novelist in his full vigour in the summer of 1866, it all looked and seemed very different. It may be right, as some have suggested, that Pierre Bezukhov's thoughts about the wickedness and horror of firing squads in *War and Peace* reflect the author's experience of July-August that year. But probably what rankled in Tolstoy's subconscious when he recalled the summer was that the incident had made no moral impression at all. He admitted to Aylmer Maude that the court martial was one of only four occasions in his whole life that he had ever spoken in public. And 'this was the time he did so with the most assurance and satisfaction to himself'. There is no evidence that he lay awake at nights worrying about the fate of the pathetic Shabunin. Tolstoy had *War and Peace* to think about. It was a wet summer, and the family were much indoors nursing colds. Tolstoy was out a lot shooting snipe. There is a death on his mind, or a potential death, as his letters reveal. His beloved Dyakov had lent him a horse, but the animal had grown weak. After a few days out on this horse Tolstoy wrote to a friend that the creature was only fit for the knacker's yard, and that the only part of her which would go home would be her hide and her collar. But, 'her death is not going to be on my conscience. I have been travelling very slowly.'

Meanwhile, preparations were under way for Sofya Andreyevna's nameday. They had a party, and asked the officers who, a month before, had presided over Shabunin's execution. There was dancing at Yasnaya Polyana, with a little hired band. They were the very musicians who had played while Shabunin was led out before the firing squad.

*   *   *   *

The man who would no more get worked up by a massacre of the Poles than he would complain to his butcher for killing meat soon put the Shabunin affair behind him. In September, he took Sofya's brother Stepan, who was becoming one of his best friends, to explore the battlefield of Borodino. He wrote to his wife on September 27, 'I have just come back from Borodino. I am very, very pleased with the trip, and even with the way I stood it, given the lack of sleep and decent food. If only God will give me good health and tranquillity, I'll write the best Battle of Borodino yet!'[23] And, in the next few months, he did.

Research went on. Some of the scholars emphasise how much Tolstoy had to read in order to write *War and Peace*. Others point out that, although he turned over a lot of material, he did not really read very closely. The events of 1805 and 1812 became for him imagined events, and where history did not fit in with what he wanted to happen, he rode roughshod over the facts. Readers of the novel, moreover, quickly notice that although he had done his homework for such setpieces as the Battle of Borodino, what makes the book live is a series of infinitely personal vignettes. The book is unforgettable and endlessly rereadable not because of the accuracy or thoroughness of its historical research, but because each character in turn is imagined with all the intensity of Tolstoy's being. He *is* each character in turn, acting them with all the vigour of his family at charades.

By this stage, the autumn of 1866, Tolstoy had decided to take

Sofya's advice and publish the novel himself in volume form. It meant borrowing a thousand roubles (some of which he immediately spent on a fur hat and boots)[24] but in the end it was a good investment. He went to Moscow to talk to an illustrator in November. The illustrator Tolstoy chose was Mikhail Sergeyevich Bashilov, who was distantly related to Sofya Andreyevna, and who was at the very top of his profession, having done famous illustrations for Griboyedov and Saltykov-Shchedrin. Tolstoy's many letters to Bashilov make fascinating reading, emphasising not merely how much he cared about the finished book, but also how vividly he saw each scene and each character in his mind's eye. If Bashilov sent a sketch which displeased Tolstoy, he got a quick letter back telling him what was wrong. They are not angry, offensive letters, but they have an eye for everything: Bagration should be wearing an astrakhan cap — the fur hat Bashilov had given him is out of period. Bashilov has made Prince Andrey slightly too affected — but he is urged not to spoil it: if that's the best he can do, he should leave it as it is. Kutuzov and Dolokhov are both splendid, but can't Bashilov make Dolokhov stick his chest out a little more? Make him more military! The advice pours out, revealing that all the characters in *War and Peace* are just as real to Tolstoy — more real, really — than characters in real life.

The title *War and Peace* was finally arrived at by March 1867. In the summer of 1867, Tolstoy revised *1805*, and cut it quite heavily. It was then announced that a four-volume work entitled *War and Peace* would soon be published. In March 1868 another notice appeared in the Moscow and St. Petersburg papers. The projected work would be now in five volumes, but anyone who subscribed to the four already in preparation would get the fifth volume free! By then, three volumes were in the bookshops and selling very well. Lest it should be thought of simply as a novel — rather than a great piece of national myth-making — Tolstoy published his famous article 'A Few Words about *War and Peace*' in the March number of *The Russian Archives*. Not long after this article appeared, a fourth volume appeared, and the fifth and sixth volumes appeared in 1869.

By now, the ending was considerably different from anything envisaged when he had started work in 1865. The urge to contradict Napoleon III, and Dostoyevsky, had become stronger than the original conception, which had been to write a preface or prehistory to the Decembrist Rising. That idea had not yet been discarded, but the book which he had now completed had taken on its own shape and developed

245

its own power over Tolstoy himself. There is a sort of exhausted anachronism about the conclusion. Pierre is not a man of 1812 preparing to grow into a man of 1825. He is much more a man of 1869, preparing to grow into he knows not what.

Chapter Eleven

The Shadow of Death

1869 - 1872

'What am I frightened of?'
'Of me,' answered the voice of Death. 'I am here!'

Memoirs of a Madman

W*ar and Peace* was published, finished.[1] Most writers feel, having completed a book, a sense of imaginative depletion. How can they ever repeat the act? The greater the book, perhaps, the greater the sense of letdown. To be in full, physical vigour and to have completed, at the age of forty-one, the greatest masterpiece in prose fiction inevitably produced a generalised feeling of gloom. This feeling was reinforced by spending the summer of 1869 reading the lugubrious philosophical writings of Schopenhauer. 'I'm certain,' he told Fet, 'that Schopenhauer is the most brilliant of men.'[2]

Now that he had conquered his gambling habit and written a book which, thanks to his wife's advice to publish it himself in volume form, had made his fortune, Tolstoy had on his hands both cash and time. Happening to see an estate advertised for sale in the province of Penza, he set off on impulse towards the end of August 1869 to look at it. It was a difficult journey, involving many changes of conveyance and finally, when the coach service gave out at Saransk, the hiring of private horses. On September 2, before he got to Saransk, he found himself overcome by exhaustion, and decided to spend the night at a place called Arzamas. He took a room at an inn, went to bed, but was too exhausted to sleep. He wrote a letter two days later describing the experience to his wife:

It was two o'clock in the morning. I was terribly tired, I wanted to go to sleep and I felt perfectly well. But suddenly I was overcome by despair, fear and terror, the like of which I have never experienced before. I'll tell you all the details of this feeling later: but I've never experienced such an agonising feeling before and may God preserve anyone else from experiencing it.[3]

The *mauvais quart d'heure* was to be absorbed and transformed into Tolstoy's inner personal mythology, and when he wrote it up as an unsuccessful short story fifteen years later, it is interesting to see what details he heightened and invented. First, the narrator of the story is not an artist, still less a great genius, but a man whose experience has been like everybody else's. As a boy he had indulged in the same filthy vices as all boys do, and as a man he had given himself up to lust. The only difference between this man (who is a civil servant) and the rest of the human race is that he has a heart more full of pity. Since childhood, he has not been able to tolerate the thought of human beings punishing each other. The sight of a serf boy being whipped threw him into tantrums, and he screamed when a pious nurse told him about the Passion of Christ. In the end, these moments of panic — taking the form of confrontation with death, and the pointlessness of existence — are resolved by religious reawakening and by reading the Gospels.

It is all a good example, in miniature, of the way that Tolstoy liked to rewrite experience and disguise from himself its true significance. After the actual night at Arzamas, he did not have a religious conversion. That was some years in the future. Likewise, though he had had moments of horror at human barbarity — as when he watched a public execution by guillotine during his visit to Paris — he was also capable of being a normal man of his time. As a soldier, he had supervised beatings, and in the recent case of Shabunin, he had not manifested any neurotic distress at the man's unavoidable fate. So the Christian pacifist version of the night at Arzamas is rewritten after the event. Tolstoy never published the story; it is an unfinished fragment, which in psychological terms makes no sort of sense. It was himself, not the reading public, that he was trying to convince.

Within the kernel of the story, however, there are two features which recur again and again from this point onwards in Tolstoy's life and which, it is believable, formed part of the original waking nightmare.

First, the title: *Memoirs of a Madman*. The narrator of the tale has just been assessed by the doctors, and after some disputing he has been declared sane. But he himself is not so sure. Nor, we may imagine, was Tolstoy. What afflicted him in that dreadful night of mental torture at Arzamas was a sense of dislocation. The mind, which had discovered in the grand design of fiction a new harmony, a peace such as it had not known before, now threatened to fly off into nightmare regions, and to afflict him with two completely contradictory horrors. The madman of the story cannot get away from himself:

> I am always with myself, I am my own torturer. Here I am, the whole of me. . . . it is myself that I am tired of, and whom I find intolerable and a torture. I want to fall asleep and forget myself but I can't. I can't get away from myself.[4]

On the other hand, although he longs for oblivion, his horror of himself is only rivalled by his dread of death. At the heart of the story there is an hallucinatory experience which was to occur to Tolstoy several times over the next few years.

> 'But what folly is this?' I told myself. 'Why am I depressed? What am I frightened of?'
> 'Of me,' answered the voice of Death. 'I am here!'[5]

The Arzamas experience was a confrontation with the hideous and inescapable fact of death. 'Life and death somehow merged into one another.'[6] He was now unable to think of anything in life without realising that all action, all feeling, all achievement, all desire would one day be swallowed up and rendered pointless by death. He need not have spent the summer reading Schopenhauer to arrive at this fairly obvious truth, but the German pessimist cannot have helped what turned out to be less an intellectual conviction than a psychological crisis.

What had begun in *War and Peace* as an exercise in mythology — a reconstruction of his personal and national history — had ended in a series of unanswerable questions: what forces move the nations? Why do things happen? Why are we here? In Tolstoy's personal life, this was quickly translated, with the help of Schopenhauer, into 'What is the point of anything?' We know that we have nothing to look forward to but death. The fatalism which characterised *War and Peace* began to get a grip on his soul. He told his wife, 'I believe in

God, in the expression in the Gospel that not one hair falls unless willed by the Lord. Therefore I say that all is predestined.'[7]

*   *   *   *

But this belief did not answer the question of what he should be doing. Presumably, had he absorbed a true belief in predestination with every particle of his being, he would simply have abandoned himself to the will of providence and perhaps spent the rest of his life as a farmer. But it is a characteristic of people who say that they believe in predestination that actually they appear to live by the will. Half the engineers, missionaries, businessmen, doctors and civil servants in the British Empire were Calvinists, but that did not stop them thinking that their own presence was essential to the smooth running of things in every corner of the globe from Saskatchewan to New South Wales. Tolstoy spent the next two or three years in a frenzy of intellectual activity, wrestling with his vocation as a novelist. In the first winter after he had completed *War and Peace* he spent much of the time in bed with influenza, and deciding that his true calling was to be a dramatist. He read plays omnivorously — Pushkin, Gogol, Molière (phrases from whose work stuck in his head for the rest of his days; whenever he needs a satirical twist in his later controversial essays he borrows from Molière), Goethe and Shakespeare. As he lay in bed, he began to think up plays of his own. This was hardly a restful experience. The characters started to jabber in his head. When he got better, he was able to indulge his passion for skating, and the idea of writing for the theatre seemed to get blown away in the icy air.

Fet, with whom Tolstoy kept up a lively correspondence throughout 1870, excited his friend's envy by getting a bicycle. *There* would be a new craze, something to occupy himself. 'I envy you,' Tolstoy wrote. 'I am depressed and writing nothing, though I *toil* painfully.'[8] That was in November 1871. Two months later, a letter to Fet revealed that Tolstoy had discovered something even more exciting than riding a bicycle: Greek.[9] The very thing!

Tolstoy had an extraordinary capacity for learning languages. To his French, German, English, rudimentary Latin, Turkish and Arabic (with smatterings of Georgian picked up in the Caucasus) he now added ancient Greek. He began with Aesop and Xenophon. Soon he was reading Herodotus and Homer. After only three months of learning the language, he claimed to have mastered a working knowledge of it. When he made this boast, during a visit to Moscow, a professor of Greek claimed that it was impossible. A volume of Herodotus was produced and Tolstoy was put to the test. When the professor who had been studying the language all his life corrected Tolstoy's reading of a word here or there with typical self-confidence the novice hotly defended his own interpretation. But the professor was compelled to admit that Tolstoy's Greek was every bit as good as he claimed. It took its toll. He worked at it so ferociously that he became ill again. His wife complained that he was muttering Greek in his sleep. He justified himself by saying that he was *living* in Athens. 'Not for nothing is this a dead language,' remarked his wife sourly, 'for it brings a man to a dead state of mind.'[10]

But for Tolstoy, it was, at that moment, everything. 'Without a knowledge of Greek,' he said — rightly, surely — 'there is no education.'[11]

*   *   *   *

His early ambition to be an educator was revived during this fallow period. As well as the children on the estates at Yasnaya Polyana, he had his own children to think about. By 1871, Sergey, the eldest, was eight, Tanya was seven and Ilya was five. Two more had been added to the brood: Lev, born in 1869, and Marya — invariably known as Masha and in grown-up life very much her father's favourite — in 1870. Pregnancy had become an almost permanent condition of life for Tolstoy's unfortunate wife. Little Lev had hardly been weaned before she feared herself to be once more with child. 'With each new child,' she wrote philosophically in her journal, 'one sacrifices a little more of one's life and accepts an even heavier burden of perennial anxieties and illnesses.'[12]

But for her husband, the thought of new minds to educate, new little beings to boss into a correct way of viewing the world was irresistibly tempting.

As so often happened when Tolstoy embarked upon something with repellent intentions, he produced sublime results. Throughout the fall of 1871, he and his wife worked on an ABC book for children. If *War and Peace* had proved him to be the Russian Homer, his ABC book is written by the Russian Aesop. He tells stories about his dogs, Milton and Bulka. He retells old Indian or Arabic legends, Bible stories and folk tales, and he makes up stories of his own, some of which, such as *A Prisoner in the Caucasus* are great works of art, elegant, concisely told, and completely simple. Some of his ABC book is still in use in primary schools in the Soviet Union today, so perfectly adapted are the stories for a young child learning to read. Moreover, although heavily moral (as we should expect), they are marked by humour and in reading them, we can almost hear the voice of him who was so popular with the children in the Yasnaya Polyana school. Tolstoy reopened the school in January 1872 and set to work teaching the children from his book. In addition to stories and legends, the book contains sections of elementary science and mathematics. But the book was to be a difficult one to publish. In the first place, Tolstoy did his usual annoying trick of summoning back the proofs, and scribbling over them time and again, so that the printers became totally confused as to what they should be setting up on the page. Another difficulty was that the censor was displeased by the book. At that time, education was rigidly controlled by the Government, and it was forbidden to start schools without permission from the Minister of Education. The fact that the Minister of Education, Count Dmitry Tolstoy, was a cousin doubtless explains why the book was not suppressed altogether, but the Government did not like the ABC book, while the literary establishment thought that the author of *War and Peace* was wasting his time with these educational concerns. Tolstoy got it in the neck from all sides.

He found the matter disillusioning, and wrote Strakhov an extremely interesting letter on March 25, 1872. Strakhov, like all intelligent liberals, had bemoaned the fact that Russia was so oppressive and intolerant. Tolstoy's reaction to this is self-contradictory:

You are right that we have no freedom for science and literature, but you see this as a misfortune and I don't. True, it wouldn't enter the head of a Frenchman, or a German or an Englishman, unless he's a madman, to pause in my place and ponder whether his methods were false or whether the language we write in and I have written in is false, but the Russian, unless he is insane, must ponder and ask himself: should he go on writing, or rather dictating his precious thoughts, or should he recall that even *Poor Liza* [a sentimental and rubbishy story of Karamzin] was read with enthusiasm and praised by somebody, and look for a different method and a different language?[13]

Tolstoy, with his enviable ability to say and see two things at once embraces the challenge of being Russian (and the restraints it puts on the writer). And while he throws up his hands in despair at the fact that he is obliged to go on writing in the Russian language, he complains in the same letter about 'our idiotic literature'. The literary language in Russian is in his view 'spineless; so spoilt that whatever nonsense you write looks like literature'. He suggests that it is only possible to write in Russian if one rejects any sort of 'literary' ambition, and tries to discover a plain, unvarnished style. It is for this reason that he has found so helpful the exercise of writing simple tales in the ABC. At the same time, he specifically hates the sort of nonsense talked by the Slavophil writers, who imply that there is something inherently beautiful in the Russian language. He wants what is 'clear, beautiful and unpretentious'. It is very much what American writers, from the era of Scott Fitzgerald onwards, felt about 'literary English'. Tolstoy looked for a new source of vigour in the language. But what is so typical of him is his double attitude. On the one hand, he thinks he might have found it if not in the language of peasants, at least in language which might be understood by the peasants (the 'deeds and language such as men do use'). On the other hand, the letter keeps open the extraordinary option of going quite another way, of abandoning the struggle to be a Russian writer and choosing some other language in which to express himself. Any Russian of his class and education could, at that period, have written just as easily in French, so the option was a real one.

*   *   *   *

Later in 1872, there occurred an incident which did, indeed, very nearly prompt him to emigrate — simply to stop being that intolerable thing, a Russian.

The previous year, he had bought an estate of sixty-seven thousand acres in Samara near Buzuluk. 'The country is beautiful,' he had written, 'in its age — it is just emerging from its virginity — in its richness, its health, and especially in its unperverted population.'[14] Tolstoy loved the nomadic people, the Bashkirs, who wandered in the hills and plains of Samara. They were living a way of life untouched by anything which had happened in the last thousand years; they were like tribesmen described by Herodotus. Also, with his great penchant for peasant minorities, with their beliefs and cultures, Tolstoy was

255

enchanted by a sect who flourished in the outlying Samaran villages of his estates — the Molokans. They were simple Bible Christians, who held the Orthodox Church, the Government and indeed most forms of human activity in abomination. They followed what they took to be a simple Bible creed, which involved imitating the prophet Elijah and John the Baptist (though not Jesus himself) in abstaining from alcohol. Their name means milk-drinkers, and this part of Russia was famous for its *kumys*, fermented mare's milk which tastes not unlike a rough yoghourt. Tolstoy loved the stuff, and had, on more than one occasion, been to Samara for the *kumys* 'cure', which meant living on mare's milk for months at a time.

In the summer of 1872, in spite of the fact that he was now a landowner there, he only had time for a brief visit. But exactly the same thing happened as had occurred when he took the *kumys* cure in Samara back in 1862: in his absence, Yasnaya Polyana suffered a police raid.

It happened that a bull ran wild on the farm at Yasnaya Polyana and gored a young herdsman. The Tula magistrate, a thrusting young liberal whom Tolstoy disliked, said that it was possible that the landlord (absent though he may have been) was responsible in law for this accident. The police arrived, and on his return, Tolstoy was placed, in effect, under house arrest, being told that he was not allowed to leave his estate until an inquest had established what had happened.

It was almost certainly at this period that Tolstoy, confined to Yasnaya, wrote his story *God Sees the Truth but Waits*, a tale which he was to add to the ABC book. It is a story which strikes a new note in Tolstoy's feelings of anger and alienation with his own country. The protagonist, Aksyonov, is falsely accused of murder, flogged with the knout, and sent to exile in Siberia. After twenty-six years he meets the real murderer, Makar Semyonich. If Aksyonov turns the murderer in to the authorities, he will be free. He does not. The murderer, before escaping through an underground tunnel, begs Aksyonov's forgiveness. But the past is beyond forgiveness. '"God will forgive you!" said he. "Perhaps I am one hundred times worse than you are!" And at these words, his heart lightened, and the yearning for home left him. . . .'[15] He dies, less in a state of Christian blessedness than in one of almost Buddhist detachment. If one tried to date this story just in terms of what we know about Tolstoy's biography, one would almost certainly think it was very late: a product of years in which he had hated the Government, expressed disillusionment with the penal system, fallen in and out of love with Christianity and bred his own new breed of religion based on Oriental detachment. In fact, *God Sees the Truth but Waits* anticipates all that. It is a good example of how, in artists' lives at least, life really does imitate art. Tolstoy was unconsciously trying on new masks which in future he would wear, not on the page, but in his own persona.

His immediate, lordly instinct, while having this trouble with a wild bull and a petty local police official, was to write direct to the Government. Old Prince Bolkonsky in *War and Peace* would have done just the same. But the Prince would not, as Tolstoy did, have expressed the desire to get out of Russia altogether. Tolstoy began to hanker after the land of the free and dreamed of living in Bournemouth. He wrote in almost apoplectic outrage to his cousin Alexandrine in St. Petersburg:

> It's dreadful to think of, dreadful to recall all the vile things that they have done, are doing, and will do to me.
>
> It's intolerable for a man like me, with a grey beard and six children, with the consciousness of a useful industrious life, with the firm conviction that I can't be guilty, with the contempt that I can't help feeling for the new courts from what I've seen of them, with the sole desire to be left in peace as I leave everyone in peace — it's intolerable to live in Russia with the fear that any boy who doesn't like my face can make me sit on a bench before a court and then in jail. . . . I'll die of fury if I don't give vent to it. . . . If I don't die of fury and anguish in jail where they'll no doubt send me (I'm convinced that they hate me) I've decided to emigrate to England forever, or until such time as the freedom and dignity of every man is assured in our country.[16]

He had all his plans set. A rough calculation told him he was worth two hundred thousand roubles. The children loved their English governess, his wife spoke English well and loved all things English. Russia, as far as the Tolstoys were concerned, had *had it*. They planned to settle on the south coast of England near the good schools and the aristocratic families.

During September and October 1872, Tolstoy bombarded his cousin Alexandrine with long, repetitive, manic letters, telling the story of the gored herdsman again and again. To add to his troubles Sofya

Andreyevna became ill with suspected mastitis. 'Only in England,' he kept repeating, 'is the freedom of the individual guaranteed.'[17] But by the end of October, the crisis was passed. The charges were withdrawn. It turned out the examining magistrate was legally in the wrong in holding Tolstoy responsible for the mad behaviour of his own bulls.*

Tolstoy's letters to Alexandrine, though they were no less long, fell to discussing matters other than the bull case and the condition of Russia. He gave her long descriptions of his children, of whom he was very fond. He was at that point singularly delighted by Ilya, a rather violent, 'sensual' boy, big for his six years, who had pleased the author of the ABC by making up a story of his own along similar lines. The story was this: a boy once asked, '"Does God have to go to the lavatory?" God punished him for asking this question, and the boy had to go to the lavatory every day for the rest of his life.'[18] These family letters are among the most delightful things Tolstoy wrote. In them the pugnacity and cheekiness which Ilya had inherited have a sort of crazy charm. He lays down the law, as he does in his 'serious' writings, but here, the laws he lays down have a *Through the Looking-glass* zaniness. 'There are two sorts of men — those who hunt and those who don't. Those who don't like children can pick them up in their arms; those who hunt have a feeling of fear, disgust and pity for babies. I don't know any exceptions to this rule. Try it out on your friends.'[19] Hilaire Belloc could have written that.

Being Russian, unless you are preternaturally stupid or wicked, produces violent inner tensions and conflicts, reflected in nearly all the great imaginative geniuses to emerge from Russia in the last two centuries. On the one hand, you know that you have been born into a 'God-bearing' nation, whose destiny is to keep burning the flame of truth while the other nations languish in decadence. (The truth may be Orthodox Christianity or the creeds of Marxist-Leninism, but the feeling is the same.) You know that the Russians are best at everything from poetry to gymnastics, and that they invented everything: ballet, bicycles, the internal combustion engine. You know that Russia has more soul than any other country — that its birch avenues, its snows, its ice, its summers are all the more glorious than the manifestations

---

* An irony of the case is that, in modern England at least, the owner of a bull who gored a farmhand would certainly be held responsible in law!

of nature in more benighted countries. There is only one drawback, which is that it is completely horrible to live there.

How can it be that the country chosen by God, or by the destiny which moves nations, or by the unseen inevitability of dialectical materialism, should have produced, in each succeeding generation, a political system which made life hell for the majority of inhabitants and which, every so often, threw up tyrants of truly horrifying stature? These are questions which have haunted in particular those few Russians who have ever been in Tolstoy's fortunate position of being able to choose whether to stay in Russia or to take the money and run. Today, we read precisely similar tensions in the utterances and writings of Soviet dissidents, and in particular Alexander Solzhenitsyn, whose hatred of his country's Government seems almost equally balanced by a fervent patriotism, a tragic knowledge that a Russian can only be himself when he is on his native soil.

A simple, though by no means exhaustive answer to the problem is: Peter the Great. He is the man who can be seen or said to have made Russia what it is. Every Russian schoolchild learns *The Bronze Horseman*. In that poem the little man, Yevgeny, whose love, whose house, and in the end whose life are swept away by floods, comes face to face with the great bronze statue of Peter, put up in the reign of Catherine the Great. All Russians have felt this to be an image of the suffering individual confronted by the heartless face of absolute power. For most Russians, this is the essence of their national tragedy; it is a tragedy which they seem pre-destined, every so often, to repeat. One thinks of the particular delight with which Stalin read the biographies of Peter the Great, his favourite historical hero.

Tolstoy, in good Pushkinian tradition, had a feeling of love-hate for Peter the Great, and his feelings of anger with the Government and isolation from Russia in all its official manifestations prompted him to plan an historical novel based on the tyrant. His feelings about Peter were much the same as his feelings about Napoleon. The idea of his novel would be to cut the superman down to size, to reveal him as cruel, vindictive, petty and, as far as his country's subsequent history was concerned, morally disastrous. It was Peter who had opened the window on to Europe. The Slavophil, 'Muscovite' side of Tolstoy could happily slay Peter for wishing to make Russia a European nation while, at the same time — lofty European and potential Bournemouth resident as Tolstoy was — attacking Peter for his fundamentally Slavic barbarism, his unshakeable tyranny, his having established a form of autocratic government from which decent people were still suffering.

Tolstoy's tremendous capacity to give himself over to an intellectual enthusiasm, to make himself the master of a subject, was thoroughly in evidence throughout 1872 as he accumulated a vast library on the subject of Peter. He made voluminous notes. In one book, he recorded in exact detail all the costume of the period. . . . 'What a period for a painter! Everywhere you look — a mystery which can only be penetrated by poetry. The whole secret of Russian life is there.'[20] Pushkin the poet had glanced at it, the seemingly terrible mystery that the Russian people almost wanted to be governed by brutes. But Tolstoy the writer of prose could not somehow get into it. It may seem paradoxical to say so, but Tolstoy had too much common sense to be able to understand it. In this sense, he was too Europeanised to get the hang of Russia — too Europeanised, and too aristocratic, independent and free. The essence of *The Bronze Horseman* is that the Russians are a slave race. The owner of two hundred thousand roubles, who would contemplate emigrating because he did not want to be bothered by the local police, had already moved out of a sphere in which this could be understood.

Also, the problem of Peter the Great and 'the whole secret of Russian life' was something quite exterior to Tolstoy. When he came into contact with it — as with the minor incident of the mad bull — he screamed with fury. The majority of Russians — then as now — lived with the presence of the autocratic regime the entire time. Those without money, and without the privileges of birth, had no choice but to submit to it. The secret of Russian life was therefore in a strange way quite alien to Tolstoy; and since he was only ever capable of writing about issues which directly affected himself, it is no surprise that the Peter the Great novel obstinately refused to come. 'I read, I take notes, I want to write, but I *cannot*.'[21] It was a desperate position.

'The period is too far removed from me,' he complained in March 1873, 'I can't put myself inside the people, they have nothing in common with us.'[22] (By 'us', he meant 'me'.) After what he claimed to be seventeen attempts to start the Peter the Great book, he decided to give it up.

*　　　*　　　*　　　*

Dostoyevsky

Pobedonostsev

Tolstoy organising famine relief in Samara, 1891

Tolstoy at home in the fields of Yasnaya Polyana. The peasant village can be seen in the background.

Tolstoy dressed as a pilgrim

Tolstoy with his daughter
Tatyana, about 1902

Family group, about 1902

Three of Tolstoy's sons (left to right, Ilya, Mikhail and Sergey) hunting wolves

The revolutionary leaders Lenin and Stalin

Priests and bishops in St. Petersburg in a procession in honour of Alexander Nevsky, the Russian warrior-saint

Aylmer Maude, Tolstoy's English translator and biographer

Sergey Taneyev, the composer with whom Sofya fell in love

Master and disciple: Vladimir Grigorevich Chertkov watches as Tolstoy writes.

Moscow, showing the river and (top left of picture) the cathedrals of the Kremlin, and 'Cathedral Square' within the Kremlin at Moscow. Tolstoy was married in the 'Cathedral' of the Nativity of the Blessed Virgin.

The Winter Palace of St. Petersburg

The only legacy of his Peter-obsession was the decision to call his sixth child, born in June 1872, after the architect of modern Russia. It was not a propitious naming. Tolstoy's wife was ill after the birth of little Pyotr, or Petyushka as they called him; Tolstoy moved the whole family to Samara for the summer, where the intense heat and fresh air did much to revivify the older children, but made life uncomfortable for the mother and baby. He survived, but only fourteen months. On November 9, 1873, Petyushka died of croup. 'I fed him for fourteen and a half months,' his mother wrote. 'What a bright, happy little boy — I loved my darling too much and now there is nothing. He was buried yesterday. I cannot reconcile the two Petyas, the living and the dead; they are both precious to me, but what does the living Petya, so bright and affectionate, have in common with the dead one, so cold and still and serious? He loved me very much — I wonder if it hurt him too to leave me?'[23]

That diary entry, surely, ranks high in the prose of nineteenth-century grief. It was their first great loss, the herald of a whole series of deaths in the family. Tolstoy, as the strangely disturbing experience at Arzamas had shown, did not need much prompting to give himself over to morbid reflections about death. Together with these reflections, there was the grey, middle-aged sense of disappointment with life. Natasha Rostova, the bright, animated essence of youthful energy, grew into the slightly frumpish and boring Natasha Bezukhova. It was a horrible knowledge, redeemed only by ideas of romantic love which were themselves, probably, illusory.

There was a good example of this truth in the life of one of Tolstoy's neighbours, back in the January of 1872. One of his neighbours, a landowner called Bibikov, cast off his mistress, Anna Stepanòvna Pirogova, and took up instead with the German governess of his children. The railroad had recently been extended into the Tula province, and in her despondency, Anna had rushed down to a piece of the track and thrown herself under a train. The corpse was taken to an engine shed which was an easy ride from Yasnaya Polyana. Tolstoy, who had never known the woman, cantered over for a squint at her mutilated remains. His early biographers relate how upsetting he found the experience without further remarking that few men would have exposed themselves to witnessing anything so horrible. The callousness is comparable to the ghoulish spirit which led him (nobody forced him) to witness the guillotining in Paris. Dickens, who loved going to mortuaries just to gaze at the waxy, grotesque inmates, would have fully understood. Tolstoy's dread of death has a love-hate quality. He did not record what thoughts passed through his head as he stood and looked at the mangled body of Anna Pirogova: nor why the desperate plight of a foolish woman should have succeeded where research into his nation's history had failed. It took time, but within a year he had started to write a novel about a woman called Anna who threw herself under a train.

Chapter Twelve
Anna Karenina
1872 - 1877

To us Russians, the most painful thing is that
in Russia even the Levins ponder over these
questions, whereas their only possible solution,
a specifically Russian one, and not for
Russians only, but for mankind as a whole, is
the moral, i.e. Christian approach to them. In
Europe such an approach is inconceivable,
although even there, sooner or later — after
floods of blood and one hundred million heads
— they will have to recognise it because in it
alone lies the solution.

Dostoyevsky, *The Diary of a Writer*

"'What am I frightened of?' "Of me," answered the voice of Death. "I am here!"' The voice which he had heard at Arzamas haunted Tolstoy and all his family in the middle 1870s. In 1874, Tolstoy's beloved aunt Toinette died, having spent the last fifty years almost continuously at Yasnaya Polyana. With her usual delicacy of feeling, she begged to be taken out of her room before she died. '"Look here, *mes chers amis*, my room is a good one and you will want it. If I die in it," (her voice trembled), "the recollection will be unpleasant to you, so move me somewhere else."' As she sank into unconsciousness, she wanted no one near her except '*cher Léon*'. Whenever she saw him, her face lit up with joy. When she died, Tolstoy felt unutterably sad 'that [he] had not been kind enough to her when she was alive'.[1] He wrote to Alexandrine, 'She was a wonderful being. Yesterday, as we carried her through the village we were stopped at every door: a peasant man or woman came out to the priest, gave him money asking him to say a prayer and took their farewell from her. And I knew, I knew that each stop was the recollection of many kind deeds that she had done. She lived here fifty years and never caused injury to anyone, not even any unpleasant feelings yet she feared death; she did not say that she feared it, but I saw that she did.'[2]

She left behind her a companion, an old woman, Natalya Petrovna, who almost immediately became deranged and, after painful scenes, Tolstoy and his wife had to get her taken into an asylum. Aunt Toinette's room was almost immediately occupied by his old Kazan aunt, Pelageya Yushkova, who was much aged and incapable of maintaining an establishment on her own; she had been living the last few years in a convent. Meanwhile, Sofya had another child, named Nikolay after Tolstoy's brother and father. He was not to live long. At only ten months, he died in howling agony of meningitis. That was in February 1875. Almost immediately afterwards, Sofya became pregnant again, and a month before her confinement, she reflected on the appalling boredom which had followed the numbness of their grief. Evenings were always the same. She sat darning, and watched her husband and his Aunt Pelageya playing 'endless horrible games of patience together'.[3] 'This year, God knows, I have struggled with these shameful feelings of boredom, and tried, all on my own, to assert my better self, and to reassure myself that it is best for the children, emotionally and physically, to live in the country, and I have managed to subdue my own selfish feelings, but then I realise to my horror that this turns into an appalling apathy and a dull, animal indifference to everything, which is even harder to struggle against. Besides, I am not on my own, I am tied to Lyovochka and the bonds have grown even tighter with the passing of the years, and I feel it is mainly because of him that I am sinking into this depression. It is painful for me to see him when he is like this, despondent and dejected for days and weeks on end, neither working nor writing, without energy or joy, just as though he had become reconciled to this position. It is a kind of emotional death, which I deplore in him.'[4]

A few weeks later, actual death returned. Sofya gave birth to a little girl called Varvara who died immediately afterwards, and not many weeks later Aunt Pelageya went the way of all aunts. As a boy Tolstoy had never much liked her. Yet, 'strange to say,' he confided in Alexandrine, 'the death of this octogenarian impressed me as never death did before. I was very sorry to lose her; she was the last link with my father's generation and that of my mother. I was very grieved to think of her suffering and there was in her death something else which I cannot describe and will tell you eventually. No day goes by that I do not think of her. That's quite easy for you others, the believers, but to us it is very hard.'[5]

To this succession of deaths in the immediate family, we have to add Tanya Kuzminskaya's poignant loss of a five-year-old daughter, and Sergey Tolstoy's loss of a two-year-old son, both in early 1873. Death, death and more death; marital disillusionment, and terrible boredom (the Russian word *skuchat'* means both to be bored and to pine or yearn): it is against this background that *Anna Karenina* was composed. It was a book which, much more than *War and Peace*, was purely a novel, but which at the same time contains all the seeds of Tolstoy's rejection of art. By the time he had finished it, he was confronting an emotional crisis, followed by an attempt at an artistic suicide every bit as final as Anna's actual suicide on the railroad.

Back in the summer of 1865 (that year in which, as he had confided to Fet, he felt at the height of his powers as a writer) Tolstoy had written a remarkable statement of his artistic creed. A prolific author called Pyotr Dmitriyevich Boborykin (1836-1921), who was unimpeachably progressive and up to date in all his views, had sent to Tolstoy his novels *The Forces of the Zemstvo* and *Setting Forth*. Both were thinly disguised pieces of autobiography and contemporary propaganda for the 'reformist' point of view. Boborykin would certainly have accepted the notion of his mentor Chernyshevsky* that the novel is just a sugar coating to make the ideas of the author palatable. This is a view of fiction which the Tolstoy who wrote *War and Peace* felt obliged to repudiate. He wrote a considered letter to Boborykin, thanking him for his two novels, explaining why he thought they were so bad. In part it was because they were sloppily composed, and poorly written. But the main thing was this: 'Both your novels are written on contemporary themes. Problems of the *zemstvo*, literature and the emancipation of women etc., obtrude with you in a polemical manner but these problems are not only not interesting in the world of art; they have no place there at all. Problems of the emancipation of women and of literary parties inevitably appear to you important in your literary Petersburg milieu, but all these problems splash about in a little puddle of dirty water which only seems like an ocean to those whom fate has set down in the middle of the puddle. The aims of art are incommensurate (as the mathematicians say) with social aims. The aim of an artist is not to solve a problem irrefutably, but to make people love life in all its countless, inexhaustible manifestations. If I were told that I could write a novel whereby I might irrefutably establish what seemed to me the correct point of view on all social problems, I would not even devote two hours to such a novel; but if I were to be told that what I should write would be read in about twenty years' time by those who are now children and that they would laugh

---

* Born in 1828, he was Tolstoy's exact contemporary, whose most famous novel was to suggest the title of one of Tolstoy's later books: *What is to be Done?*

and cry over it and love life, I would devote all my own life and all my energies to it.'[6]

There is such sunny common sense in all this that we might wonder how he could ever have come to abandon such a position. Ten years after the letter to Boborykin, the critic Mikhaylovsky pointed out a complete contrast between the expressed 'ideas' of Tolstoy, and the stuff of his life-enhancing fiction. Writing in *Fatherland Notes*, Mikhaylovsky expressed the view that Tolstoy was a brilliant thinker, as well as a novelist. The distinctive thing about Mikhaylovsky's essay is that he does not dismiss all Tolstoy's ideas (as many of his readers were beginning to do) and yearn for him to stick solely to psychological fiction. Nevertheless, Mikhaylovsky did see (and he saw it clearly, and remarkably early, in 1875) that *Anna Karenina* (at that stage unfinished) reveals, to an excruciating degree, the divisions and conflicts within Tolstoy himself. 'I shall only say that in this novel the traces of the drama going on in the author's soul are expressed incomparably more clearly than in any of his other works,' Mikhaylovsky wrote; and again, 'It is difficult even to imagine. . . . a writer bearing in his soul such a terrible dream as Count Tolstoy bears in his.'[7]

These remarks are thrown out in the course of a defence of Tolstoy as an intellectual: and Mikhaylovsky's essay is the starting point for what is perhaps the most brilliantly succinct of all studies of Tolstoy's ideas — that of Sir Isaiah Berlin.[8] Mikhaylovsky wants to kiss both Tolstoy's right hand (with which he wrote his ideas) and his left (with which he wrote his fiction). We, who might not be in the kissing business, can nevertheless value Mikhaylovsky's insight that *Anna Karenina* itself is the arena in which Tolstoy's self-conflicts and dramas are being fought.

A lot of this is inexplicable, but one element is not. Tolstoy was never so happy as when he was writing *War and Peace*. Had he been able to continue to write about the past, his happiness would have continued for much longer. But what he did not realise (indeed his imagination only functioned when he did not realise it) was that he needed to write about his own past. Then the magic worked. Paradoxically it was only by an egoistical concentration on himself that he could perform the illusion and make readers love life in all its countless, inexhaustible manifestations. In *War and Peace* he had been rearranging and rewriting his country's history as well as his own. In *Anna Karenina*, he strayed into 'contemporary themes'. What happened was that he started to use up the experience almost before he had had it. His art had always depended — sometimes to a conscious, sometimes to an unconscious degree — on drawing from life, with all the comforting possibilities of distortion, of laundering experience, which that offered. By the time he came to describe the marriage of Kitty and Levin, however, he was using not the past but the present, and something like a short circuit occurred in his brain. It is the purpose of this chapter to chronicle some of the processes which led up to this literary phenomenon.

*　　*　　*　　*

Like all Tolstoy's great works, *Anna Karenina* was a long time gestating and growing.⁹ But in this case, the longer he spent on it, the more he was involved in a semi-conscious attempt to destroy the original conception, the more he was apostasising from his view that the purpose of a novel was to make people laugh and cry over it; the more he was using the thing as 'a vehicle for establishing a correct point of view on all social problems. . . .' The delays in writing the book were not creative delays, but destructive.

In a letter to Strakhov which Tolstoy never sent, and which was not discovered until 1949, he explained the origins of *Anna Karenina*. In the spring of 1873, he happened to reread Pushkin's *Tales of Belkin*. 'Not only Pushkin but nothing else at all had ever aroused my admiration so much.'¹⁰ And in particular, he was struck by the fragment 'The guests were arriving at the country house. . . .' At once he set to work thinking up characters and events which went with this fragment. The unsent letter shows an authentic glimpse of inspiration itself. Pushkin simply acts as the catalyst for something which has been waiting there to be released.

'The guests,' wrote Tolstoy, 'assembled after the opera at Princess Vrasskaya's. . . .' Within *three weeks* he was able to write to Strakhov that the first draft of the book was almost complete.

This early version of *Anna Karenina* is simply the drama of Anna herself. In the first conception of the book, there was no such figure as Levin, no Kitty and therefore no reference to the social and spiritual problems which so preoccupied Levin in the finished book. Most revealingly, Anna began life, in his first scribblings, as Tatyana Pushkin. The story concerns the triangle alone — the woman, Gagin (the Vronsky figure) and the unfortunate husband. Anna has none of the beauty or charm which her admirers find in the published novel. She is plain with a low forehead, almost a snub nose, and no figure. 'So far and a little more and she would have been misshapen.'[11] An early note even adds the author's opinion that she is a 'disgusting woman'. The husband, who gives his consent to the divorce, rambles about, a heartbroken wretch, and dies at the end of one of these early drafts. The fate of the two lovers is uncertain. In one early version, Anna gets her divorce and settles down to a happily married life with Vronsky. About Vronsky-Gagin, by contrast, the author is uncontrolled in his admiration, praising his beauty, his charm and his many gifts. In one variant, he is actually described as a poet. All these descriptions were to be suppressed in the final version.

If it was Pushkin which set Tolstoy going, the seeds of the story itself had been sown years before. In February 1870, he had told his wife that he had the idea of writing a story about a married woman who was disgraced through a sexual scandal. His task would be to depict her 'not as culpable, but as uniquely worthy of pity. . . .' This idea faded. Presumably it was not unrelated to the fact that his sister, Marya Nikolayevna, had been in a similar position. As a family friend of the Berses, who had married young, Marya was looked upon as an almost aunt-like, or elder-sister figure to Sofya Andreyevna even before she married Marya's brother. Then, in her mid-thirties, Marya had 'gone to the bad' in the way that two of her three surviving brothers Dmitry and Sergey had done. She was animated, attractive, passionate. Turgenev liked to hint that he had had a *tendresse* for her in their youth. No less impulsive than her brothers, she had run away from her husband and got herself pregnant by a Swedish viscount. The husband (no Karenin: he had been frequently unfaithful to her) died in 1865, but Marya Nikolayevna continued for a while to live in Scandinavia while the 'scandal' died down.

'*Malheureusement le journal se tait précisément pendant les années où Tolstoï créa ses deux œuvres principales*,'* says the French edition of *Anna Karenina* sombrely, only half seeming to recognise that the two events might not be unconnected. The experience of his sister's disgrace gets put into the sausage machine, and is not spoilt by being analysed too soon, as it would have been had he kept a diary through

---

* 'Unfortunately the diary becomes silent during the very years when Tolstoy created his two main works.'[12]

this period. Memory — with all its rich powers to distort and to save — is the mother of the muses; memory, and not *reportage*.

Then again, there was the incident in January 1872, only a few *verst*s away from Yasnaya Polyana, when Anna Stepanovna Pirogova ran up the local railroad and threw herself under a train. There is a danger of isolating the suicide of Anna Stepanovna Pirogova and pushing ahead — after all, she has the same Christian name — the comparisons between her situation and Anna Karenina's beyond any point where such a comparison would hold. Two things to bear in mind with this death, when we imagine ourselves back into that engine shed of 1872, are the extreme novelty of the railroad (whereas we take it for granted) and the absolute normality of suicide (which for us is shocking). Dostoyevsky, in a famous issue of his *The Diary of a Writer*, dwells on the horrific fact that there are people who commit suicide for no apparent reason. He also makes the sweepingly theological point that 'neither man nor nation can exist without a sublime idea. And on earth there is but one sublime idea — namely the idea of the immortality of man's soul — since all other "sublime" ideas of life, which give life to man, *are merely derived from this one idea.*'[13]

Tolstoy, whose nihilism went deeper than Dostoyevsky's, and whose egotism was more self-protective, could never really see this, even though in his novels — and above all in *Anna Karenina* — life itself is so potently and lovingly drawn. Goldenweiser describes a conversation with Tolstoy when he was a holy old man. 'I can't understand why people look upon suicide as a crime. It seems to me to be a man's right. It gives a man the chance of dying when he no longer wishes to live. The Stoics thought like that.'[14]

Those who draw an immediate correlation between the suicide of Pirogova and that of Tolstoy's fictional heroine sometimes fail to notice that in the neighbour's suicide there was a motive, in the novel there is none. Film versions and précis always try to provide Anna with reasons. They tell us that she feels intolerably torn between love for Vronsky and that for her little son Seryozha. But as she says herself she has abandoned Seryozha and been perfectly happy to do so while 'another love' satisfied her. The 'decision' that Vronsky no longer loves her is completely irrational. The core of her despair is a madness which we glimpse as she lies alone on her bed four chapters before the end, dosed with opium and watching shadows dance around the room. '"Death," she thought. And such panic seized her that it was a long time before she realised where she was and with a trembling hand could find the matches to light another candle in the place of the one that had guttered and gone out. No — anything — only to live. . . .'[15] This is the sort of crazy state which Tolstoy himself was to enter during the closing stages of the novel when, as he tells us, he had to hide ropes and guns from himself for fear of yielding to temptation. His later sparring partner, Konstantin Pobedonostsev, was only one of many pens to muse upon this terrible disease which befell not just Tolstoy, but hundreds of thinking Russians at this period. Why it should have done so perhaps only a Jungian analysis of the collective unconscious could fathom. The Russians simply wanted to destroy themselves. What else explains their history in the last hundred years?

> The ancients [Pobedonostsev wrote] were accustomed to place a skeleton or a skull in the midst of their banqueting halls that they might be reminded of the proximity of death. This custom has decayed: we feast and make merry and strive to banish all thoughts of death. Nevertheless, at the back of each stands death and his threatening face at any moment may appear before us.
>
> Every morning brings news of suicides, those suicides unexplained and inexplicable which threaten to become a familiar feature of our lives. Never has there been a time when the human soul was valued at so low a price, when there reigned such indifference to the fate of men created in the image of God and redeemed by the blood of Christ. Rich and poor, learned and ignorant, age and youth which has hardly begun life, nay the very tottering infant, throw away their lives with inconceivable recklessness.[16]

The novel, in such circumstances, could not survive without reflecting the mores and concerns of the hour. Tolstoy's creed of artistic independence, expressed to Boborykin, became ultimately impossible. Like Anna reading the English novel, he chose action in preference to reading; and yet, like her, was confronted by the terrible pointlessness of existence.

The railroad itself (if we revert for one more moment to the corpse of Pirogova, and Tolstoy staring at its mangled remains) has for us a less obviously spiritual connotation; but that was not so in the nineteenth century. Tolstoy was one of those who had lapped up *Dombey and Son*, with its many images of railroads as a destruction of 'real life'; and what was true of Victorian England was no less true of the virgin soil of Russia.

The railroads have been called 'symbols of modern Russia with its interrelated process of spiritual destruction and material progress'. Alexander II had been a passionate railroad builder. Before his reign, Russia had had fewer miles of railroad track than any country in Europe — only seven hundred and fifty miles in the whole of the Empire at the time of the Crimean War. The 'boom' in the railroads had taken place while Tolstoy was studying educational method, learning Greek, writing *War and Peace*, having children. By the time of Pirogova's suicide there were over fourteen thousand miles of track in different parts of the Empire.[17] Count E. F. Kankrim (Minister of Finance, 1823-1844) had put his finger on precisely what was wrong with railroads, as far as the Russians were concerned. If you built them, it would encourage people to *travel*.[18] The size of Russia to us moderns implies a challenge that we might fly all over it, or see it from the window of a car or don our tracksuits and spend a day or week on the Trans-Siberian Express. Distance for us implies distance covered. Before the advent of the railroad — and, come to that, of roads — distance was something which almost by definition could not be covered. So, when a westernising liberal in 1836 moaned that 'we Russians' were '*solitaires dans le monde, nous n'avons rien donné au monde, nous n'avons rien appris du monde, nous n'avons pas versé une seule idée dans la masse des idées humaines*',* he was expressing exactly what the Slavophils, and the great majority of Russians, liked about their country, and still do.

In the same year that Tolstoy looked at the mangled body of Anna Pirogova, the Rector of the Riga Theological Seminary was asked to bless a new railroad bridge. In his speech, he said, 'conflicting thoughts rise up the soul when looking on a new route like this. What is it going to bring us? . . . . Will it not in part be the expeditor of that would-be civilisation, which under the guise of a false all-humanity and a common brotherhood of all. . . . destroys true humanity, true brotherhood?'[20]

So, in the very image of the train with which he begins and ends the developed story of *Anna Karenina*, Tolstoy is not able to escape the

* '. . . . alone in the world, we have given nothing to the world, we have learnt nothing from the world, we have poured not a single idea into the mass of human ideas. . . .'[19]

contemporary issues which he had originally felt were inimical to artistic creation. The railroad comes to him ready-made with foreboding.

The intense importance to Tolstoy of distance, space, virgin territory unvisited and untrammelled, is shown in the fact that the year before this suicide, he had bought that sixty-seven thousand acre estate in Samara. His love of the people there, the Bashkirs and the Molokans, heralded a new sense of inspiration, of alienation, in Tolstoy. He had always preferred Yasnaya Polyana to Moscow. He had always preferred country neighbours to the 'literary set' of St. Petersburg. He had always preferred to be monarch of all he surveyed rather than a man in a clique or a crowd. But the move to Samara provided a chance of yet further isolation from the mainstream. He was feeling precisely the sense of alienation from life which made Anna Karenina's intensely-felt existence ultimately intolerable.

As we know, Tolstoy's method of 'limbering up' before writing fiction of his own was to read an English novel. When he wrote to Alexandrine asking her for letters of introduction to the best English families, and expatiating upon the freedoms of English society, he was almost certainly deep in some favourite Trollope. He is known to have read *The Prime Minister* with fascination, and to have been inspired by the ghastly railroad suicide of Lopez in that novel. The power of English fiction to absorb the imagination shapes an important moment in *Anna Karenina* when the heroine, who has not yet quite admitted to herself that she has fallen in love with Vronsky, settles down in the Moscow to St. Petersburg train with an English novel — surely a Trollope — on her lap.

Anna Arkadyevna read and understood, but it was not pleasant for her to read, that is to follow the reflection of the lives of other people.[21]

Reading is an image of life in this novel. Hundreds of pages later, when the whole tragedy of her love affair with Vronsky has unfolded and she decides, so arbitrarily, to throw herself under a train, her life itself is described as a book. 'And the candle, by whose light she had been reading a book filled with alarms, deceptions, grief and evil, flared up with a light brighter than ever before, illumined for her everything which formerly had been dark, guttered, grew dim, and went out forever.'[22] Yet Anna's distaste for the very process of reading, when we are first introduced to it, appears to be a simple Platonic distrust of art — the characters in the novel are only the *reflections* of nature. But her objection, as the next sentence shows, is the reverse of Platonic. It is not because she wishes to see into the life of things that the novel wearies her. It is because the life of the characters in fiction somehow or another threatens her own life. She is at one and the same time too exuberant for this world, and envious of these 'reflections'. It is an extraordinary series of thoughts to place into the mind of a woman sitting in a train, trying not to think about being in love with another man. And although Tolstoy tries to make the scene relevant to the Vronsky-Anna liaison (so that the guilt of the adulterous milord becomes her guilt) he appears to be describing, with great vividness, a sensation which has no particular place in the book. '"I think there's a pain somewhere in the room," said Mrs. Gradgrind, "but I couldn't positively say that I have got it."'[23] There are many such moments of dislocation in *Anna Karenina*. 'She herself too much wanted to live. When she read how the heroine of the novel looked after a sick man, she herself wanted to move about the sickroom with noiseless footsteps; when she read how a member of Parliament had made a speech, she wanted to have made the speech herself; when she read how Lady Mary rode to hounds, or teased her sister-in-law, or amazed everyone by her bravery, she wanted to do it herself. But there was nothing to do, and while her little hands played with the smooth paper-knife, she continued to read. . . .'[24]

It is almost an enactment of Hallam's advice to Tennyson: 'You cannot live in art.' Tolstoy knew you couldn't, but he could not live anywhere else either — least of all in Russia, which was, quite simply, unbearable.

The longing to act, to do, to be a man of action rather than a man of letters was much in evidence in the period of gestation, and of early drafts for *Anna Karenina*. Eighteen seventy-two had been dominated by writing and publishing his ABC and simple stories for children, by concern for the education of the children at Yasnaya Polyana. In 1873, he spent the whole summer in Samara, and witnessed the failure of the crops there. It was the first time in his life that he was to become involved in famine relief. On this occasion, the casualties were comparatively minor. Through relations in Moscow and St. Petersburg he was able to alert the richer classes to what was needed, and two million roubles were raised for the relief of the hungry. Tolstoy liked this sort of work. For all his inability to be, either within himself or domestically, a good man, he was in love with goodness and yearned to do good deeds. He was also, as a laird and a soldier *manqué*, very good at organising things when he gave his mind to them. Distressing as it was to contemplate the plight of the poor, it provided him with the most urgent excuse to stop working on *Anna Karenina*.

*　　　*　　　*　　　*

The tortuous progress of the novel, after its first, fine, careless rapture, more than explains its ultimate shape. Since no one has ever put a satisfactory date on all the variants, it is hard to know how much Tolstoy was kidding himself when he announced to Fet (in September 1873) that 'I am completing a novel that I had already begun'.[25] We are told by his wife that by then the novel was 'all sketched out' but that he had not written anything all summer.[26] Strakhov read a version of the manuscript in July 1874. His comment reveals that it was still entirely the story of Anna and her suicide. 'The internal story of passion is the main thing and it explains everything. Anna kills herself with an egoistic aim, still serving that same passion; it is the inevitable result. . . . of the direction that was taken from the very beginning. . . .'[27] But at about the same time, Tolstoy was writing to Alexandrine that he was going to stop the novel (which he was having printed) 'so much do I dislike it; but I am busy with practical matters, namely pedagogy; I am organising a school. . . .'[28] Strakhov larded Tolstoy with praise, for 'the amazing freshness, the absolute originality' of the book, and this 'almost got me interested again. But. . . . it is terribly disgusting and nasty.'[29] By October 1874, he announced that he had definitely decided to abandon the novel.

Then, quite suddenly, he wrote to Fet, 'An indispensable purchase of land in Nikolskoye has come up for which I must borrow ten thousand for a year on the security of the land. It may be, perhaps, that you have money that you have to invest.'[30] Fet refused to lend the money — perhaps he did not have it to lend — and it was then that Tolstoy once again entered into negotiations with Mikhail Katkov, the editor of *Russkii Vestnik*.

One must not think of Katkov merely as a figure of Grub Street. He had direct political power — his power over Dmitry Tolstoy or Konstantin Pobedonostsev was of a kind which would have been less easily exercised had his earlier dreams of a representative form of government been realised. There is no reason to suppose that Katkov was corrupt, or that he was anything but sincere in his belief that a combination of Russian military strength and Russian religion would save the world. Dostoyevsky — another friend — was peddling the same idea week after week in *The Diary of a Writer*.

If one thinks of Lev Tolstoy as an essentially subversive figure in political terms, his association with Katkov might seem a little surprising. But money is money. He knew that he would be happier publishing the book with the left-wing Nekrasov, to whom he wrote, asking if Nekrasov could match Katkov's offer of five hundred roubles per sheet. It was a forty sheet novel. The twenty thousand roubles which were on offer would pay for his land in Nikolskoye and leave him its value in cash all over again. Strakhov, watching these negotiations aghast, said, surely accurately, that it was an 'as yet unheard of price for a novel'.[31]

But signing the contract with Katkov did not make it any easier to get on with the work. Between January 1875, when Tolstoy got his first payment, and summer 1877 he was writing the book, but there were very long interruptions. In the summer of 1875, for example, he was able to say 'For two months I have not stained my hands with ink or my heart with thoughts. Now, however, I am taking up the tedious, banal Karenina with the sole desire of making some space for myself more quickly — leisure for other pursuits, not only pedagogical, which I love, but wish to drop.'[32]

This highly attractive indolence and cynicism is recorded for us by the painter Ivan Kramskoy in his *Letters to P. M. Tretyakov*. Kramskoy initially visited the Tolstoys at Yasnaya and tried to persuade Tolstoy to sit for his portrait. He was surprised by how young Tolstoy seemed — only a man in his mid-forties. He had expected more grey hair, more solemnity. But there were lots of laughs. Kramskoy had been commissioned to do the picture for the Tretyakov Gallery. His normal rate was one thousand roubles per canvas. Before he could even start work, the Tolstoys (their twenty thousand for the new novel guaranteed) had beaten him down to an agreement that he would paint a group portrait of the family for two hundred and fifty roubles. Then work could begin. After this initial loss of his virginity as a subject for painters, Tolstoy always enormously enjoyed having his portrait painted, and he could write to Fet: 'I sit and chat with him and try to convert him from his Petersburg faith to the Christian one.'[33]

As has been well observed, 'Kramskoy did not dream that while he was painting the portrait of the author of *War and Peace* Tolstoy was doing as much for him and that he would reappear in *Anna Karenina* as the painter Mikhaylov.'

As well as a good eye for a face, Kramskoy had a good ear for dialogue. Here is a snatch from a walk they took together.

Kramskoy: What do you respect?

Tolstoy: The Samara wilderness, with its farmers, the Bashkirs, about whom Herodotus could have written. Homer ought to have done it and I don't know how. I'm studying. I've even learned Greek to read Homer. He sings and shouts and it's all the truth. Peace comes in the steppe.

K: But how's your novel, Lev Nikolayevich?

T: I don't know. One thing's certain. Anna's going to die — vengeance will be wreaked on her. She wanted to rethink life in her own way.

K: How should one think?

T: One must try to live by the faith which one has sucked in with one's mother's milk and without arrogance of the mind.

K: You mean, believe in the Church?

T: Look, the sky's cleared. It is pale blue. One has to believe that the pale blue up there is solid vault. Otherwise one would believe in revolution. . . .[34]

Tolstoy only had half an interest in the novel by this stage. Left hand and right hand were both trying to write at once, with peculiar results. The first four issues of *Russkii Vestnik* in 1875 contained Parts I, II and the first ten chapters of Part III. There was then complete silence until 1876, when the public were allowed to read of Levin mowing the fields, and Karenin discovering his wife's unfaithfulness. The book was not complete until 1877.

It was in the summer of 1874, that is, about a year after the novel's original inception, that Tolstoy introduced the character of Levin, and the vast subplot which was to balance, or overwhelm, the story of Anna herself. Thereafter, the simplicity of the book, its self-contained shape, was to be exploded into something altogether grander and more diffuse. 'It is Levin,' John Bayley remarks in his telling phrase, 'who liberates the novel from itself.'[35]

No one can fail to see that Levin is an autobiographical figure, and the extent to which this novel is a mere substitute for the journals which Tolstoy was not at the time keeping is aesthetically astonishing. The maid in Levin's house, Agafya Mikhaylovna, has exactly the same name as one of Tolstoy's maids at Yasnaya Polyana. Levin's wastrel brother is in every minute particular a portrait of Tolstoy's brother Dmitry, and the death of Nikolay in the novel bears strong resemblance to the death of Dmitry in Tolstoy's reminiscences. Levin's proposal to Kitty is exactly the same as the way in which Tolstoy proposed to Sofya Andreyevna. So is the painfully intimate scene in which he insists on showing his young bride his diaries, and makes her weep. Levin's increasing preoccupations with the duties of a landlord and with educating and liberating the peasants are all simple transcriptions of things which existed in the surface of Tolstoy's mind when he was writing the book. No ingestion has taken place at all. There have been gallant attempts to defend what Tolstoy himself called the 'architecture' of the novel, but by the time we are into the second half of the book it is hard to avoid agreeing with the view that it 'cannot even be called a novel, that it is a collection of photographs collected completely at random, without any general idea or plan.'[36] Turgenev, it will be remembered said, 'I don't like *Anna Karenina*, although there are some truly great pages in it (the races, the mowing, the hunting). But it's all sour, it reeks of Moscow, incense, old maids, Slavophilism, the nobility etc. . . . .' And again, 'The second part is trivial and boring.'[37]

Turgenev, however, very likely had private reasons for disliking the book. Among the legendary adulteries which formed part of Tolstoy's mental world was a Bers family secret. In 1833 Turgenev's mother gave birth to a natural daughter, almost certainly fathered by Dr. Bers, who was in turn to become Tolstoy's father-in-law. Like Anna, Varvara Petrovna went abroad to hide the scandal. Life, often so much neater than art, allowed her to return the following year, because her husband died.

Be that as it may, it is hard not to see what Turgenev meant. Even if one excepts the novel's second half from his censure — 'trivial and boring' — the extended Levin passages are not obviously justifiable in aesthetic terms. Part VI ends with Anna and Vronsky going to Moscow to establish themselves like a married couple. We wait another eight chapters before we meet Anna again, and meanwhile we have to read about Levin reading his book on rural economy to Professor Katavasov, or the death of such hitherto unheard of ('real') characters as the Countess Apraxina. There is nothing artistic, nothing planned about these interludes. We know that instead of 'getting on with his novel' he is doodling, palming us off with his own ideas and concerns.

And yet Professor Bayley is right. The book would be diminished without these extraordinarily open-ended structures. It is rather like wandering into what appears to be a new house. On our left the dining room, finished and complete, with its furniture, pictures, characters and conversation. On our right, however, we fling open the door of the ballroom and find ourselves in an open field, with the architect and builders still looking at the plans. One can make too much of this, and take too seriously Henry James's fastidious dismissal of Tolstoy's 'loose, baggy monsters'.[38] There is more 'structure' in *Anna Karenina* than in the novels of Dickens and Trollope. The Jamesian perception of the unities in fiction formed no part of the syllabus in the chaos where Tolstoy went to school. And one has to recognise, moreover, that in many of the diary passages in *Anna Karenina* — extensions of his diary mode is all they are really — there are scenes of unrivalled vividness and realism. One thinks of Kitty's *accouchement* which stays in the mind not only because of its photographic accuracy, but also because of the transparent — rather devastating — honesty with which feeling is transmuted. Levin attends — as Tolstoy did three times in the course of this novel's composition — his wife's *accouchement* and then looks down at his new-born child. 'What he felt towards this little being was absolutely not what he had expected. There was nothing gay or joyful in this feeling; on the contrary, it was a new, excruciating dread. It was the consciousness of a new area of vulnerability. And this consciousness was at first so excruciating, the fear was so powerful, that this helpless being might suffer, that he hardly noticed the strange feeling of senseless joy, and even of pride which he felt when the child sneezed.'[39]

Tolstoy's unrepentant lack of reasonableness in the face of childbirth is one of the great *givennesses* of the book. It is surely the earliest example in fiction of the specific discussion of birth control. Here, as throughout the book, he specifically flouts his own doctrine that novels should not be about issues of the day, and gives us an up-to-the-minute discussion, veiled in dotted lines between Anna and Dolly. '"*N'est-ce pas immoral?*" she said after a pause.' It is one of the best bits of the book and is a good example of the way the story is no longer a finite contrivance at which the novelist is working (in a manner which would have pleased Henry James) to contain his material, but a

280

great, open thing in which almost any modern preoccupation might find its relevance. Strangely enough in the very year that Tolstoy finished *Anna Karenina*, Charles Bradlaugh and Annie Besant were fighting a court battle to allow back into print Charles Knowlton's *Fruits of Philosophy or The Private Companion of Adult People*, a simple work of 1832 which recommended 'syringing the vagina soon after the male emission into it with some liquid'. The English judges were at one with Tolstoy and Dolly over the matter, and did not allow it to be reprinted.

How are we to explain the fact that although we recognise these divergencies and digressions for what they are, the book does have something which feels, at least the first couple of times we read it, like cohesion? The answer is of extreme relevance to Tolstoy's biographer, for it lies in the pure, unwatered egoism of the author. It has been rightly observed that Levin is not the only 'autobiographical' figure in the book, and that we can just as easily recognise Tolstoy in the figure of Anna herself. Self-preoccupation was the beginning and the end of Tolstoy's character, and it is out of the self, purely and not tirelessly, that the novel was born. 'The longer Levin went on mowing, the oftener he felt moments of oblivion, in which his arms did not seem to move the scythe, but the scythe itself, his whole body, so conscious of itself, so full of life, and as if by magic, regularly and definitely without a thought being given to it, the work did itself of its own accord. These were the most blessed moments.'[40]

This is what is happening in *Anna Karenina* itself. If we read how the book was written, we might assume that Tolstoy began with his original conception of the story, tired of it, and filled it up with a lot of his own 'thoughts' and passages from his own life. But this is not actually what happened. He was pouring himself into the book, writing it with his own sweat and blood. In order to work himself up into a sufficient level of interest and frenzy to write his historical fiction, whether the wholly fructiferous *War and Peace* or the abortive *The Decembrists* and *Peter the Great*, Tolstoy was in the habit of reading hundreds and hundreds of books, so as to have material on which his imagination could feast. Here, it is all different. He provides himself as the stuff of the story, as in the earlier much shorter pieces, *Childhood, Boyhood, Youth* and *The Cossacks*. In *The Cossacks*, he had given himself ten years to absorb and transform his experience. In *Anna Karenina*, as in his diaries, he was writing up the experience almost before he had had it. The result was to be more emotionally

281

draining than he could possibly have realised. He was in effect scouring himself for material, pouring his own feelings into the guilty Stiva, the striving Levin, the hopeless Anna. There is a crude sort of shape to the book, of course. It begins with an amoral man disillusioned with marriage, it ends with a moral man in a remarkably similar state of mind. Between this there are two railroad deaths, and an impossible attempt to live by romance. But the greatness of the book is not in its shape but its scenes, 'blessed moments', where the mower is so full of life that his movements have an existence of their own.

The great message of *Anna Karenina*, proclaimed more in the bits where the author is not proclaiming, just mowing, is this belief in *life*. Anna, who spontaneously wants to be, to live, not to view life through the lens of art or satire, is utterly unlike Karenin. She is a natural person, as is Kitty in the sickroom of her brother-in-law.

'Thou hast hid these things from the wise and prudent and hast revealed them unto babes,' thought Levin, while talking with his wife that night. Levin thought of the Gospel text not because he considered himself wise. He did not consider himself wise but he could not but know that he was cleverer than his wife and than Agafya Mikhaylovna, he could not but know that when he thought about death, he thought with all the powers of his soul. He knew also that many great and manly minds, whose thoughts on that subject he had read, had pondered it, but did not know the hundredth part of what his wife and Agafya Mikhaylovna knew.[41]

Tolstoy's daemon knew that outside the blessed moments, when the scythe moved automatically, he had nothing in him but ratiocination. He could rarely intuit. It is remarkable, for instance, that in this great love story, not one line is devoted to describing the actual development of the *affaire*. From the moment in the train returning from Moscow to St. Petersburg, we do not see Anna and Vronsky together until they are in Italy, when the thing is a *fait accompli*. He can describe their disillusionment with each other with the most chilling plausibility. But we never see them happy in their intimacy. Never having experienced such an *affaire*, he could not begin to describe it. The thing is as simple as that. The virginal Henry James gives us far more of the conspiratorial and guilty relationship between Kate Croy and Merton Densher in *The Wings of the Dove* than

Tolstoy does, with all his knowledge of 'life', of the love between Anna and Vronsky.

When scenes of intimacy are successful, they are often slotted into moments where the plot creaks with implausibility. One thinks of the setpiece when Anna returns in secret to see Seryozha. 'During the time they had been separated and under the influence of that gush of love which she had lately felt for him, she had always imagined him as a little fellow of four, the age when she loved him best. . . .'[42] And she is amazed to discover that he is actually nine. She, in fact, is not at this point consulted. It is Tolstoy who is working out how old the little boy is while Anna waits on the set and perfects her lines. Then he nods, and the camera begins to roll. The point of the scene is that, while the reader has been spared any blush-making intimacies with Vronsky, he is allowed the fullest possible view of her besotted love for her son. We are like the old servant Vasily Lukich, bursting in on the scene. 'He shook his head and sighed and closed the door again. "I will wait another ten minutes," he said to himself, coughing and wiping away his tears.'[43] The scene is deliberately 'touching', like a Victorian parlour song, or the slushier bits of Dickens. It is so well done that it has us in tears; but when we have recovered we can see what Tolstoy has been up to. It is stage-managed, and entirely different, as a rendering of intimacy, from, say, the spontaneity of the marital conversation in which Kitty and Levin are wondering whether Koznyshev will marry Mlle. Varenka.

'Well,' asked her husband when they were going home again.

'It doesn't work,' said Kitty with a smile and a manner of speaking reminiscent of her father, which Levin often observed in her with pleasure.

'How do you mean, doesn't work?'

'Like this,' she said, taking her husband's hand, raising it to her mouth and slightly touching it with her closed lips. 'It's like kissing the hand of a bishop.'

'But which of them doesn't it work for?' he said, laughing.

'For neither of them. It should have been like this.'

'There are some peasants coming.'

'No, they didn't see. . . .'[44]

There is never such a moment of erotic conspiracy between Vronsky and Anna. Anna's articulated wish to get out of the pages of a novel and into real life can't be realised by her creator, any more than his life with Sofya Andreyevna, of which we receive so many snapshots in this book, will quite consent to be wedged into fiction. Or rather Sofya Andreyevna and Lev Nikolayevich were making their own kind of fiction, a different, more lugubrious novel with an equally dramatic railroad ending. When describing moments which he had not lived Tolstoy could only — who has ever done it better? — analyse, penetrate, describe. But living, in this spontaneous sense, became more difficult.

The underlying tragedy, or logic, of *Anna Karenina* is amoral in a way that Tolstoy would later think of as 'Hindu'. The forces of life are irreconcilable and irresistible. 'Vengeance is mine' is an artistic tag, not a religious statement in this book. It is his own way of asserting control, while, with the other part of himself liking to quote Pushkin — 'my Tatyana has gone and got married, I should not have thought it of her' — a coy way of observing how the characters in a work of fiction get out of control and lead their own lives. The book prepares us for what is going to happen in Tolstoy's own life. It is on *him* that the vengeance falls; vengeance for using life, not living it, for observing, not being. What he instinctively reveres is naturalness: Levin's 'real' experience of the country rather than his liberal half-brother's theorising about it; or Kitty with her children. The counter-balance these scenes provide with those of Anna and Vronsky do not make us feel how virtuous family life is in the country compared with adultery in the city, or still worse, abroad. (This was the whiff that Turgenev caught when he thought of it as sour, reeking of incense.) On the contrary, all that matters is something much simpler than morality. It is that Anna is alive; alive to an almost vulgar degree. For most of the book, Vronsky, who is so unerringly well-observed, only exists as a piece of sex. We see him as he is, but we feel only what Anna feels.

This reverence for what is, in Tolstoy, is nothing like a Wordsworth-ian Romantic's feeling for nature. It is much simpler than that. It is being able to look at the sky as if it were a solid vault, and not to question. Tolstoy in this book is full of himself, of people, of places, of things, of grass, of sky — all just being themselves. The fact that we are alive is for Tolstoy the most interesting thing about us. And the most awe-inspiring thing is that this being — this awareness of rain on sweaty shoulders, or the agony of sexual guilt, or the excitement of love, or the warmth of a mother suckling her baby — can be snuffed out instantly, and made nothing. It is the passionate impulse to recapture life from this nothingness which impels his art.

*   *   *   *

That is why Levin and the many passages of the novel which appear extraneous to the central story of Anna and Vronsky are in the end so important not just to Tolstoy, but to us. These distinctions, of the kind made by lesser mortals — between art and life, between what should and should not go into a novel — no longer mean anything to Tolstoy. He is gasping for breath, panting to get out of his novel. And yet, though this is what (he assures us) it felt like from the inside, yet from the outside, it has the effect of magisterial *grandeur*. Tolstoy's famously blasé question — 'What's so difficult about writing a story of how an army officer gets entangled with a married woman?'[45] — would sound like some attempt at humility if it were a mere denigration of what, by any standards, must be one of the greatest novels in the history of literature. But what Tolstoy was saying was something that was not in the least humble. He was saying, 'So — O.K., I have written the greatest novel in the history of the world. But who's interested in *novels*? My task is bigger than that.' One sees the same process at work in the later novels of Turgenev where the private concerns of the characters are almost swamped — in *Smoke* for instance — by reflections on the contemporary scene.

As Tolstoy had observed when the coroner and the police bothered him over the death of his herdsman, Russia is not a place where you can be left alone. Being left alone is all that an artist wants, but countries which make this impossible inevitably and automatically create a class of articulate dissidents. 'It is unbearable to live in Russia.' It is this simple fact which lies behind and explains many of Tolstoy's more incomprehensible actions over the next thirty years. He had wanted to bury himself in Samara. He found only famine and incompetence which compelled him to become involved. And then, towards the close of 1876, the Russians began to behave in a morally indefensible fashion in Bulgaria, or so it seemed to Tolstoy. During the period when he was writing *Anna Karenina* a fever of pan-Slavism had gripped Russia. This was the idea that all Slavs, in whatever sovereign state they happened to reside, should look to Russia to protect them, their ethnic and above all their religious tradition. Dostoyevsky and other keen pan-Slavists (or, as we should call them, Russian expansionists) spoke fervently of an Orthodox revival, and of the ancient city of Tsargorod, or Constantinople, being 'restored' to the Russian Church and people by an invasion of Turkey. Tolstoy did not view the conversion of the world to Russian Orthodoxy with any particular enthusiasm. 'The God of Sabaoth and his son, the God of the priests, is just as little and ugly and impossible a God — indeed far more impossible — than a God of the flies would be for the priests, if the flies imagined him to be a huge fly only concerned with the wellbeing and improvement of the flies.'[46]

Throughout the summer of 1876, the Serbs and the Montenegrins were engaged in rebellions against their imperial masters, the Ottoman Turks. The Russians supported them, with the enthusiastic prayers of the Metropolitan of Moscow, with money and with volunteers. But in this first round, in spite of the fact (or perhaps because of the fact) that they were both Slavs, the Serbs and the Russians failed to cooperate and they were easily defeated by the Turks.

The European powers, and in particular the British (Disraeli was again Prime Minister) were anxious, once an armistice was signed, that Serbia should be protected from Turkish reprisals, but more anxious about the intentions of the Russians. It was not in the interests of any of the western powers, and least of all Great Britain, for the Russians to invade Constantinople; and it was this which they were pining to do. In November 1876, Alexander II referred to 'our volunteers who have paid with blood for the cause of Slavdom', and began to threaten that if 'Russia's just demands' were not fulfilled by the Turks, 'I firmly intend to act independently'.

The usual nonsense was gone through. Ambassadors were summoned to Constantinople. By March 31, 1877, Lord Derby, the Foreign Secretary, had found a 'peace formula', as we should now call it, which protected the interests of both the Turks and the Russians. A month later, on April 24, 1877, Russia declared war on Turkey. The war lasted about a year, and failed to result in a Russian Constantinople. The following year the Turks got a guarantee from Disraeli that the British would protect any invasion of Asiatic Turkey by the Russians. The main results of the war, which the Russians in the end won, were the creation of modern Bulgaria, and the beginning of British rule in Cyprus. So much for the aims of pan-Slavism.

Since, by now, *Anna Karenina* had become so much more than Tolstoy's novel — it was his equivalent of Dostoyevsky's *The Diary of a Writer* in which he could air his views to the huge public who bought *Russkii Vestnik* — it was inevitable that Tolstoy should devote his thoughts to the Turkish War. The outbreak of hostilities provided Tolstoy with a perfect way of rounding off his story. John Bayley notices even the very minor character Veslovsky, who has just got married, going off to the wars. 'Unobtrusive as it is, there is nothing naïf or pious about this touch. . . . So Veslovsky married recently, and now he is off to volunteer for the wars — well, well!'[47] Everything points the same way, and every touch is directed with deadly effect. John Bayley is right to draw attention to the cynicism with which the novel ends. The young men who go to volunteer to help the Serbs are all, like Vronsky, people who have something to get away from. We do not need to have it spelt out to us. Veslovsky, like everyone else in the Tolstoy *œuvre*, has found out soon enough that marriage is hell. That is his reason for taking the Tsar's shilling. Similarly, in the devastating conversation between Levin and Koznyshev about the war, the same point is made. 'In a nation of eighty millions there can always be found not hundreds, as is now the case, but tens of thousands of men who have lost their social position, happy-go-lucky people who are always ready to go. . . .'[48]

What now stands as Part VIII of the novel was on Katkov's desk by the time Part VII had gone to press. Anna had thrown herself under the train, followed by the words 'To be concluded'. But the novel never was concluded in *Russkii Vestnik*. Katkov tried to persuade Tolstoy to eliminate from Part VIII those passages which expressed cynicism or unbelief in the war effort against Turkey. Tolstoy refused to alter a word. From this time dated Tolstoy's view that the novel had an architecture, a link which was more than its characters or story could show. *Russkii Vestnik*, in its May issue, contained the following short note:

In the previous issue, the words 'To be concluded' were inserted at the foot of the novel *Anna Karenina*. But with the death of the heroine the novel proper finished. According to the author's plan a short epilogue of a couple of printer's sheets was to follow, from which readers learnt that Vronsky, in grief and bewilderment after Anna's death, left for Serbia as a volunteer, and that all the others were alive and well, but that Levin remained in the country and was angry with the Slavonic committees and the volunteers. The author will perhaps develop these chapters for a special edition of his novel.[49]

The whole episode is really quite funny. It is impossible not to feel that, simply as an editor, Katkov was right. With serial fiction, the audience wants to know what happens next. If one episode ends with a train running over the heroine's head, it is hard to see where the necessary element of suspense comes in to make readers buy the next instalment. Who, buying *Russkii Vestnik* to see 'what happens next' in Tolstoy's novel, is going to be interested in the inner life of Levin? And what reader of that arch-conservative periodical was going to want tirades against the war? Katkov obviously made the right decision, from his own narrow point of view. Tolstoy was furious, and wrote off to the editor of another periodical, *Novoye Vremya* (*New Time*), to explain what had happened. 'The masterly exposition of the last unpublished part of *Anna Karenina* makes one regret the fact that for three years the editor of *Russkii Vestnik* gave up so much space in his journal to this novel. With the same gracefulness and laconicism he could have recounted the whole novel in no more than ten lines.'[50]

This is very amusingly said, and it is a pity that we do not have more to and fro in this argument between Katkov and Tolstoy. Obviously, though Katkov was right as the editor of a periodical to turn down Part VIII, he was also right to hope that it would be printed when the novel reached book form. It is an essential part of the book, and it is essential reading for anyone who wants to understand Tolstoy himself. With an arbitrariness which does not seem to matter much (Shakespeare would have done the same, and probably did) Tolstoy gives to each of the characters in Part VIII his own thoughts, feelings and experiences, as though he were dealing out a small deck of cards. So, Vronsky remembers Anna's corpse, 'warm with recent life' and mangled as Pirogova's corpse had been when Tolstoy saw it in 1872; and all the characters in the end, except Kitty, are caught up in the inner drama which preoccupies Levin. Life is unanswerably trivial and pointless — Why am I here? What am I? An inability to answer these questions makes him want to commit suicide, but even in these very desperate moods, he felt in his soul 'the presence of an infallible judge deciding which of two possible actions was the better and which was the worst'.[51]

*　　　*　　　*　　　*

So in the 1870s we see the public and the private questions — Why am I here? What is Russia up to now? — converging on Tolstoy to produce a profound personal crisis. He was close to despair about himself, but he was a very long way from despair about Russia as a whole, and a long way from despairing about art. We must not leap ahead and imagine that Tolstoy aged forty-eight or forty-nine held the developed 'Tolstoyan' views with which he liked, aged seventy, to annoy his wife and friends.

Levin's view of Russia as eighty million *individuals*, very few of whom were much interested in Serbs, remains central to Tolstoy's common-sense spiritual quest. The highest manifestation of individualism was in artistic genius, and though he felt his own artistic career to be in ruins, he looked about hopefully at others.

He was jealously unable to see virtue in Turgenev, but in many of his other great artistic contemporaries, Tolstoy saw not only genius but hope: for the human race, for Russia. Reading *Virgin Soil* in March 1877, he was appalled. Paklin in that book says that it is Russia's misfortune that all the healthy people are bad and all the good people are ill. 'That is my own. . . . opinion of the novel,' said Tolstoy. 'The author is unwell.'[52]

But even this suggests an appetite for artists who are 'well', wholesome, and powerful in their expression of individual distinctiveness and freedom. A few months before, there had been a happy musical evening in Moscow when Tolstoy had met his great admirer Pyotr Ilyich Tchaikovsky — the beginning of something which could have been a friendship, had Tolstoy not spent the second of their meetings attacking Beethoven. Nevertheless, Nikolay Rubinstein and Tchaikovsky arranged a concert at the Moscow Conservatoire in Tolstoy's honour which he was unable to remember without 'trembling'. In Tchaikovsky's music, he would have heard those pure, wholesome strains which seemed absent in Turgenev, a wordless vision which recognised life's beauty and tragedy as inextricable.

Something of the same sort came to Tolstoy in his conversations with the poets, above all with the incomparable lyric poet Tyutchev. He described Tyutchev in these terms to Strakhov: 'He is a childlike old man of genius and majesty. Among the living I do not know anyone except you and him with whom I could feel and think so identically. But at a certain spiritual height the unity of views on life does not unite, as is the case in the lower spheres of activity for earthly aims, but leaves each person independent and free. . . . We are more strange to one another than my children are to me or even to you. But it is joyful along this deserted road to meet these strange travellers.'[53]

Fyodor Tyutchev expresses his thoughts in perfectly made lyrics, which is perhaps why he is not better known among non-Russian readers. The critics have probably been right to discern in his 'Schopenhauerian' sentiments many of the concerns of the latter part of *Anna Karenina*. Certainly, Tolstoy was reading a lot of Tyutchev at this date.

Лишь жить в самом себе умей -
Есть целый мир в душе твоей
Таинственно-волшебных дум…

[Know how to live within yourself. In your soul there is a whole world of mysterious-enchanted thoughts. . . .][54]

The spiritual solipsism which Tyutchev celebrates is balanced by a fascination with love which has its quite recognisable parallels in *Anna Karenina*. His strange poem 'Predestination' seems to speak of the impossibility of love ever being happy in terms which directly match poor Anna's wretched ravings.

И чем одно из них нежнее
В борьбе неравной двух сердец,
Тем неизбежней и вернее,
Любя, страдая, грустно млея,
Оно изноет наконец…

[And whichever is more tender in the unequal contest of two hearts, will more inescapably and surely — loving, suffering, languishing sadly, pine away at last.][55]

'In my opinion Tyutchev is the first poet,' said Tolstoy, 'then Lermontov, then Pushkin. . . . Tyutchev as a lyric poet is incomparably more profound than Pushkin.'

Tolstoy's friend Afanasy Fet had, after an interval, started to write poems again, which Tolstoy spontaneously admired. Like a true Tolstoyan man, Fet in his poems is often alone with nature, above all

alone beneath the stars, as in his lovely '*Na stoge sena noch'yu
yuzhnoi*'. On a southern night, lying on a rick and facing the night
sky, he asks the question:

> Я ль нёсся к бездне полуночной,
> Или сонмы звёзд ко мне неслись?

[Was I racing towards the midnight abyss, or were the hosts of stars
racing towards me?][56]

Stars were the theme of another poem which Fet sent to Tolstoy in
the very weeks in which he finished *Anna Karenina*. The last stanza
is singled out by Tolstoy for particular praise.

> Вот почему, когда дышать так трудно,
> Тебе отрадно так поднять чело
> С лица земли, где всё темно и скудно,
> К нам, в нашу глубь, где пышно и светло.

[That is why, when it is so hard to breathe, it is comforting to raise
your brow from the face of the earth, where all is dark and bare,
towards us, towards our infinity, where it is splendid and radiant.][57]

Tolstoy particularly liked the fact that in this poem the speakers are
not men, but the stars themselves. If he was repelled by a religion
where a lot of little flies appeared to be worshipping one big fly of
their own devising, Tolstoy had always recognised, in his life as well
as in his art, the littleness of man, the mysteriousness of existence. In
the questions which churned involuntarily and ceaselessly in his
mind, it was inevitable that he should seek, and find, religious solutions.

'Please,' he wrote to Strakhov in April 1877, as the last words of
Anna Karenina were sent to *Russkii Vestnik*, 'let's go as soon as
possible to the Optina monastery. . . .'[58]

*   *   *   *

The Optina Pustyn monastery was one of the great spiritual power-
houses of the Orthodox world. It is situated about two miles outside
the town of Kozyolsk, not far from Moscow. At the beginning of the
nineteenth century, it had almost dwindled out of existence, having

291

only three monks, one of whom was blind. But during the central years of the nineteenth century, Optina had witnessed a tremendous revival, along the pattern of monasteries on Mount Athos. A *skit*, or monastic village, had been built, where religious solitaries lived a semi-eremitical life under the direction of an elder or *starets*.

These *startsy*, who revived traditions of piety which had been all but forgotten in Russia for three hundred years, were viewed with some suspicion by the Church hierarchy. There was a danger of their becoming an autonomous spiritual force. Certainly, their wholehearted approach to Christianity had little in common with the secularised, state-established religion of the Moscow Patriarchate. At Optina, it was once more discovered that the Gospel was a demanding spiritual adventure, asking from the believer not a nominal allegiance, but a complete self-sacrifice. 'One can save oneself outside a monastery,' said one of the most famous *startsy*, 'but with great difficulty.'[59]

This saying occurs in a letter written by Starets Amvrosy (Father Ambrose) who, since the mid-sixties, had been chief *starets* at Optina. The door of the elder's cell was constantly thronged with visitors. They ranged from high-born young women who had driven over from Moscow to mock, to dispossessed pilgrims who believed that there was benediction in the man's very touch. Simple people consulted the *starets* as if he were the Delphic oracle. Should they marry? Should they sell a pig? Many came with more searching questions, and more complicated spiritual problems. The stories are legion of Starets Amvrosy turning the hearts of atheists, or shaming sinners into penitence. As a confessor and counsellor he was almost clairvoyant, with the gift recorded in other great spiritual masters (one thinks of the Curé d'Ars) of being able to see into people's past before they unburdened their souls. The Dostoyevskys visited him in 1878 when they lost a child, and Amvrosy's words to Anna Grigoryevna, which she found deeply consoling, were transcribed and used in her husband's accounts of the Elder Zosima in *The Brothers Karamazov*. The whole of the monastic part of *The Brothers Karamazov* is based closely upon Dostoyevsky's profound and pious relations with Starets Amvrosy.*

---

* The monks in the monastery, however, are reported not to have recognised the authenticity of the *starets* in the novel. (L. A. Zander, *Dostoyevsky*, p. 135, London, 1948.) See Linner, Chapter 4, for general discussion of differences between Starets Amvrosy and Starets Zosima.

It was to this place, the year before Dostoyevsky visited it, that Tolstoy and his friend Strakhov set off in July 1878. Like Zosima in the novel, Amvrosy is recorded to have been ill much of the time, and exhausted by his stream of visitors. But witnesses have reported that he was particularly fatigued by the visit of Tolstoy. Tolstoy was to visit him several times over the next twelve or thirteen years. On this first visit, he was 'impressed by his wisdom'.[60] We do not know exactly what passed between the two men, but from the surviving writings of Starets Amvrosy we know that the holy man would have been demanding and stern. Tolstoy was, emotionally, worn out, and he had no idea in what direction his life should now turn. Some such words as these, from the letters of the *starets*, were ringing in his ears as he left Optina: 'I have offered you my opinion and advice, but I do not force or seek to convince. You yourself must select what you want. The Lord Himself does not force anyone to do anything but only proposes voluntary selection, saying in the Gospel: "If thou desirest to enter into life, if thou desirest to be perfect", do such and such. However, know that these conditional commandments are so obligatory that if one does not fulfil them, one not only does not attain perfection, but one cannot inherit the blessed life of the age to come.'[61]

Chapter Thirteen
The Holy Man

1877 - 1884

At death, you break up: the bits that were you
Start speeding away from each other for ever
With no one to see.
                    Philip Larkin, *The Old Fools*

After *Anna Karenina*, Tolstoy attempted to revive his novel about the Decembrists. 'I am now deep in my reading about the 1820s,' he wrote to Alexandrine in January 1878, 'and I can't tell you the satisfaction I get as I envisage those times to myself. It is extraordinary, and pleasant, to think that a period which I can remember, the 1830s, has already passed into history.'[1]

He went to St. Petersburg and interviewed surviving Decembrists. In March 1878, he went to the notorious fortress of Peter and Paul, the prison where so many victims of the system had languished since the days of Peter the Great. 'They told me there that one of the criminals ate glass and then threw himself into the Neva. I can't tell you the strange and powerful feeling that came over me at the thought of that person. It was like the feeling I had when they brought me the handcuffs and the leg irons of 1825.'[2]

Yet somehow or another, this great work, which had been gestating in Tolstoy's mind longer since than *War and Peace*, was to be stillborn. His imagination was no longer fully engaged with the history of his own past or that of his country. Instead, it had become engaged with the eternally unanswerable questions which were aroused by his visit to the Optina Monastery. The daemon which imagined the early drafts of *1805* and *The Decembrists* had happily clothed itself in Pierre the agonised liberal; but the finished novel, *War and Peace*, had ended with Pierre the aspirant holy man. The same thing had happened with Levin in *Anna Karenina*. Tolstoy was slow to catch up with the poses of his own inner imagination, but when he did so, it was with exaggerated force.

In the spring of 1878, Turgenev in Paris had been pleased, but warily surprised, by a penitent letter which he received from Tolstoy: 'Forgive me if I have been at fault in any way with regard to you.'[3] Tolstoy begged his fellow novelist to forget all their previous quarrels and to remember only the good things which they had enjoyed together. It was the sort of letter which a postulant nun might have written to a schoolfriend before going into the cloister.

When the opportunity arose, later that summer, Turgenev visited Tolstoy at Yasnaya Polyana. He found that a tremendous change had overtaken Tolstoy. Turgenev's novels reveal the liberal humanist's ability to recognise life's mystery for what it is, and not to worry at it. He was no metaphysician. For Tolstoy, such questions as Why are we here? What is the point of living? Is there a God? What is the Good? were of consuming importance. He had, during this summer, become obsessed by them. Turgenev discovered that there was little meeting ground between the two of them. After this particular visit, he wrote to Tolstoy, 'I am glad that your physical health is good and I trust that your intellectual malady. . . . has passed.'[4] He went on to say that he had often experienced such moods of depression himself. To others, he expressed the fear that Tolstoy was going mad. For Tolstoy's part, Turgenev's urbanity and good humour were, in such circumstances, intolerable. On a rather later visit, Turgenev, carried away with high spirits, demonstrated a can-can to the children at Yasnaya Polyana. 'Turgenev, can-can. Sad,'[5] was the priggish comment Tolstoy noted down afterwards.

More tragically, the born-again Tolstoy had no time any more for his beloved cousin Alexandrine. Deeply pious though she was, he suspected her worldliness, and her occupations at Court. Initially, as Tolstoy came to believe that he was undergoing a religious conversion, he and Alexandrine had become closer. But as he expressed himself with greater and greater distaste for the Orthodox Church, she felt a gulf widening between them. By 1880, he could pay a visit to the capital without so much as looking her up or saying goodbye. 'There is a harshness, such lack of friendship, and I had rather not say it, such vindictiveness in your behaviour,' she complained.[6] He repented, and there was a reconciliation of a sort. But it was an extraordinary symptom of Tolstoy's need and compulsion to wander out into a spiritual wilderness of his own making, a latterday Simeon Stylites, that he tried to alienate even those whom he loved the best.

The outward and visible signs of his regeneration were to say the least of it bizarre. To the pleasures of lust, there were now added the more complex pleasures of religious guilt. Later, Tolstoy would claim that he had never committed adultery, but this seems an improbable boast when we notice how much he made of his new-found ability, with the dawn of religious belief, to resist the allurements of such beauties as Domna, the cook. (After his conversion, he would ask the family tutor to walk past the kitchen with him to guard him against temptation.) Inspired by the Gospel to believe that all true Christians must hate wives and children for the Lord's sake, he announced that he would like to become a monk — news which Sofya Andreyevna, pregnant for the tenth time with their son Mikhail, viewed with a mixture of emotions. Tolstoy still allowed himself, at this early stage, alcohol, tobacco, and meat — all of which he would in the course of time eschew. But he took to wearing peasant costume all the time and undertaking menial tasks which might have been performed better by artisans. The most notorious example of this, perhaps, is his belief that a Christian should make his own shoes. Fet teased him by ordering a pair of shoes made by Tolstoy. Of course, he never made a pair which anyone beside himself would admit was wearable.

When Turgenev had visited him in summer 1878, he was still in the grip of nearly suicidal melancholia:

> A rope round the neck, a knife to jab into the heart, or the trains on the railroads; and the number of those in our circle who act in this way becomes greater and greater. . . .[7]

he mused. But although with one part of himself, death was attractive — appallingly so — the deepest part of his artistic and spiritual hunger was for life. This had always been so in his books. It became so in his life. And it was this consciousness of life itself in all its vividness, as led by simple people, which led Tolstoy to a rediscovery of belief in God. 'I lived only at those times when I believed in God. . . . I need only to be aware of God to live; I need only forget him or disbelieve him and I died. . . .'[8] 'Live seeking God,' an inner voice told him, 'and then you will not live without God.'[9]

It was the devout peasants who seemed, suddenly, to have the secret of how to live. Tolstoy therefore decided that he must try and live as they did. He began to go to church, to keep the fasts, to confess his sins to the priests, and to be a good Orthodox. But no one of Tolstoy's intellectual curiosity and spiritual restlessness could be satisfied with a purely passive acceptance of Church doctrine. He began to read the Gospels, deeply and attentively, and this reading had a revolutionary effect upon his life.

Who was it who was reading the Gospels? That is, for the biographer of Tolstoy, the interesting question. Was it the little boy whose brother had told him that the secret of all goodness and happiness was written on a green stick buried in the woods at Yasnaya Polyana? That is, was Tolstoy trying to become again a little child, and to revive the primitive faith not only of his own infancy but of his nation? If so, he might have remained an Orthodox, as Dostoyevsky did. Was it, rather, this reader of the Gospel, the beady-eyed novelist who had that extraordinary capacity to see old things as if for the first time? Here we are nearer the truth, and nearer, too, to Tolstoy, the Voltairean sceptic, the eighteenth-century rationalist. We also hear, from now on, persistent echoes of the man who asserted that bronchitis was a metal.

Tolstoy decided not merely that to seek God was to live. He also decided that the only way to live was the way advocated by Jesus in the Gospels: to sell all that he had and give to the poor, to take no thought for the morrow, to reject violence in all its forms, to banish revenge, to call no man Master but God alone.

The lives of those who have been transformed by the ethics of the Gospel are, for the most part, those of a profoundly mystical character — figures who believe in some way or another that they are encountering not just a set of extraordinary ethical commands, but the presence of Jesus himself. In lives as various as Francis of Assisi, John Wesley or General Booth of the Salvation Army, for example, this seems to be an inextricable part of the experience. Tolstoy never had an encounter with Jesus, nor, as far as is recorded, did he ever believe that he had met with Jesus in prayer or had any of the mystical experiences of others who have decided that they must live as Jesus taught. Tolstoy's decision to live in this way seems to have been purely idiosyncratic and arbitrary.

This is where the Voltairean sceptic is observable. It is possible to read the rest of Tolstoy's life as an heroic attempt to live as Jesus Christ told his followers that they should live. That, up to a point, is what it was. But it is also possible to read the next thirty years as an extraordinary demonstration of the fact that the Sermon on the Mount is an unliveable ethic, a counsel of craziness which, if followed to its relentless conclusion as Tolstoy tried to follow it, will lead to the reverse of peace and harmony and spiritual calm which are normally thought of as the concomitants of the religious quest. Tolstoy's religion is ultimately the most searching criticism of Christianity which there is. He shows that it does not work.

*   *   *   *

The progress from artist to sage or holy man, which, to western readers seems embarrassing or a bit of a bore, is a fairly common phenomenon among Russian writers. Leskov did it, Gogol did it. In his own fashion, Dostoyevsky did it. We have the contemporary example of Solzhenitsyn. In almost all cases, the majority of westernised critics find, within such transformations, an artistic falling off. It is hard to judge in such a subjective matter. If we were predisposed in favour of holy men and wiseacres we might be more inclined to take seriously the later work of Russian writers. Only by an early death, it seems, such as blessed the careers of Pushkin and Lermontov, can the great Russian writer escape the desire to become a prophet.

Tolstoy's life follows this pattern, but, as we should expect, to an exaggerated degree: so exaggerated, that it is very hard not to think of his life as falling into two distinct halves, divided by the publication of *Anna Karenina*. It is right to point out, as nearly all writers on Tolstoy do, that there is a continuity between his former and his later self. Even as a young soldier, we are reminded, he was planning to start a new religion based on the ethics of Christ without the miracles. In his early stories, as in *War and Peace* and *Anna Karenina*, he holds up self-images which are transformed by some sort of spiritual alchemy. All his life he had dreaded death. All his life he had sought, for at least some of the time, a spiritual solution to the eternal questions. Yes, yes, but this is to miss the obvious point that after *Anna Karenina* there are no great novels. There were to be many magnificent novellas and short stories from his pen over the next thirty years, and one large work of fiction, *Resurrection*. But Tolstoy was never again to recapture the sustained brilliance of the first seven parts of *Anna Karenina*. The quarrel which blew up over the eighth part was symptomatic of the disaster which he knew had overtaken him. There would henceforth be an abundance of good minor stuff, and of major stuff magnificently flawed. But the author of *War and Peace* and *Anna Karenina* was tragically written out.

Why tragically? Could he not be content with having written two of

301

the greatest, if not the two greatest, novels in the history of literature? Apart from the answer being very obviously a negative, this question rather misses the point of what had happened to Tolstoy. The creative processes were still powerfully at work in him; they were to go on being thus at work for the next thirty years. But they had no matter to work upon. Just as the acids of the full stomach provide a useful work in digesting food but, in an empty stomach, start to consume the very walls of the belly and to cause ulcers, so with the creative processes. One cannot explain them. But one can point out that in the case of Tolstoy they worked in close conjunction with experience. And now the whole career had been, as it were, gobbled up and used. The childhood and early life had been Copperfielded in the 1850s. The time among the Cossacks had been laundered and transformed as befitted the bridegroom of the virginal young Sofya Bers. Then Russia and all its past, together with all Lev Nikolayevich's past, had been anatomised, distorted and revivified on the most magnificent epic scale. And finally, modern marriage and the fear of death — the two subjects closest to his heart — had been used. Chronologically, spiritually, intellectually, he was going to have to scrape the barrel in future if he was to continue his policy of writing out of experience, particularly since the experience in *Anna Karenina* had been so close to the recording of it. As we have already observed, all the great crises of the book — not merely those of Levin and Kitty, but those of Vronsky and Anna, Anna and Karenin, Anna and Sergey — are Tolstoy's own. His monomania had never had fuller, or more creative range. And it was not surprising that when the novel reached its conclusion he should suffer an emotional and spiritual collapse. In some senses, having finished such a novel, one large part of himself ceased to exist. And he had in him no particle of the Prospero, no desire whatsoever to throw away his wand. Having used himself up in one capacity, it was necessary to rediscover himself in another.

That so intelligent and self-aware an artist as Tolstoy did not know that he was, to all intents and purposes, *finished* as a novelist, defies belief. He certainly knew. And the knowledge was no mere artistic tragedy. When he tried to go back to his fourteen-year-old scheme to write about the Decembrists, the novel stubbornly refused to come. The entries — few enough — in Sofya Andreyevna's diaries reveal a pathetic anxiety to see him started once more. She knows the vital emotional importance, for all of them, of Tolstoy being able to write fiction.

October 23, 1878. The weather is windy and unpleasant. Lyovochka was just saying that he had read his fill of historical material, and was going to start on Dickens's *Martin Chuzzlewit* for a rest. I happen to know, however, that when Lyovochka turns to English novels he is about to start writing himself. . . .[10]

A stream of writings were to continue to pour forth, but not the sort of stuff which Sofya Andreyevna nor the world might admire or revere. For the first time since before *War and Peace*, he had started a diary, in the spring of 1878. Later, he was to record:

Went to mass on Sunday. I can find an explanation which satisfied me for everything in the church service. But prayers for a long life and the subjugation of one's enemies is blasphemy. A Christian should pray for his enemies, not against them.

Read the Gospels. Christ says everywhere that everything temporal is false, and that only the abstract is real. 'The birds of the air,' etc. The children Ilya and Tanya have been telling secrets: they are in love. How terrible, *nasty* and sweet they are. Started to write 'my life'.[11]

Emerging from their nursery world, the Tolstoy children now began to observe their parents not as inevitable facts of nature, but as separate individuals. They were aware of a whole world of secrets, a whole, separate past, which was never mentioned in front of the young people. Aunt Tanya Kuzminskaya, the sister of their mother Sofya Andreyevna, seemed to be at the centre of it all. Some of the children knew about Tanya's brief fling with Uncle Sergey. Others began to suspect that she and Papa — Lev Nikolayevich himself — were in love.

Much of what we know of Tolstoy's family life derives from the memoirs and reminiscences of his children. It is strange to think that none of them knew the Tolstoy we know. They never knew the anguished adolescent who had no idea of what direction his life would take. They never knew the soldier of the Crimea, or the tiresome young literary lion who quarrelled with Turgenev. Saddest of all, they never knew the author of *War and Peace*, happily married and fully engaged in the sublime act of artistic creation. Those years when Lev Nikolayevich and Sofya Andreyevna worked in partnership were now waning.

The pair the children saw on the sofa after dinner were growing apart. Tolstoy's spiritual crisis was both a symptom and a cause of that. In a family circle as large as theirs, it was no simple thing to observe. There were never just the two of them sitting there. As often as not, Sofya would be sitting with her sister Tanya, both with a baby or a young child on their laps. They were so close to one another that they would take it in turn to suckle one another's children. And the grand old man himself would be shuffling in and out, losing his temper and muttering about Gospel simplicity. In such an atmosphere it was hard for the older children to know where to place their loyalty, from where to derive their security. The inevitable pattern tended to be that the daughters began to see things from their father's point of view and the sons to sympathise with their mother. By now Sergey was sixteen and almost totally uneducated. He longed to go to *Gymnasium* and the University in Moscow, and in this his mother supported him. Ilya, too, one of the most observant of the children, did not want, at thirteen, to grow up as a country bumpkin. They would be their mother's chief supporters in the move to buy a house in Moscow. But for Tanya, at fifteen, who was more than a little in love with her father, Yasnaya Polyana was enough, and the spiritual quest in which her father was engaged was more exciting than any school or dance or theatre. Thus began that dislike of her mother, soon to be taught to some of the younger children, which was a necessary concomitant of being a fully-fledged Tolstoyan.

*   *   *   *

From now on Tolstoy's diary-self and the diary-war with his wife — in which each wrote rude remarks meant for the other's perusal — become important channels of literary energy. Viewed one way, it was a reversion to an earlier stage of creativity, to the phase before he started writing fiction. If *War and Peace*, the great non-novel, was anticipated and underpinned by the many attempts at self-chronicling represented by the early tales, by his reading of family history and genealogy, by *The History of Yesterday*, by his rules of conduct and by his journals, so the resurrection of the diary habit was an attempt (conscious or unconscious) to start storing up the next great non-novel. But it was always stillborn, never quite to be created. There were at least a dozen books of which a lesser artist would have been proud but nothing on the old grand scale of *War and Peace* and

Anna Karenina. Henceforward, art was always a distraction from the grand business of autobiography. The diaries and letters which fill such multitudinous volumes of the *Collected Works* were only part of the show. There was the daily spectacle of St. Lev or the Old Monster (varying between the two from hour to hour) laid on for the edification of the children and close intimates. There was Lyovochka the village idiot or *yurodivy*, muttering his holy thoughts, mowing (very badly) in the fields or attracting the derision of simpletons and sophisticates alike by his hamfisted attempts to make his own boots. There was the bearded prophet, doling out wise saws and advice to pilgrims with the portentous self-confidence of the *starets*. There was, still refusing to go away, the retired army officer and landed aristocrat, straight-backed and haughty, riding over his coverts, his sharp, blue eyes as ready as any good squire to spot a fox, a broken fence or a nice bit of woman.

To all this was brought the same manic creative fervour as had been devoted to the chronicles *1805* and *1812*. In *War and Peace*, the extraordinary osmosis had occurred so that what begins as an exercise in self-obsession comes to us off the page as independent and very nearly as selfless as Shakespeare. What originally animated the characters in *War and Peace* might well have been Tolstoy's ego but he is as invisible as a good puppet master when he leaves Prince Andrey gazing at the sky at Austerlitz or Nikolay Rostov hating himself for gambling, or Natasha sobbing at her folly over Anatole Kuragin. In the second half of Tolstoy's life the puppet master is suddenly revealed and all these completely inconsistent roles — squire, *starets*, *yurodivy*, lecher, saint, husband, historian, private landowner, public dissident, etc. etc., are revealed as cameo roles designed to show off the virtuoso skills of a crude but self-assured actor. This is not to say that Tolstoy was in control, or that he was hypocritically pretending to be any of these figures; merely that the instinct in a novelist of trying on masks is so strong that it will continue even after the practice of fiction has been abandoned. Tolstoy's life as a religious sage should not be compared with other religious leaders so much as with Dickens's spell of public performances of his work on stage. The effect is not unlike the famous Ealing Studios comedy where all the members of an eccentric aristocratic family — suffragette aunt, boring parson, apoplectic general, etc. — are played by the same actor, Alec Guinness. As in this movie, *Kind Hearts and Coronets*, what is in outline an essentially sad story becomes wholly farcical when we see the same face cropping up again and again in different costumes. The ideal place for such 'role play', as mid-twentieth-century jargon would term it, is in the pages of a novel. But something had happened — no one can explain what it was — which held him back from writing fiction on the scale which his genius and temperament required.

*   *   *   *

The most important upshot of the quarrel with Katkov was the response to the whole affair of Dostoyevsky. It is one of the ironies of nineteenth-century literary history that Tolstoy — with his advancing anarchism and extreme dissatisfaction with the *status quo* in Russia — should have published *Anna Karenina* in *Russkii Vestnik* under the editorship of the arch-reactionary Katkov, whereas Dostoyevsky (whose views were much closer to Katkov's) should have published the greatest imaginative indictment of political liberalism (*The Devils*) in *The Contemporary* under the editorship of the leftist Nekrasov. The last part of *Anna Karenina*, rejected by Katkov and published separately by Tolstoy as a pamphlet, excited the most violent reaction in Dostoyevsky, who devoted pages of his *The Diary of a Writer* to answering Levin's latent pacifism.

Is it for mere vengeance, for mere killing, that the Russian people have risen? And when was it that assistance to the massacred, to those who are being exterminated by entire regions, to assaulted women and children in whose defence there is no one in the whole world to intercede, was considered a callous, ridiculous and almost immoral act, a craving for vengeance and blood-thirst! And what insensibility side by side with sentimentalism! In fact, Levin himself has a child, a boy! He loves him! When this child is bathed in a bathtub it is almost a family event! Why doesn't his heart bleed when he hears and reads about wholesale massacres, about children with crushed heads crawling around their assaulted, murdered mothers with their breasts cut off? This happened in a Bulgarian church where two hundred such corpses were found, after the town had been plundered. Levin reads all this, and there he stands and meditates:

'Kitty is cheerful today; she ate with an appetite; the boy was bathed in the tub, and he begins to recognise me: what do I care about things that are transpiring in another hemisphere? *No immediate settlement for the oppression of the Slavs exists or can exist* — because I feel *nothing*.'[12]

Is this how Levin brings to a close his epopee? Is it he whom the author seeks to set forth as an example of a truthful, honest man? Men, such as the author of *Anna Karenina*, are teachers of society, our teachers, while we are merely their pupils. What then do they teach us?

This is a direct challenge to Tolstoy from the other great genius of the age. And Dostoyevsky scored a very palpable hit when he noticed that Tolstoy thought the Eastern question was unimportant because it did not affect him personally. That is precisely what was happening at this point in Tolstoy's life.

They never met, Tolstoy and Dostoyevsky. They would have had every opportunity of doing so at Father Amvrosy's cell in Optina Monastery. They were both friends of Strakhov. Had they wished to meet, there would have been every possibility of arranging such a thing. Instead, like two great monsters, they sniff and pace the ground and never come into contact. Dostoyevsky (who was not in Tolstoy's later sense of the term in the least 'aware') exposes his obsessions with Tolstoy, as with all the great questions of the day — the future of Russia, the destiny of the Christian religion, the perfidy of Turks, leftists, etc. — in the pages of *The Diary of a Writer*, a journalistic diary, designed for public consumption. Tolstoy at this period is much more inward looking. He had retreated into himself. He is on the threshold of various exercises in self-exploration and self-revelation — *A Confession* and *What I Believe* (almost, an aggressive *Just What I Believe*) — but they are doomed to be censored. No one will read them. And yet, as they pace around their prey, like two giant cats, they are sniffing at the same things, seeing the same problems, absorbing the same huge facts into their imaginative worlds.

For both of them, nothing less is at stake than the spiritual future of the human race, the very essence of what we are. For both of them, the spectacle of ignorant armies clashing in Bulgaria or the Balkans, or of the pitiful crying of the urban poor, excite religious questions. Both respond to these religious questions in violently different ways, and because Tolstoy says nothing publicly in response to Dostoyevsky, it may be assumed that all the controversial running is on Dostoyevsky's side. But this is a false assumption. Enemies and admirers of Tolstoy alike have taken his own word for it that his spiritual odyssey happened

307

as a result of rational quest. But as Dostoyevsky so repeatedly shows us in his fiction, human beings are not rational creatures, and in response to religion it is not possible, or even desirable, that they should be. Precisely during the years of Tolstoy's spiritual crisis, Dostoyevsky was reaching the climax and culmination of his religious thinking. It cannot be that the two facts are unconnected. Ever since *Crime and Punishment* and *War and Peace* appeared month by month as alternate episodes in the same periodical, the two giants had been placed before the reading public in a vast, metaphysical coexistence. It was something much bigger than feelings of pure literary rivalry, though that came into it. Rather, it is almost as though the Godhead had chosen to become incarnate in two beings, the fullness of His truth being too mysterious, and too immense for embodiment in a single human life. The boldness and profanity of the comparison is one at which even Dostoyevsky would have blushed. But what emerged from it all was not merely two quite different sorts of novel. It was two different Christs.

*   *   *   *

Anna Karenina was finished, and its author was spiritually exhausted. 'Pushkin once said to his circle of admirers, "Fancy what Tatyana has gone and done. She's got married. I would never have expected it of her." I could say exactly the same of *Anna Karenina*. My heroes and heroines sometimes take steps which I would not have intended. . . .'[13] But on another occasion Tolstoy said, 'There was nothing else she could do — struggling her whole life through with that tedious Karenin.'[14]

The sensation of characters taking on a life of their own provides the novelist with the most magnificent feelings of freedom and release; but when they vanish, and the book is published, and more characters obstinately refuse to come to life in the author's head, he is thrown back on himself, and on his family.

The routines of Yasnaya Polyana continued as before. At nine o'clock Tolstoy would shuffle down in a dressing gown on his way to breakfast. His dressing room and study were on the ground floor. Usually, on the staircase, some of the children would run out to meet him. After breakfast, he would go into the drawing room and sit with his wife. He would drink tea and she had coffee. Then he would go out into the entrance hall and swing on the parallel bars to try to use up some excess energy. At about eleven o'clock he would go into his study and 'write'. But he was not writing fiction. He would scribble down 'thoughts' on stray bits of paper, the backs of envelopes. Sometimes he would write them up at greater length. He would sit there in his study until four. 'Lyovochka works all the time,' complained Sofya Andreyevna in 1879 in a letter to her sister,

> but alas, he is writing some kind of religious dissertation to prove that the Church disagrees with the teaching of the Gospels. There will be barely ten people in Russia who interest themselves in it.[15]

Like so many of Countess Tolstoy's cruel remarks, this hits home (though as it happens, she was entirely wrong about the numbers of people who would be interested by Tolstoy's religious reflections). At this time, 'Lyovochka' was deeply isolated from his friends, from the world, from his family.

The habit of churchgoing, which might have served to unite Tolstoy with his neighbours and fellow countrymen, only increased his feeling of isolation. He would return from the liturgy in a black mood. The peasants whom he had hoped to woo as brothers and sisters in Christ all bowed to him and doffed their caps. And the church service itself was simply nonsense. 'Just listen to the words and chants they sing in the chancel,' he said one day in a disillusioned mood. 'They are absolutely not being sung for the peasants. Even I can't understand what they are singing. Take for example the "sequence" which they sing on Christmas day. . . .'[16] And he went into his study and produced a book to read the passage aloud.

This sort of thing — his studying the Scriptures and the texts of the liturgy — would go on until teatime; by then, he would be ready for a walk or a ride. He rode and walked very fast, so if you went out with him it was difficult to keep up. When he came back from his ride, he would have dinner. It was rather a stately affair, with flunkeys in white gloves and frock coats. After dinner he would go back into the study for more burrowing into the question of religion. Then, in the evening, at about eight, he would emerge and sit with the family. Sometimes he played Chopin or Beethoven on the piano. If his sister happened to be staying, he would play a duet with her. Music always moved him to tears — even if he just heard snatches of a child's practice from two or three rooms away. The children would then be packed off to bed, and the grown-ups would sit together drinking tea until midnight. Usually, there would be talk, but sometimes Sofya Andreyevna or Lev Nikolayevich would read aloud.

On the surface, it seemed a happy enough existence, but Tolstoy was not happy. The drama of his unhappiness could not be fashioned into truth by becoming a novel. It now came bursting out of him, rawly unreal, as *A Confession*.

A Confession, which has been described as 'the finest of all Tolstoy's non-fiction works'[17] and 'one of the noblest and most courageous utterances of man',[18] was probably begun in 1879. For some time, the juices had been gnawing at an emptied imagination, the stomach wall having to exercise its usual digestive function of turning experience into fiction. In the previous summer of 1878, he had toyed with the idea of writing a proper autobiography and jotted down some reminiscences of his childhood, but, like his attempt to expurgate his ancestral past in *The Decembrists*, it came to nothing.

Approaching *A Confession* 'blind', the reader will indeed be arrested by its overpowering emotional force, and might even mistake its apparently ratiocinative thrust, its burning intellectual sincerity, for a piece of argument. But for those who have followed Tolstoy's life and work in a chronological order, its ninety or so pages give off disconcerting impressions. It is not the book which its author intends us to read. Doubtless, while he was writing it, *A Confession* felt as noble and courageous as some modern readers have found it; and there is — unquestionably — a high nobility about it. But it is not, as Tolstoy so heart-rendingly believes, the record of a mind clearing, of a troubled soul coming at last to peace. Newman's *Apologia* in a different way gives off highly comparable danger signals. His insistence that joining the Roman Church was 'like coming into port after a stormy sea' (a strange way of describing the anguish he had felt ever since becoming a Catholic) is highly comparable to Tolstoy's claim at the end of *A Confession* that he has found the secret which will give his soul peace. Tolstoy's *A Confession* is outwardly the story of a thoughtless sensualist, who had put all thoughts of God, the meaning of life, soul or goodness aside. He had pursued first, as a young soldier, the sins of the flesh, and the cruel pleasures of war. Then, as a literary man, he had pursued fame and money, and had enjoyed the didactic role thrust upon the Russian writer, even though he had nothing to teach. Then he had got married and become wholly absorbed in his family. He had, however, been haunted by a terrible sense of the pointlessness of existence in upper-class society. He had known both the anguish of *ennui* so profound that he had often been tempted to commit suicide; and on the other hand, or at the same time, a terror of death which poisoned his whole life. He had turned this way and that for a solution to the questions Who am I? and What is the point of living? Philosophy (Kant and Schopenhauer) had been as impotent to help as had natural science. Finally, he had discovered that while the pampered intelligentsia and aristocracy were leading lives which were indeed pointless, and which led only to despair, there was a huge category of persons who had faith, who were able to live and who did, apparently, know life's secret. These were the peasants. He had thrown himself into adopting their Holy Orthodox faith, but he had been unable to resist thinking about it and going into it, and the more he went in, and the more he thought, the more obvious it became to him that the Orthodox Church was founded on a lie, that its insistence upon such esoteric or improbable doctrines as the Trinity, the Ascension, or the miracles of the saints, was as blasphemous as its refusal to take seriously the central moral teachings of Him whom they claimed to be the second person of the Trinity. But this liberation from the Church, this discovery that the monks and the archimandrites and the bishops and the theologians had got everything wrong, did not shake Tolstoy's faith in the honest Christianity of the peasants. Nor did it drive him back into a pure Voltairean negativism. On the contrary, it was when he realised that being Orthodox was incompatible with true Christianity that he felt a true peace, and he resolved to practise the five great commandments given by Christ in His Sermon on the Mount. Henceforth, like Levin at the end of *Anna Karenina*, he would live by this simple creed, and he would achieve salvation, that is, not some mystical or supernatural benefit bestowed upon him by the Church, but the inner certainty that he was leading a life as it was meant by God to be led.

Such, in essence, is *A Confession*. The violence of its similes, his life as a boat careering down a fast river as he tries to row against the stream, knowing that the bank is God, or the man about to fall into the dragon jaws of death, pausing to lick two drops of honey, is a taste of the Tolstoy who was now struggling to be born. They reflect the appalling conflicts which were going on inside him; and they suggest that he had undergone, or was undergoing, what in slightly outmoded modern jargon would be termed a mental 'breakdown'. Every bit of his life is seen as an aching torment. There are various moments when the unconscious egoism of a man who is lying back on the

311

analyst's couch shows a sign of painful dislocation. For example, in section eleven, where it suddenly dawns on him that 'life is evil and an absurdity' (a generalisation applying to the whole of humanity) is not necessarily true because 'my particular life of senseless indulgence of desires was senseless and evil'. Or again, in a slightly different mood, when he describes his anger with the scientists for being unable to answer the question 'Why do *I* live?'

Tolstoy writes in such a frank and readable manner that his rhetoric can deceive us into thinking that such a proposition makes some sort of sense. But who are these scientists and why should 'they' have devoted their minds either to the rather nebulous question of whether life has a meaning (not their job) or to the more specialised question of why Lev Nikolayevich should exist?

Once one is alerted to the danger signals, *A Confession*, precisely because of its artless sincerity, is revealed as a transparent piece of self-deception: transparent, that is, to everyone except the author. It simply is not true, for example, that at earlier phases of life Tolstoy thought only of sensualism, or only of fame, or only of money. Throughout his life, he had been troubled by a conflict between an unyielding, intellectual rationalism and a passionately religious temperament. He had often thought of amending his life along the lines of some simplified form of Christianity, purged of its 'dogmas'. He had often flirted with the Orthodoxy of his boyhood, yearned to lead a simple life, and to imitate the peasants. He had always — except for brief crazes and intervals — preferred the country to the town. So the picture of his slow turning-away from the life of the urban intelligentsia towards rural piety is a totally false one. Nor does his picture of, for example, the St. Petersburg intelligentsia bear any relation to what it had actually been like at the time. His claim that they were all burning to teach their readers great moral truths was as untrue of Turgenev as it was of Tolstoy's great friend, Fet, an unwavering devotee of art for art's sake.

Just as *Childhood* bore less relation to his actual childhood than it had done to the period when the book was being written, so these 'memories' of St. Petersburg society when Tolstoy was a young man are actually direct responses to what was happening at the time he was writing his confession. He is referring not to Fet and Turgenev, but to Dostoyevsky's challenge, 'Men such as the author of *Anna Karenina* are teachers of society.'

The most extraordinary claim of all is that in the early years of his marriage he regarded authorship as being of no possible importance, and that he only wrote 'insignificant work' for the sake of monetary reward.[19] Does this describe the fervent energy with which he wrote and wrote and recorrected Sofya's copies of *War and Peace*? Apparently, it is meant to. Even if there had been no financial reward, there could have been no greater possible satisfaction for a novelist than to have written *War and Peace* which is indeed one of the 'noblest utterances. . . . of man'. Tolstoy's capacity to forget had blotted it all out. Moreover, in describing his state of mind upon finishing *Anna Karenina* he reveals his extraordinary, and surely psychotic, ability to find dissatisfaction precisely in the areas which should have given the greatest and the noblest forms of pleasure. '"Very well," he had said to himself, "you will be more famous than Gogol or Pushkin or Shakespeare or Molière, or than all the writers in the world — and what of it?" And I could find no reply at all.'[20] The reason he could find no reply is that it was not a rational question. It is almost unimaginable that Pushkin, Molière or Shakespeare would have asked themselves such a question. Tolstoy thinks that by asking it he reveals his indifference to literature. In fact, it reveals quite the reverse. It shows that he had seen it all as a competition: a competition which, moreover, he had won. Having decided implicitly that he was in fact the greatest literary genius in the world, it was not like him to rest on his laurels. Having got some laurels, he proceeded to tear them leaf from leaf. There is nobility, there is grandeur here. But there is also titanic arrogance, and a peculiar destructiveness which is all Tolstoy's own. Tolstoy's question suggests that so long as there were these geniuses, his own was to be rebuked; and this attitude was to harden over the coming years as he developed his theories of art. But, once more, there is a genius whose name very conspicuously does not appear in the list, and we almost expect to hear it later on in *A Confession* when he tells us that having failed to find anyone among his own class who understood the meaning of life, his eyes were opened. 'And of such people, understanding the meaning of life and able to live and to die, I saw not two or three or tens, but hundreds, thousands and millions. And they all — endlessly different in their manners, minds, education, and position as they were — all alike, in complete contrast to my ignorance, knew the meaning of life and death, laboured quietly, endured deprivations and sufferings, and lived and died, seeing therein not vanity but good.'[21]

What is this if it is not the voice of the Devil who speaks to Ivan

Karamazov in his dream: 'I would surrender this super-celestial life, all ranks and honours, if only I could become incarnate in the soul of a seven-pood merchant's wife and put up candles to God.'[22]

It may be that part of the unconscious, motivating force for the conversion of Tolstoy was a panic-stricken longing not to be Dostoyevsky. For having steered so firmly in the direction of a seven-pood merchant's wife, and having put up candles to God, Tolstoy became convinced, and devoted the next five years of his writing life to proving that, while the peasant worshipper had somehow or other got hold of the secret of life, his or her faith was actually based on lies and misconceptions. But one must emphasise that any part Dostoyevsky played in all this must have been marginal, and unconscious. The figure who was about to be passed through the digesting machine of Tolstoy's imagination was none other than Christ Himself, and the theological outpourings which now came from Tolstoy's pen reflect his famed genius for 'making it strange'.

      *   *   *   *

Just as in his fiction, he is able to give the impression that he is Adam on the first day of creation — the first person who ever heard a new-born infant cry, who ever saw a storm or felt the heat of the sun — so in his newly-found scholarly enthusiasm, Tolstoy manages to write as if he were the first person who had ever read the Gospels. And there is in his reading something abidingly refreshing, and strange, something which the Christian reader, however orthodox, must cherish, and which will always disturb the rationalist. *A Confession* was intended as a preface to his *Critique of Dogmatic Theology*; and the *Critique* forms a natural complement to the collation of the Gospels at which he was hard at work during 1881. So, it makes sense to discuss them altogether.

It is worth making the point, perhaps, that Tolstoy, though with one part of himself a rationalist, would, with another, have sympathised with Dostoyevsky's self-professed irrationalism. And the point has been well made, by Lev Shestov, that to believe in the Gospel ethics as Tolstoy did was more fantastical than to accept, with Dostoyevsky, the Gospel miracles. Many orthodox critics have understandably found Tolstoy lacking in any transcendental sense whatsoever. But if this were true, his position would probably be easier to understand, less disturbing. There are many passages in the

Critique which confirm Shestov's view that Tolstoy was 'willing to err with Christ against all reason'.[23]

One thinks of the great invocation — of course designed to ridicule Trinitarian orthodoxy, but also a genuine prayer — to which probably the young Wordsworth would have said 'Amen'. 'O God, God inconceivable, but who art, God by whose will I live, Thou hast put in me this aspiration to know Thee, and to know myself. I have erred, I have sought out an infallible truth. I knew that I was going astray. I gave myself up to evil passions, while knowing that they were evil, but I never forgot Thee; I always felt Thy presence even in the very moment of my sins. I all but lost Thee, but Thou hast stretched forth a hand which I seized and all my life is filled with light. Thou has saved me, and, henceforth, I will look for only one thing, to grow near to Thee and, so far as it is possible to me, to understand Thee. Help me, teach me! I know that I am following the good, that I love, or want to love, everyone, that I want to love the truth. Draw nearer, Thou God of love and truth, reveal to me all that I can understand of Thee and of me.

'And this good God, this God of truth replies to me through the mouth of the Church, "The Deity is One and Three." '[24]

His rationalistic dismissal of the doctrine of the Trinity should not blind us to the genuine flights of (admittedly vague, and unsubstantiated) transcendentalism in the prayer.

The *Critique* dismisses all the traditional Christian doctrines — the Incarnation, the resurrection of Christ, the ascension into heaven, the miracles of the Gospels and of the saints. Inevitably it also therefore disposes of all the theology of grace, any suggestion that Christ has taken upon us our sin, or created a reconciliation between the human race and the Father. Nor is the dismissal made with tones of regret or humility. Tolstoy makes no bones about his assertion that the Orthodox theologians (he examines in particular the Patriarch Philaret's *Catechism* and Patriarch Macarius's *Introduction to Theology*) were knowing and deliberate liars who had perverted and distorted the simple message of the Gospel.

There is one area where Tolstoy was indisputably right, and since it is of such momentous importance for the development of his writing and thinking, it must be mentioned here, although there will be further discussion of it when he comes to write his innumerable essays on pacifism. And that is that Christ in St. Matthew's Gospel forbade His followers to take their revenge for evil done against them;

that He told them to turn the other cheek if they were struck, to forgive their enemies, and to bless those who persecute them. This is an unquestionable part of the Gospel teaching. Equally unquestionable is the fact that the Orthodox Church, like almost every other Christian denomination in history except the Society of Friends, made no bones about disavowing the plain tone of Christ's pacifist teaching. There are plenty of arguments against pacifism. Tolstoy got used to most of them, and even conceded their force. They are based on patriotism, or practical common sense, or a desire to protect the defenceless, or fear, or a combination of all these things. What they can never be based upon is the teaching of the Gospels, even though the attitude of Christ in the Gospels (and of John the Baptist) to *soldiers* appears to have been less critical than many modern-day pacifists. So there is an ambiguity. But the fundamental idea that Christians do not practise what they preach is a bullseye shot, never aimed with more immediacy or more violence, or more passion than in Tolstoy's religious writings. At an early stage in *A Confession* he said that it was, and is, impossible to judge from a man's conduct whether or not he was a Christian believer.

*　　　　*　　　　*　　　　*

Though Tolstoy was temperamentally incapable of reading Dostoyevsky's novels, and claimed that he had been unable to finish *The Brothers Karamazov*, he cannot have been unaware of the book's religious substance. All of it, in essence — the religious problem posed by the suffering of children, the mystic destiny of the Orthodox Church ('a star has arisen in the East!'), even the imaginative obsession with Christ's temptations in the wilderness, all the things which stay so vividly in our heads when we have read *The Brothers Karamazov* — had been pouring forth in disconnected outbursts in *The Diary of a Writer* throughout the late 1870s. When the Tolstoys were aware that Papa was in his study reading 'periodicals', he was surely meditating on the Dostoyevskian position. So, even if we accept Tolstoy's claim that he had not read the whole of *The Brothers Karamazov*, it still makes sense to view his religious apologia *What I Believe* as a piece of writing which has Dostoyevsky all the time in view.

   The Brothers Karamazov asks religious questions more searching than any other work of literature. As such, it sailed terribly near the wind as far as censorship was concerned. Even though Dostoyevsky was a personal friend of Konstantin Pobedonostsev, the Procurator of the Holy Synod itself, the opening sections of his novel (which Tolstoy did admit to having read) were regarded in official circles with extreme suspicion. The dialogues between Ivan and Alyosha, and in particular Ivan's exposition of how he does not accept God's world — he hands back his admission ticket — was an unanswerable statement of the theological problem of suffering. Then, in the next chapter, came the poem Ivan had never written about the Grand Inquisitor, who saw the temptations in the wilderness as an offer to Christ of three great weapons — miracle, mystery and authority. He silently rejects them all. But are not these the weapons by which the Orthodox Church (as well as Dostoyevsky's principal target, the Roman Church) has, throughout history, attracted its adherents? So, at first, it would seem, though not in fact, either in logic nor in Dostoyevsky's view. On August 16, 1879, Pobedonostsev had written to Dostoyevsky, 'Your "Grand Inquisitor" made a strong impression on me. I have not read anything so powerful for a long time. All I was waiting for was a rebuff, an objection and an explanation — but so far in vain.'[25]

Dostoyevsky was quick to reply that the book is a novel, and that even the elder Zosima's sermons 'belong to his person, that is to say, his artistic portrayal', but even so, he was equally hasty to put the Orthodox case in the next section of the novel, 'The Russian Monk'.

The best possible defence of Orthodox Christianity (small or large 'o') is placed not, in fact, on the lips of the famous Elder Zosima, but in the great speech made by the wilier, and more worldly Father Paisy, when he says to Alyosha:

"Always remember, young man, that secular science, having become a great force in the world, has, especially since the last century, investigated everything divine handed down to us in the sacred books. After a ruthless analysis the scholars of this world have left nothing of what was held sacred before. But they have only investigated the parts and overlooked the whole, so much so that one cannot help being astonished at their blindness. And so the whole remains standing before their eyes as firm as ever and the gates of hell shall not prevail against it. Has it not existed for nineteen centuries and does it not exist today in the inmost hearts of individual men and the masses of the people? Why, it is living in

317

the hearts of the atheists who have destroyed everything, and is as firmly rooted there as ever! For even those who have renounced Christianity and are rebelling against it are essentially of the same semblance as Christ, and have always been that, for so far neither their wisdom nor the ardour of their hearts has been able to create a higher ideal of man or of man's dignity than the one shown by Christ in the days of old. . . ."26

The wholeness of which Father Paisy speaks is nothing less than the everlasting Gospel, the mystery of the incarnate Christ, which continues in the world, and in men and women's hearts, even though each individual part of it, when subjected to scrutiny, might appear to have been disintegrated and destroyed. This argument goes with the whole thrust of Dostoyevsky's novel that man is a wild, irrational being, who will always gravitate in individual cases to folly or evil, and who is always going to be a prey to political and economic exploitation for the same reason. It would be wrong to look for a rational means of salvation for such a being. The means of salvation is not in the man-manipulated 'myth, mystery and authority' which religious groups might try to exploit but in the actual reality, only perceptible here as a mystery, of the Incarnate.

Tolstoy attempts, in his synthesis of the Gospels, to 'investigate the parts'. But his exegetical method, though based purely on Enlightenment presuppositions, is the very reverse of 'modern'. On the contrary, like Dostoyevsky's, it is a great imaginative recasting of the New Testament material. Tolstoy could not approach the Gospels without a compulsion to rewrite them.

European scholarship, western scholarship, which had been focusing upon the Gospels in radical sceptical earnest for the previous forty years, had achieved the results described by the anguished Father Paisy to Alyosha Karamazov. The Tübingen school in Germany had taken the Gospels to bits. The most notorious and radical of their theologians, David Friedrich Strauss, had brought to the study of the New Testament a whole package of scientific and philosophical presuppositions which enabled him to examine the Gospel stories in the same sceptical spirit which would have governed a scholar's reading of, say, Plutarch's *Lives*. Strauss took it for granted that personal immortality was an impossibility and that 'science' had disposed of the miraculous. But having dismantled the whole thing, he then wanted to put together some picture of Christ of his own. The result was his *Leben Jesu* (1838) which George Eliot translated into English, tearfully losing her simple Evangelical faith as she did so. Ernest Renan did for the Catholic world what Strauss had attempted for the Protestant. His *Vie de Jésus* of 1863 depicts a rather sugary, sentimental figure, fond of his mother, devoted to reveries by the seashore or in meadows full of flowers, someone who is in many ways a bit like Renan himself. It was not until the century was over that a bleak German sceptical mind was able to look at these lives of Jesus and their many analogues, and see them for the imaginative works which they really were. Albert Schweitzer's *The Quest for the Historical Jesus* is a corrective to the idea that Jesus *can* be discovered as a real historical character without taking into account the manner in which the Evangelists saw him. Jesus outside the Gospels only exists in the faith of the believers. This was something which, in their different ways (neither of them would have liked Schweitzer's bleakly apocalyptic Christ much, but that is beside the point), both Tolstoy and Dostoyevsky saw. Coming from a completely different religious tradition, their imaginative Christs emerge with much more terrifying wholeness than that of Strauss or Renan. In fact, knowing of Tolstoy's obsession with the Gospels, Strakhov sent Tolstoy Renan's *Vie de Jésus* in the spring of 1878. Tolstoy fasted in preparation for his reading of the book, which perhaps explains his particularly dyspeptic reactions.

If Renan has any ideas of his own, they are the two following ones:
(1) That Christ didn't know about *l'évolution et le progrès* and in this respect Renan tries to correct Him and criticises Him from the superior position of his idea. This is terrible, at least to me. Progress in my opinion is a logarithm of time, i.e. nothing, an establishment of the fact that we live in time; and suddenly it becomes the judge of the highest truth we know. . . .
The other idea of Renan's is that if Christ's teaching exists, then some man or other existed, and this man certainly sweated and went to the lavatory. For us, all degrading realistic human details have disappeared from Christianity for the same reason that all details about all Jews etc. who ever lived have disappeared, for the same reason everything disappears that is not everlasting: but what is everlasting, remains.[27]

But dyspepsia alone does not explain Tolstoy's differing attitude. For a French Catholic brought up like Renan to believe in an almost magical, insubstantial Christ — a figure pointing gingerly to his scarlet Sacred Heart from the bright statues of Breton country churches, and identified with the light wafer of the sacred host — it was shattering to faith to imagine a real, Palestinian itinerant teacher who sweated and went to the lavatory. To an Orthodox, such contrasts would be meaningless. Likewise a German Protestant who had been brought up to believe that the Bible was some kind of magic book, every word of which was authenticated by the Holy Ghost, the textual inconsistencies in the Bible were wholly injurious to faith. For the westerners, Catholic and Protestant, all hung on authenticity. For the Russians, it was not so. Neither Tolstoy nor Dostoyevsky can be taken as representative Orthodox (believers or heretics), but for both men what counted was the moral and spiritual power of Christ in the lives of men and women. Where they diverged was in their response to the essentially European question of 'authenticity'. Tolstoy, having 'gone into it all', found that it would not 'do'. He therefore self-confidently jettisoned the Church, the sacraments, the theology of grace. . . . But what emerged was not something tragic or etiolated, but something four-square and strong.

Nu i chto zh? Tolstoy had asked the question, having decided that he was a greater genius than Gogol, Pushkin, Shakespeare, or Molière. It has a sort of baby-directness. It is not the language of intellectual argument, it is the language of nursery squabbles. But on his lips it represents his extraordinary searchlight mind, which focused on what for him was the most important side of the question. And in this matter of New Testament scholarship, and Church doctrine, it is as if he asks it again. So! Some character from Germany has proved that Christ never thought of Himself as the second person of the Trinity, or that miracles are impossible. *Nu i chto zh?* Well, so what?

Tolstoy had a voracious appetite for scholarly reading, for languages, for textual work. But as far as he is concerned, nearly all the questions which caused such anguish to the European theologians were not worth asking. He brushes it all aside. What is burningly, glaringly important, is the question of how we should live. Was the Sermon on the Mount true? Did not its truth expose all that was wrong in the heart of men, all that was wrong in contemporary society? Should we not be actually living as Jesus taught us to live, banishing anger from our hearts, refusing to take vengeance even on those who wrong us, banishing lust and avarice from our lives? Is not that the path to life?

The rest, as far as Tolstoy is concerned, is simply an irrelevance.

Although, or perhaps because, he understood what the German critical school were up to, his own exegetical methods take no account of his years of study in the field. As so often in his life, one is struck by the curious way in which the 'enlightened' eighteenth-century nobleman is combined in one person with the 'original' newborn babe Lev Nikolayevich, who sees everything with shockingly fresh eyes. Pierre Bezukhov and old Prince Bolkonsky are both the co-authors of his synthesis of the Gospels. The idea that you could simply rewrite the Gospels in a shape which suited you and throw out all the bits you did not like would have offended the scholarly sensibilities of the sceptical, Protestant Germans quite as much as it scandalised the orthodox believers of the Russian or Roman Churches. But to the eighteenth-century rationalist, it was a perfectly sensible thing to do. Long before anyone had done any real scholarly work on the New Testament, Thomas Jefferson, for example, had been so certain of the rightness of his own views that he could produce a Gospel gutted of the miraculous: a marriage feast at Cana in which everybody drank good wine, but not wine which had once been water. With the same self-confidence the eighteenth-century squire in England might have pulled down the little Gothic church on his estate and replaced it with a neoclassical temple in the clean modern manner. At the same time, Tolstoy is in some ways oddly a Russian Orthodox: for example, in the way in which he treats the fourth Gospel as fully historical as the Synoptics, and does not in the least share the German belief that the first three Gospels are somehow or other closer to the source.

He lets the Gospels say what they say when it is what he would be saying anyway. There is a most revealing passage in *What I Believe* when the *nu i chto zh*-arrogance gets pushed to its furthest limit and he actually says, 'It is terrible to say, but it sometimes appears to me that if Christ's teaching, with the Church teaching that has grown out of it, had not existed at all, those who now call themselves Christians would have been nearer to the truth of Christ — that is to say, to a reasonable understanding of what is good in life — than they are now.'

The everlasting doctrine of redemption thus gets rewritten into a reasonable understanding of what is good in life. His Jesus is an eccentric countryman, violently opposed to citified bigwigs, European-isers, Tsars, Procurators, bishops and the like. Tolstoy discards all the elements in the Gospel which make no sense. No one here kneels before a transfigured Christ on Tabor; no one sees Him still the winds and waves; no women flee, terrified in the darkness of dawn at the discovery of an empty tomb. The sheer terror of the Gospels, the extraordinary sense that people were all the time being confronted with a Being who both is and is not one of them, is quite absent in Tolstoy's version. There is no demoniac seized with devils who recognise an enemy stronger than themselves; no Virgin kneeling before the angel of the annunciation, no Thomas, scarcely able to look at the figure who stands before him showing the print of the nails. There are merely a lot of stubborn idiots who won't see the plain truth about the way they ought to live.

Nevertheless, a heresy will get nowhere if it is all wrong. Tolstoy's great appeal is not in his cavalier attitudes to the text of the Gospels (anyone could do that if they had the patience or the cheek) but in his merciless spotlight on the chinks in the Orthodox armour. Even today many Christian believers assert (1) that Jesus was divine and infallible and (2) that there is no need to take any notice of the things He is alleged to have taught. This is the inconsistency which Tolstoy highlights. And he replaces in typically exaggerated form, with another pair of incompatibles, a Jesus who is not divine, but whose words *are*. Tolstoy believed Christ's words to have an absolute, unassailable, moral authority, and it is for this that modern Christians can feel gratitude towards Him. In our own day, there has been a further refinement on behalf of the clerisy. We have not merely clergymen, as Tolstoy had, who claim that there is no reason why we should even attempt to follow Christ's teachings; we also have those (the majority, perhaps, of New Testament scholars) who believe that it is impossible to reconstruct what the *ipsissima verba* of Christ actually were. So, why try? Tolstoy's approach to the New Testament is arresting because it undercuts even such evasiveness as this. Even if Christ did not say the words, they are still true, eternally true, morally and absolutely true. So, for the next thirty years, he boldly asserted.

Like many other heresiarchs, he is certain not only of what the *ipsissima verba* were, but also, precisely what is meant by them. By the time his distinctive creed was formed, Tolstoy made no bones about believing that Christ advocated a consistent anarchism, a policy of civil disobedience. 'Swear not at all' means 'Refuse to take part in judicial assemblies.' It may be that this is what Jesus taught. It may be, further, that no one who took these words of Jesus to heart could, in conscience, have taken part in the judicial procedures of nineteenth-century Russia. But — this is the point which would have meant nothing to Tolstoy — nor is it possible to reconstruct exactly what Jesus thought about law courts. The assertion that He violently disapproved of them is a good enough stick with which to beat the Establishment and to enrage the likes of Katkov, Pobedonostsev — and Dostoyevsky. 'Resist not evil.' Again, it is hard to see how anyone who had absorbed Christ's teaching of non-violence could knowingly or willingly get involved in a war. But there is no evidence that Jesus, or his precursor John, taught pacifism as such. John the Baptist told soldiers to be content with their pay, not to burn their draft cards. Jesus said that he had never known such faith, in the whole of Israel, as was found in a Roman centurion. On the other hand (another consideration which would have meant nothing to Tolstoy) scholars believe that the Gospel of Luke, from which these two examples are drawn, was deliberately compiled to give to the Romans the impression that the Christians were not subversive. So the argument comes full circle.

Even in the area of wealth, where it would seem that the Gospel of St. Lev was completely in agreement with those of Matthew, Mark, Luke and John, it is hard to say exactly whether Jesus had an 'economic policy'. If Christ had not wished us to have any money at all, why did He hold up a coin and tell us to pay our taxes? How can you pay tax if you have not saved up some money?

Tolstoy's anarchism, which became more and more extreme as the years progressed, would have struck a particularly jarring note in the ears of his Orthodox hearers. In the various legends on which the western mind likes to focus — whether of Becket and Henry II, or More and Henry VIII, or Innocent XI or Pascal versus the Bourbon Monarchy — the interest of civil rulers in ecclesiastical affairs is seen as interference. The ideal Christian Church, it is felt, is one where the secular authority has no control, and the very notion that kings or doges might have a say in the running of the Church is seen as 'Erastian' by western Christians as different as Blue Bonnets or Ultramontanes. The *Kirchenkampf* in the 1930s in Germany was but the culmination in the West of a whole series of confrontations which had been going on ever since the days of Hildebrand between the civil and the ecclesiastical powers.

But the East had fed its mind on different stories. The first Christian city, Tsargorod, or Constantinople, had, like the First Ecumenical Council of the Church at Nicea, come into being through the decree of a Christian emperor, Constantine, in western eyes a figure who symbolises a compromising of a gospel which is not of this world, in the East revered as a saint. It was he who made the Empire Christian. His cult derives from an idea of power which is found in the New Testament, that strand of thought which bids us render to Caesar the things which are Caesar's and to submit ourselves to every ordinance of man for the Lord's sake. 'The powers that be,' wrote the Apostle Paul during the reign of the Emperor Nero, 'are ordained of God.' If this were true of a pagan Caesar, how much truer it must have been of the Potentate who founded Christendom itself. Equally was it true, in Russian eyes, of the monarch of old Rus whose conversion to Byzantine Christianity in 988 marked the beginning of 'Holy Russia'. Vladimir, like the Emperor Constantine, bears the title '*Isapostolus*', which means 'equal to an Apostle'. In the West, the majority of monarch-saints are martyrs, or those who have somehow failed to exercise their monarchical authority. It was easier to be canonised in the East just for being a king. The eastern Churches have a less narrowly sacerdotal vision of humanity than those of the Latin rite. All believers, for the Orthodox, are kings and priests. Christian kings, princes and governors, no less than bishops, are God's ministers. Since all power belongs to God, and comes from God, there can be nothing wrong, by this view, in allowing the secular authority to exercise power even in the ecclesiastical sphere. So, in nineteenth-century Russia, it was a layman who was Procurator of the Holy Synod, and the Tsar who decided even doctrinal matters. In 1842, the Procurator was a retired army officer called Pratasov who was able to forbid the Metropolitan of Moscow to prepare a commentary on the Holy Scriptures. Nicholas I, himself only an army officer with no theological training, was consulted about the afterlife and decreed, rather to the consternation of his clergy, that there was no purgatory. Nevertheless, the stubbornness or ignorance of the laity is no more or less troubling than that of the clergy to the Orthodox. And eastern believers have looked askance at the various attempts at theocracy in the history of the West, where in their suspicion of 'Christian kings, princes and governors', clergymen have seized for themselves a secular influence and created such un-Evangelical anomalies as the state of Geneva under Calvin or the quasi-imperial pomps of the Vatican.

Tolstoy was no doubt reacting against the corruption and abuse which he deemed to have overcome the Court and the Church in nineteenth-century Russia. But his anarchical distrust of civil authority *per se* is deeply un-Russian. In his devotion to the Beatitudes, in his pacifism, in his distrust of material possessions and his desire to live like a beggar and a pilgrim, it is almost possible to believe that Tolstoy drew unconscious inspiration from the traditions of Russian Orthodoxy. But the anarchism was not a native flowering. It is all of a piece with his fierce independence of mind and his exaggerated sense of self. It was fed from a variety of sources: from Rousseau, from Proudhon, as well as from the American sectaries with whom he was in correspondence, most especially from the Quakers.

It also has to be said that, as well as being the least Russian, it is also the silliest of his teachings. Neither common sense, nor the New Testament (and the two are not always coincident) suggest to us that civil government is in itself an evil. No one would deny that Christ came to found a kingdom not of this world. But it is from Proudhon and not from Christ that Tolstoy derives his belief that all governments are of necessity founded upon violence. And one is bound to ask — since Tolstoy never really supplies an answer — why Christianity should necessarily consider it sinful to supply a populace with food, roads and drains, none of which, in the history of mankind, have ever been available without the intervention of some centralised authority. Tolstoy's reasons for doubting the validity of civil defence, not to mention wars or prisons, are explained very fully in his writings, though his failure to distinguish between the violence of an individual (which Christianity has always condemned) and a magistrate's duty to defend the defenceless citizens, stems directly from his anarchic understanding of the state. One has to add that when hunger befell Russia in 1891 he would immediately lay aside his anarchist principles and become once more the authoritative officer-type, organising relief on a huge scale. Likewise, his objection to owning his own copyrights was forgotten when he wished to raise money to give to religious dissidents safe conduct to the New World. The virtue of Tolstoy's deeds quite often belied the absurdity of his attitudes. And one should remember this when reading his religious stuff.

The whole bent of Tolstoy's mind is towards making things clear and simple. The New Testament, however, is neither clear nor simple. It is not really possible to approach it in the way that Tolstoy approached it, because it does not yield answers so easily. A scholar might suppose that there is simply a lack of evidence. After a hundred and fifty years of 'critical' analysis of the Gospels, no one has been able to prove even such simple questions as when or where they were written. It is as if they are in fact placed in a unique position, as if their hiddenness and mystery eluded modern scientific analysis.

A theologian might see here something providential, the master-touch of One who in the days of His flesh thanked God for concealing Himself from the wise and revealing Himself to the simple; One who in the days of His resurrection revealed Himself to Paul as the ultimate mystery. For the Evangelist Mark, the resurrection is the ultimate mystery too, a messianic secret revealed to a tiny handful of people, an empty tomb, and women running away because they were afraid. For Paul, it was a mystery of the spirit, groaning and travailing through all creation to reconcile man to God and to undo his sins, a reconciliation which took place in the darkness of Christ's Passion. To the author of Hebrews, it is a mystery: Christ is seen metaphorically as the High Priest, entering the veil of the Holy of Holies and offering sacrifice — Himself — for sin. To Evangelistic John, the pre-existent Word has become Flesh, and to the Apocalyptic John, the Son of Man from the Book of Daniel has appeared in the sky. From beginning to end, the New Testament is caught up in mystery. Its difficulties will never be solved by scholars, though there is no harm in their trying. Glints of what the mystery was, and is, are only discernible through worship.

Tolstoy had tried that, but it did not answer. His rationalistic, nineteenth-century knees lacked health until they had stopped genuflecting. But he was enough, *au fond*, a Russian Orthodox to know that he could not refuse to worship without, as it were, divine sanction. And so the Gospels themselves had to be looted and plundered and robbed of the mystery which is their essence. If he were doing so as a conscious act of blasphemy, perhaps his action would have had small effect. But all-unconscious of any impurity of motive, he laboured on, with total sincerity. With devastating clear-sightedness he kept asking the question, how is it that Christians can refuse to obey the words of Christ? He wrote from conviction. More than anything he had ever desired, he now desired to obey those words himself, to identify with the poor and the oppressed, to abandon his wealth, to live in peace and forgiveness with all men. Is it any wonder that his thoughts had such an appeal? Dostoyevsky on an imaginative level recaptured the Holy Redeemer, the Christ who against all logic and all deserving, redeems the sins of the world. Tolstoy, with no less imaginative panache, restored to the world Christ's starkest and most revolutionary moral demands.

*　　　*　　　*　　　*

While all these thoughts were brewing, two deaths occurred which were of the utmost significance in Tolstoy's life: Dostoyevsky's and the Tsar's.

Dostoyevsky died on January 28, 1881, lying on his sofa, with the copy of the New Testament which had been given to him by wives of the Decembrists thirty years before when he had been on his way to the prison at Omsk. In a scene which he could have composed himself (and in a sense did), he got his wife Anna to carry a flickering candle to the Testament and hold it to a text which fell open at random. It was the Baptist's encounter with Jesus at the beginning of St. Matthew's Gospel: 'But John restrained Him and said, "I need to be baptised by you, and you come to me?" But Jesus said to him in reply: "Do not restrain me, for this is how we have to fulfil all righteousness."' Anna Dostoyevsky in her memoirs believed that this text actually 'killed' her husband, because he took the words 'do not restrain me' to be a portent of the fact that he had no longer to live.[28]

When Tolstoy heard the news of his death from Strakhov, he wrote at once,

I never saw the man, and never had any direct relations with him, and suddenly when he died I realised that he was the very closest, dearest and most necessary man for me. I was a writer, and all writers are vain and envious — I at least was that sort of writer. But it never occurred to me to measure myself against him, never. . . .[29]

This is the best commentary on relations between Tolstoy and Dostoyevsky. There was probably no literary rivalry in the vulgar sense between the two giants. But there was an acute consciousness in each of the other, an acutely strong desire, on both their parts, not to be like each other. It would almost be a plausible exaggeration to claim that in his art — though not in his views — Tolstoy was henceforth to feel free to trespass, as it were, on Dostoyevsky's territory, to write the books which, in Dostoyevsky's lifetime, he would not have been able to write for fear of being Dostoyevskian. That is too crude and simple a way of looking at it. Let Tolstoy's own words stand.

A month after Dostoyevsky died, there was enacted a scene such as he might have written into *The Devils*. Six attempts had been made on the life of Tsar Alexander II, by nihilists and revolutionary groups. On February 17, 1880, a violent explosion had shaken the Winter

Palace, killing forty Finnish guards. The Tsar, who was entertaining the Prince of Bulgaria at the time, looked up from his whist as the chandeliers tinkled above their heads and said calmly, 'God has saved me again.' 'One is tempted,' the German Ambassador remarked privately afterwards, 'to regard as moribund a social body which fails to react to such a shock.'[30]

The reign had been blighted by these assassination attempts. After the first of them, in 1866, the liberalising, reforming instincts of the Tsar had been put firmly in check by his advisers. Count Dmitry Tolstoy, for example, heavily egged on by Katkov, was appointed Minister of Education in 1866, and caused an immediate about-turn in educational policies. He regarded the superficial materialist outlook of the young to have been caused by their not doing enough Latin and Greek, and he abolished the teaching of science in all Russian grammar schools. The police, the army, the Holy Synod were all, likewise, put into reverse gear, and foreign policy both on the Polish border and in the Russo-Turkish conflict had become more unashamedly jingoistic. The more repressive the regime had become, the wider the discontents grew; and the more violent the reactions of the malcontents, the fiercer the Government felt itself right to become.

But Alexander II had been persuaded by some of his ministers to take tentative steps towards the establishment of some form of constitutional advisory body, the first steps towards a constitutional monarchy on an English pattern. The liberalisers received the support of the Tsar's mistress (subsequently his morganatic wife, Catherine Dolgoruky) while it was opposed by the Tsarina and her conservative friends like Pobedonostsev. But there is no doubt that some such reforms would have gone through in the spring of 1881 if it had not been for the Tsar's assassination.

The Government's battle with the terrorists appeared to be gaining ground. Indeed, in February 1881, Andrey Ivanovich Zhelyabov, the leader of one of the most dangerous organisations, was arrested. One of his accomplices, Sofya Perovskaya, resolved on murdering the Tsar before Zhelyabov's interrogators blew their cover.

On the cold morning of Sunday, March 1, the Tsar signed General Loris-Melikov's reforming charter. Then he went, as he did each Sunday, to inspect the Guard, a formal, slow business, which took several hours. Then, again as he did each week, he called on his cousin the Grand Duchess Catherine.

It was part of the security arrangements that the Tsar should always return to the Winter Palace by a different route. Nevertheless, the terrorists this morning were to get their man. A mining student called Ryssakov threw a bomb as the Tsar's sledge passed by. The Emperor insisted on stopping the sledge and inquiring after the Cossack, his escort, who had been wounded. Someone in the crowd called out to Alexander himself, to ask if he was wounded. 'Thank God, no!' he called back. And at that point another anarchist, a Polish student called Hrieniewicki, threw a bomb directly at Alexander's feet. Both the legs were shattered. He whispered, 'Home to the Palace, to die there.' Escorted by bleeding Cossacks on blood-spattered horses, the poor little body of the Emperor was taken back to die in the arms of the morganatic wife on whom he so childishly doted. The liberator of the Russian serfs had died, like the liberator of the American negro, by the violent hands of an assassin.

When the news reached Yasnaya Polyana, the assassins had already been rounded up and stood trial for their lives. Having decided that all forms of civil government were wrong, that revenge in all circumstances was wrong, that taking a man's life was always wrong, it was not surprising that Tolstoy thought that the terrorists should be pardoned. The most solemn moments of life can be reduced to farce if general questions of public morality become a matter for private domestic dispute. For a long time, Tolstoy had begun to find that the only member of the household he could really 'talk to' was his children's tutor, an avowed atheist, and a rather charming young man called Vasily Ivanovich Alexeyev. To judge from Alexeyev's memories of the conversations, the great man was capable of provoking, as well as speaking, some fairly considerable nonsense. ('I once asked him what sort of music he liked best. He replied, "Simple folk [*narodnuyu*] music. And my favourite composer is — the people [*narod*]."') Without wishing to emphasise the idiocy of this sort of thing, Alexeyev is punctilious in his memoirs to show Tolstoy's eyes filling with tears as he listens to Beethoven. And it was Beethoven and Chopin that he himself played, not folk songs, when he sat down at the piano. Or again, Tolstoy claimed to Alexeyev that he did not like verse, only prose. Poets were forced to say things they did not really mean for the sake of the rhyme. But next time he went to Moscow, Tolstoy brought Alexeyev a present, a copy of Tyutchev, whom he loved to declaim. In particular, he liked to intone the lines

Молчи скрываися и таи
И чувства и мечти твои…

[. . . . be quiet, lie low and hide
Your feelings and your dreams. . . .]³¹

Tolstoy's ability to get along well with young men, almost to flirt with them, was always a source of peculiar annoyance to his wife, who — in a few words which, again, Alexeyev does not appear to have meant maliciously — just happened to overhear the things the two men were saying to each other as she listened through the study door. They were talking about the assassination of the Tsar, and agreeing with one another that the terrorists should be pardoned. It was more than she could stand. She burst into the room, yelling, as was her wont, 'Vasily Ivanovich, what are you saying?' she called. 'If it were my son and daughter in here with you, and not Lev Nikolayevich, I would order you to clear off immediately!'³²

Tolstoy took refuge in sleep, and dozed off on the study sofa. He dreamt that he was both the executioner and one of the criminals, and he woke up in a cold sweat. It is tedious to keep repeating this point, but how wonderful this faculty of completely imagining himself into the other man's shoes would be in a novelist. But Lev Nikolayevich is no longer a novelist. He has put such vanities behind him. He is a prophet. And so, his capacity to *be* the criminal, to *be* the executioner took the form of an intense and literal sympathy with all concerned.

Tolstoy was not a fool. Nor was he out of touch with what was going on at Court. Cousins and friends of his were all involved with the Court at its most intimate levels. He knew perfectly well that Konstantin Petrovich Pobedonostsev, who had recently become Procurator of the Holy Synod, had now in effect assumed the reins of power. When he had been the new Tsar's tutor, Pobedonostsev had openly stated his conviction that Alexander Alexandrovich was fundamentally stupid. But this made it all the more imperative that as Alexander III, and Emperor of all the Russias, the new Tsar should have sound advisers. It had been rightly said that Pobedonostsev exercised over Alexander III an ascendancy similar to that exercised by Torquemada over Ferdinand and Isabella or by Père Lachaise over Louis XIV. Pobedonostsev's conviction was that reforms and liberalising had gone far enough, and that the constitutional reforms of Loris-Melikov should be scrapped. It has to be said that the policy of repression of which Pobedonostsev was the architect worked. The Revolution was held off for another quarter century and more. And it could be argued that if the reactionaries had not given in in 1905, they would not have been caught off guard twelve years later by the comparatively small insurrection of the Bolsheviks. So Pobedonostsev should not be viewed as an ostrich-like fool who was blind to the 'inevitability' of revolution in Russia. In 1881, there was nothing 'inevitable' about it. Pobedonostsev was, we are told by a contemporary, a man of 'thin, dry, somewhat pinched features, cast in the Byzantine mould; cold, sharp eyes, rendered colder still by the spectacles that shield them, and whose glance is as frigid and cheerless as the cheerless ray of the winter's sun'. Pobedonostsev may have been cold, but he was not unthinking. His own memoirs are a highly intelligent defence of the conservative religious position[33] and, as his friendship with Dostoyevsky shows, he was big enough a man to 'take' from a writer of genius a degree of religious speculation which, in a lesser mortal, would have been thought wholly unacceptable.

It was to this figure that Tolstoy addressed a short note, which begins, 'I know you to be a Christian,' and asking him to pass on a letter to the new Emperor, 'written by me about the recent terrible events'. The letter is justly famous as a piece of magnificent and imaginative rhetoric; and it is a bold embodiment of Tolstoy's newly-fashioned and understood Christian belief.

> Sire, If you were. . . . to summon these people, to give them money and to send them away somewhere to America, and were to write a manifesto headed by the words: 'but I say unto you, love your enemies' — I don't know about the others but I, a poor loyal subject, would be your dog and your slave. I would weep with emotion, as I am weeping now, every time I heard your name. But what am I saying, 'I don't know about the others'? I know that at these words goodness and love would flow across Russia in a torrent. The truths of Christ are alive in the hearts of man, and they only are alive, and we love others only in the name of these truths.[34]

The words are of course directed not to Alexander III, who could barely be expected to understand them, but to Pobedonostsev. When he read Tolstoy's letter, the Emperor remarked, 'If the crime had concerned me personally, I should have the right to pardon those who were guilty of it, but I could not pardon them on behalf of my father.'[35] All Tolstoy's letter had done had been to mark him down, in the Government's eyes, as a troublemaker.

The reaction of Tolstoy's wife to the matter was one of simple outrage. She hated the anarchists, some of whom had started to write to Tolstoy, even to visit him and hang on his words. She felt a perfectly natural fear that the Government would associate Tolstoy with the murderers and revolutionaries, and that this would inevitably bring trouble to the family.

The dispute between them over the letter to the Tsar was a symptom of a much deeper rift which was growing and developing between them. On April 3, the six murderers were hanged. The children watched with a mixture of anguish, admiration and embarrassment the effect this had on their father. During May, Tolstoy noted that he had had conversations with Sergey, Tanya and Ilya about non-resistance to evil. He felt completely isolated by what he saw as their stubborn refusal to understand him. Later that summer, he announced that he wanted to make another pilgrimage to the Optina monastery. He set off on June 10, 1881, with an old peasant coat, bark shoes and a staff in his hand. Being unused to walking such long distances and having home-made shoes which were quite inadequate for the journey, he arrived covered in blisters. The return journey was done by train.

The family might reasonably have wondered what he was up to. His diary reveals his belief that 'the family is the flesh' and that he wanted to commit suicide.[36] Their mother had the more practical fear that if they remained in the country the children's education would be neglected. This necessitated buying a house in Moscow. Tolstoy by now had an income of over thirty thousand roubles per annum, two thirds of which derived from his novels and one third from his farms. In addition to the estates of Yasnaya Polyana, he now had thousands of acres in Samara, where he could escape his worldly family, hob-nob with the *kumys* drinkers (Molokans) and think simple thoughts. Initially, he was so opposed to the idea of adding to their wealth by buying a Moscow house that Sofya Andreyevna went off to take a rented house from Tolstoy's Volkonsky cousins in Denezhny Lane

(Money Lane) in Moscow. Later, in October 1882, they bought a house in Dolgo-Khamovnichesky Street. Of necessity, it was large. Yasnaya Polyana, with its small number of moderately sized rooms, was becoming uncomfortable for the eight surviving children, and all their entourage of servants, tutors and nannies, not to mention their father's eccentric visitors — the 'dark ones' who came to Tolstoy, expecting and usually receiving a sympathetic ear for their madcap views.

Tolstoy's son Ilya recalls that, by this stage of the family history, 'the world was divided into two camps . . . . with *Papa* in one and *Maman* and everyone else in the other'.[37] Yet for his sisters, whose devotion to their father was intense, there was soon to come a time when they felt that they could not serve God and *maman*. Sofya's increasing bad temper and absence of sympathy for her husband was to have the effect of alienating some of the children and making them side with their father.

By the end of Tolstoy's life, these divisions had hardened into embattled positions. In this period of childhood and adolescence it was a cause of confusion and agony for all the children. Both their parents were highly remarkable and the children realised that they owed them so much. Ilya had fully believed his mother when she said that, if they did not go to Moscow, he would never be educated. But he had no sooner enrolled at his *Gymnasium* than he realised that he knew Greek better than any boy in his class. How had he learnt it? From Papa reading Xenophon to them in the nursery.[38]

Sofya Andreyevna was happier in Moscow than she had been for a long time at Yasnaya Polyana. Friends and relations came in and out each day; she was near her own family, the Berses. But, as she admitted to Tanya, 'I cried every day for the first two weeks because Lyovochka became not just sad, but even fell into a kind of desperate apathy. He did not eat or sleep and sometimes literally wept, and I thought I really would go mad. You would be surprised to see how I have changed, and how thin I have grown.'[39]

Although the move was what family life and common sense required, it was precisely out of tune with the movements of Tolstoy's imagination at that time. With no fiction to write, he was busy making a fictitious character out of himself. While he was with the Molokans in the absolute remoteness of Samara, his fantasy knew no check. He could be a humble servant of Christ, drinking *kumys* and wearing malodorous clothes and thinking peaceable thoughts. In a town house, where servants bowed every time you passed, all this became impossible.

As a countryman, he in any case had less and less taste for city life. 'Stench, stones, luxury, poverty, debauchery. Malefactors have come together, robbing the people; they have collected soldiers and set up law courts to protect their orgies and they feast. There is nothing for the people to do except to take advantage of the passions of these others and lure back from them what has been stolen. The peasants are cleverest at this. Their wives remain at home, while they wax our floors, rub our bodies in the bath and ply as cabmen.'[40]

There is a Dickensian vision of the city here, as a seething mass of multifarious humanity, mingled with a Proudhon-like certainty that anyone with property is a thief. And there is also here a sly old country squire's hatred of town.

But Tolstoy's vision of Moscow also reflects an actual change which had come upon the city since he had known it as a young man. The census of 1864, taken not long after Tolstoy got married, reckoned the population of Moscow as three hundred and seventy-eight thousand, showing an increase of barely thirty thousand since 1833. By the end of the nineteenth century, the population of Moscow was nearly two million. Russia was ceasing to be a primarily (almost, a solely) agricultural economy. Mining, metal-work, cotton, sugar, textile manufacture, all knew an enormous increase in the last four decades of the century. Since the liberation of the serfs in 1861, there had been an inevitable drift away from the land. Peasant farmers and agricultural workers, tiring of the struggle to make a living from the land, drifted into the cities. Russia was creating its own urban, industrial proletariat — the wage-slave class who, in England, gave Marx and Engels the hope that there would be a revolution of 'the people' — in other words, not of peasants but of factory-workers.[41]

All Tolstoy's instincts were repelled by the industrialisation of Russia. He shared with John Ruskin and Henry David Thoreau a vision of human life itself being destroyed by the smoke, the noise, the squalor. At the same time, although he pined for some way in which he could be dispossessed, he had all the rural landowner's contempt for what the merchant and industrial classes had done to the towns.

As often as he could, he escaped, and went back to Yasnaya Polyana. When they were together, he and his wife had become increasingly quarrelsome. Indeed, the more he wrote about religion, the more quarrelsome he became.

The flavour of marital life at this period is caught in Sofya Andreyevna's diary entry for August 26, 1882:

It was twenty years ago when I was young and happy that I started writing the story of my love for Lyovochka in this book: there is virtually nothing *but* love in it in fact. Twenty years later, here I am sitting up all night on my own, reading and mourning its loss. For the first time in my life, Lyovochka has run off to sleep alone in the study. We were quarrelling about such silly things — I accused him of taking no interest in the children and not helping me look after Ilya, who is sick, or making them all jackets. But it has nothing to do with jackets and everything to do with his growing coldness towards me and the children. Today he shouted at the top of his voice that his dearest wish was to leave his family. I shall carry the memory of that heart-felt, heart-rending cry of his to my grave. . . . Lord help me! I long to take my life, my thoughts are so confused. The clock is striking four.

I have decided that if he doesn't come in to see me, it must mean he loves another woman. He has not come. I used to know what my duty was — but what now?

He did come in, but it was the next day before we made it up. We both cried and I realised to my joy that his love for me, which I had mourned all through that terrible night, was not dead. . . .

The doubts, however, could never be altogether stilled. The old Tolstoy, who loved his wife and wrote novels, was now a shadowy figure, glimpsed only occasionally.

Tolstoy's wife was not the only one to mourn him. The readers of *War and Peace* and *Anna Karenina* were waiting in vain for another novel from the great writer's pen. No one was more generous in his mourning than Tolstoy's fellow novelist Turgenev, whose last letter, in the summer of 1883, was an urgent plea to Tolstoy not to abandon art.

Kind and dear Lev Nikolayevich. It is a long time since I wrote to you, for I have been and am, frankly speaking, on my deathbed. I cannot recover — there is no use thinking it. I am writing to you particularly to tell you how glad I am to have been your contemporary, and to express to you my last, sincere request. My friend, return to literary activity! That gift came to you whence comes all the rest. Ah, how happy I should be if I could think that my request would have an effect on you!! I am a doomed man — even the doctors do not know what to call my malady, *Névralgie stomacale goutteuse*. I can neither walk, nor eat, nor sleep. It is even wearisome to repeat all this! My friend, great writer of the Russian land, heed my request! Let me know if you receive this bit of paper and permit me once more to embrace you heartily, *heartily*, and your wife and all yours. I can write no more. I am weary.[43]

Two months later, Turgenev was dead. In September, Tolstoy was asked by the Society of the Lovers of Russian Literature to speak at a memorial meeting in honour of Turgenev. These literary meetings in honour of great writers who had died often became the occasion for the pronouncement of some great words, *ex cathedra*, by the writer selected to make the chief speech. Dostoyevsky had made a great speech at the unveiling of the Pushkin monument some years before. Nekrasov's funeral was a similarly public occasion, with speeches made about the state of literature and the condition of contemporary Russia.

Tolstoy's second cousin Dmitry was the Minister for the Interior. When the bureaucrats got to hear that Lev Nikolayevich was planning a speech at the Turgenev commemoration, he drafted a memorandum in which he denounced the author of *War and Peace* as 'a madman, from whom one might expect anything; he may say unbelievable things and there may be a considerable scandal'. It was not long before the Governor-General of Moscow had informed the President of the Society of the Lovers of Russian Literature that their meeting in honour of Turgenev had been 'postponed for an indefinite time'.

The rebuttal came as no surprise. Ever since the assassination of the previous Tsar, the Government had become more and more autocratic and reactionary. No great public speaker, Tolstoy was probably not even particularly disappointed that the authorities should have stopped his mouth. They could not do the same to his pen.

What I Believe was finished in the autumn of 1883. In it the processes which had been at work in his earlier religious writings — *A Confession*, the *Four Gospels*, and the *Critique* — reached their culmination. Few scholars of the New Testament nowadays would

The Holy Man

'accept' his readings in their entirety. That is, they would think that on a factual level, he had misread the Greek. It simply is not true that the word νόμος (law) in the New Testament is always to be identified with civil order. 'Jesus denounced the institution of all human tribunals of whatever sort'[44] (Chapter III). Well, did He? We have already spoken of the impossibility of using the Gospels as a quarry from which we could reconstruct in such vivid biographical terms what Jesus was like. But if He did denounce all forms of human tribunal, it is odd, for example, that He never mentioned this fact to the 'ruler of the synagogue' when raising his daughter from the dead; or that He kept His mouth shut in front of Pontius Pilate. Again, even the most sceptical reader of the New Testament will raise an eyebrow to be informed that 'Jesus not only did not recognise the resurrection but denied it every time He met with the idea. . . .'[45] Fighting words, but how can they be justified? Either you take the Modernist line that it is impossible to know what Jesus said, only what the Evangelists make Him say; or you are a Fundamentalist and believe that His words are recorded in the Gospels. In which case, what are we to make of His words to the widow of Nain? Or to Martha, 'I am the resurrection and the life'? The four Gospels all in their different ways (not surprisingly, they are written from the point of view of faith) all depict Jesus as repeatedly calling men to Himself. 'Come unto me all that travail and are heavily laden.' 'Suffer the little children to come unto me,' etc. etc. Tolstoy tells us, 'Jesus never asked men to have faith in His person.'

Even to begin to unpick the many ways in which Tolstoy contradicts (or as a modern critic would say, misreads) the New Testament is to miss the point. The point is, as he says, that 'I alone understand the doctrine of Jesus.' And again, 'That is why, after eighteen hundred years, it so singularly happened that I discovered the meaning of the doctrine of Jesus as some new thing.'[46] You cannot argue with a man who writes like that.

I am lost with my companions in a snowstorm. One of them assures me with the utmost sincerity that he sees a light in the distance, but it is only a mirage which deceives us both; we strive to reach this light, but we never can find it. Another resolutely brushes away the snow; he seeks and finds the road, and he cries to us, 'Go not that way, the light you see is false, you will wander to destruction; here is the road, feel it beneath your feet; we are saved.' It is very little,

337

we say. We had faith in that light that gleamed in our deluded eyes, that told us of a refuge, a warm shelter, rest, deliverance — and now in exchange for it we have nothing but the road. Ah, but if we continue to travel toward the imaginary light, we shall perish; if we follow the road, we shall surely arrive at the haven of safety.[47]

And this road is none other than the following of Jesus's five commandments, as interpreted by Tolstoy himself. Old heresies, like old jokes, acquire their own particular kind of pathetic obsolescence. But read in a nineteenth-century context, *What I Believe* is an intensely exciting, invigorating piece of heresy. While all over Europe the clergy was agonising about whether the Book of Genesis was compatible with the discoveries of Charles Darwin, or whether Noah's Ark was historically true, Tolstoy was resurrecting the much more urgent question — is the moral teaching of Jesus true? If it is, it makes demands upon us. We must change the way we live. In our day, the shape of the battleground has altered. But one can guess that he would not have been very interested in the fact that some modern-minded bishop did not believe that Jesus rose from the dead. He would have seen why such derisory figures only excite the notice of newspapermen, while the imagination of the entire world has been moved by the Christ-like example of Mother Teresa of Calcutta. The appeal of Mother Teresa is not that she is a woman or a Roman Catholic but simply that she is one of those rare people who has taken the commandments of Jesus quite literally, and given up everything, and clothed the naked, and fed the little ones. As Chesterton once said, Christianity has not been tried and found wanting. It has hardly ever been tried.

Tolstoy wanted to try. That is what his *Credo* explains. But he was too much of an egotist and a rationalist to submit to the teachings and disciplines of a church. 'To be of no church is dangerous. Religion, of which the rewards are distant, and which is animated only by faith and hope, will glide by degrees out of mind, unless it be invigorated and reimpressed by external ordinance, by stated calls to worship, and the salutary influence of example.' But Samuel Johnson's censure of a great English heresiarch did not foresee the possibility that someone might invent a religion which was animated by no faith at all, save in the power of love; whose 'calls to worship' came from within, rather than without; but who had, by the time he finished *What I Believe*, the very distinct intention of starting a new religion. Ever since the idea of Christianity purged of its miraculous and irrational elements had first dawned on his mind while still a subaltern in the Caucasus, the idea had been subliminally present in Tolstoy's mind. Perhaps it went (as so many biographers have wanted to tell us) to the Ant Brotherhood of his childish years.

> The Church that sought to detach men from error and to weld them together again by the solemn affirmation that it alone was the truth has long since fallen to decay. But the Church composed of men united, not by promises or sacraments, but by deeds of truth and love, has always lived and will live forever. Now, as eighteen hundred years ago, this Church is made up not of those who say 'Lord, Lord', and bring forth iniquity, but of those who hear the words of truth and reveal them in their lives. The members of this Church. . . . practise the commandments of Jesus and thereby teach them to others. Whether this Church be in numbers little or great, it is, nevertheless, the Church that will never perish, the Church that shall finally unite within its bonds the hearts of all mankind. 'Fear not, little flock, for it is your Father's good purpose to give you the Kingdom.'[48]

It was only little over a decade since the Supreme Pontiff in Rome had declared himself the Infallible Vicar of Christ, a claim which was vigorously denied by the Patriarch of Constantinople, and the Patriarch of Moscow. Now, it appeared, in the autumn of 1883, Christ had raised up a new guardian of His truth on earth. And all that was lacking, as the Patriarch of Dolgo-Khamovnichesky Street put the finishing touches to his encyclical, was a devotee ardent enough to take the Gospel to the world. The Papacy of the Counter-reformation was immeasurably strengthened by the energies of St. Ignatius Loyola. The very Gospel of Christ might never have been preached beyond the bounds of Jewry had it not been for the fervour of Paul of Tarsus. Tolstoyism awaited its archpriest. And on October 15, 1883, on the steps of the house on Dolgo-Khamovnichesky Street, he rang the doorbell.

Chapter Fourteen

Real Christianity

1884 - 1887

I hope no Reader imagines me so weak to
stand up in the Defence of Real Christianity,
such as used in Primitive Times (if we may
believe the Authors of those Ages) to have an
Influence upon Mens Belief and Actions: To
offer at the restoring of That would indeed be
a wild Project; It would be to dig up
Foundations, to destroy at one Blow all the
Wit, and half the Learning of the Kingdom; to
break the entire Frame and Constitution of
Things, to ruin Trade, extinguish Arts and
Sciences with the Professors of them; In short,
to turn our Courts, Exchanges and shops into
Deserts. . . .

Jonathan Swift, 'An argument to prove that
the Abolishing of Christianity in England may,
as Things now stand, be attended with some
Inconveniences. . . .' 1708

Vladimir Grigoryevich Chertkov was at the time of his meeting with Tolstoy an army officer aged twenty-nine. He was a handsome, even a slightly beautiful, young man with watery, dark eyes, and sharp, aquiline ears and nose. His is the face of a gentle, religious aristocrat: the sort of man, in fact, who so fascinated Dostoyevsky. His father, who was very rich, was a general and an aide-de-camp to the Tsar. His mother, *née* Chernishev-Kuglikov, was an intimate with the Empress. She was a religious woman, who had come under the influence of the English Evangelical preacher Lord Radstock and undergone a 'conversion'. Vladimir Grigoryevich, having had the usual sort of aristocratic Russian youth — cards, drink, women — had also been converted by Lord Radstock's ideas. He was always very close to his mother. This conversion of Chertkov's had happened in 1879, when he was only twenty-five. He had gone to England, at his mother's prompting, joined the Piccadilly Club and the Cricket and Skating Club, read a great deal of Evangelical literature, and lodged with a sympathetic clergyman.

He appears to have started reading Tolstoy in earnest on his return to St. Petersburg in 1880, and evidently got to learn from mutual acquaintances, most notably N. V. Davydov, of the religious evolutions which were going on in the Master's mind. The final sections of *Anna Karenina* made a profound impression on him, and he longed to meet Tolstoy. Davydov thought that it could be arranged. Towards the end of October 1883, Chertkov made plans to journey to Yasnaya Polyana. He too, like Levin, wished to abandon the pursuit of worldly success, live in the country and think simple thoughts. He too, moreover, had become a pacifist. He had already resigned his commission in the army and gone to live on his mother's estate in order to teach peasant children. He felt sure that talking with Tolstoy would help to clear his mind. Then, just as he was about to set out to Yasnaya Polyana, he received a telegram from Davydov: TOLSTOY IN MOSCOW, and he boldly paid a call at the house.

For Chertkov, it felt as if he was meeting an old friend. Tolstoy, it seemed, had already heard about Chertkov from a third party (Davydov or Rusanov). Tolstoy read him some of *What I Believe* which he had just finished. Chertkov was profoundly excited. Though disturbed by the fact that Tolstoy had discarded the doctrine of grace, he was electrified by the spiritual kinship which immediately established itself between them. He visited Tolstoy several times before returning to his maternal estates at Lizinovka. 'Everything is lovely here,' he wrote to Tolstoy. 'We have just had our first fall of snow, and there is great joy. Tomorrow the boys start work in the handicraft school. It will be very lively and even more, fun.'[1] With this letter he enclosed some Evangelical books, expounding the divinity of Christ. 'I want him to read them,' he confided to his diary, 'because I want him to understand me better, so as to be able to help me.'[2] Tolstoy was not helped by the books. 'Dear kind Vladimir Grigoryevich, who are so close to me,' he wrote back, 'I got your books, and I thank you for them. I have read them and though you will think me proud, I found nothing in them. But I love you so much that I cannot but tell you the truth.'[3]

The intensity of Tolstoy's feelings for the young man must have alarmed Chertkov's mother. So must the fact that it was quite obvious that Vladimir Grigoryevich was so much under Tolstoy's spell that there was not much future for his Evangelical beliefs. Nothing that the general his father knew of Tolstoy, from Court gossip, could have recommended the association either. In the spring of 1884, while staying in the country, Chertkov started to translate *What I Believe* into English. The geographical distances between the two friends had meant that they were not able to meet as often as they would like, but they wrote such full letters to one another that Chertkov sometimes felt closer to Tolstoy when they were apart than when they were having to snatch hours together away from the family in the Tolstoy house in Moscow. He spent April in St. Petersburg with his parents, writing what Tolstoy considered a 'splendid' letter about the frivolous manner in which the St. Petersburg aristocracy celebrated Easter.

Chertkov was by now using Tolstoy as his father confessor, and in one letter, he poured out revelations about the 'dark' side of his character. Tolstoy knew so well the perils of reconciling sexual passion with a desire to be good, and remembered from his own resolutions, when he was Chertkov's age, the dangers of climbing the ladder of perfection.

> Any letter of yours disturbs me. I'll tell you my feelings when I get your letters: I am frightened and alarmed in case you should break your neck. And not because I do not trust in your strength, or that I don't value you highly; not because you have climbed up terribly high in my opinion (where you need to be) but because I think you are insecure there. I say this because I love you very much and because the work you are doing on this belltower is very dear to me. I want to give advice and am frightened of interfering. One thing I can't help saying in reply to your last letter but one. You ought to get married — i.e. I think you will be safer high up there if you tie this rope around you. I was alarmed by the words in your last letter but one. 'I have had a lot to drink and I have depraved thoughts.' I know you deliberately exaggerate what is shameful, and in this respect I always make you an example for myself. But this is frightening. Another thing — I am afraid that you are carried away by proselytism — by conversion as an end in itself. . . .[4]

Chertkov replied that he had no plans for marrying just yet, and that he was not in love with anyone. But this was obviously untrue. He was patently in love with Tolstoy, and Tolstoy with him; though not in a sexual sense.

At the end of April, Chertkov's father suffered a cerebral haemorrhage and died. Not long afterwards, evidently thinking that she could break the dangerous friendship, Chertkov's mother sent him once more to England.

The summer at Yasnaya Polyana without him was wretched. Tolstoy felt a series of crushing depressions, and quite alienated from the family.

Cranks and devotees had started to make the pilgrimage to see the author of *A Confession* and *What I Believe*. Some, like Isaak Feinerman, were political revolutionaries, who were disillusioned with socialism and came to discover more about Tolstoy's social and religious vision. Others journeyed from further afield, like the Russian-born American William Frey (born V. K. Geins) who had attempted to found various kinds of agricultural communes in the United States. Religious seekers, social malcontents, pilgrims and beggars all beat a path to Tolstoy's door. They helped to exacerbate the alienation which he felt from his family. The strangers, however wild or odd they may have been, were trying to listen to him, and understand him. But this could not be said of his nearest family. The Gospel saying was coming true: 'And a man's foes shall be they of his own household.' He tried to talk to his children but, young or old, it was the same story. 'Seryozha is impossibly obtuse. The same castrated mind that his mother has. . . .'5 'Talked with the children about how to live — to be one's own servant. Verochka said, "Well, that's all right for a week, but surely you can't live like that!" And this is what we bring our children to!'6 Letters from Chertkov were the only ray of light 'in the darkness that has thickened even more since the arrival of Tanya'. His sister-in-law, who, as a young woman had provided him with so much of Natasha Rostova's *joie-de-vivre* was now, as far as he was concerned, a bore; her husband Kuzminsky 'tedious. . . . lifeless'.7 The Kuzminskys were quarrelling a lot. So were the Tolstoys, Lev Nikolayevich and Sofya Andreyevna. Tempers were not improved by Tolstoy's (successful) attempts during the summer of 1884 to abandon one of his greatest passions: smoking tobacco. By this stage, he was also beginning to think that he should give up alcohol and become a vegetarian. Simplicity and humility were now thunderously insisted upon. He was not 'Sir' or 'Count': just plain Lev Nikolayevich, and woe betide the servant who forgot this. At table, there were outbursts of rage if the food was too elaborate for the tastes of the aspirant saint. He wandered round the village, causing a mixture of awe, gratitude, bewilderment and embarrassment as he fraternised with his peasant friends. One day he helped an old woman to rebuild her hut. Another day he would go and chop wood for some poor family. When he returned to the big house in the evening, however, Sofya Andreyevna, tired and hot, and near her twelfth confinement, taunted him with his inconsistency.

'He pumps water for the whole house,' she complained to her sister, 'and lugs it in an enormous tub. . . . He does not eat white bread, and he postively doesn't go anywhere.'8 For Sofya, this was simply playing at Robinson Crusoe, while his true work was intellectual. She was profoundly worried that, since his conversion to the simple life, the farm had run down, and he had made rudimentary efforts to make over the property at Yasnaya to his wife, so that he might technically be said to have abandoned the property. But he was still the owner of vast estates in Samara and, as yet, he still received his considerable literary royalties. Such inconsistencies were a source of moral torment to Tolstoy himself, who did genuinely desire to escape it all. For his wife, they were a crazy aberration and, with eleven children and a twelfth on the way, if was terrifying that her husband should take this view of money and possessions. The more Tolstoy attempted to imitate Christ, the more violent the atmosphere became. Such quarrels reduced him to a state of nervous exhaustion. Pathetically, he was toying with the idea of writing a novel about peasant life, but of course it would not come.

On June 18, he went out to do some mowing and returned to the house to bathe. He found his wife waiting for him, and once more she started to rail at him, asking him why, if he was so humble, he kept so many horses. He felt he had had enough, and set out for Tula, resolved — one of many such resolutions — to leave home for good and let them all stew in their own juice. But when he had got angrily half way on his journey, he turned back. He realised that he could not leave her, heavily pregnant as she was. He came up the drive. Two of his sons were playing *vint* with some bearded peasants. 'Where is your mother?' 'Oh,' said their sister Tanya, 'on the croquet lawn, didn't you see her?' 'I don't want to see her,' was the reply.[9] He went to his study, resolved to spend the night there, but the terrible sadness of it all prevented him from sleeping, and filled his heart with pity. But the pity was not strong enough to make him go and see if she was all right. He dropped off to sleep and at two in the morning, she woke him. 'Forgive me, I'm in labour, perhaps I'll die.' He took her upstairs. Labour had begun. 'What is the most joyful and happy event in a family passed off like something unnecessary and depressing,' he noted mercilessly in his diary.[10] The baby was Alexandra (Sasha) who only died in 1979 and was to keep a candle burning at her father's shrine until the end.

The confinement was a miserable one, and they all remained miserable for the next month. Sofya and Lev quarrelled. She complained at his non-stop tea-drinking, and a row flared up. But, most revealingly, this began to tempt him carnally. 'I'd like to refrain, but feel I won't in present conditions. But cohabitation with a woman alien in spirit — i.e. with her — is terribly vile.'[11] He had just finished writing this sentence on July 7, 1884, when she came into the room and started shouting at him hysterically. She said that she wanted to run away. He took her back upstairs, and tried to calm her down, 'like a sick woman' — which, having given birth only three weeks before in very difficult circumstances, she was. He then returned to his study to finish his diary entry. 'She will remain a millstone around my neck and round the children's until I die.'[12]

The following week, on July 14, he insisted upon his marital rights. She refused 'with cold spitefulness and a desire to hurt me'.[13] He immediately started to pack, and decided once more that he had to leave home. Then he woke her up and told her that she was no longer any use either as a wife or mother. 'I was wrong not to have gone away,' he added to the diary. But in fact, after all this rowing and quarrelling, she had yielded to him, and a severe haemorrhage followed. The midwife was summoned the next morning, and ordered them not to have conjugal relations for a month.[14]

The hot weather and the quarrels were having a sad effect on the children too. Twenty-one-year-old Seryozha was getting on his father's nerves. 'He was rude without any cause. I was angry and gave him a thorough reprimand — bourgeois habits, and obtuseness and spitefulness, and self-satisfaction. Suddenly he said that nobody loved him, and began to cry. God, how it hurt me. I walked about all day and managed to catch Seryozha after dinner and said to him, "I'm ashamed." He suddenly burst out sobbing and started to kiss me, and say "Forgive me, forgive me. . . ."'[15]

Into this household, so torn apart by misery and strife, there came almost each day Chertkov's letters from England, and not just letters, but cuttings from Matthew Arnold, accounts of the Salvation Army and its doings and beliefs, and helpful novels such as the anonymous *The Ground Ash*.[16]

It is a sad tale. Squire Risley, wishing to enact for their son his wife's dying wish — 'Teach him to be like Christ' — is faced with a quandary. The squire sees as clearly as Tolstoy did that the ideals of Christ are fundamentally at variance with the wisdom of this world. 'Now the character and teaching of Christ may be summed up in one short word and that word the most distasteful to the present generation. I might fairly say, but that I am unwilling to appear irreverent, that it was "spoony".* No other epithet can be fairly

* A modern equivalent might be 'wet', 'yellow', weak.

applied to a system of morals which placed all humanity in a state of helpless, abject dependence on divine grace, which declared persecution to be a blessed thing, which forbade men to resist evil, and which enjoined that he who was smitten on the cheek should turn the other to the smiter.' Nevertheless, in spite of his misgivings, the Squire places his son in the care of a fanatical clergyman called Mr. Sheen, who is so rigid in his following of the Gospel precepts that he will not even allow the little boy to name the heathen divinities in Greek lessons. When young Risley goes on to Weston, a public school, he soon learns the truth of his father's view that 'any child who attempted to keep his Baptismal vows would be thought of as a muff and a mollycoddle and a spoony and a sop and everything else that is odious and abominable in the eyes of his schoolfellows'. Needless to say, young Risley gets hell from the other boys, and from the masters, who resent his refusal to construe passages from heathen literature just as much as the boys take a dim view of his lofty attitude to their smutty talk and rough games. The final disaster occurs when Risley smashes his fag-master's statue of Apollo. All the prefects take a stick of ground ash and take it in turns to give him 'one cut apiece'. He is either hit, or cut, or thrashed, or kicked by every boy in the house. Squire Risley rushes in at this point to rescue his boy, and he is carried to matron's room in a state of great weakness. The reader imagines that he has died, but he flickers to life for just long enough to have an affecting reconciliation with his tormentors.

> 'Forgive me, Risley!' he cried, kneeling by the bedside and laying his hand tenderly on Nigel's arm. . . . 'I'll promise you one thing, at any rate, that I will never use my ground ash again as long as I live.'
> 'And will you take up the Cross instead?' asked the dying boy.
> 'Yes, that I will,' replied Sidney, 'I will try to be like Christ in remembrance of you.'[17]

And the curtain falls with everyone in tears.

This 'spoony' stuff obviously made a great impression on Chertkov, and Tolstoy, likewise, was entranced by it. 'Full of pathos, but good,' he noted in his diary:[18] while to the beloved Chertkov, he said that it was 'very good'.[19]

Chertkov had asked in another letter how Tolstoy understood the idea of getting external help from God in prayer. He recalled, in his reply, an incident which had happened quite recently when Alexeyev had still been a tutor in the household. Tolstoy arranged 'a most loathsome act' with a woman, and made a date with her. As he was going to keep his appointment with the peasant woman, he passed his son's window in the garden, and he called out to remind him that he had a lesson that day. Tolstoy came to his senses and did not keep the appointment with the woman. 'Clearly it can be said that God saved me,' he said. But he went on to point out that the temptation did not pass. It was only when he confided the whole matter in Alexeyev. 'He was a good man. He understood me and looked after me like a child.'[20]

The only thing which could save him from the lusts of the flesh, Tolstoy seems to state, was the loving affection of a pure-minded young man.

One other thing. On one occasion this year I was lying beside my wife. She wasn't asleep, nor was I, and I suffered painfully from the awareness of my own loneliness in the family because of my beliefs, and that they all in my eyes see the truth but turn away from it. . . . I don't remember how, but being sad and miserable, and feeling that tears were in my eyes I began to pray to God to touch my wife's heart. She fell asleep; I heard her quiet breathing and suddenly it occurred to me: I suffer because my wife does not share my convictions. When I speak with her under the vexation at her rebuffing me, I often speak coldly, even in an unfriendly manner; not only have I entreated her with tears to believe in the truth but I have never even expressed to her all my thoughts lovingly, and gently, yet there she is lying beside me, and I say nothing to her, and what I ought to, what ought to be said to her, I say to God.[21]

The letter seems to anticipate the opening of Meredith's *Modern Love*, even Larkin's 'Talking in Bed'. The extraordinary thing is that he should have chosen to share these extremely intimate scenes with Chertkov. Only to his brother Sergey had Tolstoy hitherto confided that all was not well with the marriage (though of course the *rows* were discernible to the whole household and to all the visitors, and were therefore notorious). To no one had he ever confided this version of the bedroom intimacies. Chertkov, whom he had known less than a year and met only a handful of times, drew this out of him. To Chertkov, as to the diary, Tolstoy was able to reveal a little of the yawning dichotomy in his soul, a split which had always existed between flesh and spirit but which had begun to be wholly polarised in his mind. The wider the split became, the less 'in control' he was. The more he strove to be like Jesus or the Buddha, the more he grew like Fyodor Pavlovich Karamazov. He might well have been thinking holy thoughts, but he was behaving like a murderer. So, juxtaposed diary entries can be as farcically contrasted, as September's.

A talk in the morning, and unexpected malice. Later she came down to my room and nagged at me until she was beside herself. I said nothing and did nothing, but was depressed. She ran out in hysterics. I ran after her. I'm terribly exhausted.

12 September. Read about Buddhism — its teaching. Wonderful. . . .[22]

And so on. He had come to believe that his family *were* the flesh which it would be impossible to live a virtuous life without renouncing. The spiritual life which called him was the life of Chertkov, who was so priggishly sure of what was right and what was wrong, and who also, like the young man in Shakespeare's Sonnets, was so admirably a cold fish, 'unmoved, cold and to temptation slow'. Chertkov, in the diaries, becomes an ideal figure, repeatedly mentioned. 'His mother hates me, as well she might. Dreamed about Chertkov. He suddenly began dancing, gaunt as he was, and I saw he'd gone mad,'[23] was an entry at the height of his rows with Sofya. 'I must be naïve like Chertkov,'[24] a thought which he had had earlier in the summer.

The open rivalry between Tolstoy's wife and his new friend was not immediately apparent. Sofya felt some relief that Lev Nikolayevich should have found a disciple at last who was well-connected, rich, presentable — she even, on occasions, found young Vladimir Grigoryevich a charmer. They had in common, *au fond*, an impenetrable and rather magnificent humourlessness, which is perhaps necessary in the spouses and companions of great seers. But rivals, in the course of 1884, they most unquestionably became.

The widow Dostoyevsky had set to work, ever since her husband's death, in preparing an Edition, a collected Dostoyevsky, and emboldened by her example, Sofya Andreyevna thought that she might do the same. This was no mere piece of oneupmanship. The Tolstoy family income, since Lev Nikolayevich had started to become a saint, had dropped violently. Stewards on his various estates, like all the stewards in Russian novels, were not slow to take advantage of their master's lack of interest in the revenues of land and villages, and the money mysteriously vanished. The farms, which Tolstoy had formerly supervised with a modicum of rough and ready efficiency, started to go to ruin. The united revenues from Yasnaya Polyana, Nikolskoye and Samara, whose capital value was hundreds of thousands of roubles shrank to fifty thousand roubles or five hundred pounds of Aylmer Maude's money. It was all very well to speak of wickedness, of laying up treasures on earth. But Tolstoy chose to ignore the parts of the New Testament which commend good husbandry, and the wise investment of talents. He was not getting the value of what he had, because he was filled with guilt about having anything. In consequence, the properties were run down, the people who might have benefited from them failed to benefit, and there was no extra money left over for any charitable purposes which might have interested him. At the same time, he went on forcing his wife to have children and, in spite of all his protests, this meant minds to be educated by tutors, and governesses, bodies to be dressed and bathed by nursemaids, mouths to be fed by cooks, tables to be served by lackeys. Where was the money to come from? Why *should* they all go and live like pilgrims or holy idiots merely because Tolstoy said so?

One does not ask these questions in the Countess Tolstoy's 'defence'. It is simply important to understand at the outset why the Collected Edition of her husband's works was so important to her. It was not just that she wished to save his reputation by putting and keeping in print those great works of his which she had so ecstatically, patiently copied. It was also that, since he had abandoned any responsibility for them, she wished to take on the role of breadwinner for a large family and two big households. She could not dig, to beg she was ashamed. But she did have it in her power to produce a Collected Edition.

But in the course of 1884, Chertkov had formed the idea of starting a small, independent publishing house himself. It would be based in the country. It would only publish 'improving' literature, and works which were accessible to the poor. From his point of view, it was obviously desirable that cheap editions of Tolstoy's work should be made available. Chertkov founded a press which he called The Intermediary and, from the first, Tolstoy was ardent in his enthusiastic support for the venture. While Sofya Andreyevna set up the publishing office for the *Collected Works of L. N. Tolstoy* in an annex of their house in Dolgo-Khamovnichesky Street in Moscow, Chertkov, aided by his young secretary (another ardent Tolstoyan, and Tolstoy's first

Russian biographer, Pavel I. Biryukov) printed *A Captive in the Caucasus, What Men Live By,* and *God Sees the Truth but Waits.* They also printed a short story by Leskov, *Christ Visits a Peasant.* Over the next few years, Tolstoy was to supply them with more 'simple' tales; most of the stories printed in Aylmer Maude's *Twenty-Three Tales* began life in this way. Chertkov may have discarded the fundamentals of his Evangelical creed, but he has retained the Evangelical's zest for publication. Evangelicals are Christians for whom the Flesh becomes the Word, and wherever they may be found, there are bookshops, bookstalls, pamphlets, literature. It may be supposed that in a country where literacy was as low as in nineteenth-century Russia, such people would not have much of a sale. But Chertkov knew what he was doing. In the first four years of its foundation, The Intermediary had sold twelve million little booklets, published at only one or one and a half kopecks. His example was one of which the Bolsheviks were justly envious. The habits of modern Soviet publishers, their desire to print good cheap editions and distribute them on a huge scale, owe much to Chertkov's pioneering work. So too does his wholly cavalier, not to say piratical attitude to the laws or obligations of copyright. On Tolstoy's recommendation they published foreign stuff too: *Oliver Twist, Little Dorrit, Bleak House, Edwin Drood, Felix Holt* (a particular favourite of Tolstoy's) and *Hypatia* by Charles Kingsley; also Matthew Arnold's *Literature and Dogma.*

But it was more than a spiritual kinship. That is not to say that it was physical, or sexual. Indeed, the whole point of young men in Tolstoy's life was that he could not have sex with them. He sentimentalised them, and got spoony about them in precisely the same way that a certain type of homosexual falls in love with young women, who excite in him not feelings of lust, but fantasies of love and beauty purged of the sordidities of sex. Moreover, lesser men than Tolstoy have felt the flattery of having a disciple; and Tolstoy's total, out-and-out egotism positively needed something akin to worship. In the days when he was slaving at *War and Peace*, this worship had been given unstintingly by Sofya. But now he hated her. And even if she had wanted to embrace his new beliefs, he could not even bring himself to explain to her what they were.

> It becomes still more difficult to find
> Words at once true and kind
> Or not untrue and not unkind.[25]

353

Marooned in Moscow in November 1884, he wrote to his beloved Chertkov, 'I would terribly like to live with you. I want to see whether you are always in that tense state you are in when I see you. You can't be like that at home. . . . I would wish you more calmness, more idleness, more good-natured, kindly and indulgent calmness and idleness. I would like to live with you, and if we are still alive, I shall live with you. Never cease to love me, as I love you. . . .'[26]

*   *   *   *

In a letter he wrote to Chertkov some months after he had finished *What Then Must We Do?* Tolstoy revealed that he had just finished reading Stevenson's *The Strange Case of Doctor Jekyll and Mr. Hyde* and found it 'very good'.[27] The famous fable of the divided self was a subject to which Tolstoy would have been qualified to bring an abundance of rich meditation and experience. In no decade perhaps more than the 1880s were the contrasts in his nature more strikingly evident. *What Then Must We Do?*, for instance, contains some of his very finest thoughts, and some of the best writing in the whole *œuvre*. It also contains some of the silliest nonsense ever written by anyone. How can one reconcile the high genius of Tolstoy (and it is not merely a literary genius, but also a very great quality of mind) with his incredible, perverse silliness? He sees the dreadful desolation in Moscow which has been caused by a combination of the callousness, greed, weakness and stupidity of the various people involved in the drama, and he announces that he has found a 'solution' to the problem. Go home, give up smoking, try to make your own shoes and give your wife twenty babies.

Tolstoy's own wife must often have wondered during these years, as she lay and watched his sleeping form, and saw the patriarchal beard draped over the sheets, or watched him sitting in his study scratchily covering page after page, whether she was looking at Count Jekyll or Lev Nikolayevich Hyde.

The children, too, were confronted with the puzzle. Hitherto, it had all been a question of Papa and his smelly friends being tiresome and upsetting Mama. The warfare between them was initially perceived as one of pure emotional torment. ('Wherever you are the air is poisoned,'[28] the children overheard him shouting at their mother one day when she was being slow to understand his doctrines of love and forgiveness.) But as time went on — and particularly for the daughters — it was possible to see that there was a genuine ideological seriousness in this mysterious, alarming figure, their father.

At first, it must have seemed little more than Father being ridiculous. Why was Papa neglecting the writings which had made him rich and famous, and getting Pavel Arbuzov, the son of the children's nurse Marya Afanasyevna, to teach him the difficult art of shoemaking? They watched him doing it for hours at a stretch, splicing bristles, knocking quarters into shape, nailing the soles. He was not good at it, but nor was he good at admitting defeat. The day he learnt to splice a bristle was as proud as the day that he had finished a great book. Prouder. 'Allow me, Lev Nikolayevich,' the shoemaker would say, tactfully, leaning over his clumsy pupil. 'No, no, I'll do it myself. You do your work, and I'll do mine.'[29]

There was all the embarrassment, as far as the family were concerned, of visitors seeing these antics. And that was the part which Tolstoy seemed to like the most. One day, Prince Obolensky, a cousin by marriage, called, and discovered that the great writer had just learnt how to drive tacks into the sole of a shoe.

'You see how well it's turned out?' he said in triumph.

'What's so difficult in that?' asked Obolensky.

'You try.'

'I'd be glad to.'

'Good, but on one condition: for every tack you drive in I'll pay you a rouble, and for every one you break you pay me ten kopecks. Agreed?'

Obolensky took the boot, the awl, the hammer and broke eight tacks one after the other. He joined in the general laughter and handed over the eighty kopecks which were given to Tolstoy's shoemaker tutor.[30]

For children, Tolstoy's humour was his most beguiling characteristic, but it could also be troubling. Tatyana recalls that if she made a criticism of someone, said that they were boring or stupid, he would always ask, 'More boring than you? Stupider than you?' 'I understood the lesson he was trying to teach me perfectly well, but I refused to accept it and would answer back insolently, "Yes, stupider than me, more boring than me, plainer than me."'[31] But this was an exchange born of intimacy between the parent and child. The irony was a shield for tenderness which neither could control. One of her most treasured memories was recovering from dangerous scarlet fever when she was only a little girl. As she began to recover, the door opened, and Father came in and sat on the bed. 'Well, Choorka, still pretending to be ill?' 'There is tenderness in his eyes and I feel I could ask him for anything he liked. But there is nothing I want. Taking his big strong dry hand I pull off his wedding ring. He goes on looking at me, smiling benevolently, putting up no objection.'[32] He would have had no objection to a child, or anyone else pulling off that ring and dissolving the union which now caused him so much anguish and torment.

The first child to sense that their father was not merely lovable but might also be right was little Masha (Marya Lvovna) when she was only fifteen. In 1885, she started to recognise the appalling poverty, the actual starvation, which was happening even on their doorstep in the village at Yasnaya Polyana, and she began to befriend the peasants who were also her father's friends. The older brothers were on the whole unsympathetic to their father, but Ilya also began to see that his father had something to say which was of lasting importance, not just about them but about life, and about Russia. When Tanya (Tatyana Lvovna), an art student in Moscow studying under Repin, wrote to her father to say that she had come to share his ideals, he wrote back ecstatically. 'Well done. . . . That is my only dream, and my greatest possible joy which I daren't hope for — namely to find brothers and sisters in my family, and not what I have seen so far — estrangement and deliberate opposition — in which I see partly contempt — not for me — but for the truth.'[33]

He had become wholly convinced that they should not be living in this way: the servants, the large houses, the money. He had renounced all that he could. He had made over his properties and his copyrights to his wife, but this had had no effect whatsoever. He was living a simple life, but surrounded by opulence. It made a mockery of his entire position.

In one of the saddest letters which he ever wrote, never sent, to his wife, he asked for a divorce. 'It's not far short of ten years since the quarrels between us would all end in my saying that we shouldn't be friends again until we came to the same view of life. . . .' Since that period, he has gone even further in his desire for renunciation of property, for simple life; but she has done nothing to understand his point of view. 'A struggle unto the death is going on between us. Either God's works, or not God's works.'[34] Tolstoy's reiterated point was not that he merely chose to live in this way, but that it was the only sane way to live. But while he wanted to learn prayer, and a governing of the passions, and manual labour, Sofya Andreyevna went on worrying about furniture, servants, society, and a pattern of education for the children of which their father wholly disapproved.

It meant that for the previous ten years the father had felt alienated from the children. And his methods of drawing close to them, where it worked with some, would have repelled others. Ilya, who became a devotee of his father at about this time and while never sharing all his ideals tried to understand them, recounts a scene when his father tried to find out if he was a virgin.

My father's delicacy in his relations with us amounted almost to shyness. There were certain matters he could never touch on for fear of causing us pain. I shall never forget how in Moscow one day I happened to run in to change my clothes and found him sitting at the table in my room writing. My bed stood behind a screen, and I could not see him from there. Hearing my footsteps he spoke without looking round.

'Is that Ilya?'

'Yes.'

'Are you alone? Shut the door. . . . Now no one can hear us and we shan't see each other, so we won't feel ashamed. Tell me, did you ever have anything to do with women?'

When I said 'No', I suddenly heard him start to weep, sobbing like a child. I too cried, and for some time, with the screen between us, we continued to shed tears of joy; and we were not ashamed, but were both so glad that I consider that moment one of the happiest of my entire life. No discussion, no reasoning, could ever have done for me what that did. The tears of a father of sixty can never be forgotten, even in moments of greatest temptation.[35]

But what if Ilya's answer had been 'yes'?

These were the sort of confessions and 'sharing sessions' which had formed such a close bond with Chertkov. In the autumn of 1886, Chertkov was married, and Tatyana noted in her diary,

Chertkov's wedding made me very gloomy. I felt my loneliness and felt regrets. Why not me instead of G[alya — i.e. Anna Konstantin-ovna Dieterichs]? Why is it not my fate to be married to so wonderful a man? I am too bad for that: I could not be as he would want. I give way to all sorts of temptations too easily; I am too lazy, too fond of myself and my useless body. All the same, though I do not love him, my heart tugs every time that I might have been in her place. . . .[36]

It is a sad thing for a girl of twenty-two to have penned. By then, she had read *What I Believe* and was trying to fashion her life after her father's ideals.

The bad relations between their parents could not be viewed merely as a grotesque domestic tragi-comedy. Tolstoy and his wife were looking at the world itself, and at Russia, with different eyes. The 'wonderful man' Chertkov, whom Tanya thought it would have been such a privilege to serve as a wife (its unrealism recalls Dorothea's feelings for Mr. Casaubon in *Middlemarch*), struck her mother merely as 'sly, malicious, obtuse and narrow-minded'. But the domestic civil war reflected the divisions at the heart of Russian society itself. As far as Tolstoy and Chertkov were concerned, it was not merely a case of Sofya Andreyevna being selfish and stubborn. It was a case of the whole governing class of Russia blinding itself to what was going on. The warfare between Tolstoy and his wife was a terrible symbol of the division in Russia itself. On the one hand, there were those who believed in the autocracy, in the Orthodox Church, and the *status quo*, who feared the violence of the revolutionary movements which threatened Russia at home, and the Turks, the British, the Germans, who threatened her stability abroad. Or there were those, perhaps the majority, who were so intent on preserving their own rich life style that they did not think at all, but were merely cynically content to allow things to go on as they had always gone on. On the other hand, there were those who, with eyes in their heads, saw things were changing, and that this Holy Religion and this great autocracy were only held together by lies and violence and oppression. It is this tension in microcosm which we witness in the Tolstoy home, and it is this which makes it so terrible. Tolstoy was not just a solipsist interested in saving his own soul. He genuinely believed — however mistaken we may now consider him — that he had found the solution to the Russian, to the human problem.

Dostoyevsky's great speech at the time of the unveiling of the Pushkin monument had excited cries of ecstasy from the crowds. 'You are a saint! You are a prophet!' Even Turgenev had wept. It was the famous assertion of the destiny of the Russian people. 'The Russian heart is more adapted to universal, all-humanitarian brotherly fellowship than any other nation,' he had told the foaming crowds.

'Not we but the future Russians, to the last man, will comprehend that to become a genuine Russian means to seek finally to reconcile all European controversies, to show the solution of European anguish in our all-humanitarian and all-unifying Russian soul. . . . to utter the ultimate words of great, universal harmony, of the brotherly accord of all nations abiding by the law of Christ's gospel.'

With the accession of Alexander III, Dostoyevsky's friend Pobedonostsev had lost no time in pushing forward a programme of Russification, and a purge of all elements in Russian society which might threaten the all-unifying Russian soul. Tolstoy's religious works, very naturally, fell foul of the censor. For example, on February 18, 1884, the police had burst in upon the Kusherev printing works and tried to seize all the copies of *What I Believe*. The head of the Moscow Civil Censorship Committee reported that 'the book must be considered an extremely harmful book as it undermines the foundations of social and governmental institutions and wholly destroys the teachings of the Church'. But the book had already gone 'up the line' and found its way, like the political writings of revolutionaries and other dissidents, into secret hideouts and foreign printing presses. This was where Chertkov was of invaluable help to Tolstoy. In 1884-5 he managed to do English translations of the major religious works and get them printed in England. German editions appeared in Leipzig, and Prince Urusov's French translations were printed in Paris.

By driving them thus underground, the Russian authorities lent a huge amount of weight to Tolstoy's religious reflections. As yet, though his name was famous abroad, *War and Peace* and *Anna Karenina* were barely known in the West. It was through his religious tracts that, for thousands of English readers, Tolstoy burst upon the world. And since Orthodoxy, in an English or American context, does not really mean anything, what struck Tolstoy's thousands of new foreign readers were firstly the lucid urgency and sincerity of his prose, and secondly the indictment which they constituted of his barbarous country. (The pattern has been continuing ever since, but the Russians never seem to learn anything, as a rollcall of dissident names from Herzen to Solzhenitsyn would testify.)

Pobedonostsev's policy of Russification was identical to that of Stalin some forty-five years later. Between April 1881 and June 1882, for example, a million Jews had fled the country, taking with them some twenty-two million pounds. Prince Meshchersky pronounced, 'When the microbes have to be destroyed, we do not pause to inquire how many microbes like the process.' The Russian press was censored 'with a bitterness which recalled the time of Nicholas I'. While pogroms in Elizavetagrad, Kiev and Odessa assailed the Jews, there were vigorous attempts to Russify the 'difficult' parts of the Empire. The Poles, the Lithuanians, the Georgians, the Ukrainians all had to face the choice between freedom or submission to the all-humanitarian Russian soul. Religious dissidents — Molokans, Dukhobors, Old Believers, and others — were forced into accepting the brotherly accord of the Orthodox Church. In Russian Turkestan, the children were forced in their new primary schools to learn Russian. On the Asiatic borders of the Empire, the Russians harried the Afghans. There was a clash between Russian and Afghan forces on March 30, 1885, which made the Gladstone Government contemplate war and there was talk of Russia invading Turkey and establishing the dream which had been so dear to Dostoyevsky's heart, the Russification of the old Empire, the re-Christianisation of Constantinople.

It was into this international atmosphere that Tolstoy's controversial writings burst, adding fuel to the emotion in which the Anglo-Saxon world most delights to indulge, self-righteous moral indignation. *Novoye Vremya* was able to make a good debating point in reply to English hostility to the fierceness of Alexander III's regime. 'The concern of England, which has beggared the population of India and Egypt, which has poisoned the people of China with opium, which destroyed, like dangerous insects, the natives of Australia and which, under the pretext of abolishing the slave trade, is now exterminating in the most wholesale fashion the numerous races of Africa — the concerns of people who do these things is certainly astonishing.' The point is well made, but it ignores, as such Russian protests always ignore — as in their 'What about Northern Ireland or South Africa?' taunts now, or their protests during the 1960s about the plight of American blacks — that though the western pot may be as black as the eastern kettle, it is not a debate which could conceivably be won by a nation that so vigorously denies freedom of expression to its people. A pen may not be mightier than a sword, but it reaches more people, and the effects of its wounds can still be felt, like those of a nuclear weapon, for generations after the sword has rusted.

It was the situation at home, and above all the plight of the urban poor in Russia, which excited Tolstoy's furious indictment of the all-humanitarian brotherly fellowship of the most holy Russias. The two decades after the emancipation of the serfs had witnessed major upheavals and revolutions in the lives of the poor. On the one hand, the immediate effect of emancipation had been to make life infinitely more difficult for the peasants, who therefore abandoned the life style which had been lived by their people for generations and poured into the cities. At the same time, the administration was desperately attempting to transform an essentially agrarian rural economy into an industrialised one, worthy to compete with the Empires of Prussia and England. The mineral resources of the Empire suddenly began to be exploited. Production of pig iron in Russia doubled between 1862 and 1886. In the twelve years after emancipation, three hundred and fifty-seven new joint stock companies were formed: fifty-three new railroad companies, seventy-three new private banks; a hundred and sixty-three major new factories. Coal production multiplied sixfold in the last decade of the nineteenth century. Oil began to be drilled in Azerbaidzhan, Baku, Tiflis. Cotton, in the regions of Moscow and Vladimir, was produced in enormously increasing quantities, with all its familiar concomitants of mills and factories, and the squalid housing of 'cheap labour'. Dickens and Carlyle and Ruskin had watched all this happening to England fifty years before. It came late to Russia, and it came even later to Tolstoy who had been so caught up in the adventure of his own existence, and so marooned in the country that, until he was forced to move to Moscow in 1881 for the children's education, his eyes had not been open to what was happening. The hallmark of his art was to 'make it strange', to see things completely afresh, an art which, when carried into the field of theological controversy, had produced a number of palpable hits, but which were obscured by the bees in his bonnet. *What Then Must We Do?* brings this quality to *reportage* of the urban scene; and, by implication, to the political sphere. It is one of Tolstoy's most impressive and unforgettable books.

The first part of the book might be defined as a Russian Mayhew, or a Muscovite Dickens. He describes, and few descriptions of urban poverty have ever been bettered. It all starts when he sees a ragged peasant, swollen with dropsy, being arrested for begging. His shock at the sight takes him to dosshouses around the Khitrov market. The first fourteen chapters of the book contain human sketches which are every bit as good as anything in his novels, animated by a sense of violent moral outrage about the divisions between rich and poor. When, having read this book, one thinks of Russia in the 1880s it will always be of these people that one thinks: the two prostitutes, dying mother of forty and ragged daughter of thirteen, who describe their profession as 'sit[ting] in the tavern', and cannot quite bring themselves to use the word 'prostitute'; the washerwoman with soapy arms, beating off the attentions of a drunken man in the filthy stench of some tavern yard; ragged boys in thin coats skating down the pavements; the old apple seller and his wife, living in a tiny room which they kept very clean, carpeted with apple sacks, and adorned with twinkling icons; another old man dying in a cellar of typhus; the fifteen-year-old prostitute, standing in the snow, smoking a cigarette, being cursed by the policeman who arrested her, 'We shall freeze to death with you here, blast you!'; and, the most Dickensian pair of all, an old-looking mother of thirty and her daughter, their faces drawn and grey, two creatures who appear to be subject to St. Vitus's Dance and who have in effect turned themselves into cigarette-making machines, their fingers twitching and moving so rapidly that you can hardly see how the cigarettes are made. For fourteen years the mother has lived in this way, constantly inhaling tobacco.

The second part of the book devotes itself more theoretically to answering the question of its title. At first, Tolstoy had assumed that it was a mere question of philanthropy. Even on this level, he found that his rich friends in society were capable of being quite thick-skinned. 'For a box at the theatre to see Sara Bernhardt they hand over the money at once, to clinch the matter. But here, of those who had agreed to give money and had expressed their sympathy, not one offered the money at once. . . .' The contrast between the riches which he saw all around him in his own circle and the degradation and poverty which existed in the Muscovite slums eventually made him recognise that Russia faced a problem much greater than could be solved with condescending acts of patronage or generosity from the rich. And in the best Biblical tradition he denounces the Ahabs and the Jezebels who are responsible for so much waste, devastation and misery. Nor is there any doubt in his mind what will happen if nothing is done to help the poor.

The hatred and contempt of the oppressed masses are increasing, and the physical and moral forces of the wealthy classes are weakening; the deception on which everything depends is wearing out, and the wealthy classes have nothing to console themselves with in this mortal danger.

To return to the old ways is not possible; only one thing is left for

362

those who do not wish to change their way of life, and that is to hope that 'things will last my time' — after that let happen what may. That is what the blind crowd of the rich are doing, but the danger is ever growing and the terrible catastrophe draws near.[37]

This in 1886: they had just thirty years to learn the truth of what Tolstoy was saying.

What Then Must We Do? is not Marxist, nor revolutionary in the political sense at all. And one of the most impressive things about it is its description of how Tolstoy grew out of wishing to patronise the poor, and discovered that it was impossible to romanticise their position. 'Among them, as among us, there were some more or less good and more or less bad, more or less happy and more or less miserable; and the unhappy were just as exist among ourselves; people whose unhappiness depends not on external conditions but on themselves — a kind of unhappiness bank notes cannot cure.'

No reader can doubt that the situation which he describes in *What Then Must We Do?* was one which actually existed, any more than they can doubt that its worst and gloomiest prophecies were fulfilled. With catastrophic consequences, the advocates of political violence were able to exploit the plight of the poor and bring about a situation which was, if possible, worse than the one which Tolstoy describes.

Where Tolstoy will probably find a mixed response among modern readers is in his own analysis of how the catastrophe could be avoided, and in his generalised reflections on the way we ought to live. The solution is at first given in one Biblical word: Repent! And on one level Tolstoy describes what is not only (to the present writer at least) obviously desirable; it is, as it happens, a description of what has been forced upon the privileged classes in the West, *faute de mieux*. Tolstoy, that is to say, advocates self-sufficiency. He questions the assumption that, for example, writers and intellectuals need other people to do their physical labours, while they provide 'spiritual' nourishment to their hearers or readers. He started to do some calculations.

It turned out that I — a very prolific writer who for forty years have done nothing except write, and have written some five thousand pages — if I had worked all those forty years at a peasant's usual work then, not counting winter evenings and workless days, if I had read and studied for five hours every day and had written only on holidays two pages a day (and I have sometimes written as many as sixteen pages a day) I should have produced those five thousand pages in fourteen years.

I came upon a wonderful fact — a very arithmetical calculation a seven-year-old boy could have made, but which I never made before. There are twenty-four hours in a day; we sleep eight, so sixteen remain. If a brain-worker devotes five hours a day to his work he will get through a huge quantity. What becomes of the remaining eleven hours?

It turned out that physical labour, far from rendering mental work impossible, improved and helped it.[38]

So Tolstoy advocates manual labour for all, simplicity of life, simple food, simple clothes, etc. The humour (deliberate) of the concluding chapters veers between G. K. Chesterton and Chekhov — unlikely poles. Many modern medics would now agree with the Chestertonianism of the

. . . . profound complexities of medicine and hygiene for people of our class are such as a mechanic might devise in order, when he has heated a boiler and screwed down all the valves, to prevent the boiler from bursting.

And when I understood all this, it seemed to me ludicrous. By a long series of doubts, searchings, and reflection, I had reached the extraordinary truth that man has eyes in order to see with them, ears in order to hear with, legs in order to walk with them, and hands and a back to work with, and that if he does not use them for their natural purpose it will be the worse for him.[39]

Many modern business executives recovering from their first bad ulcer or coronary thrombosis will probably agree with these words. Likewise anyone reading the plays of Chekhov will recognise the world that Tolstoy depicts when he says 'When we ask: What then must we do? — we do not really ask anything, but merely affirm. . . . that we do not want to do *anything*.'[40] His depictions of the idle rich in their ballrooms and houseparties are puritanical, but also extremely funny.

What I find hard to understand is why Tolstoy should attribute all the many ills which he anatomises to the existence of property. Before the curtain goes down, he has started to play all the old Proudhon gramophone records: 'Property is the root of all evil. . . .' Those who fulfil the word of God do not own things etc. etc. This has a fine sound to it. But the Leninist question has to be answered: *Who? Whom?* Who is going to *control* the lives of the happy peasants, writers and aristocrats who — in the Tolstoyan vision — are all leading pure, teetotalling, non-smoking lives, ploughing and sowing and stitching boots, and hewing wood and drawing water by day, and writing their five hours of nonsense each evening before the sun goes down? If they owned their little patch, and their hut in which all these wholesome activities took place, then it might be said that they were approaching something like a service which was perfect freedom. But if they did not own the hut, then they would always be at the mercy of the man, or the council or the corporation who did; and that is a simple fact. By asserting his silly 'property is theft' creed as though it were an immutable law of the universe, Tolstoy spoils the whole case which he is making out, because in attacking the notion of property, he makes any realistic plan for human betterment impossible. Property never has been abolished, and never will be abolished. It is simply a question of who has it. And the fairest system ever devised is one by which all, rather than none, were property owners.

Female readers who have followed the argument about the purpose of a man's body (to work) will perhaps be wondering what is the purpose of a female body in the scheme of things. The fortieth and final chapter of the treatise tells us in unambiguous tones. Not all modern readers will feel satisfied with the manner in which Tolstoy deals with 'the wonderful nonsense called women's rights',[41] nor the assumption that women who use methods of contraception because they wish to 'imitate the sham work done by men' are evading their duty and putting themselves on the same level as prostitutes. If, however, you are a woman who obeys the will of God, 'you will not, either after two or after twenty children, say that you have borne enough, any more than a fifty-year-old workman will say that he has worked enough, while he still eats and sleeps and has muscles demanding work'.[42] It is hard to see, by the time we reach the end of the book, that Tolstoy thinks women have *any* function in world except as breeding stock. Since human life is as brutish, as unfairly ordered, and as doomed to disaster as he has informed us in the first half of the book that it is, we are a little surprised to discover that he advocates women giving up their lives to producing (and feeding, most importantly; he had a horror of wet nurses) anything up to twenty babies. 'Women, mothers, in your hands more than in those of anyone else lies the salvation of the world,'[43] is his slightly peculiar conclusion on the feast of St. Valentine, 1886.

*   *   *   *

He had barely finished *What Then Must We Do?* when he returned to an unfinished story which he had begun in 1882, and polished it off in the space of not much more than a month. It was the novella *The Death of Ivan Ilyich*. Touchingly, the motive for finishing this searing tale was to have a pleasant surprise for Sofya when she returned from Moscow: a new work to be included in her Collected Edition. She was delighted, considering it the first purely artistic work which he had attempted since the completion of *Anna Karenina*.

It is one of his most disturbing stories. Very little happens in it, beyond the fact that Ivan Ilyich, who has a middlingly successful legal career and has become a judge, is confronted with the fact of his own mortality. He contracts cancer, and as he approaches the end, he views his past life as a waste of time, his future death too horrible to contemplate, and diminution and frailty and the sheer stink of his dying body with the profoundest disgust. Above all, he fears death itself. When the disease is in its early stages, he tries to put it out of his mind. 'And what was worst of all was that it drew his attention to itself not in order to make him take some action but only that he should look at it, look it straight in the face.'[44] This he is unable to do, until the very end when, after three days of screaming, and months of physical and moral torment, he is able to face death, and dies. But although he has been visited by the priest he dies without religious consolation; it is merely the acceptance of mortality itself which brings him peace.

The story disturbs, and appeals, because of its universality. 'The syllogism he had learnt from Kiesewetter's *Logic*, "Caius is a man, men are mortal, therefore Caius is mortal" had always seemed to him correct as applied to Caius but certainly not as applied to himself. That Caius — man in the abstract — was mortal was perfectly correct, but he was not Caius, not an abstract man, but a creature, quite, quite separate from all others.'[45] That is the syllogism which the tale enforces upon the reader. The generality of death becomes particular as we share Ivan Ilyich's dreadful inner torments on his sickbed. No human life would emerge with any more 'point' or justification than his. But we would not necessarily agree with a modern scholar that Ilyich is 'a man like many other men'[46] in his reaction to things. He is in fact a man very much more like Lev Nikolayevich than he is average. For example, before the illness begins, he really hates his family, and for the past twenty years, his wife has made his life a misery by her querulousness. They come together again for brief moments of amorousness and then once more the warfare between them starts up. His only happiness is snatched from his work, or his male friends, or from choosing furnishings for the house. And the illness only serves to emphasise to him the extent to which his family are strangers with him. As he lies dying, too weak even to use a bedpan without assistance, and revolted by the smell of his own breath and by his own excrement, the only individual who can bring him any consolation is the handsome young peasant servant Gerasim, whose good humour is not shaken by the smell, and who is honest enough to accept his master's illness, and not lie to him. One of Ivan's only comforts at this stage is being allowed to lie with his trouserless legs over the young lad's shoulders. 'Health, strength and vitality in other people were offensive to him, but Gerasim's strength and vitality did not mortify but soothed him.'[47] There is nothing of Everyman in this bizarre, but inescapably touching confession. But there is much of Tolstoy.

By a paradox, however, a severe illness which afflicted Tolstoy during the summer of 1886 did not produce a greater discord between himself and his wife. It had the opposite effect. He had insisted on continuing to follow the plough while suffering from a sore on his leg, and this developed into erysipelas. Tolstoy's principles and instincts forbade him to consult a doctor, but eventually a specialist from Moscow called Chirkov was brought down by the Countess to Yasnaya Polyana. By now, the ulcer on Tolstoy's shin was severe, and he had a fever of 104°. The leg was much swollen, and they began to despair of his life. A tube had to be inserted into the leg to drain off the fluid and this caused excruciating pain.

For nine weeks he was laid up, and the disciples — particularly Chertkov — were kept at bay. 'Although the last two months, when Lev Nikolayevich was ill, were an agonising time for me,' his wife wrote in her diary, 'strangely enough they were also a very happy time for me. I nursed him day and night and what I had to do was so natural, so simple. It is really the only thing I can do well — making a personal sacrifice for the man I love. The harder the work, the happier I was. Now that he is on his feet again, he has given me to understand that he no longer needs me.'[48]

These words were written towards the end of October 1886, but her services were still required. While he was on his sickbed, he had been composing a play — a work which had had to be dictated for the most part — and on October 26 Sofya Andreyevna agreed to copy out the first act.

*   *   *   *

The Power of Darkness is a play about a peasant family and their handsome young labourer Nikita. In the first act it emerges that he is the lover of his master's wife, Anisya, and in the next act, egged on by Nikita's mother Matryona, she kills her husband Pyotr. By the third act, he is married to Anisya, hating her, drinking too much, and carrying on with other women. By the fourth act, he has got with child his sixteen-year-old step-daughter Akulina. To hush the whole thing up, his mother stage-manages another murder, and the baby is buried in the cellar of their cottage. In the fifth act, Nikita gets his comeuppance, and the real villains of the piece — the older women in his life — go free.

It is a strange play to come from the pen of one who, only so recently, had been converted to a true view of life by observing the beliefs and habits of the peasantry. Their religion is superstitious and unenlightened. One thinks particularly of Matryona, an adept at fortune telling and all kinds of mumbo jumbo, insisting that they baptise the baby before sending Nikita down the cellar to murder it. His conviction that he hears the bones crunch as he tries to smother the child beneath a piece of wood is one of the less pleasant memories which one carries away from *The Power of Darkness*. These peasants are crude, cruel, aggressive, greedy, materialistic, and above all, stupid. They have all the faults of the upper class, but with none of the virtues which Tolstoy knew in a Fet or a Turgenev: no wit, urbanity, tolerance or good taste. If it were not so obviously written by Tolstoy, the friend of the peasants, one could be forgiven for thinking that it was the work of an 'enemy of the working class'. It is relentlessly horrible because it is — deliberately — comic. The ghastliness of the peasant family is presented with genuine and exaggerated gusto, and all the peasants who are caught up in this appalling cycle of crime are represented as comic morons.

Sofya Andreyevna did the copying of the various versions of the play and was really pleased with it. 'The characters are wonderfully portrayed and the plot is full and interesting,' was her reaction to the first act; but the second, where there is merely a plot between a woman and a mother-in-law to murder her stupid husband, she considered 'rather flat — it needs more theatrical effects, and I told Lyovochka so'.[49]

Alexander III was also impressed by the play. One of Tolstoy's friends, M. A. Stakhovich, went and read the play to the Tsar and the Court. Alexander suggested that it be put on by the best actors and actresses who could be found. It was, he declared, 'a marvellous thing'.[50]

This was not how the play struck Konstantin Pobedonostsev when it reached the Procurator of the Holy Synod in the spring of the following year. He wrote to Alexander III to tell him that having finished the play he had scarcely been able to recover his spirits. 'Even Zola never reached this level of vulgar and brutal realism. . . .'[51] But though Pobedonostsev was able to ban the play, his censorship came too late. Already, Chertkov had printed millions of copies in pamphlet form. 'It is a catastrophe,' Pobedonostsev wrote, 'that this minute enormous numbers of copies of Tolstoy's play have already been printed and are being sold for ten kopecks each in cheap booklet form by peddlars on every street corner.'[52]

In Pobedonostsev's mind, sedition was sedition, and it was the Government's job to put it down. At about the same time he censored *The Power of Darkness* a group of six students were arrested on charges of treason. The previous autumn they had attempted a demonstration to commemorate the fiftieth anniversary of the birth of Dobrolyubov, the radical and friend of Herzen. Their little demonstration had been rounded up and suppressed with the greatest possible brutality, and they had resolved to murder the Tsar. When they were arrested, they were found to have manufactured bombs, and to have collected other explosive devices. They were all condemned to death and hanged. When the news reached Yasnaya Polyana, it agitated Sofya Andreyevna 'so badly that it has driven everything else from my mind. This evil will beget many others. . . . Lyovochka heard the news in despondent silence. He had so often imagined it happening.'

She never wrote a truer word than when she imagined this evil begetting many others. One of the students who was hanged, and their ringleader, was called Alexander Ulyanov. On that very day, his younger brother Vladimir swore his revenge,[53] and thirty years later he arrived at the Finland Station in Petrograd to fulfil his word. By then he was known as Lenin.

Chapter Fifteen

The Kreutzer Sonata

1887 - 1890

I know for certain that copulation is an
abomination. . . .

Among all his other creative qualities, Tolstoy has (like George Bernard Shaw) an abiding capacity to irritate his reader. Doubtless it is a capacity which produced in him its own curious satisfaction. But much more than his capacity to irritate, he has a power to disturb, to unsettle, to upset. Although his targets were his own contemporaries — the Government, the Church, the westernising liberals and the literary establishment of the day, together with 'experts' and intellectuals of all kinds, medics, scientists, and theologians — he also possessed a prophetic knack. He expressed opinions about the human condition which to this day are capable of getting under people's skin and making them angry. In no area of his thought is this more apparent than in his analysis, from the late 1880s onwards, of the sexual question. Any modern reader of this phase and group of his writings can expect to be ruffled. While there are probably more people in the world today than ever before who sympathise, in broad outline, with Tolstoy's ardent pacifism, with his suspicion of alcohol and tobacco, even with his vegetarianism, there are also probably fewer than ever before who are able to stomach his views about sex. It is this non-literary fact which probably explains why almost everybody misunderstands the masterpiece of his penultimate period, *The Kreutzer Sonata*.

I wanted to say, first, that in our society generally, at all levels, there has emerged the firm conviction, supported by lying science, that sexual intercourse is something necessary for health, and that since marriage is not always a possibility, then sexual intercourse outside marriage, not binding a man to anything unless to financial payment, is a completely natural thing, and therefore not so much encouraged, as obligatory. This conviction has to such an extent become general and firmly held that parents, on the advice of the doctor, arrange debauchery for their children; governments, whose natural *raison d'être* consists in concern for the moral welfare of their citizens, institutionalise debauchery, that is, they regularise a whole class of women, obliged to perish physically and spiritually, for the satisfaction of the supposed needs of men, while unmarried people, with a completely calm conscience, give themselves up to debauchery.[1]

Modern liberal western prejudice might wish us to see these words as the product of some twisted Augustinian psyche. It is important to remind ourselves of the extent to which sexual standards had collapsed in the latter days of Imperial Russia. A modern biographer of Rasputin (much the liveliest) reminds us that Russia at the turn of the century 'enjoyed a degree of sexual openness, as opposed to licence, that by the standards of the age was extraordinary'.[2] In the one and a half pages of small type ads in the more sober daily newspapers in St. Petersburg, a reasonable proportion would concern accommodation or domestic service. But the greater part would, each day, concern treatment for venereal disease; products such as Urital Galen guaranteed to stop the most stubborn discharge in no time, and were in stout competition with dozens of other quack remedies. Nor was this limited to metropolitan sophisticates or town-dwellers. One thinks of the experience of Mikhail Bulgakov, who served as a *zemstvo* medical officer in the Smolensk province the year before the Revolution (at Nikolskoye, an estate where Tolstoy spent a lot of time with his friends the Olsufyevs) and found the whole of this rural population riddled with venereal disease. He describes it in his story *The Speckled Rash*: how it had spread to everyone, old women and children as well as men. 'It came in many insidious guises. It would take the form of whitish lesions in an adolescent girl's throat, or of bandy legs, or of deep-seated, slow ulcers on an old woman's yellow legs, or of oozing papules on the body of a woman in her prime. Sometimes it proudly displayed itself on the forehead as a crescent shaped 'crown of Venus', or, as in indirect punishment for the sins of their fathers, on children with noses that were the shape of a Cossack's saddle.'[3]

Whether a modern reader would choose to share Tolstoy's moral outlook is another question. As an analysis of what was going on in Russia, his reflections were simply factual.

It will be as well, perhaps, to discuss Tolstoy's views about sex at this period, before turning to *The Kreutzer Sonata*, because although the two are quite obviously interrelated, they are not connected in the way that most modern critics have believed.

Puritanism had been latent in Tolstoy from the very beginning; and certainly by the time he was finishing *Anna Karenina*, we find in him a profound disapproval of sexual intercourse, save for the purpose of procreation. These views had been reiterated, with a strength amounting to crudity, in *What Then Must We Do?* Two quite opposite, or apparently opposite, influences came to work on his mind in the late 1880s, and were still working with full force while he was actually writing his story: one was his desire for Evangelical simplicity, and the other was a deepening misanthropy. The two things came together in his emerging sense that the highest call which could be followed by a human being was one of total celibacy. This was a departure from his position in *What Then Must We Do?*, in which he had seen some beauty and glory in human procreation. Since then, he had been bombarded with literature from the United States of America, and was in particular impressed by the teachings of a (by now almost extinct) sect, the Shakers. He was very much taken by Dr. Alice B. Stockham's *Tokology: a Book for Every Woman*, which he had devoured at the end of 1888, and which advocated complete celibacy within the married state, and men and women living together as brother and sister. The Shakers abjured the eating of pork and the practice of sexual intercourse. They derived their convictions from a certain Ann Lee, an Englishwoman who had resided at Toad Lane, Manchester until, in 1774, the Spirit moved her to forsake her husband and seek a new life in the American colonies. There her gifts of ecstatic utterance, shouting, convulsions and visionary powers attracted a credulous following. God revealed to her directly that the Original Sin practised in the Garden of Eden had been sexual intercourse. He also revealed that Jesus Christ was Chief Elder of the Shakers and that Mother Ann was the Head Eldress. After her death in 1794, her followers worshipped Ann Lee as the second Christ and confidently expected her to return to earth on clouds of glory. Since they are not allowed to reproduce themselves, the Shakers have inevitably declined in numbers; although in the nineteenth century they attracted converts, there have been very few in the twentieth century.[4] Should Ann Lee return to earth today in the manner expected by the faithful, she would find only a tiny band of wise virgins, watching for her Parousia in New England.

Tolstoy did not share the apocalyptic hope of the Shakers, but he read their views on sex and pronounced them 'Excellent. Complete sexual restraint.'[5] Not that he was able to practise it since, as he admitted to Chertkov, 'I am a dirty, libidinous old man.'[6] Nevertheless, celibacy had by now become his ideal.

Hostile readers will consider this 'ideal' about as impressive as the tears of some incurable lecher before an icon of the immaculate Mother of God, but it has to be said that Tolstoy and the Shakers have the New Testament on their side. The pattern of his understanding in this matter is exactly parallel to his discovery of what Christ taught in relation to violence and resistance to evil. Most modern churchmen (with the exception of the Pope), beguiled by what Tolstoy would call 'lying science' and what they would call common sense, have a shrill desire to dissociate themselves from anything which smacks of 'fear of the physical' or an irrational dread of sex. For Tolstoy, the question was rather different. He wanted to recover the teachings of Jesus, and he believed them to be true. In the case of Christian pacifism there are anomalies which Tolstoy had to argue his way around.

In sexual matters, the New Testament presents a much more united and consistent ethic. True, Christ consorted with publicans and sinners, but it was to them and to the harlots that He addressed His teachings of chastity. He forgave the woman taken in adultery but told her to sin no more. And His call to chastity is more searching than any before or since. 'Ye have heard that it was said by them of old time, Thou shalt not commit adultery: But I say unto you that whosoever looketh on a woman to lust after her hath committed adultery with her already in his heart' (Matthew V.27-28). Later in St. Matthew's Gospel we are told that some are made eunuchs for the Kingdom of Heaven's sake. There is not a single passage or text in the New Testament, from any of its different writers, which departs from this ideal. The whole of the early Christian tradition, both in the New Testament and in the writings of the Greek and Latin fathers, held out celibacy as an ideal, marriage as a distinct second best in the Christian life, and sex as in general a dangerous and a bad thing.

Tolstoy's exposition of his beliefs about sex in the Afterword to *The Kreutzer Sonata* are preached in deliberately intemperate terms. But, as with his doctrines of peace, there is nothing in his ethical view (one discounts his rejection of the doctrine of grace etc.) which would not have found an echo in St. Paul, in Clement of Alexandria, in Tertullian, in St. Augustine. It is, in fact, 'mere Christianity'. The Afterword, which is one of his clearest expositions of the teaching, is much less thunderous than is often supposed by readers who have only had it described to them. His point is a rather crucial one to any Tolstoyan understanding of Christianity; and that is that Christ taught an ideal. Tolstoy fully recognises that when the ideal is chastity, not many people will be able to attain it. 'The follower of Christ's teachings is like a man carrying a lantern in front of him on a stick which might be long or short; the light is always in front of him, and is always inciting him to follow; and then it opens up to him a new space ahead, filled with light and drawing the man to itself." There is a great gentleness in this image, which the commentators do not always repeat for us.

Opponents of Tolstoy and opponents of the Bible (which in this case come to the same thing) often point out that if this ideal were put into practice, the human race would suffer the fate of the Shakers and become extinct. And they would see it as part of the sinister strand in Biblical tradition, the strand which hates mankind. God, in the Old Testament, who told the human race to be fruitful and to multiply, decided within a very short space of time that He repented that He had made man on the earth, and therefore decided to destroy the human race, preserving only a small remnant in the ark. This strand of Bible thinking can be found from the beginning of the Christian Scriptures to the end, from Noah's ark to the choirs of the elect singing around the throne of the lamb while the majority of human-kind is plunged into a fiery lake towards the close of the Apocalypse of John.

Christ's teaching about celibacy needs to be seen in this context. He held before His disciples not only an ideal of celibacy, but also a vision, inherited by Paul and the other writers of the New Testament, of a world which was shortly to be brought to an end by the 'Abomination of Desolation'. Questions of world population in the next generation but two or three are scarcely of interest to men and women who believe that any cloud passing over the sky might contain a trumpeting angel and the promised Messiah.

Tolstoy did not believe in the Parousia, nor the Last Judgement, nor any of the 'mythological' elements in the New Testament. But within his own nature there was a correspondingly 'dark' theme to which he confesses in his diary as the year 1889 develops. 'Death is ahead of me, i.e. life, so why should I not be glad?' he noted in an entry which suggests a continuing hope of immortality. 'It's just because I feel I have lost interest in — I don't say my own person or my own joys (they are dead and buried thank God) — but in other people's good; in the good of ordinary people, that they should be educated, not drink, not live in poverty; I feel my interest is cooling even towards the general good, the establishment of the Kingdom of God on earth. . . .'[8] There is typical honesty here, and perhaps if natural disasters, famines, and the worsening political situation had not shaken him out of this view in the quite near future, Tolstoy's religious position might from now on have developed along purely 'mystical' lines.

But there was in Tolstoy, as well as a natural cooling of interest in the Kingdom of God on earth, a positive glee in arguments which were absurd, provocative and irritating. Earlier in the year 1889, a happy diary entry recorded reading Voltaire with a niece. 'We roared with laughter.'[9] So, when dumbfounded critics confronted Tolstoy with the view (considering it unanswerable) that if we were all celibate, the human race would die out, it was quite inevitable that he would enjoy being forced into the ultimate rejection of humanity itself. 'You will object that this would mean the end of the human race. . . . What a great misfortune! The antediluvian animals are gone from the earth, human animals will disappear too. . . . I have no more pity for these two-footed beasts than for the ichthyosaurus.'[10] For a moment the humble Christian who loves all mankind has been taken over by the *saeva indignatio* and biting comedy of Jonathan Swift.

And, doubtless, we should bear in mind all these things as we start to read *The Kreutzer Sonata*. As so often, the story came to him by someone telling him an anecdote. He started it, laid it aside, and allowed the idea to gestate. Then followed a period of intense writing and rewriting. In this case, the anecdote came from an actor called Vasily Nikolayevich Andreyev-Burlak. He had been to see the Tolstoys on June 20, 1887,[11] and in the after-dinner circle he described meeting a stranger in a train, who had poured out to him the story of his wife's unfaithfulness. Tolstoy had immediately doodled with this tale and at that point thought of it as his story of 'sexual love'. The next year, in their Moscow house, he was again in Andreyev-Burlak's company. Tolstoy's children put on a little concert for a gathering of friends. Andreyev-Burlak came, and Repin the painter. The children's teacher, Yuly Lyasota, played the violin part of Beethoven's 'Kreutzer' sonata, with Tolstoy's son Sergey at the piano. It was very much part of the family repertoire and, as always, Tolstoy was moved by it. But now, for no more rational reason than that Andreyev-Burlak was present, Tolstoy came to associate it with the wronged husband in the railway carriage. He would write a monologue for Andreyev-Burlak to recite. Repin could paint the scene. It could be made to incorporate one of his unfinished short stories, *The Man Who Murdered His Wife*. Andreyev-Burlak could be enjoined to 'perform' this story as a dramatic monologue, rather like the public readings of Dickens.

And so the idea of *The Kreutzer Sonata* was born. And even though the actor Andreyev-Burlak died on May 10, 1888,[12] the monologue form, turning into prose fiction with a first-person narrative, remained part of Tolstoy's conception. For most of that year, 1888, he did little to the story, but in 1889, he took it up in earnest, and worked and reworked it. Throughout the summer, this was the principal thing on his mind, and the diary reflects this. The figure of the musician — the despised figure in the story whom the narrator of the story believes to have seduced the wife — thinks to himself, 'I won't go to a brothel, I may get infected there. . . .' Then, a month later, 'I must make the dying woman delirious, as she begs for forgiveness and can't believe it was he who had killed her. . . .' Two days later, on August 19, 1889, he adds, '"Fornicator" is not a term of abuse, but rather denotes a condition (the same is true of a woman fornicator, I think) — a condition of restlessness, curiosity and the need for novelty which comes from intercourse for the sake of pleasure, not with one person but many. Likewise "drunkard". One can try to abstain, but a drunkard remains a drunkard and a fornicator a fornicator — at the first lapse of concentration he falls. I am a fornicator.'[13]

A version was finished by the end of August, and a week later, having copied it, Sofya Andreyevna gave a reading aloud to the older children and the family.

The story in its finished state begins as a third-person narrative by a colourless figure making his way across Russia by train. Conversation in the carriage turns to the universally interesting subjects of sex, love and marriage. Wishing to moderate some of the intemperate views expressed by the other passengers, a certain lawyer claims that there are many people who live long married lives. But this is violently contradicted by a passenger called Pozdnyshev. 'Marriages in our day are mere deception!' he announces. And he then goes on to suppose in typically paranoid fashion that the lawyer was alluding to him, Pozdnyshev, when he spoke of some marriages passing through 'critical episodes'. Pozdnyshev then announces that he himself killed his wife.

Few announcements can be more calculated to compel an audience. The reader is as gripped as the narrator in the train by Pozdnyshev's extraordinary story. It very soon becomes clear that Pozdnyshev is a man with an insane sexual obsession. All his memories of sexual awakening in his youth are tormented with guilt, every sexual encounter is regarded as a terrible 'fall' from some ideal of purity, and the activity of sexual intercourse is described as a perverted thing which should by rights appeal only to monkeys and Parisians.

But it is for marriage that Pozdnyshev reserves his strictest censure. He is a man with a mission. He longs to disabuse his hearers and to persuade everyone that all marriages, everywhere and in every circumstance, are an obscene sham. Years before, when he was a gullible young man visiting Paris, that city of monkey-business, he saw a sign advertising a bearded woman and a water-dog. He eagerly paid his money and entered, only to discover that the 'bearded woman' was a man dressed in women's clothes, and the water-dog was a dog dressed in a walrus skin and swimming in a bathtub. Bitterly disappointed, he made his way out of the show. The showman called out to the public, 'Ask this gentleman whether or not the show is worth seeing!' And he was too ashamed to tell them that it was all a sham. This is what marriage is like, says Pozdnyshev.

Charging ahead with his narrative, Pozdnyshev allows himself many generalisations with which no sane listener could agree — such as that the emancipation of women, or university education for women, has come about solely through motives of lust by both sexes, or that most cases of adultery have been occasioned by music, that well-known aphrodisiac. This idea, which explains the title and the theme of the story, that music is the food of love, is Pozdnyshev's overriding obsession. He married a pretty woman. They had children ('a regular hell'); they came to hate one another, while lusting after one another. You know, Pozdnyshev seems to imply, the usual thing. And then there came to their house a musician called Trukachevsky who offered to accompany Pozdnyshev's wife on the violin.

From the moment this suggestion was made, Pozdnyshev became convinced that the pair were conducting a sexual intrigue. In connection with his work, Pozdnyshev had to go into the country to attend the meeting of the local council, or *zemstvo*. He remembered the look on the faces of his wife and the musician while they were playing the 'Kreutzer' sonata. He resolved to return to Moscow early from his meeting, surprise the guilty lovers and give them the only punishment which such behaviour deserves: death.

The dénouement of the tale comes with Pozdnyshev's return home. He found his wife and the musician — not in bed, but merely sitting in the drawing room having played some music. The musician escaped, but Pozdnyshev killed his wife with a curved Damascus dagger which hung on the wall.

It is strange to think of Sofya Andreyevna reading this outstandingly nasty tale to the assembled family, in the same way that she might read some harmless story by Leskov, Trollope or Turgenev. When it was over, Tanya, ever anxious to ingratiate herself with her father, said that one could not sympathise with the wife, and that she would not repent because she had not really committed any sins. Tolstoy's spirits were high, and evidently he felt happy that week with his family. Above all, it was good to be writing fiction again! 'One joyful thing I do remember is that the awareness of life through the recovery of my talent has been restored to me,'[14] one of the most touching, and revealing sentences in the whole of Tolstoy's diary. There is not the slightest suggestion in any of the diary entries that Sofya Andreyevna objected to the story, nor that anyone in the family thought that the madman in the train, who had murdered his wife because she was having an affair with a fiddler, bore the slightest resemblance to Tolstoy, any more than the wife resembled Sofya Andreyevna. If she had objected to it, how could Countess Tolstoy have borne to read it aloud to the family?

However, there were, as always, tensions in the air. Sofya Andreyevna was more taken up with little Ivan (Vanichka) than with any of her previous children. She probably knew that he was the last child she was ever going to have and at forty-four, and no less than thirteen completed pregnancies behind her, it is possible that she even hoped he was the last. There was certainly an enormous joy and consolation to be derived from this child's company — more than from any other. Since Sofya Andreyevna was much preoccupied and, with Tolstoy, so frequently out of sympathy, it is not surprising that he should have turned to his daughters for help, advice and secretarial assistance.

Marya (Masha) was the person responsible for most of the nine drafts which Tolstoy made of this novella. As Tolstoy wrote to Masha's old teacher Alexeyev on August 22, 1889, 'Of my children, only Masha is close to me in spirit. The others, poor things, are only oppressed by the fact that I am always around, reminding them of what their conscience demands of them.'[15] It is typical of Tolstoy that he has observed that most of his family find him tiresome, but that he confidently attributes this to moral weakness on their part.

The favours he showed to Masha caused eruptions in other parts of the household. Some time after the ninth version had been copied, Masha casually came into the hall and put on Tatyana's galoshes. It left Tatyana marooned in the house — the wet weather had started, and when Masha returned, there was a silly squabble.[16] But it was not really a quarrel about galoshes. Tatyana resented the fact that her younger sister was so doted upon by Papa, and the fact that her efforts to guide her life according to Tolstoyan principles appeared to go unnoticed. Had she not vowed in her diary, 'since the inception of *The Kreutzer Sonata*, not to get married?'[17] Whether she was the more influenced in reaching this decision (ten years later she broke it) by reading her father's work or by witnessing the way her parents were getting on together, we are not informed.

No one was more jealous of Masha than their mother. 'I used to copy everything he wrote, and loved doing so,' she scribbled in her diary. 'Now he carefully conceals everything from me and gives it to his daughters instead. He is systematically destroying me by driving me out of his life in this way, and it is unbearably painful.'[18]

By now, however, a worse threat had appeared in Sofya Andreyevna's life. *The Kreutzer Sonata* had been submitted to the official censor, and it was all taking a very long time. Its first failure to get past the censor was early in 1890, when Tolstoy allowed N. I. Storozhenko permission to publish it in a collection dedicated to the memory of S. A. Yuryev. But by then, copies of the story had got out, and were circulating. Lithograph copies, produced illegally by underground presses, were reproducing thousands of copies of *The Kreutzer Sonata* in St. Petersburg, making of the whole story a *cause célèbre*. Pobedonostsev, who had hitherto thought it a 'powerful work', and not immoral, had found his opinion echoed by the Tsar who thought it 'magnificent'. But the fact that it was being circulated by a seditious press (without Tolstoy's permission) made it all the more dangerous to handle. Who had got it to the underground presses, to the lithographers, and hectographers? Can we doubt it was Chertkov, via Masha? Sofya Andreyevna was understandably furious. If a major new work of fiction could be stolen in this way, what was to become of her magnificent Collected Edition of Tolstoy? It was essential for her that *The Kreutzer Sonata* should appear in Volume XIII of the *Collected Works*: essential for her financially, and even more importantly, essential from the point of view of showing the world who was the victor, herself or Chertkov, when it came to handling her husband's affairs.

Unfortunately, the story was not being read on its literary merits, but rather for its gossip value. By now it was notorious in the drawing rooms of St. Petersburg and Moscow that the Tolstoys were what is called 'unhappy', and it is hardly surprising that very scandalous interpretations were placed upon the story. Biryukov, Chertkov, and the many young men who hovered about Tolstoy and lapped up his opinions were not slow to promulgate the views of the Master, and to spread abroad his *ex cathedra* pronouncements. It was common knowledge that Tolstoy had begun to favour complete celibacy: even in marriage. . . .

One can imagine the fun which gossips and hostesses had with all this, and how galling the Tolstoys would have found it had they known the half. Chertkov, who was an intelligent reader of Tolstoy's works, felt that it was a very great mistake to give to Pozdnyshev, the murderer, so many of Tolstoy's own views, and to make a man who was slightly mad, and an obvious rotter, the vehicle for the newly discovered Tolstoyan view of sex. Might it not confuse the issue? Tolstoy, significantly, did not reply to these suggestions for a good three weeks,[19] and only did so when he had half-decided to write an Afterword, from which we have already quoted, giving the party line to the faithful.

But Chertkov had been right, and Tolstoy knew it. There was something profoundly odd, from a missionary point of view, quite self-destructive, about the way in which Tolstoy's famous 'views' are put into the mouth of such a person as Pozdnyshev. John Bayley, the most percipient literary critic to have written about Tolstoy in English, is tantalisingly brief in his analysis of the tale. He sees as a confusion behind the tale what could be regarded as its haunting strength, when he says that 'it is as if we knew that Shakespeare had hated sex, but not so much as Hamlet does; and was disgusted with human beings, but not in quite so sensational a fashion as Timon'.[20] This is well said, but perhaps it is not because Pozdnyshev is made to act as 'Tolstoy's agent in the story'. Rather the opposite. In the story, Tolstoy's imagination is liberated from his views. It is not that he abandons them or is disloyal to them. But it is rather as we see Sir Walter Scott — a high Tory in life — able in his fiction to see the limitations and absurdities of his own point of view. Remember, Tolstoy sets out, not to write a tract about sex, but a murder story, and it 'catches him', inspires him, on those two evenings with the actor, and in the innumerable drafts in the study, on a purely imaginative level. That is why he is so 'high' on September 11, 1889, in the knowledge that his talent has been 'restored'. Moreover, *The Kreutzer Sonata* is a great departure; it is unlike anything in the *œuvre* which has gone before. *The Death of Ivan Ilyich* is immediately recognisable as the sort of desolating *aperçu* which could have occurred to someone in one of the great novels. It is not so far removed from some of Prince Andrey's blacker moments, or Anna's. Nor would it surprise us in the least if we found out that Ivan Ilyich was actually acquainted with Karenin. But in *The Kreutzer Sonata*, we step outside the Tolstoyan world. If we were told merely the outline of the plot, without knowing its author, we would guess that it had been written either by Maupassant or Dostoyevsky — two authors much on Tolstoy's mind at this date. And it is this straying outside his normal territory as much as the so-called autobiographical slant to the tale which leads to our sense of displacement here, our feeling of an imagination not so much out of tune with its material as at war with it. By the time eighteen months had passed, the loyal Tolstoyan vision had reasserted itself, and he was able to write to Chertkov that any mention of the story was 'terribly offensive' to him. 'There was something nasty about *The Kreutzer Sonata*.' It was in fact, to use the title of one of Dostoyevsky's early works, 'A Nasty Story'; it does not really have a moral: if it did have one, it would be rather more Swiftian than Tolstoyan. In Pozdnyshev, the wife-murderer met on the train, there is a level of anarchic evil which is much more Dostoyevskian than anything Tolstoy had attempted before. His exaggerations and generalisations are not a reflection of Tolstoy's own views. They are a grotesque distortion of Tolstoy's own vision of sex. It is as though Tolstoy's imagination came upon Tolstoy's brain buzzing with ideas and used the phenomenon, just as it used the external details of the man's story from Andreyev-Burlak's anecdote. Thus we all know that Tolstoy was highly sexed but only those who wish to disbelieve all evidence and suppose him to have been mad (or very stupid) can really think that he would echo, with his serious mind, Pozdnyshev's view that women act so powerfully on men that it is not safe to let them out in ball-dresses: when he sees them so arrayed, Pozdnyshev tells his train companion, "'I want to call a policeman and ask for protection from the peril, and demand that the dangerous object be removed and put away. Ah! you are laughing," he shouted at me, "but it is not at all a joke."' But Tolstoy's imagination can see that it is, and that to speak in this way is deranged, dotty. We feel this nowhere more strongly than when he expects his companion to see that there is an obvious connection between sexual desire and the 'Kreutzer' sonata, or to believe that because music has power to excite passion, it is only safe that it should be performed in rooms where this passion can be given no sexual outlet. 'How can that first *presto* be played in a drawing room among ladies in low-necked dresses?' Pozdnyshev is a nut. The tension in the story (because he tells us very early on that he has murdered his wife) consists in watching him working up to the point of explosion where it seems reasonable to cancel his meetings of the *zemstvo*, and travel back to Moscow by overnight train with the sole purpose of murdering a woman he believes to be having an affair with a violin teacher. And the reason he believes it, and he is probably right, is that the violin teacher has expensive Parisian clothes and a big bottom, and sensual lips and whiskers. Pozdnyshev is in the grip of lust and jealousy. His wife probably (though it may be that she is a Desdemona — we are only allowed to see her through his eyes, which is one of the very clever things about the story) is in the grip of lust, but not jealousy. They have both been disillusioned by the experience of marriage and because of the modern doctrine that sex is good for you (here, if at all, an element of the tract creeps in) they have become victims. True, much of Pozdnyshev's self-disgust, his weeping at his first sexual experience, his addiction to sexual experience while loathing himself for doing it, his hatred of his wife, have formed part of Tolstoy's experience. But it is a gross simplification to think that Pozdnyshev is Tolstoy. On the contrary, he is the greatest indictment of the Tolstoyan view of men and women that was ever imagined. And it is almost as if he is like some terrible puppet that has got out of control on the end of Tolstoy's arm. It may very well be that when Tolstoy started to revise the story he had wanted Pozdnyshev to be a cipher for his own views (though there is in fact no evidence for this). But what happened is that all kinds of inarticulate things in Tolstoy's subconscious rose up and created Pozdnyshev as he actually is. The old pattern was at work of Tolstoy using fiction to purge and to sanitise existence. In early stories his imagination had washed experience, leaving him, for example, as an innocent and not a fornicator in *The Cossacks*. Here, the imagination was doing more disturbing work. It was unearthing, beneath all the doctrines of love and chastity, the violence and the hatred which were inseparable from sexual passion in Tolstoy's life.

Sofya Andreyevna was a woman with a violent temper, and though clever, she was not in the least logical. She was also extraordinarily vain, and when she realised that the story had become a matter of tittle-tattle in the drawing rooms, she became more than ever anxious to make certain facts clear to the world. The first, rather touching fact which she wanted to publish to the world was that she and her husband were still 'sexually active'. She therefore let it be known that her chief dread was that the true postscript to *The Kreutzer Sonata* would be another baby. What sort of a fool would that make of her? Well, none at all, as she knew perfectly well, but it would have made a bit of a fool of her husband. By now she had taken it into her head that *The Kreutzer Sonata* was some sort of attack upon her, or upon women, and so she composed a disastrously feeble little reply, a short story called *Who is to Blame?* Luckily, friends prevailed upon her not to publish it, otherwise she really would have been made a fool of. It tells the story of one Prince Prozorovsky, a lecher of thirty-five who marries a poor innocent girl of eighteen, and makes her miserable. When a painter loves her (but only Platonically) the brute of a husband becomes violently jealous and kills her. If her artless little story makes any kind of point, it is to show that Sofya Andreyevna had completely missed the point of *The Kreutzer Sonata*. So, more surprisingly, has Troyat. If one takes the view (which is barely tenable) that *The Kreutzer Sonata* is an autobiography, and that the crazy Pozdnyshev, so anxious to attend meetings of the *zemstvo* (Tolstoy despised these local councils and would have nothing to do with them) is a portrait of the author, then who comes out of it badly? Certainly not Pozdnyshev's dull little wife. No reader of the story can blame her for the fact that she arouses feelings of completely irrational anger in her husband. Troyat says, 'It is hard not to imagine the irritation Tolstoy must have felt in Sofya's presence when Pozdnyshev says, speaking of his wife, "'I watched her pouring out the tea, putting the spoon in her mouth and swinging her foot, noisily sucking on the liquid, and found myself

loathing her as though she were committing some hideous crime.'"'
But we are surely not being invited at this point to think that
Podznyshev is being reasonable? So why should Sofya Andreyevna
take offence? Because she herself has irritated Tolstoy in similar
ways? But if the story has a moral or a point, it is surely to demonstrate
that sexual passion and marriage reduce people to these conditions of
hatred. And it is the truth of this, rather than its alleged ungallantry,
which all readers find uncomfortable. Tolstoy does not say in this
story that it is a universal truth. But there is enough evidence around
us to know that it is true.

Its truth may lend power to the story, and it may be more to the
point than Sofya Andreyevna's annoying habits. But even that is by
the by. To repeat, this is a murder story. It is not, as so many critics
seem to imagine, an *evangel* placed upon the lips of the most
inappropriate preachers. It is the sort of story of unbridled and
terrifying passion of which Dosyoyevsky made himself the master.
And while it has all Tolstoy's directness, and largeness, and clearness,
there are suggestions at various points that he was actually writing
with Dostoyevsky in his eye. A question which dogged Tolstoy, in life
and in art, was that of our consciousness, our consciousness of
existence itself. One remembers Anna Karenina in the train, reading
the English novel and envying the characters their life. So, when
Pozdnyshev describes doing his wife in, he makes this highly apposite
and Tolstoyan observation: '"When people say that in a fit of rage
they do not remember what they are doing, that's twaddle, a lie. I
remember everything, and not for one second have I stopped
remembering. The more steamed up I got, the more clearly the light
of consciousness [*svet soznaniya*] flared up inside me, so that I could
not but see what I had done. I knew what I was doing for every
second."'

There follow, in the most graphic details, all his passing thoughts
and sensations as he drives the dagger home. '"I heard (and I
remember) the momentary resistance of the corset, and of something
else as well, and then the knife sinking into something soft."' It is one
of the best murders in literature. And we catch within it a sort of
literary reply to the great murder-expert himself. After Raskolnikov
has committed his second murder in *Crime and Punishment*, 'A
dreamlike and even absent-minded condition gradually came over
him; at moments he seemed to lose all awareness of self, or rather, to
lose sight of the important things in favour of trifles. . . .'[24] For

Dostoyevsky's characters, evil is like a drug on which they can get high, drunk; for Tolstoy's characters, it sharpens their hideous awareness of things. It is as though Pozdnyshev is saying to Raskolnikov, 'You may have lost your awareness of self when you did *your* murders, but I was overwhelmingly aware of self when I did mine.' He is just as self-aware as all the early and middle-period heroes and heroines. Only what — even for Anna — was a source, much of the time, of joy — the knowledge that 'I am I' — has become for Pozdnyshev (*pozdny* means 'late' in Russian and he is born out of time in his unhappy author's imagination) a source of perpetual, scorching torment. He is a soul in hell.

*   *   *   *

In March 1891, Tolstoy wrote to Strakhov in St. Petersburg asking him to buy some books — Thomas Paine's *Age of Reason* and Schopenhauer's *Parerga und Paralipomena*. As for payment, Strakhov was to get the money off 'Sofya Andreyevna who will be in Petersburg a few days, I think, to my great regret, to petition for the publication of Volume XIII. You can't imagine what a misunderstanding there has been about it — first tragic and now comic.'[25]

From now onwards, both the Tolstoys were obsessed with their posthumous reputations, and chronicled their lives even more fully than they had done before. Both — but particularly Sofya Andreyevna — seemed to have been engaged in a perpetual Dogberry-exercise, anxious to be writ down an ass. Events which are meant to be full of dignity, or pathos, had a tendency to become completely ludicrous. And the aftermath of *The Kreutzer Sonata* is a case in point. There is something inescapably absurd about Sofya Andreyevna's position. On the one hand, with *Who is to Blame?*, she wants us to believe that she has been somehow or another wronged by the story. On the other, she exhibitionistically and tirelessly petitions to be the highest authority in the Empire to make sure that the story is published with maximum publicity. And while she was pulling strings at Court to get her audience with the Tsar, she was able to let fall in all the right ears that she was afraid of being made a 'fool' of by her husband in his new role as prophet of celibacy. She may be forty-five years old but — oh, he was a beast! He could not stay away from her.

The audience with the Tsar was arranged through friends of Alexandrine. For nearly a fortnight after writing to Alexander III,

Tolstoy in his study. The sofa on which he, and most of his children, were born is behind him.

Tolstoy telling two of his grandchildren Sonya and Ilyosha 'the Tale about the Cucumber'. Photograph by Chertkov, 1909.

Tolstoy posing with peasant children

An al fresco meal at Yasnaya Polyana. Chertkov is on Tolstoy's right, his wife on his left at the head of the table. Other figures are, from the left, the family doctor (the one who looks like Lenin) Makovitsky, Sasha, Yelizaveta Obolenskaya; and to the right of the picture, Masha Obolenkskaya, Gusev and Varvara Feokritova.

Tolstoy still enjoyed riding deep into old age. This photograph was taken at Yasnaya Polyana in 1908, when he was eighty.

Tolstoy and his sister at Yasnaya Polyana

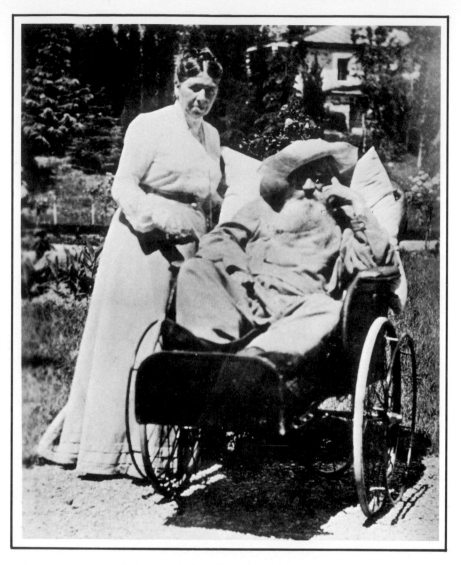

Tolstoy and his wife in the Crimea, 1904

Tolstoy with Maxim Gorky

Tolstoy and Chekhov

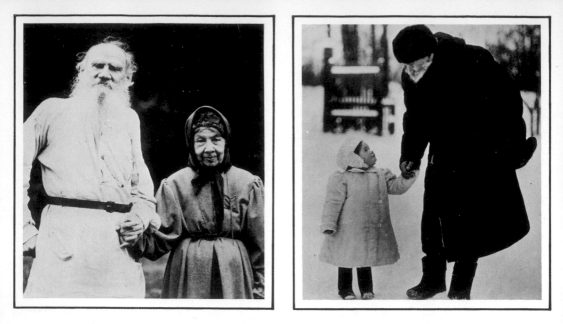

Left Tolstoy with his gipsy sister-in-law, Sasha, in 1906 or 1907. By now, he had shrunk in size to less than 5′ 4″, so Sasha cannot have been big. (*Right*) Tolstoy with his grand-daughter Tanya.

Tolstoy with his brother Sergey

Tolstoy walking in the woods at Yasnaya Polyana, 1908

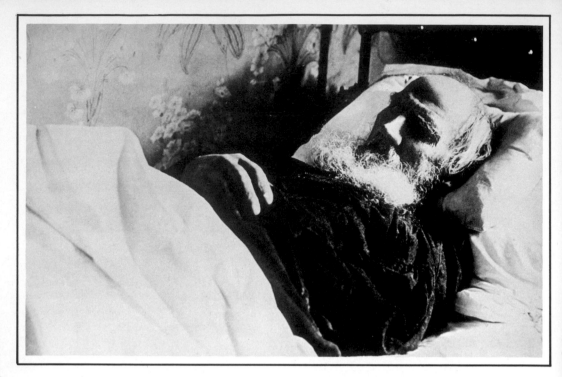

Tolstoy on his deathbed at Astapovo

Tolstoy's funeral at Yasnaya Polyana

Sofya Andreyevna despaired of getting an audience, and then, on the Saturday before Passion Sunday, she was told that her request had been granted and that his Imperial Majesty would receive Her Excellency the Countess Tolstaya.

The first impression given by the Emperor to his loyal and excellent subject was disconcerting. He reminded her of Chertkov, especially in his voice and manner of speaking. What is more, the hated Chertkov was one of the people whom the Emperor wished to discuss. 'Do you see much of Chertkov, the son of Grigory Ivanovich and Elizaveta Ivanovna? It seems your husband has completely converted him.' Sofya Andreyevna was quite unprepared for this question and for a moment lost her composure. Then she said that over two years had passed since they last saw the Chertkovs; but that she and her husband had had the idea of publishing good, moral, popular literature at a low price to replace 'the many stupid and immoral books which were being published for popular consumption'.

In a totalitarian state, all questions put by those in authority to their subjects are threats. On the one level, this is a conversation between a genial monarch and an aristocratic lady: it could be George V and the Duchess of Buccleuch. 'How's so-and-so's boy? Got a lot of cranky ideas, what?' But this is Russia, and on another level, the conversational parallels are more like some alarming telephone call from Stalin to the wife of a man of genius. How much of this does Sofya Andreyevna realise? Instinct makes her lie; she wants to underestimate the degree of closeness between her husband and Chertkov. She knows that Chertkov is politically dangerous; that religious heresy is *politically* dangerous; that Pobedonostsev's secret police have been investigating her husband and her husband's friends. The Tsar expresses his regret that Lev Nikolayevich has left the Church. '"There are so many heresies springing up among the simple people, which are having a very harmful effect upon them," says the Emperor. To this I replied, "I can assure your Majesty that my husband has never preached any philosophy either to the people or to anyone else. He has never mentioned his beliefs to the peasants and not only does he not distribute the texts of his manuscripts to other people, he is actually in despair when other people distribute them. . . ."' Again, she longs to exonerate her husband from implication in seditious conduct. At the same time, she is desperate, as a commercially astute person, to get permission to publish Volume XIII. She starts to get carried away with lies. Only the other day, Lev Nikolayevich was saying that he had completely moved away from any interest in philosophical and religious matters, and would like to write something more along the lines of *War and Peace*. 'Ah,' said the Tsar, 'how good that would be! What a great writer he is!' It would certainly encourage him to return to literature, wheedled Sofya Andreyevna, if the Tsar would permit him to include *The Kreutzer Sonata* in the Collected Edition. 'Well,' asks the Tsar, 'would you give it to children to read?' But in the event, he relented. After all, few enough people could afford the thirteen volumes of the complete set. 'It will not have a very wide circulation.'[26] Curiously enough, Chertkov met with exactly the same response twenty-five and thirty years later when he was allowed to start work on his Collected Edition of Tolstoy. Both Christian Emperor and Marxist Dictator fell back in the end upon the power of Mammon.

Nothing could have been more calculated to annoy Tolstoy. And when he heard what his wife had been saying to the Emperor, he had a little explosion of wrath. In particular he objected to her lie about manuscripts being stolen from him and published without his permission. But soon, rather to his surprise, his anger evaporated. There was, after all, something more than a little flattering about the whole incident. The Tsar of Russia wishing that he would write some more in the vein of *War and Peace*; his wife having the energy and persistence to have gone through with it all. What helped to allow the anger to die down were two very refreshingly normal impulses. First, no one more than Tolstoy himself yearned for the return of that talent which had enabled him to write *War and Peace*. No one. And second, he was touched that the incident implied that perhaps she was really quite fond of him after all.[27]

Illness, however minor, in her husband always increased Sofya's fondness and about a month later, she was able to record that 'Poor Lyovochka has inflamed eyelids and has been sitting alone in a darkened room for the past two days. He was a bit better today. Yesterday I sent for Doctor Rudnyov and he prescribed bathing the eyes in Goulard water which he sent us. Yesterday Lyovochka dictated to Masha a letter on religious matters for Alekhin (a dark one) and I was amazed by how good it was, and how totally it corresponded to my own feelings.'[28] Such moments of sympathy and correspondence between the two of them led inevitably to the dirty, libidinous old man, the fornicator (as he had variously described himself) to thinking and doing dreadful things. 'Whether I explained properly or not why the greatest sexual continence is necessary I don't know,' he wrote in his diary a week after dictating the letter whose spiritual content so impressed Sofya by its likeness to her own opinions. 'But I do know for certain that copulation is an abomination which can only be thought of without revulsion under the influence of sexual desire. Even in order to have children you wouldn't do this to a woman you love. I'm writing this at a time when I'm possessed myself by sexual desire, against which I can't fight.'[29]

Chapter Sixteen

Terrible Questions

1890 - 1893

Our feet have reached the holy places but our hearts may not have done so.

Father Sergius

The summer of 1891 was extremely hot; and for Tolstoy it was a productive one.[1] He spent the months of June doodling with the stories which would become *Father Sergius* and *Resurrection*, and talking about vegetarianism and sexual abstinence with the hordes of 'dark ones', foreign sightseers, seekers after truth and other nuisances clamouring for a glimpse of the great man. His wife, who found him 'extraordinarily sweet, cheerful and affectionate at the moment', purred contentedly to her diary. 'If only the people who read *The Kreutzer Sonata* so reverently had an inkling of the voluptuous life he leads, and realised that it was only this which made him happy and good-natured, then they would cast this deity from the pedestal where they have placed him!'[2]

It is rather a cheering thing to read from the pen of someone twenty-six years married. This very juxtaposition between the happily sexual private Tolstoy and the tormented prophet of abstinence is what gave birth to *Father Sergius*, the most powerfully erotic of all his stories. 'I love him when he is kind and normal and full of human weaknesses,' his wife said. 'One should not be an animal, but nor should one preach virtues one does not have.'[3]

Father Sergius is a famous *starets*. In his youth he had been a nobly born army officer, who abandoned his fiancée when he discovered that she had been the mistress of Emperor Nicholas I. 'His disillusionment with Mary, whom he had imagined to be a person of angelic purity, and his sense of hurt were so strong that they led him to despair; and the despair led him — to what — to God, to the faith of his childhood. . . .'[4]

Sergius does not merely become a monk, he becomes a famed master of the spiritual life, who eventually leaves his monastery to become a hermit. The first powerful moment of sexual temptation in the story occurs when he is forty-nine years old. A passing group of frivolous rich people see if they can't seduce 'Kasatsky the handsome hermit' by loosing to him a vampish (female) member of their party. She pretends that she is a stranger who has lost her way, and asks for shelter from the cold in his cell. He is so tempted by her that the only means by which he can resist is through the infliction of physical torment on himself, and he takes an axe and cuts off a finger of his left hand. She is so impressed by this demonstration that she herself is converted and becomes a nun.

Yet Sergius is not really a saint. He became a monk because he was jealous and hurt, not because his heart loved God. And now he enjoys a 'spiritual reparation' in a way which is almost as carnal as 'worldly fame'. As with his creator, Tolstoy, there is within him a perpetual sense of dislocation. Everyone else is convinced; and he is not exactly putting on an act. Yet 'he was often astonished that he, Stepan Kasatsky, had come to be such an extraordinary saint.'

Then, one day, he was visited by a merchant whose daughter had a nervous disorder. She was a plump, fair girl of twenty-two with a 'very developed female figure'. When they are alone together, the afflicted one and the saint become a woman and a man. She tells Father Sergius that she has had erotic dreams about him, and it is only a matter of minutes before she embraces him and places his hands on her breasts.

He wanders out of his cell, a completely disillusioned man; disillusioned, that is to say, with his own self-image. After a spell of wandering, he comes upon his former fiancée, now an old *babushka* with an unsatisfactory son-in-law and very little money. He realises that his renunciation of her has been priggish and ultimately ungodly. It is she who must bless him, and not the other way around.

After this *aperçu*, he becomes a wandering pilgrim, 'and little by little God started to reveal Himself to him'. Sometimes he goes alone, and sometimes he walks with the other wanderers. On one occasion when he is walking in such a group some French tourists stop and stare; and, thinking that no one in that ragged band will understand their language, one says to another '*Demandez-leur s'ils sont bien sûrs de ce que leur pélérinage est agréable à Dieu.*'*

* 'Ask them if they are really sure that their pilgrimage is agreeable to God.'

An old woman replies to them, 'As God accepts it, Our feet have reached the holy places, but our hearts may not have done so.'[5]

The gap between Tolstoy's ideals and his actual behaviour have made those who do not want to understand him dub him a hypocrite. But a hypocrite is a man who pretends that such gaps do not exist. In Tolstoy there was no such pretence.

Well, but you, Lev Nikolayevich; you preach — but how about practice? People always put it to me and always triumphantly shut my mouth with it. You preach, but how do you live? And I reply that I do not preach and cannot preach, though I passionately desire to do so. I could only preach by deeds; and my deeds are bad. What I say is not a sermon but only a refutation of the false understanding of the Christian teaching and an explanation of its real meaning. . . . Blame me — I do that myself — but blame *me* and not the path I tread, and show to those who ask me where in my opinion the road lies! If I know the road home and go along it drunk, staggering from side to side — does that make the road along which I go the wrong one?[6]

Father Sergius reveals, however, not only Tolstoy's absence of humbug — but the strange awareness which his artistic self (so long forced to play second fiddle to his prophetic soul) had of his real nature. And, as in nearly every story of his later period, we think of Dostoyevsky. What could be more Dostoyevskian than the thought that a monk who has fallen into sin comes closer to God than a pillar of rectitude?

As well as being a minor artistic masterpiece, and one of Tolstoy's most effective religious statements, *Father Sergius* is, even more than most of the Tolstoyan *oeuvre*, crammed to bursting with *him*. But Sergius is not a self-portrait any more than the child in *Childhood* is one. Sergius, in fact (his handsomeness, his connections at Court, his loftiness), is much more like Chertkov than Tolstoy. Just as in *Childhood*, the novelist is best able to explore his own nature by imagining what it would be like to be someone else. The reason that *Father Sergius* was never published in Tolstoy's lifetime is that it was too near the bone — too vivid a dissection of what was wrong not only with Chertkov, but also with the whole Tolstoyan way of looking at the world. The story derives much of its power from buried self-knowledge, its furtive, almost masturbatory mixture of self-acceptance and self-disgust. The complexity of his nature is contained here, and almost explained.

*   *   *   *

Paradoxically, the year in which Tolstoy did most work on *Father Sergius*, 1891, was also the year in which it seems least possible to blame him for the path he had chosen. It is the year in which he shines out as a hero.

More important than any of the 'dark ones' who visited Yasnaya Polyana that summer was an official of the local Tula *zemstvo* named Ivan Ivanovich Rayevsky. He had a loose acquaintance with Tolstoy dating back over many years: they had even briefly attended classes together at the Moscow *Gymnasium* in their boyhood. Rayevsky, on his visits to Yasnaya, liked to tease the 'great man' and remind him of all his inconsistencies: at one point claiming that it was wicked to own land, and at another buying huge tracts of Samara, on the very borders of civilisation; at one stage being more Orthodox than the Orthodox and observing the fasts; at another, breaking away from the Church and starting a religion of his own. Instead of taking this furiously, like the Countess Tolstoy, or solemnly, like Chertkov and the disciples, Rayevsky was able to laugh at his old friend. But he recognised Tolstoy's moral authority; after good-humoured conversations about the subject with his neighbour at Yasnaya, Rayevsky had, for example, given up tobacco; and he had become a conscience-stricken landlord, attempting to better the lot of his peasants through the activities of the local *zemstvo*. He was a practical man. It was he who first brought to Tolstoy's attention the fact that Russia was threatened with one of the worst famines in its history.

Since working out his own intellectual position on the matter, Tolstoy had remained fixed in his view (*What Then Must We Do?*) that 'relief' for the poor in terms of handouts from the rich actually exacerbated the social problem. He was therefore slow to respond to what Rayevsky was saying. Disturbed by the talk of famine, and by the evidence of crop failure in his own district, Rayevsky invited Tolstoy's three sons, Sergey, Ilya and Lev and the family tutor at the time, A. M. Novikov, to take a census of the crops and stores in a neighbouring district. Tolstoy was busy with his writing. 'It is more important to love than to feed,' he wrote airily to his fellow novelist Leskov. 'I think the most effective remedy against famine is to write something which might touch the hearts of the rich.'[7]

He had no idea what was going on, nor of the extent of the catastrophe. Very few people did, even in the Government. And this was not so much, as used to be thought, because the Government was hushing things up, as because it did not know itself, and was paralysed by the appalling communications system of Russia, by the sheer size of the place, and by the natural tendency towards secretiveness with which the country has always been dogged. In a society where the free press is censored, rumour goes unchecked. By April, stories had reached St. Petersburg that the winter grain had failed in all the eastern provinces, and the wildest stories began to gain credence. It was said that in the Simbirsk province all the children had died.[8] There were stories of the Emperor giving fifty million roubles out of his own fortune to help the starving, and of local governors, and even the Red Cross, embezzling relief funds. The Committee of Ministers was cautious in the extent to which it admitted the crisis, insisting upon the use of the terms *neurozhai* (crop failure) and *bedstviye* (calamity, misfortune) rather than the emotive *golod* (famine). Behind the scenes, ministers quarrelled among themselves. The Minister of Finance had a policy of selling cheap grain abroad and, since the harvests were bad all over Europe in that year, it was partly the export of cheap Russian grain which exacerbated the plight of the peasants. Yet when the Taxation Minister Yermolov, an underling of the Chief Finance Minister Vyshnegradsky, threatened to make clear the extent of the crisis to the other members of the Committee, he was told firmly by Vyshnegradsky, 'No one should know of this — otherwise you will spoil my rate of exchange.'[9] Durnovo, the Minister for the Interior, eventually overruled the Treasury and insisted on getting aid to the starving, but in spite of the Government's efforts, most of the aid got through too late, and it was badly hampered by bad communications, by the fact that roads in the stricken areas were often impassable, and railways had not been built, and by inbuilt suspicion of local government which had been part of Pobedonostsev's counter-reforms. Since the autocracy felt that it was selling the pass to deal with the local assemblies, the *zemstvo*s, rather than directly with the individual local nobility, the Government was hamstrung. The Government of Alexander III behaved with gross incompetence, but not, as has sometimes been suggested, with total callousness on this occasion. It was merely finding out and demonstrating the fact that Catherine the Great had long ago discovered that the country was too large to be governable. It was a fact which the revolutionaries savoured, as they stirred up panic during these years. Small wonder that there were riots, and that mobs tried to attack the grain trains as they rumbled over the border taking cheap food to Germany and Austria.

Tolstoy's interest in the matter was slow to dawn, and his conscience was slow to be pricked. But when his sons and Novikov returned in July 1891 to tell him the things which they had seen on his own doorstep, he was immediately stirred. Within two days of seeing the desolation for himself, he determined to act.[10]

The sight of a peasant *izba* in these districts was shocking to someone even as well acquainted with peasant life as Tolstoy. The stables had long ago emptied. The animals had been sold to pay for grain, and the grain had all been eaten. As winter drew on, the only fuel available for heating was human dung, and this was not always readily available since there was widespread suffering from dysentery and diarrhoea — not yet brought on by the hideous typhus epidemic which was to follow in the wake of the famine so much as by the bitter yellow bread which some of the peasants made (they called it *golodnyi khleb*, famine bread) made from tiny amounts of rye and weeds such as goosefoot. Children with bloated features and dirty yellow skin would have lolled on the doorsteps or, as the weather grew colder, huddled on the stove.

Tolstoy's son Lev was at once dispatched to their estates in the Samara district to work there, which he did tirelessly until his own health collapsed. The two eldest boys worked in the Tula province in the Chern district. Tolstoy, with Tatyana, Masha and Sofya Andreyevna moved to Rayevsky's estate Begichevka, about a hundred miles southeast of Yasnaya Polyana. They threw all their energies into setting up soup kitchens on the pattern devised by Rayevsky.

Throughout the famine, and the epidemics which followed it, the Tolstoy family were thus occupied, and although they returned home for short intervals in order to be ill, and although he continued to write, it was the practical relief of human suffering which marked the next two years of the family's life. Their example had a powerful effect, and there were many landowners, as well as sympathisers coming out from the towns, who assisted with these soup kitchens. As well as collecting, distributing and conserving food, the Tolstoys were able to set up care for the children of the villages where they worked, and basic medical supplies. Some of the time, Sofya Andreyevna helped in these makeshift hospitals, kindergartens and dining rooms. She fully entered into the need to help the destitute, and she was as disgusted as they all were by the indifference of Tolstoy's brother Sergey who greeted Lev Nikolayevich and Tatyana coldly when they appealed to him for help, and said he was just a pauper. For much of the winter of 1891-2, however, Tolstoy and his wife were apart. She was at Yasnaya Polyana dealing with the enormous correspondence which Tolstoy's public appeals were generating. She sent them as much money as she deemed wise from the profits of Volumes XII and XIII of the *Collected Works* and between November 3 and 12, 1891, she received nine thousand roubles in donations from strangers and well-wishers.

But the whole matter gave her cause not only for delight in the strange manner by which pity can beautify human character, but also fear for her husband's safety and reputation. In November, Tolstoy published an article in the liberal newspaper *Russkiye Vedomosti* entitled 'A Terrible Question' (*strashny vopros*): and that question was whether Russia was capable of feeding itself. The rhetoric of the piece was deliberately inflammatory and it lashed out at the callous Governmental incompetence which was making the crisis worse rather than better. A few days later, the conservative *Moscow Gazette* discussed the article in disapproving terms, and suggested that Tolstoy was bringing to birth a 'new political party with liberal tendencies'. She herself wrote letters to *Russkiye Vedomosti* supporting her husband and attacking the appalling contrasts between rich and poor which existed in that society. Shortly thereafter, the newspapers received notice from the Government that no more letters from Tolstoy would be published.

He would not be silent. Perhaps in part, his courage and tirelessness were strengthened by the death of Rayevsky, who caught influenza at the beginning of his campaign for the hungry and wore himself out in their service. Perhaps it was simply the natural justice of it. And the old soldier and the squire in Tolstoy were good at organising. By July 1892, he had set up two hundred and forty-six kitchens, feeding thirteen thousand people daily, and a hundred and twenty-four special children's kitchens, feeding three thousand daily. He had personally raised a hundred and forty-one thousand roubles for the relief of the poor, which included half a million dollars from America, and a quite independent donation from the English Quakers of twenty-six thousand pounds.

Through Chertkov, he had access to the English press, and he defied his own Government's censorship by printing appeals in *The Daily Telegraph*. Rumours began to reach the Tolstoys that the Government was thinking of taking action against him. Alexander III felt that he had been tricked into receiving Sofya Andreyevna. The Minister for the Interior told the Emperor that Tolstoy's letter to the English press 'must be considered tantamount to a most shocking revolutionary proclamation': not a judgement that can often have been made of a letter to *The Daily Telegraph*. Alexander III began to believe that it was all part of an English plot and the *Moscow Gazette*, which was fed from the Government, denounced Tolstoy's letters as 'frank propaganda for the overthrow of the whole social and economic structure of the world'.[11]

Sofya Andreyevna wrote to the Minister of the Interior, Durnovo, denying that her husband was planning to overthrow the Government; and she tried to write letters to the press to the same effect, but by now they were censored.[12] Priests were dispatched to Begichevka to investigate what Tolstoy was up to, and to spread abroad the idea that Tolstoy was the Antichrist. They found Tolstoy and his wife living simply in one room. They found canteens where ragged, thin-faced people were queuing up for rye bread and cabbage soup.[13] 'You think that Antichrist will come in an evil guise,' the priests told the hungry peasants. 'No, he will come to you with kindness, with bread at the very time when you will be dying of hunger. But woe to him who is seduced by this bread.' The peasants were not impressed. Sofya Andreyevna's sister Tanya wrote from St. Petersburg to say that there were rumours of a plan to send Tolstoy into exile in England. (In fact there had been, but when the proposals reached Alexander III he had written on the papers, 'No action yet'.) When a party of uniformed Government officials arrived at Begichevka to inspect the place, the peasants surrounded the house where Tolstoy was. It was a false alarm, and when he left, in the summer of 1892, crowds followed him down the road. They knew who their friends were.

It is only with the knowledge available to modern historians, and with a tragic hindsight, that we realise that the responses of Alexander III and his Government to this famine crisis could have been worse. A few statistics. Somewhere between three hundred and seventy-five and four hundred thousand people died in the famine districts in 1891-2, which constituted an overall rise in the death rate of twenty-five to thirty per cent. Many of these deaths were avoidable. But compare the famine which swept through India in 1899-1900 —

Berar, Anjer, Bombay and Punjab. There, the organisation of the Raj
was in every way superior to that of the Russians, and there was an
unquestionable desire to help the afflicted. Nevertheless, although the
casualties were numerically smaller, there was an overall rise in the
death rate of three hundred per cent. In both cases, natural calamity
was exacerbated by an inevitable measure of human incompetence
and selfishness. The story is unfortunately quite overshadowed in its
horror by other stories in Russian history. While Lev Lvovich Tolstoy
organised famine relief in the Samara district in 1891-2, there was
one very conspicuous absentee from his band of helpers: Lenin, who
was at that time in 'internal exile' there. According to a witness,
Vladimir Ulyanov (as he still was) and a friend were the only two
political exiles in Samara who refused to belong to any relief committee
or to help in the soup kitchens. He was said to welcome the famine 'as
a factor in breaking down the peasantry and creating an industrial
proletariat'.[14] Trotsky, too, took the line that it was improper to do
anything to improve the lot of the people while the autocracy remained
in power. When they themselves seized power, the chaos and
desolation were immeasurably worse. One thinks of the crop failure
on the Volga in 1921 when somewhere between one and three
million died, in spite of the fact that they allowed in foreign aid. By
the time of the 1932-33 famine in the Ukraine, the Soviet Union was
enjoying the munificent protection of Comrade Stalin. His policy was
to allow no foreign aid, and no Government intervention. At least
five million died. But Tolstoy cannot be blamed for being unable to
foresee barbarity on this scale, nor for his sense that the Government
of the Tsar must be shaken and hounded and prodded in its conscience.
His son Ilya remarks on the inconsistency between his father's view of
social welfare in *What Then Must We Do?* and the practical efforts to
which he devoted himself during the famine.[15] When one compares
Tolstoy's inconsistency with Vladimir Ulyanov's consistency, one
sees the virtue of inconsistency.

Nevertheless, nearly half a million dead is bad enough, and Tolstoy
was outspokenly critical of the part played in the whole affair by the
Government. Nor could he limit himself to complaints about the
famine. It was the whole system which was at fault, and the famine
had merely exposed the evil of it. Everywhere he went now, he heard
about, or saw with his own eyes, examples of barbarous cruelty and
injustice. Here is one example. (Tolstoy lists dozens in his letters,
essays, and other writings.) A certain landowner in the Oryol province

wanted to keep his mill pond so high that it flooded all the meadows on which the peasants grazed their flocks. They complained to him, but he got a court order which permitted him to go ahead. The women of the village at this point went down to the canal where the workmen were starting to create a dam, and drove them away. The district commissary gave orders to the police that one woman from each household in the village should be locked up — an order which it was impossible to carry out. So the landlord complained to the local governor, who sent police to the village to enforce the order, and scuffles broke out. The rural chief of police got beaten up by men who did not want to see their wives or mothers locked up. So the Government ordered a special train, and took a battalion of soldiers armed with rifles and rods, and a regimental doctor to supervise their proceedings. Twelve men were arrested, and a bench was set up in the village square. The first man was then stripped, and taken to the bench by two policemen for a flogging, while the village stood around weeping and shouting protest. After fifty strokes had been administered, the peasant had stopped screaming, and the doctor went forward to feel his pulse. The victim had lost consciousness, and the doctor decided that enough was enough. But not for the governor, who was by now really excited, and demanded that the unconscious man, whose buttocks and thighs and sides were swollen with weals and sores, should be given twenty more strokes. And this happened twelve times in the presence of the sadistic district governor.[16]

When Tolstoy witnessed recruitments in the army, and saw the poor, drunken, half-starved lads being brought into Tula from the villages in carts by the recruiting officers, he wondered how it was that they eventually came to perpetrate such outrages. When he saw soldiers in uniform, who had been trained, he was only aware of pleasant-faced young men, sitting about on trains, smoking, grinning, laughing. How could such evil be? The evil derived, Tolstoy believed, directly from the fatal human desire for *government*. If they did not have governments, they would not need armies and torturers and penal systems to enforce their will.

Tolstoy openly encouraged discussion and publication of abuses in the system. When the American journalist George Kennan went to Siberia and began to write about the treatment of prisoners there, Tolstoy wrote to him, 'I am very, very grateful to you, as is every Russian person now living, for publicising the horrors which have been perpetrated under the present Government. . . . We know

404

nothing here. We only know that thousands of people undergo the dreadful agonies of solitary confinement, forced labour and death, and that all this is hidden from everyone except those participating in these cruelties.'[17]

There was an allowable hyperbole in claiming that all Russians were grateful for having the horrors brought to light, but one group of people who did not share Tolstoy's sense of gratitude were the Committee of Ministers. Tolstoy was by now not merely taking risks. He was going much further than that. He was using his position as a famous and internationally regarded writer to challenge the lawful Government of the Emperor; to challenge its very right to exist. In 1890, his friend Nikolay Ge had exhibited a picture at the St. Petersburg Wanderers' Exhibition entitled *What Is Truth?* It was a picture of Christ before Pilate. 'The treatment of Christ as God has produced many pictures whose supreme perfection is already far behind us,' he wrote. 'Contemporary art can no longer treat Christ in this way. And now in our time people are attempting to depict the moral significance of Christ's life and teaching. These attempts have been unsuccessful until now. But Ge has found a moment in Christ's life which is important for all of us now and which is repeated everywhere throughout the world — in the struggle of the moral, rational consciousness of a man making himself manifest in the humdrum realities of life, with the traditions of a refined, good-natured and self-confident force crushing this consciousness. Such moments are many.'[18]

By now Tolstoy was preparing himself to be such a figure standing before kings and governors for Christ's sake and suffering as they had always suffered. There were many in Russia who now absorbed the simple and incontrovertible logic of his position. 'The socialists, communists, and anarchists, with their bombs, riots, and revolutions, are not nearly so much dreaded by governments as these scattered individuals in various countries all justifying their refusals on the ground of one and the same familiar doctrine.'[19]

This was a challenge which did indeed pose an extraordinary threat to a Government which was more than nominally Christian. The Emperor and his Committee of Ministers believed that their authority derived from Christ. And here was Tolstoy, reminding young readers, in the clearest terms, that you could not, in Christ's name, do what was forbidden by Christ. Tolstoy heard with a mixture of delight and fear of a young man — his case was by now typical — who refused

military service in Moscow Town Hall. He was required to take the
oath on the Gospels. He refused, pointing to the passage in the
Gospels where oaths are forbidden. Though he refused to take the
oath, they forced him to enrol, but he then refused to perform any of
his military duties. They could put him on a charge, and imprison him
for insubordination, but the challenge remained. He was refusing, not
on revolutionary, but on Christian grounds. So, after a spell in prison,
he was sent to a lunatic asylum. In those days in Russia they had not
become sufficiently advanced to use lunatic asylums as places of
political torture. When the doctors had examined him, and found him
to be sane, they were obliged to release him. And for two years, he
was sent with a party of convicts to the Caucasus, refusing at any
times to bear arms or obey military orders. In a country which was
nominally Christian, and really believed Christ to be God, what could
be done with such a man? He was eventually released. And this was
going on all over Russia.[20] If such ideas were to spread, it would
undermine everything.

Tolstoy's immediate followers became convinced in the course of
1893 that the scene of Christ before Pilate could not be far from its
enactment. Chertkov went to England, carrying with him the bulk of
Tolstoy's private papers and manuscripts, to keep them from the
hands of the secret police. But what could they do to Tolstoy? They
could send him into exile, where they could be certain that he would
be tireless in his attacks upon the wrongdoings suffered by the
Russian people. They could lock him up, as they were beginning to
lock up his followers. But locking up political dissidents can so often
rebound upon the powers that do it. . . .

The cunning and haunting truth of Ge's painting is that everyone
who sees it knows that power, in the end, is on the side of the silent,
dispossessed figure of Christ, rather than that of Pilate. And this was
the problem which Tolstoy very calculatedly and brilliantly arranged
for the Government.

In Saltykov-Shchedrin's amusing novel, *The Golovlyov Family*, it is
proposed that the tiresome young scapegrace son Styopka should be
banished to the Suzdal' Monastery to keep him out of harm's way. And
this was a suggestion which was seriously proposed for Tolstoy in the
early 1890s. Suzdal' has been described as an 'ecclesiastical Bastille'.
The point of such an incarceration would be to emphasise that Tolstoy
was a heretic. Certainly the story went the rounds of St. Petersburg
that this was going to happen, and it reached the ears of his cousin

Alexandrine, who immediately sought an audience with the Emperor.

'In a few days,' she told Alexander III, 'a report will be made to you about shutting up in a monastery the greatest genius in Russia.'

'Tolstoy?' he asked.

'You've guessed it, sir.'

'Does that mean that he is plotting against my life?'

This reply shows how stupid and how remote the Emperor was from *anything*. Clearly his ministers found it much more convenient to lump together all the revolutionaries and anarchists, and to frighten him into thinking that Tolstoy might do to him what the revolutionaries had done to his father. But evidently wiser counsels prevailed. It was said that he squashed the proposal on the grounds that such an imprisonment would make a martyr out of Tolstoy. The extraordinary fact, however, emphasised by Ge's picture, is that artists, poets and writers are and have been martyrs in Russia ever since the beginning of the nineteenth century. In a country ruled by the suppression of the truth, the imaginative writer is in a peculiar position of strength, for he or she can see through the lies without the need for evidence. Perhaps this is why there has existed at the very heart of the Russian autocracy a powerful lingering of respect for literary genius. One thinks of the courage with which Pushkin admitted to Nicholas I, of all people, that he sympathised with the Decembrists. More memorable yet is the moment when Stalin telephoned Boris Pasternak in 1934 to discuss the arrest of Osip Mandelstam. It is one of the most extraordinary conversations in the history of literature. Pasternak behaved like a fool on this occasion, but Stalin's few words down the line show the unease he felt at having made a victim out of a poet of genius. 'If I were a poet and a poet friend of mine were in trouble, I would do anything to help him.' Stalin said. Pasternak, so completely taken aback at the voice which was speaking to him in his flat really being that of Stalin, began to mutter about writers' organisations not really coping with cases such as Mandelstam's. 'But he's a genius, isn't he?' snapped Stalin. 'But that's not the point,' said Pasternak. 'What is then?' Stalin asked. Pasternak said that he would like to meet him to have a talk. 'What about?' 'About life and death,' said Pasternak. Stalin hung up. So, if he had possessed a telephone, would Pobedonostsev. Tolstoy's cousin Alexandrine had more sense than Pasternak.[21] She saw that all that was at issue was Tolstoy's genius. Any fool, as far as a dictator is concerned, can have ideas about life and death. Not everyone could write *War and Peace* or Mandelstam's poems. Stalin gave the word — subsequently changed or discarded — about Mandelstam: 'preserve but isolate'. Alexander III would love to have done the same to Tolstoy, but he could not. This was partly because the autocracy never came close to Stalin's thoroughgoing murderous brutality — or, same thing, political efficiency; partly because Tolstoy had outmanœuvred the Government. By the time his next controversial book had reached the censors, it was already circulating in thousands of lithographed copies and was being published in translation in Germany, France, England and the United States.

The book was called *The Kingdom of God is Within You.*

*   *   *   *

The Kingdom of God is Within You is an alarming book to read. It fails to hang together and, for once, the chief reasons for its inconsistencies are not merely Tolstoy's own split personality, but also the divisions and incompatibilities in society; divisions which reflected a profound shake-up in the heart of man, the heart of things towards the close of the nineteenth century. Things fall apart, the centre cannot hold. There are two warring strands in Tolstoy's book, and because it is a reasonably long book, and he made no attempt to impose a shape on it, the likelihood is that he did not himself fully see the inconsistencies. However, the fact that they are both there is witness to his unerring honesty. The first strand is a call, which would by now be familiar to anyone who had read his work, to the human race to accept the values of Christ. The familiar Tolstoyan attacks on the Church are trotted out. And he asserts, which is incontrovertible, that there is an absolute opposition between the Gospel of peace, and the practice of war and violence. The writings of American Quakers and others are quoted at great length to substantiate his point of view, and at times the essay drifts into flights of Rousseauesque optimism about the future. Because Christian values are true, and everyone knows in their heart that they are true, Tolstoy concludes that there must come a time when these values eventually overthrow the tyranny and the fear and the oppression which made nineteenth-century Russia, and the whole world, such a miserable place. 'Men of our time do not merely pretend to hate oppression, inequality, class distinctions, and all kinds of cruelty not only to men but to animals — they really do hate all this, but they do not know how to abolish it or cannot make up their minds to part with the system that supports it all but seems to them indispensable.' If only, Tolstoy argues, all men and women would obey their consciences, then the whole hateful business would be transformed. With the side of his nature which is not merely a reader of Rousseau, but also a decent individual, he believes that public opinion will eventually become so strong that wars and floggings and tortures and the oppression of the poor must, eventually, come to an end.

It may be that somewhere in the western world, there are readers of *The Kingdom of God is Within You* who believe that this idea of an evolving decent public opinion *has* brought about the good effects which Tolstoy predicts.

> Governors, police officials and tax collectors, pitying the peasants, often try to find pretexts for not collecting the taxes from them. Rich men are reluctant to use their wealth for themselves alone, and disburse it for public purposes. Landowners build hospitals and schools on their own land, and some of them even renounce the ownership of land and transfer it to the tillers of the soil or establish communities on it. Mill-owners and manufacturers arrange hospitals, schools, savings banks and pensions as well as dwellings for their work people. Some of them form companies in which they share equally with the workers. . . . All these facts might appear accidental did they not come from one common cause just as it might seem accidental in spring that the buds begin to swell on some of the trees unless we knew that this is caused by the coming of spring generally, and that if the buds have begun to swell on some of the trees they will certainly do so on all of them. It is the same with the manifestation of Christian public opinion in regard to violence and all that is based upon it.[22]

It may be that some liberal, comfortable, western reader of these words might suppose that the spring had come. There is, indeed, among decent people, an abhorrence of violence which might well have struck our great grandparents as extraordinary. There is universal lip service to the idea of 'human rights' and human equality. There is an ill-defined economic egalitarianism at the heart of all western democratic government policies, even the most 'right wing' of which feel committed to providing care for the old, and the poor, and the sick. But only the blindest and most ignorant of western readers could imagine that the buds on Tolstoy's trees had really heralded the spring. Reading his words nearly a century after they were written, we see a sort of tragedy in the fact that in Russia of all places, he felt — and was justified in feeling — that he could appeal to these feelings of decency, and to a belief in the Gospel of Christ, not only from 'public opinion' but from the Government itself.

For in addition to the 'dawnist' optimism of his essay, there is another strand which is much more frightening. As a reader of Proudhon and de Maistre, he sees that power is of its essence violent, and that governments can only continue, whatever their complexion, by possessing the means to subdue their enemies with violence. 'To seize power and retain it is necessary to love power. But love of power does not go with goodness but with the opposite qualities — pride, cunning and cruelty.' That is why he opposes any idea of revolutionary activity against the regime which advocates violent means. For this would simply be to replace one system of violence with another, one lot of violent tyrants with another lot. 'Today, let us say, the power is in the hands of a tolerable ruler, but tomorrow it may be seized by a Biron, an Elizabeth, a Catherine, a Pugachov, a Napoleon I or a Napoleon III. And the man in whose hands the power lies may be tolerable today but tomorrow he may become a beast or he may be succeeded by a mad or crazy heir — like the King of Bavaria or our Paul I.'[23]

Here Tolstoy raises the very heart of the difficulty, and he is unable to answer it. He is unable, even, to face it sensibly, and soon reverts, with tragic lack of foresight, to the feeling (how often is it uttered in pre-revolutionary situations) that 'a revolution could hardly be more disastrous for the great mass of the people than the existing order. . . .' or even to pathetically, ridiculously naïve questions. 'Without a state,' we are told, 'we should also be subject to violence and attacks from evil men in our own country. But who are these evil men in our midst from whose attacks and violence we are preserved in the state and its army?'

History would provide him with a long list of names in answer to that question; all men who understood the truth which he saw with the realistic side of his nature when he wrote, 'It has been so since the beginning of the world and is so now. *The evil always domineer over the good and inflict violence upon them.*'

The Kingdom of God is Within You, then, is a disturbed and broken thing, passages of sublime truth alternate with pages of complete nonsense; optimism of the craziest kind jostles with a ghastly realism of vision. The world would be better, Tolstoy asserts, without governments, without standing armies, without police forces and without prisons. But he is unable to show that this would abolish the proclivity of evil men for dominating the good, and for the strong bullying the weak. The essay has many historical postscripts. One cannot read it today without these postscripts intruding into one's sense of the truth or untruth of his words.

When one contemplates that within thirty years of his book being written, tens of thousands of young men were killing each other every day in the battlefields of the Somme, Passchendaele, Mons, his analysis of the folly and barbarity of war seems quite unanswerable. Tolstoy's words seem nothing but the truth. The decisions of the generals and the politicians seem nothing better than lunacy.

Or another postscript, British India. It is well known that Mahatma Gandhi began to read Tolstoy when he was in South Africa and that all his pacifist writings, especially *The Kingdom of God is Within You*, made a deep impression upon him. It was from Tolstoy that he learnt the idea of passive resistance. And it was by passive resistance, helped along by a catastrophically changed economic climate at home in England, that the Raj fell. Here, allowing for all the obvious modifications and exceptions which such a generalisation would demand, it would seem as though passive resistance did actually work. It is hard for an Englishman to write the next sentence without seeming ludicrously smug on his own nation's behalf; but it has to be said that it only worked because of a fundamental decency in the manner by which the Raj was organised. In England and in India, there genuinely had been a change of heart of the kind which Tolstoy described. Public opinion had lost sympathy with the imperial idea. And it would have been unthinkable for any post-1920s British administration to authorise a gunning down of the passive protesters. (The millions who were slain after British withdrawal during the time of partition provide their own interesting commentary on Tolstoy's ideas that governments in themselves always produce, rather than repress, violence.)

But the Raj postscript is not the one which comes first to mind, and it is not the one which comes first in historical order. Lying down in front of a train or a mounted policeman might have been a good idea in Delhi in 1946. But what good would it have done in Kiev or Moscow or Leningrad in 1936? Tolstoy had a vision of human

411

barbarity eventually being tempered by the ideals of Christ. No one could have any conception of the sufferings and horrors which were to befall Russia once Lenin and Stalin were in control. And Stalin was Lenin's natural heir, the fulfiller of his own understanding of, and belief in, unbridled and absolute power. Under Stalin, it did not make any difference whether you thought of yourself as resisting or submitting. You suffered or you got killed. Tolstoy could not conceive that there should dawn a day in Russia when there would be a government who did not merely fail to share his ideas of decency, but regard them with derision. *The Kingdom of God is Within You* is therefore an infinitely sad book to read. It is as far as an eighteenth-century rationalist can go in pointing out how human beings have fallen short of the ideals of Christ. But he starts with a neutered Christ, the Christ of Thomas Jefferson and Benjamin Franklin, a Christ purged of miracle and of terror, a Christ who can only hold out barely attainable ideals to help decent people be a little more decent. The Christ of the New Testament is a powerful figure, supernaturally conceived and understood. He is the embodiment of love itself, of God Himself, and on the Cross of Calvary, he utters the psalm which speaks of the total and, until that moment in history, unbridgeable gap between the mystery of human sin and the glory of the everlasting godhead. 'My God, my God, why hast thou forsaken me?' An English or an American rationalist or Christian Modernist may find much with which he would agree in Tolstoy's *The Kingdom of God is Within You*; but it has very little to say to the slain of the trenches, or the victims of the Russian Civil War, or the countless millions who died as a result of Hitler and Stalin's death camps, purges, and battles. To those numberless and nameless ones, perhaps, who had suffered from the oppression of unbridled evil, triumphant, irrational demonic power, Dostoyevsky's *The Devils* makes more sense.

When they looked back at the reign of Alexander III, historians could see that the famine and cholera deaths of 1891-3 had been a turning point. Pilate was weakened by the reproachful gaze of his prisoner. But the alarming thing is that the prisoner was weakened too. A step further had been taken towards mere anarchy being loosed upon the world. During the reign, every attempt had been made to strengthen the autocracy of the Emperor, and in the short term, doubtless, it was to succeed. Liberal newspapers had been silenced, or actually wound up. According to Pobedonostsev, the phantom of representative government had been exposed as the 'great lie of our time'.[24] But there was more at stake than democracy. For both Tolstoy and Pobedonostsev, the malaise which threatened the Empire was essentially religious, but both had radically opposed visions of the symptoms and the cure.

One tiny detail brings this out with ludicrous poignancy. When the Archduke Nikolay Konstantinovich, the Emperor's cousin, wrote to Alexander III asking what was to be done about the famine-stricken steppes, Pobedonostsev appended a note to the letter, before passing it on to his royal master, regretting that in his concern for the starving, the Archduke had omitted to comment on the urgent problem of church restoration in the famine areas. There is an emblematic fittingness that Pobedonostsev should have laboured so hard, and spent so much money, on the preservation of so many beautiful abbeys, cathedrals and churches which within decades were to become museums of atheism. One of his last memos to Alexander III concerns the fine old church of Ananour in Tiflis, 'which is really in a state of the most dangerous dilapidation and ruin. The doors are already sealed shut, a stone has fallen from the cupola, and the roof is crumbling away.'[25] Alexander supplied two thousand roubles for this useful work. A few days later, having been taken ill at the age of fifty in Livadia, in the Crimea, the Emperor died. Neither he nor Pobedonostsev knew, and nor could they conceivably have seen its significance if they had known, that a few yards from that crumbling church in Tiflis a young seminarian called Iosif Vissarionovich Dzhugashvili, later known as Stalin, had just begun his training for the priesthood.

Chapter Seventeen

Resurrection

1894 - 1900

Я говорил: тому что было,
Уж не бывать! уж не бывать! ....
Но вот опять затрепетали ....

[I said: What is past shall be no more, shall be
no more! . . . But, lo! They have started to stir
again. . . .]

Pushkin

Nicholas II became the Emperor of Russia in October 1894. It would have required great gifts of prescience, at the beginning of the new reign, to know that he would be the last of his line. Optimists would have predicted the very opposite. When one Russian tyrant dies and is replaced by another, there are usually thoughts of change. Nicholas differed from his father in ways which might have made a dispassionate observer believe that he would transform the monarchy, and survive. He had a much deeper understanding of international relations and of Russia's place among the nations, having travelled more than any of his predecessors since Peter the Great. Since 1893, he had been the chairman of the Trans-Siberian Railway, and the year before his accession had been spent travelling about the Empire. Even more than his father had done, he valued the expertise of the Finance Minister, Witte. He understood and valued Witte's perception that Russia had to expand as a modern, industrial society.

Liberals had further grounds for hope. Nicholas had espoused — and within months of succeeding, married — Princess Alice of Hesse-Darmstadt, a match to which Alexander III had been implacably opposed. With hindsight, we can see that he was absolutely right, and that no greater disaster ever befell the Russian monarchy than the arrival of this hysterical, humourless, German princess, and her eager conversion of herself into Alexandra Fyodorovna, the Orthodox zealot. Her paranoia, her religiosity, and her sheer inability to understand and get along with people were all unknown to the Russians when she arrived; and her calamitous association with Rasputin, her pathetic belief that the charlatan could cure her son's haemophilia — the whole sorry story — lay in the future. All the constitutionalists knew was that the courtship of Nicholas and Princess Alice had taken place at Windsor under the approving eye of their grandmother, who presided over the stablest constitutional monarchy in Europe. Surely some of Queen Victoria's political wisdom would rub off on the young pair? *Zemstvo* leaders began to hope that the new Emperor would set up representative assemblies. The *zemstvo* from the Tver province went so far as to voice this hope, to claim it, indeed, as a right, 'so that the expression of the needs and thought not only of the administration but also of the Russian people may reach to the very height of the throne'.[1]

This was fighting talk for a document which was going to be shown to Pobedonostsev. On January 17, 1895, a reception was held for deputations of the nobility, the *zemstvo*s and the cities. It was at this reception that the Emperor gave that reply which became instantly notorious. 'I am informed that recently in some *zemstvo* assemblies, voices have made themselves heard from people carried away by senseless dreams about participation by representatives of the *zemstvo* in the affairs of internal Government. Let all know that I, devoting all my strength to the welfare of the people, will uphold the principle of autocracy as firmly and as unflinchingly as my late, unforgettable father.'[2]

So much for the liberal hopes. The sentence about 'senseless dreams' is one which Lenin would echo, not only with his lips but in his life. Stalin would be the same. But, as with all official pronouncements given from an autocratic source, there is a message here given out between the lines. Tolstoy heard it clearly enough. He and his daughter Tanya were staying at Nikolskoye with their friends the Olsufyevs when they heard news of the Tsar's speech. 'An important event,' Tolstoy thought, 'which I'm afraid will not be without consequence for me.'[3]

As Tolstoy saw things, Russia at this time presented him with two alternatives. The first was to join with the revolutionaries, 'to break violence with violence, terror, dynamite, bombs and daggers'. The other alternative was to work with the Government; to attempt, by means of compromise, 'gradually to unravel the net which holds the people fast and free it'. Both these courses were equally abhorrent to

Tolstoy. 'One thing only remains: to fight the Government with weapons of thought, word and way of life, not making any concessions to it, not joining its ranks, not increasing its powers oneself. That's the one thing needful and it will probably be successful. And this is what God wants and this is what Christ taught.'[4]

He had defined the position of the refusenik. His confidence that in so doing he was recapturing the original intentions of Christ won many hearts. The Tsar, egged on by Pobedonostsev, had sent back the clear message that Tolstoyism, in practice if not in word, was now an indictable offence.

This is well exemplified in the career of a man like Prince D. A. Khilkov. During the Russo-Turkish War of 1877-8, Khilkov had been an officer in the regiment of Hussar Guards. The experience of killing a Turk in battle had been a shattering one. After the war, he became a pacifist, and was drawn to the practices and beliefs of a pacifist sect which flourished in the regions where he had been quartered on military service. The sect called themselves the Dukhobors, which means 'Spirit Wrestlers'.[5]

On his return home from life among the Spirit Wrestlers, Prince Khilkov started to read Tolstoy. From his new religious friends, he had learnt pacifism and hostility to Orthodoxy. To these were now added a distrust of land ownership. He divided his estates among his peasants, lived among them in poverty and tried to convert them to his newly found point of view.

When Khilkov's story became known to the authorities, he was arrested, imprisoned and sent into exile in the Caucasus. He had been in touch, by letter, with Tolstoy ever since 1887, though the two men had never actually met. Khilkov had worse sorrows than exile to endure. In November 1893, he and his wife were visited by his mother, accompanied by the police from Tiflis. (Tiflis, where Stalin was by now starting to get involved in underground social democratic groups such as *Mesame Dasi*, was the nearest big town to Khilkov's place of internal exile.) The police abducted Khilkov's children and told his wife that, by Imperial decree, they were no longer allowed custody of them.

Tolstoy was distressed by the story and wrote to Chertkov that Khilkov's mother probably thought that she was acting for the best. 'Surely you can see how she and everyone involved in this mad, cruel business will explain that it was all done with the best intentions?

How can one analyse the extent to which a person is being sincere or unselfish? The only thing to do nowadays is to try not to get mixed up with things like this and not to be a party to them.'[6]

The doctrine of non-intervention, however, attractive as it was, could not be pursued with consistency, in this case of the persecuted religious minorities, any more than it could be pursued in the case of the starving. Quite simply, Tolstoy had too much bigness of heart to be able to stand on the sidelines. Tolstoy got Chertkov to take up Khilkov's cause and he himself intervened with a letter to the Emperor. Khilkov, for his part, was anxious to acquaint Tolstoy with the plight of religious minorities such as the Spirit Wrestlers. Since the period of 'reaction' had set in under Alexander III (engineered by Konstantin Pobedonostsev, but enthusiastically supported by innumerable others throughout the Empire) religious orthodoxy was enforced in a manner and to a degree which now barely seem credible. In the case of mixed marriages between Orthodox and, say, Catholics and Lutherans, it now became illegal for the children to follow the religion of the non-Orthodox parent. There were strong financial and political disabilities imposed — in different regions of the Empire — on Jews, Moslems and Buddhists. Disabilities were removed if the 'dissident' consented to Orthodox baptism. But it was to the errant children of the Christian household, rather than to infidels, that the fiercest treatment was dealt out: to those who accepted the truth of Christianity but questioned the Holy Synod's right to claim for itself a religious authority. Persecution was the reward for Old Believers, themselves more orthodox than the Orthodox, as well as for the zanier extremes, such as the Molokans and the Dukhobors.

Particular disapprobation was felt for those sects, such as the Dukhobors, who refused military service. They found themselves herded into penal battalions. Someone who suffered in this way gave Chertkov the following account, which was smuggled out to England. Through the crippled translation, we can hear his voice with pathetic clarity:

From the very first day the bloody chastisement commenced. They were flogged with thorny rods, whose thorns were remaining in the flesh and were thrown in a cold and dark cell afterwards. After few days, they were requested again to do the service, and for the refusal, flogged again. And so it was going on and no end was seen. Besides, they were always hungry, because they were eating no meat and were given too little bread. They were physically exhausted; many were sick; but the doctor was refusing to admit them in the hospital, unless they would agree to eat meat. The chaplain was requiring the performance of the Orthodox rites, and they were driven to church by fists and musket butt-ends. . . .[7]

It is against a background of such stories that Tolstoy's religious and political ideas must be seen. A modern western reader who picks up, say, *The Kingdom of God is Within You* might be forgiven for thinking that its ideas are crazy. But its assaults are not upon the Orthodox Church of today, neutered in some quarters and made a vassal of an atheist state, purged and chastened in other areas by persecution. Rather, Tolstoy was attacking the cruel and powerful instrument of a spiritual despotism. When the word 'government' is synonymous with barbarism, it is understandable why Tolstoy thought it morally imperative to be an anarchist. Solzhenitsyn, eighty years later, was to say that merely to live in the Soviet Union was to be corrupted.

Whether he liked it or not, Tolstoy was caught up in the drama of his country's history. He was not a passive observer. He was part of it. For the remainder of his life his concerns grew wider in scope, larger in sympathy. He could not be silent. He could not be inactive. He could not be in any doubt where his duty lay. For his wife, by contrast, the areas of concern all became smaller and more localised. From this time onwards, her diaries, hitherto sporadic and sketchy, became voluminous, obsessive. They begin to reveal a mind hysterically out of control. From Tolstoy's point of view a great tragedy was being enacted: a Christian Empire, blasphemously claiming to act in the name of Christ, was moving inexorably towards self-destruction. For Sofya Andreyevna, there was also a tragedy to watch as her family was torn apart by illness, death and quarrels. It would not have been in her nature to move through the menopause calmly. She began to feel herself threatened, and Tolstoy gave her good grounds for such fears: threatened financially as Tolstoy recklessly signed away his copyrights; threatened emotionally as he overtly conceded that he needed the companionship of his disciples more than that of his wife.

Towards the end of 1894, the principal cause of anxiety to her was the illness of her son Lev (Lyova) who was in a Moscow lunatic asylum suffering from fits and nervous depressions. Eventually, they realised that he was suffering from malaria, but his mother did not know this. She felt confident that she knew who was to blame.

'My poor Lyova. How deeply he has suffered from his father's unkindness! The sight of his sick son spoilt his easy, sybaritic life,' she wrote cruelly.[8]

In January 1895, a group of Tolstoy's friends, Chertkov, Biryukov, Popov, Tregubov and Gorbunov-Posadov, called at Yasnaya Polyana and, after some chat, posed for a photograph. Sofya Andreyevna exploded with wrath. She claimed that they had tricked the old man 'on the sly' into having the photograph taken to make it look as though there were some Tolstoyan 'institution'. 'The public would seize upon it and they'd all want to buy pictures of Tolstoy with his disciples — that would make them laugh. But I was not going to let them drag Lev Nikolayevich from his pedestal into the mud.'[9]

She was just jealous. The wrath which followed was something which she was able to orchestrate. She could not stop it, but she could direct it, like a beaver carrying sticks to a dam. She allowed the row to continue a whole week, as she screamed, collected 'allies' from among the children or the servants, and singled out anyone who disagreed with her as an enemy or a spy. Normally, Tolstoy was provoked by his wife's bad temper into fits of no less undignified rage. But on this occasion, he behaved calmly, perhaps sensing that there was something disquieting in her overreaction. It was a taste of things to come. Even Sofya Andreyevna herself recognised that the photographer who had committed this heinous sin was a perfectly pleasant young man. When he realised how unhappy she was, he handed over the negatives and allowed her to destroy them.

'When it all gets too difficult, I fly into a rage,' she said, 'and I say harsh things which I then regret; but by then it is too late, and that makes me even more miserable.'[10]

The misery was exacerbated by the illness of the younger children. Vanya, little Vanichka the youngest, had an upset stomach and a high fever. Tolstoy, who was trying to finish a story, took the opportunity to leave Yasnaya Polyana. He and Tanya went to stay with their friends the Olsufyevs. It was on their snow-bound estate at Nikolskoye, and subsequently during a week in Moscow, that he completed his remarkable *conte, Master and Man.*

* * * *

The title of the tale (*Khozyain i rabotnik*) recalls the world of Christ's parables. The words could almost be rendered 'householder' and 'labourer' were it not for the fact that the essentially Biblical irony of the story depends upon our being free to ask, '*Who* is the master?'

At first, it would appear that the master is Vasily Andreyich Brekhunov, a petty merchant in a provincial town who is anxious, despite the fact that it is past the feast of St. Nicholas, to make a journey to a neighbouring landowner who has promised to sell him some timber at about a third of its market value. To accompany him on this business trip, he engages a peasant called Nikita, one of Tolstoy's most engaging and memorable characters. Nikita has a drink problem: at present it is under control, but it always needs watching, and that is why merchant Vasily Andreyich is able to engage him so cheaply. Nikita also has a marital problem. His wife is having an affair with a cooper. Yet, in spite of all his deficiencies of circumstance and character, Nikita is one of those who are at ease with life, like Yeroshka in *The Cossacks* or, at the opposite end of the social spectrum, Stiva in *Anna Karenina*.

It is a quality which (lacking it totally himself) Tolstoy regarded with a particularly sympathetic awe. The only other character of any consequence in the story is Mukhorty (Bay), the pony who accompanies the two men on their adventures and pulls their sleigh. It is quite inevitable, once they have set out on their journey, that things happen as they do. The snows and winds become more severe. Drifts have obscured all familiar landmarks. Darkness is beginning to fall.

They come to a village which Vasily Andreyich says must be Grishkino, 'and Grishkino it was. . . .' 'And sure enough, when they got through the snowdrift, they drove into a street. In the furthest yard, on a rope, there desperately fluttered about in the wind some hanging, frozen linen. . . .' I give this stilted rendering of the original to convey the suspense of the sentence, which is lost if (with more naturalness) we translate: 'On a rope in the furthest yard there was some frozen linen, hanging from a rope and fluttering about desperately in the wind.' In the Russian, we wait expectantly to see what was hanging from that rope. It could be anything or anyone. Tolstoy uses a familiar Dickensian trope of clothes become animate: 'shirts, one white and one red, drawers, leggings and a petticoat. The white shirt was struggling with particular desperation, waving its arms about.'[11]

We are to meet this shirt a couple of times more as the travellers circle the village, trying to find their road. The suspense becomes almost unendurable. There is no reason except the hope of making a quick buck which spurs Brekhunov along. Every instinct makes us yearn for him and Nikita to spend the night in the village. There is a tantalisingly short break in a peasant's cottage for tea (poor Nikita dare not, as his master does, touch the vodka) and then off again into the snow. When they are thoroughly lost, and it is dark, and Vasily Andreyich has blamed Nikita for everything, the little merchant thinks that he can escape on his own, leaving the peasant to perish. But he returns. And finding Nikita cold and close to death, Vasily Andreyich undergoes a transformation of vision. In a moment which is oddly reminiscent of *The Death of Ivan Ilyich*, Vasily Andreyich derives comfort merely from hugging this large peasant man. He throws himself on Nikita's body and restores it to life and warmth. 'Nikita is alive and that means that I am alive too,' he says to himself with pride.

And he remembers about money: the shop, the house, sales, purchases and the Mironov millions; it is difficult for him to remember how this same individual, whom people called Vasily Brekhunov, had been interested — as he had been — in all that.

His thoughts about Vasily, i.e. himself, are these:

'So what! [*Chto zh!* — O.K.!] In this matter he has not known. . . . he has not known anything of what I know now. I now know without any doubt at all. NOW I KNOW.' And once again, he hears the summons of him who had already called to him. 'I'm coming, I'm coming.' With joy and loving kindness now his whole being speaks. And he feels that he is free and nothing can hold him down any more. . . .[12]

Once again, as when we meet the animated shirts on the washing line, we sense the proximity of Dickens. This is a death which keeps company with those of Barkis, Jo the Crossing Sweeper, or Little Nell. But it is also full of strong Tolstoyan ironies. With the loftiness of our aristocratic narrator, we realise that there is something absurd in Vasily's pretensions to be a 'master' when his wife is of the peasant class, and he himself is only removed from that class by one generation. His claim to be Nikita's superior rests wholly on a little shop and bits of money which (semi-honestly) he has scraped together over the years. Soon we discover that the chaotic, shambling figure of Nikita is much more the master of the situation when exposed to the elements. Nikita knows how to handle a horse, and he has some sense (more than Vasily Andreyich) of where they are going. But then again, we learn that when two men are lying out exposed to the elements and dying of cold, such human distinctions count for very little. Our true master, like the *khozyain* or householder of the Gospel parables, is our Father in Heaven.

Vasily Andreyich Brekhunov (*brekhun* means a liar) dies having discovered that his life has been based on a misconception of the truth. Nikita survives to see his children and his children's children. And in the final sentences which follow Nikita's death, Tolstoy looks towards the unknown future life, of whose existence, in his non-fictional works, he had begun to concede the possibility. 'Is it better or worse for him there, where he has woken up — this time after his actual death? Is he disappointed, or has he found the very thing he has been waiting for? We shall all find out soon enough.'[13] Again, one gets the feeling that this conclusion owes a large amount to Dickens — whose novels all presuppose a state of future blessedness in which innocent sufferers are consoled — than to any elaborately worked out metaphysic. For sophisticates, the 'points' of the tale will seem too heavily laboured. I am not of their number. Tolstoy must have known, when he finished it, that he had achieved something which, in this particular mode, could not be bettered. Even those who deprecate the moralising conclusion would concede that there could be few more vivid accounts of weather in the whole of literature. These are large sayings, however, and the actual publication of the story restored Tolstoy to the levels of petty (though murderously intense) acrimony which, as a domestic figure, he found himself inhabiting.

*   *   *   *

Some husbands can't be trusted with other women or, the moment their wives turn their backs, they reach for the whisky bottle. Tolstoy's comparable weakness was a tendency, when not strictly supervised by his wife, to make impulsive and unwise decisions relating to the copyright and publication of his work. If it had not been for Sofya Andreyevna, *War and Peace* would have made him no more money than Katkov chose to pay him for serialisation. 'Volume rights', as such, would have been almost valueless in an age in which readers

425

collected serial publications and had them bound at their own expense.

Having finished *Master and Man*, Tolstoy desperately needed — most writers do — an immediate response to what he had written. This is most satisfyingly achieved by selling the work in question: it shows that the appreciative first reader is prepared to put money where their mouth is. Alone in Moscow with Tanya, Tolstoy could not show the story, as he had done so many of his previous works, to his wife. Instead, he handed it to an editor: the handsome (female) editor of the paper called *The Northern Herald*: Lyubov Yakovlevna Gurevich, who, needless to say, asked if she could buy it. The deal was struck.

When Sofya Andreyevna joined her husband in Moscow, he sheepishly admitted what he had done. There was — as he could have predicted — an explosion of fury which was volcanic even by his wife's excitable standards. She accused 'that scheming half-Jewish Gurevich woman' of having buttered him up. Since he had allowed the woman the story without payment, he might as well have given it to Chertkov for his 'cheap little Intermediary'.[14] At least, that way, the story would have reached a wider audience. This was the worst of all worlds. Chertkov's peasant readers could not afford to buy *The Northern Herald*. The Countess had lost her story for Volume XIII of the *Collected Works*. It was not a loss which she would concede without a fight.

Master and Man had already reached proof stage. In order to pacify her, and to show that he did not intend to exclude her from his literary career, Tolstoy urged her to help him correct proofs, as she had done in the past. Now, however, merely to read the thing excited in her feelings of rage and grief. He did not love her, that was it! He was indifferent to her. If he loved her, he would let her have the story for Volume XIII. Throughout the fortnight there were disturbingly tempestuous swings of emotion between the two of them. Rage would be punctuated with outbursts of physical passion. But after these frantic, often angry couplings, there would recur the debilitating sense that 'there are no mutual feelings between us'.[15]

At length, the wrangling proved too much for Tolstoy. His wife announced that she did not care what agreements had been made, she was going to *have* the story for her Volume XIII. She grabbed the proofs and started to copy them out at fever pitch, a sort of lunatic parody of the self who had laboured so faithfully to copy *War and Peace*. This was insane behaviour, and Tolstoy said so. In that case, she reasoned, he must be having an affair with the half-Jewish witch. Why else allow her to publish the tale? At this, Tolstoy lost his temper. He ran upstairs, collected an armful of clothes and said that he was going to leave the house. He would not be returning. The marriage was at an end.

To his wife, this merely proved that he was in love with Gurevich, and that he was running away to his mistress. With childish petulance, she could not allow him to leave her. If anyone was to be allowed the dramatic gesture, it must be her, Sofya Andreyevna! She would abandon him, oh yes. Although she was wearing only a nightdress and a dressing gown, she ran out into the snowy streets and the below-zero temperatures. Tolstoy, finishing his packing in a dressing room, heard what she was doing, and chased after her. He was only wearing underclothes and a waistcoat: no shirt.

As he ran after her up the pavement, she shrieked, 'I don't care! Let them take me away and put me in prison or a mental hospital!'[16]

Tolstoy dragged her back towards the house. It was not easy. They kept falling over on the snow, and as they cascaded into another drift, she would express the hope that, like the merchant in the story which had sparked off the row, she would die of exposure. She was put to bed when they got back to the house, but in the next couple of days made a number of other attempts to 'escape', running out into the street improperly clad. Those who, thickly muffled against the sub-zero temperatures, have had a taste of winter in Moscow can catch the full horror of what these escapades suggested about Sofya Andreyevna's state of mind.

Even by their own volatile standards of behaviour, these outbursts were tempestuous enough to worry Tolstoy. 'I'm sorry for her and I love her,'[17] he wrote in his diary. The gynaecologist was summoned and muttered ('cynically' in Sofya Andreyevna's view) about her 'time of life'.[18] Some medicine was prescribed. Tolstoy came and knelt by the bed, and sobbed and asked her forgiveness for his unkindness. The other children gathered around with tearful or bewildered expressions. Tolstoy's sister, now a nun, told Sofya that everything which she had said in her frenzy was true 'but that I'd gone too far'.[19]

She got her own way. The story was taken away from *The Northern Herald* and published jointly in Chertkov's Intermediary and Volume XIII of the *Collected Works*.

Her own marital and gynaecological disorders had left little time for noticing the children's illnesses. Among the sad faces anxiously encircling their mother's bed was that of little Vanya who, ever since the New Year, had shown signs of being feverish and upset in his stomach. The day after Sofya pulled off her triumph and got the rights in *Master and Man*, Vanya developed scarlet fever. A doctor came — a different doctor — and diagnosed a sore throat and diarrhoea. The next day, at eleven o'clock at night, Vanya died. He was not quite seven years old.

It was like a terrible bath of cold water cast over the heads of two scrapping dogs. When the little boy died, their quarrel forgotten, Tolstoy took his wife's arm and led her into Tanya's empty bedroom. They sat on the sofa and hugged one another, 'nearly unconscious with sorrow'.[20]

*   *   *   *

It would seem as though Vanichka was a very remarkable child, even if we allow for the pious exaggerations of his grieving parents. Sasha, his elder sister by four years, wrote, 'He was more just and wise than grown people. With some deep intuition, he sensed the truth and reached out for it as a plant reaches towards the sun. How many times, not knowing that he did it, he taught the older ones around him.'[21] This was an impression made not just upon the family, but upon visitors and friends. The famous scientist Mechnikov said of Vanichka, 'I knew, the first time that I ever saw him, that he would either die or become a greater genius than his father.'[22]

Once, when she had been combing his hair and looking at his face in the glass, his mother had been surprised by Vanichka saying, 'Mummy, I feel that I really *am* like Papa!' Such is our cynicism that we probably find accounts of Vanichka's virtue mawkish. Whether we do or we don't, we can find in his desire to imitate his father (and, perhaps, his actual uncanny resemblance to Tolstoy) a good indication of how the balance of power, in the nursery, had shifted. The older children had only come to an appreciation of Tolstoy's ideas (if at all) when they reached the years of discretion. Vanichka seemed to have imbibed Tolstoyan ideas instinctively. 'No, Mummy! Don't say Yasnaya Polyana will be mine! Everything is everyone's!' If this isn't enough to make us sick, we read, some weeks before he died, of his tying labels to his few possessions and attempting to give them away. 'To our cook, Simon Nikolayevich, from Vanya' etc.[23]

Now this angelic and attractive presence had been removed from the Tolstoy household. Doubtless, his canonisation in the eyes of the family took place partly because, during the last month of his life, his parents had been so engaged in bitter dispute that they had barely noticed the infant saint and prodigy in their midst. Sofya Andreyevna never fully recovered from this death. For once, the cliché was true and she was 'never the same again'.

'She was in the habit of taking refuge from everything in life which was painful, incomprehensible and vaguely worrying to her in her love, her passionate and reciprocated love for this boy, who was exceptionally gifted, both spiritually and emotionally,' Tolstoy wrote. 'He was one of those children sent prematurely by God into a world which is not yet ready for them, someone ahead of his time, like swallows arriving too early and freezing to death.'[24]

As he contemplated her grief, Tolstoy was astonished by his wife's spiritual purity. He admitted to his cousin Alexandrine, 'This loss was painful to me, but I don't feel it nearly so much as Sofya, firstly because I had and still have another life, a spiritual one, and secondly because Sofya's grief prevents me from seeing my own loss, and because I see something great is taking place in her soul, and I pity her and worry about her condition. Generally speaking, I can say that I am well.'[25] The rest of the family prepared for Easter. Tolstoy, who was above all that kind of thing, looked on with sympathetic condescension. He even felt entitled to be privy to his wife's Easter confession which was made to some holy-man friend of his nun sister. This 'very intelligent priest, Father Valentin told her that mothers who lost their children always turn to God initially and then return to the cares of the world. He warned her against this. 'I don't think this will happen in her case,' added Lev Nikolayevich, the spiritual expert in his summing up of the matter.[26]

During the spring, while his wife grieved and lost weight and spent much of her time in bed with influenza, Tolstoy felt himself 'becoming the bearer of God's will'. Dostoyevsky had believed that the Russian people, under their Church and Emperor, were the God-bearers. For Tolstoy, the exact opposite was true. His nation was God-less and he was the chosen vessel of Heaven who, like another prophet in another land, 'did but prompt the age to quit their clogs'.

The sadness of his own domestic scene was in itself a positive encouragement to take an interest in public affairs. (Prophets and Evangelists are often enough people for whom home has become intolerable.) Each week brought news, either from John Kenworthy, or from Chertkov, or from some other source, of further Government brutality. He wrote, with great perspicacity, in his diary: 'A man is considered disgraced if he lets himself be beaten or if he is accused of theft, brawling or not paying card debts etc., but not if he signs a death sentence, takes part in an execution, reads other people's letters, separates fathers and husbands and wives from their families, confiscates people's resources or puts them in prison. But surely that is worse.'[27]

During March, while his wife languished in bed and communed with her priest, Tolstoy visited the dissident Izyumchenko in prison (he had been sentenced for two years in a penal battalion for refusing military service) and his friend Kolkhov in the psychiatric hospital in Moscow. The doctors suggested that Sofya Andreyevna should be taken abroad for her health, but the risk was too great that, once out of the country, Tolstoy would find readmission refused. At some stages of his life, he had relished the thought of exile. But now? Exile from his friends, his books, his daughters? Marooned in some foreign house with a wife whom he pitied but no longer liked? At the end of April he sent Sofya Andreyevna off to Kiev with their daughter Tanya. 'The woman must live,' he observed smugly in his diary, 'but there is nothing to live by. She lacks the habit of, even the strength for, a spiritual life because all her strength has been expended on her children who are no longer there.'[28] In all his writings on the subject, he had made it clear that this was what women were *for*: to breed and devote themselves to children. If this made the life of the soul impossible, it was tantamount to saying that women do not have souls, or anyway not souls that matter.

While his poor trivial wife and daughter went off to Kiev, the spiritual Master decided to take lessons in riding a bicycle. His ardent disciple Popov was scandalised by this concession to industrialisation and modernity. What could be less Tolstoyan than using a machine to convey you from one spot to another? 'It's quite harmless,' thought the fountainhead, 'and it amuses me in a childish way.'[29]

Meanwhile, as he wobbled his bicycle around the arena in a riding stable or paced the Moscow streets, Tolstoy's mind moved backwards and forwards in a series of melancholic reflections. He took Sasha and a friend to the theatre and felt sorry for the little girls being so excited by the electric lights. There was only one important progress and this was not electricity, not learning to fly, but 'the establishment of the Kingdom of God upon earth'. It was not a thought calculated to enliven a matinée; and, as they paced home through the Moscow streets, the Kingdom did not look as though it were drawing nigh. Few of the faces which passed by were undisfigured by alcohol, nicotine or syphilis. 'Their feebleness is terribly pitiful and offensive.'[30]

Like nearly all men who have wanted to establish a kingdom of peace and love on this earth, Tolstoy had an ambivalent attitude towards the human race. Sometimes he was able to disguise his misanthropy as a scheme of universal improvement and sometimes not. In moods of self-awareness, he knew that he was a much less simple character than his guru-poses would allow. However much he wanted to be a secular *starets*, a self-made saint, he knew that he was (because so much more complicated) in fact much weaker than the godless hordes, his wife included, on whom he looked down with such condescension when in one of his 'spiritual' moods. 'All life is a struggle between the flesh and the spirit,' he wrote and added realistically, 'gradually the flesh triumphs over the spirit.'[31]

It was such a sombre thought as that which inspired *Father Sergius*, the short story at which he began to work around this date. Sergius the failed ascetic is one of Tolstoy's more brilliantly lurid self-projections. Into him is poured Tolstoy's everlasting war with lust. And there is also the much more insidious pleasure of being famed for a spiritual role to which he was actually unsuited. Then there is the dream of martyrdom at the hands of the authorities, exile, and a life of genuine simplicity and obscurity. If Tolstoy, like Sergius, had found employment by a *muzhik* as family tutor and general dogsbody, would the arrangement have been a success? The question (unlike those schoolroom exercises in Latin with *num* and *nonne*) is not 'expecting the answer' yes or no. However self-deceiving he may have been, Tolstoy probably genuinely believed that such a life would bring happiness. The wretchedness of relations with his wife lent sweetness to the idea of the Government sending him into exile in Siberia. The risk was quite genuine, as he increased his vocal defence of such fringe groups as the Dukhobors.

The Dukhobors were a rum lot, even by the rum standards of Russian religious eccentrics. Their origins, some time in the eighteenth century, are obscure and it is hard to pin down many details of their beliefs or customs since most of them have been illiterate. Indeed, since they object to written records or formulated dogmas, illiteracy is rather cherished by them. Even the New Testament is rejected in favour of The Living Book — that is, the guidance of the spirit in individual Dukhobor leaders. *Mutatis mutandis*, there is much in the Dukhobor position which will be familiar to the post-Barthes schools of criticism in Paris or Yale.

Some English and American Quakers who visited a Dukhobor community in 1819 were scandalised by their complete absence of interest in the historical Christ whom they considered less important than their own leader of the moment. The great thing seemed to be prophecy: the prophetic utterance of the living spirit.

The movement had its ups and downs and (inevitably) its schisms. Alexander I was tolerant towards them. (The Dukhobors were, and perhaps are, among those who believed that the liberal Tsar did not die in 1825 but, rather like King Arthur, continued a mysterious existence which would one day be known to the faithful; in this case, they believed, not that Alexander was sleeping in Avalon, but alive on the shores of the Baltic, and practising the religion of the Dukhobors.) Gradually, as the century wore on, the Dukhobor renunciation of property was compromised. By the close of the century there were many Dukhobor peasants who were, by peasant standards, rich; there were even Dukhobors who had compromised their pacifist principles by doing national service in the army. Then there was a revival of the old values, and squabbles broke out within the movement. The larger group of Dukhobors, and the more reactionary, called themselves the Large Party. They chose, 'in the spirit of Christ', a leader called Pyotr Vasilyevich Verigin, who took the title of Peter the Lordly.

Verigin pretty soon fell foul of the intolerant spirit of the times. His insistence that property and warfare were sinful got him thrown into prison in 1887, and then exiled to Shenkursk in the Arctic Circle. It was there that he read Tolstoy's religious writings and absorbed many of his teachings. The authors of the standard history of the Dukhobors make out a convincing case for believing that it was really their Tolstoyism which got them into trouble.

Peter the Lordly, who claimed for himself a divine infallibility as absolute as the Apostolic successors of Peter the Fisherman in Rome, was naturally unwilling to admit that many of his ideas were derived from books. He had no sooner read Tolstoy than he imagined that Tolstoyan ideas had been fed directly into his brain by God; and during the years 1893 and 1894 Peter the Lordly, having now been released from prison, issued a series of directives which were to have dire consequences upon the lives of his followers in the Caucasus. Their only weapons were those of civil disobedience as prescribed by

Tolstoy. Pobedonostsev, Procurator of the Holy Synod, had rather stronger weapons at his disposal.

The first thing which Peter the Lordly did was to ban the consumption of meat. This announcement led to a further schism among the Dukhobors between the Fasters (those who accepted the new teaching) and the Butchers, who lived in a cold mountain climate where it was impossible to grow grain, and who therefore depended for survival upon a meat diet.

Meanwhile, Cossack troops were sent to the Dukhobor villages to demonstrate what the Government thought of their refusal to do military service. The Cossacks were authorised to beat and violate any Dukhobor they found. General Surovzev, who supervised some of these licensed debaucheries, accused the Dukhobors of not being prepared to lay down their lives for their Emperor. They replied: 'You say wrong. We are ready to lay down our life for every man, including the Tsar: if we saw him being tortured, we would lay down our life for his sake, as well as for any other man, but we cannot murder for any man, because it is forbidden by God.'

It was an answer of which Tolstoy himself would have been proud. He first heard of their plight from Prince Khilkov, his disciple who was stationed in the Caucasus after the Russo-Turkish war. Peter the Lordly, with peasant cunning, concealed from Khilkov the fact that he had read Tolstoy, so that when accounts of Dukhobor beliefs and customs began to reach Yasnaya Polyana, the similarities between the things which Lev Nikolayevich had written and those which had been 'revealed' to Peter the Lordly were so striking as almost to appear miraculous. Tolstoy, with all his energy and learning, had spent years poring over the Greek Testament, reading the philosophers and the scholars and studying non-Christian religions before deciding that the essence of the Gospel was contained in the doctrine of non-violence and the refusal to recognise civil authorities. Celibacy and vegetarianism were later thrown in for good measure. The Church had arrogantly rejected his claim to have rescued the authentic Jesus from its maw. And yet here, in Russia, eighteen hundred years after Christ, were a group of simple, unlettered peasants, who had managed to preserve the Gospel intact. It never crossed Tolstoy's mind that it was rather less than ten years since Verigin had read *What Then Must We Do?* and other tracts. For Tolstoy, the 'survival' of the Dukhobors was tantamount to 'the resurrection of Christ himself'.[32]

He therefore needed no encouragement from his friends to start a campaign on behalf of the Dukhobors; and this had far-reaching consequences: for Tolstoy and his art; for his wife and family; for Chertkov; and, more than for anyone, for the Dukhobors. What had begun as some crazy ideas buzzing about in the heads of a few thousand peasants in the mountain villages of the Caucasus was to be a drama played out on the world stage. On October 23, 1895, *The Times* (of London) published Tolstoy's letter 'The Persecution of Christians in Russia', followed a month later by a lengthy article in *The Contemporary Review*.

Much the most energetic and well-organised of Tolstoy's informants about the struggle for religious freedom in Russia was Chertkov, who had by now become a full-time agitator. In December 1896, he and two other friends Tregubov and Biryukov drafted a pamphlet called *An Appeal for Help*. 'A terrible cruelty is now being perpetrated in the Caucasus. More than four thousand people are suffering and dying from hunger, disease and exhaustion, blows, tortures and other persecutions at the hands of the Russian authorities.'

In January, they published the pamphlet, and all three were immediately arrested. Tregubov and Biryukov were exiled to Estonia, as was Prince Khilkov, whose continued presence in the Caucasus was thought undesirable. Chertkov had already taken the precaution of sending his fanatical wife and his children to England. In February, he was allowed to follow them. He would not return to Russia for another eight years.

Tolstoy was bitterly distressed. For all he knew, Chertkov had gone forever. True, he would be able to meet up with Kenworthy and the other English Tolstoyans; and, like Herzen in an earlier generation, he would be in a stronger position to expose the evils of the Russian Government from the freedom of a country where there was virtually no censorship. Nevertheless, the idea of Chertkov's exile made the Master uneasy: 'I'm very much afraid that you'll be corrupted in England. I've just received the *Review of Reviews* and read it, and I caught such a breath of that astonishing English self-satisfied dullness that I put myself in your place and tried to think how you would get on with them.'[33]

*   *   *   *

Chertkov's sojourn in England was of great importance to the future of Tolstoy's work in Russia. Not only were the greater portion of

Tolstoy's works — published and unpublished, literary and didactic — collected by Chertkov in exile. The period of exile itself was to establish Chertkov's *bona fide* credentials later on when, under the regime of Lenin, the great ninety-volume edition of Tolstoy's works was undertaken. Such was the strength of Chertkov's personality, and his skill at organising his team of assistant editors, that this 'Jubilee Edition' (the first volumes were published to coincide with the centenary of Tolstoy's birth, 1928) continued to roll from the presses and be bound in the handsome blue cloth quarto editions throughout the blackest years of Soviet history. By the time of Chertkov's death in 1936, the bulk of the work was done. Of course, such a lavish work was beyond the pocket of ordinary Soviet citizens. But those who could sneak into a library were able to enjoy the paradoxical pleasure during the 1930s (when all other religious and revisionist literature was banned, and the Stalinist purges had destroyed all literary and religious freedoms) of reading Tolstoy's denunciations of political power, and urging of private individuals to follow conscience alone and to submit to no laws but those of God. This strange literary paradox was a fruit of Chertkov's English years.

'The Croydon Brotherhood', the Tolstoyan group founded by the ex-Methodist minister John Kenworthy, had moved to the suburb of Croydon and established a land settlement at Purleigh in Essex. The idea seems to have resembled a modern kibbutz, only without the common discipline or common sense which has made the kibbutz experiment so (comparatively) successful. The Purleigh Community, in which Tolstoy himself took the keenest interest, was not to last. Aylmer and Louise Maude tried to live there for a while, but they did not stay. There were quarrels. Kenworthy was destined to die in a lunatic asylum.

Chertkov did not join the Purleigh community. It would have been intolerable to him to belong to any organisation of which he was not the recognised leader. He lost no time, after his arrival in England, in putting money and energy into something called the Free Age Press, run by A. C. Fifield. This enterprise managed to produce no less than four hundred and twenty-four million pages of Tolstoy's writing.[34]

Finding Purleigh altogether uncongenial, Chertkov moved his centre of operations to Tuckton House, near Bournemouth, taking over the disused Christchurch waterworks nearby as his publishing house. Tuckton, a red brick edifice of fairly recent construction, became a centre of Tolstoyism. A picture of Tolstoy hung in the hall.

So zealous was Chertkov to preserve Tolstoy's manuscripts and papers that he constructed a special strongroom for the purpose, lined with steel and fireproof bricks. When, for some reason, the room had to be demolished in 1965, it took two workmen a whole week to make a tiny hole in the wall of this room. Nobody was ever allowed access to the room during Chertkov's time at Tuckton, and it was there, piecemeal, that he built up the material for his ninety-volume edition. From 1902 onwards, he began the process of copying all Tolstoy's correspondence. Meanwhile, the house became a sort of international refuge for malcontents. The anarchist Prince Kropotkin was one of the many visitors from Russia, Poland, the Ukraine, Holland, all over.

Chertkov did not limit his energies to propagating Tolstoyism among the Slavs. He made sorties to Oxford to address undergraduate societies on the subject, and he gave lectures to local clubs and Women's Institutes. It is hard to guess how Chertkov responded to the inescapably low key (emotionally and politically) of everything which went on in England. He had known it before, when he had been to London as a young Evangelical convert of Lord Radstock's, joined various London clubs, played cricket, and so on. Perhaps he was so naturally fervent a person that he never quite noticed the capacity of English liberalism to make everything vapid. A good example of what Tolstoy feared when he spoke of 'that astonishing English self-satisfied dullness' is to be found in the writings of Aylmer Maude, who had come back to Chertkov in 1897 and, finding him insufferably arrogant, quickly parted company with him. In his introduction to *What Then Must We Do?*, perhaps the most violently despondent of all Tolstoy's political reflections, an exposure of the gap between rich and poor which leaves no reader unaffected, Maude felt that the English had gone some small way towards solving the difficulty. 'Some attempt to bridge the gulf and supply mental sustenance where it is badly needed may be found in our village Women's Institutes, as well as in various amateur dramatic groups up and down the country and in the Citizen House movement at Bath.'[35] There is a sort of craziness about this which could never be translated into the Russian language, let alone the Russian context. In the year that Maude wrote it, the Great Terror was at its height, and tens of thousands of Russians were herded to their death, or sentenced to imprisonment in concentration camps.

These events lay in the future, and were quite simply unimaginable when Chertkov and his followers sat in the garden at Tuckton House and spoke of their hopes for the setting up of the Kingdom of Heaven on Russian soil. Sometimes even Chertkov allowed his mind to dwell on something more trivial. He followed the fortunes of the local football team, and presented the Bournemouth Football League with a cup. Sad to say, the cup has gone missing.[36]

* * * *

Meanwhile, one of the most immediate results of Chertkov's exile in England was that the first stage of the rescue of the Dukhobors got under way. Chertkov dispatched his old friend Arthur St. John, a former captain in the Royal Inniskilling Fusiliers, to see what he could do for the Spirit Wrestlers. The Captain arrived in the Caucasus with money from the Quakers and greetings of good will from Tolstoy and Chertkov. Perhaps, in a military career, he had witnessed odder scenes than those presented by these pathetic encampments of fanatics, some of whom practised nudism. But one may doubt it. He was greeted by emotional crowds, and not only because he brought with him several thousand roubles. There was a great amount of bowing, for the Dukhobors believe that the Deity resides in His fullness in every human being, and reverence their fellow men as Orthodox would an altar or a wonder-working icon. There was weeping and sighing. Captain St. John promised that he would do what he could, but not long after his arrival, he was arrested by the police and sent over the border to Turkey. From there he made his way to Cyprus and determined that the Dukhobors should find there 'a kind of *pied-à-terre* where we could bring them over without further delay as many as our means will at present allow'. The British High Commissioner was consulted, but there was anxiety in Whitehall. The establishment of a Russian colony on Cyprus would have provided a perfect seedbed for spies or political agitators. It was a full two years from the time of Chertkov's exile before a solution — a well-nigh miraculous one — to the Dukhobor problem was found.

Not that the Dukhobors were the only persecuted minority with claims upon Tolstoy's sympathy. No less persecuted were his old friends the Molokans, the milk drinkers of Samara. According to new edicts brought in by the Government, heretic parents could be forcibly separated from their children if they refused to bring them up in the Orthodox faith. There was a particularly sad series of cases in Samara, in which the police rounded up Molokan children and took them off

437

to monasteries. The parents were not told where their children were. There was a policy of deliberately tormenting parents, who would be told that they could see their children if they turned up to church at such and such an hour on such and such a day. When they kept the appointment, the worried parents would find in the church, not their own children, but other Molokan adults who were being forcibly instructed in the Orthodox faith. 'You are filled with sadness because your children have forsaken you,' they were told by some quisling monk, 'but so also is your holy Mother the Church because you have forsaken her.'[37]

Tolstoy was appalled by the story. 'Such things were done only at the time of the Inquisition. Nowhere, not even in Turkey, is such a thing possible, and no one could believe that such a thing could happen in a Christian country in 1897.'[38] Marooned at Yasnaya Polyana, he wired to his daughter Tanya in St. Petersburg to get in touch with their friend the distinguished lawyer Koni (a liberal who had been largely responsible for setting up the jury system in Russia) and to await the arrival of aggrieved Molokans at the railroad station. Until this alarming request arrived, Tanya had been enjoying a metropolitan interlude, compiling an album of French and German pictures, visiting exhibitions, and calling upon the great painter Repin whose pupil she became. Tolstoy had urged Repin to attempt a canvas of the Decembrists being led to execution, but in the atmosphere of the late 1890s, Repin felt that such a theme would be 'dangerous'.

With the arrival of her father's telegram, however, Tanya's practical, bossy nature asserted itself. Koni had already attempted to speak in the senate of the Molokan plight; their friends the Olsufyevs had done their best to get a letter from Tolstoy taken to the Emperor. Tanya asked Count Dmitry Olsufyev what was to stop her interviewing the Procurator of the Holy Synod himself, Pobedonostsev. Olsufyev thought it was worth a try, though Koni was more dubious. Tanya immediately went to the telephone and arranged to see 'Pob' (as her diary calls him) between eleven and twelve the following day.

The interview reflects some credit both upon Tanya and on the usually much maligned Procurator himself. In the hall of Church Government House, she was asked if she was Countess Tatyana Lvovna Tolstaya, and she admitted that she was. When she was actually shown into Pob's presence, however, he pretended to vagueness about her identity. What was the nature of her request? She told him the Molokans' plight, which he knew perfectly well already. They were suffering because of laws brought in by himself.

Pobedonostsev was taller, sturdier, more handsome than she had expected. His reaction to the sad story was one of genial reasonableness. 'It's all through the Bishop of Samara getting over-zealous. Children have been taken away from sixteen parents. There is no such statute in Russia.' Tanya, who had studied the whole matter with Koni and reread the wording of the statute that very morning, protested. 'Excuse me. I think that there *is* such a statute, though fortunately it has never hitherto been applied.' 'Yes, yes,' said Pob. 'You send me the names of your Molokans, and I shall write to Samara.'

When she took her leave, Pobedonostsev showed her out, all charm, and watched her descend his great staircase. When she was half-way down, he called over the banisters, 'What is your name?' 'Tatyana,' she said. 'And your patronymic?' 'Lvovna,' she replied. 'So! You are the daughter of Lev Tolstoy?' 'Yes.' 'The famous Tatyana!' She laughed, and she said she had never known *that* before.[39]

Afterwards, Koni explained to her how it suited Pob's purpose to receive a petition on behalf of the Molokans, but not to know until after the interview was over the identity of his suppliant. He could not acknowledge that he had received Tolstoy's appeal to the Emperor; he could not be seen to negotiate with anarchists and enemies of the Imperial system. Equally clearly, though, the persecution of the Molokans had been a blunder which served no good purpose. In this way, he could squash the matter unofficially and, as he hoped, easily.

But, as it happened, the Molokan children themselves added a complication which neither Pobedonostsev nor Tolstoy would have foreseen. When the cruel statute was revoked, and word reached the Samaran monasteries that the Molokan parents could come and reclaim their children, there were embarrassing scenes. The children, who, perhaps for the first time in their lives had eaten regular meals and slept in beds, announced that they preferred life in the monastery and refused to come home.[40]

*   *   *   *

A couple of days after her surprisingly cordial encounter with Pobedonostsev, Tanya rejoined the family circle in Moscow, where another tragi-farce was being enacted by her mother. On February 5, *What Is Art?* had been published in a separate book (the first edition) by the Posrednik House. Five thousand copies were sold within the week. It is a book in which Tolstoy allowed his knockabout, 'bronchitis is a metal' persona full rein. ('"What! the Ninth Symphony not a great work of art!" I hear exclaimed by indignant voices. And I reply: "Most certainly it is not."'[41]) The denunciatory tone is never more hoarsely vociferous than in his assaults on 'counterfeit' or 'upper-class' musical performances.

The day after publication, there was a musical evening in the Tolstoy household. Tanya remembered that 'Taneyev and Goldenweiser played a four-handed arrangement of Taneyev's overture to the *Orestes*. It is an incomprehensibly uninspired thing with one miserable little theme at the end, which is a trifle of consolation for hearing through a lengthy piece in which their hands seemed to fall just about anywhere on the keys.'[42]

The two musicians who excited these satirical opinions were in fact both successful concert pianists. Alexander Borisovich Goldenweiser was a young Jew who was deeply attached to Tolstoy's writings and way of life. Because, like Boswell, he only partially understood his great hero but was, at the same time, wonderfully literal-minded, Goldenweiser has provided us with some of the best snatches of Tolstoy's conversation — prose snapshots of his domestic life.

Sergey Ivanovich Taneyev's part in the story is rather different. Born in 1856, he was older than Goldenweiser, and had been a longstanding friend of the family. Tolstoy never greatly cared for him. As long ago as 1889, Tolstoy had dismissed Taneyev as a 'completely ignorant man who has adopted an aesthetic outlook that was new thirty years ago and imagines he is in possession of the last word in human wisdom. For example: sensuality is good; Christianity is Catholic dogma and ritual and therefore stupid; the Greek outlook on the world is the most elevated, and so on. . . . Taneyev gets on my nerves.' Nevertheless, Tolstoy's profound love of music covered a multitude of Taneyev's follies. As Tchaikovsky's favourite pupil, Taneyev deserved to be taken seriously. He was the teacher of, among others, Rachmaninov and Scriabin. Like many of his contemporaries, he took an interest in folk music, but less in the emotional fashion of the Mighty Five and more for its melodic structures. There is something abstract and intellectually impressive about this most technically adept of Russian composers. But he was never as popular as Moussorgsky, Cui, Borodin or Glazunov, perhaps because he lacked some primary emotional quality. This coldness was to play its part in his distinctive relationship with the Tolstoy household.

Tolstoy might complain about Taneyev, but in the initial stages of their friendship, there were two things for which he valued his companionship. They would often play duets together — in particular Bach, Chopin and Beethoven. Taneyev also provided Tolstoy with something for which he was always (like most Russian men) on the look-out: a good game of chess.

Things started to go wrong after the death of Vanichka. As Sofya Andreyevna emerged from the first prostrations of grief she began to lose herself in music and decided (something which she and Tolstoy were forever in the process of doing) to perfect her keyboard performances. Taneyev, who presumably found Moscow summers disturbingly quiet, would retreat to the noisier atmosphere of the country, where he could compose and practise with just the right level of distraction. He spent the summer at Yasnaya Polyana, taking rooms as a paying guest in one of the wings, and in 1896 Sofya asked him back, free of charge, if he would consent to become her tutor. She was by now fifty-two years old: that is to say, twelve years Taneyev's senior. Tolstoy was on his way to seventy. Deeply to Taneyev's embarrassment (when the truth of things slowly dawned on him) Sofya Andreyevna fell in love with the musician.

She put no check on her infatuation, and started to pursue Taneyev everywhere. She attended all his Moscow concerts that autumn and winter. In the spring of 1897, she chucked over the Lenten fast and set off to attend Taneyev's concerts in St. Petersburg.

Tolstoy, always preternaturally jealous by temperament, tried to view these goings-on rationally, but he couldn't. Rather than witness his wife making a fool of herself, he retreated more and more to the Olsufyevs at Nikolskoye-Obolyanovo — always, for some reason, a place where he could write. There he wrote Sofya a pathetic, but from her point of view intolerable letter, telling her that her obsession with the pianist was nothing but a game and that she would never succeed in making the man love her. It particularly grieved Tolstoy that all this should have blown up after the *rapprochement* between himself and his wife following upon the death of Vanichka:

It is terribly painful and humiliatingly shaming that a total outsider, an unnecessary and quite uninteresting man rules our life and

441

poisons the last years of our life: it is humiliating that one has to ask when and where he is going, and when he is playing at what rehearsals.

This is terrible, terrible, painful and disgusting. And it is happening just at the end of our life — a life spent purely and well, just at the time when we have been drawing closer together in spite of all that could divide us.[43]

With a painful irony, the Tolstoys were inhabiting much of the same territory as the fantasy which had given rise to *The Kreutzer Sonata*: a musician and a jealous husband. Unlike the mad narrator of that tale, Tolstoy did not imagine that his wife was actually having an affair with her musician; nor did he want to murder her. But he did find the association completely intolerable. He tried to be kind about it, but he was unable to react with the good humour which the situation required. Throughout the summer of 1897 while he suffered the exile and absence of Chertkov, Tolstoy penned enormous letters to his wife proposing solutions to the Taneyev problem. Both his daughters, Masha and Tanya, had indulged in unsuitable liaisons. Tanya was still entangled with some married man. Sofya Andreyevna's infatuation filled Tolstoy with similar feelings of shame. The one obvious and sensible solution — 'to persuade oneself that this will pass and that it is not important at all' — was one which Tolstoy could not contemplate without 'horror and despair'.

In all seriousness, he proposed that she must choose between her infatuation and her marriage. Either she stopped seeing her pianist or Tolstoy would leave her, go abroad, go into exile. Later in the summer of 1897, when she had had Taneyev to stay at Yasnaya without Tolstoy's permission, he issued another ultimatum. This time, however, he stuffed the letter into the leather upholstery of the armchair in his study where it was discovered, four years later, by his daughter Masha. He had decided once and for all that he would leave his wife. Their beliefs and life styles were incompatible. He longed for solitude. He was going. By the time Masha read these words, the situation had changed. The Taneyev problem had faded in the way such things do. The great escape still lay in the future. Illness had changed the complexion of family life once more, and they were all living with the consequences of publishing *Resurrection*.

*　　　*　　　*　　　*

Resurrection is a novel which has earned the disapprobation of scholars and critics, but in Russia it has always been one of Tolstoy's most popular novels. The story of the young serving maid who, after a single amorous fling with the nephew of an aristocratic house, becomes pregnant and slithers into a life of moral degradation, might just about be allowed by the highbrows. But they cannot easily admire the melodramatic plot in which Maslova, by now a prostitute on trial for murder, comes up before her first seducer, Prince Nekhlyudov (of *Russian Landlord* fame) who is a member of the jury, sitting in judgement upon her. Nekhlyudov is so outraged by the injustice of the bungled verdict that he pursues her through all the labyrinthine bureaucracy surrounding Russian prisons, accompanies her on her journey to Siberia and attempts to marry her in reparation for the great wrong which he did her in the distant past. Of all the born-again Tolstoyan heroes, Nekhlyudov is the most reborn. It is not only on the last page that new life springs up in the hero's heart to justify the title of the novel. All this, the sober critics tell us, is crude stuff, written by the old moraliser who penned *The Kingdom of God is Within You* and *What Is Art?*

Certainly, if one gives a mere outline of the plot, *Resurrection* sounds insufferable. This is not, however, the impression given off by successive rereadings. Enthusiasts for the book see it as a resurrection in a different sense, a vehicle by which he very nearly managed to escape the strictures which the Tolstoyans, and his family and the official censor had, all in their different ways, been so long imposing upon him. Here was a book where he was free to speak with that authentic voice which had been speaking in him or through him ever since *Childhood*. In terms of his own art, as well as in its religious significance, the title of the book is wholly appropriate.

The plot, which some readers find so fantastical is — like most improbable stories — something which actually happened. Tolstoy's lawyer friend Koni had been told the story as long ago as 1887 and in the family thereafter it came to be known as *Konevsky* — Koni's Story. A real prostitute, Koni told them, was on trial for murder. She was disease-ridden, wretched and abject. A young man on the jury recognised a girl he had formerly seduced. He obtained permission to interview her in prison and offered to marry her; but she died in gaol.

Readers from countries where there is a more advanced legal system than obtained in nineteenth-century Russia may conceivably be puzzled by the fact that the young man had not either declared his former association or silently absented himself from the jury, having made his reasons clear in private session with the judge or the clerk of the court. But as Koni himself found when he got to work on jury reform (and there had only been trial by jury *at all* in Russia since 1864)[44] the problem was to find anyone even remotely suitable to sit as a juror. A long trial in the provinces, for example, would ruin a peasant farmer who had to be away from his land for several weeks. After 1889, only members of the Orthodox Church were allowed to serve on juries and, although there were plenty of those about, the preponderance of those who sat on juries were those who, like the farcical jury in Tolstoy's story, lived lives which were fairly remote from Maslova and her kind.

Many of Tolstoy's biographers, as well as his wife, believed that in refashioning Koni's story into a novel, Tolstoy was in fact reliving some guilt-ridden complex about an actual girl he had seduced in his youth. Then they usually go on to point out that the girl, or girls, in question (housemaids from Yasnaya, Moscow and Kazan have all been brought forward to substantiate the theory) did not go on to become prostitutes. This is advanced as evidence of Tolstoy's tormented attitude to sex. In real life, it is repeated, these girls had their babies (or not) and settled down as perfectly contented servants, either in the same house or in some other. No shock. No disgrace. No mud and slime, except in the imagination of the novelist. But the time had long since passed — and with it the nervous crisis following *Anna Karenina* — when Tolstoy simply used art as a laundry for his own personal experiences. *Resurrection* appears dislocated and disjointed, at this imaginative level, only if we are forced to view it as a piece of autobiography. But it is not on this level that it has touched those millions of readers who have found in it things deeper, both disturbing and consoling, than anything in Tolstoy's *œuvre* except *War and Peace*.

A rougher and more off-key attempt to set the book into some sort of biographical framework is found in Strakhov's comment, in 1895, when he heard of the story and Tolstoy's interest in it: 'One way or another it will be the story of Chertkov.'[45] Nekhlyudov, as exquisite in his personal manners as in his morality, is in every way more like Chertkov than he is like Tolstoy. As most Russian readers of the story have recognised, the humourlessness of Nekhlyudov's campaigning zeal is much more Chertkovian than Tolstoyan. Viktor Shklovsky points out that we are always on Maslova's side against Nekhlyudov;

in this novel, we always see what is ridiculous about his moral poses. A survey of the chronology of Tolstoy's life, moreover, shows that the periods when he worked on the novel with the most intense bursts of energy all correspond to periods of Chertkov's absence. Had Chertkov not been exiled in 1897, Tolstoy might never have finished the book at all.

We have considered Tolstoy's interest in the Dukhobors, and told the part which he played in establishing the means by which these poor people escaped the tyranny of the Tsars and found a new life abroad. When St. John's plans for them in Cyprus fell through, the possibility arose of the Dukhobors emigrating *en masse* to Canada. Four thousand of them set out to Canada by way of Cyprus, their island sojourn claiming a quarter through dysentery and malaria. The enterprise cost some forty thousand dollars. Sixteen and a half thousand of this was raised by the Dukhobors themselves, who were able to realise the value of property. Five thousand was supplied by the Tolstoyans at Purleigh. A further fourteen hundred was contributed by the Society of Friends. But the bulk of the expense — seventeen thousand dollars — was borne by Tolstoy himself, who agreed to waive his principle of not accepting money for what he wrote, and to donate the proceeds of *Resurrection* to the Dukhobor appeal. When the bedraggled exiles arrived at the Canadian prairies, they were greeted by a delegate of the local Labour Organisation with these words: 'I do not know the name of your Emperor, but the name of your patron and friend, Count Tolstoy, is as well known in Canada as in Russia, and I hope that one of the boys now listening to me, fifty years hence, will fill, like him, with honour to his country, the literary throne of the world.'[46]

Fifty years later, as it happened, the Canadian authorities were having untold trouble with the Dukhobors who enjoyed an enthusiastic spell of reviving their traditional customs of nudism and arson; but that is another story.

*　　　　*　　　　*　　　　*

We have not really asked ourselves the question: Why? Why the Dukhobors? The 'reasons' only make sense because Tolstoy gave them sense. He could have raised an appeal, as he did in the case of the famine victims in 1891. He could have sold land, or given them inherited money of his own. When he announced his intention of giving the royalties of *Resurrection* to the Spirit Wrestlers, his wife moaned that he was giving a fortune to cranks while 'black bread will do for his children and grandchildren'. His Soviet biographer points out that at this date, Tolstoy's children and grandchildren had a fortune conservatively estimated at half a million roubles. 'White bread cost four kopecks a pound, and they could buy a trainload of the best'.[47]

It is on one level absurd to suggest that he 'had' to write a novel to save a handful of religious eccentrics, particularly a novel on this scale, and a novel which involved such labour. It was not something casually thrown together to raise money. Three intensive periods of work (1889-90, 1895-1896 and the final dynamic period of composition in 1898 and 1899) created the book. As with the great works, there was limitless patience and energy displayed to get things right (of which perhaps the most notorious is the no less than fifty rewritings of the first description of Maslova's eyes. They went through every colour in the spectrum.) He had not been working on this expansive scale since *Anna Karenina*. The impulse came from inside. It was only the notion of doing it for the Dukhobors which released his daemon into a freedom which it had not known for twenty years. The mature Tolstoy (like Sir Walter Scott who kept the very identity of the author of *Waverley* a secret) could only write fiction because he disapproved of it. The head and the guts were at war. But at its finest moments in this story, they fuse. If we want the whole Tolstoy, he is here. In the letters, the diaries, the tracts, the essays, the short stories, he is only present in bits.

Resurrection's power as a work of art and its effectiveness as a piece of political propaganda both stem from the same source. In *Anna Karenina*, life itself, the knowledge that the world was teeming with life of which our own personalities are but a part, became a torment for the heroine, a torment which is not rationally explained in the story and only makes sense in terms of some sort of brainstorm in the author; hence the disconcertingness of *Anna Karenina* as an artwork in its last few hundred pages. In *Resurrection*, this *Angst* has vanished completely. Life — what Henry James would call 'clumsy life at her stupid work'[48] — is in effect the heroine of the story. We feel it in the very opening paragraph, where nature is too strong even for the modern industrialised city which is trying to suppress the spring. 'Spring was still spring, even in the town,' we are told, as grass and leaves defy stones, paving, bricks. This life, which the earth has of itself, is felt beneath the surface of almost every page. Its first really dramatic appearance comes on the Easter night of Maslova Katyusha's seduction. The church service at midnight has been wonderfully joyful. For Nekhlyudov, it has been all of a piece with his as yet innocent love for the girl. 'The golden iconostasis glittered for her; the tapers in the candelabra and the candle stands burnt for her; these joyful chants were for her sake: "The Easter [Passover] of the Lord, Rejoice O ye people!" And everything, just everything which was good upon earth was for the sake of her.'[49]

> There in the nimbus and Comper tracery,
> Gold Myfanwy blesses us all.[50]

This scene, incidentally, could easily have been penned by the most pious Orthodox believer, and it is not always mentioned by those who find offence in the later, much more notorious description of a religious service in the prison chapel. But the two services are deliberately juxtaposed. Here, religion, sex, the classes, all are at one. The voice of love and the voice of nature, the voice of the individual and the voice of old Russia rise in a unified chorus. It is a 'natural' scene. Nature itself is ambivalent when it comes to questions of sexual morality.

That night, when they have exchanged their traditional Easter greetings — 'Christ is risen!' 'He is risen indeed!' — they are aware of the thaw and the coming of the spring. Nekhlyudov hears it from the porch of the *dacha*: 'There, on the river, in the fog, there was going on some sort of tireless, slow work. . . .'[51] When, a few pages later, the seduction happens, Katyusha resists with her lips, but her whole being says 'I am all yours.' Nekhlyudov, having made love to her, goes out into the porch and hears the ice cracking on the river with greater speed — a Lawrentian moment, but Tolstoy does not spoil it with any heaviness. 'So what [*Chto zh*]?' Nekhlyudov asks himself. 'Is it a great happiness or a great disaster which has befallen me?'[52]

No Lawrentian hero asked any such post-coital question. Sex has a natural ambivalence in Tolstoy's artistic world, something close to the idea of original sin in the Augustinian world view. Katyusha — or Maslova as we best know her, her name in the later part of her career — has made her living by it, with her marvellously attractive squint, eyes as glistening as currants and large breasts. She cannot really escape. She exudes sex and, even in the foetid conditions of city

447

prisons or in the transit camps, the men can't keep away from her. Like the spring, which is still spring even in the town, Maslova's sexuality keeps her in touch with a natural world with which it is possible for some of the men in the story, whether benign, liberal intellectuals, lounge lizards, priests or petty officials, to lose touch altogether.

Nekhlyudov's friends, the Korchagins, for example (who in an early story by Tolstoy might be presented as merely silly, with their smart clothes, new paintings, newspapers and delicate food), are creatures of such artifice. Life of the spirit — the life of the river and its thaw, the life of natural enjoyment which leads to Maslova's undoing, the life of moral awakening which saves Nekhlyudov — would be impossible for them.

Those who entertain the simple view that Tolstoy 'just' wanted to 'get back to nature' or 'just' wanted to lead 'a simple life' should look again at the universal cohesion of *Resurrection*. By the time we read the last sections, it seems to have achieved its effect almost without effort. In the first half of the book, we find the world out of joint: prisons, law courts, armies, tortures, modern cities, modern class distinction, religion all form part of the same farcical mumbo-jumbo, just as sex is reduced to a drunken, commercial transaction in a sordid hotel bedroom. In this first half of the book we are confronted with a world which is manifestly and hopelessly unnatural. It has not even been troubled by Nekhlyudov's question; when the power of sex makes him nature's servant, is this a good thing or a bad thing? Conscience itself, which for the Rousseauesque Tolstoy was always natural to man, has been silenced. Conscience is dead, not just in this or that individual but, as we realise with such force in the second half of the book, for an entire nation.

There could be no clearer indication of the way in which Tolstoy's introspective artistic method had moved on since the 'laundry' days up to and including *Anna Karenina*. Many of the most powerful scenes in *Resurrection* are those set in Siberia among the prisoners, a world of which Tolstoy had absolutely no direct experience. Many of the more vivid details are lifted from his reading.

The snapshot of the officer supervising the prison convoy is a good example of Tolstoy's eye being as sharp as ever: 'When the carts were filled with sacks on which those who were allowed were seated, the officer of the convoy took off his cap and, having wiped his forehead, his bald head and his fat nose, made the sign of the cross. "Forward

march!" he commanded. . . .'[53] Compare that account with that of the
American journalist George Kennan, whose book on Siberia and the
exile system was published in New York in 1891: 'When the sick and
infirm had all taken the places assigned them in the invalid carts,
Captain Gurgiss took off his cap, crossed himself, and bowed in the
direction of the parish church, and then, turning to the convicts,
cried, "Well, boys, go ahead!"'[54] Tolstoy adds (quite typically) the
wiping of a sweaty forehead; he makes the head bald and the nose flat.
Kennan's Captain Gurgiss is made more vividly physical, and is
realised in sharper focus. Tolstoy's use of Kennan (and it is extensive)
is one of the supreme examples of a great imagination transforming
neutral material into literature, equivalent to Shakespeare's use of
Holinshed or Proust's of the Goncourt Journals. Prosaically, one
could say that the essence of *Resurrection* in its second half is all in
Kennan. Tradition even imagines that the good 'Englishman' at the
end of the story is Kennan himself, though this figure with his Bibles
and his embarrassing sermons in prison cells seems more like
Chertkov's old hero Lord Radstock than the intelligent (and secular)
American. Russian scholars have found a third 'original' in the figure
of a German preacher called Dr. Baedeker who felt called to preach to
the convicts of Siberia.[55]

What no reader of the novel will ever forget is the vividness of
those convicts and the conversations they have among themselves. In
the first half of the book, we know that spring will come, that the ice
will break, that Nekhlyudov will seduce Maslova. It is all natural and
inevitable. In the second half of the book, we know with the same
certainty that something will happen to Russia. Things cannot go on
in this crazy, barbarous way. And it is one of the mysterious features
of the book, finished seventeen years before Lenin's train pulled into
the Finland Station, that we have no doubt at all that the oppressors
are less strong than their prisoners. It is not just hindsight which
makes us say this. The 'resurrection' which is in store for them is as
certain as the return of spring to the earth. The question merely
remains, when we have finished the novel, of how the ice will break
on the river, and how change will come to Russia.

To the virtuous political prisoner Kryltsov, talking with Nekhlyudov,
it is unfortunate that the 'politicals' are kept separate from the
criminals in their long journey to Siberia. After all, it is the class from
which those criminals have grown that the intellectuals seek to
liberate. 'And yet,' Kryltsov says, 'not only do we not know them, but

we do not want to know them, and worse than this, they hate us and think of us as their enemies. And that is terrible.'[56]

At this point they are interrupted by the hard-line revolutionary figure of Novodvorov — (Newcourt, the name means; by implication, New Regime). '"There's nothing terrible about it," said Novodvorov, who had been listening to the conversation. "The masses always revere just power," he said with his rasping voice. "At present the Government has power and so they revere it and hate us; tomorrow we shall be in power — and they will revere us."'[57]

Tolstoy was not such a fool that he could not see that the Novodvorovs would one day exercise power, simply because it was they who most wanted it. But there is another figure at the end of *Resurrection* who haunts us no less. We do not get the full measure of Tolstoy unless we realise, even now, seventy years after Lenin, that this voice is even stronger than that of Novodvorov. Whether we consider that it is so will depend more on us than on the novel. This figure, like so much in the later part of the book, is a *trouvaille* of Tolstoy's, an invention in the truest sense of the word. Into the mouth of the little old man whom Nekhlyudov meets on the ferry, Tolstoy puts a speech which is directly based on a letter which he received in October 1899 from an anonymous correspondent in Baku. The correspondent was a free man. He had no name. He was simply an individual, a *chelovek*. In his brilliant use of this figure, Tolstoy offers the clue, if they could only read it, to the innumerable people whom this novel offended.

As is notorious, his wife was offended by it, which was one of the impulses which kept him writing. So were all 'decent' people in Russian society. In Paris, the book was rejected by several publishers on the grounds of impropriety which, considering it was the decade and city which published Zola, was not bad going. Passages about large breasts and beguiling eyes were no less abhorrent to Tolstoy's Quaker friends and his many other goody-goody fellow travellers abroad. Mudie's, the lending library in London, at first refused to stock the book when it appeared in translation. In the first U.S. edition of the book, Chapter Seventeen of Part I was actually cut out altogether. In Russia itself, the bureaucracy could not be expected to like the Dickensian satire on the law, nor the depiction of brutality in prisons, nor the suggestion that draconian punishments were not merely barbaric but also ineffectual. Likewise, Orthodox fellow travellers, of whom there were many, could enjoy being shocked by

Tolstoy's deliberately blasphemous account of Mass in the prison chapel, for 'to not one of those present, from the priest and the superintendent down to Maslova, did it occur that this Jesus, whose name the priest repeated in wheezy tones such an endless number of times, praising Him with outlandish words, had expressly forbidden everything that was done there'.[58]

And in each of these cases, the objection is a collective one. If you write thus, you cannot be one of us; anathema, anathema, anathema. For Tolstoy, however, as for all great Christian artists, there is something ludicrous about believing that we can journey towards the truth collectively. Though, upon our arrival, we find ourselves together, we shall always have made the journey alone. That is the truth embodied in the nameless Melchisidech encountered on the ferry.

'I have absolutely no faith, because I believe no one; no one but myself,' the old man replied, just as quickly and decisively.

'But how can you believe in yourself?' said Nekhlyudov, joining the conversation. 'It is possible to be mistaken.'

Shaking his head the old man replied decisively: 'Not in *life*.'

'Then,' asked Nekhlyudov, 'why are there different faiths?'

'There are different faiths because they believe in other people and not in themselves. I believed in other people and I wandered about as if I was in a swamp. And I got so lost that I did not hope to get out of the swamp. Old Believers and New Believers and Sabbatarians, and all those other sects like the Molokans and the Castraters. Each faith just praises itself and so there they all are, crawling about like blind puppies. There are many faiths but One Spirit [*Dukh*]. Both in you, and in me and in him. That means if everyone believes in the spirit in himself, everyone will be united.'[59]

This man who believes so much in *Dukh*, Spirit, might strike us at first as a bit of a Dukhobor; but Tolstoy doubtless knew by now that the followers of Peter the Lordly, like the Tolstoyans of the Croydon Brotherhood, were no longer listening to the voice of the spirit within them, and attending instead to some new-made orthodoxy as interpreted by someone else. New Dukhobor was but old priest writ large. It may be thought that the old Melchisidech with no name carries individualism to the point of lunacy, as Tolstoy himself wished to do. But it is an essential part of the Christian inheritance that individualism can't be taken too far. All men, since Christ, are islands, entire of themselves.

In the years during which Tolstoy had been telling the world how it ought to behave, there had been many occasions when he had been tempted to lay down the mantle of the prophet and take up that of the hierarch. Chertkov and the Tolstoyans did, in effect, regard Tolstoy as the founder of a new religion, and themselves as the appropriate guardians of the sacred truth. But this was not how Tolstoy saw himself. In November 1888, a girl came to see him, asking how she should live, and when she had gone, he felt depressed. It was a fundamental part of his experience and belief that we are each guided by our own conscience. And yet, here came these people, like the girl, wishing to be guided, not by their own conscience but by Tolstoy's. It was all wrong.

> I tried to persuade this young lady not to live according to my conscience, as she wanted to do, but according to her own. But she, poor girl, doesn't even know if she has a conscience of her own. That is a great evil. What people need most of all is to find out for themselves and to develop their own conscience and then live according to it: and not, as everybody does, take somebody else's completely foreign, inaccessible conscience and then live without one at all, but lie, lie, lie in order to look like a person living according to some other chosen person's conscience. I truly prefer a convivial rake who never reasons and rejects all rational consider- ations to a thinker who lives according to someone else's conscience, i.e. without one. The rake may develop a conscience, but the other man will never do so until he returns to the state of the first man.[60]

'He is a Tolstoyan,' he once said contemptuously of a visitor to the house, 'that is a man with convictions utterly opposed to mine.'[61]

Boris Pasternak, whose father Leonid did such hauntingly successful illustrations for *Resurrection*, was never more truly Tolstoyan than when he made Zhivago say, 'The Gospels are an offer, a naïve and tentative offer: "Would you like to live in a completely new way? Would you like to enjoy spiritual beatitude?" And everyone was delighted, they all accepted, they were carried away by it for thousands of years. . . . When the Gospels say that in the Kingdom of God there are neither Jews nor Gentiles, do they just mean that all are equal in the sight of God? I don't believe it means only that — that was known already — it was known to the Greek philosophers and the Roman moralists and the Hebrew prophets. What the Gospels tell us is that in this new way of life and of communion, which is born of the heart and which is called the Kingdom of God, there are no nations, but only persons.'[62]

Resurrection explores and celebrates this idea with profound intelligence. Its author is under no illusions, as the Tolstoy of the pamphlets sometimes is. He knows that the tyranny of the bureaucrats, bishops, judges, procurators and generals will one day give place to the tyranny of the revolutionaries and that this will probably be infinitely worse. But the novel asserts that you don't destroy the evil of the system by replacing it with another system. Only persons can undermine systems. And the more twentieth-century leaders have ruthlessly attempted to behave as though persons were statistics, the more prophetic *Resurrection* has become. Hence its vast popularity in the Soviet Union in the days of Lenin and Stalin. Once the Politburo and the Cheka and the Gulag and the whole odious machinery of Soviet Communism had been established, there was no means of undermining it by political or military means. And yet individuals did not just survive. It was by being individuals that, in a million tiny areas, they did in effect defeat the system, as we learn from the testimony of Solzhenitsyn, Nadezhda Mandelstam and others. In books like *The Gulag Archipelago* or *Hope against Hope* we discover that human individuality, like the grass between the paving stones at the beginning of Tolstoy's novel, is ultimately indestructible.

Without it, art cannot flourish — one reason why twentieth-century art, with its love of trends and movements, has been such a strange mixture of worthless, official stuff and individual brilliance, and why so many of the best poets and novelists of the twentieth century have not been westerners busily following the latest fashion, but Russians who had reason to cherish their artistic individuality. *Resurrection* is an exciting monument in Tolstoy's own life because, in the course of writing it, he rediscovered and reasserted his artistic freedom. Whether it was Chertkov's absence, or a particularly helpful bout of hatred for his wife, or the knowledge that he was seventy years old and approaching the end of his creative life, who can tell? But with an energy which he had not been able to rouse since finishing *Anna Karenina*, Tolstoy wrote his great novel.

The undertaking disrupted the entire household, particularly in its last year of 1899-1900. Visitors, children, in-laws — anyone who could write — was enlisted to help Sofya Andreyevna to copy and recopy Tolstoy's semi-legible manuscript. Then there were interruptions when Tolstoy fell ill. Sometimes, his stomach was cripplingly painful. What did he expect, asked Sofya Andreyevna, if he sat down at the table and ate three cucumbers? On other occasions, she would insist that his *masseur* rub the small of Tolstoy's back three times a day. At other moments, the story just got stuck.

After he had reached Part III of the novel, he was seized with uncertainty about how the story should proceed. Should Maslova accept Nekhlyudov's gallant offer of marriage or not? This uncertainty held up the writing for several weeks and Tolstoy could do nothing except play games of Patience until the matter was resolved in his head. This was an habitual way with him of coping with writing problems. If the game came out, she would marry Nekhlyudov; if not, she would turn him down.[63]

There is never much likelihood of 'winning' a game of Patience. Tolstoy's instinct knew better than his mind what shape the story should take. We may only wonder that he was in any doubt, for, to the reader, it is clear that he is not only exercising his own artistic freedom in *Resurrection*. He is also reworking and resolving his relationship with the giants: as some critics would say, wrestling with the anxiety of influence. The characters of Nekhlyudov and Yevgeny Onegin could hardly be more different, nor those of Tanya and Maslova. Nevertheless, for one who had Pushkin's poem in the bone, as it is in all literate Russian bones, there could be no surprise in the dénouement of *Resurrection. 'Ya vas proshu, menya ostavit!* [I beg you, leave me!]'[64] The heroine's rejection of the hero, in terms of the simple mechanics of the plot, is purely Pushkinian.

The stuff of the story, its actual matter, is altogether un-Pushkinian. These prisoners, exiles, whores, revolutionaries and social destitutes are not the characters we should expect to find in the pages of the early Tolstoy either. They seem to belong to another novelistic world. Twenty years previously, Tolstoy had told Strakhov that he did not know 'a better book in all modern literature — Pushkin included' than Dostoyevsky's *The House of the Dead*. Dostoyevsky, by paradox, never wrote more straightforwardly, more Tolstoyanly, than in this prototype of all Russian prison stories. *Resurrection* is both a homage to Dostoyevsky's descriptions of Siberia and a proud artistic assertion that Tolstoy can write with the same vigour about prison villages, convoys and punishment blocks as he had, in his prime, written about ballrooms and battlefields.

This earlier self, the Tolstoy of *War and Peace*, is the third of the great giants, after Pushkin and Dostoyevsky, whom he confronts in *Resurrection*. There is here a deliberate and fascinated reconsideration of some of his own greatest effects, as though a composer had chosen to introduce a theme from some grand earlier symphony into a later, more tightly wrought chamber work. One obvious such occasion is the scene where Maslova (still, then, Katyusha) comes to catch a glimpse of her beloved Nekhlyudov at the railroad station. It is quite as vivid as anything in *Anna Karenina*. But in Maslova, there is always this sense that life will have its power to snatch her back from the jaws of death. She is not a 'good' person; but in a way which the moral Nekhlyudov can never be, she is good at being alive: competent in the way that an animal is competent to look after itself. Her separation from Nekhlyudov is enforced in our minds by the image, on that wet, muddy, autumn night, of her trying to catch Nekhlyudov's attention. He is in the train, just passing through. She is pregnant, ruined. He does not know about any of that. He does not know that she is pregnant; he does not even know that she is there, looking at him, as he lolls back on the velvet upholstery of the railroad car and plays cards in his shirtsleeves.

As soon as she recognised him, she knocked on the pane with a frozen hand. But at that very moment, the third bell rang, and the train slowly moved off, at first back, and then one after another the interlocking carriage began to move forward in jerks. One of the players got up with the cards in his hand and began to look out of the window. She knocked again and pressed her face against the glass. At that moment, the carriage by which she was standing started up with a jerk and pulled out. She followed it, looking through the window. The officer wanted to lower the window, but just could not. Nekhlyudov got up and, pushing aside that officer, began to lower the window. The train increased speed. She was walking with quick steps, not falling behind, but the train was gathering more and more speed and at the very second that the window was lowered, the guard pushed her aside and leapt into the carriage. Katyusha was left behind, but even so, she ran along the wet boards of the platform; then the platform stopped and she could only just stop herself falling, as she ran down the steps to the ground. She ran, but the first-class carriages were far ahead. The second-class carriages had already whizzed past her. Then, even more quickly, the third-class carriages passed, but she kept running.

When the last carriage had shot by, with the lamp behind, she was behind the water-tank and no longer sheltered from the wind, which snatched her headscarf from her head and made her dress stick to one side of her legs. . . .[65]

It is at that moment, almost literally dragging her way through mud and slime like the girl in the song, that she decides to do away with herself by throwing herself under the next train to pass. The little girl who is running along beside her, trying to keep up, calls for her to come home, but she goes unheeded. And then, as so often in this book, nature itself intervenes.

He, that is to say the child, his child which was in her, suddenly started, knocked against her, and smoothly stretched himself and then again started to push with something thin, delicate and sharp. And suddenly, everything which a moment before had so tortured her that it seemed it was impossible to live, all her malice against Nekhlyudov and her desire to be avenged on him, if only by her own death, all this suddenly receded. She calmed down, straightened herself, tied back her shawl and hastily went home.

Exhausted, wet, muddy, she returned home and from that day began that spiritual transformation in consequence of which she became what she was now. From that dreadful night, she stopped believing in God and in the good. Before that, she really believed in God and believed that other people believed in Him; but from that night, she became convinced that no one believed in this and that everything they say about God and His laws is a fraud.[66]

The popular Soviet editions of the novel to this day neuter the passage. They say merely that from that day onwards, she stopped believing in goodness, which the scenes of her life in prison prove to be untrue; and they add a sentence of propaganda about people only using belief in God as a means of deceiving others. Tolstoy's point — identical to one about himself in *A Confession* — is thus completely lost.[67] Maslova has the gift of life (which Anna Karenina loses a long time before her suicide) but she is rudderless without God. Maslova has plenty of innate decency, but no sense, as she had before, of a moral law governing her destiny. Her conscience has been stifled. Something of the same kind, the book would have us believe, has happened to Russia itself. By the end of *Anna Karenina*, we have come to doubt the simple patriotism of *War and Peace*. To Nikolay

Rostov, it was natural to love Russia. For Levin, cultivating his garden while the troops move into the Balkans, patriotism has lost its innocence. In *Resurrection*, sex itself has undergone a similar contamination. The novel ends on the stirring note of Nekhlyudov reading the Gospel of St. Matthew and deciding to go out and establish a Kingdom of Heaven on earth.

Many readers have wondered how such a thing is possible for someone who follows Tolstoy's line of complete non-involvement in all forms of political life. Nekhlyudov seems like the man censured by Pastor Bonhoeffer in his book *Ethics* (a book born out of the agonising choices of political involvement under the Government of Hitler): 'If any man tries to escape guilt in responsibility, he detaches himself from the ultimate reality of human existence. . . . He sets his own personal innocence above his responsibility for men.'[68]

The novel fails to recognise the fact which so obsessed Dostoyevsky, that if good men do not hold on to power, bad men will take it from them. Power is not a neutral thing which will simply evaporate if, as Nekhlyudov, with such incredible folly, desires, you disband the armies and let all the criminals out of gaol. Anyone with sense knows what would happen if murderers were allowed to roam free, or if small countries had no defence against large countries. St. Augustine remarked that it was a characteristic of heretics that 'they are unable to see what is perfectly obvious to everyone else'.[69]

A contemporary of Tolstoy's was to write, 'Power is great and terrible because it is a sacred thing. . . . Power exists not for itself alone but for the love of God. . . . To live without power is impossible.' These words were written by Pobedonostsev himself, whose *Reflections* contain more obvious sense than *Resurrection*. 'Only fools have a clear conception of everything. The most cherished ideas of the human mind are found in the depths and in the twilight: around these confused ideas which we cannot classify revolve clear thoughts, extending, developing and becoming elevated.'[70] It is usually suggested that Pobedonostsev censored *Resurrection* merely out of pique, because he objected to the portrait of himself as Toporov. (*Topor* means an axe and the adjective from it, *toporny*, means clumsy or uncouth.) In Nekhlyudov's interview with Toporov, Tolstoy places into the fictitious Procurator's mouth the exact words spoken by Pobedonostsev to Tanya: 'I know all about this case. . . . and I am most grateful to you for reminding me of it. The provincial authorities have been somewhat over-zealous. . . .'[71]

Certainly, Pobedonostsev would not have liked the assertion that 'in the depth of his soul he did not believe anything. . . .' or 'his attitude to the religion which he upheld was like that of a poultry keeper to the offal on which he feeds his fowls: offal is very unpleasant, but the fowl eat it and love it, therefore they must be fed on offal.'[72]

The personal slights, however, extending throughout a whole chapter, got past the censor and were published and distributed to thousands of readers. Russia in 1899 was not a nice place to live. But there have been worse places, such as Russia in 1935. It is worth remembering that the assault on Pobedonostsev (one of the most powerful men in Russia) was allowed to be read by the entire literate populace. Compare this with the fate of Osip Mandelstam, a little over thirty years later, who committed the crime of reading aloud to a disloyal friend, in what he thought was privacy, a sixteen-line poem which denounced Stalin, 'the Kremlin mountaineer'. By the standards of a later generation, the draconian 'Pob' was a softy.

But he recognised that in *Resurrection* Tolstoy had composed the most unforgettable assault on the Russian Imperial regime. Both abroad and in Russia, *Resurrection* was more widely disseminated than anything Tolstoy had previously written. For every person who had read *War and Peace* there were twenty who had read *Resurrection*; and the book makes it abundantly clear that Russia is about to explode. The medicines prescribed by it may be foolish; the diagnosis of the illness was accurate.

Pobedonostsev could not stop intelligent foreigners from reading the book and concluding that Russia was in a terrible political mess. But, as Procurator of the Holy Synod, he could not ignore Tolstoy's claim that Russia had departed, not merely from decency, but from God himself. It was in this area that the propaganda was between Tolstoy and the Government was to be waged, for, short of locking Tolstoy up and making him into a political martyr, there was little the Government could do, save take the extremest possible measures to brand Tolstoy as a godless heretic.

The trouble with the war was that both parties played into the other's hands. To be anathematised by Pobedonostsev was just what Tolstoy wanted. Part of the daemon, the impulse which kept him writing the novel, was the liberating knowledge that he was striking out on his own and annoying, not just the Procurator, but many other people as well. In England, where the book was banned by the circulating libraries, it is doubtful whether Chertkov liked the book all that much. And it must have been with unmixed glee that Tolstoy watched his wife transcribing the manuscript and correcting the proofs, her brow furrowed with disapproval. She described herself as 'repelled by the calculated cynicism of his description of the Orthodox liturgy. For instance, "The priest extended to the people the gilt image of the gallows on which Jesus Christ was executed" instead of "the cross". The sacrament he calls "*kvass* in a cup". It is scurrilous and I hate it.'[73] She did not dare to object, or she would lose the right to keep *Resurrection* for her Collected Edition. She was meant to hate it. So were the clergy, with whom Tolstoy had been enjoying a battle ever since he had published *A Confession*.

That there were imperfections in the Orthodox Church, no one would deny. Pobedonostsev imagined a self-righteous foreigner, an Englishman, coming to Russia and saying, 'Prove me your faith by your deeds!' Pobedonostsev admitted that if an Orthodox were challenged in this way 'he could only hang his head. He would feel that he had nothing to show, that all was imperfect and disorderly. But in a minute he might lift up his head and say, "We have nothing to show, sinners as we are, yet neither are you beyond reproach. Come to us, live with us, see our faith, study our sentiments, and you will learn to love us."'[74] Tolstoy, however, was a tougher nut to crack than the supercilious foreign visitor. He had been baptised and brought up in the Orthodox Church and he did not like what he found. In *Resurrection*, he depicted the Orthodox religion in as offensive a manner as he could. He said nothing of the good which poor Orthodox priests did in the towns, nor of the mystical tradition kept alive in the monasteries, such as the Optina monastery where he himself had been a grateful visitor. By inserting such crude attacks upon the Church into his novel, Tolstoy enabled the Government, in the person of Pobedonostsev, to sidetrack the terrible political assault which the book represented. The Church could respond in a manner which was calculated to make Tolstoy a suspect character in the eyes of 'ordinary Russians'.

In the Cathedral of Our Lady at Leningrad, outside the iconostasis, there are two western pulpits, the gift of some foreign potentate to the Tsars. The pulpit has no place in the devotional life of the Orthodox. When a sermon is preached it is from the steps just outside the iconostasis. These decorative pieces of ecclesiastical furniture in the cathedral have only been used once. On February 24, 1901, Metropolitan Anthony of St. Petersburg ascended into one of these pulpits and read the document which formally excommunicated Tolstoy from the Orthodox Church. It was published in the journal of the Church's Holy Synod and a decree went out through all the Empire that it was to be pinned to every church door in Russia.

Well known to the world as a writer, Russian by birth, Orthodox by baptism and education, Count Lev Nikolayevich Tolstoy, seduced by intellectual pride, has arrogantly risen against the Lord and His Christ and His Holy heritage, and has plainly in the sight of all repudiated his Orthodox Mother Church which reared and educated him and has dedicated his literary activity and the talent given to him by God to disseminating among the people teachings opposed to Christ and the Church, and to destroying in the minds and hearts of people their national faith, that Orthodox faith which has been confirmed by the Universe and in which our forefathers lived and were saved, and to which Holy Russia until now has clung and in which it has been strong. . . .[75]

There followed an itemisation of his particular heresies and a declaration that 'the Church does not reckon him as its member'.

Since Tolstoy had not reckoned himself a member of the Church for at least twenty years, one might think that all this, from the bishops, came a little late. No novel in the history of literature has ever achieved quite such an accolade, unless one considers that the Pope paid Charles Kingsley a greater compliment by placing *The Water Babies* on the Index of Forbidden Books. In the strange times in which Tolstoy was living, the denunciation of *Resurrection* by an irate, brocaded figure with a beard was a serious matter.

As Lenin knew so well, the majority of Russian people would never opt for a violent, still less for a Marxist revolution. But equally, there was an overpowering feeling that something had to be done, that things could not go on as before, that the bureaucracy was unfit to govern the Empire. Tolstoy became a focus for all this discontent precisely because he was so insistently not of any party, precisely because his howls of rage against the authorities were so irrational, and because he produced no serious programme of alternative action. He was no good at saying what should be done, but very good at saying what was wrong. Everyone with eyes in their head could see it. Pobedonostsev could see it. The fact that they excommunicated him after twenty years of attacking the Orthodox religion was just one symptom of the fact that their nerve was beginning to fail.

*   *   *   *

The edict of excommunication caused a sensation. At the time, there was a painting by Repin, 'Tolstoy at Prayer', on exhibit in a St. Petersburg gallery. It depicted the sage kneeling barefooted in the woods, a latter-day St. Francis. 'Repin painted me barefooted in a shirt. I have to thank him for not having taken my trousers off too,' Tolstoy remarked to Goldenweiser.[76]

On the day that the edict was pronounced, the Government forbade any mention of Tolstoy in the press. But crowds gathered in the gallery around this painting. People adorned it with flowers. It had become an icon.

Tolstoy himself was in Moscow that day. As he turned into Lubyanskaya Square, he saw a crowd of several thousand. 'There he is!' called out a voice and quoted with heavy irony from the deed of excommunication. 'The Devil in human form!' Cheers broke out. 'Hurrah, Lev Nikolayevich! Greetings! Hail to the great man!'[77] Dunayev, who was with Tolstoy at the time, managed to hustle him into a taxi, but this demonstration of solidarity, not to say idolatry, must have been pleasing to the newly denounced heretic. So, too, were the flood of letters, flowers, telegrams and expressions of sympathy which poured in as a result of the excommunication.

It was a common joke that there were two Tsars at that time in Russia: Nicholas II and Lev Nikolayevich Tolstoy. His novel had touched a nerve and it was providing the most glaring demonstration of the political power of art. But that power was not just political. While the crowds hurrahed and the bishops had time to wonder whether they had done the right thing in giving the book so much free publicity, Tolstoy felt — most unusual for him — an intense feeling of inner satisfaction, of artistic achievement. After *Anna Karenina*, there had been a nervous and imaginative collapse which made him revile his own genius, and hate the 'magazine story about an officer falling in love with a married woman'. With *Resurrection* he suffered no such spiritual reaction. Gorky describes him reading passages of the book aloud to a group of friends. When he had finished, he paused and looked up with a smile. He said, 'The old man wrote it well.'[78]

461

Chapter Eighteen
Sad Steps

1901 - 1905

To be Ant Brothers meant only to screen ourselves from everyone, to separate ourselves from everyone and everything.

Tolstoy, *Reminiscences*

'The public has laughed at Tolstoy's excommunication. In vain did the bishops insert a Church Slavonic text into their statement. It was all too insincere, or smelling of insincerity.'[1] This was Anton Chekhov's view, and he probably spoke for most intelligent people. In order to emphasise the boorishness of the Church authorities, Tolstoy wrote a reply to Pobedonostsev and his ecclesiastical quislings, in which he was frank in his disbeliefs, and attractively humble in his expression of belief. He admitted that he did not think Jesus was God. Indeed, he said that to pray to Jesus as if He were God was the greatest blasphemy. But he did believe in love. The more love everybody had, the closer we would all be to establishing the Kingdom of God on earth. Governments hate this sort of thing as much as the idealistically-minded young like it. Copies of Tolstoy's *Credo* were circulated in great numbers among the students and the malcontents.

Meanwhile, it looked as if the God of the Church might be displeased with Tolstoy, who became increasingly frail, and at the end of June, 1901, nearly died of malaria.[2] He had no sooner recovered from the first attack than he was struck down by a second. The doctors ordered him south for the winter, and a kind friend of Cousin Alexandrine's, the Countess S. V. Panina, offered him the run of her luxurious villa at Gaspra, on the southern shore of the Crimea. In September, accompanied by his wife, and two of his daughters, Sasha and Masha, he set out. Two Tolstoyan disciples managed to attach themselves to the party — Boulanger and Goldenweiser. They were able to note down the extraordinary popularity of the Master. As the train stopped at Kharkov, for example, throngs of students, having heard that

Tolstoy was on board, ran up and down the platform peering through the train windows to catch a glimpse. 'Get well soon! God bless you! Hurrah for Tolstoy!' The whole station echoed to such cries when the old man agreed to appear at the window of his carriage to wave to the young people.

He was well enough, as they made their journey through the Crimea, to explore Sebastopol on foot, and to point out to Boulanger war relics in the museum. But then they came upon a photograph of himself, and the place lost its savour. 'How sad. What's the point in that expensive building, and that elaborate collection of old buttons and shell fragments? All this horror should be forgotten, it's terrible, terrible. . . .'[3]

The confrontation with an old self was what horrified him at Sebastopol. Once settled in the warmth and the comfort of Countess Panina's villa at Gaspra, however, the images of former selves occasionally fascinated him.

One day, as he sat looking at the sea, with two younger literary visitors, he turned to one, Anton Chekhov, and asked 'Did you fuck a lot of whores in your youth?' Chekhov was embarrassed and mumbled. Tolstoy, momentarily aglow with the excitements of his earlier sins, said clearly, 'I was an indefatigable fucker.' The other man, Maxim Gorky, who did not expect such 'peasant' vocabulary from an aristocrat, was disconcerted by the exchange, and noted it down in his *Reminiscences of Tolstoy*.

It was a happy conjunction, this, of Tolstoy, Chekhov and Gorky all in the Crimea at the same time. Chekhov, who was within a few years of his premature death, and had just got married, had come to live at Yalta in the hope that the climate would help his tuberculosis. In his youth, Chekhov had idolised Tolstoy and been carried away by 'Tolstoyan' ideas, but his natural sense of irony and common sense had weaned him away from such dreams. Nevertheless, he saw in Tolstoy a great moral force for good, as well as the greatest of Russian writers. Tolstoy, too, profoundly admired Chekhov's fiction, and had copied the story *Darling* into his daily breviary, *The Circle of Reading*. 'Chekhov has given us an ideal type of woman in *Darling* — self-sacrificing, kindly, whose main attribute is love, and without thought of self she serves to the end the person she loves.'

'That is what Lyovochka likes!' interrupted his wife, with some justice. 'A type of woman — a she-animal, slave, lacking in all initiative, interests! Wait on your husband, serve him, bear and feed children!'[4]

The one thing Tolstoy was unable to admire in Chekhov was his dramatic bent. 'Shakespeare's plays are bad enough,' he would say, putting his arm around Chekhov and squeezing him, 'but yours are even worse!' 'There is no real action,' as he noted after a production of *Uncle Vanya*, 'no movement towards which the conversation of the neurasthenic intellectuals tend. It is incomprehensible what Chekhov wanted to say anyway.'[5]

Chekhov took all this criticism in good part. The photographs of Tolstoy in the Crimea with his family and with 'literary' visitors gives us a sad glimpse of the manner in which his last days might have been spent. He always got on best with young or younger men, and life was much happier when he was surrounded by people who revered him for his literary genius rather than for his views.

These views inevitably cropped up. But it was a different matter when they were aired with intelligent friends who had minds of their own. There was the comical moment — after he had shocked Gorky with his foul language — when he leant forward and fixed the young man with his deep-set eyes. 'I'm more of a peasant than you!' he asserted — surprising words for the low-born genius Gorky to hear from a count.[6] Gorky, who dreamed of violent revolution in Russia, and threw in his lot with the Bolsheviks, nevertheless recognised in Tolstoy something which transcended politics, and even art itself.

'Why don't you believe in God?' Tolstoy asked him one day.

'I have no faith.'

'That is not true. You are a natural believer, and you can't live without God. You will come to feel it soon. If you don't believe it is out of stubbornness or hatred, because the world is not the way you want it to be. Another thing is that people sometimes don't believe because they don't dare. That happens to the young. They worship some woman but they don't want to let her see it; they are afraid that she won't understand — they've no courage. Faith, like love, demands courage and boldness. You must tell yourself, "believe" and everything will be all right.'

Gorky greeted this speech with silence, but Tolstoy raised a finger and said, 'You can't avoid that question by saying nothing.' 'And I,' Gorky remembered, 'who do not believe in God, looked at him, I don't know why, with a great deal of circumspection and a little awe too. I looked at him and I thought "This man is like God." '[7]

How much better it would have been for Tolstoy to have died there when he was living at Gaspra — the family all around him, and reasonably at peace, and in the company of two of the greatest Russian writers, Chekhov and Gorky.

When they parted, Tolstoy kissed Chekhov and said, 'Don't write any more plays, old thing.'[8]

Tolstoy used to say that Chekhov would have been a better writer had he not also been a doctor. Chekhov's professional opinion was that Tolstoy was a very sick man and might die suddenly at any minute. In fact, when they parted in 1902, Tolstoy had eight miserable years to live, and Chekhov himself less than a couple.

His health returned and he went back to Yasnaya Polyana. From St. Petersburg, he heard that his dear 'old girl' Alexandrine had been extremely ill, and close to death. 'I too was close to death,' he wrote to her, 'but here I am still not dead and sometimes I regret it — it was so good to be dying. . . . But sometimes I rejoice, because our senile lives are simply not useless, as people often think, but on the contrary, are of the utmost importance in terms of the influence which the old can exert on other people. You, with your ardent religious feeling and heart of gold, have probably experienced and are experiencing the enlightenment that illness gives. . . . My faith and the faith of all good people (forgive me for the immodesty of including myself among them) are one and the same thing: belief in God the Father who sent us into this world to do his will. . . .'[9]

Alexandrine struggled to reply, and thanked him for his letter in which she felt that note of sincerity which had echoed between them in younger days. She was on the way out. A few months later, she died — on March 4, 1904 — and yet another link with Tolstoy's youth was severed. But they were deceiving themselves if they thought that they shared a common faith. In more vigorous days, they had reached the point of agreeing not to discuss religion, since she had failed to convince Tolstoy of the truth of Orthodoxy, and he was unable to be polite about the subject.

Nineteen hundred and three was the year in which he wrote what is perhaps his most devastating assault on institutional Christianity — *The Restoration of Hell*, a fable worthy of Swift. For about three hundred years after the death of Christ, Hell is empty, save for Beelzebub himself. Christ has led out the captive souls, and taught them a new way of living, which the Christians all follow. But after a long period of loneliness, Beelzebub hears noises above his head, and a minor devil pops down to see him. This junior tempter reveals, almost without prompting, that human beings have overthrown the teachings of Jesus in favour of something called the Church. They have taken to ignoring Christ's words, squabbling about trivialities and persecuting anyone with whom they disagree.

'But can it be that things are exactly as they were before? Are there fornicators, robbers and murderers?' asked Beelzebub, already beginning to cheer up.

The devils, also cheerful now, spoke at once, trying to show off in front of Beelzebub.

'Not exactly as they were before but better than ever!' one of them shouted. 'We can't cram all the adulterers into the old quarters,' another one piped up. . . .[10]

The piece ends with a terrible dance, in which the devils who have invented art, culture, education, medicine, socialism, drunkenness, women's rights and science all join the devil who invented the Church and parade themselves gleefully before the chief of devils. It is Tolstoy's most acidly despondent, most hilariously misanthropic piece of work.

*   *   *   *

Within months of losing Alexandrine, Tolstoy was faced with the death of his last surviving brother, Sergey. In appearance the two old men were remarkably alike. Photographs of the pair, with their long, white, Santa Claus beards, could be of twins. And yet there is something lacking in Sergey's face: to the camera, it looks merely as though Sergey lacks Lev's anguish. We know that he lacked his brother's genius. And, as far as Lev was capable of judging, he entirely lacked his brother and sister's religious feelings.

Nevertheless, for Tolstoy blood was thicker than water. It did not in the end matter to him very much that his brother rejected the great truths of Tolstoyism as so much tommy-rot. Pirogovo, the Volkonsky estate which Sergey had inherited at the time of his majority, had been run on very different lines from Yasnaya Polyana. There, the serfs were still serfs. They bowed at their master's approach. He was a strict, if benign, landlord, who, unlike his younger brother Lev, kept things neat and in order. Lawns got mown. Harvests were gathered in due season. Fences were mended. Pot-holes were filled in. His stables were still full of splendid horses. He was a hard-drinking, cynical squire. His gipsy wife Masha had been married grudgingly long after the birth of her children, and was kept in subjugation. But none of this stopped friendly, and quite frequent, visits between the two brothers. By August 1904, Sergey was dying, hideously, of cancer of the face and tongue. Lev went over to visit him for one last time, and came back to Yasnaya on August 22. There was no point in staying. His brother was in too much pain. When he died four days later, without any awareness he was dying, and without any faith, Tolstoy realised that death reduced all differences to the level of triviality. 'All is well with him just the same.'[11]

At Sergey's funeral, Tolstoy helped to carry the coffin; the last of the brothers. Now, it was just Lev and Marya who remembered the Ant Brotherhood. In his *Reminiscences*, composed a few years later, Tolstoy recalled that, much as he had loved his other two brothers, 'I was enraptured by Sergey, copied him, adored him and wanted to be like him. I was enraptured by his handsome appearance, his voice (he was always singing), his drawing, his high spirits and in particular (though it seems an odd thing to say) the spontaneity of his egotism,'[12] a highly Tolstoyan thing to admire. Memories of the boy Sergey surged back: Sergey keeping chickens, sketching and painting them to perfection, and feeding the birds by squeezing long sausages of black and white bread through the keyhole of their coop; Sergey and some village boy, at the age of about nine, tobogganing down a hill at Yasnaya Polyana and narrowly avoiding death as they whooshed beneath the feet of three horses pulling along a *troyka* in the snow. He remembered the Ant Brotherhood huddled under chairs and conversing in low secret voices. For 'to be "Ant Brothers". . . . meant only to screen ourselves from everyone, to separate ourselves from everyone and everything. . . .' What had begun, for orphans, as an emotional necessity had developed into a habit. To be born the child of privilege, with many siblings, is to enjoy a peculiar emotional advantage over the rest of the world.

Pirogovo, with its many servants, and its well-organised *seigneurial* routines, represented a way of life which was soon doomed to pass away forever, as surely as its master had done. It was here perhaps that Lev Nikolayevich conceived his remarkable story *After the Ball*. He wrote it out in a single day, the previous August, at Yasnaya

Polyana. Together with *The Restoration of Hell*, it represents the very best of Tolstoy's later genius. The extreme popularity which the tale has always enjoyed in Russia (during those periods when it has not been censored) testifies to the singular truth about that country which it embodies. The original title was *Daughter and Father*. In the story, the protagonist, who loves the young daughter of a crusty old colonel, watches her dance with her father at a provincial ball. In his devotion to the young woman, the old man seems so touching, so humane, so civilised. Everything at the ball is beautiful — the clothes, the food, the cut glass and the crystal. But the young man returns from the ball at dawn and sees the old colonel in a different light. A court martial has taken place, and a poor wretch is being punished by running the gauntlet while all the men in his regiment strike him with the knout. For all his shrieks and pleas, the colonel shows no mercy.[13]

After the Ball is written with all the prophetic passion of the later Tolstoy, but with all the observant consciousness of things as they are which had characterised the great work of his maturity. It is great Tolstoy: it ranks with the very greatest things he ever wrote. And it shows how even at the end, when he was determined with his bronchitis-is-a-metal side to get the tone of the times completely wrong, nevertheless, with his artistic sense, he was unerring. Even if no other literature survived from Russia in the first decade of this century except this one, extremely short story, we should be able to predict the Revolution, and the subsequent character of Russian life in the twentieth century. It contains all the horrible paradox that a nation which can feel so tenderly has somehow been condemned to policemen and armies and governors of the most ruthless severity. *After the Ball* seems to contain within it the secret of how one nation could produce in the same generation Nijinsky, Shostakovich, Akhmatova. . . . and the Stalinist purges.

Tolstoy's attitude to this people, with whose history and sufferings he had so long identified, suffered the most painful strains as, throughout 1904 and 1905, it underwent the experiences of war and social revolution. Beelzebub, in *The Restoration of Hell*, had been puzzled by the central and fundamental question about war: which is, how do you persuade people to do it? Killing another human being because you do not like them is understandable, perhaps — though Tolstoy does not say so. But why should you be prepared to kill another human being merely because your Government has fallen out with their Government? Easy, says the devil who invented nationalism. 'We do it like this: we persuade each nation that it is the very best in the world — Deutschland *über alles*, France, England, Russia *über alles*, and that this nation (their name is legion) ought to dominate all the others.'[14]

This diabolical view is probably endemic in nationhood, but during the 1890s, it became epidemic. In the two decades before the First World War, fervent nationalism, for reasons which no historian has ever been able properly to analyse, began to run wild, leaving the poorer nations of the world entirely at the mercy of the rampaging lunacy of the richer ones. China was one of the worst-hit nations. The full extent of British exploitation of the Chinese will probably never be known: but it was the Chinese slaves, shipped over to the diamond mines of the Transvaal, who ensured that the wealth of South Africa continued to pour into London, even after the disasters of the Boer War; just as later (though subsequent British Governments all tried to hush it up and they buried the wretches in unmarked graves) it was Chinese slaves who were bought by the British and used as cannon-fodder on the Western Front between 1914 and 1916.

The Germans and the French were no better, nor were they alone. The Russians had no business in Manchuria, nor did the Japanese; but in those days the Chinese with a civilisation infinitely more ancient and distinguished than all their exploiters put together could do nothing about it. The Japanese considered that they owned the Chinese Liaotung Peninsula, and ever since the Russians had seized it from them in 1898 the Japanese wanted to get it back. They therefore staged a surprise raid on the Russian fleet at Port Arthur on February 8, 1904. It was no Pearl Harbour. They managed to destroy only one Russian battleship. But Port Arthur was besieged, and the war which ensued was a damaging one, with dreadful consequences. The Russians came to the rescue of their fleet, the Japanese held firm, and it was January 2, 1905, before the Russians surrendered Port Arthur. By then, a hundred and ten thousand Japanese had been killed in or around Port Arthur. In the land battles, notably the Battle of Mukden in February and March 1905, the casualties were of the order of fifteen thousand Russians and twenty-four thousand Japanese killed in one month.

The war was a humiliation for the Russians; it was the first time in modern history that an Asian power had achieved a victory over a European. 'Japan in the space of a few decades not only drew level

472

with European and American peoples, but surpassed them in technological advances,' Tolstoy observed. 'The success of the Japanese in the technology not only of war but of all material advances as well has shown how clearly and how cheap these technological advances which are called culture are. It doesn't cost anything to copy them and even to invent new ones. What is invaluable, important and difficult, is a good life. . . .'[15]

These reflections came to Tolstoy in the summer of 1905 after the Japanese had routed two Russian naval squadrons off the island of Tsushima. The war excited in him painful feelings of patriotism. In spite of his devotion to the religion and the mysticism of the East, it obviously hurt his national pride that the Russians were being defeated by yellow men. He put it down to the fact that the Russians were at least notionally Christians, whereas the cruel Japanese could give themselves up wholeheartedly to the art of war. 'Although we are bad Christians it is impossible not to hide the incompatibility between the Christian faith and war. Recently (that is in the last thirty years or so) this contradiction has come to be felt more and more [that is, by him. . . .]. And therefore in a war with a non-Christian people for whom the highest ideals are the fatherland and the heroism of war, Christian peoples are bound to be defeated. . . .'[16]

This view reflects not only a touching affection for his own fatherland, but also a gentle interpretation of Russia's predicament which is quite at variance with the spirit of the times. It is the voice of an Ant Brother speaking from under a chair. Later that summer, the elder statesman Sergey Witte accepted President Theodore Roosevelt's invitation to go to New Hampshire and enter peace negotiations with the Japanese. The American President had suggested himself as the peacemaker, and they spent the month of August bountifully doling out bits of Chinese territory to the Russians and the Japanese respectively. The Russians kept the Chinese Eastern Railway and the whole of the northern part of Manchuria. The Japanese got back the Liaotung Peninsula. Witte was a stubborn negotiator on the Russians' behalf, but no one could disguise the fact that it was a Japanese victory.

The war had seriously weakened the position of the Government and strengthened the hand of the violent revolutionaries. 'How right the Slavophils are when they say that the Russian people try to avoid power, that they run away from it. They are prepared to offer it to bad people rather than be soiled by it themselves,' Tolstoy observed.[17]

Rather than regarding this national characteristic as a disastrous one, Tolstoy added, 'I think that if that is so, they are right.' Not everyone agreed with him. The year 1905 was marked by a series of disruptions whose collective effect was to change Russia forever. It was particularly noticeable (considering how comparatively small they were in numbers) how powerfully instrumental were the urban proletariat in bringing about this social disturbance.

A strike was declared in the capital, which by January 7 immobilised St. Petersburg. Then on January 9 Father Gapon had led his famous demonstration. A crowd of a hundred and fifty thousand marched on the Winter Palace. They were forbidden by their sacerdotal leader to carry red flags or socialist paraphernalia. Instead they bore icons, religious banners and assurances of their 'unshakeable trust in the Tsar'.[18] They wanted a separation of Church and state; the introduction of income tax; the replacement of indirect taxation by progressive income tax; an amnesty for political and religious prisoners. As history knows, they were greeted by violence, and several hundred people were killed by Cossack troops.

After Bloody Sunday, as it came to be known, the general strike in St. Petersburg spread to all the large towns in the Empire. In February there were peasant revolts in the Kursk and Oryol provinces. In June, just before the Council of Peace in New Hampshire with the Japanese, the crew of the battleship *Potemkin* mutinied at Odessa. In defiance of police prohibitions, a joint congress of *zemstvo* and city representatives was held in Moscow in July demanding a representative assembly, the first steps towards a democratic Parliament and constitution. Meanwhile, there were petty mutinies going on throughout the armed forces, and outbreaks of rebellion and violence among the rural poor.

The whole Empire was seething: waiting for change. Russia suddenly felt young, vigorous, violent. Milton, just before the Civil War in England which ended in the execution of Charles I, wrote, 'Methinks I see in my mind a noble and puissant nation rousing herself like a strong man after sleep, and shaking her invincible locks. . . .'[19] This was what it was like in Russia in 1905. Tolstoy, who was rereading Taine's *History of the French Revolution*, knew quite well that his own woolly theories of universal love and brotherhood would cut no ice whatsoever with people who suddenly felt as if it were in the very air the possibility of changing a hateful and oppressive political system. Aylmer Maude tells us that when he visited Russia in

1902, Tolstoy was a national hero — the man who had dared to reply to the Synod and rebuke the Tsar. When Maude returned in 1906, things were very different. 'Politics had become to most people as the breath to their nostrils, and consequently Tolstoy, who was telling them to leave politics alone, was to the Liberals a stumbling-block and to the Socialists a snare.'[20] Tolstoy's role in the Revolution was analogous to the role of the Church in modern South Africa. When the whole thing is over and everyone is wallowing in blood one will see that the various well-meaning clergymen who believed themselves to be important to the people and their struggle are, after the event, all but forgotten.

Russia was changing. It was like the moment, described so incomparably by Tolstoy in *Resurrection*, when Nekhlyudov and Maslova, as very young people, emerge from the Easter liturgy in darkness and hear the sound of breaking ice coming to them upon the midnight air. Spring and dawn and resurrection are in the sound. On October 8, 1905, a railroad strike was declared, followed by general strikes in all the major cities of the Empire. The Bolsheviks at this stage were a tiny minority party representing the interests of a tiny minority of the population. They were deeply divided amongst themselves on questions of tactics and ideology. We are not to imagine all these discontented people as proto-communists, though, as Lenin gleefully recognised, they were doing the communists' work for them. They were 'a noble and puissant nation' who had had enough. They did not yet know in any detail what they wanted instead of the present absurdly unjust state of things. But they wanted change. The Emperor was guided in everything by his unpopular German wife, a stubborn, religious maniac who by now acted upon the advice of the holy man Rasputin. The Tsar's folly in retrospect is hardly possible to believe. His reaction to the October strikes was to say that he would appoint a strong military dictator to crush out the spirit of the times. His cousin the Grand Duke Nikolay Nikolayevich was selected for this unenviable role. The Grand Duke said that if appointed to such a role he would shoot himself, and that the Emperor must accept Witte's moderate proposal for an elected *Duma* or Constituent Assembly. At least a modest start had been made. They were miles away from having a decent system of government. But at least they had a *Duma*, a place where members (albeit elected chiefly by great landlords and rich businessmen) could criticise what was going on.

Tolstoy's irresponsible view that the Russians hated power and would not soil their hands with it was ultimately a romantic fiction. Their system was so constituted that they could not get their hands on power without huge constitutional upheaval. By the time of the second *Duma*, it looked as if some sort of reform might take place, but all hopes for this were dashed by the third *Duma*. The Tsar and his little circle of advisers were solely responsible for this terrible folly. Tolstoy, with the Slavophils and religious cultivators of indifference who agreed with his point of view, were also responsible in a small measure. After the abolition of slavery in 1861, there was nothing about the structure of nineteenth-century Russian society which could not have been reformed by a gradual process of liberalisation. The state could have offered religious freedom to the people and disestablished the Church. The tax system could have been reformed so that rich merchants and big landlords helped the masses rather than the other way around. The majority of the population of the Empire were peasant farmers, who merely wanted to farm their land in peace, owning their own property and harbouring their own profits. Tolstoy could not approve of them because he regarded it as an *a priori* truth, culled from the writings of Henry George, that land should be in public ownership. But public ownership implies an all-powerful state, and Tolstoy did not want that either. His muddled political thinking, which carried away so many Russians at the beginning of the century, was understandably discarded for wilder counsels. The fact that he ever had influence at all on any wide scale is a symptom of how terrifyingly out of control Russia had become.

Lenin, watching from abroad, was completely fascinated by the 'really glaring' contradictions in Tolstoy's works, ideas and teachings. Lenin was chiefly struck by the contradiction between the incomparable artist and the 'landowner obsessed by Christ'. He was unimpressed by the 'worn-out sniveller' who beat his breast and boasted to the world that he now lived on rice cutlets. But there are other Tolstoys. 'On the one hand, there is the pitiless criticism of capitalist exploitation, the exposure of violence perpetrated by the Government, the revelation of all the profound contradictions between the growth of wealth and the achievements of civilisation and the spread of poverty, the degradations and sufferings of the working masses.'[21]

Lenin, who was more relentlessly logical than Tolstoy, saw the vast contradictions in Tolstoy's person and standpoint as symptomatic of the 'those contradictory conditions in which the historical activity of the peasantry in our Revolution was set. . . .' Lenin saw that the interests of different groups of people must ultimately find a political expression. This is common sense, and therefore Tolstoy rejected it. But with the wise and imaginative part of himself he saw that if you refuse to soil your hands with power, there will be others who are not so squeamish.

*   *   *   *

This wilful absence of common sense in Tolstoy was ultimately the death of his artistic imagination. He had been trying to hammer it on the head ever since his breakdown following *Anna Karenina*. But it would not quite die. The battered baby obstinately kept crying. In spite of the fact that Tolstoy in various moods only wanted to be a Buddhist mystic or a peasant in a field or social prophet, his artistic imagination kept breaking out — the grass between paving stones. Witness *After the Ball*, dashed off in a single day.

Bronchitis-is-a-metal hated all this and between the years 1903 and 1906 he wrote and rewrote his ridiculous essay on Shakespeare in order to convince himself that art was an unnecessary adjunct to the good life.

The first time Tolstoy was taken to the Bolshoy Theatre as a little boy, he saw nothing at all. 'I did not know that it was necessary to look at the stage sideways and I looked straight in front of me at the opposite boxes.' He recalled this fact in 1903, when he was beginning to reread Shakespeare, and the tunnel vision which the story reveals is everywhere apparent in one of the most disagreeable productions of his later years: the long essay, *Shakespeare and the Drama*, finally published in 1906.[22] He spent three years of desultory work on the subject, rereading a lot of Shakespeare and his critics in preparation for this notoriously unsuccessful and somehow embarrassing attempt to dislodge Shakespeare from his pedestal. When we consider how much else was going on in Tolstoy's life at this time, the Shakespeare essay seems all the stranger. It was published in the year in which he nearly lost his wife, and he did lose his favourite daughter. When not distracted by his own illness, or that of his family, or by quarrels which tore Yasnaya Polyana apart, or by his followers being put into prison, or by his peasants causing an affray, or by the generally deteriorating state of Russia itself, Tolstoy still had a huge amount of literary work on hand. Even if he were never to finish *Hadji Murat* and *Father Sergius*, there was all the work of propaganda to be done — denunciations of war, capital punishment, property and oppression wherever they might be found, letters to followers and disciples all over the world, a compilation of spiritual reading. Why, in the middle of all this, did he choose to write fifteen thousand words of nonsense about Shakespeare?

The most famous bit of the essay is the passage where he tries to do for *King Lear* what, in *Resurrection*, he had done for the Orthodox liturgy. That is, he describes it in such a way that it sounds ridiculous. '"How old art thou?" "Not so young, sir, to love a woman for singing, nor so old to dote on her for anything," to which the King replies that if he likes him not worse after dinner he will let him remain in his service. This conversation fits in with neither Lear's position nor with Kent's relation to him, and is evidently put into their mouths only because the author thought it witty and amusing. . . .' etc. etc.[23] Tolstoy can construct arguments in this *reductio ad absurdum* manner so readily that he does not realise how inapposite and stupid his analyses of *King Lear* actually seem. George Orwell in a famous essay[24] suggested that the reason for this was that Tolstoy was himself Lear, blind to the folly of giving away all his possessions, and preparing unconsciously for running, white-bearded and half mad, out into the heath and the storm.

The dramatic force of Orwell's essay can never be forgotten, even though none of the details exactly fit (Lear had no sons, no recalcitrant wife, no followers with the operational skill of Chertkov, who, far from allowing his master to give anything to his family, engineered him into writing wills which all but disinherited the Tolstoys in favour of the Tolstoyans. Tolstoy, far from being betrayed by his daughters, was served by them devotedly. There are many other points of difference.) We tend to remember Orwell's image of Tolstoy-as-Lear and forget the rest of Tolstoy's essay which reveals the actual clue to the reason for its composition.

After *Anna Karenina*, Tolstoy apostasised from his view that novels should make us laugh and cry and present us with the illusion of living characters. Instead, he espoused the dreary and narrowing view that an artist's function was to tell the world how it should behave. In Shakespeare, who is the archetypal artist, the man who buries himself in the passions and sympathies of his created characters, Tolstoy met his greatest reproach, the most blatant possible reminder of what he had given up when, after *Anna Karenina*, he turned to writing works of half-baked religious thought. 'Shakespeare,' it has been wisely said 'displays the dance of human passion. . . . Hence he has to be objective; otherwise he would not so much display the dance of human passion, as talk about it.'[25] Tolstoy, who in his greatest fictitious creations seems second only to Shakespeare, sets out in his petty and destructive essay to show two things. First, he tries to show that Shakespeare could not portray human characters at all. Even Tolstoy cannot deny that Falstaff is 'a thoroughly natural and characteristic personage'; ('unfortunately,' he adds, with the sour note of some governess or puritanical village dominie, 'the artistic effect of the character is spoilt by the fact that it is so repulsive in its gluttony, drunkenness, debauchery, naughtiness, dishonesty. . . .').[26] But our impression that when we read the other works of Shakespeare we are being confronted by an extraordinary range of human characters and passions is, we gather from Tolstoy, quite illusory. Othello, Iago, Hamlet, Macbeth, Cleopatra, Romeo and Juliet, all are as wildly unreal as Lear himself. There is an almost Mephistophelian arrogance in the way that Tolstoy asserts Shakespeare's inability to depict character: there is the unspoken suggestion that if you want real characters you would find them in Tolstoy's early and greater novels; and there is the vandalistic desire to dismiss the whole idea of character in literature as of any importance.

But Shakespeare arouses in Tolstoy more than a horror of what he himself had abandoned in mid-career. Tolstoy is repelled by Shakespeare's generosity of temper, his largeness of view, his tolerance, his humanistic enjoyment of people being themselves. By the time he had grown old, all these qualities repelled Tolstoy. He quotes a German scholar, G. G. Gervinus, as saying that 'Shakespeare considers that humanity should not set itself ideals but that all that is necessary is a healthy activity and a golden mean in everything.' And then he goes on to discover in Shakespeare a scorn of the common people and a belief in political oppression. The truth is that Shakespeare's plays breathe a sunny common sense, in which the personality of the artist has been subsumed in the artifact. Political and ethical views can be extracted from the plays, but never with certainty because Shakespeare did not see it as his function to boss his audiences into thinking as he did. *Shakespeare and the Drama* does not make happy reading. When we compare Tolstoy's irascible, chuntering dismissal of Shakespeare as 'insignificant and immoral. . . . cannot possibly serve to teach the meaning of life' with the late romances from Shakespeare's own pen, there is an inescapable feeling of pathos. The essay on Shakespeare diminishes Tolstoy, not least because it feels as if it is motivated by unconscious envy, but chiefly because it is so very foolish. Like an idiot blinking at the sun, he claims that there is nothing to see because he has shut his eyes. Or perhaps he simply never stopped being a little boy, staring at the boxes on the other side of the theatre, never giving one glance to the stage, and being puzzled, after two uncomfortable hours, that the audience should be so loud in its applause for something he had not seen.

*   *   *   *

Tolstoy had achieved what almost every writer sets out to achieve: celebrity. He had done so on a scale unparalleled in the history of literature, and he paid the price of achieving fame as much for his views and his hostility to the system as for his literary masterpieces. Those who live by the news will perish by the news. This certainly happened to Tolstoy; the first famous man whose death rattle was inaudible because of the rolling Pathé news cameras outside the window. He was the first of many lesser figures in the twentieth century whose loudly and publicly expressed desire to be alone attracted crowds wherever he went. A crude claim, made by many writers, is probably true. The Russian bureaucracy reckoned that foreign visitors would only want to see three things in Russia — St. Petersburg, Moscow and Yasnaya Polyana. The journey between the two capitals was effected by rail. Rather than give visitors a true impression of what road travel was like in the rest of the Empire, they constructed the tarmacadamed highway down to Tula. Pilgrims could enjoy a smooth ride and all modern conveniences on their journey to the great enemy of progress.

Observers of the literary scene in Russia since Tolstoy's death cannot fail to be struck by the contrast between his treatment and that of dissidents in the reign of Stalin and since. There were plenty of figures in the bureaucracy who would have liked Tolstoy muzzled and locked up. Perhaps an element of subtlety contributed to the fact that, unlike his disciples, he was never himself imprisoned or sent into exile for his repeated lambasting of the whole social order, and his urging upon the populace of a programme of civil disobedience.

There was also an element of personal affection for the old man. Not only was he related to many former members of the Government

480

and the Court, but he had now become old, and the Russians, even more than the rest of us, revere old age. No British Government can ever have liked George Bernard Shaw or Bertrand Russell, but once they had passed the age of eighty, they both became almost national institutions. The sight of Russell being carried into police vans protesting against the nuclear threat was not a westernised version of Gulag. It became as good-humoured and as frivolous as everything else in English public life.

A little of this irony hung around Tolstoy's last days in Russia. Many of the pilgrims came because they believed that he was the Master, who had revealed to the world the great truths about human life. And in a sense this was true. Others came to pay homage to the greatest of Russian writers, which he unquestionably was. But a good number came with a mixture of such feelings blending with the simple desire to be entertained. And Tolstoy did not fail to oblige.

One of his hundreds of visitors was the young English writer Desmond MacCarthy, who had been given an introduction and was invited to stay at Yasnaya Polyana. He approached, up the rutted drive, through the famous turreted entrance, and came up to the low-slung, two-storeyed wooden house, by the standards of English country houses little more than a villa. It was a bright, hot, summer day. On the lawn, there was a Chekhovian scene. Countess Tolstoy was taking tea with her daughters and some relations. She rose to greet her young visitor and, all politeness, offered him tea. Her husband was out in the fields, but he would be returning shortly. Her husband always liked to show guests to their rooms by himself. She hoped that Mr. MacCarthy would understand.

Everyone spoke excellent English. The tea party was agreeable and mild. As he was finishing his second cup of tea MacCarthy looked up and saw that the Master was making his entrance: the cap, the long white beard, the belted peasant shirt and felt shoes all gave the visitor instant visual gratification: this was what he had come to see.

Tolstoy was completely without 'side', and very friendly. He led MacCarthy inside the house, speaking to him as if they had been friends all their life. He led the young man to a bedroom down a surprisingly narrow corridor. The room was exactly what was expected: an iron bedstead, a washstand, everything quite clean but austere. Tolstoy announced that he liked to be in his study in the later part of the afternoon, but that they would meet again for dinner. Oh, and there was one small thing — the chamber pot. If MacCarthy did not very much object, Tolstoy liked his guests to empty their own chamber pots. He felt that it was demeaning to ask the servants to perform this office on anyone else's behalf. MacCarthy agreed that he would empty his own slops, and Tolstoy shuffled off down the corridor.

While he was unpacking, MacCarthy heard some very different footsteps in the corridor, hastier, lighter steps. They approached his door, and someone knocked.

'Come in!'

It was Sofya Andreyevna.

'I hope that you are comfortable.'

'Very comfortable, thank you.'

'Has my husband shown you where everything is?'

'Yes, thank you very much Countess Tolstoy.'

'But has he' — her voice becoming shriller — 'has he told you about the chamber pot?'

'Yes, it is perfectly all right, I do assure you. I am quite happy to empty my own. . . .'

By now Sofya Andreyevna's voice is loud and sharp.

'Always he tells the guests this nonsense. Our lazy servants, what do we pay them for if they do no work? I must ask you most *strictly*, Mr. MacCarthy, not to empty your own chamber pot. It really is too humiliating that my husband should have asked you such a question!'

The summer nights were warm. The lawn was nearby. MacCarthy was young. The chamber pot went unused.[27] But the little incident reflected in miniature the conflict which was being enacted inside the house. Should one man ask another man to empty his pot? This is a lavatorial version of Lenin's great question — *Who? Whom?* — and Russia was to answer it in Lenin's way. That is to say, it was to bypass as wholly irrelevant both the Tolstoys' points of view. To Sofya Andreyevna, it was self-evident that servants should do as they were told. To Tolstoy, each man was an island entire to himself. In political terms, neither belief is true, but it did not stop them fighting the battle to the death.

Chapter Nineteen
Last Battles

1906 - 1910

My consciousness of *me* . . .

Letter to Chertkov

Nineteen hundred and six was a year for renewing old contacts and opening up old wounds. In February, after an estrangement of nine years, Sofya Andreyevna had invited Sergey Taneyev the composer to Yasnaya Polyana. The visit was not a success. They were both 'strained and unnatural'.[1] In August, another ghost from the past resurfaced: Chertkov. His mother was ill, and the authorities accepted a plea of clemency that he should be allowed to revisit Russia to see her.

There was only time, on this short trip, for Chertkov to make a brief visit to Yasnaya Polyana. He returned to England that autumn, still tireless in his work for the cause. Mysteriously enough, Tolstoyism (like so many other religions, including Christianity) had developed more easily in the absence of the Master. Its principles were clearer than ever. As Master and disciple sat facing one another, it was not quite clear any longer which was which. Seeing a mosquito crawling across Chertkov's by now balding head, Tolstoy stretched out affectionately and swatted it. 'What have you done?' asked the horrified Chertkov. 'You have killed a living creature, Lev Nikolayevich. You should be ashamed of yourself!'[2] What had begun in Tolstoy's soul as a spiritual reverence for life had become, in Chertkov's legalistic mind, an organised code as fanatical as that of the Jains.

If 1906 was a year of renewed links with the past, it was also a year of loss. In the spring of 1906, three of Tolstoy's daughters went abroad for a holiday. After a series of miscarriages, Tanya, at the age of 42, had managed to produce a baby. The experience left her exhausted, so Masha and Sasha took her to Rome for a recuperative few weeks. While they were there, Tolstoy wrote to Masha, 'I advise you to get the most that you can out of Europe. I myself don't want anything from it.' He went on to deplore the fact that the Russians were continually borrowing bits of 'political parties, electoral campaigns, etc. Terrible!' The only consequence of all this western-isation, in his view, would be that men would more and more come to abandon the soil, 'the only basis for an honourable and reasonable life'.[3] Like so many of Tolstoy's prophecies, this was the absolute opposite of what took place in Russia over the next thirty years. Lenin failed precisely because the *kulaks* refused to abandon the soil.[4] By recognising the advantages of moderate political reform and land ownership, Tolstoy would have protected the rights of the very people he claimed to be most estimable. As it was, by opposing all forms of government, and declaring that land ownership was wicked, he with his great influence helped to pave the way for the overthrow of the society in which the peasant smallholders were beginning to flourish. The only way that Stalin could defeat the *kulaks* and impose upon them his scheme of collective agriculture was by massacre, and enforced removal of the peasants from their land. He 'moved' twenty-five million. God knows how many he killed — no less than ten million and probably many more.

A month after writing this letter, Tolstoy came near to losing his wife. She fell seriously ill in September. A Moscow doctor, Snegiryov, was summoned and discovered a large uterine tumour. She was too weak to be moved to hospital. Snegiryov had to perform the surgery in her bedroom at Yasnaya Polyana.

Before she was anaesthetised, Sofya Andreyevna held Tolstoy's hand and whispered, 'Lyovochka, forgive me, forgive me.' It seemed as though her life was ebbing away. All the children had assembled, and when the moment for surgery came Tolstoy was deeply sceptical. He thought that 'the great and solemn moment of death was approaching, that we should submit to God's will and that any interference on the part of doctors would only violate the grandeur and solemnity of the great act of death'. In all this, there was more than a wish that she had come to the end of her journey, but the children insisted that the doctors do their best. How much tragedy would have been avoided had the doctors done nothing and allowed the poor Countess to die!

Tolstoy was in a great state of agitation about the operation. He went off into the Chepyzh grove, some hundreds of yards from the house. There he prayed, alone. 'If the operation is successful,' he told the children, 'ring the big bell, twice, and if not. . . . No, don't ring it, I'll come myself.'

Half an hour later, the operation was successfully completed. Masha and Ilya ran down to the woods to tell their father 'Successful! Successful!' they shouted. He came out of the undergrowth, and stared at them. He was pale. 'Good, go back, I'll come in a minute,' he said, and went back into the wood. He returned to the house a little later, and went in to see his wife as she was recovering from the anaesthetic. 'Good heavens, what a horrible thing! They won't even let a person die in peace. A woman lies there, her stomach cut open, tied to the bed and without pillows, groaning louder than before the operation. It's some kind of torture!'[5] Whether the torture was worse for her or for him, we shall never know.

It was not Sofya Andreyevna who was to die that year. It was Masha. She, of all the children, was closest to her father. He was curiously undemonstrative with them, unable to hug or touch them. She alone was brave enough to stroke his hand or kiss him, or soothe his troubled old brow with her caresses. She, too, was the most deeply Tolstoyan of all the children. Sasha might be a vegetarian and wear simple clothes but, as she tells us in her semi-credible memoirs, she always knew that Masha was more deeply and naturally Tolstoyan. Masha had a particular rapport with peasant people. She was tireless in good works, endlessly in and out of the *izba*s with little gifts of food or clothing. Since by now Tolstoy's diary was left open on a table in Yasnaya Polyana for all the faithful to read — rather like the works of Mrs. Baker Eddy in a Christian Science Reading Room — he had to be guarded in what he said. On August 24 he wrote disarmingly of how much he had enjoyed a visit to Masha and her husband (Obolensky, whose small estate was only a few *verst*s from Yasnaya Polyana) 'I was going to say that Masha is very dear to me, but everyone reads my diaries.'[6]

During the autumn the Obolenskys came over to Yasnaya Polyana and at the end of November, Masha suddenly fell ill with a cold. By the second day it became obvious that her condition was very serious and that she had contracted pneumonia. Very quickly, and within a few days, her whole appearance changed. Her face became thin and hollow. Red spots began to inflame her cheeks, and her husband and Sasha took turns to nurse her.

Tolstoy, who was reading again the epistles of John and finding them 'wonderful', also took turns at sitting by the bed. 'There is no fear in love. . . . Beloved, now are we the children of God and it doth not yet appear what we shall be: but we know that when He shall appear, we shall be like Him.'

On her deathbed, Masha, aged thirty-six, demonstrated all her qualities of innate calm, spiritual courage and resignation. She remained conscious to the end. Her husband and her father were with her. An hour before she died, she opened her eyes, took Tolstoy's hand and laid it on her breast. She whispered, 'I'm dying.' Thus she died.

Tolstoy went to his study and wrote, 'Masha is dead. Strange, I feel neither any horror, nor fear, nor any consciousness that something out of the ordinary has occurred, not even any pity or pain. . . . I watched her all the while she was dying. It was so amazingly calm, for me she was a being in a state of revelation, preceding my own revelation. . . .'[7]

Telegrams and letters of condolence poured in. They seemed 'falsely sympathetic'. But the genuine response of the peasants to Masha's death could not fail to move him. It took a long time to carry her coffin from the house to the cemetery where lay buried Tolstoy's parents and three of his children. All the peasant women wanted to pause and say a prayer for Masha's soul, so that the coffin stopped at each house in turn. Every door had a particular memory for Masha. Here she had sat up all night nursing a child with scarlet fever. There she had sat by a woman in labour. Here she had come to weep with one newly widowed woman.

Tolstoy's favourite encounter was not at the funeral, but while he was out walking. He bumped into Kunya, who was an idiot. 'Have you heard about our grief?' Tolstoy asked. 'Yes, I've heard.' And then immediately, 'Give me a kopeck.' *How much better and easier that is*,' he told his diary.[8]

Now, at seventy-eight, he assumed that his own demise could not be far away. He looked forward with momentary religious detachment and calm to following Masha and being absorbed into the likeness of Christ. But his own temperament and situation were wildly different from Masha's. Moreover, he failed to recognise how deeply he had relied on Masha. 'Nor did I know,' wrote Sasha, 'how irreparable that loss was to us, how Father would need Masha in the tragedy that was to be played out four years later, when I was destined to take on my young shoulders a responsibility beyond my powers.'[9]

The tensions in the household continued to provide a grotesque parody of Tolstoy's quarrel with the political condition of Russia as a whole. For example, Tolstoy continued to advocate, both by the written and the spoken word, the theories of Henry George, and to insist on the wickedness of land ownership. The land belonged to all! Yet, throughout the year of 1907, there were outbreaks of petty violence and thieving which Countess Tolstoy felt unable to ignore. Her own brother, Vyacheslav Bers, an engineer, was murdered by unemployed workmen while he was helping with the excavation of a harbour near St. Petersburg, and this did not dispose Sofya Andreyevna kindly in favour of the revolutionaries. These were dangerous times. 'Lev Nikolayevich constantly compares the present situation with the French Revolution as described by Taine,' she wrote.[10] On the estates of her son Misha they set fire to the sheds which housed all his valuable agricultural equipment. A neighbour of the Tolstoys, Madame Zvegintseva, had a coachman who was set upon by prowlers and shot.

It was all very well for Tolstoy to preach brotherly love and the universality of property. What did he intend to do about the fact that the peasants had cut down a hundred and twenty-nine of his oak trees and taken away the timber? Nothing. It was not his property any more. The paradox of the situation was that, because he had signed away his estate to his wife and family, they were in the position to make the decisions; and they took a decidedly un-Tolstoyan and common-sense approach to the matter. Their nightwatchman was shot by someone coming through the woods near the house and the cabbage fields were raided. At that point, Sofya Andreyevna, with the support of her son Andrey, called in the police.

On September 7, 1907, the governor of Tula came over. It was a slightly embarrassing visit since Andrey, a pious conservative in politics and Orthodox in religion, was having an affair with the governor's wife. The police rounded up four of the peasants, and guards were stationed by the house. 'I have not been able to get rid of an ugly feeling,' Tolstoy said. The whole episode made his position more ridiculous. Not only was he in all but name the laird of a large estate and fortune, while he professed the need for dispossession; but worse, the apostle of non-violence was now compelled to accept the presence of armed guards, who stood about in the hall and on the verandahs, smoking and swearing and leaning on their guns. The fact that Chertkov tried to interest them in his pacifist pamphlets and to engage them in dialogue somehow only made the situation more galling.[11]

The old man tried to get away. Would it not be possible for him to go to live in Tanya's house? But Sofya Andreyevna would have none of it. Then, would she at least ask the police to release the peasants they had arrested? It was not a matter for discussion. Sasha, in tears, went to Andrey and begged him to relent, but the answer was firm: 'Your mother asked me to undertake the protection of Yasnaya Polyana and of your family and I am merely carrying out her request.'

So Tolstoy remained indoors, dictating thoughts to his helpers and to his secretary. Spiritually preparing for death, he revised and enlarged his spiritual lectionary, *The Circle of Reading*, passages from the Hindu and Buddhist Scriptures, from the *Philokalia* of Orthodox spirituality and from the New Testament. All members of the household took turns at copying and recopying bits of this *Circle*. But while all these religious writings were used by Tolstoy in a conscious effort to prepare for his own death, the writings of these years reveal an inability to let go, and a longing to remain on the earthly scene and to be directing operations as much as he could. *I Cannot Be Silent* was the title of a pamphlet which he dictated to his secretary Gusev and had printed in 1908. It was a protest against the reintroduction of the widespread use of the death penalty in Russia. The title was really true. He had to go on talking and writing. 'You say that you do all these horrible things in order to restore peace and order. . . . But how do you restore them? By destroying the last trace of faith and goodness in men. . . . By committing the greatest crimes. . . . You say that this is the only way of pacifying the populace and quelling the Revolution; but that is evident nonsense! It is obvious that you can't pacify the people unless you satisfy the demand for the most elementary justice. . . . that is the demand for the abolition of private property in land. . . .'[12] And so on.

He could not be silent. When the young Gandhi wrote to Tolstoy about the appalling conditions under which Indians laboured in the Transvaal, he received copious encouragement for his campaigns of civil disobedience and passive resistance. For Tolstoy, the struggle was the same, whether it was the people of Russia against their Government, or the peoples of the Transvaal against the English, or the Negro against his American oppressors. He quoted Krishna — 'Children, look at the flowers at your feet; do not trample upon them. . . .' 'What are needed for the Indian as for the Englishman, the

Frenchman, the German, and the Russian, are not Constitutions and Revolutions, nor all sorts of Conferences and Congresses, nor the many clever devices for submarine navigation and aerial navigation, nor powerful explosives, nor all the sorts of conveniences to add to the enjoyment of the wealthy, powerful classes; nor new schools and universities with countless faculties of science, nor the augmentation of papers and books, nor gramophones and cinematographs, nor those infantile and for the most part corrupt imbecilities called Art — but only one thing is needful — the law of love which brings the highest happiness to every individual as well as to all mankind. . . .'[13]

This was the sort of thing which he had been saying for the last thirty years, and he went on saying it, day after day in his letters and diaries. The more he said it, the more his disciples wanted to hear it, and the more it spread like wildfire among the Russian people, and the less notice was taken by any authority in the world who might have actually changed things for the better.

Tolstoy's full-time secretary, supplied by Chertkov, was called Nikolay Gusev. He was to be one of the most punctilious of scholars, both as an editor of Tolstoy's works, and as the compiler of a chronology of Tolstoy's life. But Gusev had not been Tolstoy's secretary for long before, in October 1907, he was arrested as a propagandist of the Revolution. He was only put away for two months. 'How I envy you,' Tolstoy told the young man when he came back to Yasnaya Polyana in December. 'How I wish they would put me in jail, into a real, stinking one. Evidently I have not yet deserved this honour.'[14]

That summer of 1907, the Government had lifted its ban on Chertkov and allowed him to return to Russia. He settled about three miles from Yasnaya Polyana, in a derelict manor house belonging to Sasha. 'It pains me to see Chertkov building such a house,' Tolstoy confided to his daughter. 'It is too big and too grand, and he is spending so much money on it!'[15]

Tolstoy did not quite realise that Chertkov needed less a house than a headquarters for a worldwide religious organisation based on Tolstoyan principles. Tolstoy's blinking incredulity as he watched the builders sawing and hammering was a miniature version of what Christ might have felt had He been able to watch His followers laying the foundation stones of the Vatican. Chertkov was moving not just his wife and family, but a whole entourage. Telyatinky — the name of the manor — was built to house stenographers, copyists, and a number of bearded persons with an unspecified function who were called 'assistants'. There was also an English photographer, who was brought over to Yasnaya Polyana at every available opportunity to photograph Tolstoy — 'from every angle', as Sasha remarked.

In spite of her impeccable Tolstoyan credentials, Sasha found the *curia* who had been imported from Bournemouth rather unappealing. 'The Russian blouses, the boots, the long beards, unkempt hair, the always earnest faces, as if people had vowed not to joke, laugh or be merry. It was only Father and sometimes Chertkov who introduced any liveliness into this group by their jokes, laughter and puns. The fact that all these Tolstoyans were splendid people and Father valued them still could not relieve the overwhelming boredom.'[16]

There can be no doubt of Chertkov's genuine devotion to Tolstoy. He was not a charlatan or a rogue. But his fanatical religious zeal (shared by his beautiful, staring, pale wife Galya) made him believe that he was entitled to possess Tolstoy, to take him over like some commodity. The return of Chertkov was inspired by a burning personal love. And with this love, there was the calculated desire to make sure that Tolstoy, before he left this earth, should entrust his mantle, quite unambiguously, to Chertkov himself. This was not merely a spiritual thing. As the Tolstoy family divided, and the children lined up behind one parent or the other, everyone was concerned with the very important matter of Tolstoy's last will and testament.

During the last years, Tolstoy wrote several wills. It need hardly be said that they were all the cause of bitter acrimony — an acrimony, as we now see, all the more pointless since, within seven years of his death, the Revolution came, abolishing all claims to personal property. The wills are also remarkable as demonstrations of the legal and professional incompetence of all concerned. Accounts have also been muddled, in modern biographies, by the existence of two Strakhovs in the story, an old Strakhov and a young Strakhov, very different in character and unrelated.

In 1883, Tolstoy had given his wife power of attorney which, in effect gave her ownership and control of all his lands and houses. These, in a series of agreements and disagreements among the children, were eventually divided up among the family during Tolstoy's lifetime in much the same way as if he had died. Ever since that time, Tolstoy had been accused of hypocrisy. Though technically having renounced his possessions, he still lived in a style which most Russians would have regarded as luxurious, and his simple vegetarian meals were served to him by a lackey wearing white gloves. One caricature in a newspaper depicted Tolstoy in a room full of valuables, labelled 'property of my wife'. He was guzzling rich food and drinking fine wine while starving onlookers held out their skinny hands in vain. It was an unfair joke, but one which arose inevitably out of the way in which Tolstoy had chosen to dispose his affairs.

Tolstoy appears to have been determined, by his will, to have disentangled himself and his heirs from the taint of property. The fact that this was legally impossible took a very long time to penetrate his brain. The first will was a note, made in his diary, that he entrusted his old friend N. N. Strakhov, together with V. G. Chertkov and Countess Tolstoy, to sort through his papers and dispose of them as they saw fit. This note was made on March 27, 1895; Strakhov died in the following year. The next note, claiming to be a will, is a letter to Chertkov in which the beloved disciple was asked to collaborate with Sofya Andreyevna in the disposition of the papers.

Since, after his return to Russia, Chertkov had been purloining all Tolstoy's manuscripts, including that of his story *Hadji Murat*, it is understandable why Sofya Andreyevna felt it unlikely that she would ever enjoy a very influential role in this 'sorting' after Tolstoy's death. On August 11, 1908, Tolstoy drew up another will, this time dictated to his secretary, N. N. Gusev. Here he expressed the wish that all his writings should be placed by his heirs in the 'public domain'.

None of these wills were legal. But what Sofya Andreyevna did not realise was that the power of attorney of 1883 did not, during Tolstoy's lifetime, give her automatic legal right over all his published works. She in effect owned his houses, his cows, and his crops. But she did not automatically own his copyright. She had no legal title to any of his works published before 1881. In fact for the last quarter-century, she had not, as she supposed, been the legal owner of *Childhood*, *The Cossacks*, *War and Peace* or *Anna Karenina*. It was essential to clear this matter up for two very obvious reasons. Firstly, until a legal document made it clear that these books belonged to Tolstoy's family, they would not, in future, be able to live on the royalties. Secondly and, for Sofya Andreyevna almost as importantly, the great Collected Edition of her husband's works could not exist if the copyrights were scattered to the winds. In September 1909, Chertkov, realising that this was the case, drew up a fourth legal will with the help of a Moscow attorney, N. K. Muravyov. This made Chertkov into Tolstoy's sole heir, but specified that none of Tolstoy's works were anyone's private property, and that they could not 'be published and copied by all without compensation'.

But this will ran into difficulties. In the first place, the lawyer changed his mind about the legality of the will. The inclusion of the phrase about the copyrights belonging to one and all invalidated the testament. In the second place, Tolstoy's conscience could not live with making an undercover arrangement. He tried to express his doubts about the morality of the case in secret letters to Chertkov. Obviously, having embarked on the crazy idea of making a secret will, and concealing all knowledge of it from Sofya, Tolstoy was compelled to be secret, even in his protestations that they should be more honest and open.

Sofya Andreyevna was now beyond reason. The children were slow to recognise how serious her psychological condition was, but her outbreaks of hysteria and paranoid fears were inflamed by the secret correspondence which she soon discovered was taking place between her husband and Chertkov. She could not get her hands on the letters, but her nose for these matters was infallible, and she was aware that letters were being exchanged. Since it was by no means clear any longer who owned the copyright to Tolstoy's works, nor who would inherit them when he died, it was understandable that she should want to watch the old man like a hawk. She did not think, however, that the letters passing between the two men were just about business matters. In her present paranoid condition it was obvious to her that they were love letters and that Tolstoy's lust for her, which had apparently at the age of eighty-one cooled, had, in reality, been transferred to the 'evil spirit in Chertkov'. She tried to explain this to her husband a few months later: 'I showed him that page of his old diary for 1851, in which he writes that he had never fallen in love with a woman but has frequently fallen in love with men.' This did not go down very well. Tolstoy turned white and flew into a terrible rage. 'Get out! Get out!' he shouted. 'I said I will leave you and I will!' Then he went to his room, slammed the door and locked it. 'Where is his love?' she asked. 'His non-resistance? His Christianity?'[17]

Tolstoy's fifth will was drawn up in very shady circumstances towards the end of 1909. Chertkov and Muravyov drafted it, with the assistance of F. A. Strakhov. This got round all the previous difficulties by bequeathing Tolstoy's literary estate to his daughter Sasha on the understanding that, when he died, she would abandon her claim to the copyright. By what justice Sasha was allowed to take away the inheritance of her mother, her brothers and sisters, it was not considered. Sasha herself expressed some doubts to Tolstoy, not least her worry about how the rest of the family would treat her after he died. 'No, I have decided it that way,' he said firmly. 'You are the last one to remain with me, and it is entirely natural that I entrust this matter with you. But in the case of your death the rights will pass to Tanya.'

This may have been Tolstoy's intention, but it was not written into the will. Can any lawyer have ever been less competent than Muravyov? The will of November 1909 makes no provision for what should happen to the estate in the event of Sasha's death. It therefore had to be redrafted in July 1910. Tolstoy copied out the whole thing himself in a little wood a couple of miles from his house, so as not to be spotted by his wife or sons. This will did allow for the literary estate to pass to Sasha's sister Tanya, and thereafter to her dependents. 'It was not easy for Father to decide on this step,' Sasha tells us, 'not easy to conceal his decision from his family. But he had firmly decided to make amends for the sin, as he called it, of having sold his own works.' It is a classic example of what Bonhoeffer called valuing our own innocence above the happiness of others.

* * * *

The will-war was an undercover operation fought by secret agents, hidden documents, concealed letters. The diary-war was a more open affair with explosives and offensives being hurled across the barricades with overt gusto. One of the sad features of the war is that it just was not worth all the pain. It might have been worth fighting such battles over the journals of the Duc de Saint-Simon, or those of the brothers Goncourt. But Tolstoy's later diaries are stupendously tedious, full of the usual old reflections about Henry George's land tax, the moral beauties of Chertkov, the love of God and the hell of family life. But these dull notebooks were the occasion of the most furious conflicts between Chertkov and the Countess Tolstoy.

Chertkov was convinced that Tolstoy's diaries were among the most important documents in world literature. He did not like the early volumes, which reflected all the Master's vulnerability, changeability and creativity. These are the records of a great imaginative genius, trying on different guises, and wrestling with the impossibility of his own nature. No. What Chertkov liked were the later diaries, the ponderous reflections of the great prophet, laced with hypochondriacal descriptions of the Master's digestive processes and his increasingly besotted devotion to his more intrusive or eccentric disciples. For some time, Tolstoy and his followers had been smuggling pages of the diary out of Yasnaya Polyana. During the years of Chertkov's exile in England, a substantial collection of Tolstoy's journals were copied and housed in Bournemouth. On his return to Russia, Chertkov arranged for the complete set of originals from 1901 onwards to be packed up and moved to his family estate at Kryokshino. (The wickedness of owning property did not apply to Chertkov himself.)

Sofya Andreyevna saw the diary question differently. Ever since the first moment of horror when Tolstoy made her read his diaries before her wedding, she had been a besotted addict. She had made copies of all the early diaries, and continued to copy out passages of interest in the later volumes, as well as keeping copious diaries of her own.

Sofya shared Chertkov's view that every sentence to drop from pen or the lips of the Master was worth preserving. But since she was his wife rather than just a preternaturally possessive hanger-on, she considered herself justified in controlling what happened to these words when they had reached the page. Furthermore, as well as loving Tolstoy more deeply than anyone else, she also hated him with a greater depth and a greater knowledge than anyone else. She could see quite clearly the story which the Tolstoyans were going to tell. She penitently believed, after he died, that her behaviour in the last year of his life had killed Tolstoy. At the same time, she could never cease to be aware that being married to Tolstoy had made her so unhappy that it had driven her mad. The injustice of being written down by posterity as a Xanthippe to Tolstoy's Socrates rankled in sane moods and insane. 'They are sure to make me out a Xanthippe,' she once said to Goldenweiser. 'You must take my side, Alexander Borisovich.'[18] In fact, Goldenweiser was one of the arch-detractors.

Tolstoy's wife therefore carried out the diary-war on two fronts. On the one hand she battled constantly to get the actual notebooks containing her husband's diaries into her own hands. This obsession, more than anything else, was what drove her crazy in the last year of Tolstoy's life. She could not banish it from her mind, and became convinced that he was hiding bits of his diary in order to send them off to his fancy-boy Chertkov. At the same time, she had been for years determined to set the record straight by writing a full diary account of her own, so that posterity might know the truth.

Countess Tolstoy's diary, at its moments of greatest emotional intensity, reminds us less of Socrates and Xanthippe than of Dickens's Fanny Squeers: 'I am screaming out loud all the time I write. . . . and so is my brother which takes off my attention rather and I hope will excuse mistakes.' This is exactly the tone of Sofya Andreyevna's louder pages. Nevertheless, her diary remains an extremely moving document, whereas Tolstoy's, oddly, is not. She remained capable of seeing why it was that anyone should be interested in Tolstoy in the first place. He had forgotten that long ago. She could see that he was a great literary genius. 'I have done nothing but copy out *Hadji Murat*,' she wrote a year before he died. 'It's so good! I simply couldn't tear myself away from it.'[19] Tolstoy's diary for the same day revealingly points out the contrast: 'Generally my state of mind is one of dissatisfaction with myself, but not of depression. I can't write but I'd like to, and I'm thinking.' By 'write' he now means 'write twaddle'. His wife's self-obsession was certainly strong, but it was outmatched by Tolstoy's own.

There is something particularly touching, and revealing, about her copying out *Hadji Murat* — the last work in which the old Tolstoyan greatness is manifest. It has had a distinguished list of admirers. For the philosopher Wittgenstein, it was one of the few works of Tolstoy which he could admire, and John Bayley has said that 'some portraits in the story are as life-giving and complete as those in *War and Peace*'.[20]

When Tolstoy said that he wanted to portray the old Caucasian warrior chief, Hadji Murat, by the technique of 'peepshows' of his various guises (Hadji Murat as husband, as fanatic, etc.), he was partially recognising within himself that the wholeness of artistic vision was breaking up. This nearly always happens to literary geniuses when they survive into old age. *Paradise Regained* is all bits. It does not aim for the cohesion of *Paradise Lost*. Hardy the novelist of comprehensive Aeschylian view gives place to Hardy the poet whose lyrics provide us with snapshots and frozen moments. *Hadji Murat* is like this.

In returning to the Caucasus for his last great work, Tolstoy turns back, like Orpheus in the Underworld, to cast a loving eye on the vanished and divided self who went with Nikolay to the Caucasus in 1851, and discovered the artistic vocation. Although the prophet Lev intervenes in the story to make us disapprove of wicked governments, violence and warfare, it is in essence as heroic a tale as one by Sir

Walter Scott. While he was writing it between 1896 and 1904, so little did its subject matter accord with mainstream Tolstoyan pacifism that he felt obliged to work on it 'on the quiet'[21] and, by the time he had completed the Shakespeare essay and persuaded himself that literature was evil or a waste of time, *Hadji Murat* was laid aside. It was his wife who cherished it. In the end, art became intolerable for Tolstoy because it made war on the ego. One thinks in this connection of that other stupendous example of great art by an old man — Titian's 'The Flaying of Marsyas'. In this painting Titian proclaims the death to self which is the prerequisite of art, as of the good life. The artist's martyrdom (different in kind from that of the political dissident or the saint) was not one which Tolstoy was prepared to undergo.

His horror, shortly after getting married, had been that marriage was the enemy of egoism. 'Where has my self gone?' he had asked, back in June 1863, 'the self I once loved and knew, that sometimes jetted out of me with such eruptive force, to my own pleasure and terror?' This was not meant to be funny when he wrote it at the age of thirty-five. He was still writing in the same vein at the age of eighty-one in a letter to Chertkov: 'However much this eighty-year-old physical being of mine and all its perceptions and doings differs from my eight-year-old physical being with its perceptions and doings of that time, my consciousness of *me*, distinct from everything else, is completely and absolutely identifiable. . . . And my consciousness of *me*, connected in the first place with my own distinct being alone, transfers its consciousness to other beings by means of what we call love. . . .'[22]

Not everyone was at the receiving end of what Tolstoy called love, least of all, in those last years, his wife. The diary-war provided a dreadful nemesis for Tolstoy's extreme egotism. While Chertkov and his wife fought over his diaries and kept records of their own, pens were scratching busily all over the household of Yasnaya Polyana and the surrounding district. More or less everyone who was literate was keeping a record. After the arrest of Gusev, Chertkov provided Tolstoy with another secretary, Valentin Bulgakov, a young student from Moscow, who was a devotee of Tolstoyism. Chertkov gave Bulgakov instructions that he should keep a full log of events and sayings at Yasnaya Polyana. The top copy was written in invisible ink, and beneath it there was a carbon which was posted every few days to Chertkov. In addition to his constant visits and letters, Chertkov could thus guarantee almost continual observation of the Tolstoy household.

Bulgakov was a good observer, and he paints the Master with rather more warts than Chertkov intended. He makes it clear that even in his dotage Tolstoy had moments of finding Chertkov a bore. He gives us glimpses of Tolstoy's jokey side. For instance, when there was to be a performance of some 'folk theatre', Sasha was longing for a part. She obviously wanted to play the young heroine, but, with true Tolstoyan humility, she asked for the part of some crone. 'Don't you want to play the part of the village policeman?' asked her father. 'No!' she replied with horror.[23]

Bulgakov's diary depicts for us more vividly than most of the accounts the underlying tension of day-to-day life at Yasnaya Polyana. At meals, the master of the house and the mistress were always bickering, or eyeing each other with suspicion. Tolstoy complained ceaselessly about the 'elaborate' diet. Sofya Andreyevna justified it 'on the grounds that a vegetarian table needs variety'. Tolstoy took to elaborate *sotto-voce* apologies to guests which were designed to get a 'rise' out of his increasingly hysterical wife.

When the painter N. N. Ge came to a meal, Tolstoy whispered, 'I think that in fifty years people will say: "Imagine, they could calmly sit there and eat while grown people walked around waiting on them — their food was served to them, cooked for them."'

'What are you talking about?' asked Sofya Andreyevna. 'About their serving us?'

'Yes,' said Lev Nikolayevich and repeated aloud what he had said.

Sofya Andreyevna began to protest.

'But I was only saying it to him,' said Lev Nikolayevich, pointing to Ge. 'I knew there would be objections and I absolutely do not wish to argue.'[24]

But, had he not wished to argue, he would not have said it. They had had the argument a thousand times. Bulgakov notices the strands of sheer hatred which run through the whole situation. He recognised eventually that Chertkov was aiming at 'the moral destruction of Tolstoy's wife in order to get hold of his manuscripts'. He saw that Sasha was consumed with malice towards her mother, and devoted herself to provoking Sofya 'as to a kind of sport'. He saw without being quite able to see. He showed, without needing to say it that, like the disappointed man in Belloc's poem, Tolstoy had reached the position where those who loved him best despised him most. George

Steiner was clearly right when he said that Bulgakov's fairness and truthfulness cost him the favour of Chertkov, and that it was for this reason that he was not made privy to Tolstoy's escape plans.[25]

The latter years of Tolstoy are so scandalously horrible, and show up all the chief actors in the drama so poorly, that it is hard not to be gripped by it. And since they were all keeping records, and since nearly all the survivors wrote histories or memoirs, it is hard for biographers to resist the temptation to tell the whole story in minute detail. It is a good example of how too much 'material' can actually distort the truth. Two of the greatest Tolstoy biographies of the twentieth century both devote infinitely more space to Tolstoy's dotage than to the days of his prime. Simmons gave nearly two hundred pages, and Troyat well over a hundred, to descriptions of Tolstoy's pathetic last days, leaving us with the impression that the most interesting thing about Tolstoy was not his literary genius but his acrimonious relations and hangers-on.

Some of the quarrels had highlighted the anomaly of Tolstoy's position, showing that his stature in the world at large as a thinker and reformer was something of which his wife had almost no conception, or that if she thought about it, the image of her husband as an anarchist prophet filled her with horror. (It was her son and ally Andrey who said at the time of the Revolution that had Tolstoy not been his father he would have liked to see him hanged for sedition.)

One such 'significant' quarrel was the one which occurred in 1909 when Tolstoy was invited to attend the eighteenth International Peace Congress which was being held in Stockholm. As one of the most famous pacifists in the world, it was inevitable that the Peace Congress should have elected Tolstoy to honorary membership, and equally inevitable that they should have asked him to attend. No one expected that he would. He was eighty-one years old. He had repeatedly refused to do any public speaking. He was known to be in poor health. While he was away from Yasnaya Polyana (and from his wife who remained there) and staying in Moscow, Tolstoy let it be known that he would attend the Congress. The organisers were extremely embarrassed when he further leaked it to the world press that he intended to address the Congress. There were rumours and counter-rumours. Some said that he was going to win the Nobel Peace Prize. But the organisers of the Congress were worried that Tolstoy's extreme anarchist views would bring their more moderate aims into disrepute. Using Chertkov and the full network of publicity which they had built up across Europe, Tolstoy let them know that he believed that the only honest course for something calling itself a Peace Congress was to advocate the abolition of all standing armies throughout the world; and this was *not* the policy of the Peace Congress.

Thoroughly satisfied with himself, having stirred up this international hornet's nest, old bronchitis-is-a-metal returned to Yasnaya Polyana to find his wife in a state of hysterical rage and embarrassment. By now, she was a psychological wreck, and had lost all control of herself. 'My mind is unhinged,' she admitted, 'it has all been a bad shock to the nervous system.'[26] Having watched her reach a fever pitch of unhappiness, screaming and shouting and threatening to poison herself with morphine he — able to say with the full confidence of moral superiority that he merely wanted world peace — backed down. He would not attend the Congress after all.

Knowing his antipathy to foreign travel, his own physical weakness, and the fact that he could not do public speaking, it is almost incredible that he had ever intended to go to Stockholm. The demon in him which loved to be provocative stirred up that row — the agitation in Sweden, the buzzing of the world press, the excitement of the secret police in Moscow, the mental torture of Sofya Andreyevna. Then, with a shrug, he could, as his disciples would see things, submit to the 'tyranny' of his wife.

So it went on, this unedifying series of horrible disputes and emotional eruptions. Tolstoy himself wrote and spoke as if it was all going on around him, and in spite of him. His propaganda exercises against the Government, his outbursts and pamphlets, brought him nothing but adulation from the crowds. The last time he and his wife travelled together to Moscow by train they were almost mobbed by five thousand people at the station shouting 'Hurrah, Lev Nikolayevich!'[27] His odious, humourless disciples infested every corner of the house, and whispered poison about Sofya in the old man's ears. No wonder she went mad. No wonder, in a way, that he did too. He was not as hysterical as she — though there were outbursts of rage. And there was within him someone who was crushed and hurt and exhausted by all the hatred in that house, and who longed for peace. But his means of escape showed quite clearly that his insatiable appetite for self-dramatisation was not yet dead.

Chapter Twenty
Escape

1910

He died when he had got too far, so far that
the masses could not follow him. . . . in a
region of eternal snows, where the night tasted
of cool stars and where he was alone with
himself and his strength. . . .
                  Alfred de Vigny on Julian the Apostate

*E*ight years after Tolstoy died, his wife was heard to remark, 'I lived with Lev Nikolayevich for forty-eight years, but I never really learned what kind of man he was.'[1]

Like many of her comments, it is an extremely intelligent one. The more evidence we possess about Tolstoy, the less he makes sense. No doubt, had he made any sort of sense to himself, he would never have become the incomparable artist he was.

When in old age Pavel Biryukov and others questioned him about his early life, Tolstoy merely tried to rehearse for their benefit memories which had become ossified into legends. Childhood flashed back to him in arbitrary bits in his last decade: a child in a bathtub, absorbed in the exact texture of the wet wood and the soap; a child with its father; a child with its aunts; but, however hard he tried to remember her, never a child with its mother. The one natural memory which, as well-balanced and unimaginative individuals the majority of us carry through life, is the icon of ourselves as unweaned children. In Tolstoy's case the 'female figure with a child' eluded him.

Now, entered upon his ninth decade of existence, he was all but alone. Alexandrine, the dear 'old girl', was gone; Aunt Toinette was gone; brothers Sergey, Dmitry and Nikolay were gone. Six out of his thirteen children were dead. At such a stage, old family links are very precious; none more so to Tolstoy than that with his sister Marya.

Unlike Tolstoy, his sister had been able to submit to the Orthodox religion as a means of purgation. It was always said in the family that, as the last-born, she had been responsible for her mother's death, and that she lived with a permanent sense of guilt about this. Whether or not this was true, there had been plenty, in her unhappy marriage, in her love affairs, to torment her essentially orthodox and deeply religious temperament. In later years (like their aunt Pelageya) she had become a nun, and settled in the austere Shamardino convent which had been founded as an adjunct to the Optina monastery by Starets Amvrosy. It was a huge place, with no less than six hundred women in it.

On one occasion when Tolstoy visited her in her convent cell, Sister Marya introduced him to an elder called Starets Joseph. He told Tolstoy that he had too much pride of intellect and that until he stopped trusting in his mind, he would never return to the Church.

Yet, in spite of the great differences between them — she, an obedient daughter of the Church, he, an excommunicated and unrepentent heretic — the two siblings were very close. 'Your brother Lev, who loves you more the older he grows,'[2] was how Tolstoy signed one letter to Marya in 1909. This was nothing less than the truth. And she, moreover, loved him. Tolstoy ribbed her about her willingness to take the vow of obedience. 'There are six hundred fools here, all living according to someone else's judgement,' he said one day when visiting her convent. But they shared a thirst for God. 'God grant that everyone might believe as strongly as he did,' she prayed after his death — even though the elders and monks forbade her to pray for Lev Nikolayevich's soul, on the grounds that by then it was in hell.[3]

More important than the outwardly religious bent which both their lives had taken, there was the deep spiritual link of their shared childhood. Aunt Masha, as she was known to the children, was a frequent and welcome guest at Yasnaya Polyana — her childhood home as well as Tolstoy's. There was an amusing occasion once when she was staying as a guest and had been placed in the large, dark, familiar room which had been occupied by her own father. It was autumn, and Marya Nikolaevna was getting on in years. Every evening, she made her devotions in the corner of the room where, from childhood memory, she knew the icons to be. But one evening she actually looked at the corner to which she had been bowing and genuflecting so vigorously. The icon had gone. There was nothing there except a cluster of large houseflies. She summoned the maid. 'What has happened to the icon?' 'All the icons have been moved to her ladyship's room,' she was told. 'There were only flies in that corner — and I only swep' 'em out this morning.' For three days she had been bowing and praying to a swarm of flies. The story reveals how every inch of the house was familiar to her.[4]

'Now there is no one left who calls me Victoria,' was the Queen's sad reflection upon the death of Prince Albert. Tolstoy and his sister clung together, as their lights went low, with a similar sense of loss, a sharing into which neither the disciples nor the children could enter. She was the last true survivor of the Ant Brotherhood. She and he were the last people living who had been held in the arms of their mother — their ever-forgotten mother, for whose image Tolstoy had searched vainly in his memory all his life.

Existence at Yasnaya Polyana had by now become intolerable for the old man. What had begun, thirty and more years previously, as a brave attempt to lead the good life and to follow the commandments of Jesus had resulted in a situation almost as acrimonious, almost as full of human corruption and wickedness as the quarrels and rivalries which erupted among the followers and patrons of St. Francis of Assisi, who had tried the same experiment six centuries earlier. Tolstoy was by now emotionally exhausted. He had believed, and still believed, that property was theft. If he had not done so, it would not have been possible for both sides in the war of the wills to have tugged at the title of his literary estate with such voracious claws. He had preached peace, and he was surrounded by daily, hourly discord. He had insisted, with fervent sincerity, that the only thing in which he believed was the law of love, which is the love of God. He was the prisoner in a nettlebed of hatred. Escape was the only answer.

His wife, who was by now seriously mentally sick, kept up a ceaseless watch, so that there was never a moment when Tolstoy did not feel himself being peered at. 'She is very pitiful to me. When I think how alone she must feel during the nights, most of which she is sleepless, and how, with a hazy, sickly awareness, she realises she is not loved and is a burden to everyone except the children, I cannot help feeling sorry for her.'[5] Nevertheless, her constant questioning of him caused him to have frequent bursts of bad temper, followed by periods of remorse. If he went to bed, he would hear her pacing about the house, in and out of the Remington room, going through every one of his papers for evidence that he was conducting some sort of conspiracy behind her back. On his study wall, there was a photograph of Sasha and one of Chertkov. Sofya took them down. Tolstoy, for a quiet life, did and said nothing about them. But on her next visit

Sasha asked him why he had allowed his wife to take down the photographs. She began to shout at her father. He turned round and walked away. 'You are acting the way she does,' he said sadly. Then he burst into tears.[6] Then he put the two pictures back on the wall. The next day, Sofya searched the house for a pistol — found one, and began firing at the picture of Chertkov. It turned out only to be a toy pistol so no damage was done.

Shortly after this, Tolstoy had a mild blackout, with pains in his chest. He began to feel she might kill him. On October 6, 1910, he had a letter from Chertkov. There was the usual routine with Sofya Andreyevna. What had Chertkov said? When he told her, she cried and wanted to know what he really said. She was then shown the letter. It proposed a visit. If Chertkov came, Tolstoy must promise not to kiss the monster. Yes, yes, he promised. But still she wept and screamed. Later in the month, she managed to find a private diary he was writing, but one of the notebooks which she had discovered during an earlier rummage was not where she had last seen it. She confronted him with this renewed evidence. 'This proves that there is a conspiracy against me.' 'What do you mean, a conspiracy?' 'Your diary has been given to Chertkov.' 'No. Sasha has it.' So it went on, this crazy existence, in which the Countess was never still, and hardly ever seemed to fall asleep.

Tolstoy bided his time, but not for much longer. He had his plans hatched, and he was ready to go. On October 21, three peasants visited the Master, and he confided in them his difficulties. He took a secret gratification in their simple attitude to the problem, and told Sasha about it afterwards with some glee. 'We do things the country way,' said Ivan the coachman. 'If any woman tries any nonsense, her husband uses the reins on her — and she gets as soft as silk.'[7]

Tolstoy still had within him some of the alacrity of a good military tactician who, seeing the moment to strike, seized it. The moment came during the night of October 27-28, 1910. As he lay awake, he realised that there was an unusual stillness in the house. Getting up and tiptoeing to her door, he discerned she was asleep. At last! Only hours before she had been pacing about, opening doors, and searching through drawers and closets. She had come into his bedroom and held a candle over his face. 'How are you?' she had demanded. But now, at last, she was still.

Tolstoy got up, and dressed, went to wake Doctor Makovitsky — his dear Dushan — and told him to pack any necessary medicines.

Then he went and woke Sasha. She was astonished to see her father standing by the bed holding a candle. 'I'm leaving immediately, for good — help me pack.' A maid was delegated to pack clothing; Sasha collected up a few manuscripts. 'You can keep those,' said her father. 'And the diary?' 'I'm taking that with me.' All the time Tolstoy was terrified that his wife would wake up. 'You stay here, Sasha,' he told his daughter. 'I shall send for you in several days, when I decide definitely where I am going. I shall most probably go to Mashenka [i.e. his sister Marya] to Shamordino.'[8]

It was six o'clock in the morning before everything was collected up in the carriage. It was still pitch dark. As the carriage moved off, Sasha jumped in and kissed her father. 'Goodbye my darling,' said the old man, 'we shall see each other soon.'

The carriage disappeared into the night.

They drove to Shchyokino station, where they had to wait for an hour for the train, at every second fearful that pursuers would come from Yasnaya Polyana. Once they were on the train Tolstoy turned to the faithful Dushan and said, 'I wonder how Sofya Andreyevna is now? I am sorry for her.'[9]

Thirty-three years before, he had described Anna Karenina, sitting in a train, trying to read an English novel, and finding it unsatisfactory because the characters had more to do than she did. Tolstoy did better on that train than read a novel. He wrote his diary: a vivid account of everything that had happened since three a.m. The extraordinary thing about the next few days of Tolstoy's life is not so much that others have given full accounts: that we should expect, for the events are dramatic and the central figure is so august and mysterious. But what is profoundly extraordinary is the fact that Tolstoy was writing the whole thing down himself. Why? Was it a crazy habit, like that of the imprisoned shoemaker in *A Tale of Two Cities* who could not stop the movement of his hands, even when the shoe was taken from him?

Or was it that events did not really happen as far as Tolstoy was concerned, however dramatic they might be, unless he wrote them down? Or was it the great storyteller's zest to make peace, at last, with his public? Over the last thirty years, there had been many admirable stories, but interspersed with much sermonising, pontificating, huffing and puffing. Did he want us, in the end, to enjoy the excitement of a good yarn, with himself — as in all his good stories — at the very centre of our attention? Or was he merely confused? Like most of his actions in the previous quarter-century, his escape from Yasnaya Polyana had the very opposite effect from the one which he professed — and probably believed — that he intended. He thought that he wanted to slip quietly away. But within hours of his escape, the news had been telegraphed to Moscow and St. Petersburg: LEV TOLSTOY LEAVES YASNAYA POLYANA was a headline which appeared almost before Tolstoy reached the first changing post on his journey. Even on the train, he did not try to keep his identity secret. Seated in the third class compartment, he could have sat quietly reading his diary, and passed for some dirty old *yurodivy*. But he engaged the young peasant next to him in a discussion about the land tax of Henry George, and then began to lecture the whole carriage about pacifism and non-violence. By the time he had got to his station — Kozyolsk — the word had spread up and down the train, and crowds of people were huddled around the door of his compartment to listen to the famous prophet's words of wisdom. The journey took six hours, and Doctor Makovitsky found it exhausting.

From Kozyolsk, they took a cab, the three of them, and presented themselves at the guesthouse of the Optina monastery. Again, Tolstoy could have said 'I am a poor old man who needs shelter — could you take me in?' But he announced himself as 'Lev Nikolayevich Tolstoy, excommunicated by the Church. I have come to talk with your elders and tomorrow I shall go to my sister at Shamardino.' The monk told him that all were welcome to stay there, and showed him to his quarters, in the monastery inn. Before going to sleep Tolstoy sent a letter and a telegram to Chertkov and to his daughter, telling them of his whereabouts. The very next morning — when Tolstoy had been away for less than twenty-four hours — a delegate called A. P. Sergeyenko arrived at the monastery inn with messages from Chertkov.[10]

There was a letter from Chertkov: 'I cannot put into words the joy it was to me that you went away.' He also gave Tolstoy an account of what had been happening at Yasnaya Polyana in his absence. Miraculously, Sofya Andreyevna slept through until eleven a.m., which must give rise to the speculation that Doctor Makovitsky, privy to Tolstoy's escape plans, had put something in her tea. Sasha, as ordered, had given her mother a letter from Tolstoy, asking his wife to understand the fact that he found his situation — i.e. living with her — intolerable, and begging her not to come after him. Sofya did not stay to finish the letter. 'Goodbye Sasha,' she had called out, with her usual unwillingness to play down the dramatic possibilities of any moment, 'I am going to drown myself.'[11] She ran down the road to the pond where the peasant women did their washing, and threw herself in. Since she had on more than one occasion tried to 'commit suicide' there before, she knew that it was never more than waist-deep. Tolstoy had no patience with this playacting any more, and he wrote a sharp letter to Sasha: 'If anyone should wish to drown it is certainly not she, but I. Let her know that I desire only one thing — freedom from her. . . . and the hatred which fills her whole being.'[12]

In the opinion of Sister Marya, it was a fatal mistake to have written this letter. Her brother Tolstoy should have stayed quietly in the monastery and not brought Sasha into things — Sasha who only made everything worse. The brother and sister met that afternoon. Tolstoy went over to see her in her cell at Shamardino. And Lev (had not their childhood nickname for him been Lev the Howler?) burst into tears on his sister's shoulders and told her all that he had been suffering in the past weeks. All he wanted now, he told her, was solitude. They decided that the best plan would be for Tolstoy to rent a small *izba* in the monastery grounds. In this way, he would be able to lead the life of religious seclusion which he had so long craved, while his sister kept an eye on him.

'Goodnight,' he said, as he left her cell. 'We'll see each other tomorrow.'[13]

But they never saw each other again. Sasha no sooner found out where he was than she set out for the Shamardino convent herself. Soon enough, they would all be on his trail! He wrote another letter, this time to his wife, in which his anger towards her had softened:

'Do not think I went away because I do not love you. I love you and am sorry for you with all my soul, but I cannot act otherwise than I am acting. Farewell dear Sofya. May God help you. Life is not a toy, we have no right to throw it aside on a whim. . . .'[14]

It is hard to know what this was supposed to mean. Tolstoy, who had been so awe-struck by the strange phenomenon of life ever since he had become conscious of his own existence, so sure of the fact that life was full of significance, had never been able to grasp what that significance was. Now, as it hastened to its close, few lives seemed more fuller than his own of sound and fury, signifying nothing.

By four a.m. he had left his room in the monastery inn, and made for the railroad station with his doctor. Discovering his room empty an hour or so later, Sasha and Varya rushed after him, and just boarded the train in time. Where were they going? The Caucasus! Or, there was a Tolstoyan colony in Bulgaria! Anywhere!

Everyone in the railroad carriage recognised Tolstoy. His ultra-private, secret escape story was in all the newspapers. The conductors tried to make things easy for the fugitives, when the second-class compartment became too much for the old man. They moved him to another compartment, and gave him gruel to drink. But he had started to shiver, and showed signs of developing a chill.

'Don't lose courage, Sasha,' he said, squeezing his daughter's hand. 'Everything is all right, very much all right.'[15]

Doctor Makovitsky said that it was essential that Tolstoy be given some hot liquid to drink, and at the next stop, Sasha was dispatched to fetch boiling water from the station master's house. The train slowed down, and the name of the station appeared on the sign-board — a name which was to live forever in literary history: Astapovo.

Sasha made her way down the platform, and was aware that she was being followed by two men. They turned out to be policemen, inquiring whether 'Lev Tolstoy was travelling with this train'. Sofya, and those members of the family who took her side, had ordered the police search.

Tolstoy was now too sick to continue his journey, and the station master at Astapovo offered to accommodate the travellers in his own house. Tolstoy could walk, with the help of someone holding each arm, but he was very weak. A crowd had gathered as he was helped to the station master's house. As he passed, they took off their hats as a sign of respect. Some bowed, as if a wonder-working icon were being carried through their midst.

Once they had got him to bed, Tolstoy slept well, and his fever abated. In the morning, he wanted to press on with their journey, but his doctor would not hear of it. Tolstoy sent for Chertkov. He also dictated a letter to Tanya and Sergey, begging them to understand that he could not send for them and not their mother: therefore he sent for no one from Yasnaya Polyana who was not with him already. 'Both of you will understand that Chertkov, for whom I have sent, is in a unique position with regard to me. He has devoted his entire life to the service of the undertaking which I have served for the last forty years of my life.' He then reclined on the pillows and began to dictate some more general thoughts to Sasha. 'God is the infinite all. . . .'

Tolstoy's wife, meanwhile, was not sure of her husband's where-abouts until a newspaper reporter telegraphed her, asking for an interview. He assumed she knew that her husband was dying of pneumonia in the station master's house at Astapovo. The children tried to dissuade her from going, but it was hard to see how they could — or as several of them were to say afterwards — why they *should*. Tolstoy in his weakened and terrified state might assert that Chertkov, whom he had known for twenty-seven years (nearly ten of which had been spent by Chertkov in English exile), had devoted his 'entire life' to the cause. But Sofya Andreyevna, who had copied and recopied all his great literary masterpieces, protected him against editors and predators, managed his household and farms and money, been his lover and his slave, and borne him thirteen children, could also have been said to have some claim on Tolstoy's gratitude and affection. The fact that it had all ended in hatred and bitterness was — Ilya, among the children, argued — all the more reason why the two tragic old people should be reconciled at the end.

Always practical, and always one to do things in style, even when distracted by madness and grief, the Countess ordered a special train to take her, her family and entourage to Astapovo. She brought with her a doctor and a nurse, and three of her children — Andrey, Mikhail and Tatyana. Sergey went ahead of the others, and was admitted to his father's presence. Tolstoy found it touching that his son had come — 'he kissed my hand', he said pathetically. But the Tolstoys could never assemble without dissension. The purpose of Sergey's visit had been to state that under no circumstances should his mother be allowed to see their father. 'It will excite him too much.'

The Tolstoyans were flocking round. They were allowed to be with the Master: Gorbunov, and Nikitin, and Goldenweiser. Chertkov, who had come on November 2, was a constant presence. Tolstoy, unaware that a special train was transporting his family to Astapovo, and completely unaware that the whole station was swarming with newspaper correspondents and photographers, and even a movie camera, suggested that his heart was too weak to stand a visit from his wife. November 2 was the last day that he wrote in his diary. 'It was a hard night,' he wrote. He had been addicted to the habit of chronicling his own existence for the last sixty-three years.[16] Now at last his pen was still and his tongue had begun to babble. 'The *muzhiks*. . . . you know how they die. . . .' he murmured as someone was trying to straighten a pillow. Then he passed into a sort of delirium. One of the sentences which he muttered in this state was 'Search, always go on searching.'

His wife had brought with her a little pillow of which Tolstoy was especially fond. Although the faithful forbade her to come into the room where he lay, they did take the pillow, and put it under his head. As soon as he recognised this object, he was aware that people had come from Yasnaya Polyana. He became agitated. Who were they? Sasha awkwardly admitted that Tanya had come to Astapovo. He was still conscious. The news that his beloved Tanya had come filled him with joy, and she was summoned to the bedside. But among these lovers of the truth, it was still felt necessary to keep up the fiction that Sofya Andreyevna was at home. Tolstoy agitatedly asked Tanya about his wife. 'What is she doing? How does she feel? Isn't she going to come here? Tell me, tell me! What could be more important than that? . . . .' He was frantic, agitated. Tanya, having been briefed to say nothing, was non-committal and left the room.[17]

Outside, on the platform, Sofya was working herself into a characteristic hysteria of rage. Questions which were of importance, such as whether she was to see her husband before he died, mingled in her mind with questions which were unimportant, such as the cost of her special train. It had been pulled into a siding. Five hundred roubles! But she would not sit in it. She paced up and down the track, and mingled with the crowds on the platform. Each train brought more crowds to the scene, journalists, and men with cameras.

Monsieur Pathé, the pioneer of newsreel movies, cabled to his cameraman Meyer: TAKE STATION, TRY TO GET CLOSEUP, STATION NAME. TAKE FAMILY, WELL-KNOWN FIGURES, CAR THEY ARE SLEEPING IN. . . .

This was faithfully done. Meyer managed to get everything but the deathbed itself on his film, which survives to this day. We can see Sofya Andreyevna agitatedly pacing up and down, and pressing her face against the window of the room where Tolstoy lay. These were decidedly not the images which she wished to be presented to posterity. She seemed to catch on by instinct to the fact that the camera can never tell the truth. Hence, when her daughters came out and begged her to return to her siding, and not to mingle with the crowds, Sofya bargained with Sasha. She begged the girl to let her go into the small porch of the station master's house while the Pathé movie camera was rolling, so that it would at least appear that she had been able to go into the house to see her husband before he died. Still Sasha refused. Her mother returned to mingle with the crowds and to talk at random with the reporters, in no fit condition to do so. Sometimes, she railed against her husband and her family, with every word taken down and misreported. Sometimes she wept and spoke only words of love for her husband.

Those who sat around the bed, who would not admit Tolstoy's wife, were even less inclined to admit representatives of the Church who had excommunicated him. Metropolitan Anthony of St. Petersburg had telegraphed on November 4, urging Tolstoy to return to the Orthodox faith. On the following day, on the Patriarch's instructions, Abbot Varsonofy, and another monk from the Optina monastery arrived with instructions to bring about a deathbed conversion for the edification of the journalists waiting outside.

As the old man sank into unconsciousness, a propaganda war raged about his head. The Tolstoyans refused to admit the Abbot to the death chamber. The governor of Tula, and various eminent representatives of the Government, sent from St. Petersburg, had also been refused admission. Tolstoy was in pain, and suffering from periodic bouts of hiccoughs. His strength was waning, and the doctor had begun to inject him with morphine. Sometimes he rallied, and appeared awake. Once, in the early evening of November 6, he sat upright. Sasha leant over him. 'Shall I fix your pillows?' she asked.

'No. I just wanted to advise you to remember that there are in the world many people beside Lev Tolstoy and you are only looking at this one Lev.' Did he really believe it? His own singularity, even when it was about to forsake him, was an obsessive preoccupation. Later that evening, he became much worse. They gave him oxygen, camphor. . . .[18]

'Seryozha!' he called to his son Sergey. 'The truth! I love many. . . . How are they?. . . .' He then drowsed off. Towards midnight, however, he had a relapse and was much worse. Only at this very last point would they open that door and allow in Tolstoy's wife.

Chertkov, who had been sitting by the bed, arose and left the room. Tolstoy's sons stood awkwardly around. His daughters were a little nearer the bed. The tiny room was crowded with people, as the pathetic figure of Sofya was allowed to squeeze through. She fell to her knees by the bed. Weeping, she whispered, 'Forgive me, forgive me!' One of the doctors was afraid she would wake the old man. What would it have mattered if she had? But she was led from the room, and stood in the freezing porch for two hours, from half-past three until half-past five on the morning of November 7. Then the door opened, and her son Sergey was standing there. He led her back into the room. 'I have never loved anyone but you,' she said to the figure in the bed. But by now he was fast ebbing away. After only a few more breaths he was gone. Sofya stood up, and leaned on the body with her head on its chest. There was no movement, no breath, no heart beat.

*   *   *   *

The most vociferous and the most respected critic of the Russian Government was silent. In all the major universities throughout the Empire, there were student demonstrations to mark the death of the great rebel. In the two capitals, there were big rallies of protest against the death penalty. All over the Empire, hundreds of thousands of people waited at the news centres and the telegraph offices to hear the news that Tolstoy was dead. In the street demonstrations which took place, all over Russia, the revolutionary movement felt itself revived.[19] When Lenin seized power seven years later, it was surely significant that an ill-informed western press should describe it as a Tolstoyan Revolution.[20] Like most journalistic reports, it could not have been further from the truth. But such was the association in the mind of the whole world of Tolstoy with revolution.

While Tolstoy's body lay at Astapovo, it received some of the attention which might have been given to an old-world corpse. (The sculptor Merkurov came to take a death-mask.)

Pasternak, the painter who had done the illustrations for *Resurrection*, came down from Moscow to do sketches, bringing with him his son Boris, the future novelist and poet. But it was not really an old-world corpse any more. It was a modern one. A Tolstoyan medical student had been asked by the faithful to inject the Master with formaldehyde to make him look better for the cameras. The photographs were taken. In death, he looks completely at peace. His death-photograph is the only one in which he does not appear to be staring at the camera with a mixture of aristocratic disdain, conceited fascination and plain animal fear, as though the black box might have been an explosive device. But the sense of peace and stillness in the dead Tolstoy's face which seems so spiritual, so calm, and so grand can probably be attributed to a cunning bit of facial massage by those who laid out the corpse and a judicious use of formaldehyde. By the time that Pathé's news cameras were rolling two days later, he was anything but natural. The train bearing his coffin arrived at the station of Zasyeka at six-thirty a.m. on November 9. There was a vast crowd waiting to see it arrive. Tolstoy's four sons carried the open coffin out into the road and it made its slow journey back to the house at Yasnaya Polyana. It is estimated that the crowds numbered three or four thousand. There were peasants with banners, 'Dear Lev Nikolayevich, the memory of your goodness will not die among us, the orphaned peasants of Yasnaya Polyana.' When it reached the house, the coffin was put on a table near the entrance hall. A high proportion of the thousands wished to file through the cramped corridors of the house to pay their respects to the corpse before the funeral, which was to take place at two forty-five p.m. Tolstoy had long ago asked to be buried on the edge of a ravine in the Zakaz wood where, all those years before, his brother Nikolay had buried the green stick on which was written the secret of how peace could come to the earth, and evil could be banished. In the end, Tolstoy had come no nearer discovering this secret than anyone else, but the return to the place of the green stick had an obvious appropriateness. Whatever muddled instincts had made him run out into the night less than a fortnight before, he had, at least in part, been running back towards his childhood, towards his sister, the last link with the Ant Brotherhood.

In spite of the fact that Andrey Tolstoy had pleaded with the Bishop of Tula to allow them a full Orthodox funeral, permission for this was forbidden by the Church authorities. Tolstoy's was therefore the first public burial in Russia since the conversion of St. Vladimir which was not attended by the rites of the Church. But it could not be described as a secular funeral. The huge crowd was full of reverence. They defied their priests by singing the ancient Russian funeral hymns. When the coffin passed them by, everyone except the police removed their hats and many fell to their knees. It is one of the most extraordinary demonstrations of public sympathy in the history of the world. No novelist has ever been given such a funeral, but it was not for his novels that they honoured him. It was for the deeds which now seem to us half mad and quixotic; it was for those volumes of his work which most readers now leave unread. Of the thousands of people who stood and watched as Tolstoy's coffin was carried through the glade and buried in that favourite childhood spot, no more than a handful had so much as heard of *War and Peace*. 'And on they went, singing "Eternal Memory."'

Notes

References are to the bibliography which follows. For example, 'Fischer 23' means that the source of my information is to be found on page twenty-three of Louis Fischer's *The Life of Lenin*. If more than one book by a single author is listed in the bibliography, the reference is amplified by the date of publication. Thus 'Bayley (1966)' would refer to John Bayley's *Tolstoy and the Novel* (1966); 'Bayley (1971)' would refer to his *Pushkin* (1971).

The following short titles are used in the notes:

JE: *The Complete Works of L. N. Tolstoy* (Jubilee Edition, Moscow 1928-1964)
Porter: Cathy Porter (ed. and trans.), *The Diaries of Sofia Tolstaya* (1985)
SW: Hugh Seton-Watson, *The Russian Empire 1801—1917* (Oxford 1967)
Simmons: Ernest J. Simmons, *Leo Tolstoy* (1949)
PRP: *L. N. Tolstoi. Perepiska s russkimi pisatelyami v dvukh tomakh* (Moscow 1978)

Since very few people have access to the complete ninety-volume edition (JE) I have attempted, in the case of references to Tolstoy's diaries and letters, to give merely the dates. Further references can then be followed up by the reader in whatever edition is to hand.

Chapter One: Origins (pp. 9-30)

1. Gusev (1954). Except where otherwise stated, all the biographical details in this book derive from Gusev's five monumental volumes.
2. JE 9.106
3. *Ibid.* 271
4. Two delightful family histories, written by kinsmen, are the books of Serge Tolstoi (1980) and Nikolai Tolstoy (1983). The latter in particular is highly recommended.
5. Crankshaw (1976) 18
6. SW 183-98 and Ulam (1981) 3-66
7. Volkonsky *op. cit.*
8. Pushkin III.7 (trans. author)
9. Ulam (1981) 65
10. JE 34.375
11. *Ibid.* 376
12. *Ibid.* 384
13. *Ibid.* 386
14. JE 9.211
15. JE 34.357
16. q. de Jonge (1972) 70
17. JE 34.395
18. Zernov (1945) 57
19. JE 32.99
20. JE 34.387

Chapter Two: Joseph and His Brethren (pp. 31-48)

1. Gusev (1954)
2. Fischer 23
3. Aksakoff 25
4. Herzen 94
5. Mackenzie-Wallace II.6
6. JE 34.370
7. Zagoskin 91
8. Zborilek 6
9. Rousseau 249
10. *Ibid.* 278
11. Vatsuro I.46
12. Nuzhin 33
13. SW 168
14. Aksakoff 25

15. SW 171
16. *Ibid.*
17. Shklovsky 81
18. Simmons 69
19. JE 46.32
20. *Ibid.* 127
21. Tolstoy's early biographers, such as Biryukov, either did not know or censored the fact that he had venereal disease. Of his modern biographers, Simmons says that 'the thought of leaving Kazan caused Tolstoy no regret', which is probably true; Martine de Courcel tells us that 'the constraints and university programmes seemed to him each day more ridiculous', a remark for which there is no evidence whatsoever. Henri Troyat imaginatively suggests that Tolstoy 'had a sudden revelation that he could no longer go on taking courses in the Law department'. This writer tells us that Tolstoy had been ill, but that the illness was 'not serious'. We are not told by Troyat what the illness was.
22. Crankshaw (1976) 73
23. Pipes 78

Chapter Three: *The History of Yesterday* (pp. 49-69)

1. Gusev (1954)
2. *Diary,* March 10, 1906
3. JE 45.182
4. *Diary,* April 17, 1847
5. Vatsuro II. 97
6. JE 4.123
7. *Ibid.* 164
8. Pushkin, *Yevgeny Onegin*, I.54
9. *Diary*, June 14, 1847
10. Pushkin, *The Bronze Horseman*, trans. Charles Johnston
11. Letter to S. N. Tolstoy, February 13, 1849
12. Letter to S. N. Tolstoy, May 1, 1849
13. Mirsky 254
14. JE I.279
15. *Ibid.* 280
16. *Ibid.* 281
17. Porter 62
18. *Ibid.* 67
19. Sterne 48
20. JE I.290

Chapter Four: *Kinderszenen* in the Caucasus
(pp. 70-98)

1. Gusev (1954)
2. JE 46.59
3. Hingley (1977) 61
4. SW 311ff.
5. *Ibid.*
6. JE 46.77
7. *Ibid.* 80
8. JE 59.169
9. JE 3.67
10. *Ibid.* 68
11. Mirsky (1949) 235
12. JE 3.74
13. *Ibid.* 86
14. *Ibid.* 71
15. JE 46.82
16. *Ibid.* 87
17. JE 59.127
18. *Diary*, November 29, 1851
19. Katarskii 103
20. Kingsmill 87
21. *Ibid.*
22. Letter to T. A. Yergolskaya, November 12, 1851
23. Eykhenbaum (1922) 75
24. JE 59.196
25. JE 1.28
26. *Ibid.* 35, 36 etc.
27. *Ibid.* 56
28. JE 45.89
29. Letter to N. A. Nekrasov, July 3, 1852
30. Letter to N. A. Nekrasov, November 18, 1852
31. Zander 53
32. PRP 1.60
33. *Diary*, January 12, 1854

Chapter Five: Crimea (pp. 99-119)

1. Gusev (1954, 1957)
2. Letter to T. A. Yergolskaya, July 5, 1854
3. *Diary,* July 7, 1854
4. *Ibid.*

5. *Diary,* July 18, 1854
6. Vatsuro I.60
7. *Diary,* January 22, 1855
8. Vatsuro I. 65
9. *Ibid.*
10. *Diary,* January 28, 1855
11. *Diary,* February 8, 1855
12. Curtiss (1965) 192
13. Herzen III. 311-312
14. Curtiss, *op. cit.* 260
15. *Ibid.* 47
16. *Ibid.* 260
17. Simmons 135
18. *Diary,* March 2/3/4, 1855
19. *Diary,* April 1, 1854
20. It reads like doggerel today but it was thought stirring at the time. S. S. Doroshenko (p. 247) has gone to the trouble of trying to link phrases in the song with certain passages in Tolstoy's diary.
21. See James
22. JE 4.56
23. *Ibid.* 67
24. *Ibid.* 78
25. Vatsuro I.65
26. *Ibid.*
27. C. S. Lewis (1979) 410
28. *Diary,* September 2, 1855
29. *Diary,* October 10, 1855

Chapter Six: Bronchitis is a Metal (pp. 120-141)

1. Gusev (1957)
2. Andrew (1982) 3
3. Vatsuro I.89
4. See Riasanovsky (1976)
5. Simmons 143
6. Vatsuro I. 138
7. Fet (1890) I. 165
8. Gustafson 86
9. Granjard 33
10. Gustafson 9
11. Fet (1890) I.225
12. Fet (1959) 67
13. JE 23.56

14. *Diary,* November 29, 1851
15. JE 19.231
16. *Ibid.* 234
17. Simmons 147
18. Mackenzie-Wallace I.117
19. *Diary,* May 15, 1856
20. Letter to V. V. Arsenyeva, November 2, 1856
21. Letter to V. V. Arsenyeva, November 8, 1856
22. Letter to V. V. Arsenyeva, November 9, 1856
23. Letter to V. V. Arsenyeva, November 11, 1856
24. Letter to V. V. Arsenyeva, January 14, 1857

Chapter Seven: Travels (pp. 142-174)

1. Gusev (1957)
2. *Diary,* February 9/21, 1857
3. *Diary,* February 11/23, 1857
4. *Diary,* February 13/25, 1857
5. *Ibid.*
6. *Diary,* February 14/26, 1857
7. Letter to V. P. Botkin, February 10/22, 1857
8. *Ibid.*
9. *Ibid.*
10. JE 45.89
11. *Diary,* March 15/27, 1857
12. Islavin 13
13. Islavin 15
14. *Ibid.*
15. *Ibid.*
16. *Diary,* April 29/May 11, 1857
17. *Ibid.*
18. *Diary,* August 26, 1857
19. Islavin 54
20. Schapiro 112
21. *Diary,* October 22, 1857
22. *Diary,* November 6, 1857
23. *Diary,* December 4, 1857
24. Islavin 45
25. Brooke 12
26. Vatsuro I.78
27. Islavin 16
28. *Diary,* May 26, 1860
29. *Diary,* July 19/31, 1860
30. *Diary,* July 17/24, 1860

31. *Diary,* July 27/August 3, 1860
32. *Diary,* July 25/August 6, 1860
33. *Diary,* July 31/August 12, 1860
34. *Diary,* August 1/13, 1860
35. See Troyat 197
36. Letter to A. A. Fet, October 17/29, 1860
37. Gusev (1957) 39
38. *Ibid.*
39. Letter to N. N. Strakhov, March 19, 1870
40. Lucas 35
41. *Ibid.* 49
42. *Ibid.* 45
43. Collins 1.38
44. de Lubac 98
45. Simmons 213
46. *Diary,* August 13, 1865
47. Woodcock 45
48. Gusev (1957) 411
49. Woodcock 234
50. Sampson 7
51. Letter to V. P. Botkin, January 26, 1862
52. Islavin 81
53. Vatsuro I.221
54. Simmons 235

Chapter Eight: Marriage (pp. 175-199)

1. Letter to V. P. Botkin, February 7, 1862
2. JE 6. 148
3. *Ibid.* 24
4. *Ibid.* 35
5. *Ibid.* 65
6. *Ibid.* 68
7. *Ibid.* 69
8. *Ibid.* 75
9. *Diary,* June 15, 1858
10. *Diary,* May 26, 1860
11. Sadly, there is no evidence to support the interesting assertion by Edwards (25) that Sofya Andreyevna was 'too aware of her sex for a girl three months short of her twelfth birthday'.
12. Gusev (1957) 384
13. *Ibid.* 470
14. Fulop-Miller 4
15. Nadezhda Mandelstam (1970) 4

16. Letter to A. A. Tolstaya, July 22, 1862
17. *Diary,* September 8, 1862
18. Porter 832
19. *Ibid.* 90
20. *Diary,* September 24, 1862

Chapter Nine: Alchemy (pp. 200-228)

1. Pipes 78
2. *Ibid.*
3. Edwards 75
4. *Ibid.* 10
5. *Ibid.*
6. Gusev (1957) 303
7. *Ibid.*
8. *Diary,* January 5, 1863
9. Porter 15
10. *Ibid.* 17
11. Shrillest of recent 'Sonyans' was Edward Crankshaw (1974). Other more moderate 'Sonyans' have included the British Cynthia Asquith, the American Anne Edwards, the French Martine de Courcel and the Russo-French Henri Troyat. Those who have taken a pro-Tolstoy and anti-Sofya Andreyevna view (Levites?) have found their patriarch in the British Aylmer Maude. Loudest and best of the Tolstoy hooligans was my late and much-lamented friend John Stewart Collis who became angry at the very mention of Countess Tolstoy.
12. Gusev (1957) 241
13. *Ibid.*
14. JE 13.284
15. Kuzminskaya 159
16. Gusev (1957) 345
17. Kuzminskaya 256
18. Gusev (1957) 361
19. Porter 38
20. Gusev (1957) 298
21. Hilaire Belloc, 'Lord Finchley'
22. Gusev (1957) 311
23. Kuzminskaya 208
24. Gusev (1957) 326
25. JE 9.133
26. Kuzminskaya 87
27. *Perepiska* I.172 (1978)
28. JE 9.147

29. JE 13.401
30. JE 9.9
31. Letter to S. A. Tolstaya, September 4, 1865

Chapter Ten: *War and Peace* (pp. 229-246)

1. Letter to A. A. Fet, January 23, 1865
2. Letter to A. A. Tolstaya, November 14, 1865
3. Porter 34
4. Gusev (1957) 121
5. Christian (1962), Gudzy (1936) *passim*
6. Knowles 115
7. *Ibid.* 116
8. Fodor 17
9. *Ibid.* 91
10. Kassin 41
11. Fodor 112
12. JE 9.161
13. *Ibid.* 276
14. JE 10.112
15. Magarshack 203
16. *Ibid.* 209
17. *Ibid.* 330
18. Jones 199
19. JE 12.316
20. *Ibid.* 320
21. Porter 40
22. Kerr *passim*
23. Letter to S. A. Tolstaya, September 27, 1867
24. Gusev (1957), for this and all other facts in the chapter, except where otherwise quoted

Chapter Eleven: The Shadow of Death (pp. 247-262)

1. Gusev (1957)
2. Letter to A. A. Fet, August 30, 1869
3. Letter to S. A. Tolstaya, September 4, 1869
4. JE 26.467
5. *Ibid.* 469
6. *Ibid.* 470
7. Letter to S. A. Tolstaya, October 27, 1871
8. Letter to A. A. Fet, November 2, 1871

9. Letter to A. A. Fet, January 7, 1872
10. Porter 45
11. Letter to A. A. Fet, January 1/6, 1871
12. Porter 46
13. Letter to N. N. Strakhov, March 25, 1872
14. Letter to S. A. Tolstaya, June 25, 1871
15. JE 21.120
16. Letter to A. A. Tolstaya, September 15, 1872
17. *Ibid.*
18. Ilya Tolstoy 46
19. Islavin 56
20. Gusev (1957) 191
21. *Ibid.*
22. *Diary,* March 13, 1873
23. Porter 50

Chapter Twelve: *Anna Karenina* (pp. 263-293)

1. Islavin 209
2. Letter to A. A. Tolstaya, June 23, 1874
3. Porter 51
4. *Ibid.* 52
5. Letter to A. A. Tolstaya, January 14, 1876
6. Letter to P. D. Boborykin, July/August, 1865
7. Knowles 91
8. Berlin, 'The Hedgehog and the Fox' in *Russian Thinkers* 72
9. Schultze, Gudzy (1966) and Stenbock-Fermor all spell out the evidence, much of which is in Gusev (1957).
10. Letter to N. N. Strakhov, March 25, 1873 (not sent)
11. JE 20.23
12. Pléiade Edition 923
13. Dostoyevsky (1984) 542
14. Goldenweiser 93
15. JE 19.371
16. Pobedonostsev 94
17. Billington 382
18. Hingley (1977) and Westwood 76
19. Billington 385
20. *Ibid.*
21. JE 19.52
22. *Ibid.* 349
23. Charles Dickens, *Hard Times*
24. JE 19.57
25. Letter to A. A. Fet, September 4, 1873

26. Porter 50
27. Gusev (1957) 111
28. Letter to A. A. Tolstaya, March 6, 1874
29. Gusev (1957) 117
30. Letter to A. A. Fet, October 17, 1874
31. Gusev (1957) 117
32. Letter to N. N. Strakhov, August 25, 1875
33. Letter to A. A. Fet, October 17, 1875
34. Vatsuro I.233-235
35. Bayley (1966) 121
36. Troyat 347
37. Knowles 22
38. James (1957) 12
39. JE 19.320
40. *Ibid.* 266
41. *Ibid.* 362
42. *Ibid.* 297
43. *Ibid.* 301
44. *Ibid.* 351
45. Gusev (1957) 176
46. Letter to A. A. Fet, April 28/29, 1876
47. Bayley (1966) 188
48. Christian (1969) 152
49. JE 20.35
50. JE 62.15
51. JE 19.362
52. Letter to A. A. Fet, March 11/12, 1877
53. Letter to N. N. Strakhov, February 15, 1877
54. Tyutchev
55. *Ibid.*
56. Fet I.23
57. *Ibid.*
58. Letter to N. N. Strakhov, April 21, 1871
59. Dunlop 59
60. Gusev (1957) 189
61. Dunlop 135

Chapter Thirteen: The Holy Man (pp. 294-339)

1. Letter to A. A. Tolstaya, January 27, 1878
2. Letter to A. A. Tolstaya, March 31, 1878
3. Letter to I. S. Turgenev, April 6, 1878
4. PRP I.188

5. *Diary,* August 22, 1881
6. Islavin 110
7. *Diary,* July 6, 1881
8. JE 23.16
9. *Ibid.* 19
10. Porter 62
11. *Diary,* May 22, 1878
12. Dostoyevsky (1984) 792
13. Vatsuro II.27
14. Gusev (1957) 257
15. *Ibid.* 196
16. *Ibid.* 218
17. Leon 194
18. Simmons 365
19. JE 23.27
20. *Ibid.* 11
21. *Ibid.* 15
22. *The Brothers Karamazov* II.17
23. q. Greenwood in Jones (1978) 112
24. JE 23.60
25. Magarshack 479
26. *The Brothers Karamazov* II.iv.i
27. Letter to N. N. Strakhov, April 17/18, 1878
28. Magarshack 498
29. Letter to N. N. Strakhov, Feb 5/10, 1881
30. SW 472
31. Tyutchev 109
32. Vatsuro II.197
33. *Reflections of a Russian Statesman*
34. Letter to Emperor Alexander III, March 8/15, 1881
35. Lowe 46
36. *Diary,* May 18, 1887
37. Ilya Tolstoy 114
38. *Ibid.* 112
39. Gusev (1957) 276
40. *Diary,* October 5, 1881
41. SW 662
42. Porter 72
43. PRP I.203
44. JE 23.317
45. *Ibid.* 320
46. *Ibid.* 316
47. *Ibid.* 312
48. *Ibid.* 327

Chapter Fourteen: Real Christianity (pp. 340-370)

1. Letter to A. A. Tolstaya, January 13, 1878
2. Letter to A. A. Tolstaya, March 7, 1878
3. JE 85.14
4. Letter to V. G. Chertkov, March 6, 1884
5. *Diary*, April 24, 1884
6. *Diary*, May 22, 1884
7. *Diary*, May 27, 1884
8. Kuzminskaya 150
9. Sukhotin-Tolstoy 111
10. *Diary*, June 18, 1884
11. *Diary*, July 7, 1884
12. *Ibid.*
13. *Diary*, July 14, 1884
14. Edwards 126
15. *Diary*, July 15, 1884
16. Pullen 96
17. *Ibid.*
18. *Diary*, July 27, 1884
19. Letter to V. G. Chertkov, August 15, 1884
20. Letter to V. G. Chertkov, July 24, 1884
21. *Ibid.*
22. *Diary*, September 12, 1884
23. *Diary*, July 12, 1884
24. *Diary*, May 13, 1884
25. Philip Larkin, 'Talking in Bed'
26. Letter to V. G. Chertkov, November 11, 1884
27. JE 85.112
28. Sukhotin-Tolstoy 96
29. Ilya Tolstoy 193
30. *Ibid.*
31. Sukhotin-Tolstoy 181
32. *Ibid.* 47
33. Letter to T. L. Tolstaya, October 18, 1885
34. Letter to S. A. Tolstaya, December 15/18, 1885 (not sent)
35. Ilya Tolstoy 206
36. Sukhotin-Tolstoy 115
37. JE 25.183
38. *Ibid.* 186
39. *Ibid.* 189
40. *Ibid.*196
41. *Ibid.* 406
42. *Ibid.* 407
43. *Ibid.* 408

44. JE 26.61
45. *Ibid.* 70
46. Christian (1969) 237
47. JE 26.85
48. Porter 75
49. *Ibid.* 77
50. Gusev (1957) 122
51. *Ibid.* 125
52. *Ibid.* 127
53. SW 474. But see also Wilson (1960), Lowe, Deutscher, Fischer, etc.

Chapter Fifteen: *The Kreutzer Sonata* (pp. 371-391)

1. JE 27.79
2. de Jonge (1982) 101
3. Proffer 19
4. Montgomery 68-80
5. *Diary,* September 17, 1889
6. Letter to V. G. Chertkov, December 31, 1889
7. JE 27.85
8. *Diary,* August 22, 1889
7. JE 27.85
8. *Diary,* August 22, 1889
9. *Diary,* February 25, 1889
10. Troyat 476
11. Gusev (1958) 672
12. *Ibid.*
13. *Diary,* August 19, 1889
14. *Diary,* September 11, 1889
15. Letter to V. I. Alexeyev, August 22, 1889
16. Sukhotin-Tolstoy 146
17. *Ibid.*
18. Porter 88
19. Letter to V. G. Chertkov, January 15, 1890
20. Bayley (1966) 282
21. Simmons 357
22. Troyat 451
23. JE 27.43
24. *Crime and Punishment* I.vii
25. Letter to N. N. Strakhov, April 7, 1891
26. Porter 211
27. *Diary,* April 18, 1891
28. Porter 621
29. *Diary*, October 30, 1891

Chapter Sixteen: Terrible Questions (pp. 392-414)

1. Gusev (1960)
2. Porter 123
3. *Ibid.*
4. JE 31.11
5. *Ibid.* 45
6. JE 23.62
7. Letter to A. A. Tolstaya, August 29, 1891
8. Robbins 64
9. *Ibid.* 35
10. Maude (1929) 300
11. Simmons 522
12. Porter 173
13. *Ibid.* 172
14. Wilson (1960) 371
15. I. L. Tolstoy (1972) 131
16. JE 24.18
17. Letter to George Kennan, August 8, 1890
18. *Ibid.*
19. JE 29.310
20. JE 29.311
21. Mandelstam (1970) 167
22. JE 32.236
23. *Ibid.* 376
24. SW 461
25. Pobedonostsev 645

Chapter Seventeen: *Resurrection* (pp. 415-462)

1. SW 549
2. *Ibid.*
3. *Diary,* January 29, 1895
4. *Diary,* February 7, 1895
5. The standard history is Woodcock and Avakumovic (1968).
6. Letter to V. G. Chertkov, March 15, 1895
7. Woodcock and Avakumovic 98
8. Porter 176
9. *Ibid.* 180
10. *Ibid.* 178
11. JE 29.33
12. *Ibid.* 44
13. *Ibid.* 46
14. Porter 186

15. *Ibid.* 187
16. Gusev (1960) 163
17. *Ibid.* 164
18. *Ibid.* 171
19. *Ibid.* 182
20. *Ibid.* 183
21. *Ibid.* 183
22. *Ibid.* 185
23. *Ibid.* 186
24. Letter to A. A. Tolstaya, March 31, 1895
25. *Ibid.*
26. *Ibid.*
27. *Diary,* April 10, 1895
28. *Diary,* April 25, 1895
29. *Ibid.*
30. *Diary,* April 26, 1895
31. *Diary,* April 28, 1895
32. Maude (1904) 164
33. Gusev (1960) 189
34. Clark (*Britain-USSR* No.68) 7
35. Maude (1935) viii
36. Clark 8
37. Gusev (1960) 351
38. *Ibid.* 382
39. *Ibid.* 376
40. *Ibid.* 389
41. *Ibid.* 390
42. Sukhotin-Tolstoy 152
43. Gusev (1960) 397
44. *Ibid.* 401
45. *Ibid.* 231
46. *Ibid.* 371
47. Shklovsky 649
48. James (1937) 134
49. JE
50. John Betjeman, 'Myfanwy at Oxford'.
51. JE 32.57
52. *Ibid.* 63
53. *Ibid.* 418
54. Kennan (1891) I.376-8
55. q. Fodor 65
56. JE 32.398
57. *Ibid.*
58. JE 32.136
59. *Ibid.* 436

60. Gusev (1960) 452
61. Goldenweiser 26
62. Pasternak (1957) 117
63. Goldenweiser 63
64. JE 32.430
65. *Ibid.* 105
66. *Ibid.* 106
67. Gusev (1960) 342
68. Bonhoeffer 210
69. Chadwick 78
70. Pobedonostsev (1965) 188
71. JE 32.181
72. *Ibid.* 182
73. Porter 371
74. Pobedonostsev 74
75. Weisbein 743
76. Goldenweiser 59
77. Simmons 642
78. Gorky (1966) 71

Chapter Eighteen: Sad Steps (pp. 463-482)

1. Chekhov (1974) 134
2. Gusev (1960) 321ff.
3. Gusev (1960) 410
4. Edwards 279
5. Gusev (1960) 411
6. Gorky 55
7. *Ibid.* 80
8. Spiers 159
9. Letter to A. A. Tolstaya, December 22, 1903
10. JE 34.111
11. Gusev (1960)
12. JE 34.345
13. *Ibid.* 122
14. *Ibid.* 110
15. *Diary*, May 19, 1905
16. *Ibid.*
17. *Diary*, March 30, 1905
18. Ulam 162
19. Wilson (1982) 125
20. Maude (1929) II.445
21. *Proletarian* (1908) No. 5
22. JE 35.216

23. *Ibid.*
24. George Orwell 72
25. Wittgenstein, q. Greer 67
26. JE 35.223
27. I was told the anecdote by John Julius Norwich, who was himself told it by Desmond MacCarthy.

Chapter Nineteen: Last Battles (pp. 483-502)

1. Edwards 397
2. Troyat 421
3. Letter to M. L. Tolstaya, March 22, 1906
4. 'It was the peasants who defeated Lenin. They were essentially small property men.' Sir Bernard Pares, *The Times,* February 5, 1930
5. Alexandra Tolstoy (1954) 431
6. *Ibid.* 448
7. *Diary,* April 15, 1906
8. *Ibid.*
9. Alexandra Tolstoy 453
10. Porter 607
11. Alexandra Tolstoy 460
12. JE 37.83
13. *Ibid.* 245
14. Gusev (1960) 156
15. Alexandra Tolstoy 452
16. *Ibid.* 458
17. Porter 536
18. Goldenweiser 59
19. Porter 633
20. Bayley (1966) 277
21. JE 74.124
22. Letter to V. G. Chertkov, November 19, 1909
23. Alexandra Tolstoy 478
24. Vatsuro II.76
25. Bulgakov (1971) xiv
26. Porter 632
27. *Ibid.* 647

Chapter Twenty: Escape (pp. 503-517)

1. Alexandra Tolstoy 519
2. Letter to M. N. Tolstaya, March 2, 1909
3. Alexandra Tolstoy 534

4. *Ibid.* 535
5. *Diary,* September 12, 1910
6. Alexandra Tolstoy 487
7. Ilya Tolstoy 261
8. Alexandra Tolstoy 541
9. Gusev (1960) 187
10. Alexandra Tolstoy 502
11. *Ibid.* 503
12. Letter to A. L. Tolstaya, November 1, 1910
13. Alexandra Tolstoy 516
14. Letter to S. A. Tolstaya, November 3, 1910
15. Alexandra Tolstoy 520
16. *Diary,* November 2, 1910
17. Tatyana Tolstoy 246
18. Ilya Tolstoy 279
19. Deutscher 119
20. *The Times,* December 12, 1910

Select Bibliography

Those wishing to survey the huge extent of books by and about Tolstoy are advised to consult the relevant volumes of Tolstoy bibliography. The range and availability of Tolstoy's works published in Russian and other languages or dialects of the Soviet Union between 1917 and 1953 can be seen in *Bibliografiya proizvedenii L. N. Tolstogo*, ed. E. E. Zaibenshnir (Moscow 1955) and others. Books and articles about Tolstoy are listed in the following:

N. G. Shelyapina and others, *Bibliografiya literatury o L. N. Tolstom 1917-1958* (Moscow 1960)

N. G. Shelyapina and others, *Bibliografiya literatury o L. N. Tolstom 1959-1961* (Moscow 1965)

N. G. Shelyapina and others, *Bibliografiya literatury o L. N. Tolstom 1962-1967* (Moscow 1972)

N. G. Shelyapina, *Bibliografiya literatury o L. N. Tolstom 1968-1973* (Moscow 1978)

David Egan and Melinda A. Egan, *Leo Tolstoy, an Annotated Bibliography of English-language* [sic] *Sources to 1978* (1979)

Garth M. Terry, 'Tolstoy Studies in Great Britain: a Bibliographical Survey' (in *New Essays on Tolstoy* ed. Malcolm Jones (1978)

My own bibliography is limited to those works which I have found especially helpful in writing this book. For the purposes of simplicity, I have divided it into three sections: the works of Tolstoy himself; studies specifically devoted to Tolstoy; and works not specifically concerned with Tolstoy, but which I have found of help or interest. In this last category, in particular, selection has been fairly rigorous. It would not be possible to understand Tolstoy without some reference to other nineteenth-century Russian writers. But although I have alluded, for example, in my text, to Lermontov, Leskov, etc., I have not thought it necessary to include their works in my bibliography except for the purposes of identifying specific quotations. Similarly, I have only given a selection of historical works. Place of publication, unless otherwise stated, is London.

1. *The Works of L. N. Tolstoy*

The standard edition of *The Complete Works of Tolstoy* is the one put in hand by V. G. Chertkov in 1928, the centenary, or jubilee, of Tolstoy's birth. This vast enterprise, which grew to ninety large, blue, cloth-bound volumes, was finally brought to completion more than twenty years after Chertkov's own death (1936) and contains the fruit of many people's scholarly labours. Ironically, considering how much they regarded one another as enemies, it grows out of Countess Sofya Andreyevna Tolstaya's edition of her husband's works, and it is an unacknowledged monument to her, as well as to Chertkov, and to two generations of Russian scholars. Because it is the only complete text of Tolstoy's works in existence, it is the one to which I refer in my notes, abbreviated, as is conventional, 'JE'.

Also invaluably useful is the twenty-volume Soviet edition of *Tolstoy's Works* (Moscow 1960).

There is an excellent selection of Tolstoy's correspondence with his fellow writers, which also prints the replies of Turgenev, Fet etc.: *L. N. Tolstoi. Perepiska s russkimi pisatelyami v dvukh tomakh* (Moscow 1978).

Every English reader owes a vast debt to Louise and Aylmer Maude for their contributions to Tolstoy scholarship. Not only does every biographer of Tolstoy stand on the Maudes' shoulders, but it was they who gave the bulk of Tolstoy's work to the English-speaking world. I first read Tolstoy in their *World's Classics* translations (Oxford) and I have had countless occasions to refer to them in the course of writing this book. In general I have attempted my own versions of the Russian when quoting from Tolstoy's fiction, but I have often relied to a large degree on the Maude translations.

A similar debt is owed to Professor R. F. Christian for his translations of Tolstoy's diaries and letters. Since these volumes contain so much useful historical and biographical information, as well as Tolstoy's own writings, I have listed them with the secondary material as books in their own right about Tolstoy.

Leo Islavin's *The Letters of Tolstoy and His Cousin Countess Alexandra Tolstoy (1857-1903)* (1929) is helpful in the same way as *Perepiska s russkimi pisatelyami* because it gives both sides of the correspondence.

2. *Books about Tolstoy or studies of his work*

Mark Aldanov, *Zagadka Tolstogo* (Brown University Slavic Reprint 1969)

N. N. Ardens, *Tvorcheskii put' L. N. Tolstogo* (Moscow 1962)

Matthew Arnold, 'Count Leo Tolstoi' in *Essays in Criticism, Second Series* (1887)

Cynthia Asquith, *Married to Tolstoy* (1960)

Michel Aucouturier (ed.), *Cahiers Léon Tolstoi I.* Anna Karénine (Paris 1984)

John Bayley, *Tolstoy and the Novel* (1966)

Isaiah Berlin, *Russian Thinkers* (1978) (This contains the famous essay 'The Hedgehog and the Fox'.)

Y. A. Bilinkis, *O tvorchestve L. N. Tolstogo* (Moscow 1962)

Pavel Biryukov, *Lev Nikolayevich Tolstoy biografiya* (3 vols. Moscow 1906-1910, revised Berlin 1921)

P, Boyer, *Chez Tolstoi: Entretiens à Iasnaia Poliana* (Paris 1950)

S. N. Bulgakov et al, *Sbornik statei o religii L'va Tolstogo* (Moscow 1912)

V. F. Bulgakov, *The Last Year of Lev Tolstoy* (1971)

B. I. Bursov, *Lev Tolstoi, Ideinye iskaniya i tvorcheskii metod 1847-1862* (Moscow 1960) *Lev Tolstoi i russkii roman* (Moscow-Leningrad 1963)

T. G. S. Cain, *Tolstoy* (New York 1977)

David Cecil, 'Some Reflexions on the Art of Leo Tolstoy', *Oxford Slavonic Papers* XI, eds. S. Konovalov and J. S. G. Simmons (Oxford 1964) pp. 60-68

Vladimir Chertkov, *The Last Days of Tolstoy* (London 1922)

R. F. Christian, *Tolstoy's* War and Peace: *a Study* (Oxford 1962)

——*Tolstoy: a Critical Introduction* (Oxford 1969)

——(ed.) *Tolstoy's Letters* (1978)

——(ed.) *Tolstoy's Diaries* (1985)

John Stewart Collis, *Marriage and Genius* (1965)

——*Tolstoy* (1969)

Martine de Courcel, *Tolstoi l'impossible coïncidence* (Paris 1980)

Rev. Alexander H. Crauford M. A., *The Religion and Ethics of Tolstoy* (1912)

The Hon. Ernest Howard Crosby, 'Two Days with Count Tolstoy' in *Progressive Review,* August 1897

Edward Crankshaw, *Tolstoy: the Making of a Novelist* (1974)

Martin Doerne, *Tolstoj und Dostojewskij. Zwei Christliche Utopien* (Göttingen 1969)

S. S. Doroshenko, *Lev Tolstoi, Voin i patriot* (Moscow 1966)

Anne Edwards, *Sonya* (1981)

B. M. Eykhenbaum, *Molodoi Tolstoi* (Prague-Berlin 1922)

——*Lev Tolstoi, kniga pervaya, 50-e gody* (Leningrad 1928)

——*Lev Tolstoi, kniga vtoraya, 60-e gody* (Moscow-Leningrad 1931)

——*Lev Tolstoi, semidesyatye gody* (Leningrad 1960)

Hugh I'Anson Fausset, *Tolstoy: the Inner Drama* (1927)

Alexander Fodor, *Tolstoy and the Russians* (Michigan 1984)

Rene Fulop-Miller, *New Light on Tolstoy* (1931)

Select Bibliography

Ettore Lo Gatto, *Storia della Letteratura Russa* (Florence 1943) pp. 306-325

Vincenzo Gibelli, *Puškin e Tolstoi* (Milan 1964)

Henry Gifford, *Tolstoy* (1982)

Alexander Goldenweiser, *Talks with Tolstoy* (1923)

Maxim Gorky, *Reminiscences of Tolstoy* (1920)

E. B. Greenwood, 'Tolstoy, Wittgenstein, Schopenhauer', *Encounter* XXXVI (April 1971) pp. 60-72

——*Tolstoy, the Comprehensive Vision* (1975)

N. K. Gudzy, *Kak rabotal L. Tolstoi* (Moscow 1936)

——(ed.) *Lev Nikolayevich Tolstoi. Sbornik statei o tvorchestve* (Moscow 1955)

—— *Lev Tolstoi* (Moscow 1960)

N. N. Gusev, *Lev Nikolayevich Tolstoi, Materialy k biografiis 1828 po 1855 god* (Moscow 1954)

—— *Lev Nikolayevich Tolstoi, Materialy k biografiis 1855 po 1869 god* (Moscow 1957)

—— *Lev Nikolayevich Tolstoi, Materialy k biografiis 1870 po 1881 god* (Moscow 1963)

——*Letopis' zhizni i tvorchestva L'va Nikolayevicha Tolstogo 1828-1890* (Moscow 1958)

——*Letopis' zhizni i tvorchestva L'va Nikolayevicha Tolstogo 1891-1910* (Moscow 1960)

Richard F. Gustafson, *Leo Tolstoy, Resident and Stranger* (Princeton 1986)

Käte Hamburger, *Leo Tolstoi: Gestalt und Problem* (Bern 1950)

Ronald Hayman, *Tolstoy* (New York 1970)

E. Heier, 'Tolstoy and Nihilism', *Canadian Slavonic Papers* XI No. 4 (1969) pp. 454-465

Laura Jepsen, *From Achilles to Christ: the Myth of the Hero in Tolstoy's* War and Peace (Tallahassee, Florida 1978)

Malcolm Jones (ed.), *New Essays on Tolstoy* (Cambridge 1978)

M. N. Katkov, '*Chto sluchilos* po smerti *Anny Kareninoi*', *Russkii Vestnik* CXIII No. 7 (July 1877) pp. 448-462

E. Kassin (ed.) and others, *Lev Tolstoy and Yasnaya Polyana* (Moscow 1978)

George Kennan, 'My Visit to Count Tolstoy', *Century Magazine* (1902)

Walter Kerr, *The Shabunin Affair, an Episode in the Life of Leo Tolstoy* (Cornell 1982)

A. V. Knowles (ed.), *Tolstoy: the Critical Heritage* (1978)

E. N. Kupreyanova, *Estetika L. N. Tolstogo* (Moscow-Leningrad 1966)

Tatyana Kuzminskaya, *Tolstoy As I Knew Him: My Life at Home and at Yasnaya Polyana* (1948)

S. Lafitte, *Léon Tolstoi et ses contemporains* (Paris 1906)

V. Lakshin, *Tolstoi i Chekhov* (Moscow 1975)

Janko Lavrin, *Tolstoy: an Approach* (1944)

V. I. Lenin, *Stat'i o Tolstom* (Moscow 1960)

F. R. Leavis, Anna Karenina *and Other Essays* (1967)

Select Bibliography

Derek Leon, *Tolstoy: His Life and Work* (1944)

Ernst Lübben, *Leo Tolstoi, der Führer von Jung-Russland* (Berlin-Leipzig 1909)

Victor Lucas, *Tolstoy in London* (1979)

M. Markovitch, *J. J. Rousseau et Tolstoi* (Paris 1928)

—— *Tolstoi et Gandhi* (Paris 1928)

Aylmer Maude, *Tolstoy and His Problems* (1902)

—— *Family Views of Tolstoy* (1926)

—— *The Life of Tolstoy* (Oxford 1929)

Harry J. Mooney Jr., *Tolstoy's Epic Vision* (Tulsa, Oklahoma 1968)

T. L. Motyleva, *O mirovom znachenii L. N. Tolstogo* (Moscow 1957)

M. V. Muratov, *L. N. Tolstoy i V. G. Chertkov po ikh perepiske* (Moscow 1934)

L. M. Myshkovskaya, *Masterstvo L. N. Tolstogo* (Moscow 1958)

George Rapall Noyes, *Tolstoy* (New York 1968)

Zoë Oldenbourg, *Anna Karenina Tolstoi* (Paris 1965)

Tikhon Polner, *Tolstoy and His Wife* (1946)

Cathy Porter (ed. and trans.), *The Diaries of Sofia Tolstaya* (1985)

Theodore Redpath, *Tolstoy* (1960)

R. Rolland, *Tolstoy* (London 1911)

S. Rozanova, *Tolstoi i Gertsen* (Moscow 1972)

A. A. Saburov, *Voina i mir L. N. Tolstogo: problematika i poetika* (Moscow 1959)

R. V. Sampson, *Tolstoy: the Discovery of Peace* (1973)

Sidney Schultze, *The Structure of* Anna Karenina (Michigan 1982)

Frank Friedeburg Seeley, '*La nemesi di* Anna Karenina', *Annali Sezione Slava* II (Naples 1959) pp. 121-146

Antoni Semezuk, *Lew Tolstoi* (Warsaw 1963)

P. A. Sergeyenko, *How Count Tolstoy Lives and Works* (1899)

Lev Shestov, *Dostoevsky, Tolstoy and Nietzsche* (Ohio 1969)

Viktor Shklovsky, *Material i stil' v romane L'va Tolstoga* Voina i mir (Moscow 1928)

—— *Lev Tolstoi* (Moscow 1963; English trans. Moscow 1978)

Ernest J. Simmons, *Leo Tolstoy* (1949)

—— *Introduction to Tolstoy's Writings* (Chicago 1969)

Marc Slonim, 'Four Western Writers on Tolstoy', *Russian Revolution* XIX (April 1960) pp. 187-204

Boris Sorokin, *Tolstoy in Prerevolutionary Russian Criticism* (Ohio 1979)

G. W. Spence, *Tolstoy the Ascetic* (Edinburgh 1967)

Logan Spiers, *Tolstoy and Chekhov* (1971)

Jonas Stadling and Will Reason, *In the Land of Tolstoi* (1897)

George Steiner, *Tolstoy or Dostoevsky: an Essay in Contrast* (1959)

Elizabeth Stenbock-Fermor, *The Architecture of* Anna Karenina (Lisse 1975)

G. Struve, 'Tolstoy in Soviet Criticism', *Russian Review* (April 1960)

Tatyana Sukhotin-Tolstoy, *The Tolstoy Home* (1950)

Alexandra Lvovna Tolstoy, *The Tragedy of Tolstoy* (New Haven 1933)

—— *A Life of My Father* (1954)

Ilya Lvovich Tolstoy, *Tolstoy My Father; reminiscences* (1972)

Lev Lvovich Tolstoy, *The Truth about My Father* (1924)

Nikolai Tolstoy, *The Tolstoys* (1983)

Sergey Lvovich Tolstoy, *Tolstoy Remembered* (1961)

Serge Tolstoi, *Tolstoi et les Tolstoi* (Paris 1980)

Sofya Andreyevna Tolstoy, see Porter *supra*

_____ *The Autobiography of Countess Sophie Tolstoy* (Richmond 1922)

_____ *The Diary of Tolstoy's Wife 1860-1891* (1928)

_____ *The Countess Tolstoy's Later Diary 1891-1897* (1929)

_____ *The Final Struggle, being Countess Tolstoy's Diary for 1910* (trans. Aylmer Maude, 1936)

Tolstoi Aujourd'hui (*Bibliothèque Russe de l'Institut d'Etudes Slaves, Tome LVII*, Paris 1980)

Henri Troyat, *Tolstoy* (New York 1967)

B. E. Vatsuro (ed. et al), *L. N. Tolstoi v vospominaniyakh sovremennikov* (Moscow 1978)

Edward Wasiolek, *Tolstoy's Major Fiction* (Chicago 1978)

E. Wedel, *Die Enstehungsgeschichte von L. N. Tolstojs* Krieg und Frieden (Wiesbaden 1961)

Nicolas Weisbein, *L'Evolution Religieuse de Tolstoi* (Paris 1960)

A. N. Wilson (ed.), *The Lion and the Honeycomb: Tolstoy's Religious Writings* (1987)

Thomas G. Winner (ed.), *Tvorcheskie raboty uchenikov Tolstogo v Yasnoi Polyane* (Providence 1974)

V. A. Zhdanov, *Tvorcheskaya istoriya* Anny Kareninoi (Moscow 1957)

_____ *Tvorcheskaya istoriya romana L. N. Tolstogo* Voskresenie (Moscow 1960)

_____ *Ot* Anny Kareninoi *k* Voskreseniyu (Moscow 1968)

3. *Books of general relevance to the life and times of Tolstoy or which are quoted in the text*

Edward Acton, *Alexander Herzen and the Role of the Intellectual Revolutionary* (1979)

A. E. Adams (ed.), *Imperial Russia after 1861: Peaceful Modernization or Revolution?* (Boston 1965)

Serge Aksakoff, *A Russian Schoolboy* (Oxford 1924)

E. Ambler, *Russian Journalism and Politics 1861-1881: the Career of Aleksei S. Suvorin* (Detroit 1972)

Joe Andrew, *Writers and Society during the Rise of Russian Realism* (1980)

_____ *Russian Writers and Society in the Second Half of the Nineteenth Century* (1982)

John W. Atwell Jr., 'The Russian Jury' *Seer* LIII (1975) pp. 44-61

P. Avrich, *The Russian Anarchists* (Princeton 1967)

Maurice Baring, *An Outline of Russian Literature* (1915)

Select Bibliography

A. J. Barker, *The Vainglorious War (1854-1856)* (1970)

John Bayley, *Pushkin* (Cambridge 1971)

Hilaire Belloc, *The Campaign of 1812 and the Retreat from Moscow* (1924)

Nicholas Berdayev, *Dostoievsky: an Interpretation* (1934)

_____ *The Russian Idea* (1947)

Reginald F. Bigg-Wither, *A Short History of the Church in Russia* (1920)

J. Billington, *The Icon and the Axe* (1966)

Dietrich Bonhoeffer, *Ethics* (1979)

Jeffrey Brooks, *When Russia Learned to Read* (Princeton 1985)

W. H. Bruford, *Chekhov and his Russia* (1948)

Henry Chadwick, *Augustine* (1986)

Anton Chekhov, *Letters* (ed. Avrahm Yarmolinsky, 1974)

Claudia Clark, 'Chertkov and the Tolstoyans at Tuckton', *Britain-USSR* No. 68 (September 1984)

Peter Collins, *Dickens and Education* (1963)

Peter Coveney, *Poor Monkey: the Child in Literature* (1951)

Edward Crankshaw, *The Shadow of the Winter Palace* (1976)

John Shelton Curtiss, *Church and State in Russia 1900-1917* (New York 1940)

_____ *The Russian Army under Nicholas I (1825-1855)* (Durham, N. Carolina 1965)

Alex de Jonge, *The Life and Times of Grigorii Rasputin* (1982)

_____ *Stalin* (1986)

Henri de Lubac, *The Un-Marxian Socialist: a Study of Proudhon* (1948)

Isaac Deutscher, *Stalin* (revised Harmondsworth, 1969)

Fyodor Dostoyevsky, *The Brothers Karamazov* (trans. D. Magarshack 1958)

_____ *The Diary of a Writer* (1984)

John B. Dunlop, *Staretz Amvrosy: Model for Dostoevsky's Staretz Zossima* (Belmont, Mass. 1972)

Jane Ellis, *The Russian Orthodox Church: a Contemporary History* (1986)

A. A. Fet, *Moi Vospominaniya (1848-1889)* (Moscow 1890)

_____ *Polnoe sobranie stikhotvorenii* (Leningrad 1959)

D. Field, *Rebels in the Name of the Tsar* (Boston 1976)

Louis Fischer, *The Life of Lenin* (1965)

R. M. French (trans.), *The Way of the Pilgrim* (1943)

G. M. Fridlender (ed.), *Istoriya russkogo romana* (2 vols., Moscow-Leningrad 1962)

L. Gerstein, *Nikolai Strakhov* (Cambridge, Mass. 1971)

Henry Gifford, *The Hero of his Time: a Theme in Russian Literature* (1950)

_____ *The Novel in Russia from Pushkin to Pasternak* (1965)

F. V. Greene, *Sketches of Army Life in Russia* (1881)

Germaine Greer, *Shakespeare* (1986)

Ian Grey, *Stalin* (1979)

V. V. Grigorenko (ed. with others), *I. S. Turgenev v vospominaniyakh Sovremennikov* (Moscow 1969)

Albert F. Heard, *The Russian Church and Russian Dissent* (1887)

Select Bibliography

Alexander Herzen, *My Past and Thoughts* (trans. Constance Garnett, 1924)

Ronald Hingley, *A New Life of Anton Chekhov* (1976)

——*Russian Writers and Society in the Nineteenth Century* (1977)

——*Dostoevsky: His Life and Work* (1978)

——*Nihilists: Russian Radicals and Revolutionaries in the Reign of Alexander II (1855-1881)* (1981)

Henry James, *The Art of the Novel* (New York 1934)

Lawrence James, *Crimea 1854-1856* (1981)

John Jones, *Dostoevsky* (Oxford 1983)

I. Katerskii, *Dickens v Rossii, seredina XIX veka* (Moscow 1966)

M. Katz, *Mikhail Katkov: a Political Biography 1818-1887* (The Hague 1966)

A. W. Kinglake, *The Invasion of the Crimea* (Edinburgh-London 1863)

Hugh Kingsmill, *After Puritanism* (1929)

Prince Kropotkin, *Ideals and Realities in Russian Literature* (1905)

Janko Lavrin, *Pushkin and Russian Literature* (1947)

C. S. Lewis, *They Stand Together* (1979)

Sven Linner, *Starets Zosima in* The Brothers Karamazov (Stockholm 1975)

Charles Lowe, *Alexander III of Russia* (1895)

D. Mackenzie-Wallace, *Russia* (1877)

David Magarshack, *Dostoyevsky* (1962)

Martin Malia, *Alexander Herzen and the Birth of Russian Socialism (1812-1855)* (1961)

Nadezhda Mandelstam, *Hope Against Hope* (1970)

——*Hope Abandoned* (1974)

Aylmer Maude, *A Peculiar People: the Dukhobors* (1904)

D. S. Mirsky, *A History of Russian Literature* (1949)

S. Monas, *The Third Section* (Cambridge, Mass. 1961)

Alan Moorehead, *The Russian Revolution* (1958)

W. E. Mosse, *Alexander II and the Modernisation of Russia* (1958)

Nigel Nicolson, *Napoleon 1812* (1985)

Dennis Nineham, *The Use and Abuse of the Bible* (1976)

M. T. Nuzhin (ed.), *Kazanskii Universitet 1804-1979: Ocherki istorii* (Kazan 1979)

George Orwell, *Critical Essays* (1946)

Maurice Paléologue, *The Tragic Romance of Alexander II of Russia* (1926)

Alan Palmer, *Napoleon in Russia* (1967)

Sir Bernard Pares, *Russia and Reform* (1907)

Boris Pasternak, *Doctor Zhivago* (1958)

M. B. Petrovich, *The Emergence of Russian Panslavism* (New York 1956)

Richard Pipes, *Russia under the Old Regime* (1974)

Konstantin P. Pobedonostsev, *Reflections of a Russian Statesman* (Michigan 1965)

A. Pushkin, *Polnoe sobranie sochinenii* (10 vols., Moscow 1963)

H. W. Pullen, *The Ground Ash: a Public School Story* (1874)

Princess Catherine Radziwill, *The Intimate Life of the Last Tsarina* (1929)

Select Bibliography

The Religious Persecutions in Russia (pamphlet issued by the Society of Friends of Russia, 1897)

Nicholas V. Riasanovsky, *Russia and the West in the Teaching of the Slavophiles* (Cambridge, Mass. 1952)

____ *A Parting of the Ways: Government and the Educated Public in Russia 1801-1855* (Oxford 1976)

____ *A History of Russia* (third edition Oxford 1977)

Richard G. Robbins Jr., *Famine in Russia 1891-1892* (New York-London 1975)

G. T. Robinson, *Rural Russia under the Old Regime* (1929)

Leonard Schapiro, *Turgenev* (Oxford 1978)

Albert Schweitzer, *The Quest for the Historical Jesus* (English trans. 1910)

Richenda C. Scott, *Quakers in Russia* (1964)

Hugh Seton-Watson, *The Russian Empire 1801-1917* (Oxford 1967)

W. T. Stead, *Truth about Russia*

Laurence Sterne, *A Sentimental Journey through France and Italy* (1952)

____ *The Life and Opinions of Tristram Shandy, Gentleman* (1972)

Christine Sutherland, *The Princess of Siberia: the Story of Maria Volkonsky and the Decembrist Exiles* (1984)

Peter Tchaikovsky, *The Diaries of Tchaikovsky* (New York 1945)

Victor Terras, *A Karamazov Companion* (Wisconsin 1981)

____ (ed.), *Handbook of Russian Literature* (Yale 1985)

E. C. Thaden, *Conservative Nationalism in 19th-Century Russia* (Seattle 1964)

D. W. Treadgold, *Lenin and his Rivals: the Struggle for Russia's Future 1898-1906* (New York 1955)

Leon Trotsky, *Kak vooruzhilas' revolutsiya* (Moscow 1924)

____ *My Life* (1930)

____ *Turgenev i krug* Sovremennika: *neizdannie materialy 1847-1861* (Moscow-Leningrad 1930)

Fyodor Ivanovich Tyutchev, *Polnoe sobranie stikhotvorenii* (Leningrad 1939)

Adam B. Ulam, *The Bolsheviks* (New York 1965)

____ *The Unfinished Revolution* (revised New York 1979)

____ *Russia's Failed Revolutions: from the Decembrists to the Dissidents* (New York 1981)

F. Venturi, *Roots of Revolution: a History of the Populist and Socialist Movements in Nineteenth-Century Russia* (trans. from the Italian by F. Haskell, New York 1960)

Prince S. M. Volkonsky, *Arkiv Dekabrista S. G. Volkonskogo* (Petrograd 1918)

Patrick Waddington, *Turgenev and England* (1980)

A. Walicki, *The Slavophile Controversy* (Oxford 1975)

Timothy Ware, *The Orthodox Church* (revised Harmondsworth 1980)

Philip Warner, *The Crimean War* (Arthur Barker 1972)

J. N. Westwood, *A History of Russian Railways* (1964)

A. N. Wilson, *A Life of John Milton* (1982)

Edmund Wilson, *To the Finland Station* (New York 1940)

Select Bibliography

—— A Window on Russia (1973)

W. F. Woehrlin, *Chernyshevsky: the Man and the Journalist* (Cambridge, Mass. 1971)

B. E. Wolfe, *Three who Made a Revolution: a Biographical History* (New York 1948)

George Woodcock, *Pierre Joseph Proudhon* (1956)

George Woodcock and Ivan Avakumovic, *The Dukhobors* (Toronto-New York 1968)

A. Yarmolinsky, *A Road to Revolution: a Century of Russian Radicalism* (1957)

Mikhail Nikolayevich Zagoskin, *Polnoe sobranie sochinenii* (Petrograd 1914)

L. A. Zander, *Dostoevsky* (1948)

A. V. Zapadov (ed.), *Istoriya russkoi zhurnalistiki XVIII-XIX vekov* (Moscow 1973)

Vladimir Zborilek, *Tolstoy and Rousseau: a Study in Literary Relationship* (Michigan 1979)

Nicolas Zernov, *The Russians and their Church* (1945)

—— *The Russian Religious Renaissance of the Twentieth Century* (1963)

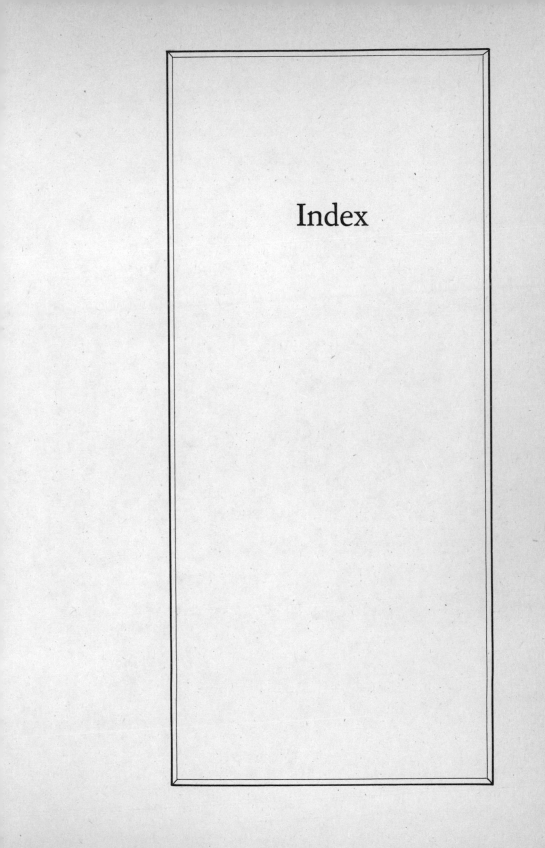

Index

NOTE: Works by Tolstoy appear under title; other works under the name of the author.

About the Author

A. N. Wilson was born in 1950. He was a scholar of New College, Oxford, where he later taught English language and literature for a number of years. From the late 1970s on, he was a prolific journalist, contributing to the *Times Literary Supplement*, the *New Statesman*, the *Observer*, the *Sunday Telegraph*, and the *Daily Mail*. For two years he was literary editor of the *Spectator*. More recently, he has concentrated largely on writing books which, along with *Tolstoy*, include biographies of Hilaire Belloc, John Milton, and Sir Walter Scott. He is also the author of ten novels; among them, *The Healing Art* won the Somerset Maugham Award in 1981 and *Wise Virgin* the W. H. Smith Award in 1983. A. N. Wilson is married with two daughters. A fellow of the Royal Society of Literature, he divides his time between Oxford and London. His most recent work is a collection of essays entitled *Penfriends from Porlock*.